Modern School Business Administration

A Planning Approach
Ninth Edition

JAMES W. GUTHRIE
Peabody College at Vanderbilt University

CHRISTINA C. HART
Peabody College at Vanderbilt University

JOHN R. RAY
University of Tennessee

I. CARL CANDOLI
University of Texas

WALTER G. HACK
Ohio State University

PEARSON

Boston   New York   San Francisco
Mexico City   Montreal   Toronto   London   Madrid   Munich   Paris
Hong Kong   Singapore   Tokyo   Cape Town   Sydney

Senior Editor: Arnis E. Burvikovs
Development Editor: Christien Shangraw
Series Editorial Assistant: Anne Whittaker
Marketing Manager: Erica DeLuca
Production Editor: Gregory Erb
Editorial Production Service: Nesbitt Graphics, Inc.
Composition Buyer: Linda Cox
Manufacturing Buyer: Linda Morris
Electronic Composition: Nesbitt Graphics, Inc.
Interior Design: Nesbitt Graphics, Inc.
Cover Designer: Elena Sidorova

For related titles and support materials, visit our online catalog at www.ablongman.com.

Between the time website information is gathered and then published, it is not unusual for some sites to have closed. Also, the transcription of URLs can result in typographical errors. The publisher would appreciate notification where these errors occur so that they may be corrected in subsequent editions.

ISBN-10: 0-205-57214-6
ISBN-13: 978-0-205-57214-4

Modern school business administration : a planning approach/James W. Guthrie ... [et al.]. – 9th ed.
p. cm.
Rev. ed. of: School business administration. 8th ed.
Includes bibliographical references and index.
ISBN 0-205-57214-6
1. Public schools--United States--Business management--Textbooks. 2.
Public schools--United States--Finance--Textbooks. I. Guthrie, James W. II.
Ray, John R. School business administration. c2005.
LB2823.5.H33 2008
379.1'10973--dc22

2007028219

Printed in the United States of America

Contents

Series Preface

■ THE PEABODY EDUCATION LEADERSHIP SERIES

Vanderbilt University's Peabody College is one of the world's foremost schools of education and human development. The Peabody faculty is in the vanguard of research and knowledge creation, while a long tradition of collaboration "on the ground" with learners, educators, policymakers and organizations ensures that, at Peabody, theory and practice inform each other. In addition to conferring a full range of graduate, professional, and undergraduate degrees, the College is committed to strengthening current educators and organizational leaders in their efforts to propel greater achievement and enhance human development.

This book and others in the Allyn & Bacon Peabody Education Leadership Series are published to facilitate wider understanding of the means by which human learning takes place and how greater learning can be fostered. Much of the nation's most forward thinking regarding learning and instruction emanates from Peabody. For example, the National Research Council's famous research synthesis, *How People Learn*, was undertaken with the leadership of Peabody faculty. Current faculty members are generating research and constructing the paradigms that will influence the teaching of reading, mathematics, and science well into the future.

Consistent with its mission and its own research, Peabody strives to model good instruction. In that spirit, each book in the Education Leadership Series has a number of instructional aids. These include full outlines of the volume's substantive material, complete tables of contents, indexes filled with significant concepts and citations, technical glossaries, chapter previews with summaries of what has been and is to be covered, extensive use of topical case studies, clearly understandable graphics, and discussion questions. These aids will enable readers to grasp the complexities associated with what 21st-century leaders need to know about such topics as leadership, finance, accountability, community relations, organizational dynamics, or education law.

Text Supplements

Each text in this series is accompanied by a **Companion Web site**. Students and instructors should visit www.ablongman.com/Peabody for test cases, simulation exercises, sample data for end-of-chapter exercises, URLs for further research and interest, added bibliographies, and other up-to-date information.

Students can find help with research projects using **Research Navigator™**, which provides access to three exclusive databases of credible and reliable source material, including EBSCO's ContentSelect Academic Journal Database, *The New York Times* Search by Subject Archive, and the "Best of the Web" Link Library. Research Navigator™ is available through Allyn & Bacon's **MyLabSchool**, located at www.mylabschool.com.

An **Instructor's Manual** with teaching resources and test items is also available to adopting instructors through their local Allyn & Bacon representative.

Education's Evolving Context

Education today must respond as never before to a set of global economic and cultural conditions. These rapidly changing conditions, and the competition they are creating, serve as a subtext for virtually every concept covered by books in this textbook series.

For most of the nation's history, it was possible for an individual to forego formal schooling and still own land, acquire relatively well-paying employment, participate in civic life as an informed citizen, and achieve a substantial degree of personal fulfillment. For many, probably most, individuals, these comfortable circumstances have changed. Modern economies render formal education crucial for individual success, social mobility, and engagement with the demands of the workforce, the environment, and government. The eventual outcome of these relatively new challenges now matters as much for a child being raised on a family farm in South Dakota as to one from a farm family in South Africa.

What has become true for individuals also applies to nations. A people once flourished or floundered based on what they could extract from the ground. Today, a nation is more likely to survive and prosper based on what it can extract from the minds of its citizens.

Readers of this series also will have to grapple with the challenges posed by global changes. Many of the divisive questions facing society as a whole have powerful implications for the conduct of education, as well.

- How can immigrants be fully integrated into American society?
- How many languages can schools reasonably be expected to offer or to use for instruction?
- How much testing is too much?
- How much should be spent on schools to ensure that all students have an opportunity to achieve the learning standards that governments set?
- How should teachers be trained and licensed?
- Should private providers be permitted to offer public schooling?
- Should the public pay for preschool and interschool programs?
- Should high school exit examinations determine graduation?
- What should class sizes be to maximize the positive effects of instruction?

These questions illustrate the complicated and interconnected policy and practical dilemmas upon which books in this series will attempt to shed light. The goal is not so much to provide direct answers to such questions as it is to arm readers with the tools that will enable them to keep pace with, and contribute solutions to, these and future problems. Specifically, this series will:

- Harness useful concepts and evidenced-based practical understandings applicable to understanding and solving emerging policy challenges and to managing and reforming modern organizations
- Provide readers with technical understanding of important components of education resource deployment, policy development, organizational development, and institutional governance and operation
- Suggest research-based means by which education institutions and practices can be undertaken to greater effect and with greater efficiency
- Enable educators to participate better in policy-related and professional debates regarding best practice

We welcome your comments and suggestions as a reader, researcher, or other user of this book, or other books in the series.

James W. Guthrie
Series Editor
Professor of Public Policy and Education

Camilla P. Benbow
Patricia and Rodes Hart Dean of
Education and Human Development

Preface

This book has a proud history, and, along with its original authors, John Ray, I. Carl Candoli, and Walter Hack, has long been held in high regard by the school business administration community. The current authors, James W. Guthrie and Christina C. Hart of Peabody College at Vanderbilt University, are honored to have inherited this mantle.

■ THIS BOOK'S PURPOSE

The purpose of this textbook is threefold. The first is to provide a school business official, or a prospective school business official, with a thorough understanding of the rapidly evolving context in which American public education now finds itself. On this dimension, the book seeks to clarify complex public policy issues at the intersection of schooling (pre-K through 12) and public management. Without clarifying and communicating these social and economic complexities—as well as the foundational knowledge at the heart of education policy and school finance—we would fail in our efforts to generate a textbook with practical utility for school business officials.

The book's second purpose is to provide the next generation of business administrators with prerequisite knowledge of key school business concepts and practices and the tools that thus enable them to leverage school management matters to further advance contemporary education operations.

A third purpose for this book is to serve as a reference work, a rich set of understandings to which school business officials can routinely turn when they desire added information on a management topic.

■ EDUCATION'S EVOLVING CONTEXT AND SCHOOL BUSINESS ADMINISTRATION

To fulfill the textbook's first purpose, four related topics are explored with considerable intensity: (1) societal interactions with education, (2) means for generating and deploying financial resources for education, (3) major public policy and education policy reform issues along with their resource and business administration consequences, and (4) means for overseeing and managing the multiple activities for which a school business official is conventionally responsible.

Since the 1983 issuance of the federal government report *A Nation at Risk*, the United States has undertaken a sustained effort to render public schools more effective. This "reform" effort is characterized by three major conditions, all of which have finance and management issues at their core.

One noticeable and significant change in the education management environment is an intensified reliance upon litigation as a means for altering education resource distribution. The "legalization" of education finance policy now takes place at an unprecedented pace in the United States. As this book goes to press, education finance lawsuits are underway, either in a discovery phase, at trial, or on appeal, in twenty states. Another twenty states have already experienced one or more such suits. Whether or not this strategy eventually renders education more effective is a matter of debate. Nevertheless, because of vastly increased personal, economic, and societal significance of schooling, advocates of all kinds want to ensure they have fair and adequate access to it. Hence, they rely upon litigation as one means available within the American political system for pursuing or protecting their interests.

Another significant contextual development since issuance of *A Nation at Risk* is a transformed perception within the policy system of education and its management. Schools were once judged by the quality, or at least the amount, of their inputs, such as expenditures per pupil, spectrum of courses and after-school activities, teacher salaries, student social and economic composition, teacher characteristics, or richness of school facilities. This perception has changed. Schools increasingly are judged by outputs, the academic achievement of their students. Enactment in 2001 of major federal legislation, The No Child Left Behind Act, strongly symbolizes and reinforces this transformation.

A third transformation is the emergence of three rationally conceived, sometimes competitively posed, archetypical strategies for rendering schools more effective. One of these reform strategies is a so-called "systemic reform" approach (Smith & O'Day, 1991).[1] Another is a conscious reliance upon market forces or greater competition among providers (Chubb & Moe, 1990).[2] A third strategy calls for intensified efforts to reinforce the out-of-school well-being of students in hopes of enabling them to perform better in school (Rothstein 2004).[3] The three strategies are not incompatible. Each will be explained in greater detail in subsequent chapters. The strategies can fit together and in a few instances, for example, in components of the above-mentioned No Child Left Behind Act, are woven together.

These three evolving conditions, (1) legalization, (2) output orientation, and (3) strategic reform considerations, have significantly altered the field of education management. This change is so fundamental and has such far-reaching implications for the study of school business administration, the undertaking of research regarding education management issues, and the preparation of school business officials particularly and education leaders generally, that an effort is made in early sections of this book to distinguish the "new" from "early" in education management thinking. Hence, the focus of this book is on "modern school business administration."

These three evolving conditions are rooted in a common societal dynamic. They have emerged from, or, at least, have been accelerated by, a remarkable change in the significance modern society accords formal education. When formal schooling played a minor role in the well-being of individuals and the future of a society, schooling was far less often the focus of litigation, outputs mattered less, and strategies for promoting school effectiveness were of lesser concern. Now that education means more, formal schooling attracts a far larger sector of interests regarding access to it, outcomes from it, and means

---

[1]O'Day, J. and M. Smith. (1993). "Systemic Reform and Educational Opportunity," in *Designing Coherent Education Policy: Improving the System*. Susan H. Fuhrman (Ed.). NY: Jossey-Bass.

[2]Chubb, John E. and Terry M. Moe. 1990. *Politics, Markets, and America's Schools*. Washington D.C.: The Brookings Institution.

[3]Rothstein, Richard. 2004. *Class and Schools: Using Reform to Close the Black-White Achievement Gap*. Washington D.C.: Economic Policy Institute.

for linking resources to outputs. It also routinely receives larger wedges of the public-sector resource pie.

One can no longer hope to understand education management by simply attending to technical mechanics; comprehension now is also rooted in understanding societal dynamics. As a result of this change, the intensified interaction between the larger society and education has altered the balance of information contained in this book. Whereas technical mechanics still count, and are covered in detail, they also must be linked to the forces that shape them and the issues they are expected to address.

■ ENHANCING READER LEARNING AND UTILITY

In the last decade, efforts to unravel what is meant by and how to assess student understanding have generated considerable dialogue among education stakeholders in general and cognitive scientists in particular. Whereas the mere recital of discrete morsels of knowledge and facts by students was generally accepted as an appropriate indicator of student understanding, more contemporary approaches stress such elements as conceptual clarity, real-world application, critical analysis, and detached reflection to appraise student understanding. In an extension of those approaches, this textbook strives to enhance reader learning and performance through combining an innovative assessment technique called *Understanding by Design*, which promotes deep understanding and meaningful application by students.

Understanding by Design. The approach to learning employed within these pages is grounded in the performance assessments developed by Grant Wiggins and Jay McTighe, two leading thinkers who advocate situating student understanding at the core of curricular, assessment, and instructional designs. In 1998 Wiggins and McTighe published the highly acclaimed *Understanding by Design*, a resource book for educators that sponsors performance assessment as a means to promote deep understanding of content by students. Wiggins and McTighe assert that individuals truly understand when they: (1) can explain, (2) can interpret, (3) can apply, (4) have perspective, (5) can emphasize, and (6) have self-knowledge. This textbook draws upon Wiggins and McTighe's six facets of understanding through the use of discussion questions, case studies, and articles from mainstream media to enhance student understanding of the topics under consideration.

The use of this approach to reader understanding yields a standard chapter outline that will guide users through the remainder of this text. Each chapter begins with a short list of learning objectives. Throughout the chapter, readers will encounter material that will be used to guide discussion. Often, this material will refer readers back to one of the opening case studies that are presented in Chapter One. In addition, each chapter will have an "In the News" feature that highlights a newspaper article, journal article, press release, or similar piece of media, which presents the issues in each chapter within a real-world context. The end of each chapter contains a chapter summary, a list of discussion questions, and web links to additional resources. In addition, key terms are defined in the glossary at the end of the book.

Acknowledgments

A textbook of this coverage and complexity seldom stands by itself. It is a product of much that has preceded it. At the turn of the twentieth century, Elwood Patterson Cubberley, Stanford professor and founding dean of that campus' education school, established a scholarly basis for understanding education finance and management. In later years, education finance greats such as Paul R. Mort, of Teachers College, R.L. Johns, of the University of Florida, and H. Thomas James of Stanford University added significantly to our knowledge regarding schools and resources. More recently, Charles Scott Benson of the University of California, Berkeley, and Walter I. Garms of the University of Rochester were towering figures in this field. We owe a debt of gratitude to all of these individuals.

We wish to express our appreciation to Peabody College's Dean Camilla P. Benbow and to Arnis Burvikovs and Christien Shangraw, of Allyn & Bacon, whose encouragement rendered this project doable. Additionally, Peabody College staff members Deborah Enright, Rosie Moody, Renée Morgan, Suzanne Vahaly, and Peter Witham were a continual source of unselfish assistance. Finally, in this regard, Joyce Hilley, who has managed the Peabody Center for Education Policy for thirteen years, continually kept the writing and production processes connected with this book on track and on time.

The authors are especially appreciative of the contributions of their Peabody faculty colleagues Dale Ballou, Mark A. Berends, Leonard Bickman, Leonard K. Bradley, Robert L. Crowson, Mark D. Cannon, John G. Geer, Ellen B. Goldring, Stephen P. Heyneman, Joseph P. Murphy, Daniel J. Reschly, Michael J. Schoenfeld, and Matthew G. Springer.

James Guthrie has benefited from the advice and friendship of a number of professional colleagues, among whom are Jake P. Abbott, California independent education executive search consultant; Jacob E. Adams, Claremont Graduate University; Gina E. Burkhardt, Learning Point Associates; Charles W. Cagle, Lewis, King, Krieg & Waldrop, P.C.; Robert M. Costrell, University of Arkansas; Ric Dressen, Edina Public Schools, Minnesota; Christopher T. Cross, Cross & Joftus, LLC; Pedro E. Garcia, Metropolitan Nashville Public Schools; Jay P. Greene, University of Arkansas; Babette Gutmann, Westat; Eric A. Hanushek, Hoover Institution of Stanford University; Janet S. Hansen, Committee for Economic Development; Gerald C. Hayward, chancellor emeritus, California Community College System; Allison Henderson, Westat; Carolyn D. Herrington, University of Missouri-Columbia; Frederick M. Hess, American Enterprise Institute; Paul T. Hill, University of Washington; Eric A. Houck, University of Georgia; James A. Kelly, National Board for Professional Teaching Standards; Joseph Jaconette, Orinda Unified School District, California; Michael W. Kirst, Stanford University; Julia E. Koppich, J. Koppich & Associates; Sabrina Laine, Learning Point Associates; Pamela Saylor Lannon, Florida education attorney; Alfred A. Lindseth, Sutherland, Asbill & Brennan, LLP; Goodwin Liu, University of California, Berkeley School of Law (Boalt Hall); Susanna Loeb, Stanford University; Robert H. Meyer, University of Wisconsin-Madison; J. Dennis O'Brien, Office of the Governor, Minnesota; Allan R. Odden, University of

Wisconsin-Madison; David H. Monk, The Pennsylvania State University; Paul Peterson, Harvard University; Michael J. Podgursky, University of Missouri-Columbia; R. Anthony Rolle, Texas A&M University; Kevin M. Ross, Lynn University; Richard Rothstein, Economic Policy Institute; Roger Sampson, Education Commission of the States; Kevin Skelly, Palo Alto Schools, California; Neil Slotnick, Alaska Attorney General's Office; James R. Smith, Management Analysis and Planning (MAP); Robert E. Stepp, Sowell, Gray, Stepp & Laffitte, LLC; Rocco E. Testani, Sutherland, Asbill & Brennan, LLC; Christopher A. Thorn, University of Wisconsin-Madison; Jason L. Walton, Lynn University; Jerry Weast, Montgomery County Public Schools, Maryland; and Patrick J. Wolf, University of Arkansas.

Christina Hart would like to thank Tracy Sturmak for her contributions to the editing process.

The authors would also like to thank the reviewers of this edition for their helpful feedback during its creation: Sidney L. Brown, Alabama State University; Theodore J. Meyers, University of Memphis; Gloria T. Poole, Florida A&M University; and Rose Tallent, Southeast Missouri State University.

As authors, we are flattered at reader interest in this volume and welcome suggestions for improving its accuracy and utility. As should be obvious in such ventures, errors and omissions are the sole responsibility of the authors.

James W. Guthrie
Christina C. Hart

Peabody College
Vanderbilt University
Nashville, Tennessee
2008

About the Authors

James W. Guthrie is a professor of public policy and education, chair of Leadership, Policy and Organizations, and director of the Peabody Center for Education Policy at Peabody College of Vanderbilt University. He instructs both undergraduate and graduate courses, and conducts research on education policy and finance. He also is the founder and chairman of the board of Management Analysis & Planning, Inc. (MAP), a California private sector management consulting firm specializing in public finance and litigation support.

Previously a professor at the University of California, Berkeley for 27 years, he holds a BA, MA, and PhD from Stanford University, and undertook postdoctoral study in public finance at Harvard. He also was a postdoctoral Fellow at Oxford Brookes College, Oxford, England, and the Irving R. Melbo Visiting Professor at the University of Southern California.

He is the author or co-author of ten books and more than 200 professional and scholarly articles. He was the editor-in-chief of the *Encyclopedia of American Education*, published in 2002.

Christina C. Hart is an advanced PhD student in the Department of Leadership, Policy, and Organizations at Peabody College, Vanderbilt University. She has an MBA in Management. Previously, she has served as a student activities director at a large, comprehensive public high school in California and as a public school administrator responsible for budgets and strategic plans.

In creating this text, the authors are proud to have updated the work of I. Carl Candoli, John Ray, and Walter Hack. Inestimable thanks go to these original authors for their contribution to our field of scholarship and to the Peabody Educational Leadership series.

School Business Administration Case Studies

■ INTRODUCTION

The following cases are illustrative and do not represent real persons or real places. They do, however, illustrate real situations and real problems. Issues raised in these cases (e.g., financial decision options, federal regulation, personal ethics, information system needs, and team management alternatives) will be a subject of explanations and analyses throughout subsequent substantive chapters.

A summary is provided at the end of this chapter, distilling school business issues with which practitioners have grappled in the six case studies.

LEARNING OBJECTIVES

In this chapter a reader will learn about:

- How a school business official can become involved with instructional issues, institutional politics, and even individual deceit.
- How often there are multiple answers to problems, and how little in life is black or white and how much is a shade of gray.
- Why a school business official and common sense are critical components of a leadership team.

 CASE 1

No Controversy Left Behind (NCLB)

It was only the first school day after Labor Day, and Harriet Alverez already felt like she had been dragged through an entire school year. Two months ago, on July 1, she had assumed her new role as Assistant Superintendent for Management Services in the Wildwood Unified School District. She had moved to town, bought a new condominium, enrolled her son in the nearby public elementary school, purchased a new professional wardrobe, and started her new job with great enthusiasm. Now, she was beginning to wonder if she had bitten off more than she could chew or had perhaps entered a world that required she know more than she knew.

Harriet initially felt she was quite qualified. She had majored in engineering studies as an undergraduate at the state university. She had worked successfully in the engineering industry for three years. She had been active in her son's school's parents' organization and that peaked her interest in becoming a teacher. She had served in another district as a high school Advanced Placement mathematics teacher for five years. The rhythm of teaching, both daily and annually, enabled her to pay attention to her family in ways that were personally important to her.

Harriet liked teaching, but her prior district had run afoul of the state in a series of surprise attendance and financial audits, and the local district superintendent had called upon Harriet to drop her classes and oversee a number of functions in the district's business office. The numbers added up for Harriet, she was a quick study, and this experience whetted her appetite for business matters. She had entered an extension service executive MBA program at a local private university. Indeed, it was a business program professor who steered her to her new position in the Wildwood Unified School District.

Wildwood was located in an inner ring suburb of a large midwestern city. It had started as a post World War II middle-class housing development and was initially populated by thousands of returning veterans who wanted its wide streets, grassy lawns, and affordable housing. Wildwood was a product of the World War II GI Bill and low-interest home loans. In the intervening half century, other subdivisions had leapfrogged over Wildwood and it had lost its once glossy tone. It now was a first stop out of the crowded city for upwardly mobile urbanites, many of whom had immigrated to the United States from other nations in Eastern Europe, Asia, and Latin America. The decidedly mixed ethnic flavor gave Wildwood a spicy sense of cosmopolitan diversity and simultaneously presented the schools with many language-related challenges.

Wildwood had one senior high school, three middle schools, and ten elementary schools. Almost all of its six thousand K–6 students were within walking distance of their elementary schools, but the district operated a bus fleet for four thousand secondary students. Wildwood's buildings were not new. The oldest elementary schools were coming up on their fiftieth anniversaries. However, they had been generally well maintained, and facilities were not the district's largest problem. Enrollments were growing, but there was still some capacity remaining from the district's last population decline that had lasted until the mid-1990s. However, Harriet had said in her successful job interview that she would undertake a careful demographic analysis to provide the superintendent and board with a better understanding of what was on the horizon by way of enrollment and capacity issues.

Now, in the midst of the current district controversy, into which Harriet saw herself increasingly being drawn, she wondered when she would find the time to get the enrollment analyses organized. This assignment would have to be pushed to the back burner while she dealt with issues stemming from the No Child Left Behind Act (NCLB), issues that seemingly came from nowhere and now were everywhere.

Congress had passed NCLB during the winter of the preceding school year. Harriet's Wildwood business manager predecessor had undertaken projections and calculated that Wildwood would be eligible to receive approximately $1 million in additional federal aid, if the act was funded as discussed in Congress. District officials had approved this estimate and had placed the anticipated revenue into their budget forecast for the forthcoming academic year, the school year that Harriet was now beginning as the district's new business manager.

Harriet had informed herself regarding NCLB. She had some questions to be sure. She was uncertain that the student achievement proficiency targets were realistic. She was not sure that 95 percent of students could, in fact, make the academic progress now expected each year. She wondered how the act's provision regarding a "highly qualified teacher" for each student would be interpreted. She could not see that the wide spectrum of state credential categories for teachers guaranteed much by way of instructional ability in teaching candidates the district routinely interviewed to fill job openings. She was particularly questioning the act's provisions whereby students in persistently failing schools might opt for other schools, possibly even private schooling, at public expense. Still, she favored the outcome orientation the legislation represented. She had seen the use of performance incentives and measurable targets in the private sector, and she favored such a strategy for schools too.

In anticipation of the NCLB mandates regarding Adequate Yearly Progress (AYP) and a trajectory of consistent added student proficiency all the way until 2014, the district had undertaken planning, and, as a result, employed fourteen additional reading and mathematics coaches and various subject matter specialists. Even before Harriet arrived, almost all of these new hires were in place in schools and were on the district payroll. Also, the district had lengthened the school day by ten minutes, a change that also had been factored into a teacher salary increase.

Then the unhappy news arrived. Now that the school year had started, the state education department recalculated every district's NCLB financial allotment and informed Harriet's office that Wildwood would now receive an additional $600,000, not the previously anticipated full $1 million. The other NCLB $400,000 would still come to the district, but it was earmarked for "supplemental services," tutorial services that low-performing students would be eligible to receive, but the use of the money was not fully at the school district's discretion. The $400,000 was more for after-school and summer tutoring than for regular school district professional employees such as academic coaches.

By Harriet's reckoning, the newly revealed $400,000 shortfall meant that half the recently employed academic coaches would have to be laid off at mid-year, or the district's reserves would have to be tapped to cover the shortfall. Harriet prepared her presentation for the upcoming superintendent's cabinet meeting, where she hoped she would receive guidance regarding one cost-saving alternative or another.

Harriet was unprepared for the hostile tenor of the cabinet conversation. It seemed as if the others present were intent on killing the messenger rather than grappling with the real problem. One of the other administrators accused her of deliberately misleading the district's officials with inaccurate financial data. The Assistant Superintendent of Instruction proclaimed that it was unthinkable to lay off the newly hired academic coaches. Did she [Harriet] not realize that researchers at the state university had determined that coaching elevated student achievement by an effect size of 2.2? The superintendent explained that tapping the restricted reserve took a super majority of school board votes and that he knew from personal exchanges with individual board members that there was not sufficient support for such a strategy. The teacher union president proclaimed that NCLB was simply a waste of public money, a political sham by which President George W. Bush hoped to keep the Republicans in power, and that the right thing to do was for the district to refuse to comply. The district's Director of Government and Public Relations informed the cabinet that a coalition of school districts had been formed with the intent of filing suit against the federal government for failing to fully fund NCLB. He advocated the district joining the suit, even if prorated legal costs would be $50,000 for Wildwood. Harriet silently wondered if the board would vote to tap the reserve for funding such a legal action.

The meeting ended without any specific direction for Harriet, and she felt quite discouraged. It was her first appearance in a Wildwood cabinet meeting and not only had she been forced to be the bearer of bad tidings, but also she could not see that any of the suggested alternatives led to viable solutions. She felt like she was trapped in a long corridor and each time she found an exit, the door was slammed shut against her.

That evening and during the next day, Harriet assessed her position and searched for alternatives. She found the research article to which the Assistant Superintendent of Instruction had referred. It had not appeared in a refereed journal. Moreover, Harriet retraced her statistics training to refresh her memory regarding effect sizes. An effect size of 1.0 represents a gain of one standard deviation. An effect size of 2.2, as proclaimed for academic coaching in the article, would mean, incredulously, that the provision of academic coaches would all by itself elevate student achievement to the 90th percentile. With outcomes such as these, one could release all teachers and rely upon a few academic coaches. Harriet realized this was spurious and she came to resent the haughty attitude of her cabinet peer who made the case for coaches.

Harriet also considered the teacher union president's comments regarding the duplicity and disutility of NCLB. She was not ready to buy this argument, as a wide bipartisan majority had enacted NCLB. If President Bush was pulling the wool over peoples' eyes, then he was bamboozling a great many Senate and House leaders of all political stripes in the process. She generally favored the outcome orientation of the legislation and was fearful that without NCLB there would indeed be students who would be left behind, and this need not and should not be.

As for the board not supporting use of restricted reserve funding, she wished only that she would be given an opportunity to make a presentation to the board to provide them with a choice. She resented having the option eliminated without explicitly trying. Her pride bridled at her role and appropriate professional access being restricted or co-opted by the superintendent.

Finally, the idea of a lawsuit struck her as unlikely to be successful. Where was the unfunded mandate? The schools were always supposed to address the learning needs of all students. The new federal law only specified what the school district should always have been striving to do. Why would it take added monies for the district to comply simply with its own historic goals and rhetorical purposes?

Harriet assessed her alternatives: It seemed to her she could do one of a combination of the following:

- She could tell the superintendent that she had reconsidered and the district should immediately strive to find a business manager replacement for her. She would stay on until an appropriate successor was identified.
- She could ask that the cabinet return to the issue, and she could confront her opposing colleagues with her points of view and her now well-informed responses. In the ensuing deliberations the chips would fall where they may. If the administrative cabinet was not a forum for open discussion, then she did not want to be part of the organization anyway.
- She could discreetly approach the president of the Wildwood Board of Education and strive to enlist his good offices in finding a solution.
- She could quietly mount a political campaign among cabinet members, striving to build a favorable coalition. Once assured of sufficient agreement, then she would bring up the issue again in a public manner.
- She could let the issue lay fallow, write a memo to the file to cover her position specifying that she had told the cabinet of the financial consequence of not facing the lost revenue.
- She could report the district's irresponsible fiscal actions to the state education department management review team.

Harriet felt alone and was not sure to whom she could turn for advice. She thought of talking to the state school business association executive. She also considered phoning the business school professor who had facilitated her getting the job in the first place. However, none of these seemed to be quite right when it came to providing counsel. Perhaps she would just have to figure out this situation herself.

For Discussion

1. Was Harriet Alverez properly prepared for her new responsibilities as a school district business manger?
2. Could Harriet have prepared with greater breadth and intensity for the cabinet meeting?
3. Should Harriet have been more confrontational in the cabinet meeting itself?
4. Should the superintendent have supported Harriet more in the cabinet meeting?

5. How should the superintendent have followed up after the cabinet meeting?
6. Should some fault be assigned to the fiscal situation in which Wildwood has found itself?
7. What course of action should Harriet take after the fact? Should she confront her colleagues, report her district, quit her job, or something else?

 CASE 2

An Ethics Matter: But What about Dieter?

Mark Walters was about as dynamic as a superintendent can be. In addition to his tall, craggy, movie star good looks; deep and confidence-instilling voice; and commanding presence; he was smooth-talking beyond comparison. He was a born salesman and promoter. After being in his presence it took individuals about an hour to realize they were not the center of the universe. He was charming, beguiling, creative, and dazzling in the use of language and his breadth of education and instructional understanding. He was an education-sector equivalent of businessman Donald Trump. He made others think they were the heroes, but his personal magnetism was overpowering. He charmed virtually every school board that employed him, and there were a lot of those as he moved often.

Mark's wife, Flora, always accompanied him in his work with school districts. He always bargained for her to become the district's assistant superintendent for instruction. She was every bit as articulate and charming as he was, so he had no trouble making the case for her employment. Districts found themselves thinking that they were fortunate to land such a dynamic duo. They got two of the best, while recruiting just once.

However, this case is not about Mark Walters or his wife Flora, as dazzling as they were. Rather this case is about Dieter Shrempf.

Dieter was the business manager in the district where Mark and Flora Walters had just been hired by the board. Dieter had met Mark and Flora as part of the interviewing process, and he had to admit that he too was swept away by the charm, wit, charisma, and intelligence of them both. His only wonderment was why they were in the job market at all. Dieter could not easily imagine that any district would want to lose a dazzling management duo such as these two.

Dieter was not suspicious by nature, indeed, his general view of life was "go along in order to get along." He did a good job keeping track of district expenditures and financial obligations. His fiscal numbers were beyond question, and he did his job without meddling. He was friendly but not gregarious. He had a few acquaintances, but generally did not fraternize with fellow school district administrators. He was an active member of the state school business managers association. However, he was not ambitious for a higher office. He did not engage in the politics that swept across the district from time to time. Dieter was Dieter, and he did not try to be anything else but a good business manager.

Dieter had the trust of the former, retiring, superintendent, whose place Mark Walters was taking. The outgoing superintendent had confided to Dieter how favorably impressed he was with Mark and Flora. He had told Dieter that he thought the district was fortunate to land a team with such obvious talent. Therefore, it was a tad unlike Dieter to do the background checking he did. However, it was he who was responsible for negotiating the employment contracts for Mark and Flora, and, between the two of them, they were about to be paid a hefty amount in salary and fringe benefits. Dieter thought it worth inquiring.

He phoned the head of the school business officials' association in the state from which Mark and his wife Flora were coming. What he learned was quite an unexpected earful.

Dieter was told that Mark and Flora had had their contracts bought out not by the last district for which they had been employed but by the last three districts for which they had worked. In each instance, they had overcommitted the district's resources and had brought the agencies to the brink of insolvency. Indeed, in their last district, the state had stepped in to prevent absolute bankruptcy, and had had to lend the district money to complete the school year and to meet the payroll.

But how, Dieter wondered, did Mark and Flora continually hide their failures so well? How did they always land on their feet? Did not anyone check the facts? Could not anyone see through their facade? Then Dieter learned yet more.

Armed with the facts from the state school business association official, Dieter began to diligently phone the districts of Mark and Flora's prior employment. However, the door was continually slammed in his face; no one would talk nor could he get a letter of reference. Dieter could not get a single negative statement that he could use in public. It seems as if everywhere Mark and Flora had failed, they had embarrassed local board members and other officials to such a degree that they had simply let the couple go, agreed not to say anything publicly if they would not sue for any severance pay. It was sufficiently embarrassing to these districts and local officials that their agencies were insolvent and they had been publicly embarrassed. They also did not want to have to admit they were further wronged by having to pay Mark and Flora any amount of salary owed on a remaining contract. In exchange for legally enforceable vows of silence, Mark and Flora were free to continue to scam other districts.

What Dieter knew was damning. However, Dieter could not prove what he knew. Moreover, the outgoing superintendent, the school board, and virtually the entire community were ardently supporting Mark and Flora. In fact, he was being pressured to consummate the employment contracts quickly. More than one newspaper article had hinted that Dieter was a bureaucrat who could not keep up with the fast pace demands that were likely to be made by the new incoming administrative team. It was suggested to Dieter that just maybe he should hurry and close the employment deal or he might find himself the target for replacement once Mark and Flora were in charge.

So Dieter went along to get along. However, he decided that he would become particularly diligent personally. His records would be even more complete; he would document every fiscal demand that the new administrative team made. If there were insufficient resources to cover the demand, he would be clear that he had recommended against the expenditure. No one would catch him napping.

Soon Dieter learned how Mark and Flora worked. They were not particularly dishonest; they were simply irresponsible. They made promises, promises that the system could not keep—a new school gymnasium floor here, an additional special education aide there, an additional assistant principal here, a district car for the itinerant music teacher there, and a consulting contract to the mayor's brother. On and on went the promises. Higher and higher soared the unbudgeted obligations. And thicker and thicker became Dieter's file.

Finally, Dieter had had enough. His personal and professional need for financial order had been strained to the maximum. He confronted Mark Walters with the uncovered financial obligations, rolling out the entire list for Mark. Mark listened to him carefully. Indeed, the absolute air of openness took Dieter by surprise. Mark was not defensive. He did say, however, that he and Flora were on the brink of delivering a huge federal grant to the district and the overhead alone would cover all of the errant financial promises. Then, a week later, to Dieter's utter amazement, the federal grant was announced, and the indirect cost allotment did indeed cover all of Mark and Flora's unbudgeted promises.

Dieter kept his mouth shut. However, his files kept building. On two other occasions Dieter confronted Mark, when the business manager thought financial obligations had amassed beyond the point of redemption. In each instance, another grant materialized, and the district's books were balanced.

Then a situation finally materialized. Mark cut a deal with the teachers' union, which avoided an imminent strike. The teachers declared Mark a hero, and the local newspaper claimed him to be a labor management genius by heading off conflict. The Rotary Club, Lions Club, Moose, and on and on all proclaimed Mark to be America's superintendent. The board was particularly gratified. They did not want to face the prospect of protracted conflict, the hiring of strike-breaking substitutes, and the criticisms of parents who did not want their children taught by unfamiliar teachers. Mark Walters was riding unusually high.

Dieter, however, knew the teacher contract's true costs. He knew that whereas the district could afford the generous labor settlement in year one, by year two the district would either have to lay off personnel or declare insolvency. In year three the consequences would be even more dire. There was no middle ground.

Dieter sharpened his pencil, and again went to visit Mark. This time Mark was testy and accused Dieter of not being a team player. He was abusive with Dieter and asserted that he was being disloyal. He recounted to Dieter all the times that the latter had been wrong. He said Dieter was always crying wolf. However, there was no wolf. Why did Dieter always have to be the skunk at the garden party? Finally Mark threatened to fire Dieter if the latter made any noise regarding the out-year costs of the teacher contract settlement.

Mark threatened to expose Dieter as repeatedly having been wrong in the past and therefore not capable of being on the district's management team. Mark further threatened to expose Dieter as not keeping accurate books. If Dieter was so good, then why had he been wrong so often in the past? How could Dieter's figures be trusted now? If Dieter had known something was wrong in the past, why had he not said something about it in public? If Dieter had remained silent so long, and

Mark had been right so often, who did Dieter think the board, the press, and the public would trust—him or the dynamic, successful superintendent?

Dieter slunk away, feeling simultaneously sad and mad; he had been suckered. He had not done what he knew professionally he should have done, and now he was trapped by his own mistakes. What should he do? The slender and distasteful options as he saw them were:

- Submit his resignation and hope to cut a deal with Mark whereby the latter would support him in his efforts to find a new job in return for Dieter remaining silent regarding the district's forthcoming financial crisis.
- Stand and fight Mark in public, amassing a solid factual argument that was indisputable.
- Expose Mark for his past deviant and irresponsible behavior.
- Tell state officials about the impending financial insolvency of the district, and the role that Mark played in the situation.
- Keep quiet and go along to get along.

For Discussion

1. Did Dieter persist sufficiently in his background check of Mark Walters?
2. Should Dieter have informed district officials from the beginning of his findings regarding Mark and Flora Walters?
3. Did Dieter do the right thing by keeping a complete file on fiscal matters where the Walters had made irresponsible promises?
4. Was it right to balance the district books by using federal government indirect costs?
5. Should Dieter immediately have informed the board when he knew that the teacher contract's settlement was highly risky in out years?
6. What should Dieter do after the fact, report the district to the state, confront Mark Walters more forcefully, quit his job, or something else?

 CASE 3

School Business Office Meltdown, and the Band Played On*

It was 8:30 p.m., and John Sample stood with his back against the scratchy stucco wall of a noisy school auditorium. He was waiting for his first meeting as a newly elected school board member to begin. Only three weeks before, he had been at a gathering of friends awaiting the outcome of the election. As results of the balloting came in by telephone, it had become evident rather early in the evening that he was to win a school board seat by a wide margin. For a few moments, he had lapsed into a long-denied reverie. During the four-month campaign, he had

*Adapted from the senior author's article in the June 1981 issue of *The American School Board Journal*.

suppressed all fantasies about winning, but on election night, he tried to imagine what his first school board meeting would be like. How would he dress? What would the issues be? How many people would attend? Would they cheer or boo when he voted? Now, three weeks after his election, he could sense that his election-night visioning was to prove uncomfortably naïve.

In an April meeting one week before the election, the school board had listed 85 school system employees (guidance counselors, arts instructors, psychologists, curriculum specialists) who would be reassigned to regular classroom teaching in the fall. Now, with all 85 employees (and hundreds of their supporters) in attendance, John's first official board meeting was sure to be memorable. The auditorium was overflowing with teachers, parents, children, and an assortment of drifters and "community activists" who appear at any public gathering in Bay City. The fire marshal estimated that more than a thousand people were present, and he continually emphasized that if the aisles were not cleared, he would call the police and close the meeting.

John was standing uneasily in a small exit alcove near the front of the auditorium. He could look out on both the audience and the stage. On the stage was a high school jazz band that, as the band director had indicated several times already in the course of the performance, recently had won first prize at a national contest. Thus, if sufficient funds could be found, he announced, the young musicians were entitled to a European concert tour in the summer.

Whatever the band members lacked in musical ability, they more than compensated for with zeal and volume. The performance was intended as a powerful message to the school board that musicians of such high quality *surely* should be accorded the utmost in professional musical instruction. As he listened to the cacophony, John struggled to remind himself that other students were learning to play Brahms and Mozart; otherwise, he would have cast his vote on the spot to disband the school district's entire music program. In observing the audience, Sample noted that no one appeared to share his view.

What was scheduled to be a thirty-minute jazz concert finally ended after more than an hour, and John's first school board meeting was called to order at 9 p.m. Aside from some cliché-riddled comments by the two re-elected incumbents and John himself (the only newcomer on the five-member body), no business was conducted until 1:30 a.m. The interim hours were filled by the angry testimony of dozens of parents and employees.

School psychologists proclaimed that they were trained to serve the psyche, and it would be wasteful and unfair to return them to classroom instruction. Art and humanities specialists explained in elaborate detail how their specific skills promoted creative fulfillment in children and how the school board, should it return these specialists to mere classroom teaching, would commit the unconscionable crime of graduating intellectually hollow automatons incapable of reading poetry or appreciating Matisse.

So the meeting went for almost four hours, as martyrs in each category bemoaned their fate and orchestrated the supporting testimony of parent groups and other constituents. Periodically, John recognized individuals at the microphone who had helped in his election campaign, and he tried to pay special attention to their remarks. The *least* he could do, he thought, was to be polite even if he disagreed with their positions. When he nodded at a speaker who had attended a kaffeeklatsch during his campaign, she returned his kindness with an obscene gesture. He realized he had been christened. No longer was he a duly elected public official charged with representing the public welfare on matters related to schools. Henceforward, he was simply "friend" or "enemy."

At 1:30 a.m., with the auditorium now almost empty, the school board moved to eliminate a number of administrative positions. John was happy with the outcome of the vote, because he had campaigned on a platform that said the school system was administratively top-heavy. In a sense it was a "cheap shot"—one can always claim that a large organization has too many administrators. But less than 60 percent of Bay City's district's licensed educators were engaged as classroom teachers—a condition John took to be outrageous and one that justified the return of the previously mentioned specialists to classroom instruction.

The intended benefit of both moves was to assist in reducing a projected $800,000 deficit in the coming school year (in other words, the school board and administration had estimated it would cost $800,000 more in the next school year to provide the same services as provided this year).

The remaining school board meetings in May were, at least by comparison, uneventful.

At an early June board meeting, the school system's business manager let fly with a staggering revelation. Whereas previously he had projected a $300,000 surplus at the end of the current fiscal year, he had revised the estimate; the district now would close its books on the school year $700,000 in arrears—a million-dollar reversal. In one evening, the projected budget deficit for the next fiscal year climbed from $800,000 to $1.5 million. With that, the business manager had both the good taste and the foresight to resign. Board members and the audience were stunned, and the board adjourned early.

In mid-June, John received an invitation to the P.T.O. council's annual banquet. The dinner was to be held in a local restaurant. The award-winning jazz band again was to be featured as the evening's entertainment. Because a petty politician needs to be in the throes of death to avoid a "must" such as a P.T.O. dinner, John attended. Approximately a hundred people were present, and, of that number, John managed to surround himself with a few supporters and friends. Throughout the awards ceremony, John's attention wandered to a foil-covered coffee can sitting in the middle of the table. It was empty. He (and others) periodically picked it up, examined it, and always returned it to its place on the table with a shake of the head or a shrug of the shoulder.

The evening drew to an awkward close because the jazz band failed to appear. Several explanations were offered for the band's absence, but none made sense. Nevertheless, John soon learned the purpose of the foil-covered coffee can. The mistress of ceremonies pointed out that audience members were expected to contribute *generously* to the send-the-band-to-Europe fund, and all present were to put money in the can. John dropped in some money and quickly told himself that he had gotten off cheap. For only five dollars, he was spared the band's music. If the truth be known, he gladly would have paid five times as much for the privilege.

After dinner, John boarded a plane for Washington and New York. He met with government and foundation officials in an effort to assess the degree to which their funds might assist Bay City in meeting the unforeseen and suddenly emerging revenue deficit. All such doors appeared politely closed, and he flew back to the West Coast with a heightened resolve to find additional budget categories to squeeze.

For example, John wondered if the district could eliminate all in-service training of teachers. This might be hazardous, because with Bay City's "no-hire" policy, it would be necessary to transfer some teachers to classes they had never taught or had not taught in years. Or, could the district cease all curriculum development activities? The effect on children probably would be minimal, but this would trigger a political outburst from various ethnic minorities. They would contend that in the absence of new materials, children would continue to be taught from white racist texts that distorted their peoples' histories. There would be some truth to that charge, too, but it was a no-win situation.

Upon getting off the plane, John went directly to a school board meeting at which a consulting firm that had been engaged to buttress the decimated business office delivered a chilling report. In reviewing previous calculations, consultants discovered a substantial *overestimate* of revenues for the forthcoming year. Consequently, what had begun as an $800,000 projected deficit and had mushroomed to a $1.5 million deficit had now grown to a deficit of between $2.5 and $3.5 million. (The district's total budget was $35 million.) As John listened to the accountants explain the miscalculations, he wondered how any organization, let alone one as tightly constrained by state law as a school district, could compensate for a 10 percent reduction in revenues in a single year.

Such were the ideas whirring in John's head as he arrived home and began opening several days' accumulation of e-mail. To his surprise, there was a high-priority e-mail, and he opened it first. It was a "mailgram" sent by a neighbor who wanted to know when the board was going to take final positive action on raising money for the jazz band to go to Europe. If something did not happen in the next week, the message noted, the students would be deprived.

On June 28, the board voted unanimously to reduce employee salaries and fringe benefits. Because the board had no confidence that their fiscal nightmare would end with a mere $3.5 million deficit, it voted to reduce employee compensation by almost $4 million. If it subsequently proved unnecessary to cut so drastically, the board easily could restore salaries and some benefits. Board members knew this was a drastic step; probably no school district in the United States had lowered salaries since the Great Depression. But the series of miscalculations and revenue revisions all had occurred beyond the legal date to fire employees. Because at least 80 to 85 cents out of every school system dollar is spent on personnel, the board's only alternative was to lower the rate of compensation.

The next several weeks were brutal. The school board met thirteen times during July, an average of twenty hours a week. Teachers, understandably upset by the proposed salary decrease, filed several lawsuits against the district. In the round of bargaining that had been completed before John's election to the board, teachers had agreed to live with no salary increase if there were no layoffs. They had not, however, contemplated a salary *decrease* policy. They began to file grievances as well as lawsuits. When the board moved to employ the best available legal counsel to defend itself, the teachers attempted to block the board from spending public funds for such purposes. In the teachers' view, the board should have been restricted to using the skeletal legal services provided to school districts by the county. The only hint of humor in this situation occurred when the superintendent suggested that, if the county counsel was so good, the board would be happy to let teachers use these services and the board would use the teachers' attorneys.

In addition to filing lawsuits, some teachers took up picketing school board meetings. Their slogan, "Fight Back, Not Cut Back," soon became etched in John's memory. The fact that, in light of the revenue problem, they were mouthing an empty phrase seemed not to diminish their enthusiasm. They chanted the words with all the fervor of Hare Krishna converts.

Meanwhile, groups of constituents intensified their efforts to preserve special programs. Minority group representatives advised the school board that the system would return to an era akin to slavery if their ethnic studies coordinators were not retained. Parents of physically challenged children dramatically presented their case for maintaining services. The fact that the district already spent twice the state average for such special schooling was of little significance. The one expenditure item that was never questioned was busing for the district's historic voluntary racial desegregation effort. John was proud of this fact; it demonstrated that a community could adhere to an ideal, a costly ideal at that, even in times that were otherwise filled with bitterness.

Repeatedly in the testimony before the board in mid-July, speakers questioned the veracity of the school system's financial plight. After a few days of planning and conferring with board colleagues and an interested newspaper editor, John proposed a Citizens' Fiscal Review Committee. This committee, to be appointed by the board, would have complete access to all school system financial records and would submit an independent report to the board and the community regarding the district's fiscal affairs. Membership on the committee was to be determined primarily by financial expertise.

The person John appointed to the committee was a young vice president of a bank. He so clearly was the best-qualified candidate that other board members concurred in his being named chairman. This appointment occurred in spite of the fact the banker had all the trappings of a conservative. He was a West Point graduate with a Harvard M.B.A and he wore vests—in other words, a rare and frequently disliked breed in Bay City. The committee eventually comprised fourteen members, five of whom represented district employee groups. A report was expected in two weeks.

The board meeting at which the Citizens' Fiscal Review Committee was announced lasted, as did most of the other public meetings in July, until 1 a.m. The next morning, John checked his answering service for the previous evening's phone calls. He recognized the names of most of those who had called, but one was new. He decided to return that call first.

A soft-voiced male answered. When John introduced himself, the caller declared that he was sorry to trouble him with petty news, but said, "I thought you ought to know . . ." He continued with the information that he had been affiliated with the school system's music program for a long time, and through his contacts he had come to suspect that the high school jazz band that was planning a European tour had not won any prize at all at the national contest. "In fact," he said, "they may have finished in last place."

Aside from the fact that he was happy to hear, even if untrue, that someone else shared his judgment of the jazz band, John considered the caller's story simply preposterous and John told him so. John recounted the great public recital at his first board meeting, the telephone calls and telegrams from parents, the fund-raising efforts, even his own contribution at the P.T.A. dinner. The caller hung up with his polite insistence that John ask the high school principal for the letter announcing the award. John agreed to do so.

In late July, as the board continued its trench warfare against the armies of waste and bureaucratic ineptitude, the board continued to hear testimony from community and employee groups. On July 22, the Citizens' Fiscal Review Committee produced its first report. The room was hushed for more than an hour while the prematurely graying chairman recited a litany of managerial error. The consulting firm's estimate of a $3.5 million deficit for the coming year certainly was reasonable, but given the state of the system's accounting, the deficit could be anywhere from $2.5 million to $5 million. Moreover, business office operations were riddled with past mistakes, unapproved cost overruns on contracts, evidence of individuals being paid overtime for days and hours not worked, no inventory of fixed or semi-fixed assets, incomplete external audits during previous years, and so on. The committee, which was supposed to establish the board's credibility, had done its job well—too well.

As the meeting ended, John quietly asked the superintendent's assistant if he would obtain from the principal a copy of the jazz band's award letter. He assured John it was unnecessary, but if it would satisfy some parent, he would be happy to get it.

August 5 was the date the Bay City school board had set for itself to adopt a final budget for the forthcoming school year. Literally hundreds of small decisions already had been made. Reductions in in-service training, curriculum development, out-of-district transportation, administrative costs, special education, and supply budgets all had been decided upon. What remained was the big decision regarding the precise degree to which employees' salaries and benefits should be sliced.

Even though steps had been taken to reduce salaries by as much as 15 percent, it now appeared that such a move would be unnecessary. By having made a number of other cuts, the board would have to reduce salaries only by approximately 4 percent. The superintendent, however, suggested another plan that, if successful, would reduce salaries by only 1.5 percent. His plan was to raise the tax rate.

The general operating tax rate was incontrovertibly frozen, unless it could be thawed by voter approval at a special election, which was not likely. The board, however, had at its disposal an override tax for the support of children's centers.

There was no ceiling on this tax, other than the caveat that whatever funds were raised through this mechanism had to be spent on pre-kindergarten-aged children. The district already had 500 such children enrolled, and the superintendent's proposal would add 150 more. The tax increase would generate approximately $900,000 in additional revenues; some of the teachers already on the payroll would be moved to teach in children's centers. The combination of no new employees and additional revenue would provide sufficient new money to ease the salary reduction burden.

The problem with what appeared to be a magic fiscal solution was that the proposal carried with it a cost for the pre-school program of $12,000 per child. This was for day care and educational services for as many as ten hours a day; the cost amounted to $15.30 per child per day. By checking, John determined that this was four times what any other system in the state spent and was substantially higher than what such services cost in the private market. In short, it appeared to be a waste of taxpayers' money. John considered it a short-range financial gimmick to solve a problem that had been building for years.

When the superintendent initially introduced the idea, two of the five board members adamantly declared that they were opposed to any tax increase. Two others vowed that they always had supported children's centers and that this was a legitimate use of tax money at a time when the funds were needed most. John declared his neutrality, waiting to see how the funds were to be employed.

For a week, board members argued with each other regarding the merits of the tax increase proposal. It would come at a time when the tax assessor had elevated overall property values in the area by an average of 10 percent. There were many elderly, retired, and unemployed residents upon whom a tax increase would impose a burden. On the other hand, teachers were being asked to accept a slight cut in pay at a time of substantial inflation.

During these discussions, John found himself increasingly opposed to the tax increase. Nevertheless, one of the board members who earlier had been the most vehement in her opposition to the tax increase began to change her mind. Gladys never gave any reasons for her new position, but Sample got a clue when she assured him one evening that her daughter's employment in one of the school district's children's centers would not constitute a conflict of interest if she voted for the tax increase. She said she had discussed the matter with the county counsel and had been assured of the legality of her position.

As the crucial meeting opened, the house was full, but the audience was remarkably calm and polite. John sensed only that the continued revelations of the system's financial trauma had prepared citizens for almost any development. As is frequently the case on complicated issues, the vote would take place not on the explicit matter of maintaining the current tax rate versus raising taxes, but on the seemingly more mundane matter of school district personnel policies. The board had to adopt new policies that evening, and such policies would specify the rate of employee pay. If the salary rate was set at 4 percent lower than the previous year, it meant that the majority of the board had decided against a tax increase. If the salary figure were set only 2 percent or so lower, then the majority had decided to impose another tax hike on the most heavily taxed school district in the state.

Board members made a series of almost perfunctory statements, heard testimony from a few members of the audience, and then moved to vote. It was a roll call, and John's name came early. He cast a vociferous "No" on the 2-percent salary plan. The next two votes were "Yes," and the fourth vote was "No." The stage dramatically was set for the tiebreaker. How would Gladys vote? She obviously was vacillating, and when her name was called, she said, "I abstain." It was a totally unexpected anticlimax.

The board then moved through a complicated series of parliamentary maneuvers, considering and reconsidering motions. The two proponents of the tax increase were furious. The woman whose daughter was a children's center teacher apparently had buckled. One of the tax proponents attended to her much the way a trainer works in the corner of a prizefighter. He hovered over her, reminding her of all the virtues of a tax increase. The entire audience waited expectantly.

By 11 p.m. the tax proponents had resuscitated themselves, and the vote proceeded in their favor. All that remained was a series of perfunctory decisions that put the budget to bed. The board had submitted a balanced budget, thus not provoking a takeover by the state. It had raised taxes, cut salaries, and reduced services. No small series of tasks for a board member whose first meeting was only three months before.

John decided to take advantage of the unexpectedly early adjournment. On his way out of the meeting, the superintendent's assistant motioned him to the side of the room, whispered a short phrase in his ear, shrugged his shoulders, and said good night.

John went home and made one telephone call before retiring. He called the jazz band informant and apologized for being rude to him earlier. John had confirmed that the jazz band had won no national prize and was not eligible for a trip to Europe. A music teacher who had since resigned had fabricated the entire matter.

As John reviewed events of the past several months, he arrived at the following alternative actions for his district:

- Strive to return teacher salaries to their position *ex ante*.
- Restore personnel levels.
- Lower the property tax rate to be competitive with surrounding districts.
- Identify a mechanism or a set of procedures that would prevent such a management meltdown from ever occurring again.

For Discussion

1. Was distributing the consequences resulting from mismanagement the right thing to do? Should taxpayers, students, and personnel all have been asked to bear a share of the pain?
2. Should the former business manager have been charged with malfeasance?
3. Was appointing a citizens' group a good thing to do to restore public confidence?
4. What should have been done to the music teacher who fraudulently claimed a prize for the jazz band?

CASE 4

Teaching Harold's Pony a New Trick: The Challenge of School-Based Budgeting

Harold Hawkins had been involved with school business matters for twenty years. He was once a high school mathematics teacher, and then made a transition to being an assistant business manager. Fifteen years ago, he was selected as the major business official for an elementary school district. Since then he had moved twice, each time assuming greater responsibility for a larger and more complicated school district. He had, however, always stayed within the same state, and thus had learned the rules well since he did not have to continually learn a new set of state-imposed regulations.

Harold had learned his job well; indeed, he was the doyenne of school business officials in his state, having been elected president of the statewide school business official association. He was good; superintendents for whom he had worked were all appreciative of his talents. He also had the confidence of the school board and was proud of his accomplishments. He liked his job, and his job liked him. He felt successful and looked forward only to a happy retirement in about three or four years.

Then, Harold encountered a challenge. He was given an assignment by his superintendent and the school board for which he was not prepared. He had worked throughout his career to ensure that all central business functions operated smoothly. He had put into place system after system, ensuring that food was served hot, buses ran on time, supplies were reordered by a schedule, payroll was almost flawless, bills were paid within thirty days, and so on. Indeed, many of his central-ized systems were adopted in their entirety by other districts because they were so effective.

Now, seemingly when everything was working to perfection, his upper-lings were upsetting his well-managed apple cart. What they wanted was for principals at individual school sites to have much more budgetary discretion than was now the case in his district. Not only that, they wanted a new financial infor-mation system that would let principals know their budget balances almost instantaneously. Also, they wanted a pupil performance information system that combined school district financial data with school-by-school academic perfor-mance information. Harold could see a train wreck ahead of him. All his past efforts at designing and polishing a perfect centralized system were about to be undone.

At first, all Harold could do was think of questions—hundreds of questions. Who would teach the principals about budgeting and accounting? How would school principals ever have time to keep track of all the accounts? Would princi-pals now need additional clerical staff at their schools, and how much would that cost the district? What about teacher salaries, were they to be determined now at the school site? What was the consequence of school site budgeting for collective bargaining? Who would manage the fringe benefits for each employee? Would schools order their own supplies? What about utility bills, would each school pay its own? Who would order food, and would each school now have its own kitchen operation? What about transportation, would there still be a districtwide bus operation? What about his forthcoming comfortable retirement?

The questions went round and round in Harold's mind. After a few days of reflection, however, Harold was feeling better. He had sorted out matters, and he now could begin to see several strategies by which he could cope with his unexpected, unwanted, and unaccustomed new assignment.

Harold thought that he might request his crack purchasing department to identify some off-the-shelf software packages that just might do exactly what his board and superintendent wanted. Surely, he was not the first business manager in the nation to face this challenge. There must be packaged programs already designed that he could either purchase or adapt to his district's needs.

His chief purchasing agent was receptive to Harold's request for help and said that he would get right on the matter. However, he asked Harold to provide him with a memo that specified the performance expectations for the new software. Harold thought that it might take a great deal of time to comply with such specifications, and could see that this would be a complicated task.

Harold thought some more. If he was going to have to write a set of performance specifications, then why not contract out for the development of the software, staff training, and other pieces of the puzzle? He could invite bids from private-sector firms and ask them to design the new budgeting, accounting, and information systems so as to perfectly fit his district's needs.

Then Harold thought even more. If he was going to have to specify all the performance ends the new systems would accomplish, why not rely upon an in-house design team and have his own school district personnel craft the new system? This way, district personnel could have the system they wanted, tailored to their tastes, at less cost than would otherwise be the case, and, finally, personnel might even be able, after working out the bugs, to market the system and make money for their district.

After a phone conversation with a business manager in a similar sized district nearby, Harold had another idea. What about bundling together several districts of similar size and complexity and form a consortium that might contract for the design and implementation of the new software needed to manage a decentralized or school-based budget system? This way, his district could fulfill its needs, and share the cost in the process.

Of course, Harold thought of a fifth option: he could retire now.

For Discussion

1. How should Harold proceed to ensure that his district has a school-based budgeting system that is effective and meets the board's and superintendent's expectations?

📁 CASE 5

Overcoming Fiscal Failures and Facing Future Challenges

North Harbor, a large midwestern city, had gained two new residents. One was Dr. Mark Turner, the new CEO of the North Harbor School District. His business manager, Howard Tremble, accompanied Superintendent Turner to his new position. They had been a team for the past ten years, having successfully cooperated to transform their former district into a managerially efficient and instructionally successful showplace. Now, they were challenged by North Harbor.

During the nineteenth-century Industrial Revolution, North Harbor became a manufacturing center bolstered immensely by its fortuitous location on a large waterway and as the hub of a vast railway network. During the prior period of heavy manufacturing prosperity, the city benefited from philanthropic donations in art and cultural institutions. Modern-day business in the city is dominated by service industries, including law, financial services, transport, health care, and insurance sectors. Still, there continues a strong philanthropic culture. Also, the city's leaders continue to take active roles in striving to improve the economy and the culture, including the schools.

The blue-collar foundation of the North Harbor workforce has increasingly found it hard to maintain employment. The city's manufacturing base continues to go offshore and local workers routinely face plant shutdowns and layoffs. This has led to high levels of poverty, rendering the once prosperous North Harbor into one of the poorest cities in the nation. Middle-class families, mainly of European descent, have largely abandoned city life for the suburbs. Despite the presence of three high-quality institutions of higher education, local area college graduates are searching farther and farther from home to find jobs and start their careers—leading to what many city leaders have labeled the North Harbor brain drain. These factors have threatened an economic and population decline in the city.

North Harbor Mayor Thomas Washington hired Superintendent Turner and his business manager, Howard Tremble. For his work, Dr. Turner was to receive an annual salary of $350,000, and Tremble was to be paid $250,000. The two men were an expensive package, and the community had never before been so generous. From the beginning, the two new hires were aware of the challenges presented by the embattled school district. Of course, both Turner and Tremble also realized that their high remuneration elevated the expectations held for their performance.

Turner and Tremble came to North Harbor after being instrumental in the turn around of Glass School District. Glass School District was comprised of 30,000 students in 56 schools. Prior to being a district superintendent, Dr. Turner was an assistant principal and high school teacher. His three major initiatives while with Glass School District were creating charter schools, increasing parental involvement, and forging business ties. In all of these endeavors, business manager Tremble was his partner. Whereas Turner handled the external relations, political dynamics, and community outreach, Tremble ensured that the internal operations of the district were fiscally sound and managerially advanced. They were a good team.

Under Dr. Turner's leadership, three alternative schools were formed in Glass City. One school enrolled returning dropouts; another accepted parenting or pregnant teenagers, and the third took in students who were chronically truant, frequently suspended, or had histories of law-related problems. The curriculum of this later school is Internet based, and its online capacities allow students to work from nonschool locations. Dr. Turner was able to negotiate an agreement with the teachers' union to create new job descriptions that included flexible work schedules and staff selection based on interviews rather than seniority.

In Turner and Tremble's last year in Glass, over $3 million was collected from sponsorships and management fees from the three charter schools. Two years after the schools opened their doors, the district showed significant increases in graduation and attendance rates.

On the parental involvement front, Turner created a district-level Parent Congress. This was a self-elected group of parents from throughout the district that met once a month with the superintendent to discuss policy issues. Turner also created paid positions for parent involvement coordinators to foster involvement. These coordinators were successful in creating tutoring and after-school programs. Based on survey data, the parents felt that they played an important role in the educational process, a feeling that was missing prior to Dr. Turner's initiatives.

As business manager in Glass, Tremble had created a financial oversight committee of corporate experts in budgeting and finance to improve the district's finances. This committee was instrumental in creating a sound fiscal policy. The committee kept the public abreast of the district's financial picture by providing detailed economic information. During Tremble's tenure as business manager, Glass voters turned down three citywide tax issues, but passed one new levy, four renewals, and one bond issue for schools. This was an amazing accomplishment in a state where 142 of the 220 local tax levies failed during the last election.

The school district Turner and Tremble were taking over had been in turmoil for thirty years. During the 1970s, the city was ravaged by race riots. An area that was once lined by homes owned by some of the wealthiest families in America was turned into a racial war zone. These riots led to a second wave of flight to the suburbs. The city was divided not only by race, but also by geography. The east side of the city and outlying suburbs became home to the "old money" elites. Irish Catholic communities dominated the west side. Those on the east side of the city sent their children to expensive private schools, while those on the west side sent their children to Catholic schools with high-profile athletic programs.

This left North Harbor City Schools with a racially segregated school district with high levels of poverty. Following the race riots, the U.S. District Court found conscious racial segregation in the district and mandated busing to reach acceptable standards of racial equality. This mandate was not lifted until twenty-five years later. Today, the 60,000 students enrolled in North Harbor schools are 70 percent African American, 10 percent Hispanic, and 17 percent white.

From Tremble's viewpoint, the most pressing problem facing the district was financing. As the property values in the city began to drop, beginning in the late 1970s, due to the decline of the manufacturing industry and the flight of middle-class homeowners, the school district found itself with a negative cash balance. Cuts began in 1990, resulting in a survey that found 70 percent of teachers were short of textbooks and teaching materials. In 1992 the state provided a $75 million loan to balance a projected deficit. With the aid of the state legislature, the district was able to avoid receivership.

By 1993, however, the district was facing a $51 million deficit and had cut 150 teachers, and 150 nonteaching staff, including 23 assistant principals. Eleven schools were closed in 1995 due to more budget deficits. The financial picture of the district became even bleaker in 1996. Faced with a $152 million debt, the state auditor placed the district in fiscal emergency. This status put the schools under state control. The district remained under state control until 1998 when the state gave control to the mayor after his determined effort in persuading voters to pass a 13.5-mill operating levy. In 2001 voters passed a $335 million bond issue and ongoing maintenance levy. However, since 2001, five operating levies failed at the ballot box, including two last years. An operating levy has not passed since 1998.

In December 2001 the five-year budget forecast called for a yearly increase of 4 percent over the previous year's budget. The actual budget for 2006 was $558 million, a 3 percent increase over the 1999 budget. In order to operate the district on the money available, the district made $35 million in staff cuts and closed nine schools. At the current budget level, the spending per student is $11,000. This is well above the state median of $8,500. The voters appear to understand the difficulties facing the district, but they seem to lack confidence in the management.

North Harbor city schools have the only appointed school board in the state. As part of the 1998 agreement giving control of the district to the city, the mayor was given the power to appoint a nine-member school board and a chief operating officer. The board, once known for its unity and solidarity, has become divided over the past two years. Last year the board was rocked by three scandals. First, the information released to the state regarding school transportation grossly overstated district bus use. The state uses this information to reimburse school districts for transportation costs. Second, the district released inaccurate attendance figures that overstated attendance by 18 percent. Finally, in June, local media broadcast a video of city employees throwing away thousands of classroom books from a warehouse that was being rented by the district. Many of those books were new or had seen very little use in the classroom. An inventory of the books was not uncovered. The board failed to take responsibility for these problems instead pushing blame on the school administration. Little has been done to increase board oversight in the district.

The structure of the board has not changed since 1998. The initial board decided to forgo committees, and that system has continued. Nationally, most school boards with districts similar in size to North Harbor have permanent committees to deal with specific issues. North Harbor's system has proven to be ineffective, especially in a district that has a half-billion dollar operating budget, a billion dollars in school buildings, and a large annual maintenance budget. As one city councilman stated, "As the board currently functions it's hard for members to provide the oversight needed. I sit there and look at this and say why would anybody want to be on this board?" Recently, the city elected a new mayor who campaigned with the promise to make education his top priority. It was his influence that brought Turner and Tremble to North Harbor.

Eighty percent of North Harbor's students are economically disadvantaged and 60 percent reside in single-parent homes. Budget cuts have increased student-teacher ratios. Teachers report class sizes of thirty-five students at the middle and high school levels. The reported student-to-teacher ratios at the elementary school level is 18 to 1, but teachers say the average class size is about twenty-six students. On the state achievement tests, beginning in the third grade and administered every year thereafter at the elementary and middle school levels, the district failed to meet the state standard of having 75 percent of the students at or above the proficient level in reading and math. In reading, the percentage stands near 50 percent at all grades and has declined when compared to prior years' results. The results in mathematics are even worse. By the eighth grade, only 31 percent of North Harbor students are scoring in the proficient range. The high school graduation rate is 50 percent and the attendance rate is 85 percent. Both of these numbers have improved over the past four years under the leadership of the former CEO, but are once again sliding, as the school board has eliminated funding for many of the programs the former CEO developed.

The schools are plagued by violence, and there is a police presence in five district high schools. Last year two brawls broke out among parents at two district elementary schools, two students were involved in shootings in school zones, and gang activity increased. Many sports programs have been cut as well as after-school programs. A growing parent group is petitioning for a voucher program in the city, citing failing schools that are not providing their children with a safe and educational environment in which to learn.

The district is finding it hard to fill teaching vacancies and blames the city residency requirement as part of the problem. In North Harbor, people must reside in the city in order to work for the city. The city is contemplating lifting the residency requirement, but opponents fear that by lifting the law the city will suffer as city employees flee to the suburbs. Studies show the city may see a 10 percent population decline if the residency law is lifted.

Dr. Turner and business manager Tremble are faced with the following problems that need to be addressed:

- How can the district increase its economic efficiency while meeting the needs of the students?
- What strategies can be employed to develop and to improve the districts public image?
- Are there governance issues within the district that lead to inefficiency and a lack of accountability? How can these be remedied?

For Discussion

1. Why turn the schools over to the mayor? Will that likely solve any of North Harbor's school problems?

2. What, if anything, should be done about the school board?
3. Should Turner and Tremble always present themselves as a team or is that a mistake? What happens to accountability when there is a team?
4. Which problem should be addressed first—fiscal insolvency, community confidence, or academic failure?

 CASE 6

Determining What a District Continually Needs to Know about Itself

Hilao Bama had recently ascended to the position of chief business officer for her K–12 public school district. She had been a high school computer science and business teacher in the district for a number of years, and then she made the transition to, and, subsequently, had been appointed, the head of the district's purchasing department. Following receipt of an executive MBA from a local public university she rose rapidly through the district's business administrative ranks, and after a decade in the business office was selected to be its chief.

Hilao's job was a big one. The expanding district already enrolled more than 75,000 students in 130 individual schools and had an annual operating budget approaching $750 million. In addition, thanks to a publicly approved building program, Hilao also had to oversee almost $300 million in capital construction budgets. Most private-sector executives with a similar span of responsibility would have been paid $200,000 or more annually. Hilao received $125,000. She knew she could make more in the private sector, but she liked her job, got along well with the superintendent and board, and liked the city in which she worked. She was ambitious, but it was tempered by her pleasure with her current job and her admiration for the people with whom she regularly interacted at work.

Hilao had studied a number of private-sector management books when she was enrolled in her executive MBA program. The ideas of Collins, Senge, Peters and Waterman, Demming, and Jack Welsh were all well known to her. She had synthesized their wisdom and understood where their counsel was and was not appropriate for a public school district. This wide reading and assimilation provided her with confidence to do her job, and she engaged easily and effectively with others—both those for whom she worked and those who worked for her.

Hilao was also well informed regarding technology and was already engaged in updating the district's administrative uses of technology, including payroll, data processing, personnel records, purchasing, and school-based budgeting.

At this time the superintendent and his cabinet provided Hilao with a new and daunting challenge. They wanted a complete overhaul and upgrade of the district's data system and had requested that she oversee the administrative team responsible for this major redesign. Hilao liked challenges, and this was a big one. However, there was little in her practical past or academic training that prepared her for this new set of expectations. As she mulled over her new assignment, these are the preliminary questions she scribbled on her pad:

- Should the district regard individual students, teachers, departments, schools, or programs as the fundamental unit or units around which to design a district-wide data system?
- What kinds of information regarding students, teachers, schools, achievement, and resources would the district routinely need to collect and from whom?
- At what center of gravity administratively should the district's data system be managed—from the business or from the academic side of the house?
- What security issues would have to be resolved when moving to a district-wide database that linked resources, personnel, and performance? Who would have access and under what conditions?
- Does any software already exist upon which the district might graft its individual needs?
- Should the district strive to solve these issues by itself or as part of a consortium of similar districts?

For Discussion

1. Did Hilao write down the correct set of initial questions? If not, what would you add or subtract?
2. How should Hilao and her information system design team strive to answer these initial questions?

Summary

This chapter presents six varying cases, all of which have consequences for business administration, school governance, accountability, and education generally. The cases display the new mode of school business. They make clear that business officials no longer have the luxury of distancing themselves from the overall operation of a school district. In the twenty-first century, school operation covers every facet of the educational endeavor—personnel, finances, management, facilities, debt service, transportation, risk management, food service—and continually touches upon issues related to policy, instruction, and community engagement.

The remainder of this book will repeatedly make reference to one or more of these cases.

CHAPTER TWO

The Rapidly Evolving World and the Problems It Presents for School Business Officials

■ INTRODUCTION

Once, the widely promulgated image of school business officials was that they occupied some dreary alcove of a remote administration building, daily donning their sleeve garters and green eyeshades, and slavishly engaging in indescribably tedious efforts to reconcile financial accounts and reschedule buses. This perspective is no longer accurate.

LEARNING OBJECTIVES

In this chapter a reader will learn about:

- An interconnected and rapidly changing set of societal conditions that serve as the current context within which school business officials must operate.
- Intensified public expectations for school and student academic performance.
- Technical uncertainty regarding instruction and education policy that impedes the capacity of schools to achieve added academic progress for their students.
- Societally imposed conditions deeply constraining the economic efficiency of modern school operation.
- Education reform strategies, to which school business leaders can contribute, holding the prospect of resolving efficiency and effectiveness challenges.
- The necessity of a modern school business official serving as an integral part of an effective leadership team, all components of which are necessary to overcome challenges schools now face.

In a modern school district, the business side is the supportive partner of the instructional side of the endeavor. An instructional decision invariably has financial and other business implications. Reciprocally, many business decisions regarding matters such as workforce size, remuneration, facility design, and operational patterns have consequences for instruction. An effective educational system demands an integrated man-agement, a team approach. The school business official is an integral part of that team.

Because of the new complexity of educational institutions, roles for school business officials have evolved into some of the most vexing jobs in educational administration. There now are more and more intense operational challenges facing school business officials and many of these challenges contribute to conflicting expectations for the role.

Playing in Traffic

School business officials, like the chief executive officer superintendents to whom they typically report, no longer have the luxury of retreating into a back office, hiding behind stacks of financial report and computer printouts, and claiming that they are responsible only for buses running on schedule, accounts being balanced, and paychecks being issued. Schooling is now too important, too public, too costly, too complicated, and the challenges too large for school business officials to be absolved from the rough and tumble of political conflict, fiscal stringency, performance pressures, and fundamental challenges involved in operating modern school systems. Stakes are intensifying, accountability is ever more complicated, enrollments are expanding, litigious threats are ever more present, stress is mounting, and institutional personnel problems are evermore prevalent. School leaders more than ever before must now play in traffic. This can be dangerous; it also can be exhilarating.

This book accepts as a given that the school business role has evolved into an unusually dynamic undertaking. The book's principal purpose is to prepare business officials to play a productive role as part of an administrative team capable of propelling student learning further and using resources even more wisely. This chapter contributes to this objective by explaining the ever-evolving societal context in which schools now operate, the elevated expectations for school and student performance, the externally imposed impediments to greater efficiency and effectiveness, and the system reforms that, if adopted, would enable schools to be better managed. In the process, this chapter offers a generalized view of modern organizational leadership and emphasizes the contributions of school business in fulfilling these leadership requirements.

Society has substantially elevated its expectations for schools. No longer is the United States satisfied with fully educating only a slender proportion of its students. Virtually every child is now expected to receive a full education. However, while performance expectations have been ratcheted up to historically unprecedented heights, the instructional technologies available to achieve these new goals continue to lag badly. In fact, little regarding public school pedagogy has changed since the nineteenth century.

Thus, the vexing situation now facing modern school business officials has come into existence. They must assist their organization in meeting vastly expanded performance goals while having little technical knowledge regarding instruction or other modern means by which such tasks can happen. This complex situation is rendered all the more daunting by society's hydraulic insistence that schools be operated in an economically efficient manner.

Fortunately, for fear that readers will learn of these challenging conditions and abandon aspirations to enter or remain in the school business field, there are means by which these problems can be surmounted. One of the principal purposes of this book is to explicate these change strategies. For all its challenges, however, participating in the business operation of modern schools can be quite rewarding materially and fulfilling personally.

■ THE EVOLVING SOCIETAL CONTEXT OF SCHOOLING

Modern microchip and transportation technologies have vastly altered the physical and lifestyle landscape of most of the world. Today, the only constant prospect facing a professional educator is sustained societal change. Technological innovations, economic transformations, means of communication, and media strategies have altered interpersonal dynamics, workforce patterns, employment requirements, product and service marketing, political alignments, health patterns, and material surroundings. Workforce changes have triggered different expectations for parents and a vast expansion of external childcare arrangements.

Interestingly, however, the worldwide technological revolution has imposed far greater workplace change on most sectors of the economy than it has for education. Professional educators have been cushioned from technological change, intensified economic competition, and dramatic workplace dislocations. This is not to say that schools are altogether escaping the consequences of modernity; they certainly are not. Witness the expanded range of services that schools now offer to assist parents, including most mothers, who now work outside the household. For example, schools now routinely offer breakfast and lunch to students.

Still, the core function of schooling, instruction, has changed little in response to this technological revolution occurring outside of schools in the larger society. However, this is a condition that seemingly cannot last long.

Government has been called on to intervene, to mitigate many of the dislocations and transition difficulties accompanying social and economic changes (e.g., Social Security, minimum wages, Medicare, pension protection, housing subsidies, and job training). Nevertheless, at the same time, antigovernment sentiment cyclically comes to the surface. All the above interactions are magnified by the lens of constant terrorist threats to physical and national well-being, privacy invasions, and restrictions of personal liberties. Seldom has the earth been so characterized by extremes of wealth, health, material comfort, and religious divisiveness.

Many varied and often conflicting social and economic programs have been proposed to ameliorate these uncertain and worrisome conditions. Public schools have not only been the setting for many of these problems, but also the proposed agency of solution. These economic, social, and material ups and downs have generally had the effect of intensifying expectation for schools, both instructionally and socially. America wants added amounts of academic achievement and simultaneously expects schools to supply many more services once supplied by families and communities.

In the News

Nearly a quarter-million city students will receive super-sized report cards this year—stuffed with details on their level of fitness, officials said yesterday. The evaluations, known as fitnessgrams, are based on tests of strength, endurance and flexibility and determine whether a student is in the "healthy fitness zone."

Roughly 235,000 students in more than 600 elementary schools and 40 middle schools took the tests this year, and officials said the program would expand to at least 200 more middle schools next year. Students do not receive letter grades corresponding to their fitness level but rather a two-page report with such recommendations as "Try to play active games, sports or other activities you enjoy a total of 60 minutes each day."

The reports are New York City's latest weapon in the battle of the bulge among school children—one in four of whom is considered obese. The tests measure body-mass index, the number of sit-ups and push-ups a student can do and jogging ability, among other things.

The fitnessgram is the Education Department Office of Physical Education's answer to the sort of complex tracking systems that the agency has implemented in other areas, most notably academic achievement. Schools Chancellor Joel Klein said fitnessgrams have the potential to "revolutionize" the way the city looks at physical education. "We even are able to correlate our students' physical health to their performance in class and on tests and to the neighborhoods they come from," Klein said. "It's a tracking system, and, as you know, I think data matters."

Klein announced the program, which began in 100 schools two years ago. "It's good for your body, and it's a lot of fun," said fourth-grader Carol Yu, 10, one of just two students who did not drop out of a jogging exercise from fatigue.

A 2003 City Council report found that half of all city elementary schools have no playgrounds and 94 percent of all schools have no athletic fields. Another 18 percent don't have gyms, and scores of schools do not have phys-ed instructors—although the DOE could not provide a count yesterday. Lori Benson, the DOE's director of physical education, said the number of phys-ed teachers has climbed steadily and would continue to grow with the introduction of fitnessgrams.

From: Andreatta, D. (2006, June 23). "Fitness report—Schools 'lean' on big apple students." *The New York Post*, p. 19. Excerpts of the *New York Post* were reprinted as a courtesy of the New York Post.

Public education has not always adjusted adroitly to these expanded expectations. Criticisms have provoked sustained pressures for school reform. Reform proposals have included increasing parent choice in selection of schools both within and among school districts, and within the public and private sectors of school operation, increasing rewards for "successful" schools, decreasing the "micromanagement" of schools by state and local district bureaucracies, empowering teachers to make more instructional decisions, decentralizing policymaking and administration to individual school buildings or subdistricts, redefining standards for teacher and administrator certification, and proposals to pay teachers and administrators for increases in student academic achievement.

In this era of ceaseless criticism and sustained political pressure for education reform, teachers, as well as administrators, school board members, and the community at large often ask each other whether they are part of the problem or part of the solution. To exercise a leadership role, school business administrators need to ask themselves the same question. In order to respond, one must explore and understand several general perspectives of school business administration: the evolving set of intensified educational expectations and the very nature of schooling itself.

In the News

Who Americans Are and What They Do, in Census Data

Americans drank more than 23 gallons of bottled water per person in 2004—about 10 times as much as in 1980. We consumed more than twice as much high fructose corn syrup per person as in 1980 and remained the fattest inhabitants of the planet, although Mexicans, Australians, Greeks, New Zealanders and Britons are not too far behind.

At the same time, Americans spent more of their lives than ever—about eight-and-a-half hours a day—watching television, using computers, listening to the radio, going to the movies or reading.

This eclectic portrait of the American people is drawn from the 1,376 tables in the Census Bureau's 2007 Statistical Abstract of the United States, the annual feast for number crunchers that is being served up by the federal government today.

For the first time, the abstract quantifies same-sex sexual contacts (6 percent of men and 11.2 percent of women say they have had them) and learning disabilities (among population groups, American Indians were most likely to have been told that they have them).

The abstract reveals that the floor space in new private one-family homes has expanded to 2,227 square feet in 2005 from 1,905 square feet in 1990. Americans are getting fatter, but now drink more bottled water per person than beer.

Taller, too. More than 24 percent of Americans in their 70s are shorter than 5-foot-6. Only 10 percent of people in their 20s are.

More people are injured by wheelchairs than by lawnmowers, the abstract reports. Bicycles are involved in more accidents than any other consumer product, but beds rank a close second.

Most of the statistical tables, which come from a variety of government and other sources, are presented raw, without caveats; and because the abstract is so concrete, the statistics can suggest false precision. The table of consumer products involved in injuries does not explain, for example, that one reason nearly as many injuries involve beds as bicycles is that more people use beds.

With medical costs rising, more people said they pray for their health than invest in every form of alternative medicine or therapy combined, the abstract reports.

Adolescents and adults now spend, on average, more than 64 days a year watching television, 41 days listening to the radio and a little over a week using the Internet. Among adults, 97 million Internet users sought news online last year, 92 million bought a product, 91 million made a travel reservation, 16 million used a social or professional networking site, and 13 million created a blog.

"The demand for information and entertainment seems almost insatiable," said James P. Rutherfurd, executive vice president of Veronis Suhler Stevenson, the media investment firm whose research the Census Bureau cited.

Mr. Rutherfurd said time spent with such media increased to 3,543 hours last year from 3,340 hours in 2000, and is projected to rise to 3,620 hours in 2010. The time spent within each category varied, with less on broadcast television (down to 679 hours in 2005 from 793 hours in 2000) and on reading in general, and more using the Internet (up to 183 hours from 104 hours) and on cable and satellite television.

How does all that listening and watching influence the amount of time Americans spend alone? The census does not measure that, but since 2000 the number of hobby and athletic non-profit associations has risen while the number of labor unions, fraternities and fan clubs has declined.

"The large master trend here is that over the last hundred years, technology has privatized our leisure time," said Robert D. Putnam, a public policy professor at Harvard and author of "Bowling Alone: The Collapse and Revival of American Community."

"The distinctive effect of technology has been to enable us to get entertainment and information while remaining entirely alone," Mr. Putnam said. "That is from many points of view very efficient. I also think it's fundamentally bad because the lack of social contact, the social isolation means that we don't share information and values and outlook that we should."

More Americans were born in 2004 than in any years except 1960 and 1990. Meanwhile, the national divorce rate, 3.7 divorces per 1,000 people, was the lowest since 1970. Among the states, Nevada still claims the highest divorce rate, which slipped to 6.4 per 1,000 in 2004 from 11.4 per 1,000 in 1990, just ahead of Arkansas's rate.

From 2000 to 2005, the number of manufacturing jobs declined nearly 18 percent. Virtually every job category registered decreases except pharmaceuticals. Employment in textile mills fell by 42 percent. The job projected to grow the fastest by 2014 is home health aide.

One thing Americans produce more of is solid waste—4.4 pounds per day, up from 3.7 pounds in 1980.

More than half of American households owned stocks and mutual funds in 2005. The 91 million individuals in those households had a median age of 51 and a median household income of $65,000.

That might help explain a shift in what college freshmen described as their primary personal objectives. In 1970, 79 percent said their goal was developing a meaningful philosophy of life. By 2005, 75 percent said their primary objective was to be financially very well off.

Among graduate students, 27 percent had at least one foreign-born parent. The number of foreign students from India enrolled in American colleges soared to 80,000 in 2005 from 10,000 in 1976.

As recently as 1980, only 12 percent of doctors were women; by 2004, 27 percent were.

In 1970, 33,000 men and 2,000 women earned professional degrees; in 2004, the numbers were 42,000 men and 41,000 women.

■ INTENSIFIED EDUCATIONAL EXPECTATIONS

It is only recently, near the end of the twentieth century with the 1983 publication of *A Nation At Risk*, that all of American public education became concerned with student performance and academic rigor. For most of the United States' 400-year colonial and national history, the nation operated its military, government, commerce, and universities by benefiting from the talents of a slender, educated elite. Before World War II, most students did not attend, and certainly did not graduate from, high school. Still, there were relatively good jobs for those who were not well educated. Johnny could quit school, work on an assembly line, earn sufficiently, marry Mary, and pursue the American dream. This fortuitous blue-collar era, as Peter Drucker, Thomas Friedman, and others have shown, is now over. These comfortable, or at least well-paying, jobs no longer exist, or if they do, they are likely to have been moved offshore.

This manufacturing-based economy worked well, or at least sufficiently, until the last quarter of the twentieth century, when microchip technology and rapid trnsportation flattened the world and rendered national boundaries of far less consequence for purpose of capital movement, commerce, and manufacturing. High-paying jobs for poorly educated workers still exist, but much fewer are located in the United States. The route to material, and possibly other forms of, fulfillment now more than ever necessitates an individual obtaining a good education.

Many American households understand this fundamental economic transformation, and the broader political system has honored their preferences for a more rigorous education system. The 2001 enactment of the No Child Left Behind Act (NCLB) symbolizes this new condition. This federal legislation has altered the centuries-long practice of judging schools by inputs, and now renders student academic performance outcomes important. As outcomes count, then inquiry in search of means for elevating outcomes also becomes important. A demand has recently been constructed for rigorous research. This is new, but it is still frustrating because the process of conducting serious educational research is only now starting and the results are still slender.

Whereas needed research about instruction and education policy has been slow in developing, the nation has nevertheless moved forward in elevating learning expectations. These heightened expectations are represented in the learning standards that have been established in almost all states. Formal learning standards serve many purposes. They provide a base on which statewide standardized assessment systems can be designed. They are part of accountability frameworks. They also contribute to the education system's eventual ability to undertake serious research regarding what works.

In addition to learning standards, most states have elevated their high school graduation requirements, reduced the number of course electives, and rendered college admission more selective. American schooling expectations are now far more rigorous for more students than in the past. However, that does not mean that every facet of society has marched in unison toward better education systems. There remain many components of schooling that are historic legacies and are comprised of anachronistic requirements imposed by the larger society upon the efficient operation of schools.

■ PUBLIC SCHOOLS "SYSTEMIC INEFFICIENCIES"

School business officials are expected to accommodate to the aforementioned new rigor, guarantee that the management- and business-related facets of a school district and school operation are undertaken to high professional standards, and ensure that instructional systems operate efficiently. This is the perfect storm of expectations to which reference was previously made. However, it is this latter expectation, efficient operation, that is the most difficult to meet.

Inefficiency. The education system is notably inefficient. During the last half century, 1950 to 2000, annual per-pupil K–12 spending in the United States increased from $2,107 to $10,054. This calculation is after controlling for inflation. In 2005 annual expenditures on public elementary and secondary education cost taxpayers approximately $454 billion, or about $55 per pupil per day. Meanwhile, the nation's student achievement improved slightly in the early to mid-1990s, and has remained frustratingly stagnant ever since.[1]

Efforts to stem the upward flow of spending, place education on a more productive path, and effectively link school resources to student performance have proven elusive. Instead, increased financial resources continue to flow to schools as a blended product of historical inertia and political pressure. Given this inability to transform resources into education production, government policies have concentrated on inputs, incentives for local communities to construct, operate, and provide equal access to schools. Whereas many issues of education equity have been addressed, policymakers and business officials have been stymied in their quests for greater productivity.

The operation of America's K–12 schooling is one of the few public activities in which governmental resource allocation bears virtually no positive relation to expected outcomes, that is, student performance. Indeed, in many circumstances, state and federal financing schemes perversely perpetuate poor pupil performance; lower achieving schools routinely receive disproportionate added resources.

These incessant spending increases and dysfunctional distributional practices are not a consequence of policymakers and professional educators being stupid, selfish, or slothful. The inability to achieve added productivity is attributable to several conditions, principal of which is technical uncertainty regarding the education production function. As of now, a sufficient amount is simply not known scientifically regarding instruction to render schools capable of powering the levels of student achievement the policy system now seeks.

An All Too Comfortable Conventional Explanation.

In education discourse one frequently hears the lament, "we know how to educate all children effectively, we just lack the (fill in the blanks: money, political will, moral commitment, etc.) to do it."

It is, perhaps, comforting to assert that more money, political will, and so on would be nice to have, but the assertion that the education profession or the policy system knows with certainty what to do to elevate student achievement does not hold water. It is not as if there exists firm knowledge regarding what to do but some oppressive conspiracy of the fully informed refuses to reveal or to pursue productive policies that would facilitate the education ends America wants.

To the contrary, the United States continues to allocate a great deal of public and private money to education in hopes of identifying solutions. Still, no local school district has succeeded in a sustained, coherent, or reproducible manner in closing, or for that matter significantly narrowing, the achievement gap between advantaged and disadvantaged groups. Although some schools have done much better than others, the best that can be said is that, at least for a time, they narrowed the gap but came nowhere near closing it. A semblance of craft knowledge may exist about how to make a little difference in the short run. However, what is not known is how to eliminate the differences in learning (and in consequent life outcomes) between economically advantaged and disadvantaged children, especially when economic disadvantage is combined with minority group status and central city or extreme rural residence.

Examples of at least partially successful programs, media stories, single-shot case studies, and anecdotes about poor and minority children who perform as well as the most advantaged students, suggest that the system can do better. However, that is not the same thing as systematically knowing how to do better. American education is in a position like primitive physicians who knew that some people recover from a disease that is usually fatal; thus, knew that the disease was survivable, but did not know by what mechanism.

Public education is not well designed for solving new and unfamiliar problems, such as how to educate a constantly changing and disadvantaged urban and rural population. No one knows how much it costs to surmount this challenge or how best to allocate resources effectively. The point of the following section is to illustrate why answers to these questions are not known now.

Why So Little Is Known

The fundamental answer to the preceding question is that *school systems are characterized by stability not adaptability*, and so are unable to adopt the classic problem-solving approach that Americans pursue when they want to address a challenge like how to go to the moon or how to conquer cancer. The existing policy and operating system for education render it difficult to distinguish the effective from the ineffective. Here is an illustrative list of impediments.

Allowing Innovation at a Micro Scale but Resisting Widespread Implementation of Systemwide Change. Teachers and principals are constantly experimenting with new ideas in their schools and classrooms. Although some of these experiments might be quirky or self-indulgent, some are probably smart and worth spreading. However, there is no ready method for identifying these innovations, assessing their value, transmitting their results to others, or combining several small ones into a broader innovation that might constitute a more productive way of teaching a whole course or grade level.

Others in the same localities—the school a few blocks away, the teacher in the next classroom, the school board—have few, if any, incentives to explore what is effective and imitate it. Teacher union leader Roger Erskine labeled this process "random acts of innovation." Former Xerox CEO David Kearns asserted the same argument when he founded the New American Schools Development Corporation, a $150 million nonprofit initiative to develop new designs for urban schools. He later discovered that innovative ideas were not sufficient: existing public education structures and practices frequently can bend with new school designs, absorbing their innocuous parts, rejecting what is uncomfortable or disconcerting, and resiliently returning to the status quo ante.

Teachers' isolation from one another is one factor retarding the spread of innovation, but other sectors of the economy (e.g., medicine) have overcome similar isolation. These sectors have done so by institutionalizing the search for new ideas, formally testing the most promising, and aggressively spreading information about success. The whole academic medical establishment exists for this purpose, as do the knowledge management mechanisms inside innovative companies such as 3M. Precious few have this innovation and dissemination assignment in public education.

Resisting Innovations that Involve Trade-Offs between Labor and Capital. The idea of education as a craft activity with a teacher directly instructing a group of students is firmly entrenched in folklore, law, and policy. State laws controlling class size and teacher licensing ensure that the lion's share of spending will be on salaries, and limit the amounts of money that can be spent on new instructional materials and other resources. Teacher hiring and compensation generally consume spending increases. Purchases of technology are possible only at the margin, as add-ons to existing budgets. As a result, even vendors of new instructional methods carefully avoid suggesting fewer teachers could do the same work or that funds allocated to salaries could be deployed differently. These restrictions limit what can be spent on new ideas and ensure that innovations will be constrained financially and by teachers' workstyle preferences. School business officials will routinely find themselves subjected to pressures to preserve the status quo and eschew the novel.

Providing the Same Funding and Rewards for Unproductive as for Productive Activities. Until recently, public schools were presumed permanent, regardless of whether or not children assigned to them learned. Standards-based reform initiatives, including the NCLB, have at least raised the possibility that unproductive schools could be punished and productive ones rewarded. However, few states or localities have determined how to do this. School districts have not created the databases on which such decisions can accurately be made, and they are still constrained by politics and tenure laws from making purely performance-contingent decisions. When it comes to particular programs, districts are similarly ill equipped to measure effectiveness (not to mention cost-effectiveness), or act on performance data. Although programs come and go and the stocks of schools in a particular locality change over time, transitions are caused more by funding availability, population shifts, and fashion than by systematic judgments regarding a school's effectiveness.

In public education, flows of people and money are molasses-like slow and sticky, and movements are seldom driven by the search for higher performance. Tenure and licensing requirements ensure heavy spending on permanent staff, and collective bargaining agreements and union political dynamics facilitate the preferences of senior teachers and shape how funding is distributed within a district. The people most likely to seek more effective uses of finances and human resources—school principals and within-school department heads, and school business officials—do not fully control funds or have much to say about who is employed. Although states fund school districts on a per-pupil basis, the pupil–dollar link is broken at the district level, where money is allocated to programs and staff categories, rather than to units whose productivity can be measured. Moreover, families in most districts have little say over schools and programs to which their children will be assigned; even when parents can choose, issues of racial balance and enrollment capacity often constrain movement.

Remaining Ideologically Resistant to Experimentation. Education historians routinely chronicle the faddish waves that wash across the landscape of American schooling. Books such as David Tyack's *The One Best System*, Larry Cuban's *Tinkering Toward Utopia*, or Raymond Callahan's *The Cult of Efficiency* make clear that many of the fundamental activities and operating conditions characterizing our present-day schools are a product of forceful advocacy, but seldom a result of systematic empirical research.

One does not have to bank upon historic hoaxes such as phrenology, efforts to convert left-handed students to right-handed practices, left/right brain instructional strategies, and

Frederick Taylor's "scientific management" to make the argument. Within the lifetime of many readers of this chapter, contemporary schools have been subjected to unproven, unproductive, unsustainable, costly, and sometimes harmful practices such as Classrooms Without Walls, SMSG Mathematics, Individually Proscribed Instruction, the "Sixty-Five Percent Solution," Self-Esteem Management, and small school and school district consolidation.

In the early part of the twentieth century, during the Progressive Era, reformers strove mightily to insulate schools from the alleged evils of excessive partisan politics. School boards in big cities became appointed. Where elections were retained, school board positions were rendered nonpartisan and elections were held off cycle. Ironically, now, at the beginning of the twenty-first century, mayoral takeover of public schools is seen by some as a panacea for solving urban school problems.

In the same time frame, the number of America's school districts has been reduced from 127,000 to the approximate 14,000 that characterize the early twenty-first-century governance landscape. The principal argument for such dramatic consolidation was that small schools were economically inefficient and denied students the full curricula offering of larger schools. In the 1960s, former Harvard president James Bryant Conant championed larger high schools, attributing the nation's low levels of academic achievement to diseconomies of high school scale. Now, the Bill and Melinda Gates Foundation has launched a major national policy initiative to persuade school districts to reduce the size of high schools and render them smaller and more personable. The new label is Small Learning Communities (SLC). The return to yesteryear may be a good idea. However, one senses that the philanthropic foundation sponsors are more advocates than analysts and the SLC idea may succumb to faddism, deservedly or not.

In the News

Shelburne Falls—Governor Mitt Romney and state education leaders are urging the tiniest school systems in Massachusetts to stop clinging to their independence for sentimental reasons and consider merging or sharing resources with other districts. The state officials want to avoid the scenes playing out in schools like Buckland-Shelburne Elementary, where about a third of the classrooms are no longer needed because of declining enrollment and instead used to store basketballs, gym mats, and salmon-breeding tanks.

The 220-student school, which may close at the end of the school year, is a part of the Mohawk Trail Regional School System, one of many school systems fighting to survive as enrollments shrink and operating costs soar. Although it is a regional school system, Mohawk Trail illustrates some inefficiencies the state wants to fix. It serves eight towns, but in a splintered fashion. It serves six towns as the K–12 district, but two others as the seventh through twelfth grade district. Those two towns, which refuse to give up all local control, run their own elementary school district.

Massachusetts has always had small school districts statewide, about a third serve fewer than 1,000 students, but now the Romney administration is taking aim at what seems to be an overly localized system. Earlier this year, Romney recommended cutting about $1.3 million in state funding to 23 school systems, mostly small ones, with large drops in enrollment. Under the governor's proposal, Mohawk Trail would lose nearly $100,000 in state aid next year, partly because its enrollment has continued to decline, from a peak of 1,800 students a decade ago to fewer than 1,500.

Next month, the Office of Educational Quality and Accountability, which reviews school systems for the state, will push the state to find more incentives to get small school systems to consolidate instead of spending millions to run their own administrations.

Key lawmakers have been skeptical of Romney's proposal, saying they doubt legislators would agree to reduce funding for school systems. Many lawmakers also don't like the idea of usurping local control from school districts by forcing consolidation. Towns within a regional school district frequently squabble about school spendings, and a few regional systems have split up.

From: Sacchetti, M., & Vaznis, J. (2006, March 14). "When classes turn tiny." *The Boston Globe*, p. A1. Copyright © 2006 Globe Newspaper Company.

Up, down, round, and round. Education policy and practice seemingly are trapped in a never-ending spiral, moving from one fad to another, and then back. What follows is true, though difficult to believe. One hundred years ago, student homework was widely touted by some education theorists as being bad for students. Indeed, claims were made that homework was injurious to student health, known to trigger disease. As recently as fifty years ago, in 1956, the school board of Santa Cruz, California, banned homework, preventing teachers from making homework assignments. Alfie Kohn and others have recently raised the same flag again. Another recent book now asserts that homework contributes to childhood obesity.[2] In retrospect, such a claim is absurd. But how does education get itself into these predicaments?

This vulnerability to fads persists because intellectual leaders of public education, including superintendents and researchers in central offices and schools of education, resist experimentation by which other fields distinguish more- from less-productive methods.

Educators generally resist the rigorous scientific methods necessary to compare the productivity of one well-defined method against another. To them, it is more important to respect the uniqueness of each student and each teacher than to discipline practice, even temporarily, in order to allow rigorous tests. (Clinical trials, which within medicine both provide evidence on the efficacy of well-defined therapies and allow physicians in practice to blend scientific findings with patient uniqueness, have not been readily accepted in education.) Educators also resist random assignment to alternative treatments, a second requirement for experimentation, on grounds that they cannot expose a child to anything that might be risky. (This precious ethical position seems to assume that there is no risk of harm or failure in whatever treatments to which children are exposed absent a clinical trial.) Taken together these overly rigid positions limit what can be tried and what can be learned.[3]

Consequence of Not Knowing

Engineers, architects, physicians, pharmacists, and scores of other professionals and craft workers such as electricians, pilots, and plumbers routinely are expected to adhere to high standards of research reliance and craft practice. Not to do so places them in substantial professional jeopardy, and exposes them to charges of tort and product liability. Today, for example, an engineering design for a new Tacoma Narrows Bridge would be subjected to careful technical review, and remedies for past aerodynamic and structural mistakes would be incorporated amply into modern designs.

Education policy proposals and classroom innovations are seldom subjected to the same intensity of technical review or held to rigorous standards of scientific evidence. Hence, the vulnerability of education policy and practice is subject to the coming and going of fads.

Illustrating What Is Important but What Is Not Known

Here is an illustrative list of currently unanswered, at least not yet scientifically addressed, but hugely consequential education policies issues:

- What is the nature of effective early childhood education? What long-term effect on academic achievement and other performance dimensions can it have? What are its relative costs and long-term benefits? And how much should be invested in its operation relative to other alternative reforms?
- What is an effective teacher? What training is necessary to prepare an effective teacher? What should state credentialing expectations be to promote effective teacher training and recruitment?
- With what sustained professional development activities should teachers be supplied or mandated to obtain? Who should pay for such activities?
- What is an effective class size, for what grade levels, and for what kinds of students? What is the relative benefit of investing in this treatment compared to other possible investments?
- What is the optimum size of a school? What are the trade-offs between operational economies of scale and individual student engagement? To what degree does school size influence student academic achievement? Does the school configuration or the size and condition of the physical facility itself matter?
- Are there any best or preferred practical means for instructing in mathematics, science, language arts, foreign language, art, and so on?
- What is the role, if any, for instructional supplies and materials? Can technology be deployed to enhance instruction or to dilute the labor-intensive nature of American public schooling?
- What are appropriate performance incentive systems? Should incentives be applied to individuals or to teams? Should incentives encompass administrators? By what means should student achievement or performance be gauged when designing educator incentive systems? What is the optimum mix of professional appraisals and peer judgments relative to empirical performance measures in an educator pay for progress scheme?
- By what means can an education accountability system best be designed? What is an effective governance system? What are the consequences of unfettered or even structured parental choice? What data system can best serve education policy?

■ WHAT TO DO WHILE WAITING FOR SCIENTIFICALLY VALIDATED ANSWERS—AN IMMEDIATELY ACTIONABLE REFORM AGENDA

School leadership teams, including school business officials, do not have the luxury of doing nothing. One cannot wait for next year's scientifically validated answers. There are children to be schooled, textbooks to be ordered, buses to be purchased, and one has to be pragmatic. Nevertheless, keeping the following six school reforms in mind as eventual targets for change will enable business officials to see at what they should aim in the long run in order to render schools more effective and to enable resources to be deployed more wisely.

These recommended reforms, targets for change, are adopted from successful public and private sector organizations with appropriate modifications so as to fit schooling.

Transparent Public Funding. Without public funding, decent education would be beyond the reach of millions of families. The commitment to public funding is based on the widely validated understanding that all Americans, even those who can afford to pay for education on their own, benefit from having a literate electorate and a competent, mobile workforce.

Though nobody can say for sure how much money is required to provide every child an excellent education, it is obvious that very low or erratic funding levels can put the goal of general public education at risk.

Unfortunately, disadvantaged children, and the neighborhoods in which they live, are usually the weakest competitors for centrally controlled resources. School districts, like other government agencies, allocate their funds and attention in response to political pressures. In school districts, this comes from articulate and engaged families seeking the best possible schooling for their children, and senior teachers who expect their loyalty to be rewarded with assignments to the most attractive schools. Because money and experienced teachers are always in short supply, the most influential families and neighborhoods often win in this competition for resources, and the less fortunate ones lose.

The most direct response to politically driven spending distortions is to attach funds to individual pupils, so that all enrolled students will have the same baseline amounts spent on them. A situation where all students in a district benefit from the same level of spending would improve on the current arrangements. However, as subsequent chapters will suggest, the struggle to find effective schools for disadvantaged children almost certainly requires weighted-student funding, to ensure that the neediest get the most.

The rationale for public funding implies more than using tax dollars to build buildings, pay salaries, or offer just one form of instruction even if it is ineffective for many students. It requires support for every child's education, in a way that overcomes poor families' financial disadvantages. As the following section of this chapter illustrates, current methods of supporting public education that attach money to buildings, teachers, transportation, and administrative functions are not traceable to students and hardly meet the lofty goal that initially justified public funding.

Concentration of Resources Near the Student. If public education is to be adaptable—to the distinctive needs of particular children and to promising new models of instruction—it needs flexible resources. It must be possible to spend money differently on different children, and to reallocate spending in ways required by promising new methods of instruction. This implies that decisions about spending should be standardized as little as possible, and controlled by people who know children and are responsible for their learning. It also implies that as little money as possible should be obligated to long-term commitments and fixed expenditures.

Unfortunately, today's public education system is built on substantially different premises. Resources are anything but flexible, due to long-term commitments to buildings, tenured employees, and programs established by national and state legislatures. Money is allocated to programs, for example, vocational education, tutoring, transportation, in-service teacher training, and to salaries. Spending decisions are made by the state or by a school district central office on behalf of all schools. Schools do not receive cash other than small amounts (normally less than $50,000 per year) for supplies, copying, small purchases, and field trips. Schools often cannot choose their own teachers: district officials assign them from a central office to individual schools.

Thus, at the state and federal level, the question is never "how much should we allocate for the education of a student," but rather "how big an appropriation can the supporters of teachers, or vocational education, or computer literacy, swing for [name the interest group] this year?"

A public education system that continually sought to find and use the most effective method for every student would need a dramatically different approach to spending and decision making. To be capable of reallocating funds from less to more productive uses, the system would need to avoid linking funding to specific employees, equipment, or programs. To support adaptation to students' needs, money would have to be controlled in close proximity to the student, by those directly responsible and accountable for providing instruction and attaining results.

These requirements differ sharply from current practice, and meeting them would require changes at every level. States would need either to consolidate all K–12 appropriations into one per-student allocation, or allow districts to combine separate accounts. Districts would also need to consolidate many different accounts, some now mandated by the state and others created for their own purposes,[4] and distribute finances directly to schools. In order to put as many consequential decisions as possible near the student, districts also need to reduce automatic spending on their central offices to a modest amount, just enough to pay for financial administration and management, school performance assessment, and investment in new schools. Districts could also provide optional services and charge fees. The section below on a school-friendly environment will describe the functions of the central office in greater detail.

Strategic Reliance upon Community Resources. People who have been involved intimately with schools serving the most disadvantaged youth know they require more time and money, and a more comprehensive commitment to youth development, than normally attaches to the concept of school. The division between education and social service institutions is yet another barrier that prevents communities from doing all they can to educate their children

Student-based public funding, especially if weighted for student needs, can provide some of the needed extra operating support. If basic state and local support were allocated such that all funds followed children and all students brought exactly the same amount to the school they attended, then categorical program funds could provide extra amounts to support more intense education programs for disadvantaged students. The combination of federal Title I, state categorical programs, and funds for education of the handicapped could support a substantial amount of extra student weighting.

This situation exists in theory, but not in practice. Districts often underfund schools serving disadvantaged children, and then barely bring those schools up to spending equality by adding on state and federal categorical funds. Within districts, the amounts spent on pupils who share a particular characteristic, for example, low-income status, now vary tremendously, depending on which school a child attends. Current practices, which seem to violate the intent of Title I comparability and nonsupplanting requirements, are nonetheless legal due to a loophole that allows districts to ignore differences of higher average salaries paid to teachers serving advantaged pupils.

Schools serving disadvantaged children might well be able to expand their hours and days of student contact if separate social service agencies' youth budgets were combined. This would require as wrenching a change in social services as in education, since it implies that agency funds would be used at the point of delivery by individuals responsible for children's overall development, rather than controlled centrally and used to pay salaries for a fixed set of adult providers. If this could be done, poverty area schools might evolve into charter youth service agencies whose core task is instruction, but which also have other flexible resources. Such schools would then be more like parishes than government agencies, able to draw from a wider array of expertise—and to spend more money—than is available to support their purely instructional roles.

Despite the constant agitation about it, the question "How much spending on public education is enough?" is difficult to answer in the absence of a public education system in which funds from all sources can be used flexibly, ineffective activities must be abandoned, and resources can flow to more effective uses. It probably takes more to educate some children than others. However, it also takes less money to operate a highly efficient system, where virtually all funds are applied directly to instruction and student services, than an inefficient one, where spending is dominated by political and bureaucratic considerations.

Rewards and Sanctions for Performance. If public education is constantly to seek more effective methods of instruction and better matches between children and teaching methods, everyone in the system must face strong performance incentives. Though teachers and administrators all hope their efforts will benefit children, they have other concerns as well—for example, complying with rules, avoiding conflict with coworkers and superiors, working in ways that satisfy themselves, and preserving time and energy for private pursuits. Strong performance incentives do not eliminate these other motives, but they can profoundly affect individuals' priorities.

Educators are neither more nor less dedicated to their work than other professionals—doctors, lawyers, engineers, and so on. In all other professions, pay, job security, work satisfaction, and prestige are strongly linked to performance. The physician who invents a successful new surgical procedure reaps huge rewards professionally and financially. Once a promising new method is developed, other physicians have strong incentives to learn and adopt it: early adopters can also reap financial rewards and those who use outmoded methods risk malpractice claims. Concepts of "best practice" have genuine operational meaning in medicine, law, and other professions. Other professionals face similar performance contingencies: a lot to gain from innovation and a lot to lose from failure to pursue the best.

In other professions, practitioners experience some stress and strain, and some competent people ultimately find they cannot "make it." These negative results are not good in themselves, but they are necessary means to attain intellectually aggressive practice and high overall performance.

Today in public education, most professionals are insulated from strong performance contingencies. Teachers are tenured, often so early in their careers that their full performance potential has never really been developed or demonstrated. Pay is contingent on seniority and completion of coursework that might or might not enhance performance. Choice of workplaces and other privileges are also based on seniority, and tenured teachers, regardless of their pay level, can be terminated only for egregious performance or outrageous behavior. On the other hand, ambitious young people cannot advance ahead of the seniority scale, no matter how hard or brilliantly they work or how scarce their skills. Consequently, concepts of "best practice" have little operational meaning in education, are hard to specify, and, even when discussed, receive little more than lip service.

Above all, even the least productive public schools can count on student enrollment. Free movement of children in search of programs that are effective for them could create strong performance pressures for schools. Choice could also allow educators with strong ideas about how to meet the needs of a particular group of students—particularly at the secondary level where student motivations and needs become diverse—to compete for students and the dollars they bring.

School districts traditionally operate a fixed set of schools, a set that changes only when student populations grow or decline dramatically. Even in localities with extremely low-performing schools, districts invest new money and reshuffle staffs to strengthen existing schools rather than closing weak schools and starting new ones. NCLB is pressing districts to think differently about the status of schools, making any school's existence and right to admit students increasingly contingent on performance.

A public education system designed for constant improvement would make all commitments to individuals and organizations contingent on performance. At a minimum, it would leave room in employment relationships to reward spectacular performers and to develop alternatives to its lowest-performing schools. A school district bent on the highest possible performance would not guarantee anyone a permanent position or insist students remain in a bad school. It would terminate any arrangement for which there was a higher-performing option clearly available. On the other hand, it would be constantly open to new options.

These requirements differ sharply from current practices and would imply profound changes in school district missions and capacities. Instead of making permanent commitments to people and institutions, a district would make contingent commitments, limited in time and renewable only after review. Instead of limiting their own options, such districts would constantly expand them, looking for a better instructional model for a given group of students, a better school leader or contract provider, and a better source of teachers.

As in other fields, this focus on performance would not all come at the expense of incumbent teachers and school leaders. Many would stand out spectacularly and be able to claim better professional opportunities and more pay. Most could adapt to higher expectations; though, as in the case of physicians learning new procedures, it might require an investment of personal time and even money.

Without such an evidence-based orientation, no stakeholders in public education, from school board members, to the teachers in the classroom, can say with confidence that they have done the best possible for the children in their charge.

Openness to New Ideas and People. If it were clear how to provide effective schools for all children, a public education system would have the simple challenge of administering proven models. However, in the face of profound uncertainty, public education needs to be open to many possibilities. Although the teachers and administrators employed by a school represent a significant share of the community's relevant expertise, they do not have all of it. Private schools, museums, youth service centers, arts and music organizations, churches, colleges and universities, and companies that invest heavily in training all have significant expertise and ideas. Surely these will not all be different or better than those available within the traditional school system. But as public education strives to identify and implement new ideas for solving pressing problems, it cannot afford to ignore alternative sources of ideas.

The same is true for teachers and school leaders. In many localities there are as many trained principals and teachers *not* working in the public school system as in it. There are, moreover, people with skills that are rare in the career teaching force (e.g., expertise in physics, laboratory science, higher mathematics, music, dance, and visual arts). Individuals experienced in managing day care centers, private schools, museum educational programs, and other training programs know a good deal about managing instruction and creating a positive environment for students. Professors and management consultants know things about turning around troubled organizations and surviving in a performance-pressured climate that public school employees have had little occasion to learn. A former head of Brooks Brothers Clothier, hired amid budget chaos in St. Louis, Missouri, took just eighteen months to reduce the overall workforce from 7,000 to 5,000 before leaving with the comment that schools are about students and learning, not adults and employment.

Any combination of these skills might produce a school that is excellent for one purpose or another, or create capacities to provide great instruction in particular areas. Public education needs to be open to such people, organizations, and ideas. It can apply the same expectations about performance and respect for public values to such outsiders as to school district careerists, but it would be self-defeating to impose arbitrary limits on what they attempt.

Although it is true that not just anybody can teach or lead a school well, it is also true that current entry requirements for those positions are not guarantees of competence. While these requirements often develop capable people, they also certify people who cannot perform the job, while screening out many who could. Current state teacher and principal licensing requirements protect incumbents and establish education schools as gatekeepers, but their contributions to improved school performance are uneven.

A performance-driven public education system would need the freedom to provide schools with whatever means necessary to improve student outcomes, and to create circumstances conducive to all schools' success. Even the best charter school laws fall short of this requirement, partly because of caps and partly because charter schools usually receive considerably less money per pupil, and fewer in-kind donations from government (e.g., free facilities, state-supported teacher pensions) than do traditional public schools. In effect, charter school operators are told to take it or leave it.

New Data Systems. There are few twenty-first-century operations as outmoded as education data systems. The following vignettes are real. Regrettably, that does not make them right.

Wal-Mart managers routinely know more regarding the location and commercial status of a toy bear manufactured in China, from the original point of purchase manufacturing specifications to the vendor's ocean shipping arrangements, to local store delivery and shelving and time of final placement into a customer's shopping basket than school district administrators know regarding the day-to-day status and school progress of their enrolled students.

A big-city school district is handicapped in participating in a major performance experiment because it cannot specify names and school addresses of its middle school language arts teachers.

Few of America's school principals can specify within 20 percent the total operating budget for their individual school.

This is not the place to put forward a full design for a modern education data system, one that productively could link resources with actions and outcomes. However, it is possible to provide guidelines for such a data system. Here is a set of beginning ideas. A modern education data system should, at a minimum, be consistent with the following illustrative ten commandments:

1. Impose minimal data collection burdens upon contributors, collecting only information useful for guiding either policy or practice.
2. Concentrate on information collection from fundamental operational units, classrooms, departments, schools, and other instructional units.
3. Use individual enrolled pupils as an informational building block.
4. Link an individual student with measures of present and prior academic performance as well as measures of individual SES, race, poverty, attendance, awards, and misbehavior.
5. Reliably link students with present and past assigned classroom teachers or other instructors.
6. Link students with their course and grade transcripts.
7. Disaggregate and apportion actual expenditures to the classroom, department, and school level in categories such as labor (administrator, teacher, specialists, classified salaries, and fringe benefits), supplies, technology, instructional materials, utilities, transport, food, district administration, debt service, district and school indirect costs, rent, consultants, and out-of-classroom activities such as child care and athletics.
8. Account for instructor time by function (reading, physical education, writing), grade level, and subject matter.
9. Extend student records chronologically across school levels, school districts, and into higher education and postsecondary activities.
10. Collect school status characteristic data for each student (e.g., school size, class size, teacher characteristics, peer characteristics).

 CASE 5 REVISITED

Overcoming Fiscal Failures and Facing Future Challenges

The voters in North Harbor School District appear to understand the difficulties facing the district, but they seem to lack confidence in the management. Consider the six school reforms proposed in this chapter. Select those that would help restore the public's confidence in the management. Which should Howard suggest be implemented in the short term (three–twelve months) and which in the long term (two–four years)? Provide a rationale for your choices.

Summary

The preceding six education reforms are not the private preserve of business officials alone. They must be pursued simultaneously at federal, state, and local levels, and, at the local level, it will necessitate the participation of other actors such as school boards and entire administrative teams. Indeed, some parts of the changes will necessitate collective bargaining as well.

However, this complexity illustrates one of this book's major points. Rendering a modern school system effective is not a job for the lone ranger. School business officials must be considered as a part of a larger administrative team. Team members assuredly will have individual roles to play and must be held accountable for relatively unique contributions to the organization's overall well-being. Still, the point is that modern complexity must be addressed by modern business strategies. This translates practically to the individual responsible for the accurate recording and distribution of resources, the school business administrator, being a crucial leadership team member.

Discussion Questions

1. Review the "In the News" article regarding student fitnessgrams. Discuss whether schools should be tracking individual student fitness. Is this practice a violation of a student's privacy? Elaborate on the advantages and disadvantages of such a practice.
2. Consider the multiple roles schools are required to fill in the contemporary education context. To what extent should society rely on schools to address societal concerns such as the physical health of students? Identify your personal beliefs regarding what services schools should or should not be providing and what schools are capable of doing.

Web Resources

National Center for Education Statistics—
    http://nces.ed.gov
United States Department of Education Institute of Education Science—
    http://www.ed.gov/about/offices/list/ies/index.html
United States Department of Education's No Child Left Behind Resource Center—
    http://www.ed.gov/nclb/landing.jhtml?src=pb

Notes

1. Postsecondary education institutions are probably even more inefficient, but that is not the subject of this book.
2. Sara Bennett and Nancy Kalish. (2006). *The case against homework: How homework is hurting our children and what we can do about it.* New York: Crown.
3. The Education Sciences Institute Act, enacted by Congress in 2002, is enormously important in combating educators' reluctance to undertake experiments. The Institute for Education Sciences (IES), established by the act, has made significant strides in

altering the paradigm within which the federal government now finances research. Randomized field trials are now the mode for major federal education research funding.

4. One middle-sized urban district studied by the Center on Reinventing Public Education at the University of Washington in Seattle maintains 200,000 separate financial accounts.

CHAPTER THREE

What School Business Officials Do

■ INTRODUCTION

How can school business officials grapple with the perfect storm of elevated performance expectations, the relative absence of technical know-how regarding instruction, and persistent mandates for efficient school operation? Amid these challenges, how can school business officials also contribute to the development and operation of an evidence-based and continuously improving school organization illustrated with the six reform principles described in Chapter Two?

LEARNING OBJECTIVES

In this chapter a reader will learn about:

- General perspectives regarding twenty-first-century educational administration.
- The historic evolution of the school business official role, including the impact of the scientific management movement and the Progressive Era.
- The functional hierarchy of school business officials' activities, ranging from skilled technician to team player to being part of the cabinet.
- Operations for which business officials are conventionally responsible.
- The business administrator as a component of an administrative team.
- Significance for business officials of a trend toward school site management.
- Consideration of the school business official as strategic planner.
- Alternative school district planning models.

These are the modern day challenges, and these challenges are intensifying the expectations held for school business officials. However, school business officials are not alone in having to make this transition to a different role. Virtually all of educational administration is itself being challenged to adapt a different orientation. The next section describes this new operating perspective for school administration.

■ THE CHANGING CHALLENGE OF EDUCATIONAL ADMINISTRATION

Regardless of precise title or position in the management hierarchy, school officials increasingly are expected to adopt a different orientation. It is an orientation toward outcomes rather than processes. This new perspective involves other features as well. Figure 3.1 below displays the evolutionary trajectory outlook for America's school leaders.

In order to cope with the above-listed educational administrative trends, five leadership perspectives or educational management frames of reference are emerging. These involve: (1) sustained strategic explorations of the external environment; (2) pursuit of internal organizational of management initiatives contributing to effective operation; (3) acting consistent with verified substantive knowledge regarding instruction and education; (4) continually striving through systematic appraisal of trial and error efforts to ascertain what can operate better for one's schools and districts; and (5) an ability to integrate these foregoing terms of reference into a coherent management style.[1]

School business officials are no exception to this set of evolving perspectives. They too will have to engage in a never-ending quest to understand emerging external developments, practice good internal management, continually acquire new knowledge of learning and instruction, undertake measurement and analyses of what they are now trying, and construct a coherent management style. However, a better understanding of future trajectories sometimes stems from examining the past. Thus, what follows is a capsulated history of the school business official role.

Leadership Dimensions and Operational Orientation	Twentieth-Century "Inclusivity" or Equality as Dominant School Policy Objective	Twenty-First-Century School Organizational "Effectiveness" as a Dominant Objective
Leadership outlook	Incremental and tactical	Combining strategic (external) perspectives with internal actions
Dominant organizational consideration	Regulatory compliance	Performance enhancement
Administrative and authority structure	Centralized, hierarchical and bureaucratically specialized	Horizontal, school-centered, distributed decision discretion
Relations and communication with parents and students	Paternalistic and directive	Customer or client orientation to parents
Service provision	Virtual public monopoly	Mixture of public and private
Source of innovation	Central authority	Operating units
Resource allocation decisions	Made centrally	Operating unit discretion
Accountability	Bureaucratic and procedural	Professional and outcome-driven

FIGURE 3.1 Evolution of School Leaders

■ HISTORIC EVOLUTION OF THE SCHOOL BUSINESS FUNCTION

At the beginning of the Republic, business facets of local school operation were directly and personally managed by a board of education or its local government counterpart. When the superintendency initially appeared among large-city school districts in the 1830s and 1840s, and was then reinvented at the end of the nineteenth century, most superintendent appointees were charged only with overseeing instruction within a school district. Even with the superintendency as an accepted professional position, business affairs typically remained under the direct authority of local school boards. The latter recruited, interviewed, and employed teachers, established individual teacher salaries, oversaw building construction and maintenance, and entered into contracts with vendors. They also often took a keen interest in the morality and religiosity of their employees.

At the turn of the twentieth century, as the U.S. population grew and many rural districts were consolidated into larger operating school district units, ever heavier demands were placed on an educational system originally designed for an agrarian society. Industrialization and concomitant urbanization concentrated the population geographically, increased the variety and specialization of skills demanded for workforce participation, and provoked schools to assume broader community and social services functions.

Because of the rapid expansion and the changing character of the educational program, many of the finance and business functions of the school board were gradually relegated to a professional business officer, though that individual was not always subordinate to the superintendent of schools. These were frequently business-oriented administrators who served in a multiple-control or hydra-headed organization; both the superintendent and the business administrator individually reported to the board. Vestiges of historic lay control of fiscal and business matters, though increasingly rare, can sometimes still be seen in the form of school fiscal officers, treasurers, and comptrollers, in tandem with a superintendent-academic reporting directly to school boards.

In the early 1900s considerable interest was generated in "professionalizing" school administration. Professor N.L. Englehart Sr., of Teachers College, Columbia University, was influential in identifying school business administration as a specialized area of general school administration and in designing academic preparation programs for individuals interested in such positions. Englehart's efforts were reinforced by the infusion throughout America's manufacturing sector of the so-called scientific management movement, a product of the efficiency and time and motion studies of industrial engineering pioneer Frederick Taylor. Taylor's ideas were influential beyond the private sector. It was thought at the time that schools too could benefit from the industrial engineering outlook, time and motion mentality, scientific management principles that Taylor espoused.[2]

Simultaneously, in the 1920s, as the school superintendency grew to almost universal institutional acceptance, the function of school business administration gravitated toward and became subordinated to a general superintendent of schools, a Chief Executive Officer (CEO). This migration in authority was assisted by reforms accompanying the Progressive Era when plentiful efforts were undertaken to insulate education and school boards from partisan politics and big city political machines. Gradually, today's unitary management control model, wherein only the superintendent reports directly to the board, became dominant. All other administrators, including the school business administrator, report to the superintendent.

Professionalization among school business administrators has had a second side. As early as 1910 the National Association of Public School Business Officials was formed; later it became the Association of School Business Officials International ASBOINTL. This organization remains vital and aspires to upgrade the performance and professionalism of school business officials. It embraces both education- and business-oriented professionals in the field.

■ CONTEMPORARY SCHOOL BUSINESS ADMINISTRATION FUNCTIONS

What are the essential day-to-day operational functions with which school business officials must grapple?

Administrative Position Vacancy

San Alamito Unified School District
Office of Human Resources

JOB DESCRIPTION: Business Manager

DEFINITION: The Business Manager is responsible for the development and supervision of the fiscal functions for San Alamito Unified School District. The person manages the operations of the business service department, and coordinates and supervises the business service fiscal team.

EXAMPLES OF DUTIES: Supervises, coordinates, and directs the functions of the business services department. Supervises Director of Child Nutrition. Supervises Purchasing Department. Develops, reviews, and analyzes the district's budget. Supervises the balancing and reconciliation of the district's accounting records. Advises district staff in the development of cost-effective business practices. Instructs school personnel and program managers in the development of the budget and accounting systems. Monitors and provides regular, ongoing oversight of the district budget. Assists and advises in the preparation and review of state and federal reports, including interpreting regulations and implementing changes in school finance. Develops and interprets financial and statistical information for the Board of Education, Superintendent, site administrators, and program managers. Serves as chief trainer in budget and business issues as they relate to the district operations. Serves as the liaison for business services with the San Alamito County Office of Education. Provides support to the staff on business software and related computer issues. Performs related duties as required.

EXPERIENCE: Five years' experience working as a fiscal manager in a school district/county office/or other governmental agency; experience with online/real-time technology; experience working with senior management personnel and supervision of staff.

EDUCATION: Minimum required bachelor's degree in accounting, business, or closely related field. Prefer candidates with construction/state building accounting experience and a master's degree.

It is generally accepted that the primary operational function of schools is that of sustaining and extending teaching and learning. It follows then that the general function of educational administration is to stimulate, develop, organize, and implement systems that deliver effective teaching and learning. School business administration, as a subsystem of educational administration, in turn embodies activities that enable teachers, administrators, and policymakers to make the best educational decisions while weighing the business implications. School business administration may not only provide for the most economic purchase of textbooks, but also to do so in terms of the most effective textbooks, given the purposes of those who make these kinds of instructional decisions. Thus, instructional or educational specifications are an integral part of the business decision. Textbook selection also has business implications, because if dollars are spent on a given textbook series, those dollars cannot be spent on other goods or services. These are known as opportunity costs.

Given a finite amount of available resources at any given time, it is important to consider economy, efficiency, effectiveness, and opportunity. School business administration contributes to teaching and learning by providing information and services that involve issues such as:

- What educational needs have business implications?
- What are the nature and cost of feasible alternatives to meet a given educational need?
- What is the most efficient means to provide each alternative?
- What is the cost-effectiveness of each alternative (to what extent does each alternative meet the educational need, and how does this equate to the expenditure involved)?
- What is the relative priority of each expenditure decision to all of the other expenditure decisions in the school system?

In simple form, a concept of the function of school business administration might be described as providing the most effective and efficient business operations for the most effective and efficient educational programs and services in a school system. An operational description of this function is that the school business administration provides and supports:

- A structure in which qualified educational personnel identify and specify program needs.
- Alternative program specifications, services, and materials for these needs.
- Cost-utility or cost-effectiveness analyses of these alternatives, supplying these data to program decision makers.
- A process for procuring or providing appropriate personnel, material, and equipment to implement selected programs as specified, providing these at the least cost.
- Appropriate performance and cost data for evaluation of the selected programs.
- Recommendations for the modification of present programs and policies or proposals for new policies.

This concept of the function of school business administration implies that educational decisions involve two important reciprocal perspectives: program decisions have business implications, and school business decisions have program implications. If a gymnasium roof leak threatens to buckle the floor and funds need to be transferred from a textbook account to the maintenance account, this business decision has implications for instruction. Likewise, if an extra field trip has been approved, this instructional decision has business implications because a bus driver must be hired and added operating costs are incurred.

The concept also implies that nearly all persons in the school system make decisions that contribute to the school business administration function. The function is not the exclusive domain of boards, superintendents, and school business administrators. Teachers, custodians, central office staff members, clerks, and school district fiscal officers also make decisions that have business implications. If their decisions are to approach the optimum, the decision makers should relate their choices to both business and instructional implications.

Below are conventional areas of responsibility for school business administrators:

- Accounting and reporting.
- Budgeting and financial planning.
- Capital fund management.
- Cash management.
- Community relations.
- Construction management.
- Data processing.
- Educational resources management.
- Facilities management.
- Fiscal audits and reports.
- Food services.
- Human resources management.
- Information system implementation and oversight.
- Insurance and risk management.
- Non-certified personnel management.
- Office management.
- Plant operation and maintenance.
- Purchasing.
- Security services for the district.
- Transportation.
- Warehouse and supplies management.
  (Stevenson & Tharpe, 1999, pp. 17–18)

The preceding activities can be disaggregated into even more specific tasks. For example, pupil transportation responsibilities include areas of routing and scheduling, school bus housing, maintenance and repairs, and transportation personnel (which may include recruiting, assignment, and staff development). Accounting and reporting responsibilities can be subdivided into many separate but related tasks. Payroll divisions use accounting, budgeting, and appropriation data, but often are separate given the size and crucial nature of the task. Human resources management may include collective bargaining, fringe benefit management, and oversight of grievance processing.

New and situationally unique tasks have always expanded the conventional responsibilities. Large urban school systems usually organize and staff a division of security personnel. Today nearly all medium-sized school systems employ such personnel or contract with private firms for such services. In many instances, electronic surveillance devices are used rather than the typical night guard, but responsibility for this form of security is frequently assigned to the school business office.

Purchasing and supply management have expanded into specialized tasks. Full-time persons or separate offices are responsible for purchase planning (development of educational specifications) and the purchasing agent functions, warehousing, product testing and evaluation, inventory and control, and so on.

A Good Business Manager Can Save You Money

Across the country, in almost every state, school districts are experiencing a shortage of financial resources. Local taxpayers are refusing to increase local property taxes, state legislatures are refusing to provide additional revenues, and the federal government is attempting to reduce or limit funds for education. There is a growing pressure to make sure that each dollar spent for education is spent astutely. Due to this environment, boards of education face a difficult problem: Where will the dollars come from?

There is no one professional better equipped than the school business manager to help boards of education wisely spend public dollars and find new dollars. Unfortunately, many activities of the school business manager go unnoticed. School board members as well as other school administrators may be unaware of the annual revenue produced each year by a competent school business manager.

Discussed below are some tips for how a business manager can save a school district money or increase revenue, thereby freeing up dollars for additional educational uses. Investing in a school business manager can be one of the smartest moves a school entity can make, as a smooth-functioning school business office can produce revenues far in excess of the cost of the business manager's salary.

- When paying invoices, use as long a grace period as a creditor will grant or take advantage of an early payment discount. Timing a debt issue properly and negotiating appropriate fees may result in a large savings for the school district.
- A properly operated and monitored system can also save a school district dollars in auditors fees and losses due to pilferage and theft.
- Familiarity with current local trends and laws regarding the financing of education can save a school district large sums of money by having the school district prepared and positioned for necessary change.
- Ensuring that grant reports are filed in a timely fashion will ensure funds are received in a timely fashion.
- When a school enters into a construction project, developing a cooperative relationship with an architect who will ensure a wise use of district funds and supervise the work in progress can reduce potential costs.
- Without accurate accounting information, it is impossible to hold individuals responsible for their budgetary decisions.
- Being familiar with the types of insurance for protection from financial loss can save money by not overbuying or duplicating coverage.
- Due to their access and familiarity with payroll information, school business managers serve as a vital part of the employee negotiations team, which may help curtail negotiations costs by reducing the hourly fee of outside consultants.
- Maintaining an accurate portion control system for food services helps to increase profitability or reduce losses.

As this article demonstrates, there are a wide variety of opportunities large and small that can generate money or institute savings. It is only through a better understanding of the functions of the school business manager and the school district business office that school districts will be able to fully realize their revenue potential.

From: Nowakowski, B.C., & Schneider, R. (1996, July). A good business manager can save you money. *School Business Affairs*, 62(7), 43–44, 46–47.

▪ A HIERARCHY OF SCHOOL BUSINESS FUNCTIONS—FROM JOB ENTRY TO LEADER

Because of the widely varying sizes of contemporary American school systems, the complexity of educational programs, historical precedents, and state law, there is considerable variation in the nature of the position that includes the business administration function. In relatively large cities, the position is frequently designated as Assistant or Associate Superintendent in Charge of Business. Other similar titles include Director of Business Affairs, Associate Superintendent for Business Services, Director of Administrative Services, and Administrative Assistant.

Regardless of titles, however, there is a skill or technical capacity hierarchy that characterizes school business official positions.

Technical Contributor. The initial level of skill required for the school business administrator is technical in nature. The school business administrator performs in skill areas such as budget development, purchasing, accounting, warehousing, building maintenance and operation, facility planning and construction, security services, transportation, data and information management, and food services. At this role level, a relatively discrete function is performed. The administrator applies specialized knowledge to responsibilities and problems assigned by the superintendent.

In the technically oriented role level, school business administrators serve as a second set of hands for their superintendents. They act for the superintendent in business affairs and exercise influence over others in the system as a delegate of authority.

Team Player. The second level of skills reflecting the increased professional status of the position is that of a member of a team. At this level, the school business administrator is a specialist among specialists. The task is not only technical; it also necessitates relating to the responsibilities and skills of others in the system. At this level, the administrator is no longer exclusively the agent of the superintendent, but is additionally a coordinate administrator who directly relates his/her functions to that of other administrators. At this level, the school business administrator specifies the business implications of group and individual proposals and decisions. The business administrator advises the board, the superintendent, the central office, and the principals.

Planning Leader. The third level of the school business administrator role is conceptual and strategic. The dominant feature of this role level is participation in planning and policy development and execution. It is important to note the centrality of planning to achieve appropriate policy development and execution. Without ultimate policy goals, planning is an empty concept. Such responsibilities clearly demand well-developed conceptual skills and a capacity to understand strategic planning.

At the conceptual level, the business administrator provides more than consultant help to other administrators. The school business official can begin to enhance the transformational goals to which reference was made in Chapter Two. Here is where the business administrator can assist a school system in rendering its financial decisions transparent, placing resources close to the student, building a modern information system, and so on. In seeking to design and implement such reforms, business managers can become active members of the administrative planning team.

As a planner, the business administrator lends expertise to the team by creating, structuring, leading, and participating in planning the school business administration function and by relating this planning to the several other structures developed by fellow administrators.

As a result of this relationship, the school business administrator is involved in long-range instructional and curriculum planning and is not merely informed after the fact by others of technical consequences flowing from each new program. The business administrator is involved in long-range staff personnel development programs rather than, for example, being instructed to develop alternatives to increasing the personnel budget by 30 percent over a three-year negotiated contract. Planning long-range pupil personnel programs rather than, for example, being given responsibility for establishing shuttle bus service among the district's several school sites during the school day, is a critical aspect of the school business official's role.

■ CONCEPT OF AN ADMINISTRATIVE TEAM

The notion of the administrative team was probably widely established in practice before it attained visibility in the professional and scholarly literature. As implied in the foregoing discussion, teams may be drawn together on many different bases. A superintendent who assumes primary or nearly complete responsibility for planning needs to be surrounded by competent and dedicated technicians. The organization will then appear to be "lean, efficient, and well directed." In one sense, this is analogous to the relationship of a general with an army or a quarterback with a team. The point is to look beyond the simple existence of the team. The organizational context within which the team operates must be considered.

Since the latter part of the twentieth century, the conventional structure of the administrative team has been modified by three growing and interrelated reform concepts. First, site-based management is evermore widely utilized as a means of bringing the focus of management back to pupil, teaching, and learning outcomes. Thus, key decisions related to these outcomes are made at the site and by persons most directly influenced by them.

A second, and complementary, concept is that of the recognition of school business decisions as a process to be engaged or influenced in part by a spectrum of professionals at the school site, especially teachers and principals.

A third and related reform is the expanding array of school choices available in many communities. The National Center for Education Statistics (NCES) estimated in 2007 that 25 percent of all households with children in the United States were enrolling their school-age offspring in schools of choice, for example, magnet schools, charter schools, or private schools.

Given these concepts, the nature of the administrative team incorporates a decentralized function wherein central office administrators act as support personnel to teachers and principals as well as line officers in terms of the functions that are centralized.

■ ROLE OF THE SCHOOL BUSINESS ADMINISTRATOR ON THE TEAM

In one sense, all of the preceding discussion in this chapter has been a prologue to a description of the role of the school business administrator. The major dimensions of that role include the school business administrator as: (1) a general administrator, (2) an administrative specialist, (3) a member of the administrative team, and (4) a planner on that team.

As a general administrator, a school business official employs processes that have long been associated with and are common to the role planning: deciding, programming, stimulating, coordinating, and appraising. The position of school business administrator calls for expertise in the specific area of business affairs in the administration of schools. Therefore, these common processes are employed and applied to specific tasks within the general area of business affairs. These tasks include budgeting, purchasing, plant planning and construction, school-community relations, personnel management, plant operation and maintenance, security services, transportation, food services, accounting and reporting, investing and asset management, and office management.

The overall objective of school business administration is to contribute to the development and implementation of general policies and administrative decisions that provide the most effective, efficient conduct of business affairs and optimize the chance for reaching educational goals. The objective is clearly implementative—that is, maximum utilization of fiscal, personnel, and physical resources to attain educational goals. The six transformational principles described in Chapter Two were provided to illustrate the kinds of education reforms that a school business official can continually assist a district in pursuing.

School business administrators do not operate in isolation. They must relate to many individuals, offices, external and internal groups, and other government agencies in order to attain educational goals through the appropriate administration of the school system's business affairs. The administrative team best provides the structure of these relationships. It is important that the business administrator relate unique skills and responsibilities to administrative problems and policy questions that are identified and defined by the broadly based administrative team. The business administrator must advise the team of the business implications of policies and decisions and is, in turn, advised of their effect on other of the district's task areas.

The school business administrator must have a cooperative relationship with building principals. The administrative team approach calls for both line and staff relationships with field administrators. The business administrator usually is perceived as performing a staff function. However, in school-site management settings, the business officer may also perform as a line officer, in that principals are often responsible to this position for business affairs conducted in their individual school units.

📁 CASE 2 REVISITED

An Ethics Matter: But What about Dieter?

Business services, the territory covered by Dieter Shrempf, is an area that most educators know relatively little about. The intricacies of budget codes, alternatives for refinancing long-term debt, and purchasing policies for obtaining bids are generally the province of the school business manager and are less open to observation or scrutiny of others. Thus, it is not surprising that questionable actions of the superintendent went undetected by all other school district personnel except Dieter. While collecting evidence confirming the irresponsible actions of the superintendent, Dieter chose to remain silent about his suspicions. Dieter faces the ethical dilemma of exposing the

> questionable actions of the superintendent and his wife and risk being fired
> or maintaining his silence. What are the legal implications in this dilemma?
> What impact might Dieter's decision have on the community? What are the
> moral and ethical implications if Dieter does not expose them? Was it ethical
> for Dieter to conduct a background check on the new superintendent and his
> wife without permission from the outgoing superintendent and was his
> decision to do so his professional responsibility?

ROLE OF THE SCHOOL BUSINESS ADMINISTRATOR UNDER SITE-BASED MANAGEMENT

Chapter Two suggests the utility of rendering financial decisions transparent and placing decision making about resources close to students. In many practical ways these provisions translate to school-based or site-based management. Hence, the *site-based management* theme, which is a common thread throughout this book, is introduced here and is expanded and amplified in subsequent chapters. Special treatment is provided when discussing the budgeting function in Chapter Nine.

The business administrator-principal relationship has increased in visibility and importance with the advent of demands for principal accountability for program and educational outcomes. If principals are to be held accountable for results, it follows that authority for some measure of program decision making must be delegated to them. Consequently, some states have mandated that principals prepare or participate in the preparation of budgets and be given the authority to administer them. Clearly, such mandates require a close and effective working relationship between principals and business administrators as "building" or "site" budgeting is inaugurated and operated. They also require that principals have cooperative relationships with administrators of staff personnel, pupil personnel, instruction personnel, and all other cabinet officers who conduct a support role.

The school business functions performed by principals who have moved toward autonomy in developing and being accountable for programs in the building under their supervision are similar to the functions appropriate to the school district as a whole. Budgeting is a key responsibility. At the building level, this usually includes budget categories related to current expenses or instructional funds and accounts. (Different terminology is used in several states for these items.) Instructional supplies, materials, equipment, texts, library books, and the like are frequently budgeted at the building level. Some decentralized systems also provide individual building personnel budgets for teachers, aides, and custodians.

Most school districts that have moved to site-based budgeting have retained centralized and district-level budgeting for capital outlay, maintenance and administration, and other funds and accounts that are districtwide rather than individual school building functions.

Maintenance can be an exception. An unusual but interesting practice is to convert a school district's maintenance unit into an internal service account and then to provide each school with its own formulaically determined maintenance budget. Then the principal can contract with either the district maintenance unit, or, if possibly believing that an outside vendor can do a better, faster, or less expensive repair, the principal is authorized to outsource the maintenance or repair activity.

In situations in which considerable budgeting autonomy is granted to the principal, considerable school business administration responsibility follows. The principal must develop and maintain a purchasing subsystem that coordinates with that of the school district. The functions of recruiting, selecting, orienting, and appraising personnel need to be accomplished within the general personnel policies of the school system. When fiscal autonomy is exercised, an accounting system must provide the principal with financial information needed to make reasonable decisions. Principals who make purchases from their own budgeted funds must adopt procedures that assure the school and staff of the most suitable materials at the best possible price. The school business administrator's role of providing staff development in business affairs to both principal and staff in each building is a necessary and effective practice in the development and conduct of building-level budgeting.

The business function affects the principal as well as other members of an administrative team. Consequently, a cooperative relationship between the principal and the school business administrator is crucial. The administrator helps the principal comply with systemwide policy in business affairs and advises the principal with regard to decisions involving personnel, purchasing, and so on.

The *planning approach* is an important concept that permeates the role of the school business administrator. School district business decisions touch pupils, teachers, principals, the administrative team, the superintendent, the board of education, and the community as well as the school business administrator. The administrative officer best positioned to provide a planning perspective and to coordinate a planning structure for business affairs is the school business administrator. The school business office must continue to exercise monitoring and control functions regardless of an organization's trajectory. Indeed, the regulatory function becomes even more crucial and demanding under the site-based management concept because it creates many additional budget centers and activities that must be monitored. The business office, as an important support staff of the school system, has a major role in the planning needed to develop the concept.

■ PLANNING AS STRATEGY AND PROCESS

The continuing evolution of educational systems from small, fragmented, ineffective organizations numbering over 127,000 nationally to much larger, centrally controlled, but often inefficient and overlapping, bureaucracies has forced a recognition of the business administration function as an integral part of the operation of the modern educational system. At the same time as the consolidation of thousands of small school district operating units was taking place, new expanded school systems were beginning to recognize the difficulty and financial enormity of the business function. The growth of the central business office has been an attempt to respond to the pressures for adequate business procedure application to the administration of the educational enterprise. This educational enterprise often commands the largest single budget in a community. Indeed, the current annual expenditures for public elementary and secondary education in the United States are projected to grow to more than $600 billion in 2008 (NCES, 2006).

From the early development of school business administration through the very recent past, the focus of the business office has been largely on day-to-day operations of the school system. True, there have been attempts to perform planning activities, but these have been largely short-range efforts and have all too often been virtually extracurricular attempts by concerned individuals to determine directions and implications of selected or anticipated actions. There is little in the literature or in field practice to suggest that any great effort has been expended on the orderly, systematic, coordinated creation of alternative plans for school districts to use as guidelines for future actions.

This paucity of planning is best reflected in the manner in which many school systems have had to adopt "crash" programs to achieve certain goals and in the way accumulated pressures have led to dislocations in educational programs. The planning void in the utilization of modern technology has been particularly acute. Hence, this book devotes an entire chapter, Chapter Four, to the dynamics of planning.

Technological progress has provided tools to upgrade the business function in educational systems and has provoked an awareness of the need to develop planning procedures. The gathering, sorting, storing, and interpreting of data that once required inordinate amounts of energy, time, and resources have now become almost a by-product of sophisticated business equipment and informational processes utilized by most educational systems. The time is already at hand when organizations are in danger of being overwhelmed by the deluge of data, much of which are irrelevant or at least unusable by the system.

This deleterious condition does not result because these data are inaccurate, but because there is a lack of sophistication in the application of planning procedures. Most school systems now have the means to generate volumes of statistical summaries, ranging from demographic to financial to student to personnel information. The difficulty arises when school system personnel attempt to utilize these data for analytic purposes, long-range planning, or specific task assignments. Quite often, because of the naiveté with which most tasks are approached, the data become worthless.

One often hears the phrase "garbage in, garbage out" to describe the use of exotic machines for the production of answers to irrelevant questions. It seems that many educational systems are suffering from a technological gap flowing from a wide disparity between the capacity of electronic systems to perform routine, merchandisable tasks and the ability of people to assimilate the information for the improved operation of the system.

As a result of the many pressures impinging on the educational system, the planning function is rapidly assuming a top priority with school administrators.

The emerging role of the school business administrator will include planning activities such as the development of alternative strategies for identifying resources that will permit totally different kinds of educational programs to operate in the future. The school business administrator must be able to project the impact of societal change that leads to educational modifications. Predictions of the composition of the school clientele must be utilized to develop alternative schemes for meeting educational needs. Present resources have to be analyzed and means devised for gathering and allocating new resources in the future. A comprehensive knowledge of the economic forces at work, along with an ability to predict accurately future economic potential, will be most important.

The era of planning will demand far greater capacity to conceive, to conceptualize, to negotiate, and to compromise on the part of the school business administrator. At the same time, it will provide a great opportunity to create, to affect, and to participate in a uniquely American invention—the U.S. public school system.

■ ALTERNATIVE STRUCTURES FOR EDUCATIONAL PLANNING

Development of an educational model conducive to planning rests on the validity of the following assumptions:

- The comprehensive planning role must be separated from operational roles so that resources are available to carry out the planning task. Those charged with comprehensive planning obligations cannot, in addition, devote the time and energy needed for the operational duties of the system.
- Planning encompasses the total system and its needs, not only the planning of facilities or any other specific segment.
- The diversity of skills needed to mount a planning function mandates a team effort, not a one-person show.
- Resources needed for planning are crucial to its success and are a continuing part of any budget.

Preferably, the superintendent should be the chief planner and should actively participate in planning activities, particularly at the decision-making level. Key members of any planning team should include the financial planner, curriculum planner, facilities planner, and program evaluations specialist.

Decisions as to programs, facilities, organization, resources, and time should be the task of the planning team. The school system should operate its educational programs on the basis of desired outcomes as identified and codified by the planning effort. Changes, modifications, alternatives, and evaluation of program effectiveness should all be the responsibility of the planning staff. Decisions as to continuation of programs, shifts in emphasis, initiation of new and different programs, priorities in the application of resources, and allocations should be planning tasks.

Because the foregoing implies a staff of such size that it is not realistically possible for the many smaller school systems, alternatives must be devised.

A Planning Coordinator. One alternative, again dependent on the size of the system, is to establish a one-person planning office with the main task of generalized planning and coordinating total systems planning. This office can draw on specialized personnel in other divisions of the school system for contributions to the development of a total plan. Persons in various components of the school system, for example, the business office, the curriculum office, and so forth, need to be provided with sufficient resources to enable them to channel time and effort into the planning process.

Outside Consultants. Another alternative presently utilized by many systems, particularly in the development of facility plans, is to contract either private consulting firms or university planning teams to develop educational plans. While this method of planning does provide a school system with a set of master plans for implementation, it is not without weakness.

- While the objectivity used by the outside consultant is a strength, lack of complete knowledge of a school system can be a weakness.
- Although the outside agency has expertise in the planning process, increased capacity of the local school system must be a main objective to ensure continued success.

- There is a danger in accepting a master plan based on present data and then following it blindly without giving consideration to changing variables and their effects on the plan.

Interdistrict Cooperation. A third planning model is for groups of districts to pool their planning resources and to share the services of a planning staff. This not only provides smaller districts with planning services, but also tends to encourage cooperative efforts in curriculum areas not feasible for a small district.

A combination of the preceding alternatives may prove the most desirable. The educational system must develop a planning capacity of its own and should call on specialists from the field to supplement and complement its own staff. In this way, expert advice on particular problems can be made available, while, at the same time, local personnel can give continuity to the planning process.

The least desirable way of conducting the planning function is to expect current staff to attempt to plan while, at the same time, resolving all existent operational decisions entrusted to them. Although this is most common, it is not the most efficient or productive use of human resources.

Summary

School business functions and tasks antedate the superintendency. In their earliest manifestation, they were largely control functions to see that public monies were spent for their intended purposes. School business administration was separated from the instructional function in both structure and process. Only when public education became larger and more complex and demands for reform of local and municipal government were finally heeded did school business administration become professionalized and then integrated into the superintendency.

The function of school business administration has traditionally been defined in terms of tasks such as budgeting, accounting, purchasing, maintaining and operating buildings, and providing similar services to support the instructional program. It has been seen as a part of the superintendency, with the school business administrator as a member of the administrative team.

In recent years the emergence of the concept of site-based management and the educational reform movement has given an impetus to a reconceptualization of school business administration.

Rather than functioning as a subunit of the superintendency that provides a service to instruction, school business administration can be viewed as a function exercised by many persons in the school organization. Superintendents, central office personnel, principals, and teachers are involved in making educational decisions. Instructional decisions have business implications and business decisions have instructional implications. Thus, the school business administration function permeates the whole school system.

This new complexity and the need to cooperate suggest that collaboration of all decision makers in the system with the school business administrator is imperative if decisions are to be cost-effective. That is, educational goal achievement should be maximized with the lowest possible cost. Persons with educational expertise should make the decision as to where the trade-off point between goals and cost is to be fixed.

Discussion Questions

1. Identify a major decision related to school business administration in a system, and then trace the planning activities (or lack of them) that went into the decision. Try to identify and describe the several planning activities.
2. Interview administrators in small, medium, and large school systems. Identify where and with whom most of the responsibility for school business administration lies. Try to draw generalizations as to the comparative structures.
3. Discuss the pros and cons of restricting school business administrator positions to those who have taught and have had appropriate educational administrative positions.
4. Identify a major instructional decision and trace the development or evolution of the decision. Point out at each step the presence or absence of inclusions of school business implications.

Web Resources

National Center for Educational Statistics—
     http://nces.ed.gov/

References

National Center for Educational Statistics. (2006). *Projections of educational statistics to 2015*. Washington, DC: U.S. Department of Education. Retrieved February 16, 2007, from http://nces.ed.gov/programs/projections/tables/table_34.asp?referrer=report.

Stevenson, K.R., & Tharpe, D.I. (1999). *The school business administrator*. (4th ed.). Reston, VA: Association of School Business Officials/Rowman and Littlefield Publishing Group.

Notes

1. These five frames of reference for leadership serve as an organizing paradigm for the companion volume in the Peabody Education Leadership Series, *Successful school leadership*, James W. Guthrie & Patrick J. Schuermann, Boston: Allyn & Bacon, 2008.
2. See David B. Tyack, *The one best system* (Cambridge: Harvard University Press, 1970, and Raymond C. Callahan, *Education and the cult of efficiency*, (Chicago: University of Chicago Press, 1962) for a full explanation of this influential movement in American educational management.

CHAPTER FOUR

Planning

■ INTRODUCTION

This chapter on strategic planning is placed early in this book because of the significance of the subject for the business operation, actually all operations, within a school or school district. Strategic planning offers a set of procedures by which those responsible for the leadership of a complex organization, including schools, can come closer to shaping their destiny rather than simply and continually reacting to the realities imposed upon the organization by the day-to-day exigencies of the external world.

LEARNING OBJECTIVES

In this chapter a reader will learn about:

- The advantages strategic planning holds as a dynamic management instrument for an education agency.
- The definition of strategic planning and tactical components comprising the planning process.
- Who should be engaged in planning.
- What comprises a reasonable planning time frame and time horizon.

Strategic planning initially assists an organization in identifying the "right things to do." Having accomplished that purpose, strategic planning also can assist an administrative team in getting things done right. The purpose of strategic planning is to render an organization more effective, to enable it to achieve its goals more completely and more efficiently, and better respond to its clients. As mentioned above, it can also protect an organization against the inevitable threat of externally generated surprise circumstances.

Strategic planning entails systematic review, and possible redeployment, of an agency's resources. This is often a remarkably complicated and resource- (e.g., time) consuming undertaking. It can involve sophisticated analytic and technical procedures, political acumen, widespread employee participation, forceful leadership, and a measure of intuition.

Inclusion of the word *planning*, however, should not deceive a reader. Strategic planning of the variety described and illustrated in this book is far from a hollow or bureaucratic paper-and-pencil exercise.

Certainly, planning reports can be ignored and "put on the shelf" to gather dust. However, if undertaken with appropriate expertise and commitment, and if designed to engage virtually every component of an organization, the strategic planning process possesses the potential to rattle an organization to its fundamental roots and render it dramatically more responsive and effective. A strategic plan is a powerful tool by which policymakers and managers can fine-tune an already responsive and high-performing agency or reorient a runaway organization.

■ WHAT IS STRATEGIC PLANNING?

The etymological roots of *strategy* stretch to classical Greece, where the original term concerned military leadership. A *stratagem* was a means for gaining the upper hand over an enemy. Often this involved an artifice or a major element of deceit. The deceptively hollow wooden horse used by Greek soldiers to gain access to the city of Troy was a stratagem. Gaining higher or more easily defended ground, surprising an unprepared combatant enemy, or severing an opponent's vital supply route are examples of military strategies.

Achieving a strategic objective often requires substantial forethought. Through the planning process, numerous detailed actions are specified. These are often referred to as *tactics*. As an aside, the 1944 Normandy invasion may well represent the most complicated human planning effort in history. Staying with this example, troop movements, logistical arrangements, aerial bombardment, compilation of intelligence, sabotage, civilian propaganda efforts, and so on, may comprise tactical details. However many and varied they may be, when motivated by an overarching strategy, the cohesive purpose of aligned tactics is to achieve an organization's goals.

Developing strategic objectives and the means for achieving them, what we refer to in this chapter as *strategic planning*, has evolved substantially from its Greek and military origins. Strategic planning presently is employed by a wide spectrum of private, not-for-profit, and public-sector organizations in order to achieve objectives more effectively, for example, enhance profits, expand services to clients, and be more responsive to constituent preferences.

Any effective organization, that is, one that purposefully is pursuing and achieving its announced objectives, engages in strategic planning. A simple business with only five or ten employees, in order to remain effective, must plan. A small, locally operating social agency, in order to fulfill its mission or adjust to a changing environment, must assess its current status and give thought to the future. Not to do so risks becoming an anachronism and obsolete. Even a family household must occasionally undertake long-range planning in order to satisfy current desires and secure the future for its members.

Planning, in these instances, may be informal and unilateral. The head of a household simply may take stock of current family needs, speculate regarding future desires, assess current and prospective resources, and arrive at a conclusion regarding next-needed actions. All of this might be done without once putting pencil to paper.

Similarly, the head of a small business may undertake an informal assessment of sales trends, current operating costs, personnel performance, and profits, stir into the mixture an informed appraisal of market developments, and arrive at a conclusion regarding future business directions.

Such simplified and informal efforts contain many elements of strategic planning, and they may suffice to promote the ends of the organizations involved, in these examples, a family and small business. These planning exercises involve important dimensions such as assessing the current status of the "organization," determining desired performance levels, possible alterations in the external environment, and arriving at a set of alternative actions. However, these simplified efforts are missing several critical components that characterize strategic planning for a large organization.

Effective strategic planning for a complex agency depends additionally upon the presence of: (1) specific organizational goals, (2) a capacity for objective, independent judgment, and (3) technical expertise. These components are not themselves sufficient, but they are necessary conditions.

Making Organizational Goals Explicit

The head of a household might assume that family happiness and security are important goals. The owner of a small business might assume that making a sufficient profit is the major objective. However, for larger organizations, particularly public-sector agencies, strategic planning necessitates that goals be made explicit. Only in this way is it possible to assess organizational performance and subsequently align or realign resources effectively.

The objectives of an education system or agency can be classified either as end goals or instrumental goals. End goals are the final outcomes or products that the system or agency attempts to achieve. High academic achievement, vocational preparation, good citizenship, and racial understanding are all potential end purposes of a school or school district. These can be regarded as strategic objectives. An organization's progress in achieving such objectives can be systematically assessed. Also, such objectives should determine rational allocation of organizational resources.

Instrumental goals, or means, are those outcomes that, while perhaps being desirable in themselves, are pursued by an organization because their accomplishment facilitates achievement of end goals. For example, a school district might regard parent participation or citizen satisfaction as objectives it desires to maximize. These probably are good things to do regardless, but there exists an additional motivation to accomplishing them. Arguably, parent participation is a means that might enhance student achievement, an end goal. Increased citizen satisfaction with schools might secure a stable stream of resources for the district. In this light, parent participation and citizen satisfaction are instrumental objectives. Ends are strategic goals and instrumental goals are the means to achieve the strategic goals. The latter are intended to promote the former.

In the absence of explicit ends, or strategic goals, it is not possible to undertake a complete planning effort for a large organization. At a minimum, strategic goals are needed by an organization as: (1) criteria with which to determine the degree to which it currently is succeeding in its mission or missions, (2) targets toward which to orient subsequent allocations of resources, and (3) foci around which to organize personnel and incentives.

▮ THE IMPACT OF POLITICS ON GOAL SETTING AND PLANNING

Establishing an organization's purposes often involves politics. There exists an infinite range of useful things to do in this world and a finite quantity of resources, including human time, with which to accomplish such good purposes. Consequently, decisions almost inevitably must be made regarding ends to be pursued and resources to be allocated. Who will pay, who will benefit, and who will participate are important questions, and they are the stuff of politics. If it is a public organization receiving and responsible for allocating public resources, that is, tax revenues, then goal setting is subject to the added complexity of government regulation regarding both rightful participants and the decision process.

Because of the political complexity involved, simply admonishing policymakers and managers to make organizational goals explicit is probably insufficient. Specifying goals is difficult, and the larger and more heterogeneous the public served by an organization, the more difficult it becomes to reach agreement among participants and to be specific. Also, reaching agreement regarding goals is frequently more difficult to accomplish in a public-sector agency than in the private or not-for-profit sectors. Lastly, the more directly linked the agency is to the electoral process, the more complicated goal setting can become.

As vast, complex, and beleaguered as it is, General Motors Corporation probably can establish its strategic goals more readily than the National Aeronautic and Space Administration (NASA). Although not directly linked to the electorate, NASA, a federal executive branch agency, is nevertheless subject to the immediate political pressures of the presidency and Congress. A locally elected school board, especially for a medium- or large-city school district, may have even greater difficulty than NASA in agreeing upon its strategic agenda. This is so because at least NASA has the luxury of a relatively prescribed zone of activity, space exploration. A local school district seems to have to wrestle with virtually every issue but space exploration.

In a small, specialized government agency, for example, a mosquito abatement control or a transportation district, it may be relatively easy for elected policymakers to reach consensus regarding goals. However, in a general government, for example, a county or municipality, or even a value-laden special service such as a public school district, community college, or university, efforts to reach agreement on or to establish priorities among specific purposes can provoke intense conflict.

Public agencies are intended to be sensitive to the needs of their citizen clients, and elected officials generally desire to be responsive to constituent preferences. If the policy charter for a government agency is broad, as in the case of a city, or if the population to be served is large and possessed of diverse views regarding the nature of the service, as is generally the case in a heterogeneous or big-city school district, there is an opportunity for substantial disagreement about goals. Ironically, the more democratic and inclusive the political process, and the more representative the resultant policymaking body, the greater the prospect of disagreement regarding agency goals.

A reader unfamiliar with the political dynamics of a public K–12 or higher education agency in the United States might be surprised at the potential range of disagreement regarding organizational purposes. At first glance, it might appear reasonable to expect schools to be concerned with maximizing student academic achievement. However, American society expects much more of schools and colleges, both explicitly and implicitly. Societal cohesion, civic participation, economic productivity, national defense, patriotism, social mobility, employment opportunities, and moral integrity are all social purposes to which schools are expected to contribute. Reasonable people can arrive at varying conclusions regarding which of these goals is of greater or lesser significance.

Implicitly, schools may be expected to meet yet another agenda of objectives. Some cynics assert that policymakers desire schools to serve unseemly purposes, such as ladders to further their own personal political careers, pulpits for publicly promoting privately held ideologies, "warehouses" for youth until they are needed in the labor market, or as trainers of an unquestioning and docile workforce.

The spectrum of potential purposes for a K–12 or higher education agency, public or private, is remarkably broad. The intent here is not to suggest that one goal or set of goals is to be preferred over another. Rather, the point is that the objectives an organization attempts to maximize, either through a set of explicit decisions or by default by making no decisions, will influence internal allocation of resources.

A school district that desires to enhance student academic achievement, promote acceptance of its graduates to colleges and universities, encourage graduate school enrollments or reduce student dropout rates, may allocate its funds and efforts quite differently from one that has as its prime, if unprofessed, purpose serving as the employer of last resort for a labor pool of unskilled political constituents.

Small agencies, or those serving homogeneous populations, are likely to reach agreement with relative ease. In more complicated settings, a set of political compromises must be struck in order to reach accord on organizational purposes. This should not be interpreted as improper or bad. Indeed, a political system is operating effectively when it resolves disagreements peacefully, which otherwise might escalate into painful and protracted conflicts.

Political compromise may necessitate multiple or vaguely worded agendas for an organization. For example, many school districts specify that their purpose is educating the whole child. This is at once a noble and an empty statement. No one can easily argue with such a high-minded aspiration. On the other hand, how would an organization know if it achieved its purpose?

However, from the perspective of strategic planning, even amorphous goals are to be preferred over the condition in which no explicit agreement is reached regarding agency objectives. In the latter situation, an organization either pursues too many goals or has no direction whatsoever. In such anarchical situations, an agency frequently will fragment its resources to the point of being ineffective. In not being able to pursue a reasonably concentrated explicit agenda, it risks not being able to achieve any purposes.

Under ideal conditions, an organization will already have derived an explicit agenda of purposes that can be used to guide a strategic planning effort. In the absence of such an agenda, planners may have to stimulate policymakers and managers to make their goals explicit. The least desirable scenario entails strategic planners, engaged from outside an organization, having to assume or infer an organization's purposes. This involves substantial risks. A resource mobilization plan directed at maximizing externally imputed objectives might be rejected by those in power as inconsistent with their implicit purposes. Under these conditions, planning can dissolve into a hollow paper-and-pencil undertaking. It is externally proposed plans or plans imposed from a super ordinate agency that are most at risk of being placed on a shelf and gathering dust.

Even though less than fully desirable, when planners have to assume organizational objectives, all is not necessarily lost. Sometimes policymakers, themselves unable to craft an agreement, will acquiesce to or adopt goals specified by a group of outsiders in whom they have confidence. A highly stressful alternative is for a planning team to impose direction, or purposes, on an organization through external political pressures. Here, a planner leaves the domain of the technician and dramatically enters the realm of planner as politician. On occasion, public officials are badly embarrassed, and may even have to resign, because they fail to understand that an appropriately legitimated comprehensive planning effort can create a potent wave of political momentum capable of unseating those in power. This is true even if the planning team is comprised of individuals from outside the operating agency itself.

Because of possible political consequences, a school administrator, including a business official or other public-sector manager, is well advised to utilize strategic planning for purposes of his or her own, as well as the organization's, well-being. If a strategic planning effort is mandated from the outside, then accede to it gracefully, cooperate with it, shape it for productive purposes, perhaps attempt appropriately to influence it, but do not resist it unless prepared to expend substantial political resources, and perhaps even lose.

If an organization's political leaders believe their agency is performing well and simply desire an affirmation of this condition, then they should seek planners from outside whose legitimacy or credentials are impeccable. Even here there is risk, however. Such outsiders may uncover some heretofore unknown and unfavorable condition. The answer in such uncomfortable circumstances is to know the planners sufficiently to have confidence that they will bring the bad news carefully to the attention of leaders and discuss its consequences before informing others.

■ KEY CONSIDERATIONS IN THE PLANNING PROCESS

When a business official or other education leader is to engage in the planning process, three key considerations must be made. These include a regard for the level of intergovernmental complexity at play in the endeavor, the need for objectivity in the planning process, and the degree of technical sophistication essential to thoughtfully approach the enterprise.

Intergovernmental Complexity

Public schools particularly, and to some degree private and independent schools as well, seldom have the luxury of freely determining their own purposes. They operate in a complicated societal and governmental matrix. The United States is a mosaic of overlapping authorities: national, state, and local. Consequently, a strategic planning effort in a school district or school should be unusually mindful of the purposes that are imposed at higher government levels, state and federal. For example, states have statutorily specified learning objectives, objectives reflected in state standardized achievement tests. Similarly the federal No Child Left Behind Act demands of states and local districts that they achieve Adequate Yearly Progress, measured in terms of academic achievement. No planning endeavor can bypass or neglect these high-level mandates. This ability to focus both within the school context and simultaneously on issues within the external environment is a key principle of administrative leadership.

Objectivity

In addition to relying upon explicit objectives, full-blown planning projects undertaken for formal organizations differ from ad hoc assessments and seat-of-the-pants extrapolations of a household or small business on yet another dimension: efforts to achieve objectivity. Objectivity, in this context, refers to the absence of prejudice, a condition of independence, a lack of conflicting interests, or an open-mindedness on the part of those conducting analyses and generating alternative recommendations.

Ensuring objectivity has important implications for the *who* of planning, a topic covered in the prior chapter and illustrated further in this chapter. However, a reader should keep in mind that at crucial junctures, independent judgment is an indispensable aid to strategic planning.

Planning rests on several platforms, where obtaining informed unbiased counsel may be crucial for the success of the undertaking. Examples include assessing potential markets for service, measuring current productivity, evaluating congruence between present personnel and those likely to be needed in the future, judging relations between an organization and its clients, and predicting future regulatory environments. A few illustrations may assist in making the point more concrete.

Enrollment projections are pivotal for understanding the numbers of students likely to present themselves for educational services in the future. These projections are also fundamental for extrapolating likely future revenues and expenditures and the need for personnel and physical facilities. Given the crucial nature of this technical planning dimension, it is important not only that those entrusted with the tasks be competent and experienced, but also that they not have a tightly vested interest in the outcome. It would be inappropriate to rely upon building contractors and architects to undertake enrollment projections or teacher or faculty bargaining agents or citizen tax relief representatives to undertake revenue projections.

Technical Sophistication

When undertaken appropriately, planning also relies upon a degree of technical sophistication that surpasses the ability of many informal or small organizations to obtain. Much of the "technology" is involved in two components of planning: (1) understanding an organization's relationship to specific dimensions of its external environment, and (2) understanding the internal allocation of an organization's resources.

External Environments. Ways to assess an organization's relation to specific dimensions in the external environment are varied. The following questions illustrate the type of considerations a planning team must make in regards to the broader environmental context. What is the current market for a product or service and how might it change in the future? Is there a new technology on the horizon that will likely eliminate the demand or perhaps create a demand for a different set of goods or services? What portion of existing and likely future demands can an organization control and under what conditions? What do current clients think about an organization's products or services? How do they perceive the organization? What changes would customers or clients like to see undertaken to serve them better?

Questions such as these lend themselves to technically derived answers. These dimensions can be made more specific for educational organizations and can be contrasted with a different set of questions that generally must be answered in other ways.

For an operating educational organization, the clientele to be served drives the system. Consequently, having adequate knowledge of the current cohort of students and projections of future cohorts is critical. Enrollment projections and student flow models can be constructed and regularly updated. No school, district, or educational system should be without such systematically generated information regarding the ebb and flow of its likely future clientele.

In the United States, where elementary school attendance is virtually universal, projecting enrollments in the early grades is a relatively easy undertaking. This is particularly true in large districts or in a state as a whole. In and out migration, private school enrollments, and possible fluctuations in birthrates must all be taken into account, but these are not difficult technically, assuming adequate information. These data must, of course, be finely tuned by the addition of information regarding building permits, developer plans, housing starts, interest rates for housing loans, and an assortment of local particulars.

Predicting enrollments for secondary schools, private schools, and higher education institutions is more difficult, but still can be accomplished with great accuracy. Indeed, predictions can be, and are, made for all such institutions by entire states and nations. Technical projections of future school populations serve as an important basis for revenue and expenditure analyses as well as assessments of future personnel and facility needs.

Enrollments can be thought of as an "input" to schools from the external environment. Another component of the external environment to which education systems must be alert is the "market" for education products. Here the concern is the relationship between the external environment and school "outputs." What kinds of jobs are likely to develop and how should educational institutions react to future labor needs? What are the views of parents, citizens, and employers regarding the current performance of schools? Various analytic and survey techniques can be employed to answer questions such as these.

In the News

Bentonville High School opened in 2000, but the school district's growth already has prodded an addition set to open next year. The 300,000-square-foot expansion will double the facility's size, making it the largest school in the state. In Springdale, Superintendent Jim Rollins said his district is seeing growth that will double its student population of 15,000 by 2016 and increase the number of schools from 21 to nearly 40. And in booming Rogers, the public school district's 10-year capital building plan has become little more than a loose guide. Rogers's rapid growth makes it impossible for serious planning that's more than three to four years out. The building plan's original $80 million estimate continues to increase with raised building expectations, said David Cauldwell, business manager for the Rogers Public School District.

Such eye-popping statistics can keep school leaders up late at night pondering solutions for the challenges that come with the region's extraordinary growth rates and changing demographics.

State law mandates Arkansas school districts submit three-year and 10-year plans for construction of school buildings. And officials from Northwest Arkansas' four largest school districts say that predicting growth areas and corresponding classroom construction is often the difference between spending millions and alienating parents with repeated school zone boundary changes.

In addition to prioritizing land purchases and school construction, superintendents must balance the frequent boundary changes that end up pulling students away from former classmates and altering the demographic makeup of the schools. "To build a school, you don't get up one morning and start hammering and nailing," said Fayetteville Superintendent Bobby New. "It's at least a three-year process." Superintendents also have to find enough teachers and maintain overall quality.

"It's not getting larger that's our challenge," Rollins said. "Our challenge and our focus is to get better, and to do that we've got to personalize the teaching process no matter what their background so they can come forward and become proficient and advanced through their learning."

Diversity

The number of Hispanics moving into Rogers and Springdale is radically shifting the racial makeup of some elementary schools. David Cauldwell, business manager with the Rogers School District, said the percentage of Hispanic students ranges from 10 percent to 60 percent in individual Rogers schools. Several Rogers elementary schools with large percentages of Hispanic students also include high percentages of poor- to moderate-income families, Cauldwell said.

Hispanic families tend to live in the same areas of town, Cauldwell said, which means the district sometimes must choose between having schools with little racial diversity and busing students away from their neighborhoods. "The school board is real concerned about that," said Cauldwell. "To bus someone past their neighborhood to go to another school probably is not as good." Rogers school leaders pour more dollars into schools with more low-income residents, Cauldwell said.

Projections

The Springdale School District keeps tabs on such growth by watching the Springdale planning and community development department and tries to acquire land beyond the growth area in a wagon-wheel fashion, said Rollins. "If this is your existing boundary for established attendance areas," Rollins said, pointing to an imaginary boundary line, "then you want to move beyond that. It gets to be a very complicated process—moving out away from the existing population to serve new subdivisions as they come into place." Fayetteville employs a full-time geographic information systems worker to track growth, student movement and other development in the school district, New said.

The mapping software shows glimpses of future growth trends, as well as student population and boundary changes. One of New's maps shows the number of students per school if Bates Elementary School had never closed. Bates would have 194 students, according to the projections, while other schools would vary from 300 to 658. Fayetteville schools save costly overhead for school construction, maintenance and administrators by consolidating students into larger schools. "It would have been administrative incompetence for us to allow this kind of knowledge to go unexecuted," New said.

Brick and Mortar

Rogers began a long-term capital improvement plan in 2002, budgeting $80 million to build four elementary schools, one kindergarten-through-seventh-grade school, one sophomore campus and one junior high school, as well as renovations to another sophomore campus by the 2008–09 school year.

The Rogers school district chose to remodel its existing sophomore campus by renovating about 100,000 square feet of existing space and adding about 230,000 square feet in new classrooms. All four of Northwest Arkansas' largest school districts are building schools on the outskirts of their towns.

Acreage is more available in outlying areas and, if positioned correctly, the newer schools can cut down on bus and car traffic, said Bentonville Superintendent Gary Compton. Compton and Springdale's Rollins agreed that school districts would prefer to have 20 to 50 acres of affordable acreage with electricity, water and sewer readily available. "But in the pace of growth we're finding that our needs outstrip our infrastructure," Rollins said. So the district has reached into agricultural areas.

The Springdale school district spent $685,440 on the construction of sewer systems for 144 acres in southeast Springdale. The district plans to open an elementary school, a middle school and a high school on the land it acquired from developer Tom Terminella, who is building three subdivisions nearby. For a time, school leaders worried sewer service wouldn't be available when the district's southeast

elementary school opens during the 2006–07 school year.

Rollins said his district recently purchased property for an elementary school at East Monitor and Scott Hollar roads east of Springdale on land he expects the city will annex someday. Bentonville's Compton said he actively pursues property to his district's far western boundaries to keep some traffic out of "gridlocked" Bentonville. "Right now everything moves into Bentonville in the morning," Compton said. "We have lots and lots of parents that choose to drive their kids to school and that's why we have traffic and safety problems around every school. If I can spread traffic out a little bit, move traffic to the west, that's a good thing, too."

Unfurling a map of the Bentonville district's 160 square miles, Compton pointed to 18 different yellow dots marking properties he's considered purchasing for schools, most of which he's walked and used an all-terrain vehicle to survey. After doubling its square footage next fall, projections show Bentonville will need a second high school around 2010.

From: Morasch, C. (2006, February 26). School leaders scramble to keep pace with needs. *Arkansas Democrat-Gazette*, Special section.

Internal Environments. Technical procedures also assist in better understanding internal allocations of an organization's resources and the status of its "productivity." A private-sector firm may desire information regarding internal allocations in order to reduce production costs and overhead, and, thereby, improve profits. A not-for-profit or public-sector organization may wish to assess internal allocations in order to determine if it can improve or expand the range of services offered to clients. Here the analytic techniques of the cost accountant come into play.

Ratio analyses are particularly useful. Here, an organization can make three kinds of comparisons. It can compare its costs for an operation or object with what it paid for the same undertaking in the past—historical comparisons. Another kind of comparison, horizontal comparison, is between an organization's costs for an operation or object with the expenditure figures from a similar organization, for example, another school district or charter school of similar size and purpose. A third kind of comparison involves assessing an organization's cost for an operation or object with expenditures for similar endeavors but in different agencies. For example, a school or district can compare its food costs on a unit basis with a college, hospital, or prison.

An organization also may desire to examine the extent to which it is currently meeting its strategic goals, and frequently this may involve substantial technical sophistication. This is especially true with schools. Measuring student outcomes can involve awesome complexity regarding sampling, item selection, test construction, and analysis of out-of-school influences on achievement.

Technical sophistication, thus, has a role in planning in order to understand both internal and external conditions of an organization. Moreover, such techniques, for example, demographic analyses, flow models, financial accounting, ratio analysis, survey research, opinion polling, and outcome measurement may be applied both to current and future conditions. Taken in isolation, absent consideration for an organization's purposes, politics, and people, these technological dimensions may prove relatively useless. However, when combined appropriately with other planning components, technical tools can crucially strengthen final plan analyses and outcomes.

■ SUMMARY DESCRIPTION OF PLANNING

What is planning? It is a composite of socio-political processes and analytic techniques designed to enhance an organization's performance and relationships with its external environment, and ratchet up the efficiency of its internal resource allocation. It combines analysis with more generally obtained information and judgments regarding matters such as demographics, politics, and technology. The outcome is an organizational action plan that takes into account likely future changes and orients the agency's resources toward achievement of mutually agreed upon organizational objectives. A good long-range or strategic plan can congeal an organization and concentrate the energies of personnel at all levels upon the organization's path to success. Obviously, such a plan has implications for a business leader's actions.

To summarize, in order to be effective, a comprehensive planning effort must:

- Be oriented toward achievement of explicit organizational goals.
- Be undertaken in circumstances that permit analytic objectivity and independence.
- Involve appropriate levels of technical sophistication.

■ TIMING: WHEN SHOULD PLANNING BE UNDERTAKEN?

Planning is, or at least should be, a cyclical activity. To be maximally effective, an organization's long-range or comprehensive plan should be systematically revisited. Not only does this enable planners to update data and extend projections, but also it enables policymakers and organizational leaders to reassess the assumptions upon which a long-range plan is based. It probably is better for an organization to construct a strategic plan at one point in time, than never to do it at all. However, the primary benefit of a major planning effort is not only initially to chart, but also thereafter to maintain a direction for an agency. When an organization continually engages in planning, the chance is good that it is transforming itself into a strategic organization. In these instances, strategic planning morphs into strategic thinking, the ultimate goal of an effective agency. The term *strategic*, when used in this context, is the same as a continuous learning organization, an agency that relies upon data and analysis continually to reinvent and reinvigorate itself.

If comprehensive or strategic planning, when undertaken at its best, is cyclical, when should the cycle begin? The easy response is "at any point and perhaps the sooner the better." This may not be the most realistic or even the best answer. There are stages in the life of an organization when initiating a comprehensive strategic planning effort makes more sense than at other times. Also, initiating a comprehensive planning undertaking has symbolic and political consequences. Therefore, selection of the starting point, and the manner in which it is announced, should be carefully considered.

If an organization is judged to be out of control, ineffective, or unresponsive to client expectations and constituent preferences, then launching a strategic planning project with substantial publicity may be desirable. High visibility and use of a prestigious planning team can focus attention on, and build and create, a powerful anticipation for improved project or agency results. All this, in turn, may assist in changing an organization. When radical reform is the purpose, then finding the most appropriate time to announce the planning project is crucial.

Leadership transitions offer a particularly attractive opportunity in the life cycle of an organization to launch a planning project intended to create major change. For example, a dramatic planning point occurs when a major management shift takes place (a new school board majority is elected or a new superintendent is selected, replacing a long-term incumbent) or a dramatic organizational shock has occurred or is about to occur (a drastic revenue ceiling has been imposed, enrollments are predicted suddenly to explode, or consolidation with a neighboring district has been mandated).

The foregoing examples represent major organizational shifts and are relatively infrequent events. They offer particularly attractive opportunities for policymakers and leaders to gain leverage for organizational change. An alert business official or other education leader will be quick to take advantage of such openings or points of inflection and use them to launch a comprehensive planning effort.

If no dramatic public event appears available as a coincidental opportunity to begin a planning project, there is an alternative—make announcement of the planning project itself the major feature. Those initiating the plan, desiring the organizational reforms, can utilize the planning project and the identification of the planning team as a publicity centerpiece. However, business system leaders should be sensitive to the fact that one or a series of highly visible events create expectations for change that can be damaging to an organization and its leadership, if not fulfilled.

If an organization is judged to be performing reasonably well and comprehensive planning is envisioned as a tool for fine-tuning its operation, then a less dramatic launching may be appropriate. Here the intent is not to use the plan for major reform leverage, but simply for minor course redirection. In such circumstances, it is often useful to begin the planning project coincident with natural recurring events in the life cycle of the organization. In this manner, no undue publicity is accorded the event, and anxiety levels are not elevated unproductively.

Among the less dramatic and naturally occurring openings for educational organizations is the beginning of the school year. Educational organizations generally are oriented to an academic year beginning in the autumn and ending in late spring or early summer. It makes good sense to initiate a comprehensive planning project so as to permit its recommendations to be considered and acted upon by all appropriate constituents in time for implementation at the beginning of the academic year. This often means launching the undertaking the preceding summer.

An added advantage of beginning during the summer is that this is frequently the least busy time for various administrative officials and professional educators. In the absence of the day-to-day pressures of dealing with pupils and parents, they may be able to devote time and reflection to planning and analysis that otherwise would not easily be available.

In addition to school years, budget cycles, legislative openings, and calendar years, other naturally recurring organizational beginnings offer additional points at which to initiate a planning project.

A comprehensive action plan is usually based upon a medium-length time horizon, for example, five years. That means projections, analyses, and goals are oriented toward a period five years into the future. For example, a planning team engaged by an education agency might begin enrollment projections for the year 2010 and carry them through to 2015.

Pupil projections act as a foundation for many other planning components, and five years is a reasonable basis upon which to project dynamic conditions such as an organization's revenues and expenditures. Personnel planning (hiring instructors) may necessitate longer-range projections. In this case, a ten-year horizon may be appropriate. Facilities' planning often requires an even more extended set of projections, fifteen or twenty years.

As is probably obvious, the further into the future a projection extends, the greater the kind and range of undetermined events that can influence the outcome and the less accurate predictions are likely to be. In order to be maximally useful, a strategic plan should be updated on a regular basis so as to take into account dimensions such as new instructional techniques, intensified state or local mandates, alterations in the environment, or changes in client preferences. Systematically reassessing the information upon which a strategic plan is based reduces the range of unknown factors, renders projections more accurate, and thus enhances the utility of the plan.

■ WHO SHOULD COMPRISE THE PLANNING TEAM?

The prior chapter provides an introduction to this topic and stresses the role that an able business leader may play in the process. However, before addressing this topic in detail, it is important to distinguish between the "Planning Team" proper and the many other individuals and groups who because of their positions will participate in the planning process.

If appropriately conducted, a comprehensive planning process will involve almost all top-level policymakers and leaders and managers in an organization and a representative sample of other employees, clients, and, in a public-sector organization, citizens will be contacted as well. All of these individuals will be needed to supply information, offer opinions, and make decisions; however, these are not necessarily members of the planning team.

A Planning Team

The planning team should consist of a group of individuals selected for the skills, knowledge, and experience they can contribute to the undertaking. The team leader (head planner) should possess a comprehensive understanding of the institution involved, be it a corporation, a state education agency, a school district, or individual school. In addition, the team leader should possess knowledge of the components of a strategic planning project, both technical and procedural. It is not necessary that the leader be able to conduct every part of the study by oneself. However, this leader should have sufficient management skill and experience to know quickly if a member of the team is not performing correctly or is incapable of completing an assignment. Given these qualities, it is often a school district's business official who is best placed to head a planning effort.

In addition to a head planner, a comprehensive planning team in education should be comprised of individuals with technical talents in enrollment forecasting, demographics, finances, personnel systems, pupil outcome measurement, survey research and opinion polling, data management, research design, statistical methods, curriculum and instruction, graphic design, and report writing.

Each of these competencies need not represent a separate full-time individual. One person can sometimes encompass more than one field of expertise. Also, experts can be engaged on a part-time or consulting basis. However, regardless of how many individuals or how much of the time of any one individual is occupied by a planning assignment, a comprehensive planning effort is likely to draw upon all the above-listed technical areas prior to completion.

In addition to leadership and technical expertise, a strategic planning team needs individuals on it who are insightful regarding organizational and political dynamics. Such individuals can contribute productively to analyzing the results of technical studies. Also, periodically it is useful to conduct a policy audit. This is an analysis of an organization's effectiveness in communicating and implementing policy directives.

Inside or Outside?

From where should the planning team members come, inside or outside an organization? An answer to this question depends upon several conditions. The purposes for which a comprehensive planning project is being initiated will necessarily influence the prospective composition of the planning team.

Assuming a large organization is possessed of substantial technical capability, it still may be advisable to rely upon outsiders to undertake the planning. The decision revolves around the degree to which radical change is envisioned or the added legitimacy of an objective outside observer is desired. Depending too heavily upon insiders risks a conflict of interest and a desire on the part of those currently employed to protect the status quo. On the other hand, if marginal or incremental changes and modest redirection are the anticipated end product, then relying upon insiders may prove appropriate. In the latter case, the assumption of available inside expertise is crucial.

If an organization does not possess on its staff the previously listed range of technical skills, then there is little recourse but to engage the services of outsiders. However, when the decision is made to utilize outside planners, to obtain technical competence, gain outside legitimacy, or to stimulate change, or all three, then the bonafides of those involved are critical. Keep in mind that comprehensive strategic planning, particularly in the public sector, is also a political undertaking. The qualifications, experience, and institutional affiliation of the planning team, particularly its leader, will enter into the political equation. They will influence not only the quality of the strategic planning effort, but also the manner in which its recommendations are accepted and eventually implemented.

Of course, a compromise or fusion of inside and outside talent is possible. Here again, the anticipated or desired strategic planning outcome is an important influence on the decision. Radical reform suggests exclusion of insiders below the policy or highest management levels. Findings and recommendations of the planning team are too subject to insider influence to take the risk, if substantial organizational change is desired.

Public or Secret?

To what degree should organizational leaders reveal the existence of a strategic planning effort and the composition of the team? In fact, a comprehensive strategic planning project is sufficiently visible throughout an organization that there is little realistic prospect of disguising its existence. This is true even in a private-sector agency, but is particularly accurate in a public-sector organization. Furthermore, the more troubled the organization, the more widely is observed the fact that it is not meeting its goals or serving its clients, the less likely a strategic planning project can be kept secret.

When a chief executive or a policy board desires new ideas or suggestions for new direction, it can sometimes convene a high-level task force and, if it wants, keep it a secret. In such circumstances, secrecy protects the initiators from embarrassment. If it does not desire to adopt the suggested ideas, it is not saddled subsequently with having to explain publicly why they rejected the advice of a prestigious body of individuals.

Of course, secrecy in such instances also has its costs. In addition to the usual tension accompanying surreptitious activities, keeping a high-level organizational task force secret often squanders the visibility and legitimacy to be gained from the prestige of its members, if the initiators, in fact, turn out to concur with its recommendations. As is often the case, there are trade-offs and decision makers are called upon to anticipate the future without complete information.

Unlike task force activities, strategic planning can seldom take place surreptitiously. Data gathering, analyses, inquiries regarding outcomes and opinions, and the overall sweep of employee and client involvement militate against secrecy. An organizational leader probably errs in attempting to engage in strategic planning secretly. The covert effort will eventually be discovered and the planning team's outcomes compromised by the subsequent suspicions. Strategic planning is better conducted openly, and members of the team should be known to those involved and with whom they will interact.

■ WHY UNDERTAKE COMPREHENSIVE PLANNING?

In the most global terms, planning is done to render an organization more effective. However, there are more detailed responses to such an inquiry. Strategic planning is appropriate for undertaking an assessment of an organization's performance and ensuring that it is headed in desired directions. In this fashion, policymakers and managers fulfill their multiple responsibilities to owners, shareholders, or the general public.

An organization that is unevaluated risks being out of control. Private-sector firms expected to generate profits for their owners have a more universal criterion, namely money, against which to assess their success. Even so, private-sector agencies can stray off course, for example, begin to lose their market share, fall prey to shoddy production quality, or lag behind competition in customer service. Consequently, the evaluation that a comprehensive strategic planning project can offer is of value in ensuring sustained productivity. Strategic planning has an added feature beyond assessment. It not only provides policymakers and managers with a scorecard on past effectiveness, but also can suggest a map for future direction.

All that has been stated immediately above regarding private-sector firms is especially true in public-sector organizations where the "bottom line" (expected outcomes) is not nearly so easily specified or measured. Every organization should have a regularly employed evaluation system, a feedback loop that continually informs policymakers and managers of the level of performance. Strategic planning extends the usefulness of such an evaluation mechanism by systematically linking organizational outcomes to specific agency purposes, internal resource allocation, and consumer or client satisfaction and preferences.

Strategic planning is also appropriate for determining whether or not the external or internal environment is undergoing changes that potentially could alter an organization's purposes or the manner in which it operates. It is important for an organization to undertake a periodic assessment of the external environment in which it operates. Only in this manner can it be assured of anticipating important changes in sufficient time to adjust to them successfully.

Rapid influx of non-English-speaking students, construction of a nearby public community college, growing taxpayer resentment, or dramatically expanding use of charter or nonpublic schools illustrates environmental alterations with significant portent for a local school district's operation. Strategic planning involves systematically scanning an organization's environmental horizon for trends and developments with potential influence. This is the case for changes likely to occur in both internal and external environments.

Systematic planning can inform an organization of important pending developments within itself. For example, a school district learning that 25 percent of its teacher workforce will reach retirement age within the next five years is in a position to plan and mount a comprehensive recruitment program. With sufficient advance notice, a school board perhaps can allocate funds to plan a recruitment campaign, develop an appropriate orientation for new teachers, inform master teachers of forthcoming training responsibilities and schedule their time accordingly, establish new linkages with teacher training institutions, and so on.

Changes in the external environment can also mean important future changes for an organization. For example, for a school district to have to accommodate to an enrollment decline of 20 percent over the next five years undoubtedly would be difficult. Layoffs, possible school closures, and declining revenues all provoke policy and management headaches, not to mention personal hardship for individual employees, parents, and possibly pupils. However, as painful as contraction can be for an organization, forewarning is far more likely than ignorance to facilitate planning that can mitigate distressing developments.

Knowing that a major change is going to occur does not by itself ensure ability to cope. However, ignorance of a pending development almost inevitably guarantees inability to formulate and mobilize resources in support of a timely and rational solution.

The larger the organization, the longer it typically takes to change direction. Thus, large organizations, such as big-urban school districts, particularly should utilize strategic planning in order to sense pending changes in their environment.

Strategic planning is appropriate when an organization's effectiveness is in question and those responsible for its management, its leaders, desire reform. Organizations can drift for a variety of reasons, lack of vision on the part of policymakers, poor leadership, lack of appropriate incentives, poor employee selection and training, misreading of client preferences, failure to adjust to environmental shifts, bad decision by business officials, and so on. Regardless of the explanation, dissatisfaction may begin to build, elected officials are unhappy, stockholders become distressed at low returns to their investment, parents express dissatisfaction with pupil academic performance or discipline, or employers become disturbed with the level of training they experience with entry-level employees.

On occasion, the dissatisfaction may be irrational. In 1957 the Soviet Union launched its first orbital space vehicle, *Sputnik*. The United States was caught technologically flat-footed by a series of prior federal government decisions regarding space. National embarrassment dictated a scapegoat be found, and the schools' alleged lack of academic rigor and discipline eventually was the target. A result was an awesome outpouring of school reform rhetoric and a flurry of high-level task forces, congressional bills, and school district flagellation. A similar set of activities ensued in the aftermath of the 1983 public release of *A Nation at Risk*, a high-level U.S. Department of Education report that triggered education alarm bells that have echoed for decades, most recently setting the stage for the 2001 enactment of the No Child Left Behind Act.

Aside from the source of displeasure, or its validity, organizations come under fire from time to time. Strategic planning offers a systematic and comprehensive means for assessing the degree to which an agency really is off course and generates alternative means by which redirection and reform may occur.

Lastly, an organization may, genuinely and accurately, believe itself to be operating effectively, and, nevertheless, desire the reassurance and feedback of an outside assessment. Under such circumstances, all or a portion of a strategic planning endeavor may be useful.

 CASE 5 REVISITED

Overcoming Fiscal Failures and Facing Future Challenges

Recall administrative teammates Superintendent Dr. Mark Turner and Business Manager Howard Tremble. Their task as newly hired administrators is to transform troubled North Harbor School District. Apply what you have learned about strategic planning in this chapter and create a brief memo for Howard to present to the board with suggestions regarding formulating a strategic plan to set the district on a course to managerial efficiency and instructional success. In the memo to the board, give attention to the planning team, the mix of inside versus outside, making the venture public or secret and why it is essential to initiate a strategic planning cycle now.

Summary

Strategic planning is a tool by which education policymakers and leaders can assess an organization to determine whether it is performing appropriately, and, thereafter, decide either that only fine-tuning and minimum redirection are in order or that substantial reform is needed.

Strategic planning relies upon a mix of technically sophisticated procedures and social and political analyses to arrive at a picture of an organization's current performance relative to its goals, the manner in which it allocated its resources internally, its relationship to external environments, and likely alterations in its external and internal conditions. The outcome of these procedures is a strategic plan that, if propelled forcefully by an agency's policymakers and managers, most assuredly school business managers, or outside political pressures, can result in sustained productivity or dynamic reform for an organization.

Whether comprised of outside experts, employees of the organization itself, or some combination, a strategic planning team consists of individuals knowledgeable about a wide range of technical procedures as well as experts in organizational dynamics and politics. A respected team leader is a crucial component.

The timing of a strategic planning effort is also important. Major transitions in the life of an organization often provide particularly advantageous openings to launch a planning project. Similarly, the completion of a planning effort should be timed to coincide with events that encourage change. In another sense, strategic planning should never stop. A plan, once forged, should be systematically evaluated, updated, and, where appropriate, altered.

Once underway, comprehensive strategic planning insinuates itself so deeply into the important interstices of an organization that any posture other than openness regarding the undertaking is ill advised. Finally, the ultimate organizational objective is not so much formal planning, though this is good. Rather, the ultimate goal is to imbue an organization and its employees, particularly its leaders, with a predisposition to strategic thinking.

Discussion Questions

1. As a litmus test for readiness to embark upon strategic planning, to what degree does your current education organization benefit from: (1) specific organizational goals, (2) a capacity for objective judgment, and (3) technical expertise? In which of these dimensions would your organization be most challenged? What can you as a strategic leader do to ameliorate this condition?

2. Reflect on your career in educational leadership. List one significant end goal that you have for yourself and several supporting instrumental goals that will help you achieve it.

3. Based on your past experiences with strategic planning or goal-setting activities, in what ways have you felt the impact of politics on the process and outcomes of these goal-setting endeavors?

4. When considering the technical sophistication necessary for successful strategic planning, both internal and external environments need to be considered. Provide one example of how you can assess an important aspect of your current organization's external and internal environment for the purpose of meeting current goals.

5. At this point in the life cycle of your organization, do you feel your institution would benefit from a new strategic planning initiative? Why or why not?
6. What are the stated mission and vision statements/purpose statements for your school district? To what degree do you feel components of these purpose statements are able to be accurately assessed?

Web Resources

Austin Independent School District strategic plan website—
    http://www.austinisd.org/inside/initiatives/strategic_plan/
New Jersey State Department of Education strategic plan website—
    http://www.state.nj.us/njded/strategic/
U.S. Department of Education, Ed Performance and Accountability
    Strategic Plan 2002–2007—
    http://www.ed.gov/about/reports/strat/plan2002-07/index.html

CHAPTER FIVE

A Legal and Regulatory Context for School Business Administration

INTRODUCTION

The principal purpose of this chapter is to persuade school business officials to regard laws and regulatory procedures as opportunities to enhance, not as merely restraints upon, the effectiveness of their organization.

LEARNING OBJECTIVES

In this chapter a reader will learn about:

- The expanding legal context within which school business officials routinely operate.
- The bases and distribution of constitutional authority allocated between federal and state governments.
- Authority delegated by states to local school districts.
- Legal instruments and procedures at the disposal of school business officials.
- Significant regulatory issues.
- Compliance and monitoring issues to which a school business official must be alert.

It is assumed that administrators should possess and act from a knowledge of law relevant to their professional field. However, this assertion has often previously been interpreted as "know school law sufficiently to keep out of trouble." However comforting, this limited concept of school law is now inadequate for contemporary business administrators.

The school business administrator's role and responsibilities must be carried out with the knowledge of legal constraints as well as legal authority and powers. In the past much attention was given to the former. Frequently, business administrators were noted for their ability to know and cite scores of laws, opinions, findings, and cases that they used to convince superintendents, principals, and teachers that requests could not be met or were clearly illegal. Many boards and superintendents depended on the business administrator to keep the system out of trouble by knowing and respecting the constraints.

At the same time, however, school systems and their administrators possess or have access to considerable authority and power that can be used legitimately to achieve the goals of the educational program. In the past these powers were not always fully exercised, and school systems and their administrators tended to be confirming and reactive. In today's context an understanding of law can assist administrators in finding new and productive approaches to performing their functions.

With the growing intensity and complexity of social and economic problems in the twenty-first century, as illustrated in Chapter Two, the call for effective performance and accountability is intense. Major social, and, hence educational, changes have redefined legal responsibility and authority in the public schools. School personnel are no longer exempted from lawsuits as *in loco parentis* protection crumbles. School systems have been challenged in court for ineffective instruction. Fiscal accountability legislation has been enacted to hold superintendents liable for miscalculating estimated available revenues and expenditures. Courts have granted or recognized new powers in professional negotiations for teachers' organizations. At the same time, legislatures have extended the power of school systems in areas of fiscal management such as investing active and inactive funds, interfund transfer and borrowing, and purchasing and leasing authority.

However, merely planning for and reacting to the present is inadequate. Given the nature of changes in the environment, planning for the future today is essentially planning for tomorrow's present. Examples from the recent past suggest how changing environments create changes in the legislative and judicial context. There is a strong likelihood of additional and unique legislation and litigation in several areas.

The civil rights of school system employees and students are constantly being redefined in both state and federal courts. The extent of the rights of privacy related to a student's locker is balanced with the responsibility and authority of school officials to protect other students from drug traffickers. The rights of an individual teacher or student carrying the AIDS virus or HIV are balanced with the responsibility of the school systems to provide a safe environment for students and staff.

State education finance systems are under constant judicial assault from plaintiffs alleging inequitable and inadequate funding. State intervention in local school district management has been initiated in many states where financial mismanagement or even "educational bankruptcy" has been charged.

The right of choice by parents in issues related to educational vouchers and tuition tax credits has emerged in the recent past and is likely to reappear in the future. In 1999 Florida enacted a statewide school voucher law that granted tax support for students in low-achieving schools to attend private or parochial schools. As expected, the legislation was challenged on the premise of separation of church and state, the relative advantages provided for wealthy families versus poorer families, and the effect of the tax credit on tuition levels. In early 2000 the Florida Supreme Court ruled the legislation to be unconstitutional. Many states, including Minnesota, Washington, Wisconsin, Ohio, Colorado, and Illinois, have implemented similar plans; all are being contested.

■ LEVELS OF APPLICABLE LEGAL AUTHORITY

There are three levels of understanding regarding legal authority and powers. First, the administrator must know the setting in terms of legal constraints, fiscal controls, and regulatory procedures.

Second, a school business administrator must recognize personal limitations in interpreting the law and should utilize expert legal counsel. In some states, the city or county attorney has responsibility for providing legal counsel to a school district. Many states have enacted permissive legislation to enable boards to obtain legal opinions on specialized functions such as issuing school bonds or entering into construction contracts. The administrator should also use the offices of the state's attorney or attorney general to obtain current opinion on knotty legal questions within the state.

A third area in which legislative and judicial concepts apply in the planning function of the school business administrator is that of acquiring a legal orientation as to the powers and authority exerted within the several levels of government and the relationships among these levels. In an overly simple model, one can accept the notion that authority should accompany responsibility and that authority is implemented through the exercise of power. Thus, knowing where responsibility resides, an administrator can begin to ascertain where and what kind of authority and exercise of power is appropriate. Such an orientation provides the administrator with a base for concluding legal generalities. Thus, a school business official is not solely dependent on specific statutory law or the state education code, but instead has a legal framework into which the specific laws and legal problems fit.

■ LEGISLATIVE-JUDICIAL ORIGINS OF SCHOOL BUSINESS ADMINISTRATION

Public education is a function of government and school business administration is an instrument of government. Hence, one must initially look to the allocation of responsibility and authority by government to determine how school business affairs are to be administered. A wealth of professional literature provides a comprehensive description of the allocation of responsibility, authority, and power among levels of government in regard to public education. Thus, a brief summary of that body of knowledge provides background for the legal setting of school business administration.

The allocation of control in education, through law, is expressed by the term *jurisdiction*. This term means "authority that is legitimated through law." The exercise of power without legal authority is unlawful; hence, the concept of jurisdiction is central to distinguishing between lawful and lawless acts of school administrators. In the U.S. education system, the hierarchy of legal jurisdiction is determined in two ways: (1) by the source or level of law, and (2) by the authority of varying government agencies. Because school law is an outgrowth of the basic scheme of the entire legal system, its place in that system must be understood in terms of universal principles that determine legal jurisdiction (Valente & Valente, 2004).

Valente and Valente (2004) identified four sources and levels of law:

1. *Constitutions.* These are charters that establish fundamental structures and powers of state and federal governments. Courts provide interpretations of constitutional intent over periods of time and changing social conditions.
2. *Statutes.* The second echelon of law is provided in legislation. Statutes develop the specifics of organization and policy. They are developed over time, and thus new legislation frequently replaces or amends earlier enactments. Courts rule on the constitutionality and the interpretation of statutes.

3. *Judicial Law.* Because legislative enactments apply to the entire citizenry, courts rule on disputes between citizens under the universal law. In so doing, judges interpret the law and apply it to specific cases. Frequently, they develop general principles to supplement the law but within the law's intent.

4. *Administrative Law.* In terms of sheer volume, the largest body of law is that developed by administrative agencies created by statute. In education, administrative law is created by state boards of education, state departments of education, county boards of education, local boards of education, administrative units of the previously mentioned bodies, and similar entities (pp. 9–11).

■ LEGAL BASES OF FEDERAL RESPONSIBILITY AND AUTHORITY

The American scheme of government is a variant of federalism. There is a reasonably specific division of powers between the central government and the several constituent states. Through the instrument of the U.S. Constitution, a federal government was created by virtue of the states delegating powers to the central government. As a result, the federal government has only those powers that the states either expressly or by implication delegate to it; all other powers are reserved via the Constitution's Tenth Amendment to the states and to the people.

Because no specific reference is made to education or schooling in the U.S. Constitution, federal government powers in education must be derived from implied powers. To date, the so-called general welfare clause has been the primary source for federal government involvement in public education.[1] The federal government has used two discrete premises to legitimate its educational legislation and litigation. The civil liberties premise is developed under federal constitutional law and statutes that prohibit the abridgment of civil liberties. These include guarantees of fundamental freedoms such as speech, press, association, and religious exercise, as well as the guarantee of freedom from discrimination on the basis of race, sex, and physical impairment.

The curriculum or program premise is based on the presumed significance of specified educational programs as instruments to achieve other federal government goals. Thus, to promote the national defense, the National Defense Education Act of 1958 authorized federal dollars to improve the teaching of the sciences and related programs. The Vocational Education Act of 1963 sought to improve vocational education programs in order to reduce unemployment and increase productivity, and the Elementary and Secondary Education Act of 1965 (ESEA) sought to develop improved educational programs to help eradicate poverty. The Education Consolidation and Improvement Act was passed in 1981 to reduce administrative burdens and consolidate other ESEA titles along with parts of the National Science Foundation Act and the Higher Education Act. The No Child Left Behind Act, passed in 2001, alters the fundamental paradigm by which the federal government provides funds to schools. This act makes clear that from now on schools will be judged by outcomes not processes.

■ LEGAL BASES OF STATE RESPONSIBILITY AND AUTHORITY

Because authority over matters of public education was not directly delegated to the federal government, it is an activity reserved to the states. States have plenary power in these matters—subject, of course, to the limitations mentioned previously in connection with federal and judicial authority.

Most state constitutions place ultimate responsibility of public education at the state level with state educational agencies dictating a range of issues—from curriculum to facilities—to school districts. The state (usually through legislative action) has the authority to modify or abolish school districts and change the powers delegated to the districts.

Responsibility for public education in a state may be thought to originate in the legislature. It is here that basic educational policy is created and financial systems, appropriations, and controls enacted. However, with education growing in complexity and magnitude, legislatures have created state boards of education and charged them with the responsibility of developing specific education policy complementary to the basic policy enacted by the state legislature.

In most states, the executive responsibility in matters of education is delegated to a state superintendent of public schools or a comparable officer. The official is often known as the Chief State School Officer or CSSO. Frequently, this official is appointed by the state board of education (although in some states an appointment by the governor or the legislature is required) or is elected. The superintendent and staff—usually known as the state department of education—have the responsibility of implementing the policies developed by the legislature and the state board of education.

The judicial function in public education at the state level is split. State school legislation is subject to interpretation by the state court system, but the state board of education holds quasi-judicial power insofar as it maintains an evaluative function over the whole state school system.

This structure of educational governance at the state level exerts a unique influence on school business officials in local school districts. They are state officials incumbents in a position approved (and often certified) by a state agency. Local school business officials must operate within general and specific educational policies created by the legislature and the state board of education and administered, supervised, and evaluated by a state superintendent and state department of education.

As a result, business administrators must know the character of these policies and regulations; must monitor their development, modification, and interpretation; and, perhaps more importantly, must know and appreciate the processes employed in order to intervene effectively in their genesis and implementation. This requires a state leadership role for local school district business administrators. They must assume the responsibility of providing expertise in state policy formulation. The rationale for this is the principle that those who are affected by a policy should have a voice in its development. Planning for involvement is crucial if this approach is to be taken.

A second type of state-level influence on the school business administrator is that exerted by agencies of general rather than specialized educational governance. Although educational appropriations and the mechanisms for allocation are specifically designed for the public schools of a state, frequently they are administered, monitored, and evaluated by general government offices. Thus, school business administrators must be familiar with state government accounting and auditing procedures and requirements. Certain state-level procedures for purchasing, issuing bonds, and employing civil service personnel must be followed in public school systems because they are state agencies.

In judicial matters, the school business administrator of the local school system is bound by rulings of the state courts. However, a business official must also be familiar with the opinions of the state's attorney or attorney general, as these constitute valuable (but not infallible) directions of possible subsequent court action.

■ STATE RESPONSIBILITY AND AUTHORITY DELEGATED TO LOCAL SCHOOL DISTRICTS

In all states (with the exception of Hawaii) considerable responsibility and authority in the conduct of public education are delegated by the state to local school systems. In general, states create the educational programs and local school districts operate them. These processes are predicated on the concept that the state is plenary—it delegates to school districts of its own creation the authority to operate these programs.

It is imperative that all school administrators know the process and the substance of delegated responsibility and authority within their own states and localities. This important legal knowledge is necessary for developing and expanding the planning role.

■ LOCAL SCHOOL DISTRICT RESPONSIBILITY AND AUTHORITY

The most important exercise of school district authority is found in the local policies developed to implement state policies. The local district executes the state policy as a quasi-corporation of the state. However, to implement the policy fully, administrative machinery must be established.

■ LEGAL INSTRUMENTS AND CONCEPTS USEFUL IN SCHOOL BUSINESS ADMINISTRATION

Legislation, judicial decisions, and administrative procedures evolving from the three levels of government provide useful specific legal boundaries and conditions that may or must be used by the school business administrator. The previous section contained exhortations for a thorough understanding of these ideas. In the following chapters pertaining to the task areas of school business administration, further reference is made to specific legal facets of each area. The purpose of this section is to provide an overview of some of the most important legal concepts that are general in nature and apply to many if not most of a school business official's several task areas.

Board of Education Minutes

State statutes determine whether it is obligatory for a board of education to maintain records, and, if so, what must be included in the records. However, the official records of the board are ordinarily *prima facie* evidence of its actions. Minutes of a board may be corrected and supplemented. It has been held that board minutes constitute the only legal evidence of board action (*Lewis v. Board of Education*, 1961).

Contractual Authority and Contracts

Because school districts are agencies of the state charged with the conduct of state functions, it follows that they must be provided authority to do so. State statutes provide limited contractual authority to school districts.

Although patterns of limitations vary among states, restrictions usually include requirements that contracts be made by designated agents at legal board meetings, that contracts be written to include specified data, that contracts exceeding a given amount be awarded after competitive bidding, and that a specified indebtedness ceiling be respected.

Common essential elements in all contracts include considerations of the legal capacities of the parties, the legality of the substance of the contract, proper offers with mutual consent to terms, and an enforceable agreement (Valente & Valente, 2004, p. 417).

Competitive Bids

Although states do not uniformly require competitive bidding, nearly all school districts use this procedure in some form. Boards may use competitive bidding at their own discretion if law does not mandate it. If a board so elects, it is then obligated to state clearly in any advertisement that bids are to be competitive, and thus the board binds itself to accept the lowest responsible bid. If the advertisement merely invites bids, the board is not obligated to accept any of the bids; if in its advertisement a board offers to accept the lowest bid, it must do so unless substantial reasons are given for the rejection.

If competitive bidding is used, it is necessary to provide a "common standard" upon which appraisals of bids are to be based. Failure to do so eliminates the basis of real competitive bidding. Thus, rather definitive plans and specifications must be provided to prospective bidders in order to enable them to ascertain a precise bid on a specifically designated activity or product. This practice incorporates an enlightened business principle as well as a legal requirement.

Boards of education may solicit bids on alternatives of essentially the same work. In essence, several bids are requested, and the board exercises its discretion in selecting the lowest responsible bidder on the best alternative. Contractors are free to submit bids on any or all of the separate alternatives and thus compete freely.

Many states require competitive bidding and further specify that the contract be awarded to "the lowest responsible bidder." It has been held that this does not require the board to accept the lowest dollar bid. Instead, the board can exercise its discretion in determining which bidder is most responsible and how this is equated with the dollar bids. In exercising this discretion, boards must act in good faith, must not act capriciously, and must conduct appropriate investigation to enable them to make a decision based on substantial facts.

Often a board, in its advertisement for competitive bids, declares its intention to award the contract to the lowest responsible bidder, but subsequently finds none of the bids acceptable. It has been held that despite the original declaration, a board may reject all bids, but in doing so the board must indicate substantial reasons for its action. This is another illustration of the board's exercise of discretion with justification.

When the board accepts the bid of a contractor, it has been held: (1) that the contractor must be notified, (2) that a definite offer must be submitted, and (3) that there must be a definite acceptance. This is contrary to the popular belief that the board merely has to extend a contract to the contractor.

The law protects contractors who, in the process of submitting bids, make errors in their bids. The general principle is that of not permitting one of the parties to profit by the mistake of another. Thus, the contractor may withdraw an erroneous bid and is not obligated to enter into a contract with the school district.

In like fashion, boards of education may make slight or superficial alterations in specifications once a contract is let. The degree of change, however, must be such that it does not substantially alter the character of the building or item and thus destroy the equity of competitive bidding on the original specifications.

■ REGULATORY MATTERS

There are a variety of operating dimensions around which school districts are the subject of federal and state regulation. There are too many categories of restraint to be catalogued completely here. However, the following section illustrates areas of principal regulatory concern for school business officials.

School Monies

A considerable portion of the responsibility borne by a school business administrator is aligned with money management. Fiscal matters in the business administrator's office include gathering, holding, investing, and expending monies.

School monies themselves are classified in several ways. The most generic classification is by function. Income monies are designated as revenue or nonrevenue. Nonrevenue monies are those that do not add to the assets of the school system. These are typically monies derived from bond issues (which must be eventually repaid), monies derived from the sale of school property (and so the form of the asset is changed but not increased), or monies derived from loans (which must be repaid). Revenue monies are those that add to the assets of the school system; they include taxes, transfer payments or subventions, gifts, fines, fees, and interdistrict tuition payments. Chapters Six and Twelve concentrate more extensively upon revenues and investments.

Control Systems for School Fiscal Policy

The discretionary power of local school boards, and hence of a school business administrator, is severely limited. As indicated in the first section of this chapter, the state, through the exercise of its plenary power, specifies general policies, then delegates to school districts those powers that must be exercised at the local level to implement the state's educational program. In terms of fiscal policy, the state usually specifies the nature of local taxes, procedures that local school boards may use to levy taxes, and quantitative limitations. The state also specifies other sources of revenue that may be obtained and used as well as how these revenues may be expended.

The budgetary function in school systems is a crucial one, and it lies at the heart of state fiscal policy for schools. As will be seen in Chapter Nine on budgeting, this process is used to determine not only the amount to be expended in a given area or account, but also the total amount of revenue needed to support the program. Because of the crucial nature of the latter decision, states usually establish precise procedures to ensure adequate decision making at appropriate levels. Budgeting authority dichotomizes school systems into two groups:

1. Fiscally Dependent Systems: those in which school boards must obtain a budget approved by another local governmental body, such as a city council.
2. Fiscally Independent Systems: those in which the board can act (within state controls) without approval from other local bodies.

Administrator responsibility in accounting, auditing, and reporting is also limited. Usually a state-specified accounting system is mandated to provide uniform reporting and controls. Common definitions of revenue and expenditure areas are mandated. Frequently, state-specified or state-administered auditing procedures are employed to monitor the accounting function in a state's school systems. Most state accounting systems rely upon the U.S. Department of Education promulgated uniform code of accounts.

State law frequently specifies control procedures regarding transferring monies within and between state-specified funds. Also, states have some explicit provision for carrying balances from the end of one fiscal year to the beginning of the next.

Several areas of fiscal policy and money management seem to make headlines nearly every year. One of the most visible problem areas is the gathering and use of "extracurricular" monies. Formerly, most states considered the administration of such monies as beyond the jurisdiction of legislatures. However, in more recent years, states have required school boards and administrators to abide by fiscal control procedures when handling extracurricular monies as well as when handling monies generated from school taxes.

Due to economic and fiscal stringencies of recent years, there is increased evidence of fiscal accountability legislation at the state level affecting practices at the school district level (Hoff, 2005). States impose ceilings on taxes levied by the district. Voter controls are also used. Budgeting procedures and levels are imposed on school systems by restrictions on proportions of increase, and budget approval procedures. Some states have established actual expenditure ceilings on much the same basis. The latter fiscal controls have been initiated either in the legislature or by initiative of the state's voters.

Tort and Tort Liability

The legal posture of school districts on the question of tort liability has changed dramatically over the past several decades. The concept of sovereign immunity ("the king can do no wrong") has been breached in many states, and now school districts stand liable, in varying degrees, for torts.

> . . . [A] tort is a civil wrong for which a court will award damages. A tort may be committed against either a person or his property and may range from direct physical injury to a person (assault or battery) to damage to an intangible asset such as a person's reputation (libel or slander).
> . . . [A] civil action for a tort is brought by the injured person for the purpose of obtaining from the wrongdoer compensation for the damage he has suffered (Peterson, Rossmiller, & Volz, 1978, p. 200).

In general, tort liability has been derived from common (judge-made) law. Fault is a primary consideration. Tort liability occurs when a person causes injury due to intention or negligence. Key questions that must be answered in tort claims are:

• Did the sued party have a duty of care under the law to avoid the injury suffered by the claimant? If so, was that duty actually breached?
• If a breach of duty occurred, was it the proximate (or direct) cause of the injury? If so, is the sued party shielded by a privilege or immunity conferred by law?
• Finally, if there is liability, does the law place a dollar limit on the money damages that the claimant may recover (Valente & Valente, 2004, pp. 116–17)?

It is imperative that the school business administrator knows the state statutes as well as case law and legal opinion on the nature and extent of tort liability. This knowledge provides some guidelines regarding legality and amount of insurance coverage as well as substantive advice to school personnel in matters of reducing exposure to tort suits. School district financial resources are clearly in jeopardy if the district is sued for the contributory negligence of one of its employees, as in the case of a school bus driver in North Carolina (*Simmons v. Columbus County Board of Education*, 2005).

The rule of sovereign immunity that traditionally protected school districts from liability is eroding, or, in some cases, has been completely abolished. A proliferation of litigation against school districts and school officials has prompted school district officials to purchase liability insurance. This type of insurance minimizes the exposure of school districts and their agents to any type of litigation seeking fiscal damages.

Conflict of Interest

Common law has long held that a school board member, as a public official, cannot consummate a contract that results in a conflict between personal or pecuniary interests and the interests of the school system. Frequently, board members are (or are related to) potential school system vendors or contractors. Questions are raised as to whether these simultaneous interests are in conflict, and, if so, in what way and to what degree.

The general principle of conflict of interest is easily understood, but difficulty arises in applying the concept to specific situations. Courts in different states have handed down almost diametrically opposed rulings on essentially similar cases. Differences center on two major considerations:

1. What constitutes personal interest? Some courts find conflict of interest only in cases of direct and pecuniary interest, whereas others find on the basis of any personal interest, even indirect.
2. What is the degree of taint of contract? Some state courts have held that contracts in their entirety are invalidated if any part bears conflict of interest. Courts in other states have declared that such contracts are void only under certain circumstances.

Similar patterns of variation are found in rulings on questions related to contracts with board member spouses, and, in cases of nepotism, the employment of relatives by the board of education.

Given this checkered pattern of judge-made law, it is incumbent on the school business administrator to be familiar with the posture of the state courts in which the school in question is located. It is important to ascertain the nature and consistency of state court rulings on the various kinds of conflict of interest cases. Opinions of attorneys general are also enlightening, although they do not stand as case law.

Race and Sex Discrimination

Decisions with regard to noninstructional or classified employees in most school systems are strongly conditioned by compliance with the Civil Rights Act (1964). The enactment of this legislation provided for the withholding of federal funds from school districts that discriminated against African Americans.

Adherence to the legislative directives of the Civil Rights Act illustrates the important role of the school business administrator in monitoring all federally funded financial assistance in order to ensure school district compliance. If there is a possibility of noncompliance, federal funds may be withdrawn, which would precipitate major budgeting problems.

A similar pattern of constraints pertains to matters of gender discrimination. *Title IX—Prohibition of Sex Discrimination in the Education Amendments (1972)*—establishes the parameters of this antidiscrimination legislation.

Sec. 901 (a) No person in the United States shall, on the basis of sex, be excluded from participation in, be denied the benefits of, or be subject to discrimination under any educational program or activity assistance. . . .

Interpretation of specific institutional and program restrictions has varied among the cases heard. Litigation of the most visible kinds of cases, such as whether girls must be given opportunities to play on boys' baseball teams, has not clarified the legal mandate.

In the News

Russell Johnson, a 45-year-old pipe fitter from the river city of Gadsden, Ala., never intended to be a champion of women's athletic rights. Lauren Cruz, a 15-year-old high school sophomore from Alhambra, Calif., was not steeped in gender-equity statutes, either. But Johnson and Cruz are at the forefront of a new phase in the evolution of Title IX; each recently filed a federal lawsuit accusing the local school district of discriminating against the girls' high school softball team. Their lawsuits seek better fields, locker rooms and equipment—facilities and services that would be comparable, they say, to those already afforded the boys' high school baseball teams.

There have been dozens of such suits in recent years nationwide, centered on claims of shoddy, weed-strewn ball fields for girls' teams or inadequate girls' locker rooms—with the vast majority of cases settled in favor of the female athletes. While the familiar battles over Title IX take place at colleges and universities, the battleground has been extended to high schools and middle schools. It is not only lawsuits that have become more common. At the federal Department of Education, the agency responsible for enforcing Title IX, the number of complaints involving sex discrimination in high school and even middle school athletics has outpaced those involving colleges by five to one since 2001.

"High school is where the Title IX action is," said Bob Gardner, the chief officer of the National Federation of State High School Associations. "The colleges get all the attention, but Title IX isn't about the nation's elite college athletes. It's about providing a grass-roots gateway to sports that benefits millions." Increasingly, people have decided to take it into their own hands to determine exactly how wide that gateway should be.

In Owasso, Okla., a local firefighter, Ron Randolph, sued his school district for discrimination under Title IX and received a settlement that led to the construction of a state-of-the-art softball complex and spawned 13 similar suits in Oklahoma.

In Kentucky, a landmark suit concerning a high school softball team coincided with the state athletic association's decision to annually review all 284 member school districts for Title IX compliance—a process that often leads to fines and penalties for the noncompliant and has brought about the construction of more than 70 softball fields.

In Indiana, where there was a state championship in pole vaulting for boys but not for girls, Steve Allen, whose daughter Tori was a top pole-vaulter, sued; the Indiana high school association agreed to add a girls pole vaulting state championship.

In Arlington, Va., a suit against the county school district by Kenneth Boehm, whose daughter Christine played field hockey, led to a settlement in which the district agreed to make a lengthy list of improvements to facilities for field hockey, girls gymnastics and softball.

In Cheatham County, Tenn., a complaint to the federal Department of Education led to an investigation and new lights for the softball field, paid for by the school district.

Another complaint to education department's Office for Civil Rights concerned the West Linn-Wilsonville School District in Oregon, which later agreed to build a $390,000 softball batting cage and to construct restrooms, dugouts and training facilities that were more like those for the boys' baseball team.

The new focus on Title IX in high schools might be tied to a significant increase in sports participation for high school girls. In 1972, when Title IX was enacted by Congress, there were 295,000 girls participating in high school sports, or roughly one in 27. Now, there are more than 2.8 million girls, or approximately one in three.

While the most common Title IX complaint involves the disparity between the fields and the facilities for softball and baseball, there are many other ways that schools' athletic departments can be in violation of Title IX. The law and related regulations cover much more than only fields and locker rooms.

Perhaps the most misunderstood factor is the use of money raised by booster groups. This money, often contributed by parents or local sponsors, is frequently used for a particular, high-profile sport like football, with some booster groups raising as much as $40,000 in a season. But for Title IX purposes, any money spent on any team, even by a private booster group, is treated as if it were public money appropriated by the school district. It is the obligation of the district to ensure that outside financing does not tip the balance, making the athletic experience inequitable for girls or boys. Many school districts have convinced booster groups to contribute to a variety of sports instead of only one or two, but that remains a controversial policy in many places.

Among other athletic department matters covered by Title IX is equal access for boys and girls to a school's training staff and weight rooms. Scheduling is often a major issue; schools are not permitted to have either the boys' or girls' teams use all the desirable evening or weekend times for games or the most popular after-school times for practice. Gymnasiums must be shared. The mode of transportation to games or practices must be fundamentally equivalent.

Coaching salaries also must be comparable. The schools must make an effort to publicize girls' teams the way they publicize boys' teams. Title IX even covers the cheerleaders, who are not supposed to cheer more often for boys' teams than for girls' teams.

Monitoring compliance is left to local school boards, activists, the courts or the Department of Education's Office for Civil Rights, which generally investigates after it receives a complaint. It does conduct periodic independent compliance reviews. Many women's rights advocacy groups would like to see the Office for Civil Rights be more aggressive in pursuing high schools that are not in compliance with Title IX.

The full impact of Title IX is yet to be determined.[2] Decisions spelling out specific compliance requirements foreshadow the direction of future trends among federal courts in applying Title IX's prohibitions. Recent federal court cases have given parents of children sexually harassed in schools a right to sue their school districts.[3]

It is obvious that the school business administrator, who has some responsibility for budgeting educational and support programs, must know the school district's points of vulnerability as they address Title IX issues. The financial implications of Title IX are many. School districts found in violation of the federal statute face paying damages awarded to victims in addition to jeopardizing federal funding. Complying with the statues of Title IX has schools taking proactive measures, such as expansion of athletic programs for females and provisions of athletic equipment for females that is comparable to that of males. School business administrators will have to monitor carefully the school district's compliance with federal laws in order to minimize unexpected financial fallout.

Due Process

With the advent of wide and comprehensive civil rights legislation and litigation, due process has become highly visible in the public schools. Teachers and others in the school system have substantive rights that cannot be abridged, conferred on them by federal and state constitutions. These include federal constitutional and statutory rights (e.g., freedom of speech, religion, association) as well as those secured in the state constitution and laws. However, unique rights and privileges not specified in the federal Constitution are protected only by the states conferring them. States will often enact statutory due process procedures to ensure provisions of these rights. Procedural due process is derived from the due process clause of the federal Constitution's Fourteenth Amendment. The amendment confers the substantive rights just mentioned and also provides procedural protection against illegal deprivation of these rights.

Due process has no simple definition. It varies with the circumstances involved. Factors that must be considered include the nature of the right, the danger of the denial of the right, and the nature of remediation. Two major questions must be addressed:

> *Application of this prohibition requires the familiar two stage analysis: one must first ask whether the asserted individual interests are encompassed within the Fourteenth Amendment's protection of "life, liberty or property"; if protected interests are implicated, one then must decide what procedures constitute "due process of law." (Ingram v. Wright, 1977)*

Few school-related circumstances jeopardize life, but allegations of the denial of liberty-related rights without due process have become frequent. An example is the denial of the right of seeking a livelihood by citing inappropriate work habits, thereby jeopardizing opportunity for future employment (*Kingsford v. Salt Lake City School District*, 1981).

The denial of property-related rights includes denial of employment as ensured by some legal entitlement under laws, regulations, contracts, and the like. Most of these allegations relate to property interest in continued employment and state statutes specifying processes required for termination of employment.

The second stage of the analysis suggests that if protected interests are encompassed, then courts must decide what constitutes due process. Valente and Valente (2004) cite the following procedures:

- The affected party must be given fair and reasonable notice of the charges.
- The affected party must be accorded a hearing.

- The hearing should be set promptly but sufficiently in advance to afford a fair opportunity to prepare for the hearing.
- The party is accorded the right to be represented by legal counsel.
- The party is permitted to present oral and written evidence at the hearing.
- The party and his or her counsel are allowed to confront and challenge all evidence against him or her, including written documents and testimony of adverse witnesses.
- An impartial tribunal must conduct the hearing.
- The party is entitled to have an official record, usually by stenographic transcript, of the hearing.
- The party should be allowed appeal to higher legal authority, including access to courts to redress legal errors (p. 197).

School business administrators most frequently have personnel responsibilities with classified and noncertificated personnel. Consequently, due-process-related problems and responsibilities fall in the areas of employee evaluations, promotions, transfers, and dismissals. State statutes and school system policy must be carefully reviewed to determine what procedural rights are conferred. Obviously, substantive rights of these employees must be honored, but the incidence of denial of federal constitutional rights is relatively low. All administrators in school systems are well advised to make certain the board of education has incorporated due process procedures in its policy and that it conforms to the constitutions and statutes of the federal and state governments.

■ COMPLIANCE RESPONSIBILITIES AND PRACTICES

The present chapter has dealt with those school business functions that the legislature and courts have said the schools must do, must not do, or may do. Another important consideration is related to compliance: the degree to which the mandatory and permissive functions accepted by the school system are actually carried out. On occasion, school systems, communities, and even state legislatures have refused to comply with legitimate but unpopular legislative or court mandates. An example of this is the challenge by states for compliance with federally enacted affirmative action measures. School business administrators may be placed in demanding and even sharp role conflict situations when questions of compliance are raised.

Acceptance of Compliance Responsibilities. Compliance is an integral part of legislative and judicial mandates. Governmental agencies and their officers and agents have the inherent responsibility to implement the authoritative policies and carry out the directives of their units. Frequently, oaths of office include explicit language concerning this obligation. Problems of compliance arise when communities or administrators are guilty of malfeasance or nonfeasance.

Fixing Compliance Responsibility. Compliance responsibilities exclusively fixed with school business administrators are relatively few. Most school-related compliance responsibilities are fixed at the state and the local board of education levels. These bodies have the responsibility to see that they carry out federal mandates in such actions as the Civil Rights Act of 1964, federal court desegregation orders, the Education for the Handicapped Act, and school prayer decisions. State legislatures and local boards of education usually delegate the responsibility for implementation to subordinate agencies or administrators. Thus, responsibility becomes blurred or confused, and noncompliance becomes a major problem.

In the News

The parents of a former Edwardsville High School student sued the Edwardsville School District in federal court this week, alleging the district failed to accommodate their daughter's special needs or evaluate her properly. Thomas and Glenna Loch had asked that their daughter receive special services because she had diabetes and emotional anxiety. She missed dozens of days of school, then stopped attending altogether the latter half of her sophomore year.

The suit alleges that she was unable to return because teachers singled her out for needing to visit the nurse often and to get water and use the bathroom during class. Those actions aggravated her emotional problems, the complaint said.

After their daughter stopped attending Edwardsville High, the Lochs enrolled her at a community college. They asked that the district still consider her an Edwardsville student and give her credit for the college classes. The parents also requested a hearing from the State Board of Education to determine if the school district was correct in ruling their daughter ineligible for special services. A hearing officer from the Illinois State Board of Education ruled in September that she was not eligible for special services because her diabetes, if controlled, would not keep her from attending school. She also ruled there was no evidence that emotional issues kept the student from making academic progress.

The suit, filed this week, requests reimbursement from the district for community college tuition, "reasonable damages" for emotional pain and suffering and attorney fees.

From: Aguilar, A. (2006, January 12). Parents of special needs student sue school district. *St. Louis Post-Dispatch*, p. B4.

Noncompliance might occur because the administrator chooses not to comply or is inept in understanding the mandate or in carrying it out. Another reason for noncompliance is that the policymaking body or subordinate responsible for the administrator chooses not to comply or is inept in understanding the mandate.

Federal programs invariably carry compliance requirements. The Education for All Handicapped Children Act (1975)[4] concerned education for the handicapped and required school systems to provide programs and services to specified handicapped students. School business administrators have considerable responsibility for appropriate budgeting, purchasing, accounting, and reporting mandates contained in the legislation. In districts utilizing the federal school lunch programs, legislation mandates eligibility criteria, revenue sources and guidelines, nutritional specifications, and accounting procedures.

State compliance requirements are demonstrated in pupil transportation policies. States frequently specify pupil eligibility for the state transportation subsidy. In addition, the district, in order to obtain the subsidy, must comply with requirements in the areas of vehicle specifications, driver qualifications, routing specifications, and vehicle purchase and maintenance procedures.

Perhaps the area of the most important stringent state compliance requirements is that of fiscal management. States frequently require school systems to use standardized budgeting, purchasing, accounting, auditing, and reporting systems. Procedures, calendars, and forms for these aspects of management are mandated by the state agencies involved.

At the local school system level, the school business administration function often assumes responsibility for compliance with local policy mandates. Consistent and uniform application of local board policy in the areas of the master contract with the teachers' negotiation body is perhaps the largest monetary responsibility in many systems. Business administrators assume compliance responsibility for the board of education in contracts with vendors. When boards contract for use or rental of school facilities by outside individuals or groups, business administrators have compliance responsibilities thrust on them.

Monitoring Compliance. Because legislative and judicial mandates have compliance requirements that fall into the areas of responsibility of other administrators besides the school business administrator, it is important that a comprehensive systemwide monitoring program be developed. In the example of the Education for All Handicapped Children Act, the administrative team should be involved in monitoring the several aspects of student eligibility, staffing requirements, program specifications, facility requirements, and other obligations, as well as those responsibilities accruing to the school business administrator. Because lack of compliance might result in the withdrawal of funding, the role of the school business administrator is twice impacted by the mandates—in terms of overall school system planning as well as specific legislative responsibilities.

The monitoring function implies an additional and generic responsibility for the school business administrator: spelling out the nature of school-business-related legislative and judicial mandates to the administrative team. These are aggregated with additional mandates identified by other members of the team and are transmitted by the superintendent to the board of education with: (1) implications for program and funding, and (2) the consequences for compliance or noncompliance.

Summary

Because schools are agencies of the state, a school business administrator must be knowledgeable in legislative and judicial matters that involve public education. All school administrators must have a generalized knowledge and appreciation of the legal bases in order to see the gestalt and thereby relate specific legal principles to the total legal concept. The derivation of legal power to enact educational policy, the exercise of plenary power by the states, and the delegation of power by the state to local school boards are among the fundamental legal concepts underlying the governance of public schools.

Because school business administrators are typically given the responsibility for executing local school district policies, it is necessary for them to know the policymaking structure and how they can relate administrative procedures to such policy. The chapter covers several specific concepts that the school business administrator uses. These include the minutes of the board of education—the legal voice of the board; contractual authority—the power and constraints on contractual obligations; competitive bids—the procedures and principles necessary to protect the school system and satisfy the law; school monies—to protect the resources of the school system and use them as intended; control systems for school fiscal policy—those fiscal controls designed to provide fiscal accountability; torts—civil wrongs for which a court will award damages; conflicts of interest—contracts that result in conflicts between interests of school system personnel and the interests of the school system itself; race and sex discrimination—where there is denial of rights provided under federal statute or administrative law; due process—where there is denial of rights provided under the Fourteenth Amendment of the Constitution or a comparable provision in a state constitution; and compliance.

The authors contend that these legal and judicial concepts underlie nearly every action of the school business administrator, who is obligated to know many of them specifically (e.g., what size purchase requires a competitive bid). As a school official with fiduciary duties, the school business administrator must also be generally aware of others in order to know when to obtain legal assistance (e.g., what kind of investments can be made with the proceeds of a bond issue).

Discussion Questions

1. Obtain a copy of your state's school code (codification of state law pertaining to schools) and determine the specific legal requirements in matters of board of education minutes, contractual authority, competitive bidding, accounting, investment of funds, budgeting, and related business functions.
2. Review the policy handbook of a school system and determine the legal bases of the school business-administration-related policies that have been established.
3. Interview a school superintendent or school business official in order to identify and discuss with the class examples that have influenced school business administration in your state of:

   a. Legislation (both state and federal).
   b. Case law (both state and federal).
   c. Judicial opinion (opinions of the state's attorney general or state's attorney).

Web Resources

Access Network at Teachers College, Columbia University, New York—school funding and education reform in 50 states—
   http://www.schoolfunding.info/litigation/litigation.php3

Association of School Business Officials International updated legislative issues—
   http://capwiz.com/asbo/issues/

National Conference of State Legislatures School Finance Litigation—
   http://www.ncsl.org/programs/educ/LitigationMain.htm

Nation Center for Education Statistics, Education Finance Statistics Center Litigation—
http://nces.ed.gov/edfin/litigation

U.S. Department of Education, Lead & Manage My School: Standards, Assessment and
Accountability—
http://www.ed.gov/nclb/accountability/schools/edpicks.jhtml?src=rt

U.S. Department of Education, Office of Special Education and Rehabilitative Services—
http://www.ed.gov/about/offices/list/osers/osep/index.html

References

Hoff, D.J. (2005, June 8). Schools feel pressure of efforts to increase fiscal accountability.
Education Week, 24(39), 1 and 24.

Peterson, L.J., Rossmiller, R.A., & Volz, M.M. (1978). *The law and public school operation*.
New York: Harper & Row.

Valente, W., & Valente, C. (2004). *Law in the schools* (6th ed.). New Jersey: Prentice Hall.

Notes

1. A reader should understand, however, that there exist other possible theories or justi-
   fications for federal government engagement with education. For example, Goodwin
   Liu of the University of California Berkeley School of Law argues for the expansion
   of federal government action in education under the "National Citizenship" notion
   contained in the Constitution's Fourteenth Amendment.
2. See Carleton, D., *Student's guide to landmark congressional laws on education*, (Westport,
   CT: Greenwood Publishing, 2002) for a detailed discussion of Title IX.
3. See *Oona R.-S. v. Santa Rosa City Schools*, 1995, and the 1992 unanimous Supreme
   Court decision in *Franklin v. Gwinnett County Public Schools*.
4. In 1990 the official name of the act was changed to the Individuals with Disabilities
   Education Act (IDEA).

CHAPTER SIX

Education Revenues: Magnitude, Sources, and Characteristics

■ INTRODUCTION

For their existence, schools rely on a spectrum of resources such as human talent, political capital, public commitment, legal support, leadership, and money. However, of all conceivable resources, money is the most significant because it is the most fungible. Money can be exchanged for or used to enhance virtually all other forms of capital. Hence, this and several following chapters concentrate on various facets of money for public schools.

LEARNING OBJECTIVES

In this chapter a reader will learn about:

- The public-policy justification for paying for elementary and secondary education through public taxation rather than private contribution.
- The magnitude, sources, and significance of public education revenues.
- Technical characteristics of taxes such as: basis; equity; liberty; efficiency; impact; incidence; yield; administrative costs; compliance; and economic, social, and political effects.

Discussion of education finance can be classified into the following stages: (1) generating, (2) distributing, (3) internally allocating, (4) spending, and (5) accounting for money. All these facets are important to the role of a school business official. This chapter is concerned with the first phase, generation of money for public education, and with *taxes* primarily used to do so.

This chapter will enable a school business official to have a firm grasp of the sources of the school district's public revenues. A reader will receive details regarding taxes' bases, equity, liberty, efficiency, impact and incidence, yield, administration and compliance costs, and economic, social, and political effects. The chapter also describes processes by which property is taxed. This chapter first defines general characteristics of taxes and then describes how they apply to each of the three most general taxes. Next, tax limitation movement of the late twentieth century is discussed, along with illustrations of alternatives to taxation for education. The chapter concludes with a comparison of U.S. revenue generation schemes and those of other industrialized nations.

■ THE JUSTIFICATION FOR PAYING FOR K–12 PUBLICLY

Education is supported chiefly by broad-based taxes (taxes based on widespread activities and conditions), but other methods of financing are conceivable. User charges (known as tuition when applied to education) come to mind. If education were primarily a personal investment or what economists label a consumption good—that is, if it did not have a preponderance of favorable social consequences—then rightfully students or their families should be expected to bear the major cost burden. If, however, schooling's benefits accrue principally or additionally to the larger society, rather than to the individual, society should pay all or part of the costs through taxes. At present, education in the United States is taken to be a social good. Thus, public elementary and secondary schools of all states are tuition-free, supported primarily by local and state taxation. The judicial system has repeatedly protected the free nature of public elementary and secondary schooling.

Postsecondary education provides an interesting contrast. At least until the beginning of the twenty-first century, most, but by no means all, of the benefits of postsecondary education have been determined to flow to the individual rather than the larger society. Postsecondary schooling confers advantages such as higher lifetime income, hedging options in one's career, and greater job choice and job fulfillment. Because of its high ratio of private, as opposed to public, benefits, the United States generally expects higher education enrollees to contribute personally to their college costs.

If elementary and secondary education is to be paid for publicly, then there must be a system of taxation. A number of states have dedicated revenues from a portion of a tax or particular tax to education (e.g., a specified percent of the sales tax or taxes on mineral extraction such as oil, gas, or coal). However, these narrowly based tax sources have proven insufficient to meet resource needs of this largest single object of state and local governmental expenditure—education. As a result, education finance has rested primarily on broad-based taxes such as income, sales, and property taxes.

■ TAX CHARACTERISTICS

For the 2007–08 school year, general revenues of public elementary and secondary schooling in the United States are estimated to approach or exceed $600 billion. Approximately 45 percent of these revenues are provided by local governments and are raised through property taxes. State revenues account for a little more than 45 percent of what schools spend. Federal funds and private contributions comprise the remainder.

Sixty-eight percent of the revenues provided by state governments results from general formula assistance that includes revenue from state income and sales taxes (U.S. Bureau of the Census, 2006). From where does all of this money come? How is it raised? What concerns are there about the process of taxation? These questions frame the bulk of the content in this chapter.

Basis of Taxation

There are four bases, or criteria, for levying a tax: (1) wealth, (2) income, (3) consumption, and (4) privilege. These all involve money—the first three directly; the fourth, indirectly.

Wealth. A tax on wealth is based on the ownership of property. The most common example is the property tax; the amount of which is linked to the value of property owned. Another example is the federal estate tax that is based on the size of a deceased person's estate. A third example is provided by localities and states that tax the holding of personal property such as an automobile, airplane, or boat. Note that the size of the tax bears no relation to the income generated by the property owned, but is based only on value of the property.

Income. A tax on income is linked to the taxable income of individuals (or corporations). Taxable income is income after allowable expenses and deductions. One of the virtues of an income tax is that the amount of the tax is related to the income used to pay it.

Consumption. A tax on consumption is usually known as a sales tax, particularly if it applies to all or most sales. If it applies only to purchases of a particulars class of items (such as "sin" taxes or taxes on goods such as alcohol and tobacco), it is often known as an *excise tax*.[1] Import duties on particular goods are also excise taxes. Many states have enacted lottery statutes. A lottery can best be viewed as a product sold by the state and an excise tax on that product. (The proportion of lottery revenues paid in prizes is the product, and the difference between total revenues and prizes, plus operating expenses, is the tax, which is conveyed to the state.)[2]

Privilege. A tax on *privilege* is a tax levied on the right to engage in an activity regulated by government. It usually takes the form of *license fees*. These fees may be related directly to commercial gain, as in the case of a retail store license, a medical license, or a license to operate a taxicab. On the other hand, they may have no direct relation to money, as with a dog license, a driver's license, or a hunting or fishing license. The number of licenses required by state and local governments is large, and the money collected in fees is substantial.[3] Imposition of license fees is usually defended as being a regulatory function of government rather than a tax, with the license fees paying costs of regulation. This is only partially true: fees are often much greater than costs. Governments also sell exclusive or semi-exclusive rights to engage in specified commercial activities within city or regional boundaries. These are called *franchises* or *concessions*. An example is a franchise granted to a utility or cable TV company.

Governments raise money by other methods that cannot strictly be labeled taxation. Higher levels of government transmit intergovernmental aid to lower levels. For example, both the federal government and state governments grant financial aid to local school districts. Governments charge fees for service. For example, a municipal government may operate an electric utility and sell power or operate the municipal sewer system. Since a fee for service is a charge for a specific product (electricity) or activity (sewage disposal), it cannot strictly be called taxation.

Equity

Since taxes are a burden imposed on all by the will of a political majority, they should treat all who are affected in an equitable manner. This may conflict with other considerations, as indicated later, but it is a worthwhile goal. What should determine whether or not a tax is equitable?

Horizontal Equity. In economics, horizontal equity implies that a tax should treat equals equally. For example, two individuals with the same amount of net taxable income should pay the same amount of income tax. Two persons who own property of equal value in the same neighborhood or jurisdiction should pay the same amount of property tax. This is a relatively simple criterion and easy to judge. Most taxes are relatively equitable on this criterion; exceptions regarding the property tax will be discussed later. Unfortunately for those establishing tax criteria, not all persons are equal. It is thus necessary to establish rules for tax treatment of unequals—a more difficult task.

Vertical Equity. Striving to treat unequals fairly (and perhaps equally) is known as vertical equity. In education finance, the principal application of this principle is not so much through taxation as it is through subsequent revenue distribution. In a subsequent chapter a great deal will be explained regarding distribution formula weightings for various costly or handicapping student and district conditions that represent efforts to achieve vertical equity.

Benefit Principle

An obvious criterion for examining the fairness of a tax system is that individuals or households should pay in proportion to benefits received, or in proportion to their contribution to the cost of whatever activity is supported by the tax. A prime example of a tax based on the benefit principle is the Federal Highway Trust Fund, supported by gasoline taxes. The money in the fund is deployed to construct and maintain federally aided highways, and the amount contributed by each person, which is a fixed amount per gallon of gas, is related to an individual's or company's use of those highways.

The benefit principle is difficult to apply in education, however. At first blush, it would appear as if only parents benefit from the public provision of education. However, public school advocates argue that entire communities, regions, and nations benefit from strong schools—in business recruitment, in trained workers who pay taxes, in civically engaged members of the community, and in general increased productivity.

Measurement. Taxes based on the benefit received or on the contribution to cost seem so eminently reasonable that there is a temptation to endorse this principle as a basis for all taxation. However, it is often difficult to assess either benefits received or contribution to cost. For example, should police costs be charged to the person protected from or saved from robbery or murder, on the basis of benefit received, or to the felon, on the basis of contribution to the cost of law enforcement activities? Or are there benefits to an average citizen from safer streets and homes that cannot be allocated on any strict accounting basis? There is general agreement that most police expenses cannot be allocated on a benefit or cost basis.

Measuring Education Benefits. Taxation based on the benefit principle for public education presents a particular problem. As previously discussed, if schooling benefits accrue mainly or largely to society and less to the individual, then society should pay all or most schooling costs through taxes. But then how are benefits received or contributions to cost to be measured and how are taxes to be implemented? If education is primarily a personal investment or consumption good, then schooling benefits can more easily be measured and taxation can be based on the benefit principle. But in this case, it is students or their families that should pay schooling costs not society, and taxation is not necessary. This is the postsecondary education situation as mentioned previously.

"Free Riders." What about national defense costs? There is a different problem here: no individual operating only out of logical self-interest would pay taxes for a pure public good such as national defense, because there is no easy way for governments to defend citizens who pay for national defense without also defending those who do not pay. This is known as the free-rider problem. In addition, there is no rational way of calculating either individual benefits from or costs of national defense. Allocation of taxes on this basis is not feasible. Rather, the total budget is decided on a collective basis through congressional and executive branch actions, and resources are generated through taxes based on criteria other than benefits received.

Welfare costs present yet another problem. Here, individual benefits are clear—welfare payments to persons. However, the folly of charging individuals a tax equal to the amount of welfare benefits received is obvious. Welfare has income redistribution as its principal goal. Taxation based on benefit received would directly contradict this goal.

For these reasons, most taxes cannot be allocated on the basis of benefit received or contribution to cost. An alternative equity criterion must be applied.

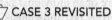

CASE 3 REVISITED

School Business Office Meltdown, and the Band Played On

John Sample's limited experience in education management did not prepare him for the announcement that the school district faced a deficit of $2.5 to $5 million. Given the perilous fiscal condition of the district, the superintendent suggests the tax rate be raised. Knowing that a tax increase would only "Band-Aid" the financial problems of the district and further knowing that the public would be against a tax increase, what are some creative ways that John could suggest to raise money for the district? He has already unsuccessfully met with representatives from government and foundation officials to ask for assistance with additional funds. Consider making a list of alternatives and sharing with your classmates.

Ability-to-Pay Principle

Tax Burdens. An alternative method for determining whether a tax is equitable is to examine the burden that a tax imposes on individuals. Besides determining that the tax system should treat equals equally (horizontal equity), it is also reasonable that those with greater means contribute more to the tax system than those with lesser means (vertical equity). The idea behind the ability-to-pay principle is that individuals should pay in proportion to the burden that the provision of the public good or service taxes imposes, which is based on the individual's ability to pay the tax. When the tax system requires individuals with the same ability to pay to bear the same amount of taxes and requires individuals with less ability to pay to relinquish fewer taxes, then the tax system satisfies both horizontal and vertical equity.

Measuring Ability to Pay. The difficulty that arises from application of this principle is determining an individual's ability to pay. Potential indices to measure the ability to pay coincide with the previously listed four bases for levying a tax: income, consumption, wealth, and privilege.

Income-based measures are the most commonly used means to determine an individual's ability to pay. Some disadvantages of such measures are that income may not be easily measurable (in-kind income or a farmer's produce from a family plot) or observable (gratuities), and that these measures could assign the same tax liability to a retired individual with low income but high wealth accumulation and a college student with low income and high debt. Further, although annual income is the more common measure, a construct of lifetime income might be a more complete measure on one's ability to pay. Regardless of the basis for levying a tax, taxes are paid mostly out of income; so current income-based measures most accurately reflect an individual's purchasing power at the time a tax is levied.

◼ PROGRESSIVE AND REGRESSIVE TAXES

Taxes Relative to Income. In judging equity of a tax by the ability-to-pay principle, one must compare the amount of tax paid with the appropriate measure of an individual's ability to pay. This is most commonly income. Suppose that for a given tax, individuals with incomes of $20,000 pay an average of $200 in tax, and people with incomes of $40,000 pay an average of $400 in tax. Each income group is therefore paying an average of 1 percent of its income in tax. This is said to be a proportional tax. Whether such a tax is a property tax, a sales tax, or an income tax, the comparison is the amount of tax paid with the income of the payer of the tax. A proportional tax would, on the surface, appear to meet the ability-to-pay standard, for each person pays the same percentage of his or her income in tax.

Next, suppose that those with $20,000 in income continue to pay $200 in tax but those with $40,000 pay $300. Now the lower-income group is paying 1 percent of its income, but the higher-income group is paying only three-quarters of 1 percent. Note particularly that although the higher-income group is paying more dollars, it is paying a smaller percentage of its income than the lower-income group. A tax with this characteristic is called a *regressive tax*.

Finally, suppose that the $20,000 group continues to pay $100 but the $40,000 group pays $800. Those with higher incomes are paying 2 percent of their income, those with lower incomes only 1 percent. Such a tax is called a progressive tax because the rates progress toward higher percentages at higher incomes (see Figure 6.1, which displays a proportional, regressive, and progressive tax imposed on four individuals that each generates the same amount of revenue).

Tax Equity. Which of these types of tax (regressive, proportional, or progressive) comes closest to meeting the ability-to-pay criterion? In considering this, one must realize that there is a basic income amount households need in order to maintain a minimum standard of living. Families whose incomes are at this subsistence level often spend all of their income for necessities and have little left to pay taxes. At the other end of the scale, extremely wealthy households find they are unable to spend all of their income on goods and services. They clearly have excess income, which could be used for investment or for paying taxes. Under these circumstances, it is evident that a regressive tax is not based on ability to pay. In actuality, a proportional tax is not either. A progressive tax, at least theoretically, leaves untouched the monies necessary for a minimum standard of living.

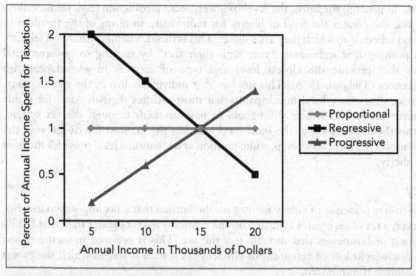

FIGURE 6.1 Tax Characteristics

However, there is no agreement on how progressive a tax must be in order to be equitable. If it is close to being proportional, it is probably unfair to poor people; if it is extremely progressive, it is probably inequitable to wealthy people. The broad band of disagreement between these extremes results partly from lack of consensus on how much life's necessities cost.

Another reason for adhering to the equity principle of progressive taxation is an unwritten tenet in the American ethos that government should intervene to reduce extreme income inequalities. One way to do this is to tax a greater percentage of wealthy households' income than that of the poor. On the other hand, many political conservatives would argue that it is the rich who invest in businesses, create employment opportunities, and thus fuel the free enterprise system. Progressive taxes reduce the money available for such investment, decreasing general prosperity and incidentally the future income available to be taxed. An alternative way to redistribute income, used extensively in the United States, is to make payments to low-income people through programs such as Temporary Assistance to Needy Families (TANF) and Medicaid. These transfer payments are discussed later in this chapter in connection with the incidence of taxation.

Liberty

The benefit principle of equity provides for the greatest freedom of the individual because individuals are taxed according to services that best fit their personal preference profile. The ability-to-pay principle subjects individuals to taxation not based on their preferences, but (most commonly) based on their income. Thus it is possible for a voter majority to increase the progressivity of the tax system to force the high-income minority to provide services for the majority. This is known as macro decoupling. The converse, micro decoupling, will be explained in a subsequent section.

Federalism. In general, the lower the level of government jurisdiction (e.g., municipality) enacting a tax, the greater the level of liberty for individuals, in terms of the freedom to choose the tax schedule to which they are subject. This is the idea behind Charles Tiebout's hypothesis positing that individuals "vote with their feet" by moving to governmental jurisdictions that provide the closest level and type of services in accordance with one's preferences (Tiebout, 1956). This implies that individuals live in the nation, state, county, service district, or local municipality that most satisfies their demand for a mix of government services and their willingness to pay for them through the tax system. Based on this theory, taxation at the local level achieves the greatest liberty because the individual chooses the local tax system, while taxation at the national level provides the least amount of liberty.

Efficiency

The ability-to-pay principle of equity focuses on the burden that a tax imposes to individuals. However, a tax often creates a burden on the economy that is greater than that felt by the individuals or businesses that directly pay the tax. This is referred to as the excess burden or deadweight loss of taxation. An efficient tax system is one in which the excess burden of taxation is minimized.

To help understand the excess burden of taxation, Figure 6.2 displays a demand and supply curve of a good with and without a tax on consumption that is a constant dollar amount (this depicted condition is common with excise taxes).[4] The demand curve demonstrates that as the price of a good falls, individuals consume more of that good. The demand curve also represents the value that consumers place on a good and demonstrates that some individuals place a higher value on a good than others. The supply curve represents the price that a company or producer is willing to sell a given quantity of the good or the marginal cost of producing the good. The intersection of these two curves represents the equilibrium price (P) and quantity (Q) of the good without a tax. At this equilibrium, some consumers would be willing to pay more for the good than the equilibrium price. The consumers' surplus represents this willingness to pay that exceeds the equilibrium price. This area is represented in Figure 6.2 by the regions ABFG. Similarly at this equilibrium, some producers would be willing to sell their product for less than the equilibrium price. This is referred to as producers' surplus or economic profits and is represented by the areas CDEH.

The demand and supply curves of a good are drawn with a tax on the supply of the good. The tax is applied as a constant dollar amount as is common for excise taxes. The areas ABFG and CDEH represent the consumers' surplus and producers' surplus before the tax, respectively. After the tax is imposed, the areas BCEF become tax revenue for the government. The consumers' surplus and producers' surplus change to the areas A and D, respectively. The areas GH (the shaded area) represent the excess burden of this tax.

When an excise tax is imposed on producers of a good, the supply curve shifts up by the amount of the tax. Now there is a different price that the consumers pay for the good (P_C) and that the producers receive for the good (P_P). This difference is equal to the tax. The amount of revenue collected by the government by this tax is equal to the value of the tax per unit ($P_C - P_P$), multiplied by the quantity purchased or sold (Q_T), which is represented as the areas BCEF. Because the tax causes the price that consumers pay to increase (from P to P_C), the consumers' surplus falls from the areas ABFG to the area A. Similarly the producers' surplus falls from the areas CDEH to the area D. The excess burden of this

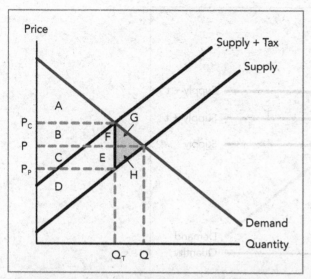

FIGURE 6.2 The Excess Burden of Taxation

tax is the original consumers' and producers' surplus, minus the new consumers' and producers' surplus, minus the tax revenue, which is the areas GH. The excess burden demonstrates that the decrease in consumers' and producers' welfare exceeds benefits to government of this tax. The goal of efficiency is to reduce this excess burden.

The "Square Rule." Now consider a case in which a good is sold at a fixed price for all quantities.[5] What happens to the excess burden when the tax doubles? Figure 6.3 on page 108 demonstrates that when the tax doubles from t to t′ (read: t-*prime*), then excess burden quadruples. In general, size of the excess burden increases with the square of the tax. This is referred to as the square rule. An important efficiency consideration that arises from this rule is that taxes should not be levied on a single good or narrow class of goods, but instead should be imposed on a broad range of goods and services. It is more efficient to place a small tax on a large set of goods, then a large tax on a small set of goods.

When an excise tax or any tax of a constant value per quantity of t is levied, the excess burden of taxation is equal to the area C. When the tax is doubled from t to t′, the supply curve shifts to the top line in the figure. The excess burden then becomes the areas ABC. This is four times as large as the area C because the area of the square B is twice the area of either of the triangles A and C. This demonstrates that doubling the tax quadruples (2^2) the excess burden.

Price Elasticity of Demand

The efficiency of a tax depends on the sensitivity of quantity consumed of a good to changes in its price. The price elasticity of demand for a good is defined as:

$$\varepsilon_D = \left| \frac{\text{percent change in quantity}}{\text{percent change in price}} \right|$$

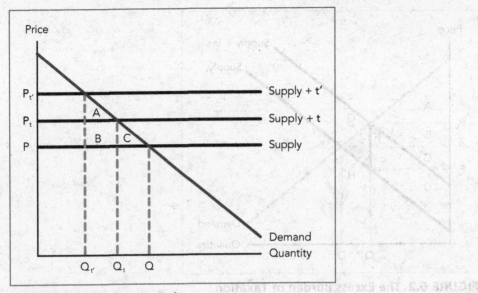

FIGURE 6.3 The Square Rule

If the price elasticity of demand exceeds one ($\varepsilon_D > 1$), so that the percent change in quantity exceeds (in absolute terms) the percent change in price, then the demand for that good is elastic. If the price elasticity of demand is less than one ($\varepsilon_D < 1$), then the demand for that good is inelastic. If the price of a good changes, but quantity that consumers purchase remains constant, then price elasticity of demand for that good is zero or perfectly inelastic.

Figure 6.4 demonstrates effects of an excise tax on a good with a perfectly inelastic demand (again assuming that the price of the good is fixed or that the marginal cost is constant). Because demand is perfectly inelastic, the demand curve is a vertical line. When a tax is imposed, the supply curve shifts upward. In this case, there is no excess burden of taxation. In general, there is a smaller excess burden of taxation for goods with inelastic demands. Therefore, a second important efficiency consideration is that taxes should be levied on goods with inelastic demands.

With a demand curve that is not perfectly inelastic, a tax results in the excess burden equal to the area A as the quantity purchased falls to Q_t and the price the consumers pay rises to P_t. When the demand curve is perfectly inelastic, a tax increases the price the consumers pay to P_t, but the quantity purchased does not change (Q). There is no excess burden of taxation for a good with perfectly inelastic demand.

Balancing Equity and Efficiency. Examples of goods with inelastic demand are goods and service necessities such as certain groceries, milk, and bread. These are items that individuals will continue to purchase at similar quantities regardless of price. An efficient tax would then be an excise tax on all grocery items. However, this would likely be a highly regressive tax because low-income families tend to spend a higher percentage of household budgets on these items, which would make this tax inequitable. This example highlights conflicts that often arise between equity and efficiency principles.

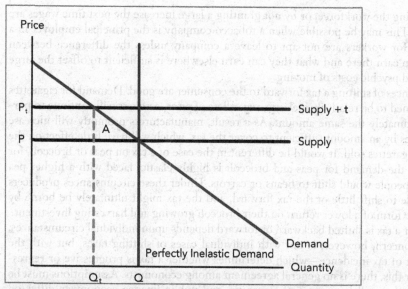

FIGURE 6.4 Inelastic Demand and the Excess Burden of Taxation

Impact and Incidence

The discussion thus far has implied that the burden of taxation rests on those who physically or consciously pay the tax. This is not necessarily true. Business firms of all kinds are taxed, but, ultimately, of course, individuals or consumers bear the burden of taxation. To discover whether a tax is progressive or regressive, one must determine upon whose shoulders actually falls the ultimate burden of paying the tax. The actual taxpayer—individual or firm—is said to bear the impact of the tax.[6] Those individuals who ultimately experience the burden of a tax are said to bear its (economic) incidence. This is an important concept to grasp: those who bear the impact of the tax are not always the ones who bear the incidence or burden of the tax.

Tax Shifting. Discovering the tax impact is a trivial matter, for it is easy to record who actually pays. Discovering the tax incidence is much more difficult. There are no firm guidelines, and economists can only make reasonable assumptions. For example, suppose a federal excise tax is levied on cigarette production. On which individuals will the burden of this tax ultimately fall? There are three main possibilities. The tax may be shifted forward to cigarette purchasers in the form of higher prices. It may be shifted backward to the cigarette manufacturer's employees in the form of lower wages. Or it may not be shifted, but remain with the owners of the manufacturing corporation (its stockholders) in the form of reduced profits or lower dividends.

In economists' language, the burden may be borne by consumption, labor, or capital. What will happen in individual cases depends upon specific circumstances. Not shifting the tax is a last resort of a corporation, to be used when other strategies fail. To some extent manufacturers may be able to shift a tax backward (probably not by reducing wages but by reducing the workforce, or by not granting a large increase the next time wages are negotiated). This may be possible when a tobacco company is the principal employer in a community, for workers are not apt to leave a company unless the difference between what they can earn there and what they can earn elsewhere is sufficient to offset the large economic and psychic costs of moving.

The chances of shifting a tax forward to the consumer are good. Demand for cigarettes is often assumed to be relatively inelastic; regardless of price, smokers will continue to purchase approximately the same amount. As a result, manufacturers promptly will increase product prices by an amount sufficient to cover the tax, which will have little effect on the number of cigarettes sold. It would be different in the case of a tax on peas or broccoli, for example, for the demand for peas and broccoli is highly elastic; faced with a higher pea price, many people would shift to beans or carrots. Under these circumstances producers would be able to shift little of the tax forward, and the tax might ultimately be borne by owners in the form of a lower return on their broccoli growing and harvesting investment.

Whether a tax is shifted backward or forward depends upon individual circumstances. The main concern, however, is not with individual cases of shifting taxes, but with the overall effect of tax incidence—which determines whether a tax is progressive or regressive—and for this, there is no general agreement among economists. Assumptions must be made about what will happen on the average, and public finance economists differ on which are the most reasonable assumptions. There is, however, a modest amount of agreement, which will be reported in a later discussion of specific taxes later in this chapter.

There have been attempts to discover the progressivity or regressivity of the U.S. tax system as a whole. One example is a study by Joseph Pechman (Pechman, 1985, p. 48).[7] He calculates that for 1980, the sum of all federal, state, and local taxes in the United States had an incidence roughly proportional throughout a wide range of incomes, with most people paying approximately 25 percent of their incomes in taxes. Actual distribution of tax burdens depends upon one's assumptions about the extent to which certain taxes are borne by capital, labor, or consumption.

Pechman computes tables based on a variety of assumptions, but there is surprisingly little difference among them. The table incorporating the most progressive assumptions indicates that the lowest income decile pays about 33 percent of its income in taxes. However, the second decile pays about 23 percent; the highest decile, about 29 percent, with everyone else in between. The most regressive set of assumptions suggests that the lowest decile pays about 51 percent of its income in taxes; the second decile, about 28 percent; the top decile, about 26 percent; and everyone else between 25 percent and 27 percent. Regardless of assumptions, it does not appear that the wealthy manage to escape taxation. The top one percent of the population in income pays about 28 percent of its income in taxes under the most progressive assumptions, and about 22 percent under the most regressive assumptions. A brief summary of similar studies and the assumptions used is found in Fullerton and Metcalf (2002).

Transfer Payments. As previously stated, it is generally impossible to assign benefits of expenditures from tax monies to individuals. The exception is cash payments to individuals for welfare, unemployment compensation, Social Security, and so forth. Economists call these transfer payments because they represent neither income nor expenditure in the economy as a whole. They simply involve taking money out of the pockets of some individuals and putting it into the pockets of others without the provision of goods or services. Pechman finds, not surprisingly, that the lowest-income groups receive more in transfer payments than they pay in taxes. Analyzing the effect of transfer payments across all income levels, he finds that the U.S. tax system is progressive in the total range of incomes if one uses the most progressive assumptions (see Table 6.1). If one uses the least progressive assumptions, the tax system is progressive for the lowest 70 percent of incomes, roughly proportional for the next 29 percent of incomes, and slightly regressive for the top 1 percent of incomes. Based on these data, the U.S. tax system as a whole may be relatively equitable.

This is not to imply, however, that the system is equally equitable in every state or community, or among particular individuals. Tax laws in each state are different. Some states rely heavily on income taxes, while others rely on sales taxes. The burden of the property tax varies substantially from one community to the next. Particular individuals must pay based on their liability for each tax, which may bear little relationship to their income. One can speculate on progressivity and regressivity only in overall terms, not in individual ones.

Yield

The yield of a tax is its ability to generate revenue. In evaluating a tax it is useful to compare its yield with those of alternative taxes and with costs of administering the tax. Some taxes are incapable of large yields. For example, the dollar volume of paper clip sales is so small that even a 100-percent excise tax on paper clips would yield relatively little revenue. On the other hand, the federal individual income tax yields an amount sufficient to cover more than half of federal operating costs. For the fiscal year ending in 2006, federal individual income taxes raised $997.6 billion. Federal expenditures were $2,708 billion (U.S. Bureau of the Census, 2007). In general, the more broadly based a tax, the greater its potential yield. Thus, an excise tax is generally not capable of as great a yield as a general sales tax. The cost of administering a tax is discussed in the next section, and yield and administration costs are compared there.

Table 6.1 Transfers and Taxes as a Percentage of Adjusted Family Income Less Transfers under Two Incidence Assumptions

The population is arrayed downward in ascending order of income for the income deciles.

Income Decile	Most Progressive Assumption			Most Regressive Assumption		
	Taxes	Transfers	Taxes Less Transfers	Taxes	Transfers	Taxes Less Transfers
Lowest	32.8%	98.3%	−65.5%	50.8%	101.3%	−50.5%
Second	22.6	58.3	−35.7	28.3	54.7	−26.4
Third	23.8	34.7	−10.9	28.3	34.8	−6.5
Fourth	25.1	23.7	1.4	28.4	23.7	4.7
Fifth	25.9	15.3	10.6	28.9	15.6	13.3
Sixth	26.1	10.9	15.2	28.6	10.5	18.1
Seventh	26.4	7.6	18.8	28.9	7.8	21.1
Eighth	27.4	5.7	21.7	29.8	5.5	24.3
Ninth	28.3	4.3	24.0	29.9	4.4	25.5
Highest	28.6	2.6	26.0	26.3	2.6	23.7
Top 5%	28.5	2.1	26.4	25.0	2.1	22.9
Top 1%	27.9	1.1	26.8	22.0	1.1	20.9
All Classes	27.5	10.0	17.5	28.5	9.9	18.6

Source: Pechman, Joseph A. (1985). *Who paid the taxes, 1966–85?*, p. 53

Income Elasticity of Yield

A tax yield that increases at a greater rate than that of incomes is said to be elastic, and a tax yield that increases at a slower rate is said to be inelastic. For example, suppose there is an excise tax on soap of one cent per bar. If individuals' average income increases, is the yield of this tax apt to increase, and, if so, how rapidly? Soap demand changes only slightly with changes in income. Even if the incomes of all people doubled, people would probably use only a little more or a little more expensive or luxurious soap. Thus, one would expect tax yield on soap to increase less rapidly than incomes, and would thus term the tax as inelastic.

The income elasticity of yield is defined as follows:

$$\varepsilon_T = \frac{\text{percent change in tax yield}}{\text{percent change in personal incomes}}$$

If the percentage change in tax yield is equal to percentage change in income, then income elasticity of yield will equal one. An elastic tax has yield elasticity greater than one; an inelastic tax has elasticity less than one. Yield elasticity of a tax on soap of one cent per bar might be expected to be low, perhaps in the neighborhood of 0.2.

In contrast, the personal income tax is an elastic tax (Institution on Taxation and Economic Policy, 2005). Elastic taxes are of significant advantage to governments in a period of expanding real income.[8] The reason is that government tax income increases more rapidly than income in general, whereas government expenses (given a constant level of services) tend to increase at about the same rate as that of incomes in general. This means that in an expansion period the government has a continuing excess of income, which it may use to finance new programs or pay debt. Ramifications of this phenomenon are discussed shortly in connection with the political effects of taxes.

In general, a progressive tax is an elastic tax and a regressive tax is an inelastic tax. This follows from the definition of a progressive tax as one that collects a higher percentage of a wealthy person's income than a less wealthy person's income. If incomes of all persons increase, a progressive tax will take a greater percentage of the incomes of all (as noted later in this discussion of the income tax). When average incomes increase, a progressive tax has an increased yield both from increases in income (assuming no indexation) and from increases in the percentage of that income that is taken. Thus, yield increases faster than increases in income. This connection should be clear in the case of the income tax. It is not as close and direct in the case of taxes not based directly on income, but it exists nevertheless.

Cost of Administration and Compliance

The cost of administering a tax is the cost to government of levying and collecting the tax. The cost of compliance is the cost to the taxpayer of complying with tax requirements. A federal tax of one dollar a pack on cigarette manufacturers would have a relatively low cost of administration. The reason is that there are only a few cigarette manufacturers. It is easy to require manufacturers to report monthly to the government the number of packs of cigarettes produced during the previous month. The number is multiplied by "X" dollar(s) per pack, and a check for the total accompanies the report. At a relatively low cost, the government can audit to ensure correct reporting of the number of packs produced.

The cost of *tax compliance* varies greatly. Usually it should be low. Perhaps the tax with the lowest compliance cost is the property tax. Individual property owners receive a tax bill yearly or semiannually and write checks for the amount. No additional effort is required. The process may be made even easier if a mortgage lender requires property taxes be paid monthly as part of principal and interest payments. At the other extreme is the individual (or corporate) income tax. Careful sets of books must be kept, supporting evidence must be filed, accountants must often be hired to prepare tax returns, and occasionally time and expense are necessary in substantiating the return.

Economic and Social Effects

Tax Neutrality. If a tax is designed only to raise money, its economic and social effects should be neutral. That is, imposition of a tax should not affect economic decisions made by individuals, nor should it affect social well-being. (Note that this discussion pertains to effects of tax imposition, not effects generated by spending tax proceeds for governmental purposes.)

Some taxes have more substantial economic effects than others. An excise tax on a particular commodity will serve to increase its price (if the incidence of the tax is passed forward) or decrease profit (if it is shifted backward). Either situation is apt to result in decreased consumption of the commodity—an economic effect. In the 1990s a "luxury tax" was imposed on costly personal sailing vessels and motor yachts. The consequence was to drive dozens of boat manufacturers out of business. These taxes, now rescinded, were not neutral; they shaped consumer behavior.

An important alleged social effect of the property tax has been abandonment of low-rent housing in cities because property taxes (on top of other expenses) exceed rental income. This can happen when assessed valuation of property is not changed to reflect reduced rentals obtainable on it. A result may be an increasing shortage of adequate housing for a city's poor.

Some states have higher taxes than others. New York consistently has had the highest total taxes, as a percentage of personal income, in the nation. Industries tend to move from highly taxed states. (This is, of course, only one reason industries move. And, conversely, they are often held to their present location by investments in plants.)

Intended Tax Effects. Many economic effects of imposing taxes are unintended. Often, however, taxes have an intended social or economic effect. For example, an import tax is levied on foreign goods to protect a domestic industry. The fact is that most taxes have important social and economic effects. Insufficient federal taxation to cover federal expenditures leads to deficits and an increase in the national debt. If debt increases faster than economic expansion (as it did in the mid and late 1980s and early years of the twenty-first century), borrowing necessary to service debt may result in higher interest rates for home buyers and consumers of other materials goods. Higher interest rates, in turn, tend to discourage borrowing for expansion or capital construction. This can particularly affect an industry, such as housing and auto purchase, that is highly dependent upon debt financing.

An excise tax on tobacco is intended, among other things, to discourage smoking, and an import tax on shoes is intended to protect a domestic industry. An income tax credit for installing home insulation is intended to encourage energy conservation. A problem with taxes designed for such specific effects is that they may, as a result, become less equitable. Balancing equity, efficiency, yield, and desired economic and social effects is a difficult task. Social and economic effects of specific taxes are discussed in subsequent sections.

Political Effects

Taxes are at once the nemesis and lifeblood of public officials. Without tax revenues, they are unable to provide governmental programs that attract votes. However, officials' votes to raise taxes can be politically fatal. Consequently, in a period of increasing incomes, such as the one the United States has had for the majority of years since World War II, an elastic tax is favored by elected officials. When incomes increase, tax yield increases even faster, providing money for new programs without necessitating higher tax rates. Public officials can both have their cake and eat it too. This has generally been true of the federal government's tax structure, which has had yield elasticity greater than one. Many new federal programs have been undertaken in the last forty years, financed mainly by federal tax structure elasticity.

Many states have had a combination of taxes that on the whole is inelastic, forcing frequent increases of tax rates.[9] This is a no-win proposition for public officials, and it is understandable that they have been attracted to state income taxes, which are generally elastic. Forty-one states, plus the District of Columbia, have broad-based personal income taxes, compared with only thirty-three in 1960.[10]

Of course, elasticity is not a one-way road. An elasticity of greater than one implies that when income decreases, tax yield will decrease even faster. The U.S. economy has been blessed with more periods of expansion than of contraction, but a recession can be disastrous for a government that has based its operations on the expectation of ever-increasing tax revenues. An example is New York, where the halcyon days of the 1960s became the nightmare of the 1970s. Governmental commitments to new and extended programs had been made with an expectation that tax revenues would increase to cover needs. When a recession hit, revenues were grossly insufficient. A state that had based much of its finances on borrowing against future revenues suddenly found its access to capital markets severely restricted. Some agencies and political divisions of the state were in even worse shape, with New York City seeking federal loan assurances and teetering on the brink of bankruptcy for years.

International Comparisons of Tax Systems

Most industrialized and developing countries also have an individual income, general sales, and property tax. The value-added tax (VAT) used in many European nations is simply a general sales tax collected by a different method. Instead of all businesses involved in the manufacture and distribution of a product being exempt from the tax except the retailer, each business in the chain pays a portion of the tax. A wholesaler, for example, buys products from a manufacturer and pays the manufacturer a VAT based on the stated percentage of the sales price (that percentage approximates 20 percent or more in many countries, significantly higher than U.S. sales taxes). The wholesaler sells products to retailers at a higher price, and collects from those retailers VAT at the same rate. The wholesaler must then remit to the government the difference between the taxes collected from retailers and the taxes paid manufacturers. Thus, wholesalers pay a net tax based only on the value they add to products by performing wholesaling functions. VAT is similarly collected from each link in the chain of production and distribution. The total collected is equal to what would have been collected from a retail sales tax at the same rate.

Table 6.2 demonstrates the variation across nations in reliance on different forms of taxation. While the United States generates less tax revenue as a percentage of gross domestic product (GDP) than the Organization for Economic Cooperation and Development average, the United States generates relatively more revenue from the property tax and personal income tax than the average OECD member nation. Although the United States draws less revenue from a general consumption tax (relative to GDP) than the average OECD country, expenditures on education are not adversely affected.

Table 6.2   International Comparisons of Tax Revenues and Expenditure on Educational Institutions as a Percent of GDP

The OECD average is unweighted. OECD classifications: the personal income tax is no. 1100, the general consumption tax is no. 5110, and the property tax is no. 4000. Property tax includes taxes on immovable property, inheritance and gift taxes, and taxes on financial and capital transactions. Total tax revenue includes Social Security. The taxation statistics are based on 2004; the education expenditure statistics are based on 2003. Expenditures on educational institutions are from public sources for primary, secondary, and postsecondary nontertiary institutions.

	Personal Income	General Consumption	Property	Total Tax Revenue	Education Expenditure
Austria	9.7%	7.9%	0.6 %	42.6%	3.6%
Australia	12.6	4.1	2.7	31.2	3.8
Belgium	13.8	7.1	1.8	45.0	4.0
Canada	11.7	5.0	3.4	33.5	3.1
Czech Republic	4.9	7.4	0.4	38.4	2.8
Denmark	24.7	9.7	1.8	48.8	4.2
Finland	13.5	8.6	1.1	44.2	3.7
France	7.4	7.4	3.3	43.4	4.0
Germany	7.9	6.2	0.9	34.7	2.9
Greece	4.8	8.5	1.5	35.0	2.4
Hungary	6.8	10.9	0.9	38.1	2.8
Iceland	14.3	10.8	2.5	38.7	5.0
Ireland	8.2	7.4	2.1	30.1	2.9
Italy	10.4	5.9	2.5	41.1	3.6
Japan	4.7	2.5	2.6	26.4	2.7
Korea	3.4	4.4	2.8	24.6	3.5
Luxembourg	6.7	6.0	3.0	37.8	3.6
Mexico	–	3.7	0.3	19.0	3.8
Netherlands	6.1	7.3	2.0	37.5	3.1
New Zealand	14.6	8.9	1.8	35.6	3.0
Norway	10.4	8.5	1.1	44.0	4.6
Poland	4.1	7.5	1.3	34.4	4.0
Portugal	5.5	7.9	1.6	34.5	4.2
Slovak Republic	2.8	7.7	0.6	30.3	2.6
Spain	6.2	6.0	2.8	34.8	3.0
Sweden	15.8	9.2	1.6	50.4	4.3
Switzerland	10.2	4.0	2.5	29.2	3.9
Turkey	4.6	7.1	1.0	31.3	2.5
United Kingdom	10.3	7.0	4.3	36.0	3.4
United States	**8.9**	**2.2**	**3.1**	**25.5**	**3.8**
OECD Average	9.1	6.9	1.9	35.9	3.5

Source: Swiss Federal Tax Administration, Division Tax Statistics and Documentation, Tax burden 2006: International comparison, Organization for Economic Cooperation and Development, Directorate for Education, Education at a Glance 2006, Table B2.1b

Summary

Taxation is the main method of revenue generation for public services, especially education. General taxation for education occurs because it is generally believed that a community as a whole benefits from a well-educated citizenry and workforce. There exist multiple dimensions of taxation as well as separate theories of taxation. All taxation is based on one of four bases: wealth, income, consumption, or privilege. Taxes can be assessed proportionally, progressively, or regressively. Each tax assesment has a different level of yield and a different elasticity; that is, a different rate of response to changes in the grater economy. Three main categories of taxes are income, sales, and property. Each tax has its own strengths and weakness in generating revenue. Each tax can also be differentially assessed. Businesses sometimes pay taxes at differential rates than residents or citizens. This is intended to bring vertical equity into the tax system by taxing different classes of producers at different levels. Proponents of flat or proportional taxes advocate horizontal equity, whereby everyone is taxed the same. All taxes can be reduced through the political process. *Tax limitation* is the term used when growth rate of taxes is held constant for citizens and consumers.

Discussion Questions

1. Taxation is complicated because taxes impact citizens repeatedly and differentially. Consider yourself to be a small business owner who also owns a home and has children. Create for yourself an optimal basket of taxation that addresses levels and limitations of property, income, and sales taxation. How would this optimal basket be different for a single professional just out of college and living in a rented apartment?
2. Describe the benefits of a value added tax over a general sales tax. Which tax is most fair to consumers? Which would be more stable for school funding purposes?

Web Resources

Congressional Budget Office—
    http://www.cbo.gov/
National Conference of State Legislatures Budget and Tax Center—
    http://www.ncsl.org/programs/fiscal/index.htm
National Tax Association—
    http://www.ntanet.org/
U.S. Bureau of the Census, Federal, State, and Local Governments Public Elementary–Secondary Education Finance Data—
    http://www. census.gov/govs/www/school.html

References

Advisory Commission on Intergovernmental Relations (1995). *Significant features of fiscal federalism* [Table. 3.5], *1995*, p. 131.

Advisory Commission on Intergovernmental Relations. (1992). *Significant features of fiscal federalism, 1984*. pp. 14–17.

Ballard, C.L., Shoven, J.B., & Walley, J. (1985). General equilibrium computations of the marginal welfare costs of taxes in the United States. *American Economic Review*, 75(1), 128–35.

Brunner, E. J., & Imazek, J. (2003). Private contributions and public school resources (Working Paper). San Diego: San Diego State University.

Duncombe, W., & Yinger, J. (2001). Alternative paths to property tax relief. In W. Oates (Ed.), *Property taxation and local government finance*. Cambridge, MA: Lincoln Institute of Land Policy.

Elissa, N. (1995). *Taxation and labor supply of married women: The tax reform act of 1986 as a natural experiment* [Working Paper No. 5023]. Cambridge, MA: National Bureau of Economic Research.

Fischel, W. (2004). Did John Serrano vote for Proposition 13: A reply to Stark and Zaaslof's "Tiebout and tax revolts; Did Serrano really cause Proposition 13?" *UCLA Review*, 51(4), 887–932.

Florida Department of Revenue. (2006). Retrieved January 31, 2007, from http://www.myflorida.com/dor/property/exemptions.html.

Fullerton, D., & Metcalf, G.E. (2002). Tax incidence. In A.J. Auerbach & M. Feldstein (Eds.), *Handbook of public economics*, Vol. 4 (pp. 1787–1872). Amsterdam: Elsevier.

Gurwitz, A.S. (1980). The capitalization of school finance reform. *Journal of Education Finance*, 5(3), 297–319.

Hausman, J.A. (1985). Taxes and the labor supply. In A.J. Auerbach & M. Feldstein (Eds.), *Handbook of public economics*, Vol. 1 (pp. 214–68). Amsterdam: Elsevier.

Institution on Taxation and Economic Policy. (2005). Principles of taxation. *Policy Brief #9*. Retrieved January 31, 2007, from http://www.itepnet.org.

Jorgenson, D.W., & Yung, K. (1993). The excess burden of taxation in the U.S. In A. Knoester (Ed.), *Taxation in the United States and Europe* (pp. 11–136). New York: St. Martin's Press.

Netzer, D. (1971). Property taxes. *Municipal Finance*, 44(2), 36.

Netzer, D. (1966). *Economics of the property tax*. Washington, DC: Brookings Institution Press.

New York State Department of Taxation and Finance. (2006). *New York state sales and use: Tax rates by jurisdiction*. Albany, NY: Author.

New York State Office of Real Property Service Municipal Profile. (2003). *New York City: Summary of exemptions by roll year, 2003 assessment rolls*. Albany, NY: Author.

Pechman, J. A. (1985). *Who paid the taxes 1966–85?* Washington, DC: Brookings Institution.

Tiebout, C.M. (1956). A pure theory of local expenditures. *Journal of Political Economy*, 65(5), 416–24.

U.S. Bureau of the Census, Governments Division. (2003). *State government finances: 2002*. Washington, DC: Government Printing Office.

U.S. Bureau of the Census, Federal, State, and Local Governments. (2006). *State government tax collection: 2005*. Retrieved January 31, 2007, from http://www.census.gov/govs/www/statetax05.html.

U.S. Bureau of the Census, Governments Division. (2006). *Public education finances: 2004*. Annual Survey of Local Government Finances. Washington, DC: Government Printing Office.

U.S. Bureau of the Census (2007). *Statistical abstract of the United States: 2007* [Table 461, Table 464]. Washington, DC: Government Printing Office. Retrieved February 20, 2007, from http://www.census.gov/compendia/statab/federal_govt_finances_employment/.

Notes

1. A sales tax commonly takes the form of an ad valorem tax, which is a tax on a percentage of the price of the good. Alternatively a *unit* tax is a fixed dollar amount per unit of the good. Many excise taxes are examples of a unit tax.

2. Forty states plus, the District of Columbia, had lotteries as of 2006. Total lottery revenues in 2002 were $39.3 billion. The tax (the total revenue minus the prizes minus the cost of administration) equaled 34 percent or $13 billion. In all of the states (except Delaware), the lottery proceeds constituted less than 5 percent of total state revenue (U.S. Bureau of the Census, Governments Division, *State Government Finances: 2002* Washington, DC: Government Printing Office, 2004; Education Commission of the States, 2006). In 2004 Tennessee implemented a state lottery, and North Carolina enacted a lottery in 2005. Some states, including Georgia and Tennessee, use the lottery proceeds to fund specific education programs or provide higher education scholarships.

3. Revenue raised by license fees totaled $35 billion nationwide in 2002 or about 3.2 percent of total state revenues (U.S. Bureau of the Census, 2002).

4. For the discussion of efficiency, a tax on consumption and its effects on the price and quantity of goods and services are described. Similar arguments can be made for a tax on income in which the service is an individual's labor, the quantity is the amount of labor supplied, and the price is the wage. Analogous arguments can be made for taxes on the other bases as well. Students new to economics will notice that the demand and supply curves in these examples do not curve. This is for the sake of simplicity.

5. This is equivalent to a constant marginal cost for all quantities. This is done for ease of exposition to understand the basic principles that can be seen by focusing on the consumers' side of the market. Similar arguments apply to the producers' side.

6. This is also referred to as the statutory or legal incidence.

7. Table 4-4. The most progressive assumption is Pechman's Variant 1c; the most regressive is his Variant 3b.

8. In 1985 the federal income tax began indexing for inflation. Prior to 1985 expanding nominal incomes caused by inflation resulted in increases in government tax income without increases in the tax rates.

9. For 1970, the Advisory Commission on Intergovernmental Relations listed eighteen states with tax structures of low elasticity (0.80 to 0.99) and twenty-three states with medium elasticity (1.00 to 1.19). Only nine states had tax structures with high elasticity (above 1.20). The lowest was Ohio, with an elasticity of 0.80; the highest was Alaska, at 1.47, followed by Wisconsin, at 1.41 (1977).

10. In 2004 Alaska, Florida, Nevada, South Dakota, Texas, Washington, and Wyoming had no individual income tax. New Hampshire and Tennessee had limited income taxes (Federation of Tax Administrators, 2004).

CHAPTER SEVEN

Distributing State Education Funds

■ INTRODUCTION

This chapter concentrates on state revenue distribution. It assumes knowledge regarding revenue generation, covered in the preceding chapter. It leaves matters of federal government education funding and within school district resource allocation to following chapters. It concentrates on the policy mechanisms by which states allocate educational funds to districts, and the implications of those methods.

LEARNING OBJECTIVES

In this chapter, a reader will learn about:

- The role of the school business official in determining district revenue eligibility.
- Values appropriate for appraising state education finance distribution schemes.
- Historical methods for allocating state funds to school districts.
- Current policies for distributing state educational funds to districts as well as each approach's strengths and weaknesses.
- Political dynamics shaping school finance distribution schemes.
- Alternative finance distribution proposals such as voucher plans.

■ SCHOOL BUSINESS OFFICIALS AND STATE SCHOOL FINANCE DISTRIBUTION

Means by which states generate and distribute education revenues for school districts are determined principally as a function of statewide political dynamics. However, it is a professional responsibility of school business officials to understand the potential outcome of these political machinations. A school business official should be available to inform local officials, both education and public, regarding the consequences to the district of proposed alterations in revenue and financing schemes. This way, local officials can better act to protect or enhance local interests. It is for this reason that knowing the general principles upon which revenue distribution systems operate is important. This chapter provides explanations of these operating principles.

The detailed calculations by which a specific local school district's revenue eligibility is determined are explained in greater detail in a subsequent chapter on local school district budgeting. However, a reader should understand that the manner in which a local school district's state revenue eligibility is determined is by the school business official completing a set of state-provided worksheets. The bottom lines of these worksheets provide local officials with estimates, usually quite accurate, of forthcoming state revenues. These worksheets are the mechanical or formulaic outcomes of the state school finance distribution principles on which this chapter concentrates.

■ PUBLIC POLICY VALUES IMPORTANT FOR APPRAISING FINANCE DISTRIBUTION

When financing public schools, states are concerned with equity, adequate provision, and efficiency of education. There is also a concern with liberty or choice. The modern practice of education finance has also begun to ask important questions about adequacy, including the achievement levels to which students should be expected to perform. The emphasis on these values has shifted over time. There has been more formal attention in education finance paid to equity. This is the dimension with which this chapter section begins. In addition, the practical consequences of these public policy values in operation is illustrated by providing a reader with a historic explanation of the means in which state school finance distribution plans have evolved in response to concerns for maximizing value.

Equity

The goal of school finance that is labeled *equity* is more commonly expressed as *equality of educational opportunity*. This expression recognizes that it is not reasonable to expect, and, perhaps not possible, to educate all students to the same level. They and their parents have different preferences and students themselves have different innate abilities.

There are many possible definitions of equal educational opportunity, but in practice the concept has been defined most often as assuring equal dollars per student or assuring sufficient resources to provide comparable programs for students when their different individual needs and costs of providing them have been taken into account. The first goal, identical resources, horizontal equity, for each student, is technically easy to construct. It may not be politically easy to achieve.

Accomplishing the second goal, ensuring "adequate" resources tailored to the needs of each student, vertical equity, is difficult to achieve both conceptually and politically. To meet this goal, one must take into account three separate kinds of inequalities among school districts—differences in wealth, in student educational need, and in educational costs. Separate remedies are appropriate for each, and the three must be combined in constructing a school finance program that is truly equitable. Each will be discussed in turn.

Wealth Equalization

As illustrated in Chapter Six, the United States relies heavily on property taxes to support public schools. Although this was equitable among local taxpayers (ownership of property, at one time, was an accurate measure of ability to pay taxes), it was inequitable among communities. A property-rich community with a lower tax rate could finance a better education than could a property-poor community with a higher tax rate.

The situation is illustrated in Figure 7.1, the first of a series of illustrations of wealth equalization systems presented in this chapter. The horizontal axis of the chart represents community wealth expressed in dollars of property value per pupil. The numbers on this scale are purely arbitrary, used to illustrate the concept. The vertical axis represents dollars of expenditure per student.

Assume that communities of the state differ in wealth per pupil, but that they all decide to make an equal sacrifice in providing education by levying a property tax at a rate of fifteen mills.[1] There is no other revenue available to schools besides receipts from this tax. The line OP, extending diagonally upward from the origin, represents receipts from this tax for districts of different wealth. For example, at a tax rate of fifteen mills, district A with $100,000 of property value per pupil will raise $1,500 per pupil (15 mills means $0.015 per dollar of property value; $100,000 × .015 = $1,500). District B, with property value of $200,000 per pupil, will raise $3,000 per pupil at the same tax rate. In other words, the amount raised is directly related to community wealth. So when there are variations in wealth, districts that levy the same tax rate raise widely differing sums per pupil.

Several points are of note here. One is that the range in value of property per pupil among districts within a state is usually much wider than illustrated in this figure. It might range from approximately $10,000 per pupil to over $500,000 per pupil. Thus, the range in amounts raised per pupil by the property tax is great. At a tax rate of fifteen mills, the $10,000 district raises $150 per pupil and the $500,000 district raises $7,500 per pupil.

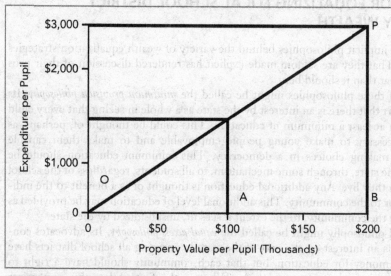

FIGURE 7.1 No State Aid

On the other hand, the range can be deceptive. The vast majority of districts in the state might typically have property values per pupil ranging from, say, $50,000 to $200,000. Even so, this means a range of four to one in ability to raise money through taxes.

The concept of tax rate representing equal sacrifice is an abstract one. If houses are worth $100,000 on average in district A, and $200,000 in district B, a tax rate of fifteen mills will mean that householders in district A will pay $1,500 in school taxes and those in district B will pay $3,000. Presumably, differences in home values represent differences in homeowners' wealth and in their ability to pay taxes, although it is not that straightforward. Homeowners in district B do pay more money in taxes, although their tax rate and presumably their sacrifice are the same.

These are averages. In district A there may be two homeowners, each with two children in school, one of whom owns a home with a value of $40,000 and the other with a home valued at $100,000. The first pays $600 in taxes at a fifteen-mill tax rate; the second pays $1,500, yet the children of both receive the same education. And, of course, the homeowner who has no children also pays taxes, even though he receives no direct benefit from the schools. The principle involved here might be expressed as "from each according to his ability; to each according to his needs" (Marx & Engels, 1848).[2]

Finally, others besides homeowners pay taxes. Commercial and industrial enterprises also pay, usually at the same rate. This means that the two communities, A and B (with property values of $100,000 and $200,000 per pupil), might actually have houses of equal value. The difference might result from a substantial industrial base in the second town. In that case, homeowners in both towns would pay the same amount in taxes, but the school district in the second town would have twice as much to spend per pupil. This would seem to be particularly egregious, although it could be argued that the presence of industries in a town makes it a less desirable place to live.

■ MEANS FOR EQUALIZING LOCAL SCHOOL DISTRICT PROPERTY WEALTH

There are three implicit philosophies behind the variety of wealth equalization strategies used by states. That they are seldom made explicit has rendered discussion of their pros and cons less clear than it should be.

The first of these philosophies might be called the *minimum provision philosophy*. Its proponents assert that there is an interest by the state as a whole in seeing that every child is provided with at least a minimum of education. This could be thought of, perhaps, as the amount necessary to make young people employable and to make them capable of intelligently making choices in a democracy. This minimum education should be guaranteed by the state, through some mechanism, to all students, regardless of the school district in which they live. Any additional education is thought of as a benefit to the individual student, or to the community. This additional level of education may be provided as a local luxury by the community, to the extent it sees fit, unsubsidized by the state.

The second philosophy might be called the *equal access philosophy*. Its advocates contend that there is an interest on the part of the state in ensuring all school districts have equal access to money for education, but that each community should have a right to decide the amount of education to provide. Whereas the first philosophy emphasizes equality of provision, this philosophy puts its emphasis on equality of access to funds.

The third philosophy is more comprehensive, and might be called the *equal total provision philosophy*. Its supporters claim that all public education must be provided to all students in the state on an equal basis, regardless of geography or a community's ability to pay. A question within this camp concerns whether the provision of education is measured traditionally, by fiscal inputs, or instead by academic or social outcomes.

Minimum Provision Programs

Flat Grant Program. When states began to appropriate money to local communities to assist with schooling costs, intergovernmental grants took the form of equal amounts of money to each community, regardless of number of children or ability to raise money locally. Subsequently, funds were distributed on the basis of equal dollars per pupil to each district. At the turn of the twentieth century, thirty-eight states distributed so-called flat grants using a school census as a basis for apportionment. Other states used enrollment or average daily attendance (Cubberley, 1905, p. 100). Since the school-census basis (a count of all school-age children in a district) provided districts with state money whether or not children attended school, it provided no incentive for districts to retain children in school.

Ellwood P. Cubberley, in 1905, was the first to write persuasively of the problems of school finance. He was concerned with the manner in which flat grant formulas favored cities, where school districts could afford to operate schools longer, and where larger class sizes were possible. School costs were higher in rural areas, where it was frequently necessary to employ a teacher to instruct ten or fewer children. Cubberley's solution was to allocate to each district an amount for each teacher employed. This, of course, still did not equalize wealth. Cubberley's plan can best be described as another variety of flat grants, with the teacher as the unit of distribution instead of the student. Today, no state depends primarily on flat grants as a means of financing its share of educational cost. The last state to rely upon such a method, Connecticut, adopted an equalizing plan in 1975.

Figure 7.2 on page 148 illustrates the operation of a flat grant program. The graphic is similar to Figure 7.1; the only difference is that the state provides a flat grant of $1,000 per pupil. A horizontal line at $1,000 shows this. Each district receives this much regardless of its wealth or the rate at which it decides to tax. Now, assume that each district decides, nevertheless, to levy a tax at a rate of fifteen mills. The result is the total amount of money available per student shown by the sloping line. District A now has $2,500 per pupil to spend; district B has $4,000. The amount district B has is shown by the vertical line BOP to consist of the portion BO, which is the $1,000 flat grant, and the portion OP, which is the $3,000 raised by taxes. The absolute difference in expenditures is exactly the same as before: $1,500 per student. However, the ratio of expenditures has lessened. Without the flat grant, district B spends twice as much as district A. With the flat grant, it spends 60 percent more ($4,000/$1,500 = 1.60).

The flat grant approach adheres to the first philosophy in assuming that a specific minimum of schooling should be guaranteed to every citizen. It assumes further that the state, in its wisdom, can determine the costs of this minimum education and will allocate that dollar amount as a flat grant. Schooling in excess of this minimum is held to benefit only the individual recipient or the community in which one resides. It is therefore a local luxury to be indulged in as each community sees fit, but not to be subsidized by the state. Under this philosophy, the flat grant is a satisfactory wealth equalizer. It does not equalize for differences in need or cost, but that is a different matter, to be discussed later. Since

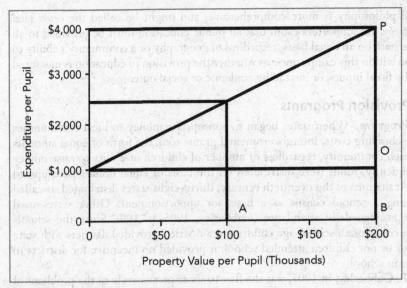

FIGURE 7.2 A Flat Grant Program

the amount of the flat grant is presumed to be sufficient to cover the education level the state believes to be minimally necessary, and, furthermore, since it is provided to all students equally and is raised by taxes levied at a uniform rate on all residents of the state, there is nothing inherently unequal about it.

Foundation Program. One practical problem with flat grants is that states seldom have sufficient revenue to provide an adequate amount per student. For example, Connecticut, in the last year in which it used the flat grant (1975), provided $235 per student (plus some categorical aids); average expenditure per student in Connecticut at the time was $1,507 (Harris, 1975). The reason states typically cannot find the necessary money is that they have allocated use of the property tax exclusively to local communities. It is rare to find a statewide property tax. George D. Strayer and Robert M. Haig described a solution to this problem in 1923. In a report to the Educational Finance Inquiry Commission, based on a study of New York State, they proposed a system that has the effect of capturing a portion of the local property tax for state purposes, without that being openly evident. Their proposal has since become known as the foundation program, or the Strayer-Haig plan.

Just as with a flat grant, the state specifies a dollar amount per student to which each school district is entitled. Presumptively, this is the amount of money per pupil necessary to guarantee a minimally adequate education. At the time of the foundation plan's invention or conception, there were few systematic efforts to ensure that the dollar amount prescribed, in fact, was sufficient to provide a foundational level of schooling. More often than not, the foundation dollar amount was a political product. Knowing what they were willing to tax or what level of revenue was available, state legislatures would first establish the revenue pool, and then, through division, determine the per pupil amount of the foundation.

The state requires each district to levy a property tax at a fixed rate (called required local effort) and provides only the difference between the amount raised by that tax and the guaranteed expenditure level. Thus, a property-poor district will generate little with the tax at the specified rate, and the state will provide generously. A district richer in property will generate almost as much as the dollar guarantee and will receive little equalization aid from the state. A property-wealthy district will generate more than the guarantee and will receive no subsidy from the state.

If the state requires each district to levy a property tax at a specified rate in order to receive state money, and counts proceeds of that local tax as part of the guarantee, the required property tax is, in effect, a state tax. If the required local tax rate is relatively high, a substantial amount of money will be raised. This, combined with state money, enables the legislature to establish a guarantee level sufficient for what is assumed to be a minimal education. Some states do not require the district actually to levy the tax at the specified rate, calling it instead a computational tax. It is then a device used only in determining dollar amount of state aid to a district. A few property-poor districts may then levy a lower tax than this, raising less money per child than the guarantee and subverting the intent of the foundation concept.

Foundation program operation is illustrated in Figure 7.3. The horizontal line LE depicts the dollar amount of the foundation guarantee, supposedly representing the cost of a minimal program. The section labeled "Required Local Effort" is the amount raised by the local property tax at a required rate of ten mills. The section labeled "State Aid" is supplied by the state, at a foundation level of $2,000. For district A, the required local effort (RLE) raises little money, and the state contribution is high. District B raises most of the guarantee locally, while district C raises more than the guarantee and receives nothing from the state. The solid sloping line at the top (MN) is the total amount that would be raised if all districts chose to levy an optional local tax at the rate of five mills, in addition to the required tax.

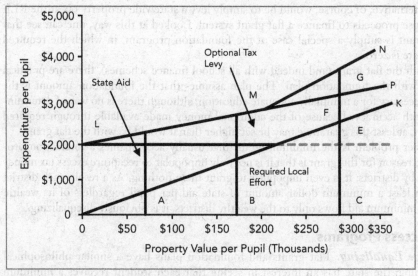

FIGURE 7.3 A Foundation Program

District B can raise more than district A, and district C can raise more than district B. The line becomes steeper at point M because districts beyond that point already raise more than the guarantee by using only the required rate, thus making the total amount they collect that much higher. That is, the slope of the line OK is ten mills, the slope of the line LM is five mills, and the slope of the line MN is the sum of those, or fifteen mills.

It may be argued that it is unfair that some districts, because they happen to be rich in property, have more money to spend from levying the required tax rates than do property-poor districts. If the required tax is indeed a state tax, then the amounts raised above the guarantee should be returned to the state to be used elsewhere. This concept is called recapture, and the effect of it is shown by the dashed lines in Figure 7.3. District C would raise, at the required rate, the amount shown by the line CF. It would return to the state the amount EF, leaving it exactly as much as every other district. Because of this, if it levied an additional optional tax at the same rate as the other districts, it would raise the amount EG. With recapture on the ten mills of RLE, the line LMGP shows the amount generated by districts at a fifteen-mill tax rate.

The underlying philosophy of the foundation plan is the same as that of the flat grant: the state should provide for an adequate minimum educational program, defined as a specified number of dollars per student, and districts may raise money above that guarantee if they wish, as a local luxury, without help from the state.

A state education financing system such as this, including recapture, would provide complete wealth equalization if the underlying philosophy were accepted. States, however, have been unwilling to employ the recapture concept. To do so is to admit publicly that the required property tax is a state tax rather than a mechanism open to local option. In addition, the amount of taxes exported from a local district is highly visible. Recapture has been attempted in only a few states, and repealed in some of those. For example, in 2004 in the trial court decision in *West Orange Cove Independent School District v. Nelson*, the Texas statewide recapture and redistribution plan was declared a statewide property tax, prohibited constitutionally in Texas, and voided.

An alternative, of course, would be to simply levy a statewide property tax at the RLE rate, and use proceeds to finance a flat grant system. Looked at this way, one can see that the flat grant is simply a special case of the foundation program, in which the required local tax rate is zero.

As with the flat grant (and indeed with all school finance schemes), there are practical problems with the foundation plan. The plan assumes that the foundation amount is the amount necessary for a minimally adequate education, although there is no way of determining this with accuracy. Because of the additional money made available through required local effort, at least this guarantee may be set higher than it would be with the flat grant.

Another problem is the minimum grant that usually accompanies a foundation program. The reason for this grant is that it is not only unpopular to recapture excess tax money generated by districts; it is even unpopular to grant them nothing. As a result, each district receives at least a minimum dollar amount of state aid per pupil regardless of its wealth. Since this minimum aid flows only to the wealthy districts, it is obviously disequalizing.

Equal Access Programs

Percentage Equalizing. Flat grants and foundation plans have a similar philosophical underpinning: the state has an interest in seeing that each student receives a minimum education, and it undertakes to guarantee this on an equal basis. Percentage equalizing has a different philosophy. Essentially, it defines equity as equal access to money for education, and it also holds that the amount of education to be purchased by a community should be determined by that community.

With percentage equalizing, each district determines the size of its own budget, and the state pays a share of that budget determined by the district's aid ratio. The aid ratio is defined by means of a formula usually written in the form:

$$AidRatio = 1 - f(y_i \div \bar{y}) \tag{1}$$

where

y_i is the assessed valuation per pupil of the district
$\bar{y}$ is assessed valuation per student of the state as a whole, and
f is a scaling factor that is usually set somewhere between 0 and 1.

For example, if property value per pupil of the district were $20,000 and that of the state $80,000, and the scaling factor were 0.5, the aid ratio for the district would be:

$$1 - .5 \times (20,000 \div 80,000) = .875 \tag{2}$$

This means the state would provide 87.5 percent of the budget of the district, with the district expected to raise the remaining 12.5 percent from local taxes. If the district had instead an assessed valuation of $80,000 per pupil (the state average), the aid ratio would be 0.5, and the state would provide half of the district's budget. It is easy to see that with this particular scaling factor, when a district's assessed valuation becomes twice that of the state, the aid ratio becomes zero. Above that point it becomes negative, the implication being that the district should instead send some tax money to the state. This is recapture, as discussed in connection with foundation plans, and it has proved no more popular in percentage equalizing states than in foundation states.

Just as the flat grant is a special case of the foundation plan, the foundation plan can be thought of as a special case of the percentage equalizing plan in which the budget to be participated in by the state is set at a particular figure instead of being allowed to fluctuate.

Adoption of percentage equalizing was first urged by Harlan Updegraff and Leroy A. King in 1922, about the same time Strayer and Haig were recommending the foundation plan (Updegraff & King, 1922). However, Charles S. Benson popularized it in 1961, and most of the eight states that enacted it did so shortly thereafter (Benson, 1961). It is interesting that the Strayer-Haig plan became part of the school finance plan of the majority of states, whereas percentage equalizing was never widely adopted. However, a plan with a new name but an identical purpose—power equalizing—evolved in 1970, and its concepts were adopted by many states.

Power Equalizing. Power equalization is a wealth equalization concept described by John E. Coons, William H. Clune, and Stephen D. Sugarman in their book *Private Wealth and Public Education* (1970). The authors concern themselves not with equalizing expenditures per pupil, but with equalizing ability of local districts to support schools. They argue strongly for the virtues of subsidiary, by which they mean making decisions at the lowest appropriate level of government feasible. This implies that the local district should make decisions on school expenditures. (Indeed, the three authors argue that the individual family should even make these decisions, leading to a concept called family power equalizing.) Coons, Clune, and Sugarman put forth their Proposition 1, which states:

> *Public education expenditures should not be a function of wealth, other than the wealth of the state as a whole.*

This argument formed a substantial part of the legal reasoning exhibited in *Serrano* and other school finance equal protection cases.[3]

The philosophy behind power equalizing is the same as that behind percentage equalizing: the ability to raise money should be equalized, but the decision as to how much money to raise should be left to the local district. Under power equalizing, the state establishes a schedule of tax rates, with an amount per pupil guaranteed to a district for each level of tax. Such a schedule might look like this (the guarantee at other intermediate tax rates is obtained by interpolation):

Tax Rate (Mills)	Guaranteed Revenue per Pupil
5	$1,000
10	$2,000
15	$3,000
20	$4,000

This schedule is the simplest power-equalizing schedule, and amounts to a guarantee of a specified number of dollars per pupil per mill levied.

However, power equalizing is more general than percentage equalizing because it is not necessary to have the linear schedule implied by the guarantee of an amount per mill per student. For example, it would be possible to have a large guarantee per mill for the first ten mills, and a much smaller guarantee for mills in excess of ten. This would tend to move districts toward a levy of ten mills, where the high marginal increase in revenue per student would suddenly decrease. A few states (Michigan is an example) have done this, but most states enacting power equalizing have adopted the simple linear schedule.

The power equalizing ideas of Coons, Clune, and Sugarman were influential. By 1984 eighteen states had adopted some form of power equalizing as an important feature of their school finance system (Education Commission of the States, 1984).

Guaranteed Tax Base. A third name for plans based on the equal-access philosophy is the guaranteed tax base, or GTB. The state guarantees each district the same assessed valuation per student. The district calculates the tax rate necessary to raise its budget, using as an assessed value for the purposes of calculation the guaranteed valuation per pupil times the number of pupils. It then levies this calculated rate against the actual assessed valuation. The state compensates for differences between the amount actually raised and the amount that would be raised at the guaranteed valuation.

At this point it should be emphasized that percentage equalizing, power equalizing (with a linear schedule), and GTB plans are mathematically identical.[4] They are simply different ways of saying the same thing, emphasizing different facets of a general idea of equal access to funds. They are illustrated in Figure 7.4.

This graphic represents a percentage-equalizing plan with a factor f of 0.5 and an average state assessed valuation of $100,000. Alternatively, it could represent a power-equalizing

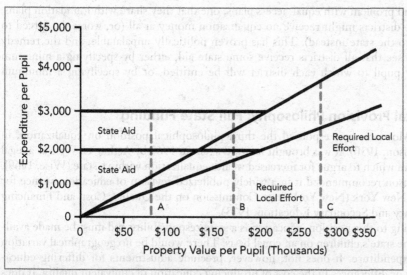

FIGURE 7.4 Percentage Equalizing, Power Equalizing, and Guaranteed Tax Base Plans

plan with a guarantee of $200 per pupil per mill of tax. Finally, it could represent a GTB plan with a guarantee of $200,000 assessed valuation per pupil. There is no difference in operation among the three plans. Figure 7.4 shows the results of two different tax rates. The solid lines and upright type show a tax rate of ten mills; the dashed lines reflect a tax rate of fifteen mills. The actual tax rate of a particular district, of course, could be any amount, but the principle is the same. Note that in each of the two instances, lines representing state aid and local effort are graphically the same as those previously provided in Figure 7.3 for the foundation plan. District A receives $2,000 per pupil at a ten-mill tax rate, and $3,000 per pupil at a fifteen-mill rate. At the ten-mill rate, it provides $750 from local taxes and the state provides $1,250. At the fifteen-mill rate, the district raises $1,125 and the state provides $1,875. District B provides much more from its own taxes and the state aid is much less, but it receives the same total amount per pupil at each tax rate as does district A. District C raises more money from its own taxes than is guaranteed by the state, and receives no state aid.

Like previously described state financing plans, these plans have suffered from practical problems. One is that since the emphasis is on a school district deciding the size of its own budget, there should be no restriction on the size of this budget. However, to guarantee that the state will share in any budget, no matter how large, is a frightening prospect for lawmakers and state officials, who fear wholesale raids on the state treasury. Consequently, the state usually limits the expenditure per student that will be equalized by the state. As long as this limit is substantially above the average expenditure, there is little cause for concern. Frequently it is set much lower. Then most districts simply are guaranteed the maximum state guarantee per student. This is the equivalent of a foundation plan with a guarantee at that level and a required local tax rate equal to the tax rate associated with that guarantee under the plan in use.

A second problem with equal-access plans, one that they share with foundation plans, is that some districts might receive no equalization money at all (or, worse, be forced to contribute to the state instead). This has proven politically unpalatable, and the remedy has been to see that all districts receive some state aid, either by specifying a minimum amount per pupil to which each district will be entitled, or by specifying a minimum aid ratio.

Equal Total Provision Philosophy: Full State Funding

Henry C. Morrison first espoused the third philosophical position on equalization, in 1930 (Morrison, 1930). It was brought forward again in 1967 by Arthur C. Wise as a legal position from which to argue for increased wealth equalization within a state (Wise, 1969). Charles Benson recommended it in a widely publicized revision of education finance for the state of New York (New York State Commission on the Quality, Cost, and Financing of Elementary and Secondary Education, 1973).

According to this position, education is a state responsibility and must be made available to all the state's children on an equal basis. There would be no geographical variation in school expenditure. It does not, however, preclude adjustments for differing educational needs or differences in the cost of producing education of equivalent quality. It does mean that, other things being equal, students will be recipients of equal monetary provision. The only means by which this can be accomplished operationally is for the state to mandate the expenditure level, and equity demands that the expenditures be supported by statewide taxation. Therefore, this method of financing the schools has become known as full state funding or full state assumption.

Full state funding does not necessarily imply state operation of the schools, but merely a state guarantee of equal amounts of money per pupil to each district. It has been clear in states that have *de facto* or *de jure* full state funding that the result is substantially greater state control.

Only one state, Hawaii, has *de jure* full state funding. Education has been operated by the state since statehood and there are no local districts. Other states have approached full state funding as a *de facto* position, even though their school finance system is nominally quite different. New Mexico and Florida have foundation plans with low required local effort. Almost all of the districts in the state generate less than the state guarantee through the required local effort and thus receive state equalization aid. Both states have rigid restrictions on optional extra millage. The result is a system in which all of the schools in the state are funded on the same basis as if there were a full state funding scheme in effect.

California is an interesting case which will be discussed in more detail later. California's Proposition 13 passed in 1978, limits property taxes to 1 percent of property value for all purposes. With few exceptions, each school district's share of these taxes is less than is necessary to operate the district and the state makes up the difference. There is little possibility of an optional local levy. However, the state does not guarantee districts the same amount of money per student. Rather, guaranteed revenue per student for each district is based on what a district actually spent in 1977–78, adjusted for inflation. The effect is full state assumption without equalization (although, as will be shown later, there have been significant advances toward equalization in California).

An interesting way of distributing money in a full state assumption scheme has been suggested by Thomas Parrish and Jay Chambers (1984). This is a precursor to "adequacy" solutions. They developed a resource cost model that separates education into homogeneous programs. For each program, experts determine required inputs: teachers, aides, supplies, and so forth. For each district, a cost is developed for each kind of input. The district is then provided by the state with the amount of money necessary to buy inputs for the programs required for its students. This is, then, a method for providing equitably for educational provision within a system of full state funding, taking into account differences in needs and costs. Criticisms of this model are provided later.

Management Analysis and Planning, Inc. (MAP) devised a similar system for Wyoming. Here a variation was employed by which panels of education experts designed instructional programs intended to deliver state-specified objectives. Thereafter, funding is guaranteed by the state.[5]

Full state assumption would appear to solve most of the problems previously discussed in connection with the other formulas. The marks of a true full state funding plan are that all educational funds are raised by statewide taxes (which could include property taxes) and that the money is spent equally on similarly situated students. Disallowing any local supplementary aid eliminates the tax and expenditure discrepancies that haunt practical application of the other plans. However, such a high degree of equity has a price. The legislature, having provided all education revenues from state sources, will want to see that the money is spent judiciously. It is almost inevitable that full state assumption will bring increased state control over education.

In Florida, for example, where *de facto* full state assumption was enacted in 1973, the state at the same time enacted a requirement that most of the funds generated by the presence of students in a school be spent on those students in that school. Since students in different programs (the mentally retarded, the physically handicapped, those pursuing career education, etc.) generated different amounts of state money, this requirement mandated a school-by-school, program-by-program accounting system with auditing by state officials. The result is a dilution of local school officials' initiative.

Which Philosophy Is Best?

Read the "In the News" article about the manner in which spiraling energy costs impact school districts in Iowa. School business managers anticipate cutbacks will be needed if the cost of fuel does not fall. This illustrates the point that every distribution formula has a "blind spot"—an unexpected circumstance that is not adequately accounted for in the funding scheme. This should not come as a surprise. As previously discussed, social, economic, and political factors have great influence on decisions about public matters, specifically education finance. Below is a consideration of the pros and cons of the various methods described above. These are theoretical considerations; each state will have particular legal, social, cultural, and economic contexts that may make one approach more palatable over others.

In the News

High fuel prices are sending a pre-winter chill through tri-state schools. And school business managers in Iowa,

Illinois and Wisconsin speak of cutbacks if costs don't fall. The Western Dubuque Community School District already operates on "lean cash reserves," said Dan Wegmann, business manager. "We don't have any magic formula that's going to offset the expense to the district," he said. "We can't take buildings that were built back in the '60s and '70s and retro fit them into modern, energy-efficient buildings." Western Dubuque's newer buildings have geothermal heating systems that help control energy costs, but most district buildings use less-efficient boiler systems.

The district also serves the largest area in the state. "We also have an enormous amount of cost with transportation and busing," Wegmann said. "Obviously, this year, the high cost of diesel fuel is hitting us hard." The effects could become serious. "If we go over budget, it has a huge impact on what we do next year," he said. "Unfortunately, it does fall back on the programs and what Western Dubuque can offer students."

Last year, Wegmann budgeted $150,000 for natural gas. This year that number rose to $190,000. Last year's diesel budget was $158,000. This year it's $250,000. Dubuque Community School District Finance Director Ron Holm said the district increased its energy budget by 15 percent. The district typically spends $1.5 million per year for heat, light and fuel. "What that means is, as you are forced for energy, you've got to cut your expenditures someplace else," Holm said.

Sen. Tom Harkin, D-Iowa, introduced School Energy Crisis Relief Act legislation Thursday to aid the state's school districts with soaring natural gas and transportation fuel bills. The U.S. Department of Energy has warned that natural gas prices in the Midwest could jump as much as 71 percent this winter.

Districts must dip into their general funds to cover the costs. Many are also turning down thermostats, turning off lights, and turning to more energy-efficient means of heating and cooling, such as geothermal systems. Like Western Dubuque, Dubuque Community is investing in geothermal heating and cooling.

Common sense cost cutting, like using more energy efficient light bulbs, helps, but only goes so far, Wegmann said. "These old buildings are barns. The heat controls entire wings, not individual rooms," he said. "I think we're doing about as much as we can to control our costs." In Illinois, the Galena School District had to increase its transportation budget by 10 percent and heating budget by 15 percent, according to business manager Paul Seymour. "In the short run, we'll sign the bill and suck it up," he said.

Platteville, Wis., schools would make any home improvement guru proud. Platteville's parking lot lights are on timers. Many bulbs have been changed from 48 to 32 watts. A centralized computer controls classroom temperatures. While he doesn't want to be "alarmist," district business manager Art Beaulieu knows every district has a difficult battle at hand. "Do you cover it with higher taxes or budget cuts elsewhere? Do we let textbook cycles go further? We did that once already," Beaulieu said. "Most people in Wisconsin are at their bare bones. They've cut all they can."

From: Fuerste, M. (2005, November 11). Energy costs fuel budget concerns: School districts are doing all they can to cut corners, not programs. *Telegraph Herald* (Iowa), p. A3.
Copyright 2005 Woodward Communications, Inc. *Telegraph Herald* (Dubuque, IA).

The philosophy of equal total provision—that the state should furnish on an equal basis all public education in the state—is the most egalitarian. Not only is all funding equal, but taxation is also equal, since the source of funds is statewide taxes. The minimum provision philosophy equalizes expenditures and taxation only for that portion of expenditures deemed necessary for a minimum adequate program. Expenditures for other purposes are unequalized. The difference between minimal provision and equal total provision is actually one of degree. Full state funding does not equalize any educational services furnished outside the public schools, whether by private schools or by individual tutors. However, there is a great difference between equalizing all the many things that the public schools offer and equalizing only a minimum program.

The equal-access philosophy is quite different. Power equalizing, percentage equalizing, and the GTB make no attempt to equalize expenditures on education. They simply equalize access to those expenditures. One could think of the equalizing of expenditures as student equity, and the equalizing of access to funds as taxpayer equity. Full state funding does both; the foundation plan does both (but to a limited extent); and power equalizing is concerned only with taxpayer equity. The distinction is an important one. Most of the school finance equity lawsuits have raised the constitutional issue of education as a state function that must be furnished on an equal basis to all.[6] It seems much easier to find a plan providing student equity that meets this criterion than one that provides only taxpayer equity.

▪ NEED EQUALIZATION

The foregoing discussion of wealth equalization contains the "other things being equal" assumption—that all students are alike in their need for education. This is manifestly untrue. Many students have unusual learning problems that require costly special teaching methods. The mentally retarded, emotionally disturbed, blind, and deaf are only a few such categories. In addition, many normal children can benefit from a program that is more expensive. This is particularly true in the area of career or vocational education. Fortunately, these differences in needs can be incorporated into a wealth-equalizing scheme as part of a comprehensive state aid plan. The ways in which this is done can be categorized as entitlement, reimbursement, and organizational schemes.

Entitlement

These wealth-equalizing schemes entitle a school district to an amount of aid that is specified in advance, independent of the actual costs to the district of operating programs for students with special needs. (Of course, the amount is presumably related to costs of such programs.) A number of approaches fall into this category and include the following.

Weighting Systems. Imagine a foundation plan that guarantees a given number of dollars per student. Implicit in such a plan is that all students should have the same basic amount spent on them. If one wishes to spend different amounts on students with special needs, one can do this by counting each such person as more than one student. For example, educable mentally retarded students might be weighted 1.5 compared with the 1.0 weighting of so-called normal students. Weighting presumably represents the ratio of the cost of providing a basic special program to that of providing a basic normal program.

Usually the normal student in the middle elementary grades is weighted 1.0 and all other weights are related to this standard. The sum of all weighted students is obtained, and this weighted student count is used as the basis for calculating state aid. Simply by substituting weighted students for actual students, one can use this method with any of the wealth equalizing plans that have been discussed. This means that practically, as well as conceptually, it is possible to separate need equalization from wealth equalization.

Weighting schemes assume that the cost of a special program bears a fixed cost relationship to the cost of a normal program. This is assumed to be true both within districts and among districts. The state compensates districts on this basis, but without otherwise dictating the content of programs.

If a weighting plan for need equalization is to be equitable, it is necessary to have an accurate determination of the program costs for special categories of students relative to the program costs for normal elementary students. This constitutes a major difficulty in using weighting plans. Because there is not yet an agreed upon technology for educating each category of student, it is difficult to agree on the extra cost involved. Even if it were possible to agree on the technology, local district cost-accounting methods are undeveloped. However, research economists are beginning to approximate such costs with increasing accuracy by relying on an econometric technique known as "cost function analysis" (Duncombe & Yinger, 2005; Schwartz, Steifel, & Bel Hadj Amor, 2005). However, even here, the above-mentioned caveat regarding accurate local-level cost accounting as a base for such analyses still applies.

Another difficulty with pupil or program weights is that they need frequent revision in order to remain consistent with actual cost differences. But this is where circular reasoning enters the argument, for this year's weights will depend on the amount spent last year. The amount spent this year will depend on the money available, and, therefore, on the weights used.

If the specified weight allocates a state aid amount more than the per-pupil cost of a special program, school districts will tend to misclassify students into special programs, and then use the unneeded funds for other programs, including those for normal students. This happened in Florida where several small rural districts placed the majority of their students into either mentally retarded or vocational programs. The remedy for such abuses is a state quota which can be unfair if it prevents enrollment in special programs of students who actually need special assistance. Another remedy is state auditing of student placements.

Approximately twenty-two states use weighting schemes in their state aid programs. In Florida, there are thirty-three separate programs with weights that vary widely. A reader should not conclude that these weightings are a product of scientific validation. A few examples are as follows:

Program	Weight
Grades 1–3	1.234
Grades 4–9	1.00
Grades 9–12	1.116
Educable mentally retarded	2.30
Deaf	4.00
Hospital and homebound, part time	10.00
Vocational education	1.17 to 4.26

Flat Grants for Special Programs. About ten states fund one or more special programs through a flat grant of a specified number of dollars per pupil in the program. The implicit philosophy is that the excess cost of educating a child in such a program is that specified number of dollars in every district.

Individually Calculated Entitlements. The imprecision of weighting and flat grant schemes means that some districts receive more and others receive much less than they need for special programs. Computers have made it possible to calculate an entitlement for each program for each district in a state. For example, in California, such a system operates for special education. Each student who may be entitled to a special education program is examined and an individual education program (IEP) established for the student. The program, in other words, is tailored to the student. Special education and related services are provided by a local plan area, which may consist of a single district or a group of districts that have agreed to cooperate to provide the required full range of services. By summing the IEP requirements of all children in the local plan area, the district(s) can establish a need for personnel and other services. Entitlement for instructional personnel is based on the number required and the average costs of their salaries and benefits in the local plan area. To this is added an entitlement for support services (including administration, supplies, maintenance, etc.), based on a ratio of such costs to the costs of instructional personnel in the local plan area. The result is a total entitlement for special education. From this is subtracted any federal aid to which the local plan area is entitled. The remainder is provided by the state. (Remember that California is a state that has *de facto* full state assumption of educational costs.)

Reimbursement

Reimbursement schemes compensate districts for actual costs of providing for special needs. Districts account for special program expenditures, deduct state-defined costs of educating normal students, and receive state reimbursement for all or a portion of the extra costs. Approximately seventeen states have excess cost reimbursements for instructional programs.

A major advantage of this approach is that districts are reimbursed only for the actual excess cost of programs; this eliminates the previously mentioned misclassification incentive. Another advantage, particularly from the legislature's view, is that money is restricted to categories for which grants are provided. This necessitates state definition of types of reimbursable expenditures, a cost-accounting system, and a reliable state audit, all of which are restrictions on district freedom. Another advantage of the excess-cost system is that the amount granted is tailored to a district's expenditure pattern. This is better than the assumption, as in a weighting system, that costs in all districts are the same proportion of normal costs.

A disadvantage of the excess-cost system, if the state pays all or most costs, is that there is little incentive for districts to operate an efficient program. This often leaves the state with the necessity of specifying a maximum dollar limit on the amount of aid per student to be granted. This may be unfair to high-cost districts, while providing no brakes on the expenditures of a low-cost district. Another disadvantage is that districts are not reimbursed until expenditures have been made, reports submitted to the state, and expenditures audited. Often a district is hard-pressed to find money to start a new program because of this delay.

Organizational Arrangements

A third manner of providing services for special students is to assign special program responsibility to an intermediate education district. The main advantage of the larger district is organizational. Because of economies of scale, intermediate districts can afford to provide programs for handicapped students that individual districts might find too costly because of the few students in the district with that handicap. A disadvantage is that it is not practical to use this approach for all special programs. Students must be transported from their usual schools and this inhibits mainstreaming. Also, additional transportation costs may outweigh the economies of scale gained by concentrating handicapped children in one place. Finally, local district authorities may fear loss of control over an important part of the education of their children.

■ OVERVIEW

There is a place in a well-designed school finance system for each of these methods of need equalization. Weighting is heavily dependent upon arbitrary cost factors, inviting misclassification of students or a failure to offer specific programs. It is probably best used where there is little or no possibility of either type of subversion, for example, when weights are used for various levels of education. That weights are arbitrary (e.g., high school students may be weighted 1.25) is not important from an equity standpoint as it would be for special programs, because all students experience each level of schooling.

Certain special programs, such as those for the multiply handicapped or severely mentally retarded, are probably best handled by an intermediate education district, state schools, a consortium of school districts, or private contracting. These services usually require a large investment in tools and equipment, and such an arrangement can spread these costs over a large pupil population.

Districts should also be allowed to contract with intermediate education districts for special programs. Such services will then be offered by an intermediate district only if it can convince local officials that it can offer better services or operate at a lower cost than they can. The state would offer aid through weighting or other entitlement methods to local districts for special students who are, for example, blind. The district would use this money either in operating its own program or in contracting with the intermediate district, whichever it found more effective or less expensive.

Most special needs should be handled through programs providing reimbursement for excess costs. Such programs offer little incentive to misclassify students into programs or not to offer the programs as there is with weighting. Districts can spend different amounts to meet needs without being rewarded or penalized. The biggest problem is that the state must establish a maximum allowable reimbursement to prevent districts from operating needlessly expensive programs. An alternative is to reimburse only a percentage of the excess cost which gives the district a stake in how much is spent.

Alternatively, these special needs can be handled through an individually calculated entitlement program such as that described earlier. Such a system appears to provide reasonably adequate safeguards against improper classification of students, and there is an incentive toward efficiency in that the district does not receive more money if it spends more or less money if it economizes.

Finally, there can well be special needs that the state will simply ignore in its financial scheme, or for which it will perhaps pay a small fixed amount per pupil, allowing districts to provide for them out of money to which they are entitled for regular students. This would be the case for experimental or inexpensive programs.

Cost Equalization

Equalization may be needed to balance differences among districts in the cost of providing educational services of similar quality and kind. There are several reasons for cost differences. They divide rather well into two categories: (1) differences in the amount and cost per unit of supplies and services that must be purchased by the school district, and (2) differences in the amounts districts must pay to attract and retain employees of comparable quality.

Supplies and services may differ in cost for various reasons. The school district in a mountain area may have to pay a large annual bill for snow clearance. The mountain district may also use more fuel for heating and find that its unit cost for fuel is higher. A sparsely settled rural area may be unable to avoid small classes and high busing costs. Land cost for school sites is much higher in cities, as is the cost of vandalism. In general, extra costs tend to be higher in rural and highly urbanized districts, and lower in suburban districts.[7]

Salaries constitute 70 to 80 percent of the average school district's budget. Thus, differences in the costs of hiring and retaining employees of equivalent quality are even more important than differences in the cost of supplies. There may be differences in the cost of living among districts, resulting from variation in rents or housing prices, food, and so on. More important, however, are differences in the attractiveness of a school as a place to teach and a community as a place to live.

It is easier to recognize cost differences than it is to measure and subsequently compensate districts for them. All states compensate districts for costs of necessary bus transportation in some manner. This is because such costs vary so widely. Usually compensation is on a cost-reimbursement basis. A district records the transportation cost of eligible students. Record keeping for such purposes is usually complicated. In fact, accounting for the transportation reimbursement, a small part of total state payments—is frequently more complicated than all the rest of the district's cost accounting combined. The state then reimburses the district for a portion of these transportation costs. In New York, state reimbursement is 90 percent of costs. There is clearly little incentive for New York districts to economize on transportation costs. In Florida, on the other hand, each district's transportation costs are estimated by means of a regression equation, with density of population used to predict a district's transportation expenditure. The district is paid this estimated cost. If it manages to transport students for less than the estimate, it may use the extra funds for other purposes. If it spends more than the estimate, it must make up the difference from its own sources. This approach encourages efficiency in operating transportation systems. Florida's is an entitlement approach, whereas New York uses a reimbursement system.

States also subsidize cost differences for necessary small schools; schools that must exist because transportation distances to larger schools would be too great. Students may be weighted with those in the smallest schools given the highest weightings. These students are counted like those weighted for need differences. Alternatively, small-school students may be treated separately with a special formula specifically for them.

As previously noted, the major cost variation is in salaries necessary to attract teachers and other employees of equivalent quality. Some states have dealt with this challenge by using a state salary schedule, not for paying teachers individually but for placing the teachers of a district in order to determine the amount of state aid to be received. Teachers are each placed in the column and step of the schedule appropriate to training and experience, the total teacher salaries that would be paid if the teachers had been on the state salary schedule is determined, and this amount is used in making an adjustment to the amount of state aid to be received by the district. In effect, this compensates a district that has more teachers near the high end of the schedule for that fact, while not compensating it for paying higher salaries than the state schedule.

Whether this is an equalizing measure or not depends on whether one views placement of teachers on a salary schedule as something under district control. The general principle of cost equalization is that districts should be compensated for differences in costs that they cannot control but not compensated for discretionary differences. If a district has declining enrollment, it cannot hire new teachers (except to replace some of those who retire or leave), and the teaching staff each year tends to move farther up the salary schedule. The district has little current control over this. On the other hand, if there is expanding enrollment the district hires teachers, and it has a good deal of control over whether it hires experienced teachers or those near the beginning steps of the schedule. State aid confers greater help on districts that hire experienced teachers. Since wealthy districts are more able to hire expensive teachers in the first place, this kind of state aid may be anti-equalizing.

Florida adjusts a district's state aid entitlement by cost-of-living differences. Each district's foundation aid level is adjusted by a cost-of-living index. Districts with lower costs of living have lower foundation levels. A cost-of-living index is a poor indicator of actual cost differences in hiring employees of comparable quality, for differences in the attractiveness of the district as a place to work and live are also important to teachers. Nevertheless, it is generally considered to be a more effective way to compensate for differences in cost than the state salary schedule approach.

The most complicated attempt to adjust for differences in cost has been Jay Chambers's cost-of-education index (1980). This approach involves gathering information on all items resulting in cost differences among districts. Some of these items would be the result of conscious choices made by the district such as the choice to have fewer pupils per classroom. Others would be outside the control of the district such as amounts of snow that must be cleared. A schedule is prepared in which those items of cost not under the control of the district are shown at their actual cost to the district, and those under "district control" are shown at the state average cost. The total cost of operation of the district is computed on this basis. This would be the total cost if the district were in its current situation but made average decisions. State aid is based on this.

One of the principal troubles with the Chambers approach is that many costs represent items that are not completely under district control. Although the district cannot control the amount of snow that falls, it can decide the extent and frequency of snow clearance. The major item, of course, is teacher salaries, and the extent to which the district controls this depends on, among other things, the rate at which it can hire new teachers. Some districts have little control over teacher costs; others have a great deal. Collective bargaining brings other problems. It is not clear how much control a district has over collectively bargained salary costs and this probably varies greatly from district to district.

A second problem with the Chambers approach is that it requires massive amounts of data from each district in the state. The procedure itself is sufficiently complicated that it is difficult to explain to legislators and laypeople.

Another area of frequent attempts at cost equalization is that of declining enrollment. Here, the problem is short term. Typically, such declines result in one or two fewer students in each class; this makes consolidation of classes difficult. A district continues to use the same number of teachers and classrooms, resulting in an increase in per-student cost. Over time a district can make reductions, remedying the short-term problem. In economists' terms, this is the result of marginal costs being substantially less than average costs. This works on the up side too, with a few additional students not increasing district costs very much; but state aid formulas have always given districts as much help for additional students as for existing ones. However, there are cries for help when enrollment declines.

Approximately half the states have tried to provide additional aid to districts suffering enrollment declines. One alternative is to permit a district to choose either the previous year's or the current year's enrollment as a basis for claiming state aid. Growing districts use the current year's enrollment figure; districts with decreasing enrollments use the previous year's figure. A variation allows districts to use either current enrollment or a moving average of the previous three, four, or five years. Either method provides temporary relief for a district faced with enrollment declines, but does not put off the day of reckoning indefinitely.

A different approach, used in a few states, is to offer a hold-harmless provision, which guarantees the district no less total state aid than it received the year before. If the district has declining enrollment, this could be thought of as the equivalent of counting "phantom students." If the save-harmless provision disappears after a short time, the effect is similar to that of the plans just discussed. If it continues indefinitely, as it has in New York, it can result in districts being paid on the basis of enrollment many years before, even though current enrollment is less than that.

Adequate Provision and Cost Adjustments

"Modern" education finance concerns itself with this issue through a different set of mechanisms than historically has been the case. Indeed, "adequacy" is now a challenge of sufficient proportion. However, it was dealt with in past times chiefly through added programs. Here is a historical glimpse.

From 1950 to 1970, the major concern of state school finance officials was to provide resources necessary to meet rapidly increasing demands on schools. Not only were enrollments burgeoning, but also the public was demanding more services. Programs such as vocational education increased the average cost per student at the same time that the number of students was increasing rapidly. The result was that state governments were under persistent pressure for new money. There was also concern with efficiency and equality during this time, but those goals often had to be subordinated to a continuing need to finance expansion.

This post-World War II period of growth was accompanied by a labor shortage as well as a money shortage. Teachers were in short supply, and the economic system responded, as is typical, by increasing the price, thus encouraging more people to enter the profession. Teacher salaries increased faster than salaries of workers in general. Some saw this as an increase from grossly inadequate salaries to a decent living wage, while others believed the new salary levels exorbitant.

Increased labor costs were added to other costs incurred from growing numbers of students and expanding program demands. Average cost per student increased tenfold, from $100 in 1940 to $1,000 in 1970; total elementary and secondary public education costs increased eighteenfold, from $2.26 billion to $40.27 billion during the same period.

Large increments of state monies were injected into education in the 1950s and 1960s, and this was generally matched or exceeded by increases in local revenues. Most of the state money and almost all of the local money were in the form of additional general aid, money that could be used for any district purpose (as opposed to categorical aid, which can be used only for specified purposes). From 1950 to 1970, expenditure restrictions were relaxed or eliminated, either by the legislature or by direct vote of the people. For example, many states had tax rate limitations, but local elections to permit school districts to tax above this limit regularly passed by large margins.

Post-World War II legislation increasing costs seldom increased equality. Although most states had equalization programs (and most were spending more on education than ever before) these higher disbursements did not lessen expenditure inequalities within states.

In addition to general aid, states provided categorical aid for a variety of special programs, such as education of mentally retarded and physically handicapped children. Several states even attempted to alleviate environmental handicaps such as poorly educated parents or poverty and ghetto living conditions. Other categorical aids went for construction of many badly needed new schools, particularly in suburbs in the fast-growing states. These suburbs frequently were unable to raise enough money locally and state assistance became crucial.

During the late 1960s and the 1970s, there was considerably less emphasis on adequate provision. The strongly felt need to improve the U.S. education system that arose with *Sputnik* in 1957 had spent itself as the United States achieved its goal in 1969 of putting a man on the moon. The concern was instead with equity—with seeing that all pupils had an equal chance to acquire an appropriate education. Even so, expenditures per pupil rose more rapidly than the economy grew.

Between 1965 and 1980, expenditures per pupil rose from $607 to $2,529—a 345 percent increase, including inflation, and a 70 percent increase in constant dollars (NCES, 2005). During this same period, the national income per capita went up 42 percent in constant dollars. One reason for the rapid increase in expenditures per pupil was the rapid decline in the number of pupils during this decade and a half. Marginal cost in education is considerably less than average cost, because an additional student or two does not require an additional teacher. For this reason, a decline in pupils translated into an increase in cost per student. In addition, attempts to improve equity usually were accomplished by leveling up, increasing money for the low-spending districts while taking nothing away from the high-spending ones. Thus, a rapid increase in expenditures per pupil accompanied attempts to improve equity. However, it is not clear that the increase in expenditures per student resulted in a more adequate education. In many cases, teachers taught smaller classes but continued to use the same techniques.

With the early 1980s came an increasing concern with adequate provision. The realization that test scores had been declining for some time pervaded the national consciousness, drawing increasing cries for school improvement. A series of reports in 1983 highlighted the problem and provided a rallying point.[8] The new push for more adequate schools did not manifest itself in the form of additional general aid for the schools. Instead, there were attempts to deal directly with the problems of improving schools by increasing "time on task," lengthening the school day and the school year, improving the curriculum, providing special assistance to teachers, reducing class size in the early grades, and employing a wide variety of other tactics. These changes were claimed to cost money, and the money was usually provided in the form of categorical grants—money that could be used only for specified purposes. In some cases the new programs were mandated by the state, whereas in others the categorical money was offered as an incentive for districts to institute specified new programs.

▮ OTHER GOALS OF DISTRIBUTION SYSTEMS: EFFICIENCY

Efficiency has long been a goal of those who finance education. It is expressed as a desire to obtain adequate education for as little money as possible. The goal is laudable, but difficult to attain. The problem is that there is little agreement on what education is to accomplish, how it is to be accomplished, and how accomplishments are to be measured. In the past, those concerned with school efficiency merely advocated imposing spending limits, theorizing that educators having a restricted amount of money will use it more wisely. During the post-World War II period of rapid school expansion, the goal of efficiency was muted, but enrollment declines in the 1970s, coupled with a continued rapid rise in expenditures per student, prompted reinstitution of limits. In the 1980s legislatures adopted a more active role by providing categorical money as an incentive for school improvement. Districts must often apply for the money, supplying detailed plans to the state education department for spending it.

▮ POLITICAL DYNAMICS AND EDUCATION FINANCE DISTRIBUTION

By now, a reader should suffer no delusion that education and politics are somehow separate activities. Schooling involves too much money, too many employees, and too many clients not to be intimately engaged with the mainstream political dynamics of the nation and of each political subdivision within states. The following sections disentangle these political dynamics and provide a reader with explicit means for understanding the warp and weave of political interests as they engage with finance distribution schemes.

▮ SPENDING LIMITS

Spending limits have usually taken the form either of restricting amounts of money available to a district or of making money available in the form of categorical aid that must be spent on programs considered desirable by the legislature rather than leaving expenditures to local discretion. Restrictions on amounts of money have taken the form of tax rate limits, annual budget votes, or direct expenditure or revenue limits.

Tax Rate Limits

The most common form of restriction is the tax rate limit. Until recently, most states outside the Northeast (where budget votes are the norm) had such limits. The tax rate limit is a maximum rate that may be applied to a district's assessed valuation to raise money for school purposes.

These limits have numerous flaws. If a uniform limit is applied across a state (the usual situation), districts that have the same full valuation of property per pupil, but different assessment ratios will raise different amounts of money per pupil. These differences have led to state boards of equalization, which adjust local assessed values to a uniform assessment rate for school purposes.

Even if the tax rate limit is based on full valuation rather than assessed valuation, there are vast differences in the amount of money per pupil that can be raised by different districts levying the tax at the allowed limit. This is because there are great differences in the amount of property value per pupil among districts. Even though general state aid programs are designed to alleviate these differences, they sometimes are inadequate for this purpose. The result is that districts must levy taxes at a rate above the limit. States usually provide for districts to raise their tax rate limit by a vote of the people in the district. In addition, for certain special purposes they may provide for a school board to levy taxes above the tax rate limit without a vote of the people. Such override taxes are often used for special education, for free or subsidized meals for needy children, and for community services.

Annual Budget Votes

Annual votes on the school district budgets have long been a custom in northeastern states. The school board proposes a budget, indicating total estimated expenditures, revenues expected from all sources other than local taxes, and (by subtraction) the amount to be raised from local taxes. Theoretically, this direct vote should be a useful mechanism for adjusting expenditures to voters' preferences. However, it sometimes does not work, partly by design of the school board. Even voters who want to inform themselves thoroughly before voting usually find it extremely difficult and thus may not be able to vote intelligently. The information furnished to the voters typically does not compare the coming year's proposed expenditures with the current year's actual, does not put expenditures in per-pupil terms, and does not adequately explain proposed changes.

Also, elections are sometimes delayed until autumn, which threatens voters with a delayed school opening if they do not pass the budget. New York law provides that a district that fails to pass a budget election can operate on an "austerity" budget. This budget is austere only in excluding auxiliary programs of particular interest to parents: interscholastic athletics, nonrequired transportation, and school lunches. On the other hand, whatever the district agrees to pay the teachers as a result of collective bargaining is automatically included in the budget, and taxes are raised to pay these salaries. Thus, the budget is austere for the public but not necessarily for educators.

Direct Revenue or Expenditure Limitations

Failure of tax rate limits or budget votes to provide meaningful limitations on school district expenditures has led some states to adopt more direct controls. Typically, the state limits the amount each district can spend per student. This is the most direct form of control, and, if established uniformly on a statewide basis, would result in equal expenditures per pupil statewide. However, it is neither politically possible nor desirable to establish such uniform limits. Some districts have higher costs per student for providing the same amount of educational services for reasons that are beyond their control. These include high costs for transporting pupils, for heating and snow removal, and for salaries of personnel in high-wage areas. Such districts would have insufficient money if the limit were uniform statewide.

The political justification for permitting disparity is as follows: Establishing a uniform limitation would either result in some districts being forced to reduce their expenditures drastically (if the limit were established only slightly above the median expenditure), or constitute no real limitation (if established near the level of the highest-spending district). As a result, when legislatures institute such limitations, they usually set each district's current rate of expenditures as its ceiling and provide for a yearly increase to allow for inflation. There may be a provision that allows low-spending districts a greater inflationary increase than high-spending districts, thus gradually squeezing the expenditures of the districts together. Such a provision is made for purposes of equity, however, rather than efficiency.

Categorical Aid

Limits discussed above have represented a confession by the legislature that it does not know how to make the schools efficient, but that it hopes school professionals will find ways to do so if sufficiently motivated. It is unlikely that these limits will promote efficiency. The bureaucratic imperative is toward expenditure expansion, not cost containment. Faced with a shortage of funds, school professionals will often make decisions designed to encourage citizens to open their pockets (such as curtailing interscholastic athletics) rather than trying to find ways to operate more efficiently.

Recognizing revenue or expenditure limitation flaws, many legislatures have opted to decide which are the priority areas for spending money on education, and then to provide funds for these specific purposes. Much of the recent increase in school funds has been provided through this mechanism. Such categorical programs take away local discretion and substitute decision making at the state level. It is difficult to establish regulations at the state level that accommodate all the different local situations. Whether categorical aid, with its accompanying restrictions, contributes to efficiency is open to question, but at least it forces districts to concentrate more on areas considered high priority by the legislature.

Choice

The three main values affecting public school policy noted in Chapter Two are equity, efficiency, and liberty (or choice). Most of the history of public education has been one of narrowing choice. By delegating local communities, or school districts, responsibility for education, states initially gave these communities wide latitude to choose the kind, amount, and quality of education to be provided. The first compulsory attendance laws began to circumscribe this freedom of choice. No one argues that this restriction of choice was bad. As noted, these three goals tend to conflict with one another, and each must be balanced against the others. Compulsory attendance is a restriction of freedom in favor of equity and adequacy.

However, as states have given more aid to local school districts, they have tended to exercise more control. Nowhere has this been clearer than in California, which in 1978 escalated from a local contribution of more than half of the total expenditure to a situation where the state in essence funds all education. School boards have found that their freedom to make decisions about most matters has been greatly circumscribed. It is clear that the legislatures have not necessarily been cavalier. They believe that they must exercise a prudent concern for the public funds they are granting to school districts. But the result has been a movement of control to the state as the proportion of school expenditures furnished by the state increased during the 1970s and 1980s.

Local school districts have also restricted the freedom of choice of parents and children. Most school districts tell parents what school their child will attend, which teacher he or she will be taught by, which subjects will be taught, and which textbooks will be used. In the elementary schools in particular, parents have little choice regarding the education of their children.

It need not necessarily be this way. Some school districts allow parents to send their children to any school in the district, or to one of several others besides that in their attendance area—subject, of course, to the availability of space. It is not clear, aside from bureaucratic convenience, why all school districts do not do this. But this is only a beginning. There have been a number of proposals to increase choice in the public schools.

■ VOUCHERS AND TUITION TAX CREDITS

Nobel laureate economist Milton Friedman first proposed the voucher plan in 1955. It is a radical concept in that it proposes dismantling the present system of publicly operated schools. It is conservative in an economic sense in relying on the private market rather than on government. Friedman described his plan thus:

> Governments could require a minimum level of education that they could finance by giving parents vouchers redeemable for a specified maximum sum per child per year if spent on "approved" educational service. Parents would then be free to spend this sum and any additional sum on purchasing educational services from an "approved" institution of their own choice. The educational services could be rendered by private enterprises operated for profit, or by nonprofit institutions of various kinds. The role of the government would be limited to assuring that the schools met certain minimum standards such as the inclusion of a minimum common content in their program, as it now inspects restaurants to assure that they maintain minimum sanitary standards. (pp. 127–128)

Voucher proponents assert that the plan has a number of advantages. Parents would be allowed to place their children in schools of their choice, instead of being forced to use schools and teachers for which they might have no enthusiasm. The injection of a greater amount of private enterprise would make schools more efficient and promote a healthy variety. Salaries of teachers would become more responsive to market forces. On the other hand, there might be more segregation by economic class.

In fact, an equivalent of the voucher plan operated in higher education for more than thirty years. The "G.I. Bill," more formally, the Service Man's Readjustment Act, enacted immediately after World War II, provided a higher education subsidy for any veteran who could gain entrance to a postsecondary program. It paid full tuition, regardless of tuition level being charged by the institution, and subsistence for the veteran and his family. It has been widely regarded as one of the most successful federal programs in the field of education, and many veterans who otherwise would not have gotten additional education became college graduates.

On the other hand, there were serious problems with the G.I. Bill as it formerly operated. A number of private for-profit schools opened just to educate veterans. Audits showed that their curricula were inadequate and their instructors incompetent, and that they granted degrees without requiring the veterans to complete prescribed courses. Fortunately, the majority of veterans selected established schools that furnished a reasonable education. Nevertheless, the potential for abuse is present when the free market is allowed to operate unfettered.

In any case, voucher plans have not been widely accepted in U.S. elementary-secondary education. For several years during the 1960s and early 1970s, the Office of Economic Opportunity and the U.S. Office of Education attempted to promote a trial of a voucher system somewhere in the United States. The closest they came was a limited experiment in the Alum Rock School District, near San Jose, California, involving no private schools. Results were inconclusive.

The late 1900s saw added attention to vouchers; Wisconsin and Ohio approved voucher plans in Milwaukee and Cleveland. Privately funded voucher plans have existed in New York and in San Antonio, Texas. Also, the U.S. Supreme Court has approved public funding of private schooling in the landmark *Zelman* v. *Simmons-Harris* case in Ohio. None of these are large endeavors. They still, however, may prove to be historically important.

Tuition tax credits constitute another proposal for subsidizing private schools. The family sending its children to private school is allowed a credit equal to their tuition on its federal income tax return. Note that this is a deduction from the tax, not from income, and is thus of more value to the family. The notion is more fully discussed in Chapter Six.

▪ FAMILY POWER EQUALIZING

Coons, Clune, and Sugarman recognized a problem with their proposed system of power equalizing. Although it met their criterion that the amount spent on a child's education should not depend upon neighbor's wealth, expenditures might still depend upon neighbors' decisions. A rural family desiring and willing to pay for an excellent education for its children might find its neighbors preferring low taxes and low school expenditures. To remedy such forced inequity, Coons, Clune, and Sugarman proposed family power equalizing (1970). In this modified voucher plan, several levels of educational quality would be available in a community's schools. Each family would then be free to choose the quality level it preferred for its children and would be taxed accordingly. Children would attend the school whose per-pupil expenditures were linked to their parents' choice of tax rate. Family power equalizing has had no warmer political reception than Friedman's voucher plan.

▪ MAGNET SCHOOLS

Public school advocates have been understandably reluctant to forego control over education, as is implied in the Friedman voucher plan. There has also been no observable inclination to adopt a scheme of differential taxation as suggested by Coons and colleagues. However, many districts (particularly those in large cities) have allowed and encouraged an option within public schools. They have established magnet schools. Each such school emphasizes a different feature of education. One may concentrate on the arts, another on science and mathematics, a third on "basics" and firm discipline. Parents are allowed to apply to these schools for their children. The concept has been widely discussed in districts faced with the alternative of busing to promote racial desegregation (Smrekar & Goldring, 1999; Goldring & Smrekar, 2000).

Magnet schools have much to recommend them if they are operated well. A major problem is that they tend to be feasible only in large districts containing a large number of schools. The usual balkanization of school districts in the suburbs makes such schemes difficult. Private schools envisioned in the voucher plans would not suffer from this problem because they draw pupils without regard for district boundaries. In rural areas, however, all of these plans to increase choice are limited by population sparsity, which makes it difficult to establish special schools, public or private. Telecommunications may alleviate this difficulty in the future, allowing instruction of pupils in widely scattered locations.

■ COMPREHENSIVE STATE SCHOOL FINANCE PLANS

Each of the plans described above is only a part of a general school finance plan for a state. The overall plan should foster adequacy, equity, efficiency, and choice. Because these goals tend to conflict with one another, each is usually compromised to some extent in order to foster the others. In addition, school finance plans are designed in the political arena, and these result in accommodations to powerful actors, whether they are school districts or elected officials. Finally, there is usually a wide variety of districts in the state—in size, special needs, and unusual situations—and the plan needs to make reasonable accommodation to these dimensions. The result is an overall school finance plan of fearsome complexity. It is not at all unusual to find no more than a handful of individuals in a state who understand the entire plan, and most of these are in the state education department. Such complexity makes it easy for inequity and inefficiency to insinuate themselves into the system, generally unrecognized.

Summary

There are a number of ways a state can distribute education funds to school districts. Three philosophical orientations to the issue of disbursement are: minimum provision, equal access, and equal total provision. Minimum provision plans, such as flat grant or foundation-level programs, are designed to provide a similar base level of funds to districts with an option for local supplementation. Equal-access plans attempt to make tax paying more equitable by using the power of the state to equalize either total funds or tax bases. Plans such as guaranteed tax-base formulae fall into this category. Finally, total provision adherents advocate for total state control of the entire education enterprise with no district butt-in. These last two categories raise the issue of recapture, in which money raised by a district is taken by the state and used to support other districts.

Discussion Questions

1. After reading this chapter, discuss the seeming relationship between local community wealth and educational quality. Discuss whether you believe that this controversial issue can be resolved through policymaking.

2. Discuss the relative merits of foundation programs, flat grants, and other revenue distribution methods we have learned about in this chapter.

3. Refer to the "In the News" article regarding high fuel prices and their impact on school budgets. Devise a short-term and a long-term plan to address increased energy expenses for an urban school district located in the Northeast. Consider the political and social implications of your plan. Do you think the federal or state legislature should provide school energy crisis relief? Why or why not?

Web Resources

Education Finance Statistics Center—
http://nces.ed.gov/edfin/

National Conference of State Legislatures National Center on School Finance—
http://www.ncsl.org/programs/educ/NCEF.htm

National Center for Education Statistics—
http://nces.ed.gov/

Public School Finance Programs of the United States and Canada—
http://nces.ed.gov/edfin/state_finance/StateFinancing.asp

References

Benson, C.S. (1961). *The economics of public education*. New York: Houghton Mifflin.

Chambers, J. (1980, Winter). The development of a cost of education index: Some empirical estimates and policy issues. *Journal of Education Finance, 5*, 262–81.

Coons, J.E., Clune, W.H., & Sugarman, S.D. (1970). *Private wealth and public education*. Cambridge, MA: Harvard University Press.

Cubberley, E.P. (1905). *School funds and their apportionment*. New York: Teachers College Press.

Duncombe, W., & Yinger, J. (2005). How much does a disadvantaged student cost? *Economics of Education Review, 24*(5), 513–32.

Education Commission of the States. (1984). *School finance at a glance*, 1983–84.

Friedman, M. (1955). The role of government in education. In R.A. Solos (Ed.), *Economics and the public interest*. Rutgers, NJ: Rutgers University Press.

Goldring, E., & Smrekar, C. (2000). Magnet schools and the pursuit of racial balance. *Education and Urban Society, 33*(1), 17–35.

Harris, M.A. (1975). *School finance at a glance*. Denver: Education Commission of the States.

Marx, K., & Engels, F. (1848/2002). *The Communist manifesto*. New York: Penguin Classics.

Morrison, H.C. (1930). *School revenue*. Chicago: University of Chicago Press.

National Center for Educational Statistics. (2005). *Youth indicators, 2005: Trends in the well-being of American youth*. Washington, DC: U.S. Department of Education. Retrieved January 31, 2007, from http://nces.ed.gov/programs/youthindicators/Indicators.asp?PubPageNumber=11&ShowTablePage=TablesHTML/11.asp.

New York Commission on the Quality, Cost, and Financing of Elementary and Secondary Education. (1973). *The Fleischmann report: On the quality, cost, and financing of elementary and secondary education in New York State*. New York: Viking Press.

Parrish, T.B., & Chambers, J.G. (1984). *An overview of the resource cost model (RCM)*. Stanford, CA: Associates for Education Finance and Planning.

Schwartz, A.E., Steifel, L., & Bel Hadj Amor, H. (2005). Measuring school performance using cost functions. In L. Steifel, A.E. Schwartz, R. Rubenstein, & J. Zabel (Eds.), *Measuring school performance and efficiency: Implications for practice and research* (pp. 67–91). American Education Finance Association 2005 Yearbook. Larchmont, NY: Eye on Education.

Smrekar, C., & Goldring, E. (1999). *School choice in urban America: Magnet schools and the pursuit of equity*. New York: Teachers College Press.

Updegraff, H., & King, L.A. (1922). *Survey of the fiscal policies of the state of Pennsylvania in the field of education*. Philadelphia: University of Pennsylvania.

Wise, A. (1969). *Rich schools, poor schools*. Chicago: University of Chicago Press.

Notes

1. A mill is an old English coin, no longer in use, the value of which is a tenth of a cent, or $0.001. A tax rate of fifteen mills ($0.015) is a tax of 1.5 cents per dollar of assessed valuation. This is equivalent to a rate of $15 per $1,000 of assessed valuation, $1.50 per $100 of assessed valuation, or 1.5 percent.

2. Property value is discussed here without distinguishing between full value and assessed value. Although taxes are levied on assessed value, the illustrations assume uniform assessment rates—that is, the assessment of all properties at full value.

3. See the discussions of *Serrano* and other equal-protection suits in Chapters Five and Twelve.

4. A proof of the equivalence of percentage equalizing and a guaranteed valuation per pupil is given in Garms, Guthrie, & Pierce (1978: 194–195). *School finance: The economics and politics of public education*.

5. A follow-up to the Wyoming study, which updates the model, can be found at http://www.edconsultants.com/documents/2001–02%20WY%20reports/WYFinal.pdf.

6. See Chapter Five for a more detailed discussion of the legal positions involved in these lawsuits.

7. See Garms, Guthrie, & Pierce, *School finance: The economics and politics of public education*, chap. 15, for a description of city schools, financial problems.

8. At least fifteen reports critical of U.S. education were issued within a year. Prominent among them were Adler (1982), Boyer (1983), Goodlad (1983), and the National Commission on Excellence (1983).

CHAPTER EIGHT

Managing Capital Projects and Fiscal Resources

■ INTRODUCTION

The term school finance connotes processes by which money for the support of schools is raised and distributed. However, once these monies are in the hands of individual school districts, business administration captures more accurately processes by which monies are or should be allocated, invested, and spent. This chapter discusses facets of school business management that impinge directly on the conservation and effective use of fiscal resources intended for capital purposes.

LEARNING OBJECTIVES

In this chapter a reader will learn about:

- The distinction between operating and capital financing.
- Public policy justification for employing debt for funding capital projects.
- School business official's role in the planning and oversight of capital projects.
- The process of siting, funding, and constructing school facilities.
- Ways by which a school system can incur debt.
- Conditions under which enrollment growth can present fiscal and physical challenges to school systems.

■ DISTINGUISHING OPERATIONAL AND CAPITAL FUNDING

In education finance a useful distinction is made between resources deployed for the sustained running of an organization, called operational funds, and those that are specified for capital purposes. Chapters Six and Seven concentrate on the generation and distribution of operational funds, those intended to sustain an organization. This chapter concentrates on capital funding. The principal difference is that capital funding is for physical projects or equipment that are relatively enduring. That is, they will likely serve multiple generations of users. The facts that they are long or longer lasting and are used for more than one budget cycle suggest that there should be a different set of arrangements by which such financial resources are generated.

Put most boldly; imagine a newly constructed school intended, with proper maintenance, to have a useable life of at least fifty years. It is hardly fair to ask the initial generation of student users, and their taxpaying parents and fellow citizens, to pay for the new school, millions of dollars in costs, when many subsequent generations will also take advantage of the school. The principal difference between operational and capital funding is that the latter stretches payment for a facility or other equipment over the lifetime of likely multiple users. Conversely, operational funds are for short-range routinely consumable items such as supplies and labor.

School business officials seldom have the luxury of concentrating on and becoming expertly knowledgeable regarding operational funding alone. Almost assuredly, from time to time, they will also have to prepare for and oversee a capital project. Informing a reader about capital funding matters is the purpose of this chapter.

■ CAPITAL CONSTRUCTION

Capital construction can make enormous demands on a school district's fiscal resources, yet much of it is outside the normal current-expenditures budget and tends to be ignored in school finance discussions. The ebb and flow of school construction is tied tightly to demographic trends, which are outside the immediate control of school personnel. Additionally, projecting and planning for this growth are at least partially beyond the capacity of local school districts and placed in the hands of other city or county officials. As a result, projecting growth becomes a process that is prone both to error and misinterpretation.

Demography and School Construction

From World War II to the end of the 1960s an unprecedented number of new schools were built in America. Rapid increases in student population, combined with migration from farm to city and suburb, necessitated construction of thousands of new elementary and secondary schools. Financing this construction placed a heavy burden on capital markets. Moreover, not all resulting schools were well constructed. Even now, at the beginning of the twenty-first century, school superintendents are facing renovation and repairs to hastily built post-World War II facilities.

Decreasing birth rates in the 1970s resulted in substantial reductions in school construction. Although some areas, primarily in the Sunbelt, continued to expand in school-age population, most districts in the North and upper Midwest witnessed a decrease in number of students. This was particularly true in older cities and close-in suburbs. How to close unneeded schools became a primary problem for superintendents and school boards. Invariably, parents agreed that for economic reasons schools should be closed, but "not in my neighborhood."

By the beginning of the twenty-first century, the school enrollment cycle once again was on the upswing. In some ways, the dynamics are much the same as after World War II. Instead of Baby Boomers, school planners are faced with the "Baby Boom echo" as the children of Baby Boomers fill school rolls. School planners also face other demographic pressures related to increased enrollment. One of these pressures is migration into the United States as immigrants and their children gain access to public schools. Finally, there is another big population shift as many Americans move away from locations in the industrial Northeast to southern and western states.[1] School enrollments grew by about 5.5 percent between 1983 and 2006. In 2007 public schools enrolled approximately 48.3 million pupils. This is the highest point in the nation's history. Figure 8.1 indicates that K–12 student enrollment is expected to increase to 50 million by 2014 (NCES, 2006).

If a district is facing enrollment surges after enrollment declines, accommodating new students may be as "easy" as filling currently underused schools to capacity, or by reactivating mothballed schools. In other cases, however, new students are enrolling in communities that must create schools to hold them. School districts have established schools that operate year-round with four staggered tracks of students to increase the capacity of school buildings. Plans have even been adopted to create schools comprised entirely of modular building units ("portables") that can be established quickly in rapidly expanding subdivisions.

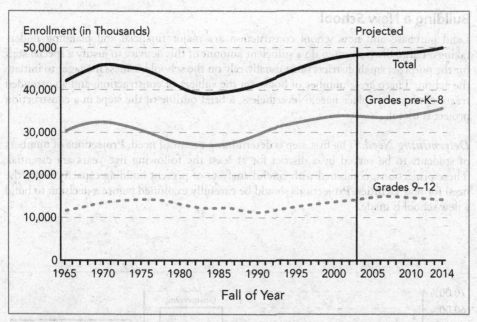

FIGURE 8.1 Actual and Projected Numbers for Elementary and Secondary Enrollment, Total and by Grade Level: Selected Years, 1965–2014

Note: Includes kindergarten and most pre-kindergarten enrollment.

Source: Hussar, W. *Projections of education statistics to 2014* (NCES 2005–065), Tables 1 and 4 and U.S. Department of Education, National Center for Education Statistics (NCES) *Digest of education statistics 2054* (NCES 2005–079), Table 37. Data from U.S. Department of Education, National Center for Education Statistics, Common Core of Data (CCD), "State nonfiscal survey of public elementary/secondary education," 1986–2002 and "Statistics of public elementary and secondary school systems," various years.

The following graphic (Figure 8.2) displays a one-time snapshot of governmental contributions to facility construction.

Capital outlay unevenness has important implications. Because construction of a new school is such a large investment, it is worth spending the time and effort necessary to be sure it is done properly. Borrowing is frequently utilized for capital outlays. Financing capital expenditures completely out of current revenues would mean large fluctuations in tax rates. In many communities, capital costs are raised through the issuance of bonds which must be passed through referenda. In rapidly growing communities, the ever-present "school bond construction referendum" tries the public's patience and politicizes even operating expenses. The mechanism of bonds is discussed in greater detail below.

An important characteristic of capital expense is unevenness of expenditure. Construction of a school in one year may cost millions of dollars, with expenditures in succeeding years being almost zero. Only the largest districts, such as New York and Chicago, can manage to smooth out these capital expenditures and spend about the same amount each year.

Building a New School

Land purchase and new school construction are major financial and planning undertakings. Large districts often do a sufficient amount of this activity to justify a special staff for the purpose; small districts must usually rely on the school business manager to initiate the action. There are a number of books on the subject of construction, and an extended treatment is out of place here. Nevertheless, a brief outline of the steps in a construction project is useful.

Determining Need. The first step is determining extent of need. Projections of numbers of students to be served by a district for at least the following five years are essential. These projections, combined with careful analyses of present building capacity verify the need for new facilities. Projections should be carefully examined before a decision to build a new school is made.

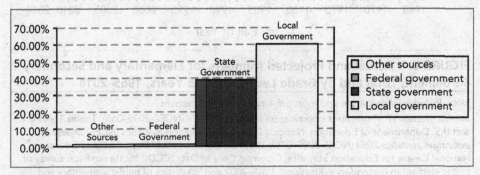

FIGURE 8.2 Percentage of Capital Outlay, 2002 (NCES)

Below are alternatives to consider prior to constructing new facilities:

1. Space presently underutilized because of inconvenient arrangement of facilities could be remodeled.
2. Utilization of space in nonschool buildings nearby. This is particularly true for classroom uses that are not part of K–12 instructions, such as day care. Nearby church-school classrooms have often been used for this purpose.
3. Consolidation of selected operations with a neighboring school district that has space. An example would be special education classes that are smaller than necessary in each district.
4. Increase the number of periods in a normal day at the high school level, thus increasing classroom utilization.
5. Multitrack year-round schooling, using selected models, can increase the capacity of a building by 20–25 percent.
6. Students may be reassigned to fill in underutilized classroom space.
7. Mobile classroom units (MCUs) may be used at schools to increase capacity. Some districts have constructed entire schools out of MCUs.

Determining Location. If, after a survey of options, it is decided that construction is the most appropriate solution to actual or potential overcrowding, the next step is to determine the new building's likely location.

Additions to present schools may be the least expensive alternative if space is available on a site and if shared facilities (multipurpose room, playgrounds, etc.) are adequate for the additional student load. However, this lower cost may be balanced by higher transportation costs if a sufficient number of students reside in a part of the district where there are no schools. Thus it is vital that an enrollment projection include not only how many students are to be served, but also where they live and will likely live in the future. Necessary data may often be obtained from city or county planning departments; electric, telephone, and other utility companies; and major residential builders and commercial developers.

Land Acquisition. Assuming that it is desirable to build a school at a new site, a district must proceed to purchase land. The simplest solution is to find a parcel of land in the middle of an area about to become a subdivision and agree with the owner on a price. Where large subdivisions are being built, a district often does this well before it will be necessary to construct a school. The district may be able to negotiate a good price for the land by cooperating with the developer, who should realize the increased value that closeness to schools brings to houses.[2] California is a case where state government and other local governments foster this cooperation. Each developer is required by state law to file an Environmental Impact Statement (EIS). This statement must be accepted by the city or county, which may require developers to deed a school site to the school district (or pay the district a specified number of dollars per house) before the EIS will be approved.

However, it is more likely that a suitable site must be assembled from parcels owned by a number of individual owners. A developer ordinarily does this by secretly obtaining options on each necessary parcel before making any purchases, to prevent owners from discovering what is occurring and holding out for a high price. It is difficult for school districts to deal in secrecy, particularly in states with open meeting laws. However, the district has an ultimate weapon not possessed by the private developer—power of condemnation, also called eminent domain.

Districts proceed in different ways on land purchases, some doing all purchasing through negotiation and others using condemnation exclusively. Condemnation has one advantage: a court, relieving a district of allegations of overpayment, sets the price. Negotiation, however, is often more appropriate when establishing cooperative arrangements with developers of a large area, or where special concessions important to the owner and unimportant to the district (such as payments spread over a number of years) would result in a lower price. Each situation must be approached on its own merits. In any case, the district's legal counsel must be involved at every transaction step.

Architectural Planning

Having selected a site, the district must begin architectural planning. A good architect can plan imaginatively and save the district money; a poor one can be a catastrophe, ill consequences lasting for the life of the building. Architects should not be selected on a bid basis. Most architects' fees are standard (indeed, state law may specify what they shall be), and any architect who promises to charge a lesser fee should be viewed skeptically. Rather, an architect should be selected on the basis of past performance in other situations. The firm, for it is seldom an individual architect, should certainly have built schools before. Stories abound of the famous architect who builds his first hospital, which is beautiful on the outside and absolutely unworkable on the inside. Firms should be invited to present sample photographs of their work, along with descriptions of the size of the firm and the kinds of expertise it offers.

After a preliminary screening, district personnel should visit schools designed by firms under consideration and talk with administrators, teachers, and maintenance personnel. This will narrow the choice to a few architects, who should then be interviewed on preferred work method, current office workload, and particular employees to be assigned to the project. It is important that these individuals' personalities be compatible with those of the district personnel who are to be most closely involved in the project.

The school district should next develop educational specifications: the number of students to be housed and the kind of educational programs to be offered. The more careful and complete such specifications, the more likely an architect will be able to design the kind of school a district prefers. Avoid an architect who says, "Tell me how many students you want to house, and I will design a school for you with no further worry on your part." *Development of educational specifications is one of the most important parts of designing a school and should involve teachers, supervisors, and administrators.* It should not be rushed, for time must be allowed for reconciling differing views. Often, square-foot-per-student figures will be used in political debate; school districts with square foot specifications greater than the state average will be tagged as extravagant, while districts with lower than state average figures will be tagged as unsympathetic.

With educational specifications in hand, an architect confers with district representatives to develop preliminary ideas. At this point it is desirable to keep the district delegation small so that it can reach tentative agreement on many facets of the plan in a reasonable time. A number of sessions may be necessary, and the district may need to gather additional data or refine its educational specifications. At some point the architect presents preliminary plans, usually consisting of plan view and elevations. When these have been sufficiently modified they will be ready for formal approval by the school board.

The architect can now develop detailed drawings and specifications. It is important from this point forward that the district's maintenance supervisor be involved, for the decisions made here can save or cost the district many thousands of dollars over the life of the building. District representatives should carefully review detailed final drawings. Errors found at this point are easy to correct. Found during construction, errors result in costly change orders; if not found until after the building is completed, they are even more costly to correct.

Bidding

The district now advertises for bids. Contractors interesting in bidding will obtain building plans from the architect, estimate labor and materials necessary, and obtain commitments from subcontractors. Typically, the general contractor does all carpentry, performs some of the other work, and supervises and coordinates all construction. Subcontractors are usually obtained for electrical work, plumbing, site grading, mechanical work, and a number of other jobs.

At a date and time advertised, general contractors' bids are opened and read. The district is generally required by law to accept the bid of the lowest qualified bidder, but this need not necessarily be the lowest bid. The architect should be present, and should carefully review the two or three lowest bids. The financial status of the general contractor should be determined, if possible, and the contractor's performance on other projects ascertained. The same is true of each subcontractor, who must be listed in the bid. An architect before recommendation of the bid award must assess many other items. If recommending someone other than the lowest bidder, the architect should present good reasons, for there will probably be a challenge from the lowest bidder before the school board. The board need not award the bid to anyone, although it usually will if the lowest acceptable bid is at or below the architect's estimate. Frequently an architect will specify alternatives, with a separate bid on each alternative, in order to be able to adjust total contract size to the funds available in case a bid exceeds the estimate. This complicates the selection of a bidder, for the lowest bidder on the base contract may be high on some alternative additions.

Construction

Construction now begins, under supervision of an architect, who visits the project site several times a week to ensure plans are followed and to resolve problems in interpretation of drawings or specifications, and to develop change orders where necessary. However, it is difficult for an architect to be on the site at all times, and shoddy workmanship can be covered up by subsequent construction before the next visit. Thus, it is essential for the district to hire a full-time inspector. This should be a person thoroughly experienced in all facets of building. This individual should be on the job any time work is underway and should insist on inspecting all work before it is covered. This is a crucial role; opportunities for concealing poor workmanship or perpetrating outright fraud are great, and the potential cost to the district is much more than what will be paid to the inspector in salary.

Design-Build Construction. Private and nonprofit organizations increasingly rely on design-build (or managed) construction for large buildings or projects, such as industrial plants, commercial developments, or hospitals. This involves services of a project architect and a prime contractor. The architect in this instance is not charged with both overall design and detailed drawing and specifications for the entire structure. Rather, once the functions to be performed within the proposed building are clearly known, the architect prepares requests for bids for various packages or components of the project: excavation, foundations, structural steel, heating and ventilation, interior finishes, and so on.

Bidders are provided with functional specifications, but not with detailed design drawings other than significant dimensions of the overall undertaking. Rather than simply expressing a dollar amount for which they will complete the component, a subcontractor also submits an overall plan with construction specifications for the component. In effect, bidding subcontractors complete detailed work of an architect and structural engineer.

The design-build format has at least two advantages. It expedites construction of the overall project. Construction can begin early without being impeded just because the architect has not completed all drawings for every phase. More important, the managing contractor and architect have the advantage of subcontractor experience. By issuing over-all performance specifications, but not detailed drawings, potential bidders can take advantage of their practical experience and offer better designs than otherwise might be the case; designs that often are less expensive to implement.

Design-build construction for public schools may not be possible in states that need to review detailed plans. Under such arrangements, whatever time was saved by the design-build mode would be lost by state review procedures. However, should managed construction become more widely adopted in the private sector, a means may be found to permit wider public sector use of similar techniques.

Completion and Preparation for Use

The final construction step is formal acceptance of a building after the architect has certi-fied to the school board that construction is complete and satisfactory. Final payment may be made soon thereafter, although the general contractor may withhold a percentage for a legally specified period against the possibility of liens filed by employees or subcontractors for nonpayment.

This is not the final step in preparing a new school for students. The most important remaining activity (begun well before completion of construction) is purchase of equip-ment for the building. This involves careful planning to ensure that everything will be delivered in time. Lists of items must be compiled and crosschecked. Detailed specifica-tions are drawn, based both on the educational needs expressed by principal and teachers and on the desires of the maintenance supervisor. These frequently conflict, for mainte-nance personnel prefer standardized equipment so as to minimize the problem of spare parts and of training mechanics, whereas teachers frequently want something unique, believing it will be more convenient or provide for better instruction. Equipment for a new building is a capital expense, usually paid for from proceeds of the bond funds used in building construction. Equipment other than that for a new building, such as additional desks for an existing school, is also a capital expense, but is usually purchased from current revenues instead of from bond funds. These capital expenditures from current revenues are usually minor compared with those from bond funds.

Surplus Facilities. Many districts, because of previous enrollment declines or population shifts, have underused or unused buildings and properties. This is a smaller problem currently than in the 1970s for school enrollments nationwide are trending upward again. However, in older sections of the nation, and particularly in older cities of those sections, enrollments may still be declining. Surplus schools and property are a fiscal problem primarily because they are a political problem. Everyone is for more efficiency, but not for closing a school in the neighborhood. The result is often underutilized schools and small class sizes. The most difficult problem facing a school board and superintendent is often that of deciding to close a school.

Assuming a decision has been made to close a school, what is to be done with it? Sometimes the district itself can use the building and site for administrative offices or for special programs. However, unless the activities involved are being moved from rented facilities, this may simply mean shifting the surplus space to another spot in the district. (That may be good, if one part of the district is growing.)

In some cases, it is possible to convert surplus facilities to other community uses. A community hall, playground, library, and park are examples. The city, county, or state may need office space. In many states, law requires the district to offer the surplus property to other governmental agencies before it may market it publicly, and it may sell the property to another agency at lower than market value. This is often advantageous to the taxpayer who supports both governmental entities, but that is scant comfort to the school district, which receives less cash than it might if it sold the property on the open market.

Unfortunately, nonschool uses for a surplus school may be limited rendering sale difficult. Often the site is abandoned for school purposes because the clientele has moved away as the area becomes commercial or industrial. Even so, it is sometimes possible to find uses that make it possible to sell the property for a reasonable sum. Near Rochester, New York, Xerox Corporation bought a surplus school for warehousing purposes. In a number of cases, surplus schools in inner cities have been redeveloped into attractive apartments.

▪ SCHOOL DEBT AND ITS MANAGEMENT

There are three categories of debt, and they apply equally to individuals, school districts, and corporations. The first category is the amount owed for items recently purchased and received but for which payment has not yet been made. For an individual, examples are a charge account at a department store or an amount owed for current purchases on a credit card. For school districts, this category of debt is known as accounts payable and is normally paid out of current revenues within a month or two of receipt of goods and invoice. Thus, it need not be considered further as part of debt management. Of course, if a district should be unable to pay its accounts on time, it might try to stall creditors (dangerous if you want to engage with them again), or borrow from a bank. Borrowing converts this debt into a second category.

This second type of debt is the sort that individuals incur when they borrow on a short-term basis to pay for purchases, or pay less than the full balance on their monthly credit card statement. This is short-term debt. One can think of this kind of borrowing as meeting a cash-flow problem, whereby money comes in too slowly at one time of year and more rapidly at another time. This is particularly apt to happen with school districts, where tax receipts or tax-supported credits often arrive in school accounts from a county or municipal treasurer in large sums once or twice a year while expenses continue on a more uniform basis throughout the year. Districts faced with this problem usually borrow from a bank or other lending institution on a short-term basis, repaying loans when tax receipts arrive. The district guarantees to pay interest at a stated rate. Such loans must typically be repaid within twelve months, and this period constitutes the dividing line between short-term and long-term debt.

Finally, long-term debt is incurred almost exclusively for purchase or construction of capital assets. An individual incurs such debt when borrowing from a bank to buy a house or an automobile, giving the bank a mortgage. School districts borrow also, but special circumstances dictate the use of a different evidence of indebtedness, called a bond. A bond is simply an acknowledgment that money has been borrowed. The district promises to pay a specified rate of interest on the debt and to repay the principal amount at a stated time. But there is not just one loan. Rather, bonds are issued in multiples of $1,000 or $5,000. Since the amount borrowed at one time may be several million dollars, there will be many bonds, and many individuals or corporations can own them. In addition, bonds can be sold by one person to another. The school district owes interest and principal to whoever owns the bonds at the time payment becomes due.

Another difference between a bond and a loan to an individual is that an individual typically pledges property as security. If payments are not made, the bank can seize the property, automobile, or other physical asset and sell it, keeping what it is owed, plus expenses, and returning the remainder to the owner. School land and buildings are public property and cannot be seized for sale. Thus, the bond usually pledges the full faith and credit of the district. This means that the district is legally bound to tax its property owners a sufficient amount to pay principal and interest on the bonds, and it can be compelled to do so through court action. Because of this call on the taxes of property owners, school district bonds are relatively safe investments. However, it is possible that local conditions could cause a district to default on its bonds. In 1983, as a result of complications related to Proposition 13 and collective bargaining contracts, the San Jose, California, School District declared bankruptcy. The decision of the bankruptcy judge preserved bondholders' rights (employees forfeited negotiated pay increases), but until his decision there was serious concern among the district's creditors. The risk of default by a district is estimated by bond buyers and is reflected in the credit ratings and interest rates districts must pay when they borrow.

Reasons for Borrowing

Should a school district borrow? Some people believe any form of borrowing is wrong, or perhaps even sinful. However, there are several good reasons for borrowing under appropriate circumstances.

First, it is sometimes simply good business. Frequently a vendor will give a cash discount for prompt payment. A typical bill might state, "Discount 1.5 percent 10 days, net 30 days." By paying 20 days sooner than required, the district can save 1.5 percent of the purchase price. Figured on the basis of 360 days per year, this is equivalent to an interest rate of 27 percent per year charged by the vendor. If the school district can pay the bill promptly, it should do so. Even if it does not have the money to pay promptly, it can probably borrow funds for less than 27 percent and it will save money in the process. Of course, this type of borrowing must be monitored carefully, for if more is borrowed than is necessary, extra interest costs may negate the savings.

Districts could eliminate the need to engage in short-term borrowing to ease cashflow problems by levying a higher tax than is currently needed and amassing a reserve fund to meet cash needs during the year. In most states, however, this is illegal. The law requires that property tax rates each year be sufficient only to make up the difference between budgeted expenditures and receipts, with receipts including all cash available at the beginning of the year. The reason for this is the basic principle of taxation that a government should not have tax revenues available until it is ready to spend money. In general, it is believed that individuals should have the right to use or invest cash themselves rather than giving it to government sooner than needed.

Of course, short-term borrowing can be abused. New York State provided a prime example during the 1970s. As a result of political pressure, the legislature voted a one-time large increase in school funding, hoping it would find the revenue to continue this in future years. However, there was insufficient money in the state's coffers to pay for the increase even in the year in which it was voted. The state solved the problem by a stratagem based on the difference between the fiscal years of the state and the school districts. This enabled the state to pay districts one year out of the following year's receipts. The strategy also necessitated borrowing by districts until they received the state money, and borrowing by the state to pay districts before it actually had tax receipts in hand. All this borrowing was a bonanza for banks and increased the cost of doing business for school districts and the state. Nevertheless, not much thought was given to it until normal state receipts fell short of meeting state obligations to local school districts. In the spring of 1976, at the last possible moment, the state was able to borrow the necessary $4 billion, part of it from state employee retirement funds. If the state had been unable to borrow this money, many school districts would have defaulted on their short-term loans, something that did not happen even during the Great Depression of the 1930s.

Management of Short-Term Debt

Short-term debt, usually incurred to solve cash-flow problems, may be a loan from a local bank, as is usual when needs are small or for a limited period. Where needs are more substantial, districts may sell notes. These are similar to bonds, for they are promises to pay, but they have a short life (typically no more than twelve months) and do not pledge the full faith and credit of the district. Because they do not commit the district to tax itself for repayment, electoral approval is not necessary and borrowing is not subject to bonding limits.

As security, notes pledge the revenue to be obtained from some future assured source. If they are secured by a promise to repay from taxes to be received at a later time, they are known as tax anticipation notes. Those secured by future state aid payments are called revenue anticipation notes, and those secured by revenue to be obtained from sale of bonds are called bond anticipation notes. Although notes are transferable, they are not usually bought by a dealer for resale, as are bonds. Rather, they are bought by the bidder who quotes interest cost, usually a bank.

In addition to notes, which solve cash shortages expected to last for several months, a district may borrow directly from a bank for periods of one day to several weeks. The other side of the cash-flow coin is that at certain times of year a district may have substantial cash surpluses. Usually, keeping the money in bank savings is the least profitable way of investing it, with the exception of leaving it in a checking account, where it may draw no interest at all.

Large districts typically have an employee whose duty is investment of idle funds and usually also short-term borrowing as part of the cash-flow problem. This investment specialist estimates the cash position for each day several months in advance, taking into account anticipated revenues and expenditures. Then investments are made in such a way that the necessary amount of money, and not too much more, will be available to meet the district's day-to-day needs. The specialist makes only short-term investments—those less than a year in maturity—typically in certificates of deposit, bankers' acceptances, treasury bills, and so forth.

To earn the most from funds, the specialist may even invest any cash left at the end of the business day overnight, and have it back again the next day. This is done through repurchase agreements with banks. Banks are required by law to have a specified percentage of assets available at all times in cash. They strive also to be as fully invested as possible. At the end of a business day they may find that their cash position is below requirement. Because government auditors always appear after business hours and without warning, the bank must borrow money overnight to cover its requirement, and it does so by means of repurchase agreements.

There are other types of repurchase agreements, all involving short-term borrowing. Unfortunately, as with many other transactions, one must be careful to deal with reputable companies and take reasonable precautions. The city of San Jose, California, lost $60 million when two New York securities dealers went bankrupt and the securities San Jose presumably owned as a result of lending them money were never found. Small districts usually cannot afford a specialist in short-term investment. However, even these districts can improve their cash flow management. School district revenues and expenditures are more predictable than those of a private business, both in timing and in amount. A business manager can therefore easily construct a calendar displaying predicted revenues and expenditures for each day of the school year, and from these projections, estimate the excess or shortage of funds in the district's possession for each day. Using this information, the manager can plan to invest idle cash during periods of excess for appropriate periods in, for example, certificates of deposit that earn more than bank savings, and to borrow on a short-term basis only the amounts needed for the minimum period necessary to keep money in the district's accounts. Most small districts do not do this, or do it poorly, and, as a result, operate less efficiently than necessary.

Long-Term Debt

Because long-term debt commits a school district to repayments over many years, it usually must be approved by a vote of the people, frequently by a super majority (votes of 60 percent or two-thirds are common). In addition, there are usually state restrictions on the total debt incurred. This limit is typically 5 or 10 percent of the value of assessed real property in the district. The intent is to prevent present district residents from saddling future residents with too large a debt, and to ensure that ability to repay present bonds is not overly diluted by future issues. Long-term debt may usually be incurred only for purchase of land and construction and initial equipping of buildings.

One reason for long-term borrowing is that school building construction is costly. To tax property owners sufficiently to pay for the entire construction cost during the year it is accomplished would usually mean prohibitively high tax rates, and in any case would result in extreme fluctuations of tax rates from year to year. By borrowing, the school district spreads costs over a period of years, giving more stability to tax rates.

An alternative, possible in some states, is to pass a special tax levy that will be in effect a specified number of years. The trouble with this method for major construction programs is that construction will not be possible until some years after initiation of such a levy. School districts are seldom able to convince the public to pass such a levy sufficiently in advance of the need (and may, in fact, not be able themselves to project the need sufficiently). The idea is enticing to some because no money is borrowed and thus no interest need be paid. However, presumed savings are illusory. Taking money away from taxpayers prematurely means they are prevented from using the assets for their own ends, which might include earning interest on it.

Long-term borrowing is also defended as a reasonable way of spreading costs among generations. A school building will last many years, typically from thirty to well over sixty. It seems unfair to force the present generation to pay the entire cost of buildings that will be used by future generations too. If people always lived in the same place, this kind of generational inequity could be excused on the same basis whereby we defend parents paying for the education of their children. Since individuals move while school buildings stay, it is more equitable to allow a school district's future residents to pay part of the building's costs. Thus, bonds are the most frequently used method of financing new school construction.

Authorizing Bonds

Steps involved in authorizing, approving, and issuing bonds are numerous and complex. Each step must be conducted with complete legality; otherwise, the bonds will not be salable. For this purpose, a district should engage a financial consultant specializing in bonding. Such a consultant:

1. Surveys the issuer's debt structure and financial resources to determine borrowing capacity for future capital financing requirements.
2. Gathers all pertinent financial statistics and economic data, such as debt-retirement schedule, tax rates, overlapping debt, and so forth, that would affect or reflect on the issuer's ability and willingness to repay its obligations.
3. Advises on timing and method of marketing: the terms of bond issues, including maturity schedule, interest payment dates, call features, and bidding limitations.
4. Prepares an overall financing plan specifying a recommended approach and a probable timetable.
5. Prepares, in cooperation with bond counsel, an official statement, notice of sale, and bid form and distributes same to all prospective underwriters and investors.
6. Assists the issuer in obtaining local public assistance and support of proposed financing.
7. Keeps in constant contact with rating services to ensure that they have all the information and data they require to evaluate credit properly.
8. Is present when sealed bids are opened and stands ready to advise on acceptability of bids.
9. Supervises bond printing, signing, and delivery.
10. Advises on investment of bond proceeds.

In addition to a financial consultant it is necessary to engage bond counsel. This is a specialized law firm that reviews legal details of bonding procedures to ensure that bonds are indeed a legal obligation of the district. Each purchaser of a bond expects to find attached to it an opinion by bond counsel (often printed on the back of the bond) that there can be no reasonable legal challenge to the indebtedness represented by the bond. The school board's attorney cannot serve this function, for purchasers will want an opinion signed by an independent law firm. Indeed, sophisticated purchasers may insist that the opinion be written by one of a very small number of recognized bond counsels. The same firm may serve the functions of both financial adviser and bond counsel, if it has marketing as well as legal skills.

The bond election is the moment of truth when the district determines whether it will be possible to borrow money. District officials will, of course, have done all they can to ensure a successful outcome. From 1940 to 1960, over 80 percent of school district bond elections passed with the required majority, but since then passage has become increasingly difficult. The percentage of bond elections that has passed declined from 75 percent in 1960 to 35 percent in 1986 (Wirt & Kirst, 2005). Interestingly, the percentage of dollars approved has risen to almost 80 percent over the same time period.

Fortunately, the need also decreased; there were fewer children to be educated. However, the demographic pendulum is now swinging the other way, and, with increases in school-age children, one can expect schools to issue more bonds and to be better able to convince the electorate to pass them. In any case, the need must be justified and documented, and then presented to voters in a convincing manner.

In the News

It was supposed to be temporary—the long white trailer on the school blacktop, sporting a lopsided California license plate and wired to a propane tank. But a year later, the trailer's eight wheels haven't budged from McNair Elementary School in Compton. Inside, three kitchen workers still wash, slice and simmer food for the school's 540 students. The school's kitchen, a few steps from the makeshift one, sits in disrepair.

McNair's $10,000-a-month trailer-turned-kitchen is among the most dramatic examples of construction delays that have vexed the Compton Unified School District since it launched an ambitious three-phase plan in 2002 to modernize 28 of its aging campuses and build two more. The district began with $80 million in funding from a successful bond measure. Today, not even through its first phase, only three of the 28 projects are complete, and the district may have to borrow $20 million to $30 million to finish the others. The superintendent has suspended

construction while the district figures out how to handle the funding shortfall.

Officials say the rising cost of construction, state money that never came through, and numerous change-order requests caused funds to be used up faster than expected. Despite delays, the district has renovated about 1,500 classrooms, said Alvin Jenkins, director of facilities for Compton Unified. But officials concede that the district probably tried to tackle too much at once without monitoring progress on each campus. "The problem with this district," Compton Supt. Jesse Gonzales said, "is it went for quantity over quality."

Two independent audits criticized aspects of the district's handling of its finances and cited incomplete and subpar construction work. A November audit by the Los Angeles-based Del Terra Group found that renovations at many schools resulted in, among other things, poorly positioned thermostats, water pooling in light fixtures, disconnected fire alarm systems and rooftop air-conditioning units that were inadequately secured against earthquakes. District critics seized on the audit as evidence that officials fumbled the $80-million bond measure passed by the city in 2002 to begin construction. "My property taxes have already gone up as a result of the bond," fumed Alan Polee, whose 7-year-old son is a second-grader at McNair. "What have they done with the money?"

The district broke ground on the undertaking four years ago with high hopes and a much-needed goal: refurbishing Compton's decades-old campus facilities, many of which were falling apart. Lighting at some schools was more than 50 years old; some sewer and electrical systems more than 100. Problems soon arose. The $400 million that the district estimated for project costs in 1998 ballooned to $600 million six years later as a result of inflation and escalating construction costs, district officials said.

From: Proctor, C. (2007, January 1). Compton school projects suspended. *Los Angeles Times*, Metro Desk Part B, p. 1.

Selling Bonds

Assuming district voters approve a bond issue, the next step is to find a purchaser. School districts do not sell bonds directly to individuals. Rather, they sell an entire issue to a dealer, usually a bank, brokerage firm, or syndicate composed of several banks or brokers. Availability of bonds is advertised and bids are received. The bid resulting in the lowest net interest rate to the district is accepted. Frequently, bids will differ only in the second or third decimal place (7.244 percent versus 7.235 percent, for example), but this difference of 0.009 percent on a $10 million bond issue amounts to a difference of over $13,000 in interest paid over twenty years.

To obtain the best bid, the district needs at least two things: a rating of its credit by one of the bond rating agencies and a bond brochure describing an issue. Both have the goal of assuring prospective purchasers that interest and principal will be paid in full and on time. There are two important bond rating agencies—Moody's and Standard & Poor's.

Moody's and Standard & Poor's. They use different codes to express the risk of a bond issue, but both agencies rate issues on a scale from highest quality to extremely risky. If a district has sold more than $1 million in bonds fairly recently, it is probably already rated by one or both agencies. If it has not, or if the district's fiscal condition has changed markedly since it was last rated, the financial adviser will ask agencies to review the rating. A small improvement in the rating can result in markedly lower interest costs over the life of the bonds, and is well worth pursuing.

In making a rating, the bond analyst tends to look beyond the issue itself to the aggregated local economy and its burden of debt. The analyst's interest is in the "debt capacity" of the issuer (the maximum amount of debt that can legally be issued by the governmental unit) and in the untapped margin of debt capacity still available. The analyst is also interested in a quantification of "indirect debt," composed of bond issues for which the issuer may be a guarantor, and "overlapping debt," the sum of all debt issued by all local governments in an area. Usually expressed in per capita terms, overlapping debt includes the individual citizen's proportionate share of city, county, school district, and other special district debts outstanding.

Preparation of the bond brochure is the financial consultant's responsibility. The district should not attempt to do it unaided. Nonprofessional brochures are immediately apparent to purchasers and tend to alienate sophisticated buyers. A professional knows what information prospective purchasers need and knows how to emphasize the most positive facets. A properly prepared brochure may also result in lower interest costs, which will repay many times the cost of preparing the brochure.

Economies of scale are immediately apparent in bonding. The cost of an election, of bond brochure preparation, and of printing bonds is almost the same regardless of issue size. The cost to bidders of the analysis necessary to make a bid (again reflected in the bid) is also almost independent of the size of the issue. The larger the issue, the lower the cost of all these fixed items per dollar of indebtedness. In addition, it is extremely rare for a small district to receive a high rating by agencies, and frequently they will not rate such a district's issue at all. A low rating will result in higher interest, and no rating may even mean no bidders. In this case the issue is usually privately placed with a local bank at a higher interest cost.

There is an alternative for small districts—the Municipal Bond Insurance Association. A school district can secure a commitment from the association to "guarantee unconditionally and irrevocably the full and prompt payment of the principal and interest to the paying agent of the bonds," with the result that rating agencies will give the issue a higher rating than otherwise. Districts pay a premium to the association for this guarantee, the amount based on the association's estimate of the issue's risk. It might seem that the premium would not be much less than the cost of higher interest rates if the issue went to market at the lower rating. The association, however, by specializing in small, fiscally sound districts, has been able to charge a premium sufficiently low to save money for these districts.

As with all other steps in the bonding process, care must be taken in the printing. The financial consultant assists in this. If the bonds are not correct in every detail, purchasing banks or brokers will discover the error and bonds will have to be printed again. The bonds are then sold by the bank or broker to individuals or other institutions. The bonds may either be coupon bonds, whose coupons bondholders clip and return each six months to receive their interest payment, or registered bonds, the interest paid to the registered owner at the time each payment becomes due. Most bonds are now registered (Rabbinowitz, 1969).

Interest and Principal Payments

A school district could borrow, say, $5 million for twenty years through the sale of bonds, with interest payable semiannually and the entire principal falling due twenty years hence. Such a bond is called a term bond. This places a large repayment burden on the district at that future time, and to meet its commitment to redeem the bonds the district would have to establish a sinking fund into which it annually placed sufficient money (including interest on the fund) to add up to $5 million by the end of the twenty years. Bonds are not repaid, as are mortgages where each monthly payment is partly principal and partly interest. Instead, each individual bond is a term bond, with only interest paid on it until maturity. Typically, not all bonds of an issue will have the same maturity date. Instead, bonds are scheduled for sequential maturity dates: some may be only five-year bonds while others are twenty-year bonds.

Table 8.1 Schedule of Principal and Interest Payments on a $5 Million Twenty-Year Bond Issued at 6 Percent Interest

Year	Interest Payment	Principal Payment	Total Payment	Principal Remaining, End of Period
1	$300,000	$135,000	$435,000	$4,865,000
2	$291,900	$145,000	$436,900	$4,720,000
3	$283,200	$155,000	$438,200	$4,565,000
4	$273,900	$165,000	$438,900	$4,400,000
5	$264,000	$175,000	$439,000	$4,225,000
6	$253,500	$185,000	$438,500	$4,040,000
7	$242,400	$195,000	$437,400	$3,845,000
8	$230,700	$205,000	$435,700	$3,640,000
9	$218,400	$215,000	$433,400	$3,425,000
10	$205,500	$230,000	$435,500	$3,195,000
11	$191,700	$245,000	$436,700	$2,950,000
12	$177,000	$260,000	$437,000	$2,690,000
13	$161,400	$275,000	$436,400	$2,415,000
14	$144,900	$290,000	$434,900	$2,125,000
15	$127,500	$310,000	$437,500	$1,815,000
16	$108,900	$330,000	$438,900	$1,485,000
17	$89,100	$345,000	$434,100	$1,140,000
18	$68,400	$365,000	$433,400	$775,000
19	$46,500	$390,000	$436,500	$385,000
20	$23,100	$385,000	$408,100	$0

Maturities are scheduled so that the sum of principal and interest payments for the district is about the same each year. These are called serial bonds. An example is given in Table 8.1 for $5 million borrowed at 6 percent interest, with the first payment at the end of the present year, the last payment at the end of twenty years, and annual interest payments on the balance immediately prior to each principal repayment. Note that the sums of principal and interest are not precisely the same each year, for this would require paying a fraction of a thousand dollars in principal each year, but the schedule created here assumes that principal payments are in multiples of $5,000. A given number of bonds mature each year, as shown by the schedule and as stated on the face of each bond. Owners of bonds that mature in a given year present them for redemption and are paid face amounts. Except in the last year, annual payments are between $433,000 and $439,000.

The entire issue of bonds schematized in Table 8.1 has a 6 percent coupon rate. This means that the school district will pay 6 percent annually on the principal amount of each bond. The bank or broker, however, will make an independent decision on the effective interest rate for each maturity date that will be necessary to attract buyers. The broker will establish this effective interest rate by selling at a higher or lower price than the par value of the bond.

In the case of a discount, for instance, the buyer may buy a $1,000 bond for $960. Nevertheless, interest of $60 per year is paid by the school district (6 percent of $1,000), and this amounts to 6.25 percent interest on the purchase price. In addition, when the bond matures the owner will receive the full $1,000, or $40 more than was paid. This further increases the effective interest rate. If the bond matures in ten years, the effective

Table 8.2 A Ten-Year Bond at Differing Coupon Rates

Year	Principal Amount	Rate	Bond Years (1) × (2)	Interest Cost (3) × (4)	Offering Price	Production (2) × (6)	Yield to Maturity
(1)	(2)	(3)	(4)	(5)	(6)	(7)	(8)
1	$350,000	6.00%	$350,000	$21,000	$10.04	$3,513,300	5.60
2	$400,000	6.00%	$800,000	$48,000	$10.07	$4,026,000	5.65
3	$450,000	5.90%	$1,350,000	$79,650	$10.05	$4,524,300	5.70
4	$450,000	5.85%	$1,800,000	$105,300	$10.04	$4,515,750	5.75
5	$500,000	5.90%	$2,500,000	$147,500	$10.06	$5,032,000	5.75
6	$550,000	6.00%	$3,300,000	$198,000	$10.10	$5,555,000	5.80
7	$600,000	6.10%	$4,200,000	$256,200	$10.11	$6,066,000	5.90
8	$650,000	6.20%	$5,200,000	$322,400	$10.16	$6,604,000	5.95
9	$700,000	6.30%	$6,300,000	$396,900	$10.21	$7,144,200	6.00
10	$350,000	5.50%	$3,500,000	$192,500	$9.59	$3,357,200	6.05
	$5,000,000		$29,300,000	$1,767,450		$50,337,750	

yield to maturity of the bond will be 6.55 percent; if it matures in twenty years, the yield to maturity will be 6.36 percent. The bank will make these calculations for each maturity date, setting a price on the bonds maturing in each year that will yield the effective interest rate it believes necessary to attract buyers. The sum of these will be the anticipated receipt from sale of the entire issue. The amount bid by the dealer may be more or less than the par value of the bonds, and the difference between anticipated receipts and amount bid is the dealer's gross profit. The award of the bid is based on net interest cost to the district.

It is also common for dealers to adjust bond coupon rates (within limits stipulated by the school district) as another way to establish a yield to maturity that will be attractive to investors. Table 8.2 displays a ten-year bond with different coupon rates. Table 8.2 also displays calculations made to determine net interest cost to the district, bond offering price to individual investors, yield to maturity based on offering price, and calculations necessary to determine dealer profit. A brief explanation should clarify details of the table.

Principal and interest payments are assumed to be made at the end of each year. Actually, interest payments are usually made semiannually, but for simplicity annual payments have been assumed. The principal amount due at the end of each year is shown in column two, with the total amount of the issue being $5,000,000. Column three displays a separate coupon rate (the rate of interest paid by the district on the bond's par value) for bonds that mature in different years, ranging from 5.50 percent to 6.30 percent. In column four the principal amount is multiplied by the number of years to maturity. Column five multiplies the coupon rate by bond years to provide the total interest paid during the life of bonds of each maturity. Column five is the total interest paid during the life of the bond issue. This amount, less any premium paid by the dealer on the purchase, divided by total bond years, results in the net interest cost to the school district. In this case, the dealer offered to buy the bonds for $5,001,000, thus paying a premium of $1,000. The calculations at the bottom of the table show that the net interest cost to the district is 6.0288 percent.

$$\text{Net Interest Cost} = \frac{\text{Total Interest Cost} - \text{Premium}}{\text{Bond Years}}$$

$$= \frac{1,767,450 - 1,000}{29,300,00}$$

$$= .060288, \text{ or } 6.0288 \text{ percent}$$

$$\text{Profit} = \text{Production} - \text{Amount paid for issue}$$

$$= 5,033,760 - 5,001,000$$

$$= \$32,760$$

The dealer decides what yield to maturity must be offered to attract buyers. In general, the longer the maturity, the higher the yield to maturity must be. The dealer will decide what offering price will be attractive. Knowing offering price, desired yield to maturity, and years to maturity makes it possible, using a bond table or a special calculator, to calculate the coupon rate necessary for the bond. This rough calculation usually produces an uneven interest rate. For example, the dealer may decide to sell bonds maturing in three years at an offering price of 100.50. The price of a bond is always expressed in terms of the percentage of par value at which the bond is priced. Thus, a $1,000 bond priced at 100.50 will cost $1,005.00. Using this calculation, the coupon rate is 5.8837 percent. This rate is then rounded off to 5.90 percent and the offering price recalculated to 100.54.

Production, the money gained through sale of bonds at each maturity, is shown in column seven. It is a product of the principal amount and the offering price divided by 100. The total of column seven is the total anticipated by the dealer from the sale of the bonds, and this, less the amount paid for the bonds, is the dealer's gross profit.

Note that the dealer plans to sell most of the bonds at a premium. Those with a ten-year maturity have been tailored for a particular customer, who for tax reasons prefers to buy a low-coupon bond at a discount rather than a higher-coupon bond at a premium. This customer still receives a higher yield to maturity than any other purchaser.

Money to pay principal and interest on bonds is usually set aside by the district in a special bond interest and redemption fund. Each year a tax is levied sufficient, along with any balance in the fund to pay the interest on all outstanding bonds and to redeem all bonds that mature during the year. Bonds are a legal obligation of the district, and neither the school board nor voters can refuse to levy the tax necessary to pay them. The decision made at the time the bond issue was approved by voters binds the district as long as any bonds of the issue are outstanding.

Money from sale of bonds is received almost immediately, usually within three weeks of the bid date, but is spent over a period of perhaps two or more years as construction progresses. Meanwhile it is invested in whatever ways are allowed under state statute. Typically, it may be put into other government securities. It is interesting that it is frequently possible to invest idle funds at a higher interest rate than it is necessary to pay on them. Doing this is called arbitrage. Investment must be carefully planned, of course, so that portions can be liquidated as necessary to make payments on construction contracts.

Ways of Financing Capital Improvements

The way most school construction is financed presents several problems. One of them is the increased difficulty in passing bond elections. As mentioned, the rate of approval of bonds by the public plummeted in the 1970s and early 1980s. People may be reacting to the general taxation level by rejecting new taxes on which they have an opportunity to vote. That a number of states have passed laws or constitutional amendments restricting tax increases testifies to this (Fischel, 1998).

Another problem is that the cost of borrowing has increased substantially. Shortly after World War II, interest rates on municipal bonds averaged only 1.3 percent; by 1967 the rate was 4 percent, in 1976 it was 6.8 percent, and by 1985 it was about 9.5 percent. Part of this upsurge reflects a general increase in the interest cost of all money for reasons that have to do with the national and world economy. Part of the increase, however, has been the result of a narrowing of the gap between the interest rates of municipal bonds and those of taxable bonds. Interest on municipal bonds is not even reported as income to the IRS, and is thus completely untaxed. Such income is of great benefit to highly taxed individuals, who are thus willing to buy such bonds at an interest rate lower than they would pay for a taxable bond. Some of the major money sources are now eligible for tax breaks on ordinary interest, among them life insurance companies, mutual savings banks, and pension funds. Nontaxability of municipal bonds thus becomes unimportant to them, and lower yields then make them unattractive. The clientele for municipal bonds is now limited chiefly to commercial banks and highly taxed individuals. But even to these buyers, the reduction of maximum tax rates accompanying the federal income tax reform of 1986 reduced the attractiveness of municipal bonds. Both of these occurrences have narrowed the difference in interest rates, and thus the subsidy conferred by the federal government on local governments.

Another problem with the usual way of financing school construction is the limit set by all states on the amounts a school district can borrow, usually expressed as a percentage of assessed valuation. The intent is to prevent present voters from saddling future residents with unmanageable debt. Rapidly growing school districts have found themselves reaching this borrowing limit with no way to satisfy the needs of unhoused students. Then too, many states do not aid districts with construction but force them to do it on their own. The property-poor district, perhaps able to have a good instructional program because of aid provided by an equitable state system for current expenditures, may find it cannot afford to build schools to house the program. Although this may seem as inequitable as the current-expenditure inequities attacked in *Serrano* and its progeny, it is far less often litigated, and facilities inequities remain in many states.

The most complete answer to the problem of equity is for the state to assume total responsibility for school construction, an experiment that has been tried with varying success in California, Florida, and Maryland. In California the 1978 passage of Proposition 13 made it impossible for school districts (or any other level of government) to increase the property tax rate, which was frozen at 1 percent for all governmental purposes. Thus, bond elections could not be held, and districts could not borrow money through that mechanism. Prior to Proposition 13, the state had had an aid mechanism for helping school districts that were property poor or fast growing. It called for state loans to those districts, to be paid back over thirty years by a specified tax levy, with the unpaid balance at the end of that time forgiven. After passage of Proposition 13, the loan program became a grant program. The state provided all of the money for construction, and the whole process became highly centralized.

A district's need for school housing is determined by enrollment projections overseen by the state. The district must submit detailed plans of each school in the district, so the state may determine, through its square footage guidelines, how many students present schools will accommodate. The difference between capacity and need is what the district is entitled to from the state. The state also supervises every detail of planning and construction. The whole process generates an enormous amount of paperwork, which has overwhelmed the state agency. Construction authorizations and grants of construction funds have fallen far behind actual needs, particularly in fast-growing school districts.[3]

There are, of course, alternatives for financing school construction that reside between extremes of full state assumption on the one hand and complete local effort on the other. New York provides state funds on a percentage equalizing basis. The district decides what it wants to build and how much it wishes to spend. The state shares the cost of construction with the percentage share depending upon district wealth. This system allows much more local discretion in school construction, but is of little comfort to the district that is unable to pass a bond election or has reached its legal bonding limit.

Summary

In addition to day-to-day operations, school systems are responsible for siting, planning, building, and maintaining schools. The process for doing this is an intricate one, influenced by the open and public nature of government. Accurately planning school sites to match projected enrollments presents a particular challenge to school systems and local governments. The construction of facilities usually requires the accumulation of debt. Most often, this is done through municipal and local bonds. As a result, school construction relies heavily upon local wealth and capacity to fund school construction.

Discussion Questions

1. Describe the school construction process. With reference to the politics of education discussed in previous chapters, define the ways that local politics can enter into the process of school construction.
2. Obtain a copy of a school district's plan for capital improvement. By examining the plan, what can you determine to be the priorities of the school district?
3. Bonds are harder to pass than they previously were. What tactics would you take for passing a bond referendum at the local level? Who would be members of your coalition? By what mechanisms would you hold these coalitions together?
4. School districts are identifying unique ways to utilize existing facilities rather than construct new facilities. What alternatives to constructing new facilities can you identify for a school district? Consider school districts in various locations, such as urban, rural, and suburban.
5. See the "In the News" article regarding the Compton Unified School District. How would you imagine taxpayers would respond to the suspension of projects? How should school district administrators respond to taxpayers? Should the school district take proactive measures to address anticipated taxpayer reactions? Why or why not?

Web Resources

Great Schools by Design—
   http://www.archfoundation.org/aaf/gsbd/index.htm
Moody's—
   http://www.moodys.com/cust/default.asp

National Clearinghouse for Educational Facilities—
   http://www.edfacilities.org/
North Carolina School Design Prototype Clearinghouse—
   http://www.schoolclearinghouse.org/
Standard and Poor's—
   http://www.standardandpoors.com/
What Schools Cost—An American School Board Journal Special Report—
   http://www.asbj.com/specialreports/0603Special%20Reports/0603index.html

References

Fischel, W. (1998). *School finance litigation and property tax revolts: How undermining local control turns voters away from public education.* Lincoln Institute of Land Policy Working Paper.

Lee, D. (2004, February 21). Complications arise in funding of Cary school. The (Raleigh) *News and Observer*, 81.

National Center for Educational Statistics. (2006). *Projection of education statistics to 2008.* Washington, DC: U.S. Department of Education.

Rabbinowitz, A. (1969). *Municipal bond finance and administration.* New York: John Wiley/Interscience.

Wirt, F.M., & Kirst, M.W. (2005). *The political dynamics of American education.* Richmond, CA: McCutchen.

Notes

1. Some have noted that this represents a reversal of the population shift known in the 1920s and 1930s as the Great Migration, where large numbers of African American citizens moved from the American South to the industrial cities of the Northeast and Midwest both to find employment and to escape Jim Crow legislation.

2. In Cary, North Carolina, developers offered a free school in exchange for preferential student assignment patterns that would keep the school as a neighborhood school for the subdivision in question. See Lee (2004).

3. An Arizona court in *Hollins v. Shofstall* declared capital outlay unconstitutional. C-253652 (Arizona Superior Court, June 1, 1972) rev'd 110 Ariz 88, 515 P.2d 590 (1973), but the Arizona Supreme Court overturned the decision.

CHAPTER NINE

Budgeting

■ INTRODUCTION

A school or school district budget is a translation of educational needs into a fiscal plan that, when formally adopted, expresses materially the educational program a community is willing or able to support financially for the budget period.

LEARNING OBJECTIVES

In this chapter a reader will learn about:

- Fundamental organizational purposes of budgeting.
- Crucial linkages between planning and budgeting.
- Universal budgeting principles and processes.
- Modern budgeting concepts.
- School site budgeting mechanics.
- Budgeting pitfalls.

The generation and continual appraisal of priorities, and a sustained search for alternative means to accomplish them, are the essential purposes of effective budgeting in schools. However, school budgeting is no longer a routinized or formulaic endeavor. Or, at least it should not be. The external environment now intrudes more forcefully upon schools than ever before. A reader need only peruse the following partial list of external influences upon schools to realize that budgeting is now a different endeavor than in the past. Consider the following conditions for budget purposes: fluctuations in student population, the changing demographic patterns of enrollment, cycles of economic inflation and deflation, increasing demands for accountability, state- and federal-mandated programs (e.g., special education mandates, Title IX restrictions, OSHA requirements, handicapped accessibility, asbestos removal, affirmative action, mandated class size, education reform, and No Child Left Behind legislation), Proposition 13-type tax-cutting initiatives, and professional negotiations. All of these have added to the need for more complex budget planning. In short, the rate of change in the educational environment calls for periodic, intensive examinations of alternative ways to allocate school funds. Additionally, multiyear projections of budgetary needs are essential to provide needed continuity in the allocation process.

Traditional methods of budgeting have not provided adequate insight to weigh alternative plans for funding education. Past definitions of the term budget often reflect a traditional mentality for budget development.

In a more dynamic view, the school budget is simultaneously an instrument of educational planning and an instrument of organizational guidance and control. It reflects organizational patterns by categorizing the elements of a total plan into sectional, campus, and departmental components, allowing costs to be more easily estimated. It then forces a coordination of these elements by reassembling costs into a whole so that a comparison can be made with total revenues. This very process requires an orderly planning that otherwise might never take place.

Budgeting, then, compels a community, school board, administrators, and staff to plan together what needs to be accomplished, how it will be done, and who will do it.

Some benefits of strategic budgeting are:

- It requires a plan of action for the future.
- It requires an appraisal of past endeavors in relation to planned activities.
- It necessitates the formulation of work plans.
- It necessitates projecting expenditures and estimating revenues.
- It mandates orderly planning and coordination throughout the organization.
- It establishes a system of management controls.
- It serves as a public information system.

Building on the work of theorists and planners such as Deming and Senge, the basis for a good strategic budget must be the vision developed for the district by a cooperative effort involving as many of the stakeholders as is reasonable. This is usually completed as a result of a committee chosen, from all of the various stakeholders of the system, to be as representative as is reasonable. The development of such a vision is a difficult task and must be grounded in the reality and promise of the district.

The purpose of this chapter is to illustrate how this budgeting vision can be fulfilled.

■ THE STATUTORY BASES FOR SCHOOL SYSTEM BUDGETING

Each of the states is vested with *plenary* (Latin for *ultimate*) control over educational policy within the sphere of its jurisdiction. Courts have uniformly held that education is essentially and intrinsically a state function; the maintenance of public schools is, in legal theory, a matter of state and not local concern.

Subject to constitutional limitations, a state legislature has plenary power with respect to educational policy. It may determine matters such as the ends to be achieved and the means to be employed. It may determine types of schools to be established, means of their support, content of their curricula, and the qualifications of teachers. It may do all of these things with or without the consent of the localities, for, in education, the state is the unit and there are no local rights except those safeguarded by the Constitution.

For many purposes, even local school board members are state officers. This plenary power allows the state to mandate that districts develop budgets and to determine the format, calendar, and procedures for the budgeting process. The state mandates budget categories.

This is also related to the state's mandated system of financial accounting, auditing, and reporting. The budgeting process is also utilized to establish tax rates. For a more detailed discussion of the legislative and judicial context, see Chapter Five.

■ BUDGETING CONCEPTS

Budget processes can be plotted on a continuum ranging from a centralized set of processes that rely little upon strategic planning to an emerging set of decentralized concepts that emphasize educational planning and evaluation as the basis for budget development. The discussion that follows contrasts centralized budgeting systems with decentralized procedures now being pioneered by adventuresome and experimental districts throughout the nation.

Concepts of Budgeting Not Viable for Contemporary Needs

Mechanical Budget. The mechanical type of budget can be set forth on two sheets of paper—one presenting the estimated yearly receipts of an institution and the other displaying how the money can be divided in order to operate a school. Under this concept, budgeting is strictly a revenue-and-expenditure operation, a bookkeeping chore, required by law, that is the product of intense activity near the end of the fiscal year and then is quickly forgotten until the end of the next year. This type of budgeting forces expenditures to fit income expectations and pays little attention to needs. Any planning done is negative, calculating what can be eliminated or what can be padded so that the budget will balance. The object of this budgeting mind-set often is to keep costs at a minimum without regard for needs or educational achievement.

Yearly Budget. The annual budget approach attempts to construct a school budget in a short (three-to four-week) period for presentation to the board of education and to the community. It is almost a refinement of the mechanical type, in that it necessitates quick decisions on expenditures and revenues and little effort is made to evaluate its impact. Decisions on staffing, salaries, programs, supplies, and services are often made with little consideration of educational needs or evolving educational opportunities. The challenge is to get the budget document completed and approved before the deadline date. Usually, this method attempts to adjust the previous year's document to include items such as pay increases, enlarged staff, and increased numbers of students, but does not consider changes in program, availability of new materials, differing needs, and emerging concepts. Once completed, this type of budget may become a straitjacket that provides little opportunity for shifts in priority.

Administration-Dominated Budget. This concept views the development of the budget as strictly a management responsibility. Little or no staff help is requested. The central office provides an impression that budgeting is a dauntingly complex process and that only a "chosen few" are sufficiently sophisticated to participate. The prevailing philosophy seems to be that if fewer people know about the budget, there will be less conflict and fewer questions. Often, value judgments are made without proper evaluation and with few options offered to those immediately affected. This tight-ship approach is symptomatic of authoritarian systems and hastens a rigid system that has contributed to the expansion of collective bargaining, citizen involvement, and student awareness.

Centralized Budget. The centralized concept of budgeting treats all schools in a system as if they were only one. It regards the district as a school system not a system of schools. While it is an efficient way of developing a budget, little consideration is permitted for differing needs among the various schools and communities served. Allocations are made on a mechanical per-pupil basis, and little attention is given to existing resources or to any backlog of requests. Decisions concerning such issues as teacher-pupil ratio, supplies, materials, texts, and curriculum are made by formula at the central office, and all schools must conform. This concept tends to treat the entire system as a homogeneous unit rather than recognize that even the smallest systems are heterogeneous, made up of diverse communities with unique needs, abilities, and capacities.

■ BUDGET DEVELOPMENT

The functional model of budget development is based on a sequence of steps beginning with an educational plan, an expenditure plan, and ending with a revenue plan. The continuous budgeting concept is based on the several steps of the functional model, but incorporates continuous evaluation and modification. The participatory budget concept involves relevant groups in decision making. A fourth concept draws on elements of the three models previously described, but incorporates considerations of organizational, political, and economic environments.

Functional Budget

The concept of functional budget development requires that the planners attempt to determine the educational objectives of a school district as the first step in the budget process. The educational plan is then translated into a budget and presented to the community for reaction and adoption. The outcome is usually a compromise between what people are willing to pay for and what the planners think is needed. It represents the best program of education the people of a community will buy at a particular time. Using the functional approach, the budget committee considers the educational plan first. It translates the qualitative and quantitative aspects of the educational program into planned expenditures and then communicates these to the taxpayers, who provide the resources.

Continuous Budget

The concept of continuous budget development considers budgeting an integral part of daily operation. Immediately upon adoption of a budget, work starts on the development of the next budget document. Strengths and weaknesses in the operation of the present budget are appraised and proposed budget plans are made. Educational plans are conceived on a long-range basis. Hastily formulated educational programs are not considered. All program plans are developed in the context of proposed financing for implementation. With year-round budget development, various areas of the school can be better coordinated, and the board of education can be given time to consider an addition or deletion on the basis of educational merit as well as of cost. The continuous consideration of the budget is not an automatic operation. Certain administrative devices must be used, including: (1) scheduling discussions of the budget throughout the year at staff, teacher, and board meetings; (2) setting up "tickler" files around the system to stimulate people to think about and make suggestions concerning the budget; (3) establishing a calendar that distributes the various phases of budget making over a twelve-month period; and (4) requiring reports that force consideration of items that should be included in the budget.

Participatory Budget

The participatory budget concept recognizes two basic principles. First, schools, as tax-supported institutions, must consult citizens in the planning process if they expect to obtain continuing and expanding support. Second, persons who teach in schools using equipment and facilities should be given the opportunity to suggest procedures and materials that they believe are most effective.

Education is big business. If we think of it as an investment that develops our human resources, then it is one of the largest, most important undertakings in the United States. Yet school costs are small compared with some other expenditures. As an example, public education expenditures for grades kindergarten through twelve are running about 3 percent of the gross national product, considerably less than the amount spent on autos, alcohol, and defense each year. Public education is the largest governmental unit controlled and administered at the local community level. People in the community must be convinced of the desirability of a particular educational program before they will support it. By the same token, teachers must believe in and understand a plan before they will contribute actively to its success.

The participatory concept of budget development involves and provides the interplay of the school staff and public representatives at the various levels of budget making. A combination of formal and informal methods is used to encourage involvement in budget development.

Teachers and other staff members are asked to submit individual requests for needed supplies and equipment. In addition, staff participation on formal committees dealing with budget development is encouraged. Many schools also conduct staff hearings and in-service meetings on the budget.

Citizens are involved as members of advisory committees and study groups. The budget hearing to report committee findings is one of the best ways to keep all citizens informed. Public sentiment is, in the long run, in favor of clear, unbiased presentations of problems and honestly sought advice and suggestions.

Attempts to involve teachers, staff, and citizens often fail because of inadequate planning and a lack of role definition. Clear delineation of the advisory nature of the participants is important before any work is completed. All participants deserve to know the disposition of their proposals and the results of their efforts. Staff and citizen participation help create a better understanding of education for the future and assist in giving direction and scope to budget development.

Alternative—Rational/Political/Economic Budget

There are those who insist, with some justification, that existing budget theories have a number of problems. First, these theories cannot satisfactorily explain disequilibrium and decremental decision making. Second, rational behavior is defined so narrowly by both rational and public choice theorists that evidence of inefficiency is interpreted as irrational and unresponsive behavior, and, moreover, as indicative of bureaucratic pathology.

In this view, the notion persists that a series of conditions affect rational budget development, among them the political realities of a given situation and the need to respond to pressures and demands that are often far removed from rationality. Another impact is the set of economic conditions that ultimately affects the rational budget process. Included here are market conditions and the stability or instability of particular areas because of conditions not able to be controlled.

Still another variable that affects the rational budget process is the impact of organizational behavior when it comes to employee justice. Because education is such a labor-intensive activity, this variable can have significant impact on the budget process. It is important that the rational/political/economic budget process seeks to incorporate the key elements of several approaches to budgeting. It is an effort to recognize the realities of emerging conditions while preserving existing budget theory.

■ THE BUDGETING PROCESS

The educational plan is the starting point of the budget process. The school budget is the educational plan translated into dollars. The school budget can be conceptualized as an equilateral triangle, with the educational program as the base, and expenditures and revenues as the other two legs (see Figure 9.1). If any one of the three sides is shortened, the other two must also be shortened. Only when the three sides meet is there a budget document.

For many, the budget may be seen as both a needs and a working budget. In the needs budget, program costs are projected as if all educational needs are to be met. The working budget is the final document, drawn according to educational priorities, and serves as the financial plan throughout the year.

Specifically, the needs budget calls for cooperatively defined educational plans, both short and long range. The development should involve the staff and community and be initiated at the building level under broad guidelines established by the central office administration. The educational needs must be translated into financial terms. As the community and staff gain experience in this type of activity, the level of sophistication in budget development increases. Important considerations for the development of a needs budget are:

- Special programs.
- Innovations.

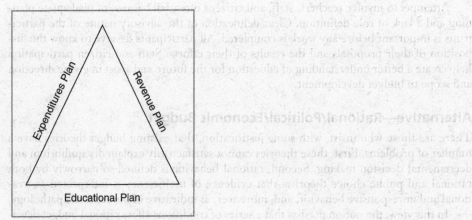

FIGURE 9.1 Budget Process

- Staff increases or decreases.
- Salary adjustments.
- Operations and maintenance.
- Fixed costs.
- Supplies and equipment requests.

A further step in the development of the needs budget is the determination of resources required to meet the budget. The total spectrum of local, state, and federal sources must be considered. Decisions should be made as to the disposition of the budget. Plans should be made for staff and community involvement in the important step of budget appraisal.

The working budget is actually a further refinement of the needs budget. The needs budget is more idealistic, in that it lacks the realistic parameters that surround the working budget. The working budget calls for the establishment of program priorities. Again, the staff and community are involved. Costing must be developed for each priority level. Determination of the amount of support from each source must be figured. At this stage, the working budget can be established. It should include appropriate documentation throughout. Approval by the board of education is absolutely necessary, and approval by the community is desired. A plan for budget appraisal should be made, such as the following (each state may have a unique fiscal year).

The Budget Calendar—Fiscal Year

Month 1	Budget year begins
Month 3	Quarterly revision—to incorporate accurate revenue and enrollment figures (present budget)
Month 4	Population (enrollment) projections
	Staff needs projections
	Program changes and addition projections
	Facilities needs projection
Month 5	Staff requisitions and supplies
	Capital outlay preliminary requests
Month 6	Budget revisions (present budget)
	Central staff sessions on needs
	Maintenance and operations requests
Month 7	Rough draft of needs budget
Month 8	Meet with staff and principals to establish priorities
	Citizen committees' reports and reviews
	Central staff and board of education budget sessions
Month 9	Budget revision (present budget)
Month 10	Working budget draft
	Meet with staff and community groups to revise working budget
Month 11	Final draft of working budget
Month 12	Budget hearings and adoption of working budget

For budgeting to be most effective, three critical conditions should exist—annularity, comprehensiveness, and balance.[1]

Annularity. A budget, an organization's resource allocation plan, is intended to cover a fixed period, generally a year. This need not be a calendar year, beginning January 1 and ending the subsequent December 31. Indeed, few school districts utilize a calendar year. The budget year is generally known as a fiscal year. The fiscal year for the majority of U.S. school districts begins July 1 and concludes at the end of the following June, in the next calendar year. However, some districts utilize a fiscal year that coincides with the academic year or with their state's legislative appropriations cycle.[2] The fiscal year for school districts is usually specified by the state.

Regardless of the precise period, or even if it is a two-year period, the important principle is that there is a previously agreed-upon span of time over which resource allocation and financial administration occur. Also, in order to be maximally useful, the fiscal year should not be altered frequently. Select a fiscal year and stay with the decision. Otherwise, public confidence, recordkeeping, and fiscal analyses are jeopardized.

Comprehensiveness. An organization's budget should encompass all fiscally related activity, on both resource and expenditure sides. A budget may contain a variety of funds and accounts, such as instruction, administration, maintenance, and transportation. It may well keep track of expenditures in more than one way, that is, by function, such as physical education, as well as by object of expenditure, such as instructional salaries. What is important is that the budget and the budgetary process encompass all revenues received by an organization, regardless of source or purpose, and all that an organization spends, regardless of source and purpose. If a budget is not comprehensive, organizational resources may be accrued or utilized for purposes outside the educational plan. This is certainly inefficient and impedes the path toward productivity and accountability.

Balance. This is the third critical budget assumption. What is received by way of resources must not exceed what is spent. This is not to assert that all organizations must always live within their immediately available resources. Certainly resources can be borrowed and paid back later. Borrowing money to construct a long-lasting building makes good sense (as illustrated in Chapter Eight). The point is that a budget assumes explicit organizational acknowledgement of resources and obligations, and the two must match. If they are out of balance, again an organization is out of control.

 CASE 1 REVISITED ────────────────────────────────

No Controversy Left Behind

Recall the case of Harriet Alvarez, Assistant Superintendent for Management Services in Wildwood Unified School District. She favors the strategy of performance incentives for teachers, particularly as NCLB mandates greater accountability and highly qualified teachers. Implementing a pay-for-performance program whereby teachers would earn large bonuses for improved student outcomes seems like a viable plan with great promise. A policy such as this would need to be researched, piloted, evaluated, implemented, and re-evaluated. How would Harriet budget for this process assuming no growth in revenue? From where could Harriet obtain these funds? What budget items could she cut? Where could she look for external funding?

Staff Personnel

Fluctuating enrollment and lower teacher turnover have forced many school districts to reduce the number of professional personnel employed. The difficult task of reduction in force is often guided by state statutes, the courts, and local negotiated agreements. Consequently, knowledge of how legislation and litigation relate to reduction in force for school personnel has become imperative for the development of sound school policy and management.

Accurate pupil population projections are the basis for planning staff needs. With the previously mentioned restrictions, it is difficult to utilize mathematical formulae for projecting staff needs. If the school system is utilizing site-based budgeting, the building staff will coordinate the deployment of staff under guidelines furnished by the central office staff. Categories that could be utilized in adjusting staffing to innovation might fit the following headings:

- Position title.
- Category.
- Same.
- New.
- Upgrade.
- Downgrade.
- Eliminate.
- Cost.

Now that the period of declining student enrollment has ended, districts must face the emerging student enrollment growth issue. The opportunity for controlling staff growth suggests that campus personnel decisions be made such that student needs determine what personnel will be added and that the central office staff be limited in that growth process. This will permit a controlled staff growth pattern and will limit the numbers of staff to be added to the district's payroll.

■ PLANNING, PROGRAMMING, BUDGETING, EVALUATION SYSTEM

Some of the principles of the planning, programming, budgeting, evaluation system (PPBES) have long been recognized in the writings of professional educators. However, often the principles were fragmented, and little attempt was made to make the total concept operational.

Essential components of PPBES are as follows:

- A careful specification and a systematic analysis of objectives.
- A search for the relevant alternatives—the different ways of achieving the objectives.
- An estimate of the total cost of each alternative—direct and indirect costs, initial costs, those to which the alternatives would commit the organization for future years, and those costs that cannot be measured in dollar terms.
- An estimate of the effectiveness of each alternative—how close it comes to satisfying the objective.
- A comparison and analysis of the alternatives, seeking that combination of alternatives that promises the greatest effectiveness, for given resources, in achieving the objectives.

PPBES is not a panacea; it is not a substitute for the experience, intuition, and judgment of educational planners. Its aim is to sharpen that intuition and judgment by stating problems more precisely, discovering new alternatives, and making explicit the comparison among alternatives.

Although computers may facilitate PPBES, they are not the decision makers. Decisions will continue to come, as they should, from the educational planners and from the political process, influenced by value judgments and pressures from various interested parties as well as by the process of systematic analysis. PPBES, through systematic analysis, seeks to aid the educational planner by being clearer and more explicit about objectives, assumptions, and facts; by trying to distinguish relevant issues from irrelevant ones; and by tracing out the costs and consequences of the alternatives, to the extent that these are knowable.

Computers and machine-like analysis cannot, by highly abstract mathematical or economic techniques, solve the value-laden problems of educational financing. However, these persons, machines, and techniques may make important contributions to the budgeting process.

PPBES and systematic analysis are not limited to cost accounting or to economic considerations in the narrow sense. PPBES should not neglect a wide range of human factors, and it should not attempt, naïvely, to measure factors that are really immeasurable. Wherever possible, relevant, quantitative estimates are to be encouraged. Good systematic analysis does not try to assign numbers to every element of a problem, does not ignore the intangible, and does not rule out subjective evaluation and the appropriate use of judgment. On the contrary, the very name PPBES reminds us that the question of who benefits and whom it costs are questions involving values as well as analysis.

The term program budgeting is not equivalent, in this context, to PPBES. Program accounting and program budgeting are basic conceptual elements of PPBES, but are limited to accounting and budgeting systems emphasizing categorization schemes by programs.

Five major categories of data must be developed in order to estimate, evaluate, and report within the multiyear framework of PPBES. They pertain to pupils, programs, personnel, facilities, and finance.

Pupil Data

It has been pointed out that one of the major ingredients of PPBES is program evaluation. The criteria developed in each district to evaluate programs will vary and may include not only classroom test results, but also other pupil statistics, such as dropout rate, college entry rate, job entry rate, or return-to-school rate. The school districts implementing PPBES will find it necessary to record such statistics in a consistent format and report these statistics in specific time frames and against specific programs. The districts should also be prepared to utilize these statistics in the preparation of new programs, as well as in the evaluation of current programs, and to maintain such statistics for long periods to develop behavior patterns, trend reports, and long-range pupil-need evaluations.

In the multiyear financial planning portions of PPBES, the districts will find it necessary to project pupil enrollment data, not only in numbers of students, but also in socioeconomic changes within the community.

Program Data

Goals, objectives, evaluation criteria, and program memoranda pertaining to each individual program operating in the school district must be recorded, stored, and reported for the successful operation of a school district PPBES. This is true for the education program (e.g., math, English, social studies) as well as the special programs (counseling, career guidance and ancillary services, transportation, maintenance, custodial).

Personnel Data

At least two major clusters of information on school district employees are required by PPBES: payroll information and assignment information. Within the PPBES framework, a district may choose to distribute first-grade teachers' pay to several different first-grade programs, while charging all of the kindergarten teachers' salaries to a single pre-school program. If a high school Spanish teacher works two periods a day as a counselor, is also assigned as an assistant football coach three months of the school year, and teaches driver training on Saturdays, specific portions of this teacher's salary must be prorated to the Spanish program, the counseling program, the athletic program, and the driver training program. The allocation of personnel assignments and costing is a necessary part of PPBES.

Facilities Data

The expenses involved in the operation of each school district facility must be recorded in order to accommodate the reporting requirements of PPBES. This requires the development of location and sublocation codes and the assignment of these codes to such items as inventory supplies, equipment, custodial and overhead costs, maintenance projects, and construction projects in the school district.

Financial Data

(In addition to program-oriented budgeting and accounting, traditional and often state-mandated line-item budgeting and accounting should be maintained by responsible levels (school districts, subdistricts, buildings) as long as it is required.) It should be emphasized that in order to preserve data comparability for state, federal, and local analysis by existing functions—such as instruction, administration, and transportation—budgets can be cast by line item within the function format and in a program format.

A caution should be inserted here to allay the fears of educators who are unfamiliar with school fiscal affairs. Accounting, enriched by cost accounting and budgeting, is crucial for the successful operation of PPBES, but it is merely a tool of the organization, not an end. Educational decision makers must guard against forming conclusions about instructional activities solely on the basis of costs. Costs must be weighed against benefits and values held by citizens for the development of their children.

▮ ZERO-BASED BUDGETING

Arthur Burns, former chair of the Federal Reserve Board, is generally credited with first using the term zero-based budgeting publicly, in 1969. The concept of zero-based budgeting (ZBB) was initiated in the private sector by Texas Instruments. It was begun as a means of answering the traditional question of how to allocate resources. Rather than conducting endless revisions of existing budgets, Texas Instruments decided to start each year from ground zero, review all activities and priorities, and, from this, develop a new and better blueprint of allocations for the coming budget year. In 1979 President Jimmy Carter issued an executive order directing each agency head, under the direction of the Office of Management and Budgeting, to submit budget materials following the new ZBB format.

In the hands of a competent principal, ZBB can be used to improve budget planning, control expenses, and justify funds to support various program alternatives. Some ZBB advocates promise more than they can deliver and minimize potential misuses of the concept, such as creating excessive paperwork and forms, reducing staff morale, and overemphasizing quantification in the evaluation of instructional programs.

The ZBB process can be simplified into the following basic steps:

Define Decision Units. A decision unit is the lowest practical organizational unit that is knowledgeable about the spending request and its impact. This unit will very likely be responsible and accountable for implementing the proposal, if approved, and has some flexibility in choosing between two or more spending options. In a school district a decision unit would be, for example, a building administrator or a department chairperson. As a first step, all possible decision units should be identified and the nature of their responsibilities and operation defined to prevent conflicts and ensure complete budgeting for the total educational setting.

Develop Decision Packages. A decision package identifies in a definitive manner a discrete function or operation that can be evaluated and compared with other functions, including:

- The goal to be achieved or the service to be performed.
- Alternative means of achieving the goal.
- Alternative levels of effort that will achieve the goal.
- The cost and benefits of each alternative.
- The technical and operational feasibility of each alternative.
- The consequences of not funding a particular function.

Decision packages are of two basic types: (1) mutually exclusive packages, which identify alternative means of performing the same function, with the best alternative finally chosen and the remaining packages discarded; or (2) incremental packages, which illustrate different levels of funding for a specific function. The incremental packages will show costs from a base level to a maximum level of cost for any one function. Normally, each division package should represent one year's effort for a person, or $10,000 of expenses. Any lower figure requires too much paperwork for the possible gains.

Rank Decision Packages. This process provides information necessary for the appropriate allocation of resources. The ranking should include all decision packages in order of decreasing benefit to the organization. The initial ranking should occur at the lowest decision-unit level. This permits the unit administrator to evaluate the importance of his own activities and to rank the decision packages affecting the unit accordingly. In the educational organization, the packages would then be ranked by each succeeding administrative level, and, finally, by the board of education.

Approve and Fund Each Activity or Decision Package to the Level of Affordability. Inherent in this fourth area is the subjectivity of the definition of affordability. Taxpayers and boards have been known to disagree frequently on the definition of this word.

▪ ADVANTAGES AND DISADVANTAGES OF PPBES AND ZBB

Educators may have a tendency to reject ZBB because it appears to be a close relative of PPBES. It should be understood that ZBB is not simply a derivative of PPBES. PPBES has five weaknesses that are corrected by ZBB:

- PPBES concentrates on what will be done, but not on how to do it.
- Budgeting, as defined by PPBES, is a cost calculation based on the decisions made in the planning and programming steps, whereas there are, in reality, many policy decisions and alternatives to be evaluated during the actual budget preparation.
- PPBES does not provide operating tools for managers who implement the policy and program decisions.
- PPBES does not provide a mechanism to evaluate the impact of various funding levels on each program and program element, nor does it establish priorities among the programs and varying levels of program effort.
- PPBES concentrates primarily on new programs or major increases in ongoing programs and does not force the continual evaluation of ongoing program activities and operations.

PPBES cannot perform these five tasks; the fact that these tasks are inherent in ZBB is, therefore, a distinct advantage of ZBB. The advantages of ZBB are:

- ZBB controls staff expenses.
- ZBB focuses management processes on analysis and decision making rather than on quibbling about incremental requests.
- ZBB combines planning, budgeting, business proposals, and operational decision making into one process.
- In ZBB, managers have an ongoing requirement to evaluate, in detail, their operations, efficiency, and cost-effectiveness.
- With ZBB, all expenditures are evaluated, and discretionary and penalty cost exposures are specifically identified.
- ZBB offers mechanisms to trade off manpower and expenses between decision units.
- In ZBB, top management has a follow-up tool to determine the level of achievement of each program relative to the cost and effectiveness of the program.
- In ZBB, the ranking sheet can be used to adjust the budget during the operating year.
- ZBB identifies similar functions among different staffs for comparison and evaluation.
- ZBB provides management training and participation in decision making.

What disadvantages or problems might occur as an organization moves from the traditional budgeting practices to a zero-based format? The most common areas of difficulty are the following:

- ZBB is threatening.
- Administration and communications are more complicated because more people are involved in decision making.
- ZBB requires more time in budget preparation.
- ZBB places emphasis on work measures and evaluative data that are often unavailable.

- ZBB forces management to make decisions.
- The large volume of decision packages inherent in ZBB makes ranking difficult.
- ZBB involves the evaluation of dissimilar functions which is not feasible.
- Evaluation of the "priority" or "required" packages can become a political nightmare.

District Use of ZBB

There is little doubt that a systematic budgeting system such as ZBB can assist local school districts in stemming the tide of rising budgets. Furthermore, ZBB is a tool that can be used to increase management and program effectiveness.

Assuming that ZBB is a worthy tool, how does a school district move from the traditional line-item budgeting to the new model? The concept is astonishingly simple, but the mechanics of implementation are considerably more complex. Three conditions are necessary to successful implementation:

- A genuine commitment to and support of the concept by top district management.
- Support of the concept of building-level planning and the building-level management team.
- Adequate technical assistance for all management levels.

Assuming the acceptance of these conditions, the school district should be able to implement a ZBB approach. The prime factor, as noted earlier, is the development of the decision package. These decision packages have features identical to many aspects of PPBES; however, there are three important differences:

- ZBB forces consideration of alternative courses of action.
- ZBB forces identification of varying levels of effort.
- ZBB forces the ranking of decision packages by progressive levels of management.

Zero-based budgeting, if adopted by a local school district, forces a rigorous evaluation of all programs. Once each program has been subjected to the evaluation procedures, it may be continued or begun at current or proposed funding levels, continued at current or proposed funding levels with modifications, expanded, reduced, or eliminated.

Whatever choice a district makes, it should not expect ZBB to be a panacea. Excessive expectations can be harmful. However, properly carried out, ZBB can have a significant effect on the budget.

■ DECENTRALIZED BUDGETING

The trend today is toward decentralization, which permits schools to be more responsive to the needs of a local area. Because of recent demands for greater involvement of principals and teachers in instructional decision making, educational efficiency and cost effectiveness, and limits on spending for only high-priority programs, several new concepts of budgeting have been introduced in school systems. Site-based budgeting has been inaugurated to extend to the involvement of principals and teachers. Planning, programming, budgeting, and evaluation systems are being employed to relate measurable educational objectives to the cost-effectiveness of alternate programs. Zero-based budgeting has been used to ensure the funding of highest priority programs before lower priority programs are incorporated in the budget.

Site-Based Budgeting

One of the major challenges facing today's school business official is providing increased fiscal flexibility at the building level. This fiscal flexibility requires the staff and principal of a specific building to become more intimately involved in day-to-day budgeting and budget control processes. Historically, training programs have not provided teachers and principals with the background needed to understand the nuances of budgeting and fiscal resource allocation. This section has been prepared as a basic guideline to enable principals and other educators to appreciate and understand building-level fiscal approaches associated with educational decision making and problem resolution.

A departure from traditional centralized administrative methods is possible when buildings, their staffs, and community members have the capacity to shape and administer the budget of a particular building and have the necessary expertise to match student needs with available resources. Underlying this section is the realization that pupils vary. Building principals and staffs must recognize these differences (e.g., cultural, ethnic, and socioeconomic), and serve pragmatically the varying levels of their students by utilizing strengths of staff and community and by deploying fiscal resources to meet priority issues. A carefully planned appraisal of pupils' performance and needs should be conducted in the local district before building priorities are established.

Implementation of the building budget process is dependent on the principal's capacity and skill to coordinate the various planning and operational components of a total educational program. Inherent in the process is the principal's ability to cooperate with a limited number of dollars to meet specific educational needs. This is not a simple process. It is often new and different, and it may take effort on the part of building-level administrators to redefine traditional roles by absorbing and applying fiscal management techniques encouraged by the site budgeting process, a process that allows the building staff to be proactive rather than reactive. The process forces planning and operational educational decisions to be made at the level closest to the student—the building level.

The site-budgeting process also encourages imaginative principals to proceed with the development of unique educational programs. Only the professional training and capacity of principals and their staffs limit it.

With site-based budgeting, instructional supplies, materials, equipment, texts, and library books are frequently budgeted at the building level. Some decentralized systems also provide individual building personnel budgets for teachers, aides, and custodians. Most school districts that have moved to building or site budgeting have retained centralized and districtlevel budgeting for capital outlay, maintenance, administration, and other funds and accounts that are districtwide rather than individual school building functions.

The role of the central administrative staff is also changed under site-based budgeting. Central administrators become support rather than line personnel. They become facilitators to be utilized by building staffs and the community to enhance further educational concepts unique to a building's service area. Therefore, a close dialogue between community members and school staff is encouraged.

Indicative of the national move toward site-based management, several of the states, Texas and Kentucky among them, have mandated that all budgets be prepared on a site-based management basis, in which the various campus budgets with specifically identified provisions are developed for the campus staff and community to participate in budgetary decisions. This, of course, is a significant and far-reaching development in the area of school budgeting and promises to bring significant change to the status quo in the arena of educational budgeting. Although this is a recent phenomenon, it is indicative of the massive restructuring now going on in educational organizations and portends continued change for the future. It is consistent with the accountability movement and provides the campus the opportunity to make budgetary decisions for which they are held accountable. This development has changed the operating procedures for the business offices of most school organizations.

In the News

New York City—Schools Chancellor Joel I. Klein yesterday laid out the first specifics of his ambitious plan to change the school financing system so that schools of similar sizes and demographics get roughly the same amount of city money per student. In a briefing at the Education Department headquarters, Mr. Klein said that many high-poverty schools, with 75 percent or more students eligible for free or reduced-price lunch, were likely to experience changes over the next several years—with 330 such schools likely to get a greater share of city money and 323 potentially in line for less. Similarly, 130 schools where fewer than half of the students are impoverished face a reduced share of city money, he said, and 129 such schools may get a bigger portion.

"I think it's important to the city that we can say that we are being equitable, we are being transparent and we are treating kids who are in a similar situation the same," Mr. Klein said. He said there was no pattern as to which schools would gain or lose in the new system, and did not discuss individual schools or neighborhoods that would be affected.

The new plan, announced by Mayor Michael R. Bloomberg in his State of the City address, will allocate money to schools by assigning different weights to categories of students based on factors like grade level, academic ability, poverty level and English language proficiency. While the weights are intended to provide additional money for the neediest students, Mr. Klein said the city eventually would provide extra money for the highest achievers, too. Currently, school budgets are not so directly tied to student characteristics, and the chancellor said that in some cases, the difference in city allocations to nearly identical schools was as much as $2,000 per student.

The mayor's announcement had immediately raised anxieties in some wealthier neighborhoods, where higher-paid veteran teachers have tended to cluster in better-performing schools. The city now covers these salaries, providing schools with a fixed number of teachers regardless of how much they are paid. Seeking to allay fears that such higher-paid teachers would be redistributed to lower-performing schools, Mr. Klein said yesterday that the city would impose changes gradually, and would buffer schools with high payrolls against sharp cuts. He also said the city would hold a series of hearings within the next month to get public feedback before final decisions were made on the specific dollar weights for different types of students.

But even as Mr. Klein sought to show that he was moving prudently, a leading expert on the city's school budget sharply rebuked his plans. The expert, Noreen Connell, who leads the Educational Priorities Panel, a non-profit group, said that the changes would initially make the budget system more complicated, and would be harmful long term by making it overly expensive for schools to retain veteran teachers.

Robert Gordon, the Education Department's managing director for resource allocation, who is designing the new system, said it would maximize the amount of control that principals have over their budgets, allowing them "to retain their most experienced teachers if that is what they want to do." And he said the chancellor's phase-in plan would shield schools from abrupt change. "We are committed to stability," he said. "At the same time, moving forward, school leaders can and should begin to manage accurate budgets just as businesses and families do." He added, "What the critics want is budgets that lock in inequities forever." At his briefing, Mr. Klein said the new system would deny educators an excuse for failing to lift student achievement. "One of the things I hear from principals is, 'Well, how can you hold me to the same standards as others, when the funding allocations are not equitable, are not transparent and they are not fair?'" Mr. Klein said.

At the heart of the chancellor's effort is a desire to simplify an enormously complex budgeting process in which schools receive money through dozens of different formulas. The chancellor's plans would deal only with city tax dollars, which make up about 45 percent of the system's overall budget, and unrestricted state money, which brings the total dollars involved to about two-thirds of individual schools' budgets. The remaining one-third of the budget is provided by the state and federal governments, but that money is earmarked for specific programs.

In the chancellor's view, school budget decisions historically were made arbitrarily by superintendents often influenced by politics or patronage. But some school system veterans argue that some of what the chancellor views as inequity instead reflects well-reasoned policy decisions that were made under previous administrations. For example, Mr. Klein's office acknowledged yesterday that among the schools that now seem to have unfairly large budgets are struggling schools that were part of a special Chancellor's District, created by former Chancellor Rudy Crew in an effort to turn around some of the system's most troubled campuses. Those schools received a large influx of resources, including higher pay for teachers.

Indeed, the teachers' union president, Randi Weingarten, invoked the Chancellor's District yesterday in criticizing Mr. Klein's plan. "We have always embraced and fought for the idea of putting more money into high-needs schools, such as with the old Chancellor's District," she said, adding, "The chancellor's plan will hurt kids and educators alike because it will destabilize good schools and give principals a disincentive to hire experienced teachers simply because they cost more."

Site-Based Budget Components

School Budget Composition. Despite the mystique that may surround the so-called intricacy of school finance and school budgets, it is possible to simplify the process. The educational system is charged with providing instructional and related services to its clients. This is accomplished by delivering programs directly to students. The delivery process invariably involves professionally trained educators meeting with students and their parents, either in groups or individually, to accomplish this task. In addition, the process includes the provision of support services to facilitate teacher-learner relationships. These support activities are defined as direct instructional support (e.g., pupil personnel, psychological, sociological) and non-instructional support (e.g., maintenance, custodial, food service, transportation).

Education budgeting is mostly budgeting for personnel. In Chapter Two, a long explanation was provided for the labor-intensive nature of public schooling in America. Approximately 80 to 85 percent of a school district budget is allocated to personnel. Another 10 percent of total costs is typically allocated to relatively fixed spending (such as utilities, fringe benefits, insurance, and interest) over which little control can be exercised. The remaining 5 or so percent of the total budget is allocated to supplies, materials, and equipment used in the system, including instructional as well as non-instructional materials.

It is important to the educational process to develop a mechanism that permits more than the limited 5 or so percent of resources to be used for unique student needs as identified at the building level. A growing number of educators feel this is best accomplished through a flexible system of allocating personnel and resources at the building level.

Many school districts are restricted in personnel deployments by union contracts that specify pupil-teacher ratios and determine class size. However, a reader should understand that union collective bargaining contracts are not permanently fixed in stone. Issues can be re-opened when contracts are scheduled for renewal. A contract is a two-way road. District needs can also be placed on the agenda and renegotiated. Moreover, many union contracts permit deviation from contract language for specific educational purposes. At the least, the specific use of professional personnel as determined by the educational needs of the student body of a particular building can be approached with reasonable flexibility. The application of staff strengths to highest priority educational needs is the most important task faced by the building principal. Similarly, the allocation of non-instructional personnel (e.g., aides, clerical) can enhance an educational program. It is appropriate that this allocation be made at the building level.

Conversely, the application of non-instructional support services, such as maintenance, transportation, data processing, food services, payroll, and purchasing, is often best accomplished at districtwide or even regional or state levels because of the potential reduction in unit cost for such services.

Nonstaff Budget Components

The portion of the typical school budget allocated to non-personnel items is roughly 15 percent. Of this, some 8 to 9 percent is utilized to pay for fixed costs that allow for little flexibility. Minor savings can be affected in selected areas, for example, utilities, by setting thermostats at a lower level or by reducing the number of light fixtures in buildings. One of the most effective conservation measures is to place all buildings on separate measurement systems, budget for utilities at the building site, and permit building inhabitants, teachers, administrators, and so on to share with the district any savings they invoke behind what was budgeted for utilities. However, even with such conservation measures, net savings are seldom much less than the increased cost of energy.

Similarly, healthy and hazard insurance costs, interest charges, and fringe benefits are all undergoing dramatic increases, leading to the speculation that the fixed-cost portion of the school budget will continue to rise in the coming decades. Certainly, legislative mandates and contractual agreements will not lower the impact of fixed costs.

Budget Component Summary

The following outline is a summary of the components that comprise the school budget. It does not follow the prescribed accounting manual; rather, it is a recognition of the three major delineations identified here.

I. Personnel (80 percent of total budget)
    A. Instructional
        1. Professional—teachers, administrators, specialists (certificated)
        2. Classified—aides, clerical and technical personnel
    B. Non-Instructional
        1. Professional—engineers, administrators, specialists, analysts, accountants
        2. Classified—custodians, skills craftspeople, cooks, bakers, clerical and warehouse personnel, drivers, technicians
II. Fixed Costs (approximately 10 percent of total budget)
    A. Utilities
    B. Insurance
    C. Fringe Benefits
III. Other Costs (5 to 10 percent of total budget)
    A. Supplies and Materials
    B. Equipment (new and replacement; upkeep and repair)

The foregoing emphasizes the restrictive nature of the school budget and the limits of what can be considered discretionary resources. The next section presents a model for building-level budgeting that permits flexibility in the allocation of resources.

 CASE 4 REVISITED

Teaching Harold's Pony a New Trick: The Challenge of School-Based Budgeting

The success of a school-based budgeting process is dependent upon the principal's ability to understand and effectively manage a budget. Many principals lack significant training in the budgeting process and the nuances of fiscal management. As the school district's business manager, Harold Hawkins has been tasked with decentralizing the district's budgeting process by allocating a great deal of budgetary discretion to principals. Harold is very concerned and slightly irritated. Review the strategies for implementing school-based budgeting that Harold has contemplated. What do you foresee will be the pros and cons of these strategies from the principals' perspectives and from the perspective of the district as a whole? How can Harold assist the principals with leading a school-based budget without engendering resentment or resistance?

■ SITE-BASED BUILDING ALLOCATION PROCEDURES: A MODEL

Staff Allotments

Assuming that a school system makes a decision to share budget prerogatives with building principals, staff, and community, and that after careful study, it is decided that the direct delivery of educational services is appropriately the purview of the building, what then can be presented as a model for such a decision?

Based on the experiences of districts that have studied the process and implemented it for a number of years, it is believed that union agreements, contract language, community expectations, staff and principal capacity, and student needs must be considered in developing a model that is sufficiently flexible to serve diverse school systems. For purposes of such development the following assumptions are made:

- That classroom teacher-pupil ratios are fixed by union contract.
- That the building is administered by a non-teaching principal.
- That a variety of noncertificated instructional personnel are part of the staff.
- That instructional specialists in art, music, physical education, and media are available on either a full- or part-time basis.
- That deployment of teaching personnel can be either through self-contained scheduling or by team/departmental/differentiated procedures.

Given these assumptions, how does the school system provide flexibility to principals and their staffs so they can direct their best effort toward meeting educational needs of students?

Although the number of teachers assigned to a particular building is often based on a negotiated agreement that specifies a formulaic ratio of students to teachers, the deployment of staff does not necessarily have to be entirely on the self-contained classroom concept at the elementary level or predicated on each class meeting daily for one period at the secondary level. Optimum use of teaching staff is possible when professional staff is assigned to areas of staff strength and when support personnel are used for tasks better performed by classified staff.

The model assumes such staff deployment but goes beyond it to include the potential of diverting resources according to specific needs at the building level. The following two examples illustrate the proposed model for elementary and secondary schools.

Example 1:
Elementary Staffing Assumptions:

- Student enrollment of 600 students.
- Non-teaching full-time principal.

- Contract-specified 1:25 teacher-pupil ratio.
- Music/art/physical education/media personnel assigned centrally.
- Secretarial/clerical personnel assigned on a 1:300 student ratio.
- Instructional aides assigned on a 1:100 student ratio.

Staff allocations as determined above are:

- Twenty-four classroom teachers.
- Two secretary/clerks.
- Six aides.
- Principal.
- Assorted specialist personnel in music, art, physical education, and instructional media.

Additionally, all staff allocations are based on actual personnel employed or equivalent salary amounts. For example, an equivalent salary amount for teachers is the average for teaching in the district. The average salary is $52,000 per year. As the staff, community, and principal develop educational priorities for the school, several important objectives are adopted. These include:

- The need for consultative assistance in teaching basic skills (e.g., reading and mathematics).
- A need for programmed materials.
- A priority for increasing the number of aides from six to nine.

In terms of dollars, the plan calls for the following:

- One reading specialist at $52,000.
- Materials totaling $14,000.
- Five aides at $18,000 each totaling $90,000.
  Total $156,000

To generate the needed resources ($156,000), the building staff determines that it can provide basic classroom instruction with twenty-one rather than twenty-four classroom teachers. Because the building qualifies, by contract, for the twenty-four teachers, the equivalent dollars (or 3 @ $52,000) are allocated to the building to be used in meeting program objectives. This amount is the average teacher's salary multiplied by the number of positions not filled.

The principal is then able to employ a reading specialist and five aides and provide for the programmed materials. (In the event that only one opening is available, an existing staff member could be assigned the reading specialist role, and, with equivalent funding for one position, accomplish the same objective.)

The potential of this example is limited only by the limits of human ingenuity. Several districts have, under this model, provided great program diversity to their elementary programs.

Example 2:
Secondary Staffing Assumptions:

- Enrollment of 1,500 students.
- Principal and three assistant principals.
- Contract calls for maximum pupil-teacher ratio ranging from 1:28 in English to 1:50 in physical education.

- Vocational programs meet state/federal guidelines.
- Clerical staff assigned on a 1:150 student ratio.
- Media professionals assigned on a 1:750 student ratio.

Staff allocations based on the above are:

- Eighty teachers (including/vocational education staff).
- Six counselors.
- Two instructional media (library) staff.
- Four administrators.
- Ten clerical staff.
- Ten instructional aides.

The building staff, community, and principal have the following priorities as part of the educational plan for the coming academic year:

Priorities

- The establishment of four study centers, each to be staffed by a professional trained in English, math, science, and social science as well as two aides.
- A program of video- and audio DVD materials to be initiated at a cost of $10,000/year.
- Materials totaling $18,000 needed for initiation of the program.

Absorbing four teaching positions can staff the proposed four centers. Using the money generated by staff reductions, the building can meet the identified priorities as follows:

Added Cost

- Assign four center leaders from existing staff $0
- Employ ten aides at $15,000 each $150,000
- Purchase center materials $18,000
- Develop tape library $10,000
  Total $219,000

Many variations of this example are possible. The model provides that buildings receive personnel resources according to contract, either in the form of staff or equivalent dollars based on the average teacher's salary. It is important to indicate that existing staff members are not discharged to create equivalent dollars. Only when attrition creates openings is the model usable. Given normal conditions, however, such opportunities are readily available.

Foundation Allotment

A second frequent item of concern to principals is the utilization of the resources allocated for supplies, materials, and equipment. The model provides for block grant allocations to buildings for these items on the basis of an amount per student. This allocation replaces the line-item amounts generally found in school accounting procedures. The building principal, the staff, and the community determine the type and number of line-item allocations. They determine how much will be allocated to capital outlay, how much to textbooks, how much to library books, and how much to general supplies.

Once that determination is made, the central office must be notified how the block grant has been distributed so budget control mechanisms can operate for the protection of the total system. On a periodic basis, usually weekly but sometimes daily, building administrators receive printouts or can go online and receive electronic updates indicating the status of each of the supply, materials, and equipment accounts they have identified, the amount of encumbrances, and the current status of available budget funds. Should there be a need for shifting of funds from one account to another during the year, a simple form or set of electronic procedures will handle that transaction. In this manner, resources are allocated equitably throughout the school system on a per-pupil basis, eliminating central office judgments as to how these resources are to be expended. The central office engages in oversight to ensure that building totals do not exceed the amount of a block grant.

Internal shifting of resources to meet emergency needs is within the purview of a building principal. The foundation allowance provides for teaching, supplies, textbooks, instructional materials, replacement of equipment, new equipment, or whatever the building educational plan calls for. Limits on foundation allowance are the same restrictions that face all school systems.

Categorical Funds

Many school systems receive categorical funds by virtue of qualifying for one or more of various state or federal special purpose programs. These may be Title I funds, Chapter III funds, bilingual funds, or migrant funds. They are intended to meet specific kinds of needs found in school buildings and school systems. All categorical funds in the model are allocated on a per-pupil basis to buildings. The use of categorical funds must be incorporated into the total educational plan of the building. Typically, categorical funds are used to employ staff, buy supplies and equipment, and hire specific consultative and other help. They are deployed to individual buildings in the form of block grants earmarked according to the specific category for which the funds are received. They must be utilized for that particular kind of program, but the development of those resources in the form of either personnel or materials is under the purview of the building staff.

Grants

Many school systems receive philanthropic grants or have devised internal grant systems for addressing particular educational needs. Much the same as the categorical funds allocation, the grant allocation is funneled to the building level in the form of a block allocation. The use and dispersal of these funds are dependent on the educational plan devised at that building.

A model of this type creates a need for greater fiscal management sophistication on the part of principals, who do possess this potential and have often been eager to assume such leadership responsibility. It is, therefore, an evolving model that can be utilized and changed to accommodate particular characteristics of a school system.

Site-Based Budget Control Procedures

Coordination of fiscal information between the central finance office and school buildings is a key step in the implementation of the budget process. It is the responsibility of the finance office to develop, with the cooperation of building principals, budget control procedures. The procedures concentrate upon: (1) an equitable method of distributing building funds (autonomous funds) on a yearly basis; (2) sufficient time for building principals, students, and parents to plan for the best use of available resources; (3) a systematic monitoring of all building funds; and (4) the establishment of a purchasing process to accommodate building budget expenditure requests.

Distributing Building Funds. Each year before the board of education accepts the school district's budget, a decision must be made as to how much money should be allotted to buildings as autonomous funds. In order to maintain equity between buildings, the amount is based on the number of students enrolled per building. Enrollment figures are projected in January for buildings and usually adjusted on the fourth Friday count submitted to the state for state aid monies.

Program assumptions related to dollars required also become a variable to be considered in fund allocation. A distinction among elementary, middle, junior high, and senior high fiscal needs is one method of approaching the problem.

In the area of initial allowances, specialized programs requiring expensive equipment and large quantities of consumable supplies generally necessitate larger allocations for junior and senior high schools when compared with elementary schools. Differences based on programmatic emphasis (e.g., an all-student requirement involving industrial arts or home economics in the junior high) will cause fiscal differences even between junior and senior high school program costs.

Another dimension to autonomous funds involves the unique use of personnel and the budget. A model for utilization of certificated personnel, presented earlier, was predicated on flexibility in staffing buildings, thereby allowing building staffs to design a variety of differentiated staffing arrangements.

Fiscal appropriations for additional supervision, clerical support, and extra personnel beyond normal classroom needs are important to consider when defining building programs. Supervision may vary from elementary lunchroom duties to ticket-taking at a senior high school basketball game. Funding decisions for these purposes must consider revenues generated locally, such as ticket sales, as well as contractually determined rates of reimbursement. The ability to generate revenue for paying supervisors for extra assignments like ticket-taking is greater at the secondary level. Because of size, elementary schools usually have more difficulty in meeting supervisory needs. A secondary school with three or four times the staff may find the task much easier. Therefore, a difference in autonomous dollars allocated for supervisory aides may vary per student from elementary to junior high to senior high. Clerical support will also vary, depending on student enrollment and responsibilities unique to elementary and secondary operations. However, the unit cost of clerical support throughout the district is defined by contract.

An internal accounting system is established at all levels of building operations. Such a system allows individual buildings additional fiscal flexibility. Class and club activities are a few areas found in the internal accounts of buildings, the larger of which are found in high schools. Therefore, principals and their staffs are charged to plan the wise use of both autonomous and internal account funds to meet student needs.

Planning the Use of Funds. For building principals to involve staff, parent organizations, and student organizations in the budget process, initial direction and ample time must be provided by the central finance office. The degree of group involvement in the budget process will vary based on the management abilities of the principal.

Projections made the previous year are the basis for original allocations. Final budget revisions are made according to the official fourth Friday enrollment of each building.

Most building principals have learned to prepare for a slight gain or loss in monies by placing from 10 to 15 percent of their projected budget in a contingency account. The impact of gains or losses is felt in the contingency account and not necessarily in accounts affecting building operations.

As an example, a secondary principal and staff plan courses based on projected enrollments. If more students are actually taking a course on the fourth Friday, an adjustment is made internally to provide the instructor with extra resources. On the other hand, a decrease in a specific course's enrollment would cause a proportionate decrease in funds. This secondary building makes per-pupil adjustments not only on the fourth Friday in the fall, but also on an internally designated fourth Friday in the spring semester.

Once adjustments for enrollment are made, a regular monitoring of the budget is accomplished with the aid of data provided by the finance office. (The details of the monitoring process are discussed in the next subsection.) Using detailed budget reports identifying building accounts and monies budgeted, encumbered and expended, the principal, staff, parent organizations, and student organizations can begin to note trends between projected budget figures and actual expenditures. Decisions are made during the year to revise original budget projections in accordance with actual budget expenditures. The principal is held accountable by the finance office for any budget revisions made while the budget is being implemented. A few principals have delegated budget monitoring to the head secretary or school fiscal officer.

As semesters and fiscal years pass, budget histories are established. These financial histories, based on monies budgeted and expended, are useful in providing fiscal projections for succeeding years. Building account histories coupled with finance office direction early in September provide the basic information and time needed to complete budget projections by the end of March.

Between September and March, building principals and staffs are busy with day-to-day operational matters. In order to involve staff, parents, and students in the planning of the following year's budget, the building principal must establish a time line. The time line is determined by the data available, staff awareness of student needs, existing resources, and community expectations. Building priorities are established through extensive deliberation among various publics and must be consistent with school district goals.

In April or early May, decisions related to the new budget must be finalized by all parties concerned. Although all members involved in the budget process may not agree with final allocations, they must at least understand the rationale for projecting the following year's budget. The final budget document must reflect: (1) adequate time and information for determining client needs, (2) school district goals and building priorities, (3) use of past fiscal budget information (reports), and (4) a concerted effort by all parties to operate within the budget for one fiscal year.

Monitoring Building Funds. Once a building budget has been approved by building planners and revised in accordance with student enrollment, the monitoring process becomes extremely important. Fiscal accountability between a building administration and the finance office (central administration) is based on a successful, routine flow of information between both parties.

The process of aiding the fiscal information flow requires an extension of most school districts' accounting systems to include autonomous fund accounts at the building level. Secondly, a direct relationship between accounts and data processing must be established.

Finally, internal auditing procedures must be established at the district and building level to make certain that expending of the autonomous budget takes place as planned.

One district uses a six-digit accounting system that supplies fiscal information to decision makers at the board of education, central administration building, and outside agency levels. Building principals report budget figures on a document that allows a differential in excess of 250 accounts. The sizable number of accounts available to buildings for budgeting purposes permits principals and their staffs to monitor more completely their own expenditures. For example, a differentiation among monies budgeted for looking at a building's account structure can quickly identify repairs, supplies, and equipment in a computer information systems class.

A periodic (weekly) budget report from the finance office is provided electronically to each building principal. The building code number precedes the account number, followed by a brief description of the account. Monies budgeted, encumbered, and expended are itemized on the report. Close monitoring of the report allows a building's budget committee to make revisions (transfers of monies) at any time there is a need. Generally speaking, revisions are needed when planned expenditures exceed monies budgeted. The correction should be made when, for example, industrial arts becomes overdrawn; the deficit should be handled from funds within the same industrial arts account structure. The managing of deficits in this manner puts part of the pressure of fiscal management on the staff member directly involved with the account.

With the rapid development of computer software and with the advent of the personal computer, it is now possible for each building and department to have at their disposal instant budget data merely by communicating with the mainframe from wherever the campus is located and through the use of appropriate identification numbers. Data are entered daily and are instantly available to all who need the data. In this manner, control over budget is simplified and every manager has the information on which to base expenditure decisions.

In some instances, unforeseen circumstances cause certain accounts to become quickly overdrawn. An example might be the home economics supply account. Alternatives are: (1) transferring monies from another home economics account, or (2) carrying the deficit over into the next fiscal year. As the reason for the deficit is discussed in budget projection meetings, the need to increase an appropriation may emerge; this would cover the prior year's deficit.

Carryover is a unique feature of the autonomous fund budgeting process. All funds allocated to buildings but unexpended should be carried over from one year to the next. This allows buildings to accumulate funds in order to purchase items that exceed any one year's allocation. For example, a $2,500 copy machine for office use may be purchased after funds in the office's equipment account have been carried over for two or three years. Principals have the option of carrying over funds in specific accounts or transferring such funds to a general building account for carryover purpose. The building budget committee can then reapportion these monies on the basis of need. Without the carryover budget feature, long-range planning takes a backseat to a traditional building fiscal philosophy that implies "spend it now on anything; otherwise, you may not have another opportunity."

Establishing the Purchasing Process. After planning budget allocation, account code assignment, and record bank establishment, the building personnel begin to identify items to be purchased. Items identified are generally categorized as supply, textbook, furniture, equipment, or repair. A purchasing form is completed at the building level. The proper account number, a brief description of the item, the vendor, and the cost are noted. Once signed by the principal, or other designee, the form is forwarded to the purchasing department. There, a purchase order number is assigned after all other segments of the form have been checked for accuracy.

A situation occasionally emerges when sudden price changes necessitate cost column revisions. If this situation occurs, building personnel are notified immediately before the order for purchase is submitted to the vendor. The total purchasing process from building to purchasing department to vendor takes from three to four days. When a situation necessitates much quicker action, a telephone transaction among the building, the purchasing department, and the vendor may take place. All telephone transactions are quickly followed up with the appropriate paperwork. Generally, equipment breakdowns requiring immediate repair are permitted as verbal transactions.

The purchasing department is an integral part of the building's fiscal planning process. Annual requisition forms identifying items commonly used by all buildings (e.g., pencils, copying paper, first aid supplies, machine oils) are sent to buildings in the spring. Although autonomous funds are used for purchases, large-quantity buying of items by the purchasing department permits buildings to receive lower costs per item. Central supply and warehousing capacity are essential for such economy of scale. In summary, the purchasing department staff serves as expediter between buildings and vendors, maintaining credibility between the school district and vendors on items requiring the bidding process. Additionally, good business procedures are maintained by developing standardized equipment, and supply and materials lists for use by all schools.

Site-Based Community and Staff Involvement. The budget process varies little from other sound management techniques implemented by school administrators. Management processes designed to provide useful and timely information to educational decision makers become one of the frameworks on which school districts succeed or fail. In educational programs offered by the district, activity in the areas of planning, operations, communication evaluation, and finance is continually assessed, adjusted, or discontinued based on information matching available resources (e.g., monies, staff, facilities) to current student needs. Constantly keeping abreast of existing student needs requires the district and individual school buildings to involve as many stakeholders (e.g., parents, staff board members, community leaders, and students) as possible in decision-making processes that affect educational programs.

An administrator cannot afford the luxury of rationalizing away the need for community engagement. When the community is not involved in decision making, there is a tendency to arrive at decisions that are not community supported. Involvement of staff, students, and community is best accomplished through organized activities. Techniques utilized to involve stakeholders vary by situation. Some schools utilize parent organizations as the vehicle; others develop formalized mechanisms such as Community Involvement Committees or Community Advisory Committees. It is crucial for the building to have such participation. The following is a brief outline of events that make a point of involving various stakeholders in the budget process.

Defining the Limits of Dollars Available. The finance office must serve as a catalyst to the other four general areas of the district by projecting expected revenues and anticipated expenditures over a period of one to three or more years. In the process, fixed factors (e.g., enrollments, staff salaries, utility rates) may be considered by groups like the board, citizen advisory committees, bargaining units, and building involvement committees (e.g., parent, student, or community organizations). Once the big picture of financial resources related to "fixed charges" (generally 93 to 94 percent of a total budget) is communicated to stakeholders, decisions related to the other 6 to 7 percent of a budget can be made. To make the best use of the remaining portion of the projected budget, an amount must be allocated to meet overall district concerns and priorities, while the balance is distributed to buildings.

Involving Stakeholders at the Building Level. Once dollars per student or per program have been clearly defined for building administrators, they, in turn, can begin involving stakeholders in preparing the building's budget. Generally, the building budget committee is made up of teaching staff representatives, community and parent delegates, and selected students (more common in secondary schools). The committee's charge is to plan a program budget, keeping in mind the school district's goals and student needs assessment information. As weeks of the process unfold, time is spent discussing the points of view of all stakeholders regarding the building's program priorities. Initial "dreams" requiring far more money than is appropriated to a building give way to short- and long-range allotment of funds. All parties quickly learn negotiation skills. Ultimately, this budget process creates useful spin-offs for other areas of the building's decision-making process. If the budget process allows for meaningful involvement, the result is a committed group of stakeholders ready to see to the successful implementation of programs based on a budget attained through mutual agreement.

Monitoring an Approved Building Budget. Periodic budget reports should be available to any group of stakeholders throughout a fiscal year. Openness expressed by having a budget report at faculty meetings, student meetings, and parent organizations or community organization sessions is a key to seeing that the money is expended as planned. Invariably, unforeseen expenditures over a fiscal year require revision of building budgets. A building that predicates the preparation of the budget on involving stakeholders and continues a policy of open review throughout the year will have little difficulty in explaining the need to revise initial budget priority projections. In contrast, lack of management skill on the part of the building administrator during preparation and monitoring of the budget generally leads toward allegations of misappropriation and misuse of public funds, and, ultimately, a lack of trust in the administrator as a professional.

In conclusion, involvement of stakeholders in the budget process helps to foster a feeling by the community in general that they have a say in how "their" dollars are spent in educational programming. Staffs operating in buildings are no longer totally dependent on central administrators providing instructional materials, supplies, and equipment for meeting the needs of students they are teaching. And, most important, students in a building or classroom have the benefit of a planned process to identify their unique needs and to provide available financial resources to meet those needs.

Summary

Long-range fiscal planning and the establishment of goals for future programs are a logical outgrowth of budgeting. The natural extension of this, in turn, is the development of better educational program plans and the synthesis of these plans into broad fiscal plans.

The resulting fiscal plans, because they are based on educational programs, will strengthen and unify the budget process. When these activities are accomplished, not only will school system operations be much more comprehensive, but there will be meaningful bases and systematic techniques for planning, reviewing, modifying, and carrying out educational programs. This, we think, will help both the superintendent and the school board to weigh the value and effectiveness of educational programs and to balance and decide on the essential policy alternatives available to them. It will also help interested citizens to understand and evaluate the services their school system provides.

Discussion Questions

1. Develop a budget calendar that allows involvement by community, staff, and student body, but still fits the proper time sequence for each of the budget steps.
2. Develop a line-item and a programmatic type of budget for some phase of the school program. How would each type of cost allocation lend itself to program cost analysis?
3. Develop a site-based budget for an elementary school. Indicate parameters on spending decided by central administration.
4. Outline a zero-based budgeting system for a high school.
5. Relate the activity of budget building to a community information program or system.

Web Resources

The Milwaukee Public Schools have a comprehensive budget webpage—
http://mpsportal.milwaukee.k12.wi.us/portal/server.pt?space=Opener&control=Open
Object&in_hi_ClassID=514&in_hi_ObjectID=444

The Oregon School Board Association publishes a website for understanding the school budget—
http://www.osba.org/covered/budget/index.htm

Notes

1. The authors are grateful for Aaron Wildavsky's explanation of these assumptions.
2. The federal government's fiscal year begins October 1 and concludes September 30 of the subsequent year.

CHAPTER TEN

Federal Governance and Education Finance

■ INTRODUCTION

In December 2001 President George W. Bush signed the No Child Left Behind Act (NCLB). This legislation reinforced a twelve-year long federal government educational reform drive initiated by his father, President George H.W. Bush. The senior Bush's efforts began with the 1989 National Governor's Summit in Charlottesville, Virginia, and evolved thereafter through three presidential administrations.[1] The 1989 Charlottesville Summit was only the third time in U.S. history that all state governors had been formally convened. The meeting resulted in the United States agreeing to its first ever set of national education goals. These goals, however symbolic, contributed to enactment twelve years later of NCLB. This latter piece of federal legislation marks a significant transition in American education.

LEARNING OBJECTIVES

In this chapter a reader will learn about:

- Constitutional language that gives the federal government entrée into education issues.
- Current and historical acts and legislation that mark federal involvement in education.
- The manner in which legislation is crafted and enacted at the federal level.

- For the first time in American history, virtually all public schools are judged on students' academic performance. Until NCLB, school systems were expected only to demonstrate *how* federal funds were used, and not *whether* use of funds resulted in elevated student academic achievement.
- For the first time in American governmental history, academic performance was formally measured for a spectrum of student subgroups, which included African American, Hispanic, Asian/Pacific Islander students as well as students in poverty and students with other documented special needs. Although federal education legislation and funds previously targeted populations of poor and minority students, no legislation had ever before specified so clearly that a school or school system was successful only when it raised academic performance for all students.

- Finally, for the first time in American history, schools are held accountable for underperformance in student learning through a graduated series of incentives and sanctions that ultimately allow students to transfer from one school to another if their regularly assigned school continues to underperform. Until NCLB, school systems were sanctioned for failures of accounting and reporting on use of funds, not lack of students' achievement or academic improvement.

NCLB illustrates several long-standing themes permeating federal legislative impulses in public education. NCLB reflects a commitment to equal opportunity, a connection among education and economic performance and social mobility of citizens, and a distinct American pragmatism that focuses on results more than inputs or processes. NCLB represents a fundamental change in the way the federal government supports public education.

Few endeavors of this significance escape controversy. Opinion regarding NCLB and the federal role in education reflects two opposing perspectives:

1. A sense of relief that the federal government is *fulfilling a responsibility* to ensure all students have access to a high-quality education after years of side stepping what had become a crucial issue for American's civil and economic rights.
2. A sense that the federal government has *overstepped its bounds* by becoming involved in a sphere conventionally reserved for state and local governments.

Proponents of each perspective claim a constitutional and legal precedent (West & Peterson, 2003; Karp, 2003). How can genuine observers of public education history and policy and legitimate advocates for children so variously construe the federal role in education? This is a key question in this chapter. Other related questions include:

- What is the federal role in American public education, especially regarding finance?
- From where is constitutional authority for federal action in public education derived?
- What policies and legislation have shaped federal educational policy throughout U.S. history?

Answers to these and similar questions are rooted in prior policy pursuit of equality, efficiency, and liberty. Federal governments historic commitment to each of these ideals has shaped public education's modern policy context. This chapter explores this history. In addition, this chapter explains the constitutional foundations for federal involvement and political dynamics behind federal policymaking.

All This Controversy for Seven Percent?

Federal educational expenditures have ebbed and flowed. Enactment of the 1917 Smith Hughes Act authorized federal appropriations that eventually amounted to 1 percent of U.S. total K–12 revenues. The Elementary and Secondary Education Act (ESEA), toward the end of the 1960s, expanded federal spending to approximately 8 percent of the K–12 total. Since the Vietnam War, however, federal spending has generally comprised 7 percent of K–12 school system budgets (NCES, 2003). Put another way, 93 cents out of every dollar spent on U.S. public education comes from state and local governments. Why, then, is there such controversy regarding federal policies when their impact is financially negligible?

State officials have asked this question as well. During the Clinton administration, both Kansas and Oklahoma considered opting out of federal education programs over a concern with federal intrusion into states' rights (Zehr, 1998; Pitsch, 1996). The issue of federal involvement was so intense that in 1995 Oklahoma Senator James Inhofe publicly requested the state's entrant into the Miss America competition, Shawntel Smith, to stop giving the impression she supported federal education reform efforts, citing the erosion of local control triggered by standards-based reform (Schmidt, 1995). Despite such controversy, federal education funds, as well as accompanying rules shaping use of those funds are important for a number of reasons:

Guaranteeing Opportunity. Federal funds support specialized students with unusual instructional needs. Antipoverty efforts and other targeted programs can be costly and expensive, and may not meet full approval of local electorates. Left to their own preferences, some local communities might underinvest in educating selected student or in pursuing selected subject or skill categories. Therefore, federal policymakers intervene to ensure all students have opportunities for educational access.

Countering Underinvestment. Federal education funds support approaches and ideas that state or local governments may not have sufficient economic incentives to attempt. Imagine, for example, that the nation's supply of highly skilled scientists or individuals possessed of a keen ability to speak languages other than English was so short as to jeopardize national defense or the nation's balance of international trade. It is unlikely that individual states would enact programs to meet such shortages. These are national needs, and on several occasions Congress has enacted and funded programs to solve problems such as these.

Capturing Scale Economies. The federal government acts in areas where states may not have sufficient capacity to address issues of concern. Some functions risk diseconomies of scale if performed by smaller units and beg to be undertaken more efficiently by a central authority. Data collection and research and development activities are good examples. Congressional action establishing the Department of Education in 1867 made prominent mention of the agency's role in collecting useful statistics for sustaining and improving the nation's schools. This task, though performed unevenly over time by the federal education authority, nevertheless falls naturally to a central government. States and smaller units of government are ill-positioned to gather and analyze information from across the nation. Hence, the present-day cabinet-level Department of Education systematically collects, analyzes, and publishes information on education in the United States. The general justification for such activities is to meet national needs likely to be neglected by states acting independently or to introduce economies made possible by centralized authority.

Undergirding each of these federal government endeavors is the fact that, although 7 percent is a low percentage, it adds up to a great many real dollars. Figures 10.1 and 10.2 illustrate increased federal spending on education in billions of dollars. Since 1965, federal investment in elementary and secondary education has increased by over $60 billion. Some will argue, as will be discussed in other chapters, that increased federal investment has not yielded elevated academic achievement. Another perspective argues that increases in education spending in general have gone to teacher salaries, maintenance, inflation, and other costs not specifically related to student academic achievement (see, for example, Hanushek, 1996; Hanushek & Rivkin, 1997).

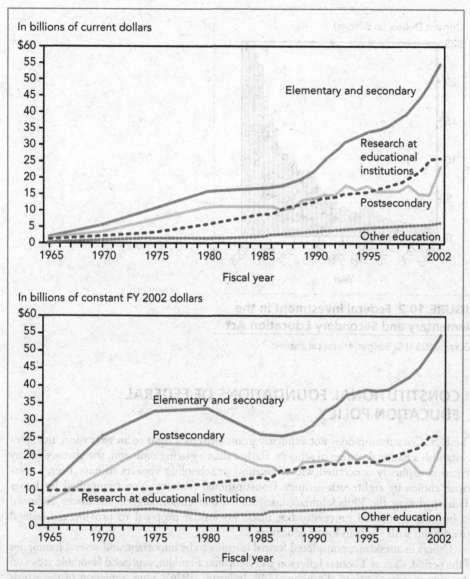

FIGURE 10.1 Federal On-Budget Funds for Education by Level or Other Educational Purpose: 1965 to 2002

Source: U.S. Department of Education, National Center for Education Statistics; U.S. Office of Management and Budget, *Budget of the U.S. government,* fiscal years 1967 to 2003; National Science Foundation, *Federal funds for research and development,* fiscal years 1965 to 2002; and unpublished data.

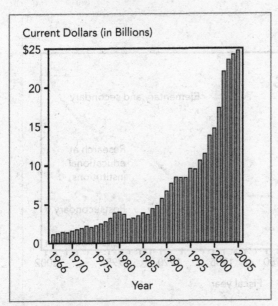

FIGURE 10.2 Federal Investment in the Elementary and Secondary Education Act

Source: 2005 U.S. Budget, Historical Tables.

■ CONSTITUTIONAL FOUNDATIONS OF FEDERAL EDUCATION POLICY

The U.S. Constitution does not explicitly grant citizens a right to an education, nor does it establish a national system of schools. Rather than a glaring omission, the absence of any provision explicitly concerned with education or schooling appears to have been a conscious choice by eighteenth-century Constitutional framers. Notes compiled by James Madison during the Philadelphia constitutional convention suggest members discussed establishing a national university but made no formal proposal to provide the federal government with a role in lower education.

Others in attendance considered formal learning to be important, and several luminaries of the period, such as Thomas Jefferson and Benjamin Franklin, expressed favorable views on education in other settings (Franklin, 1749; Jefferson, 1976). Thus, omission of the words *schooling* and *education* from the Constitution might not have been a casual act or oversight.

Nevertheless, it was only in the mid-nineteenth century that state-enacted compulsory attendance laws triggered present models of public schooling (Guthrie et al., 1975). Thus, those attending the 1787 constitutional convention had little experience with government provision of education, and their negative disposition toward King George III and the strong British monarchy prejudiced them further against granting a national authority right to control such a potentially influential undertaking as schooling.

Given this context, exactly how did founding fathers express a preference for a limited federal government? Mention was made of this dynamic in Chapter Five. Thus, this is an abbreviated explanation.

The U.S. Constitution's Tenth Amendment specifies ". . . powers not delegated to the United States by the Constitution, nor prohibited by it to the States, are reserved to the States respectively, or to the people." This provision reflects social contract theories of government intensely important to constitutional framers (Baker, 1947). The right to individual self-determination was held to be an inalienable quality of each human being, one that should be ceded to representative governing bodies only with strict limitations. Hence, the Tenth Amendment explicitly asserts that national government is to be imbued only with powers expressly granted to it. All other authority is to be held by states or by individuals, unless specifically denied by the Constitution. The Tenth Amendment's ending, "or the people," makes clear that the citizenry is the ultimate source of governing authority.[2]

The effect of the absence in the Constitution of a proclamation of express national responsibility for education and schooling, when coupled with language of the Tenth Amendment, is to cede plenary (ultimate) legal authority for public education to state government. As a result, each state constitution, as a condition of entry into the union, contains an education clause explicitly acknowledging state authority over education and schooling. As will be evident later, it is these clauses that have become the focus of a series of school finance litigation cases.

Because of these federal and state constitutional arrangements, the federal government has no widespread specific responsibility for operating education programs. (Direct federal administration of institutions such as the armed service academies, Gallaudet College for the Deaf in Washington, D.C., and the Overseas Dependent Schools are limited exceptions.)

The federal government's constitutional authority to finance and regulate education programs is derived from implied powers contained in several sections of the U.S. Constitution. Over the centuries since ratification, numerous judicial interpretations of constitutional provisions have expanded the scope of the federal government's education authority. These implied powers have been reinforced by court decisions regarding the general welfare clause and other parts of the First Amendment and both due process and equal protection clauses of the Fourteenth Amendment.

The First Amendment—General Welfare Clause

Article 1, Section 8, Clause 1, of the Constitution is commonly referred to as the general welfare clause. It states, "The Congress shall have power to levy and collect taxes, duties, imposts and excises, to pay the debts and provide for the common defense and general welfare of the United States." For a century or more following adoption of the Constitution, this was a controversial provision. Proponents of a limited national government, such as James Madison, desired a narrow interpretation, whereas advocates of a strong central government, such as Alexander Hamilton, argued for a broad view of the clause. In the 1930s, U.S. Supreme Court decisions substantially altered the nature of the debate. In a case involving New Deal legislation sponsored by the Roosevelt administration, the nation's highest court ruled that Congress had authority to interpret the general welfare clause as long as it did not act arbitrarily (*United States v. Butler*).

The U.S. Supreme Court also held that the clause could be interpreted differently from time to time as conditions necessitate redefinition of the nation's general welfare (*Helvering v. Davis*). Debate has since shifted to whether or not a particular policy proposal is useful, instead of whether Congress possesses authority to implement it. Consequently, federal education programs are viewed as falling within the implied constitutional authority of Congress. This is not to assert everybody always agrees on the wisdom of a particular legislative proposal or a new federal education program. Contemporary education initiatives can still provoke heated debate at the federal level.

The First Amendment—Contractual Obligations

Article 1, Section 10, of the Constitution has been judicially interpreted to allow the federal government to restrict the ability of states and local boards of education to impair contractual obligations. The Supreme Court has held that "a legislative enactment may contain provisions which, when accepted as a basis of action by individuals, become contracts between them and the state or its subdivision" (*State ex rel Anderson v. Brand*). The constitutional provision regarding contractual obligations and legal principles derived from it have also been applied to controversies between teacher unions and school boards over tenure rights and retirement agreements.

The First Amendment—Church-State Relations

The Supreme Court has held that the First Amendment was intended to create a wall of separation between church and state. Consistent with this view both state and federal courts have repeatedly struck state efforts to provide direct financial subsidies to religious schools. The U.S. Supreme Court evolved a three-pronged test to determine whether a sectarian school aid plan violates the wall of separation: (1) the statute must have a secular legislative purpose, (2) the statute's primary effect must neither advance nor inhibit religion, and (3) the statute and its administration must avoid excessive government entanglement with religion (*Lemon v. Kurtzman*).

Application of these principles served, until the last decade of the twentieth century, to discourage state aid to church-related elementary and secondary schools. However, with the 1983 Supreme Court decision in *Mueller v. Allen*, matters began to evolve in a different direction. The *Mueller* decision approved a Minnesota statute providing state income tax deductions for school fees, both public and nonpublic. Advocates of federal aid to religious schools took this to be a signal that the Court was increasingly disposed toward their cause. A 1985 decision in a New York case, *Aguilar v. Felton*, counseled caution. Provision to church-related schools of federally funded compensatory instructional services authorized by Chapter One of the *Education Consolidation and Improvement Act* was restricted by this decision. However, at the opening of the twenty-first century, the nation's highest court seemed more disposed toward use of public funds for private and religious schools. In the 2001 case of *Zelman v. Simmons-Harris*, the Court ruled that publicly funded education vouchers provided to students might be redeemed at religious schools, saying:

> We believe that the program challenged here is a program of true private choice, consistent with Mueller, Witters, and Zobrest, and thus constitutional. As was true in those cases, the Ohio program is neutral in all respects toward religion. It is part of a general and multifaceted undertaking by the State of Ohio to provide educational opportunities to the children of a failed school district.

The Fourteenth Amendment—Equal Protection

The Fourteenth Amendment, adopted in 1868, was one of three constitutional amendments intended to free slaves. It stretched the mantle of the first ten amendments to protect the civil liberties of citizens from state encroachment (LaMorte, 1974). The Fourteenth Amendment contains two clauses of particular importance to federal authority over education: (1) the so-called due process clause, and (2) the equal protection clause.

The equal protection clause served as the basis for one of the most significant reforms ever undertaken in American public education: overturn of dual school systems for whites and blacks, which evolved from slavery and were supported statutorily in seventeen southern states and the District of Columbia. In 1954 the U.S. Supreme Court issued a school desegregation decision that overturned the "separate but equal" doctrine, which had dominated U.S. race relations since the 1896 decision in *Plessy v. Ferguson*. In *Plessy* the Court had let stand an 1890 Louisiana statute segregating races on railway cars as long as, presumably, facilities were equal. In *Brown v. Board of Education*, by far the most noted of the desegregation cases, the Court stated:

> We conclude that in the field of public education the doctrine of "separate but equal" has no place. Separate educational facilities are inherently unequal. Therefore, we hold that the plaintiffs and others similarly situated for whom the actions are brought are, by reason of the segregation complained of, deprived of the equal protection of the laws guaranteed by the Fourteenth Amendment.

The *Brown* decision, in conjunction with implementation decrees and numerous lower-court decisions, was resisted, sometimes violently. The eventual result, however, was a dismantling of the *de jure* racially segregated school systems that had long characterized public schooling in the South. More subtle discriminatory mechanisms that contribute to *de facto* segregation have not lent themselves so easily to legal remedy (Wilkinson, 1976; Orfield, 1978; Kirp, 1982; Walters, 1984).

In the News

Is There Constitutional Authority for NCLB?

There is little dispute over whether NCLB represents an unprecedented level of federal involvement in the affairs of our public schools. However, there is disagreement between the law's supporters, who hail this federal intrusion into state and local education as effective national reform, and its detractors, who argue that the intrusion consists of a set of politically motivated mandates that are detrimental to our schools. The language of NLCB speaks to the sweeping authority intended by its passage: "The purpose of the title is to ensure that all children have a fair, equal, and significant opportunity to obtain a high-quality education and reach, at a minimum, proficiency on challenging state academic achievement standards and state academic assessments." To accomplish this, NCLB sets extensive requirements for states, including establishing an accountability system and staffing schools with high-quality professionals.

This level of federal intrusion into a domain typically under state control raises legal questions because Congress must act within the limits of federal authority established by the U.S. Constitution. The Constitution reflects a careful balance between the powers of the federal government and those of the states. James Madison argued, "The powers delegated by the proposed Constitution to the federal government are few and defined. Those which are to remain in the State governments are numerous and indefinite." The Constitution defines this balance in the 10th Amendment: "The powers not delegated to the United States by the Constitution, nor prohibited by it to the States, are reserved to the States respectively, or to the people."

Past court decisions, most notably *San Antonio* v. *Rodriguez* (1973), have declared that the Constitution does not establish, either explicitly or implicitly, education as a right or delegate the authority over schools to the federal government. Instead, education is within the domain of state and local governments. As the U.S. Supreme Court said in the celebrated 1954 *Brown* v. *Board of Education* opinion, "Education is perhaps the most important function of state and local governments."

If the federal government is not specifically authorized by the Constitution to delve into matters of education, what other grounds could there be that would satisfy the 10th Amendment's conditions for the assignment of powers? For the authority to legislate as broadly as it has in NCLB, Congress relied on a provision in the Constitution that provides power unlike any other defined in that document: the spending clause. In archaic-sounding language, the spending clause (Art. I, sec. 8, cl. 1) states: "The Congress shall have Power To lay and collect Taxes, Duties, Imposts and Excises, to pay the Debts and provide for the common Defense and general Welfare of the United States . . . ." The spending clause is the basis not only for NCLB but also for most federal education policies, including those that prohibit discrimination—Title VI (race, ethnicity, and national origin), Title IX (gender), and the Individuals with Disabilities Education (IDEA) Act and Section 504 of the Rehabilitation Act (disability)—and those, like the Family Education Rights and Privacy Act, that protect student privacy. Any future federal education reforms, including a national curriculum, national tests, or national licensure standards, will almost certainly have to be crafted as spending clause legislation.

From: McColl, A. (2005, April). Tough call: Is No Child Left Behind constitutional? *Phi Delta Kappan,* 86(8), 604–10.

The equal protection clause has also been used as basis for a constitutional challenge to school finance arrangements in many of the fifty states. Chapters Five and Twelve explain the legal logic and practical consequences connected with this judicial reform strategy. Suffice it to state here that the practical outcome, though not wholly unsatisfactory, has been nowhere near the legal success of the school desegregation suits. Indeed, reform efforts in racial desegregation and school finance simultaneously display the power and limits of the federal government's ability to influence public education. Because of the complexity of the United States' multi-tiered and many-faceted system of government, the results of these efforts have not been nearly as successful as advocates had hoped, or as devastating socially as opponents had feared.

The Fourteenth Amendment—Due Process

The Fourteenth Amendment's due process clause states, "nor shall any State deprive any person of life, liberty, or property, without due process of law." This clause also provides a major legal vehicle through which the federal government can influence public education. Generally, the due process clause must be weighed against society's need to protect itself.

Though continually being redefined judicially, so-called police powers are inherently within the authority of government at all levels. For example, teachers and other school employees are not free simply to do or teach whatever they would like if such actions jeopardize society's need to protect itself. Courts have generally enforced the Smith Act, which makes it a crime punishable by fine and imprisonment to advocate forceful overthrow of the government. These rulings have established a limitation regarding what can be taught in public as well as private schools. As Morphet, Johns, and Reller (1985) stated:

> . . . those who insist that the federal government should have no control whatsoever over the curriculum of public schools seem to be unaware of the inherent police powers of the federal government relating to matters of national concern.

The federal government's ability to influence America's system of schooling is not limited to its legal authority. Influence is also possible through means such as financial inducement, demonstration projects, and dissemination of information and research findings, evaluation efforts, and moral persuasion. These are discussed in subsequent sections of this chapter.

Despite this limited authority, the federal government has had a history of influence in education. In the mid-twentieth century, federal authorities inaugurated numerous education programs that presently provide services throughout all fifty states, trust territories, thousands of local school districts, and schools. It is these programs that are usually included when one considers the "federal role" in the provision and support of education. In actuality, the federal government has assumed a considerable role in matters of public education since the earliest days of the republic. It is unlikely that even a single American public school is presently untouched by federal education policy. Sections below review federal involvement in issues of equity, efficiency, and liberty that have had financial implications for American public schools.

■ THREE PILLARS OF SCHOOL FINANCE AND FEDERAL INVOLVEMENT

Policymaking at all levels, including the federal government involves combining practical ideas with ideals in order both to solve problems and convince the public that a solution is consistent with its idea of "America." Viewed in this light, the three value streams of equality, efficiency, and liberty can be articulated in the following manner.

Equity. A federal value of equal opportunity is expressed in U.S. foundational documents. In public education, equity is usually referred to in terms of opportunity; that is, every student should be assured a right to educational opportunity, but not a right to any specific level of personal educational attainment or academic achievement. This means that students should have access to schools and colleges and not be deterred from educational opportunities by race, creed, wealth, or selected other markers. Federal equity policies have directed funds toward students living in poverty as well as students of color and other minority groups in order to ensure educational opportunity is distributed equally throughout society.

Efficiency. A federal value of efficiency recognizes, sometimes, that federal action is the most cost-effective and quickest way to accomplish a task. In education, efficiency impulses have focused on state institutions of higher education and students' financial aid to acquire educational services. Historically, federal actions to ensure equity have included providing land directly to states to support education, funds directly to students to subsidize college costs, and data and feedback to school systems to support more effective education. In addition, federal policies may reflect a view that pre-existing government bureaucracy needs to be rescued from itself and simplified or streamlined to provide federal funds to local districts in a more efficient manner.

Liberty. A federal predisposition toward liberty stresses the idea that citizens as well as state and local governments are free to make choices without coercion. In public education, the federal role in enhancing liberty has involved walking a tight rope and serving as an adjudicator between rights of governments and rights of individuals. The federal government has supported liberty by providing funds directly to students, litigating cases thought to limit state or school system autonomy, and providing results-oriented directives for systemic improvement while leaving states and systems free to innovate, what some have termed "top down support for bottom up reform."

Equity—Ensuring Access

Although many scholars think of federal involvement in equity issues along the lines of race, such as the 1896 *Plessy* or 1954 *Brown* Supreme Court decisions, the federal government has been striving to ensure educational access for almost the entire history of our nation. One of the federal government's first attempts to ensure access to educational opportunity was initiated before the U.S. Constitution was even ratified.

Land Survey Ordinance and Northwest Ordinance—Using Land to Ensure Access to Schools. In 1785, even before ratification of the Constitution by all original colonies, central government policy on education was being made. The Land Survey Ordinance of that year provided for several sections of land in each township within newly formed territories to be reserved for support of public schools (Campbell, Cunningham, Nystrand, & Usdan, 1990). Specifically, Section 16 of each plot was to be reserved for schools, and, in a symbolic commitment to separation of church and state, Section 29 was reserved for religious purposes.

The 1787 Northwest Ordinance continued support of access to public education in what was to become Michigan, Indiana, Wisconsin, Ohio, and Illinois. These early ordinances signaled a federal commitment to public education that was to continue throughout American political history. This commitment is summed up best in a sentence from Article 3 of the Northwest Ordinance, which reads:

> *Religion, morality and knowledge being necessary to good government and the happiness of mankind, schools and the means of education shall forever be encouraged. These two ordinances demonstrate federal government's historical commitment to use its greatest resource (at that time, land), as a lever to ensure citizens would have access to schools and educational opportunities.*

Morrill Act—Using Land Grants for Higher Education. Vast amounts of undeveloped land remained one of the federal government's greatest resources into the 1800s. In 1862 Congress passed the first Morrill Act, named after Senator Justin S. Morrill of Vermont, the bill's major proponent. This statute allocated 30,000 acres of federal land to each state for each of its two senators and each representative to which it was then entitled. Income from the sale or rental of these lands was to be used for establishing agricultural and mechanical arts colleges. These "A & M" colleges were to contribute to the new nation's supply of artisans and technicians. Such institutions were also to instruct students in military science and tactics.

Each state benefited from this program. Not all recipients have been public institutions, however. Cornell University in Ithaca, New York, and the Massachusetts Institute of Technology in Cambridge, Massachusetts, are both examples of prestigious private institutions that have received aid from Morrill Act proceeds. So-called land-grant colleges received additional aid upon passage of the Second Morrill Act of 1892 and the Hatch Act of 1897.[3]

Head Start—A Popular Foray into Education Policymaking. Creation of Head Start, through President Lyndon Johnson's antipoverty legislation, The Economic Opportunity Act of 1964, represents a textbook example of the federal government creating legislation to fulfill needs that state and local governments ignored. Head Start was created as an independent agency to develop poor children so that they would be better prepared for school. Head Start was aligned with the Johnson administration's commitment to equity, while acknowledging the meritocratic nature of public education. While results from Head Start have been mixed, the program has remained popular with legislators as well as the general public.[4]

Elementary and Secondary Education Act (ESEA)—A Federal Plan for Education Support. Another piece of landmark federal education policy was passed in 1965. Unlike Head Start, the Elementary and Secondary Education Act (ESEA) was specifically directed to supporting public education for low-income students. Like Head Start, ESEA revenue is distributed widely across the nation.

Historically, the bulk of ESEA funds have been dedicated to "Title One," which seeks to support students in poverty. Since its 1965 passage, the ESEA has been the main lever by which the federal government seeks to influence K–12 educational policy. Both Bill Clinton's Improving America's Schools Act of 1994 and George Bush's No Child Left Behind Act of 2001 were reauthorizations of ESEA in which specific new approaches to education were added, such as use of standards and assessments to determine if schools receiving federal money were attaining concomitant student achievement gains, and a system of rewards and sanctions for states, districts, and schools receiving funds and that could not demonstrate improved results. Currently, under NCLB, the federal government annually invests over $20 billion on America's schools because of ESEA.[5]

One ESEA legacy is research into the effects of remedial action and family background on student academic achievement.[6]

Emergency School Aid Act (ESAA)—Federal Money as Incentive for Desegregation. From 1955 through the 1960s, judicial pressure was exerted upon southern schools to dismantle dual school systems. Throughout much of this period the Justice Department and the Office of Civil Rights, both within the executive branch, also attempted to pressure school districts to undertake racial desegregation. Beginning in 1968, the Nixon administration attempted to dilute judicial and executive branch mandatory desegregation pressures and proposed substituting more federal inducements for voluntary desegregation of local school districts. Proponents of racially integrated schools were skeptical of such a strategy, but Congress in 1972 nevertheless enacted the Emergency

School Aid Act (ESAA). The intent of this legislation was to assist local school districts in racially integrating schools by providing federal funds for in-service training of teachers, employment of teacher aides and instructional specialists for desegregated classrooms, or whatever else local school officials reasonably contended would assist their districts in voluntarily desegregating schools. Appropriations for this statute reached their peak in the late 1970s, totaling approximately $300 million.

Impact Aid—*Just Compensation for Military Communities.* At the outset of World War II and again in the early 1950s with the Korean War, local officials frequently found school districts faced with virtually unmanageable growth problems. Nearby military bases and other federal installations expanded quickly, and adjacent public schools often would have to absorb hundreds of additional pupils in a short period. Worse, federal installations were not subject to local taxation. To compensate for this condition, Congress enacted in 1940 and subsequently renewed the Lanham Act, P.L. 81-874. This in lieu of tax statute compensates local districts for loss of property tax revenue resulting from the "impact" of federal activity. Hence, these funds have come to be known as impact aid. Local school districts annually conduct a census among pupils to determine eligibility. Thereafter they use funds they receive as though they were general revenues.

Public Law 94-142 (*Education for All Handicapped Children Act*)—*Letting More Students through the Schoolhouse Door.* Throughout the 1960s and the early 1970s, increasing political pressure was brought to bear on state legislatures to correct injustices to handicapped students. Many states were not providing school services for severely handicapped students, and other states were underfunding such programs. Following several important state court cases in which it was held that handicapped children deserved equal protection of the law, state legislatures as well as Congress enacted programs to ensure better schooling for the handicapped (*PARC v. Commonwealth*, 1971; *Mills v. Board of Education*, 1972).

The Education for All Handicapped Children Act (EHCA) of 1975, was one result of the congressional activity. This federal statute distributes funds to states and ultimately to local districts for education services to various categories of handicapped schoolchildren. In accepting funds, states and districts must agree to follow a rigorous set of federal regulations in educating eligible students. One of the policies in place today because of EHCA is that every identified student's instructional program be guided by collaborative development of an IEP, or individual education plan. These plans ensure that each student's special circumstances are considered when making educational decisions.

Many local school officials express annoyance at the high level of distrust implied by the unusually legalistic procedures, such as the paperwork required to initiate, implement, and assess an individual student's IEP. Handicapped advocates reply that past abuses speak poorly for the integrity of local education officials and contend that firm federal regulations are altogether necessary to ensure handicapped students are treated fairly. Nevertheless, EHCA brought many more students into the classrooms of American public schools, guaranteeing access to educational opportunity was now distributed more widely than ever. In addition, the spirit of EHCA, that students should be placed in the "least restrictive educational environment," also known as "mainstreaming" is reinforced by provisions of No Child Left Behind, which make academic improvement of special needs students a precursor for school and school-system success.

Bilingual Education—Access for Non-English Speakers. Increasing immigration, particularly from Spanish-speaking and Asian nations, began to challenge resources of selected local school districts after the mid-1900s. Children of many new Americans had only limited, if any, ability to speak and read English. Ironically, these youngsters were compelled by statute to attend schools whose medium of instruction, English, was for them unintelligible. In San Francisco, site of a heavy influx of non-English-speaking Asians, students and their parents filed suit against the school district in order to receive language assistance in school. The case, *Lau v. Nichols*, eventually was decided in favor of plaintiffs. Based on Section 601 of the 1964 Civil Rights Act, the U.S. Supreme Court found that non-English-speaking students were discriminated against and mandated that the school district provide multilingual instructors and other educational assistance to these children.

The legal precedent became established that school districts were responsible for assisting limited- and non-English-speaking students. To defray added costs of such services, several state legislatures enacted categorical school aid programs and Congress added Title VII to the Elementary and Secondary Education Act. The latter provision allocates funds, through states, to local school districts for bilingual instruction. Federal appropriations were never large, to the point that many state and local officials consider bilingual education to be an "unfunded mandate" from the federal government. Again, however, this commitment to non-native English speakers is reinforced through provisions of No Child Left Behind that make the academic success of (what are now termed) English language learners a precursor for school and school-system success.

Efficiency—Ensuring Best Use of Public Resources

A second pillar of education finance is that of efficiency. Some federal initiatives to improve efficiency of public schools are as follows.

Vocational Education—Making Public Schools Work for American Business. In the early twentieth century, as the United States moved toward World War I, Congress, concerned about availability of skilled workers to supply both American industry and the war effort, passed the Smith-Hughes Act of 1917. The statute authorized federal funds to states to establish secondary school programs in agricultural and industrial trades and homemaking. States were required to match federal funds. This act established a precedent for matching grants that has become a major lever used by federal officials to induce program cooperation by state and local agencies.

The Smith-Hughes Act was controversial. John Dewey observed in 1917, upon passage of Smith-Hughes: "It settles no problem; it merely symbolizes inauguration of a conflict between irreconcilable opposed educational and industrial ideals." Indeed, the tension in education policy between providing both academic and vocational course and the practice of "tracking" students based on their perceived abilities is present today.

The federal government's initial concern for vocational education has been strongly sustained. Congress enacted the George-Reed Act in 1929, the George-Ellzey Act in 1935, the George-Dean Act in 1937, and the George-Barden Act in 1946. The 1963 Vocational Education Act, promoted by President John F. Kennedy, established a different direction for vocational education, a direction that has been pursued with systematic reauthorizations. The Clinton administrations School-to-Work Act reflected a commitment to vocational education as well as the policy innovation of required matching funds.

During the Great Depression of the 1930s, Congress established several antipoverty programs containing significant educational components. Frequently, vocational training was a prominent feature of these undertakings. For example, the Civilian Conservation Corps and the National Youth Authority both provided vocational training for unemployed depression youth.

In 1965, as part of the Johnson administration's War on Poverty, the Federal Job Corps was established to enable out-of-school and out-of-work youth to gain job skills. Depression-era education programs were operated directly by federal agencies such as the War Department (now the Defense Department) and the Federal Security Agency, an ancestor of the present-day Department of Education. The Job Corps was operated by a variety of private organizations under direct contract to the now-defunct Office of Economic Opportunity.

Compared with programs in surrounding local school districts, these federally funded and operated vocational training endeavors were unusually expensive, costing up to twenty times as much per enrollee as public school vocational training. Local and state public school officials insisted they could perform the same function more efficiently. Such complaints, along with changing economic conditions, eventually terminated these poverty-relief efforts, and virtually none of them remains today.

National Assessment of Educational Progress (NAEP)—Developing the Nation's Report Card. In 1966 the federal government funded an effort to assess the national performance of students and school graduates—the National Assessment of Educational Progress (NAEP). Initially this undertaking was contracted by the Department of Education to the Education Commission of the States, in Denver, Colorado. At that time appraisers of performance were prohibited from making state-by-state comparisons. In 1983 the NAEP was moved to the Educational Testing Service in Princeton, New Jersey. In 1987 a highly visible national study panel chaired by Tennessee governor Lamar Alexander and Spencer Foundation president H. Thomas James issued *The Nation's Report Card*, a report that recommended massive changes in governance and procedures for the NAEP. The panel proposed, for example, that state-by-state test score comparisons be undertaken (Alexander & James, 1987).

This massive achievement-assessment program tests thousands of students throughout the nation. It is not an endeavor that individual states could easily organize or afford to operate for the entire nation. It falls more naturally to the federal government to conduct such an undertaking.

Data Collection and Dissemination—Making Innovation Available to All. There is less financial incentive to engage in research when potential results may advantage a host of others besides the initiating agency. Under such conditions, a tempting strategy is to wait and hope to piggyback on the research funded by another. Educational research and development can be viewed in this light. Why should one state expend its scarce resources on basic research on, for example, human learning when there is no reasonable way to restrict useful results to its boundaries? Under such circumstances, there is likely to be an underinvestment in an activity that might otherwise enhance educational efficiency and the productivity of the entire economy. To avoid such a condition, the federal government has long supported educational research and development.

In 1954 Congress passed the Cooperative Research Act, which authorized federal funds for educational research in institutions of higher education. The U.S. Office of Education, one of several agencies constituting what was then known as the Department of Health, Education, and Welfare (HEW), administered this statute. In 1965 main features of the Cooperative Research Act were incorporated into Title IV of the Elementary and Secondary Education Act (ESEA). The latter act substantially expanded the amount of federal money available for education research. Additionally, it established twenty regional educational laboratories and twelve university-based research and development (R & D) centers. The aim was for new ideas to be developed in the R & D centers and transformed into practical applications and distributed to school districts by the regional educational laboratories. This research, development, and dissemination strategy was patterned after a highly effective model utilized by U.S. agriculture.

In 1975 federal education-research functions were transferred to the new National Institute of Education (NIE), then within HEW, and, subsequently, a part of the Department of Education. By the late 1970s, however, federal expenses accrued from the war in Vietnam, large outlays for domestic social programs, and diminished political affection for public schools had reduced education research appropriations. Several of the R & D centers and regional laboratories were closed, and funding for the remainder was insufficient to support large-scale research projects. Though the NIE continued to be the major funding source for education research throughout the 1970s and early 1980s, its institutional impact was minimal in many areas, and there were even serious suggestions for its dissolution (Finn, 1983b). By 1985 the NIE had been folded back into the Department of Education and was known as the Office of Educational Research and Improvement (OERI). With NCLB, OERI was reconstituted into the Institute of Education Sciences (IES).

National Defense Education Act (NDEA)—Funding for National Needs and Priorities. In 1957 the Soviet Union launched the first successful earth-orbiting satellite, *Sputnik.* The event rocked America's sense of technological superiority. U.S. public education served as a convenient scapegoat for popular frustration and disappointment. The nation subsequently regained its poise and launched a massive federal program that resulted in moon landings and other space successes of the 1960s and 1970s. Education also benefited, with enactment of the 1958 National Defense Education Act (NDEA). This statute utilized federal matching funds as an incentive for local school districts to upgrade instruction in science, mathematics, and foreign language. Higher-education institutions also participated, through expanded financial support for college students entering the teaching fields of science and math. The NDEA was successful in helping schools meet intensified public expectations for American scientific and technological supremacy.

In the 1960s the National Science Foundation (NSF) funded fellowships and advanced training programs for science and math teachers at many colleges and universities. The NSF also funded a number of science and math curriculum-revision projects that substantially influenced secondary school instruction (Marsh & Gortner, 1963).

In the early 1980s the mass media and professional periodicals began reporting increasing shortages of qualified secondary school math and science teachers (Guthrie & Zusman, 1982). Fear of losing a competitive economic position in international sales of high-technology products and techniques motivated President Ronald Reagan in 1985 to propose and Congress to enact the Education for Economic Security Act, embodying many of the same purposes as the 1958 NDEA.

In 1966 Congress passed a Sea Grant program providing colleges and universities with added federal funding to expand marine research. In 1987 the Reagan administration proposed to provide land-grant institutions with added funding to conduct research in electronics and other high-technology areas.

Education Consolidation and Improvement Act (ECIA)—Reforming the Reforms. Sometimes, the federal government uses its role in education policy to attempt to improve its own efforts. In 1981 Congress accepted a Reagan administration recommendation and consolidated many existing education programs into two major statutes of the ECIA. Chapter One of this act continues the major feature of the 1965 ESEA—federal funds for compensatory education for students from low-income families into a limited number of the so-called block grants, wherein states and districts would be permitted greater discretion over spending. Interest groups comprising the educators and others who were benefiting most directly from the categorical aid resisted consolidation for fear their particular programs would lose ground to local spending priorities under a block grant (Kirst, 1986).

In 1981, when the Reagan administration initially proposed deregulation and consolidation, several major programs were discussed for inclusion, among them special education and compensatory education. The eventual compromise was to preserve the categorical integrity of major programs and to combine many smaller authorities. ECIA Chapter Two was the result. This foray into more innovative federal funding for education programs harked back to the tradition of local control in public education. Although the ECIA was eventually reformulated into the more recognizable categorical aid of ESEA, the precedent of using federal funds in more creative ways to spur change continues in NCLB. The failure of ECIA was due more to a lack of capacity of state and local officials to handle the massive change in the federal paradigm than to any specific problem with the policies proposed by ECIA.

A Nation at Risk—The Bully Pulpit Changes the Course of Education Research. In 1983 Terrell Bell, then Secretary of Education, and the National Education Excellence Commission released a report. Titled *A Nation at Risk*, the report decried declining performance in American public schools and the seeming lack of will for substantive education reform. Although the report proved controversial, and although it did little to nothing to change education legislation, the report had an electrifying effect on the education research community. The report kicked off an era of research into excellent and effective schools that continues to this day. With hindsight, one can see that *A Nation at Risk* spawned the research base that undergirds federal policy today, such as No Child Left Behind. *A Nation at Risk* is an object lesson in the ability of the executive branch of government to use the bully pulpit to alter the course of education policy.

New American Schools and Comprehensive Schools Demonstration Project—Creating a Context for Innovation. During the administration of George H.W. Bush, education policy focused on the implementation of a standards and assessment paradigm. Part of this effort was the creation in 1991 of the New American Schools Development Corporation (NASDC), an organization that was intended as an incubator for education innovation. NASDC was to transition from being federally funded to becoming an independent organization. Its task was to create and support models that created whole school change, or "Comprehensive School Reform" (CSR) as opposed to simply reforming schools through the categorical programs found in ESEA.

Federal legislation enacting the Comprehensive School Reform Demonstration Project supported NASDC by offering schools and school systems block grants for adopting one of

NASDC's Comprehensive School Reform (CSR) models. In this manner, the federal government provided a laboratory for a new approach to school reform (Education Commission of the States, 2005). This strategy has generally been found wanting. Few school boards and central office administrators are in a position to adopt a radical reform. Public education is woven so tightly into the fabric of American politics that dramatic, rather than incremental, change is almost always the only change that can occur. New American Schools Development Corporation has repeatedly reinvented itself, but has not been, and probably cannot be, a major factor in changing American education. The federal government's measurement of outcomes and provision of rewards and sanctions for results strategy, embedded in NCLB, provide a brighter promise of provoking change.

America/Goals 2000—Using ESEA to Implement a New Education Paradigm. Both the Bush and Clinton administrations relied upon the ESEA to bring a new reform strategy to pubic schools. Using the funding from the ESEA as an incentive, both administrations sought to implement federal legislation that demanded state standards and assessments for all states, with a system of rewards and sanctions for performance attached to the assessments.

Liberty—Offering Choice

Confronted with large numbers of returning soldiers after World War II, Congress enacted the Service Man's Readjustment Act, which provided financial assistance to veterans to acquire postsecondary schooling. This statute, the G.I. Bill (described in detail in Chapter Seven), was a forerunner of voucher plans in that federal funds flowed to the individual and he or she decided upon an institution to attend. Although aid was for postsecondary schooling, and, therefore, did not provoke intense questions of aid to nonpublic schools, the G.I. Bill set a precedent for the federal government to use the individual as a unit of assistance and not just an institution. This precedent was acted upon in the 1975 Higher Education Act that made a radical policy shift in providing federal student aid for higher education directly to students. Previously, federal student assistance had been funneled through institutions. This change enabled students to use their aid dollars in a more portable manner, thus giving them more control of their higher education decisions.

In the 1980s the Reagan administration proposed a tuition tax credit plan, which would benefit elementary and secondary as well as postsecondary institutions (Catteral, 1983b; Jacobs, 1980; Mazzoni, 1988). Controversy over such an arrangement has been more intense than that concerning the G.I. Bill. Tuition tax credits expand choice by permitting households to deduct all or a portion of nonpublic tuition payments from federal income taxes. The allowable dollar amount is a credit against federal income taxes owed, not simply a deduction from income. Many private school officials and parents of private school children favor such a plan. Conversely, many public school advocates oppose the plan. Opponents fear that federal private school subsidies will undermine public schools, and they allege that the plan will violate First Amendment prohibitions of aid to religious schools (Huerta & d'Entremont, 2007).

Prior to 1983, tuition tax credit proposals had passed in the U.S. Senate on six separate occasions. In 1979 the House of Representatives enacted a tuition tax credit plan by a narrow margin, but President Jimmy Carter's threat of a veto, given Democratic control of the Senate at the time, was sufficient to stifle the bill. President Reagan's administration again proposed such a plan, but the prospect of huge federal budget deficits in the 1980s dampened prospects for congressional approval (Whitt, Clark, & Astuto, 1986). Aside from economics and politics, however, the constitutionality of such a plan is perhaps enhanced by the U.S. Supreme Court's decision in the previously mentioned cases of *Mueller v. Allen* and *Zelman* v. *Simmons-Harris.*

Another mechanism for enhancing choice in education is the use of vouchers. Voucher plans are described in greater length in subsequent chapters. Suffice it here to mention that people have been advocating federal vouchers for several decades, and there was even a small federally funded voucher experiment in the 1970s. Reagan administration voucher proponents repeatedly proposed that Chapter One of the ECIA be revised to empower compensatory education funds to be allocated to households of low-income students so that they can decide as consumers how best to remedy their education deficit (McEwan, 2004).

No Child Left Behind—A Policy Shift on Three Levels

No Child Left Behind focuses on results and represents a commitment to efficiency in federal education policy. Sanctions for underperforming schools reflect a (relatively new) federal understanding that schools must be changed wholesale, rather than one program at a time. NCLB makes provisions for educational choice for students if a school demonstrates a failure to improve. In this way, NCLB connects to impulses toward liberty outlined in legislation such as the higher Education Act, Regan-era initiatives, and present-day privately supported voucher programs.

■ MAKING AND IMPLEMENTING MODERN EDUCATION POLICY

Conventional wisdom holds that federal policy for almost any endeavor, not simply education, is a consequence of political interactions among the three components of the so-called "iron triangle"—the education agencies of the executive branch, congressional committees, and interest groups. The idea for a new piece of legislation may arise from any of these groups or from a large number of other sources, such as a new book, a study supported by a philanthropic foundation, a journalist's article, or an academic research project. This process is termed agenda setting, and there are a number of theories that discuss how to approach this process from a theoretical perspective. Once an executive branch agency or a member of Congress is interested in sponsoring an idea, drafting the concept in bill form is relatively easy, either by counsel in an executive branch agency or by the Legislative Drafting Service in the House or Senate.[7]

Identifying potential supporters of an idea and then negotiating compromises may be necessary before important factions agree to support a bill. The more important a bill, the more groups likely to be affected, the larger the federal appropriation involved, and the greater the likelihood of controversy. Many more bills are defeated than enacted. In many cases an idea must be submitted repeatedly over a number of years before eventually proving sufficiently understood and popular to be adopted. Also, whereas an idea may stem from many sources and be initiated by any one component of the triangle, conventional wisdom holds that eventually the other two components must also agree before passage will occur. Brokering multifaceted agreements necessary to ensure enactment of a bill is an art form seldom fully appreciated by the public.

Making a Bill into Law

Conventional high school civics textbooks explain that policy is made by the legislative branch and implemented by a politically sanitized executive branch agency. This is but another form of the frequently promulgated myth that a clear distinction can be made between policymaking and policy administration. In fact, political conflicts left unresolved in the enactment process almost inevitably are reflected in efforts to implement legislation. Consequently, administering federal education policy is far from a mechanically simple, politically sterile, technocratic undertaking (Bailey & Mosher, 1967; Jones, 1984).

Once an education bill has been approved by both houses of Congress, it is often necessary to convene a conference committee, composed of members from both House and Senate, to resolve differences between the two houses' versions of the bill. Assuming presidential approval, the bill is then a public law and is numbered as such. For example, Public Law 94-142 (Education of All Handicapped Children) denotes the 142nd bill to become a statute in the ninety-fourth session of Congress. Thereafter, the specified administering agency within the executive branch is responsible for drafting regulations to implement the new statute.

Implementation and Administration

Regulations are necessary because it is not generally possible in the enactment phase to write a statute so that it will cover every practical contingency connected with implementation and administration. Also, political dynamics of enactment frequently necessitate a degree of ambiguity and vagueness. The higher the abstraction, the greater the probability that political agreement can be reached. "Accomplish good and avoid evil" is an admonition so vague as to be vapid. However, few oppose the principle. As soon as legislation becomes specific, detailing which groups will receive how much money for what purposes, prospect of political conflict increases. Thus, to dampen controversy and attract a greater number of supporting votes, authors of legislation sometimes leave legislative wording deliberately vague, and it is up to those who draft regulation to tidy up the rules of administration. If the statute is ambiguous, interest groups may lobby as assiduously to influence regulations as they did to influence the initial legislation itself.

An education bill is likely to fall within the administrative province of the Department of Education. This cabinet-level department was created in 1978 upon the recommendation of President Jimmy Carter. Previously the U.S. Office of Education (USOE) as well as the National Institute of Education (now the Institute of Education Sciences [IES]) were agencies within the Department of Health, Education, and Welfare (HEW). The latter is now the Department of Health and Human Services (HHS), reflecting the separation of education.

The Department of Education legal counsel is responsible for drafting regulations. In this process, it pays particular attention to the legislative history of a bill. This is derived from committee hearing recording and committee reports in both the House and the Senate. Whatever debate accompanied passage of a bill on the floor of each house also becomes part of the legislative history, as does the conference committee report, if any. From such records the intent of the bill is more fully deduced and prescriptions for administration are drafted that are intended to guide actions of state and local officials as they implement legislation. Regulations specify purposes for which federal funds can be used, state and local plans that may be required by the Department of Education, and rules by which local projects will be audited.

Regulations, once drafted, are submitted to appropriate congressional committees for approval. Also, they are published and distributed in the *Federal Register* to gain the reaction of educators and others in the field. When the approval process is complete, regulations are inserted in the Federal Administrative Code and carry the weight of law. Often, guidelines are provided to assist state and local officials in interpreting regulations and the statute itself. Federal guidelines are typically written in straightforward language and provide examples of procedures and programs to assist local administrators (Kirp & Jensen, 1987).

Appropriation

To this point, explanations have focused on procedures concerned with enacting and implementing authorizing legislation, the substantive bill that specifies purposes of the federal education program and authorizes funds to be spent. The actual dollar amount Congress will allocate to purposes for which spending is authorized is established through an "appropriations" process. This endeavor is a virtually separate legislative track involving interaction with executive branch budget officials and relying heavily upon the Congressional Budget Office and appropriations committees and subcommittees in both the House and the Senate. It is not sufficient for policymakers, professional educators, and members of the public merely to have a sophisticated understanding of the dynamics of authorization politics. Knowledge of appropriation politics, which is characterized by a separate political culture, is also necessary. A thorough reading of a book such as *The New Politics of the Budgetary Process* is useful in gaining a comprehensive view of this important area (Wildavsky & Caiden, 2003).

Gaining Administrative Compliance

Federal officials are eager that education funds be spent in compliance with statutes and regulations. Inducing compliance is a topic that has been addressed by experts in public administration (Berman & McLaughlin, 1978; Knapp, 1983). A few of the strategies utilized by the federal government are listed here. Keep in mind that the United States bureaucracy is multitiered, with each layer wanting to guard its historically evolved prerogatives.

The major strategy pursued with education programs is to require state and local agencies to submit in advance a plan for the use of federal funds. The plan must comply with guidelines for the legislation involved. Thereafter, it is assumed that local administrators will operate in a manner consistent with a submitted plan. Periodically, state officials may audit a local or state agency, either the Auditor General of the Department of Education or the General Accounting Office (GAO) of Congress. The purpose of an audit is to ensure program spending is consistent with locally submitted plans and federal regulations.

 CASE 5 REVISITED

Overcoming Fiscal Failures and Facing Future Challenges

As Howard Tremble reviews his options for generating school change, he realizes the federal government may be able to play a role in bringing additional funds to the district. How could Howard creatively use federal funds to bring about districtwide reform? Which problems in the school district should Howard target for federal funds?

Another stratagem is to require local or state matching of federal funds. The reasoning is that a requirement of a mix of monies will commit local officials to the success of the federally subsidized endeavor as if it were wholly their own. Yet another strategy is to empower local clients or program recipients to pressure local districts to ensure compliance. There are at least two expressions of this strategy. One is to be found in Education for All Handicapped Children Act, wherein parents of handicapped youngsters can request a "fair hearing" with local officials and even be represented by an attorney in the process. Such an adversarial process is intended to protect clients' statutory rights and to provide them with a lever for gaining local district compliance. Somewhat more subtle is the creation of school-site advisory councils and parent advisory councils such as are recommended or required by a number of federal and state program regulations. The idea here is that parents—presumed program benefactors—will advise and appropriately oversee the actions of local education officials. NCLB's No Child Left Behind's empowerment of parents to transfer children when confronted by a persistently failing local school is another strategy intended to gain administrative compliance with policy purposes.

Summary

Federal involvement in education policymaking has increased substantially over the last two hundred years, as has federal investment in educational programs. Federal investment in education rests at around 7 percent of total investment for education. Federal involvement usually addresses one of the following issues: promoting opportunity, ameliorating underinvestment, and capturing economies of scale. Within each of these motivating ideas, issues of equity, efficiency, and liberty can be found. The No Child Legislation of 2001 represents a culmination of a number of federal efforts to spur educational reform. NCLB's accountability structure is well in tune with the language and structure of the standards-based reform movement in education that began to emerge in the late 1980s. The process of enacting federal education legislation involves a number of players in the executive and legislative levels to design, pass, implement, and fund education policy.

Discussion Questions

1. From your reading of this and other chapters, craft an argument of federal involvement in public educational policymaking. Base your argument in legal cases and constitutional arguments. Determine your level of comfort detailing a rationale for federal involvement, and assess the strengths of your argument with classmates. Conversely, craft an argument for states to control education policymaking. Share this rationale with others and assess its strengths and weaknesses.
2. Assess No Child Left Behind from a federal perspective. How does this legislation complete the arc of legislation that has come before it pertaining to education?
3. Determine a time line and a path for federalizing American curriculum. How would such a curriculum be crafted? What special interests would advocate for the defeat of such legislation? Under what authority could such legislation be crafted?

Web Resources

Head Start—
    http://www.acf.hhs.gov/programs/hsb/
Institute of Education Sciences—
    http://www.ed.gov/about/offices/list/ies/index.html

No Child Left Behind—
http://www.ed.gov/nclb/

The Federal Register—
http://www.gpoaccess.gov/fr/index.html

References

Alexander, L., & James, H.T. (1987). *The nation's report card.* Cambridge: National Academy of Education.

Baker, E. (Ed.). (1947). *Social contract: Essays by Locke, Hume and Rousseau.* Oxford, UK: Oxford University Press.

Bailey, S.K., & Mosher, E.K. (1967). *The ESEA: The Office Education administers a law.* Syracuse, NY: Syracuse University Press.

Berman, P., & McLaughlin, M. (1978). *Federal programs supporting educational change: Implementing and sustaining innovations, Vol. 8.* Santa Monica, CA: RAND Corporation.

Burtless, G. (1996). *Does money matter? The effect of school resources on student achievement and adult success.* Washington, DC: Brookings Institution Press.

Campbell, R.L., Cunningham, L.L., Nystrand, R.O., & Usdan, M.D. (1990). *The organization and control of American schools.* Englewood Cliffs, NJ: Prentice-Hall.

Catteral, J.S. (1983b). *Tuition tax credits: Fact and fiction.* Bloomington, IN: Phi Delta Kappan Educational Foundation.

Education Commission of the States. (2005). Comprehensive school reform. Retrieved February 25, 2007, from http://www.ecs.org/ecsmain.asp?page=/html/issue.asp?issueid=27.

Finn, C.E. (1983b). Why the NIE cannot be. *Kappan,* 64(6), 407–10.

Franklin, B. (1749). Proposals relating to the education of youth in Pennsylvania. Retrieved February 25, 2007, from http://www.archives.upenn.edu/primdocs/1749proposals.html.

Guthrie, J.W., & Zusman, A. (1982). Teacher supply and demand in mathematics and science. *Kappan,* 64(1), 28–33.

Guthrie, J.W., Craig, P., & Thompson, D. (1975). The erosion of lay control. In *Public testimony on public schools, National Committee for Citizens in Education.* Berkeley, CA: McCutchan.

Hanusheck, E.A. (1996). The quest for equalized mediocrity. In L. Picus & J. Wattenbarger (Eds.), *Where does the money go?* (pp. 20–43). Thousand Oaks, CA: Corwin Press.

Hanusheck, E.A., & Rivin, S.G. (1997). Understanding twentieth-century growth in U.S. public school spending. *Journal of Human Resources,* 32, 35–68.

Huerta, L.A., & d'Entremont, C. (2007). Education tax credits in a post-*Zelman* era. Legal, political and policy alternatives to vouchers? *Education Policy,* 21, 73–109.

Jacobs, M.J. (1980). Tuition tax credits for elementary and secondary education: Some new evidence on who would benefit. *Journal of Education Finance,* 5, 233–45.

Jefferson, T. (1976). Bill for the general diffusion of knowledge. Reprinted in J.S. Pancake (Ed.), *Thomas Jefferson, revolutionary philosopher: A selection of writings.* Rootberry, NY: Barron's.

Jencks, C., & Smith, M. (1972). *Inequality: A reassessment of the effect of family and schooling in America.* New York: Basic Books.

Jones, J.R. (1984). The role of federal government in educational policy matters: Focus on finance. *Journal of Education Finance,* 10(2), 238–55.

Karp, S. (2003, November 7). The No Child Left Behind hoax [speech]. Retrieved February 25, 2007, from http://www.rethinkingschools.org/special_reports/bushplan/hoax.shtml.

Kirp, D.L. (1982). *Just schools.* Berkeley: University of California Press.

Kirp, D.L., & Jensen, D.N. (1987). *School days, rule days: The legislation and regulation of education.* New York: Falmer Press.

Kirst, M.W. (1986) *The federal role and chapter I: Rethinking some basic assumptions.* Paper prepared for Research and Evaluation Associates, Washington, DC.

Kirst, M., & Meister, G. (1983). *The role of issue networks in state agenda setting* (Institute for Research on Educational Finance and Governance Project Report 83–80A10. Stanford, CA: Stanford University.

Knapp, M.S. (1983). Cumulative effects of federal education policies on schools and Districts: Summary report of a congressionally mandated study. Washington, DC: Department of Education.

LaMorte, M.W. (1974). The Fourteenth Amendment: Its significance for public Educators. *Educational Administration Quarterly,* 10(3), 1–19.

Marsh, E., & Gortner, R.A. (1963). *Federal aid to science education: Two programs.* Syracuse, NY: Syracuse University Press.

Mazzoni, T. (1988). The politics of educational choice in Minnesota. In W.L. Boyd & C. Kerchner (Eds.), *Politics of excellence and choice* (pp. 217–30). London: Falmer Press.

McEwan, P. (2004). The potential impact of vouchers. In A.R. Rolle (Ed.), *Peabody Journal of Education, Special Issue: K–12 Education Finance: New Directions for Future Research,* 79(3), 57–80.

Morphet, E., Johns, R.L., & Reller, T.L. (1985). *Educational organization and administration: Concepts, practices and issues.* Englewood Cliffs, NJ: Prentice-Hall.

National Center for Educational Statistics. (2003). *Federal support for education: Fiscal years 1980–2003.* Washington, DC: U.S. Department of Education.

Orfield, G. (1978). *Must we bus?* Washington, DC: Brookings Institution Press.

Pitsch, M. (1995, June 7). Goals 2000 fails to gain firm foothold. *Education Week.*

Pitsch, M. (1996, May 1). To placate conservatives, measures alter Goals 2000. *Education Week,* Retrieved February 25, 2007, from http://www.edweek.com.

Sabatier, P. (Ed.) (1999). *Theories of the policy process.* Boulder, CO: Westview Press.

Schmidt, P. (1995, October 11). Miss America's platform ruffles partisan feathers. *Education Week,* Retrieved February 25, 2007, from http://www.edweek.com.

Smith, M., & O'Day, J. (1991). *Putting the pieces together: Systemic school reform* (CPRE Policy Brief). New Brunswick, NJ: Eagleton Institute of Politics.

Walters, R. (1984). *The burden of Brown: Thirty years of school desegregation.* Knoxville, TN: University of Tennessee Press.

West, M.R., & Peterson, P.P. (2003). The politics and practice of accountability. In M. Peterson & M. West (Eds.), *No Child Left Behind? The politics and practice of accountability.* Washington, DC: Brookings Institution Press.

Whitt, E.J., Clark, D.L., & Astuto, T.A. (1986). *An analysis of public support for the educational policy preferences of the Reagan administration.* Charlottesville, VA: University Council for Educational Administration, University of Virginia.

Wildavsky, A., & Caiden, N. (2003). *The new politics of the budgetary process* (5th ed.). New York: Longman.

Wilkinson, J.H. (1976). *From* Brown v. Baake. Oxford: Oxford University Press.

Zehr, M.A. (1998, October 28). School-to-work opponents unable to block funding. *Education Week*, Retrieved February 25, 2007, from http://www.edweek.com.

Zigler, E., & Muenchow, S. (1992). *Head Start: The inside story of America's most successful experiment.* New York: Basic Books.

Notes

1. President George H.W. Bush's education legislation, America 2000, as well as President Clinton's Goals 2000 legislation were each built upon a policy foundation that included standards, testing, rewards, and sanctions. For an academic perspective on this, see Smith & O'Day (1991). See also Pitsch (1995).

2. Contemporary Americans assume the Supreme Court to be the final arbiter when the executive branch and legislative branch reach an impasse or when otherwise there is policy system gridlock. Interestingly, Baker (1947) asserted that constitutional framers did not view the Supreme Court in this overarching role. Rather, the final arbiter of decision making was seen to be citizens, not institutions.

3. Congress passed Morrill's first effort in 1858, only to be vetoed by President James Buchanan. Morrill's "reply to President's veto of Land Grant Bill" is an articulate justification of federal encouragement of education.

4. See http://www.heritage.org/Research/Education/bg1755.cfm for a summary of research. Most researchers agree at this point that Head Start imparts initial gains to poor children, but there is controversy about whether those gains continue into late elementary or middle school. See also Zigler & Muenchow (1992).

5. http://www.ed.gov/about/overview/fed/10facts/index.html.

6. For an early example of this work, see Jencks & Smith, (1972). For a more recent treatment, see Burtless (1996).
   NASDC history can be found at http://www.naschools.org/contentViewer.asp?highlightID= 6&catID=105.

7. There is a wide body of research on what is termed agenda setting at the federal level. For one overview, see Sabatier (1999). For alternatives to the "iron triangle," see Kirst & Meister (1983).

CHAPTER ELEVEN

Accounting, Auditing, and Reporting

■ INTRODUCTION

Accounting, auditing, and reporting have been associated with school business administration since its inception in the nineteenth century. Since 1990, however, the nature of these tasks has changed considerably. In their initial century-long period of development, accounting tasks were oriented to control; that is, public monies had to be accounted for to assure school district patrons that tax dollars were being spent in the proper amounts and for the proper purposes.

LEARNING OBJECTIVES

In this chapter a reader will learn about:

- The definition of and purposes served by school accounting systems.
- Background and evolution of school accounting.
- Fundamental accounting concepts and procedures.
- Significance of fund accounting.
- School accounting cycles.
- Contemporary accounting practices.
- Generally Accepted Accounting Procedures (GAAP).
- Purposes of and practices involved with audits.
- Comprehensive Annual Financial Reporting (CAFR).

More recently, since the end of the twentieth century, accounting purposes have been expanded to incorporate contemporary accountability concepts. With this additional orientation, accounting, auditing, and reporting are now used to provide necessary data and interpretation to determine costs and benefits within the financial frameworks of educational institutions.

A school business administrator employs accounting techniques to describe: (1) the nature, sources, and amounts of an institution's revenues; (2) the allocation of revenues within the institution to various programs (or funds and accounts); and (3) the actual expenditures in these programs. These data are then related to program outputs or educational outcomes, so that other district officials and citizens can understand the financial implications of program decisions and the program implications of financial decisions. In this way, district decision makers and managers, and the schools generally, are accountable to the public, and the public has information upon which it can exercise decisions in areas of financial policy.

 CASE 4 REVISITED

Teaching Harold's Pony a New Trick: The Challenge of School-Based Budgeting

The most difficult task when moving from centralized fiscal processes to school-based financial responsibility and accountability is to change attitudes as to the propriety of the move toward school-based management. The reluctance or desire of site staff to implement school-based management processes that are typically centralized will hasten or delay success and/or failure. Principals may become disgruntled and feel overwhelmed when tasked with the complexities of reporting financial data, conducting audits, and managing multiple fiscal accounts. As the district's business manager, Harold has a fiduciary duty to ensure that principals comply with appropriate accounting, auditing, and reporting standards and regulations. How can Harold assist the principals with leading an expansion of school-based fiscal management without engendering resentment or resistance? What type of staff development, mentoring, outside training, or other provisions should Harold consider utilizing to make the transition smooth?

Because of this recent and significant movement toward a program budgeting type of accountability for the public, there is now an additional level of the accounting, auditing, and reporting task: an internal accountability prerequisite to integrated and comprehensive planning.

This book promotes the planning process as a central part of education administration and planning as a team effort. Planning inputs from individual specialists within the administrative team are interactive. For example, programmatic and financial facets of a staff personnel administrator's proposal can have an effect on the proposal lodged by the administrator in charge of instruction. There must be a timely flow of accurate and appropriate information within the planning team. Each member is accountable to the team in order that individual plans and specific proposals can coalesce into an integrated educational program, which, in turn, can be proposed to and evaluated by the public.

School policymakers and administrators have responded to the public demand for accountability not only by implementing program-oriented accounting systems, but also by decentralizing educational policymaking and administration. The major vehicle used to accomplish decentralized administration is a greater site-based orientation, described in previous chapters. This concept requires the implementation of an accounting system that provides budgeting, revenue, expenditure, and accounting data at the level of the building or operating unit. These data are necessary for effective planning of the operation of the program as well as for holding the staff and administrators accountable for decisions delegated to them.

Thus, school accounting is manifest in several ways and places throughout the school system. It is an important means of providing vital information for districtwide as well as site- or building-level financial decisions. It is crucial in providing a structure for holding the institution as well as specific policymakers and administrators accountable for their decisions and performance. Lastly, school accounting is an important vehicle for providing information to the public to use in formulating basic policy or responses to specific ballot issues pertaining to the school operation.

■ SCHOOL ACCOUNTING: A DEFINITION

> *School accounting has been defined as: . . . recording and reporting activities and events affecting personnel, facilities, materials, or money of an administrative unit and its programs. Specifically, accounting is concerned with determining what financial records are to be maintained, how and by what officer they will be maintained, and the procedures, methods, and forms to be used; recording, classifying, and summarizing activities or events; analyzing and interpreting recorded data; and preparing and issuing reports and statements that reflect conditions as of a given date, the results of operations for a specific period, and the evaluation of status and results of operations in terms of established objectives.* (Adams, Hill, Lichtenberger, Perkins, & Shaw, 1967, p. 260)

Several components of this definition deserve to be highlighted.

First, accounting deals with activities and events that affect both operational inputs (money, material) and the school's program.

Second, the process of accounting incorporates acts of recording, classifying, analyzing, and interpreting data.

A third concept expressed in the definition is that of recording conditions as of a given date and the evaluation of the status and results of operations in terms of established objectives.

From this definition and these conceptual characteristics it is apparent that the accounting function is an integral part of the planning process employed by the educational team.

■ SCHOOL ACCOUNTING PURPOSES

Accounting serves several purposes in schools. Among the most important are:

- Maintaining an accurate record of significant details of the business transactions of the school system.
- Providing a basis and medium for planning and decision making by both policymaking and administrative bodies at local, state, and federal levels.
- Providing a control mechanism to ensure appropriate use of resources in the educational enterprise.
- Expediting the process of setting priorities; establishing, analyzing, and selecting alternatives in the budgeting process; and establishing an operational blueprint for the school system.

- Providing a medium for reporting financial conditions to patrons of the school district as well as to other constituents and agencies at the local, state, and federal levels. This is done for purposes of planning and policymaking, accountability, control, and comparative study.
- Providing basic information to calculate and extend school district budgets, tax levies, and state and federal subventions or transfer payments.

■ EMERGENCE OF SCHOOL ACCOUNTING SYSTEMS

School accounting had its genesis in public accounting, which, in turn, sprang from business accounting. Thus, several basic principles of the latter can be appropriately used to design or evaluate accounting systems to be used in public schools. A primary difference between public school accounting and business accounting (other than the absence of a profit seeking in public-sector endeavors) is the presence of legal restrictions or controls on the sources and procedures for obtaining revenue for public education and on the purposes and processes for expending those revenues.

Fiscal controls placed on the school district by state government typically limit revenues to taxation, gifts, tuition, fines, fees, and transfer payments from state and federal governments. In many instances, specific controls are specified in state laws. Strict control over expenditures tends to be the rule rather than the exception in most states. For example, in some states, teachers' salaries may not be paid unless a valid teaching certificate is on file, in the appropriate school district office, for any individual on the professional payroll; or public monies may not be expended for paying the moving expenses of the superintendent.

States exercise their plenary legal authority over the school districts as quasi-corporations by specifying the accounting and other fiscal procedures to be used. Typically, states require a public school fund accounting system; all districts in a state conform to a common financial recording system with common funds, accounts, definitions, and procedures. Usually, a series of funds are established, including discrete sources of revenue to be used for specified purposes with each fund typically a unique entity. Within each fund, the uniform accounting laws typically provide for a group of accounts that define, as legal restrictions, those transactions that may be made within the given fund. For example, in Ohio the expenditure for replacing a computer used for instruction must be charged to the 740 account—equipment replacement—in the general fund. However, purchase of an additional computer to be used for instruction in a new school built with monies from a bond issue must be charged to the building fund—account 640, equipment.

School accounting systems, with their rather rigid state controls, serve another major purpose. The designation of funds and the construction of school budgets around the funds provide the baseline decisions and information needed to determine tax rates. In many states, public officials or agencies empowered to levy taxes, use these financial data to designate required tax rates that in turn, are extended by the tax department in the appropriate jurisdiction. For example, three basic property tax levies are calculated in Ohio: the current operating levy (required by the general fund budget), the bond retirement levy (required to finance debt service), and the permanent improvement levy (for financing capital improvements with current revenue).

■ BASIC CONCEPTS IN SCHOOL ACCOUNTING SYSTEMS

The craft of accounting comprises an organized body of knowledge and an orderly application of procedures. Three basic concepts are used in the accounting function in public school systems. School personnel with responsibility for general and fiscal policy decisions and those with responsibility for executing them must apply the concepts in order to utilize the information resources afforded by an accounting system. Frequently, specific terms used in an accounting context carry meanings quite different from those used (or misused) in lay language.

The Accounting Equation

The first concept is related to describing an organization's financial status at a given moment. *What a school system or an individual is worth is equal to what is owned minus what is owed.* The basic accounting equation is stated as:

$$Owned - Owed = Net\ Worth$$

Accounting terminology translates the equation by substituting standardized terms.

- Assets are things owned.
- Liabilities are things owed.
- Equity is the difference between things owned and things owed, and, thus, equates with net worth. When applied to school accounting, the term fund balance is used.

Thus, the equation becomes:

$$Assets - Liabilities = Equity$$

If a school system has $500,000 in its bank account and owes $450,000 for teachers' salaries, its equity equals $50,000. The equation can be stated in several different forms with the preceding example:

$$Assets = Liabilities + Equity$$
$$(\$500,000 = \$450,000 + \$50,000\ or\ \$500,000)$$

$$Liabilities = Assets - Equity$$
$$(\$450,000 = \$500,000 - \$50,000\ or\ \$450,000)$$

$$Equity = Assets - Liabilities$$
$$(\$50,000 = \$500,000 - \$450,000\ or\ \$50,000\ )$$

Because the accounting equation is an algebraic expression, it can be added to or subtracted from, provided the same amount is added to or subtracted from both sides of the equation.

In the following example, suppose that the school system increased its assets by $100,000.

Using the equation Assets = Liabilities + Equity, assets would be increased by $100,000, so it would be necessary to add $100,000 to the other side of the equation. The actions and reactions of adding to or subtracting from any of the elements of the equation are governed by the following concepts:

- One asset can be increased, while another can be decreased by an equal amount. Invested funds, for example, can be converted to cash. Thus, the amount of assets remains the same, although investment assets decrease and cash assets increase.
- An asset can be increased, while a liability is increased by an equal amount. Material that was ordered has been received, but has not yet been paid for. The assets have been increased by the value of the material, but the liabilities have been likewise increased because the school system now owes the vendor for the material.
- An asset can be increased, while equity is increased by an equal amount. Fines, charges, and gifts received increase assets and, at the same time, increase the school system's equity.
- A liability can be increased, while another can be decreased by an equal amount.
- Money can be borrowed to pay a vendor's bill.

It must be recognized that changes in the equation may be made in combinations of the preceding actions and reactions, because a single transaction may result in several simultaneous changes.

Because school accounting involves the reporting and recording of activities and events affecting the school system over a period of time, it is essential that the ongoing and changing financial condition be recorded. Therefore, it is necessary to introduce a dynamic character or capability into the accounting system. This is accomplished by adding two elements to the basic accounting equation:

$$Assets = Liabilities + Fund\ Balance + Revenues - Expenditures$$

Revenues result from transactions that increase assets without increasing liabilities or from transactions that decrease liabilities. Revenue increases eventually increase fund balance. Typical revenue transactions are receipts of local property taxes, state subsidies, and grants or gifts. Monies obtained from a loan or a bond issue are not revenues, as they entail the creation of a liability in that they must be repaid.

Expenditures result from transactions that decrease assets and fund balance or that increase liability and fund balance. Typical expenditure transactions are the many expenses of conducting the educational program: teachers' salaries, instructional supplies and equipment, support services, and supplies. Payment of a loan is not considered an expense, as it decreases liability and assets but fund balance remains the same.

■ THE ACCOUNTING PROCESS

The financial status of a school system changes as it transacts business that effects changes in its accounting equation. It is these transactions that are recorded, classified, and summarized in the accounting process. Transactions are originally recorded in a journal, and, from it, are posted to accounts. Accounts are established for each asset and liability and for

ASSETS		= LIABILITIES	+	FUND BALANCE	+	REVENUES		− EXPENDITURES	
Debit	Credit	Debit	Credit	Debit	Credit	Debit	Credit	Debit	Credit
Increase	Decrease	Decrease	Increase	Decrease	Increase	Decrease	Increase	Increase	Decrease

FIGURE 11.1 T Accounts for the School Fund Accounting Equation

equity. Because of the unique nature of school district accounting specified by individual states that mandate discrete funds and accounts, public school system accounting procedures use the term fund balance rather than equity.

Accounts reflecting the action and reaction of the several transactions are commonly known as T accounts. The concept of debits and credits is built around the way data are recorded in each account. The left side of the T account is the debit side, while the right is the credit side. (See Figure 11.1.)

The derivation of the words debit and credit in the accounting context can provide an important insight into this concept. Tidwell (1974) states:

> The Latin word debeo means "owe." The history of the use of this word as it applies to accounting began when the only transactions necessary to be recorded were those with customers or suppliers. A charge against a person who owes appears on the left side of the account with that person. The left side of the account is the "debit" side.
>
> The Latin word credo means, "trust," or "believe." The history of this word as it applies to accounting began at the same time as the word debit. The amount shown as owed to a person who trusts us appears on the right side of the account, which is referred to as the credit side. (p. 35)

To keep accounts in balance, or to maintain the accounting equation, there must be an equal use of debits and credits for each transaction. As indicated earlier, a single transaction might have two or more debits and two or more credits. However, the total amount of debits must still equal the total amount of credits. In a series of transactions, the total debits must be equal to the total credits. The fact that the accounts are self-balancing through equal entry of both debits and credits identifies such a system as double-entry bookkeeping.

An application of the concepts of the accounting equation and double-entry bookkeeping with debits and credits can be illustrated in a simple example.

A school district has a balance of $100,000 when it opens its books at the beginning of the fiscal year. Over a period of time during the school year, it completes a series of transactions, and they are to be recorded in the accounting system. In chronological order, the opening balance and succeeding transactions are:

1. $100,000 in the opening balance is recorded.
2. $500,000 in local taxes is received.
3. $450,000 is paid for teachers' salaries.
4. $1,000,000 is borrowed from a local bank.
5. $100,000 in supplies is ordered and received from a vendor.
6. $150,000 is paid for salaries of noncertificated personnel.

	ASSETS =		LIABILITIES +		FUND BALANCE +		REVENUES –		EXPENDITURES	
	Debit	Credit	Debit	Credit	Debit	Credit	Debit	Credit	Debit	Credit
	Increase	Decrease	Decrease	Increase	Decrease	Increase	Decrease	Increase	Increase	Decrease
(1)	100,000					100,000				
(2)	500,000							500,000		
(3)		450,000							450,000	
(4)	1,000,000			1,000,000						
(5)	100,000			100,000						
(6)		150,000							150,000	
(7)		100,000							100,000	
(8)	500,000							500,000		
(9)		1,000,500	1,000,500							
	2,200,000	1,700,500	1,000,500	1,100,000		100,000		1,000,000	700,000	

FIGURE 11.2 Illustration of the Application of the Accounting Equation and Double-Entry Bookkeeping

7. $100,000 is paid to vendor for supplies.
8. $500,000 in state aid is received.
9. $1,000,500 in principal and interest on loan is repaid.

These transactions would be recorded as shown in Figure 11.2.

Opening balance (1): $100,000, so Assets are debited and Fund Balance is credited.

Transaction (2): The school system receives $500,000 in taxes, so Assets are increased by a debit and Revenue is increased by a credit.

Transaction (3): The school system pays $450,000 in teachers' salaries, so Assets are decreased by a credit and Expenditures are increased by a debit.

Transaction (4): The school system borrows $1,000,000 from a local bank, so Assets are increased by a debit and Liabilities are increased by a credit.

Transaction (5): The school system orders and receives a $100,000 purchase of supplies from a vendor, so Assets are increased by a debit and Liabilities are increased by a credit.

Transaction (6): The school system pays $150,000 in salaries for classified personnel, so Assets are decreased by a credit and Expenditures are increased by a debit.

Transaction (7): The school system pays $100,000 to the vendor for the supplies previously ordered and received, so Assets are decreased by a credit and Expenditures are increased by a debit.

Transaction (8): The school system received $500,000 in state aid, so Assets are increased by a debit and Revenues are increased by a credit.

Transaction (9): The school system pays $1,000,500 in principal and interest on the $1,000,000 borrowed previously, so Assets are decreased by a credit and Liabilities are increased by a debit.

To be certain that transactions have been properly analyzed and recorded, and that debits and credits have been equally applied, a trial balance is calculated.

■ SCHOOL FUND ACCOUNTING AND OPERATION

Accounting in public schools employs basic concepts in common with private-sector accounting. However, given the mission of the public schools and the statutory constraints and directives applied to them, the accounting procedures diverge somewhat from private-sector practices. Sources and levels of revenue for the schools are relatively fixed by law and tax administration practices. Expenditures are likewise controlled. Thus, public schools use "fund accounting" that designates several funds, each having its own discrete purpose and appropriate expenditures and its own discrete source of revenues. Public school accounting is built around separate accounting systems for each fund. Most states have a fund for current operations—variously termed educational, general—for teachers' salaries, instructional materials, and so forth. Similarly, many states designate a building or capital outlay fund for fixed assets, such as site, buildings, and equipment. Bond funds are established to pay principal and interest on school bonds that have been floated. Each of the separate funds is a separate accounting entity.

The remainder of the discussion on accounting is devoted to an examination of how the accounting process is applied. It is built around the business administrator's responsibility for and in the accounting cycle.

Everett, Lowes, and Johnson (1996) identify ten basic steps in the cycle:

1. Journalize transactions.
2. Post transactions.
3. Prepare a trial balance.
4. Prepare a worksheet.
5. Prepare financial statements.
6. Journalize closing entries.
7. Post closing entries.
8. Balance, rule, and bring forward balances of balance sheet accounts.
9. Rule temporary accounts.
10. Prepare post-closing trial balance. (p. 17)

While monitoring accounting responsibilities, a school business administrator must adhere to legal mandates and constraints. States usually exercise their plenary authority in requiring an accounting for school district resources by specifying the data, forms, and procedures to be used; and by assigning individuals fixed responsibilities in accounting and related functions. In many states, these functions involve responsibilities shared among superintendents, boards of education (or their counterparts) or board secretaries, treasurers, clerks, school business administrators, and other local or state officials or agencies. Thus, it is extremely important that job expectations and working relationships be constructed carefully and clearly to avoid confusion, role conflict, and muddled role expectation.

The movement toward site-based management (with budgeting, purchasing, and accounting responsibilities given to principals and directors of various discrete operating programs) highlights the problems of clarifying responsibilities and fixing accountability. Administrators in these kinds of centers have had decision-making authority delegated to them. It is necessary not only to clarify this authority and accountability, but also to relate it to the rest of the system. Thus, the decentralized accounting mechanism for a given cost center must be an integral part of the accounting machinery of the whole school system.

Program-oriented budgeting and accounting systems have been developed with this capability. Funds and accounts can be disaggregated such that appropriations and expenditures can be identified by programs, courses, teachers, and objects in a given building or cost center. The major point is this: If management of educational programs is site based, the accounting system likewise must be site based.

The accounting challenge is not met simply by a precise set of job descriptions and elaborate computer software. Ongoing working relationships must be developed and maintained if the organization so necessary for effective school fund accounting is to function. Accurate and reliable accounting data must be accompanied by an integrated decision-making system acting on the data. Site-based accounting data and decisions must be related to central administration and board of education accounting data and decisions. Thus, all levels must see the larger scene as well as that scene in which they play. Unfortunately, in the past many principals knew little of fund accounting and how accounting-based decisions impacted their roles.

■ THE ACCOUNTING CYCLE

Several discrete and sequential steps characterize the accounting process.

Initiating Transactions

The accounting cycle begins with the initiation of a financial transaction. This may occur in many different sectors of the school system. It may be the certification that taxes are to be collected, the consummation of a contract for construction of a building, or a teacher's requisition for art paper. In most systems, this latter type of transaction is the most prevalent.

The approval procedure for requisitions is usually a local administrative decision of which the business administrator must be knowledgeable. When the approved requisition data are committed to a purchase order, the school system becomes liable for its payment. Many state-mandated accounting systems require that funds be encumbered, or "earmarked," to pay this obligation, and, thus, subtracted from an asset account. When a school system recognizes revenues as soon as it gains a right to them and recognizes an expenditure as soon as liability occurs, the system may be said to use an accrual basis of accounting, rather than a cash basis, the latter records only financial transactions involving cash receipts and disbursements.[1]

Thus, the encumbering process finalizes the contracting or purchasing act and initiates the accounting act by providing the document and data for the journal, a book of original entry in the accounting process. The contract or purchase order becomes a voucher, a business document that provides evidence of a business transaction.

Journalizing Transactions

The accounting office continuously gathers all vouchers generated by a school system. These are analyzed in terms of debits and credits, and are recorded in the general journal. This volume of original entry records all transactions in chronological order (hence, the term journal). Specific data on each page of the general journal include the date of the transaction, the specific accounts affected by the transaction, an explanation of the transaction, the posting reference, which indicates the specific location of the posting in the ledger(s) and debits and credits to all accounts affected by the transaction. The concept of debits and credits discussed earlier is applicable to the general journal as well as to ledgers of the several different accounts.

After the opening entries have been recorded in the general journal, they are posted to the appropriate accounts in the general ledger. The general journal entries include the date, account identification, explanation, posting reference (the account number in the general ledger where the transaction will be posted), and whether the entry is a debit or a credit.

The General Ledger

A ledger is a group of accounts. All asset, liability, expenditure, revenue, and fund balance accounts comprise the general ledger. In practice, the simplistic examples of accounting concepts presented earlier have given way to more complex forms of recording and analyzing these data. The asset account in the accounting equation has been replaced by a whole series of asset accounts including cash, taxes receivable, and revenue receivable from various local, state, and federal sources. Liability accounts can run literally into the hundreds in some states. Equity, or fund balance, accounts are used in each individual fund of the accounting system and reflect differences between current assets and current liabilities in these individual accounts.

Revenue and expenditure accounts were originally created to reflect a unique feature of governmental and school district accounting. Because revenues available to school systems are relatively fixed through local property tax levies, state aid appropriations, and rather predictable amounts of other income, and because there are rigorous state controls over expenditures, it is both possible and necessary to build in safeguards for raising and expending school system monies. Two related types of accounts that assist in financial planning are known as revenue and expenditure summary accounts.

These summary accounts and their functions are:

- Estimated Revenue Summary: summarizes all revenue estimated to accrue during the given fiscal year.
- Revenue Summary: summarizes all revenue actually received.
- Appropriations Summary: summarizes the total amount appropriated by the board, including authorization of fixed amounts for specific purposes during the given fiscal year.
- Expenditure Summary: summarizes all expenditures incurred, including those paid and unpaid, that result in benefits enjoyed during the given fiscal year.
- Encumbrances: summarizes all encumbrances that are chargeable to and included in an appropriation for the given fiscal year.

Revenue and expenditure summary accounts provide a school administrator with information on the nature and amount of expenditures established in the appropriations, the nature and amount of expenditures to date, and the nature and amount of expenditures that are not yet encumbered. Revenue and expenditure summary accounts provide important planning tools for the school business administrator.

Posting the General Ledger

Transactions entered in the general journal are posted to the appropriate accounts in the general ledger. This process brings together or summarizes all similar accounts. The general ledger is comprised of individual accounts. Each account incorporates data regarding its designation (cash, accounts receivable, and so forth), its account number (usually the state-mandated code or classification system), date of the transaction, explanation, the posting reference (designation of page or electronic location of the transaction in the general journal), and the designation as to whether the transaction was a debit or credit to the particular account (same designation given the transaction in the general journal).

Recording Budgets and Appropriations

At or near the beginning of the fiscal year, school systems adopt budgets and appropriations for operations during the coming fiscal year. These basic financial decisions are transactions and must be recorded. The appropriation is used to establish estimated revenues and expenditures. These data are entered in the general journal and general ledger in a fashion similar to the entries that originally opened the books. The journal entry account title in the operating or current expense fund would be "Estimated Revenue" and would be a debit amount. The equal credit amount would carry the title "Fund Balance."

When the general journal entries for estimated revenue are posted to the general ledger, the same account titles and debit and credit assignments are entered as were entered in the general journal. Subsidiary ledger forms for the revenue ledger include account descriptions and numbers for each of the several revenue sources. Estimated expenditures or appropriations are entered in a similar fashion.

Recording Transactions

The preceding sections covered the principles of accounting, how the books are opened, and how budgets and appropriations are recorded. The latter two functions are performed only once each year to prepare for the entry of the normal daily transactions.

Processing Accounting Data

Manual, machine, and electronic data processing have all been used in accounting systems in recent years. The basic principles of school accounting apply, however, in any of these. The latter two types of processing have advantages over manual accounting in terms of speed, multiple use of a given entry, and mechanical or electronic reliability.

Accounting machines are frequently used in small school systems. Through the use of carbons, multiple carriages, and the like, a few well-trained people can maintain relatively complex accounting systems. Larger school systems generally rely upon online computer-based accounting systems with capabilities for numerous and complex accounting functions.

In the News

An examination of the Yonkers beleaguered school system exposed a sluggish, paper intensive bureaucracy prone to unnecessary spending, sloppy recordkeeping and inadequate oversight, according to the results of an independent audit.

The Board of Education, which manages the school district, the state's fourth largest, still does most of its business on paper, registering each purchase and personnel transaction in forms that are kept in binders and cabinets, essentially within anyone's reach, the audit says. The few functions that are automated rely on a system so obsolete that its files cannot be read by today's computers.

Yonkers schools, which have been undercut by perennial budgetary woes, a bitter desegregation battle, cronyism and scandal, have had little opportunity to update or modernize the system. Like New York's other major cities, Yonkers finances its public schools through the city budget, not through property tax levies, and year after year there is a push and pull between parents and educators on one side and city officials on the other about how much to spend on education.

Workers use index cards to track everything from inventory to vacation, overtime and sick days for the schools' 3,800 employees, and must fill out cumbersome forms every time someone is hired, fired, transferred or suspended. The forms are passed from person to person until they reach the one in charge of entering the information into the payroll system, a process fraught with opportunities for error and fraud.

The audit was commissioned by Mayor Philip A. Amicone. "All of this is aimed at one result: improving our system and providing our system with accountability," Mayor Amicone said at a news conference. "There has to be accountability for the taxpayers, and there has to be accountability for the children. They need to know, and their parents need to know, that the money that should go into teaching is going into teaching and is not being wasted in unnecessary administrative costs."

What auditors found was a system that was hard to supervise, since it was nearly impossible for anyone to promptly obtain and share information. Further, important decisions and projects were bound to be delayed because workers gave every transaction equal weight, regardless of complexity, urgency or cost, the auditors concluded.

Because the school district relies heavily on paper, about 40 percent of its operating costs pay for the time supervisors spend correcting the mistakes that inevitably show up in many of the forms they review, the audit says. Besides, policies intended to provide checks and balances are not followed, mostly because the process is too difficult. "The system needs a complete overhaul," Mr. Badillo, supervisor of the audit, said, calling for more internal controls. "There is, of course, a lack of technology in the whole process," he added.

It is hard to tell how much money has been wasted by the schools over the years, in part because it is unclear how many of the school district's employees were doing duplicate work or handling jobs that could have been performed with the push of a button. Auditors estimate that the Board of Education could save up to $13 million by becoming computerized. With that, a staff reduction will be inevitable, but the mayor said he hopes to achieve it through attrition rather than layoffs. A second audit of the Board of Education, by the state's comptroller, is under way.

From: Santos, F. (2006, April 7). Audit calls Yonkers school system archaic. *The New York Times*, p. 3. Copyright © 2006 The New York Times Co. Reprinted with permission.

■ SCHOOL ACCOUNTING IN CONTEMPORARY PRACTICE

Observers of contemporary school accounting readily note marked contrasts between concept and practice. These differences are due to the use of simplistic examples to convey an abstract concept—for example, use of T accounts to show relationships between and among debits and credits and among assets and liabilities. In contemporary practice, T accounts are not used in school fund accounting. Instead, state-mandated accounting systems have tended to be single-entry cash accounting systems with required encumbrance procedures. Often they were built around state-mandated line-item budgeting systems. However, change is increasingly apparent in both state and school system procedures.

Many states have integrated mandated or permissive program-oriented budgeting systems into their required accounting systems for school districts. This not only reflects good management techniques, but also attempts to improve fiscal and management accountability to school decision makers and administrators and the publics they serve.

Contemporary budgeting practices include the movement from line-item to program-oriented budgeting. Generally speaking, spending budgets are developed around the basic funds, and, within each fund, major program areas are identified. In the Ohio school accounting system, for example, the general fund contains major functions (program areas) that include instruction, supporting services, community services, extracurricular services, nonprogrammed charges (payments to other governmental units), contingencies and inter-fund transfers, and other functions. Subsets of instruction are regular instruction (elementary, middle/junior high school, high school, other regular), special instruction (e.g., academically gifted, mentally retarded, physically disabled), vocational, adult/continuing, and other instruction (Montgomery, 2005). All funds and functions within each fund reflect similar breakdowns into smaller units of school system programs.

Within each function, objects of expenditures are classified. Major objects are employees' salaries and wages, employees' retirement and insurance benefits, purchased services, supplies and materials, capital outlay, capital outlay-replacement, and other objects. Each object is further specified. For example, supplies and materials subsets include general supplies; textbooks; library books, periodicals, newspapers, films, and filmstrips; food and related supplies and materials; supplies and materials for operation, maintenance, and repair; supplies and materials for operation and repair of motor vehicles; and other supplies and materials.

Contemporary program-oriented accounting systems often must accommodate site-based management, budgeting, and accounting. This is done through the inclusion of the operational unit or cost center in the accounting systems. Transactions are attributed to the appropriate administrative unit in the school system. Many transactions occur at the districtwide level: for example, collection of taxes, salary contracts for the superintendent and others who serve districtwide concerns, and liability insurance. Some transactions may be attributed to a given division or department (e.g., pupil transportation, teaching personnel), while others may be attributed to a given school. Thus, the accounting system attributes each transaction to one (or more) cost center. Individual school systems assign code numbers to each cost center.

Special cost centers have been designated as special projects and are often supported by restricted monies that are earmarked and must be accounted for separately from the more general programs of the school system.

Beyond operational units and cost centers, even greater detail is provided when subject areas and subsets thereof are identified. This permits an expenditure to be traced not only to a given school, but also to a given subject taught in a specific school and at a given instructional level.

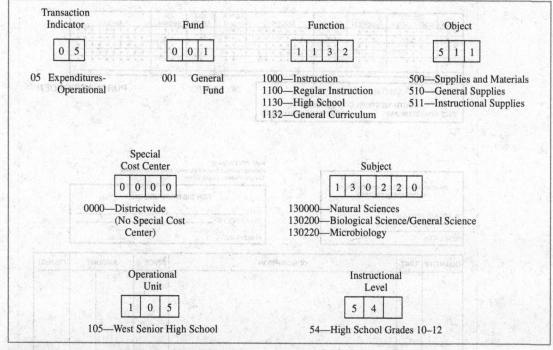

FIGURE 11.3 Coding an Expenditure Transaction

For example, in contemporary practice, when Mr. Jones, a West Senior High School microbiology teacher, requisitions and receives a set of microscope slides for his class, the accounting system will ask:

1. What kind of transaction is this?
2. What fund is affected?
3. What function does it meet?
4. What kind of object is it?
5. Is it in a special cost center?
6. What is its subject?
7. To which operational unit should it be attributed?
8. To what instructional level should it be attributed?

Using the example of the Ohio accounting system and the purchase of the microscope slides, the transaction for budgeting, purchasing, and accounting purposes is illustrated in Figure 11.3.

A similar logic is applied to other school system transactions. In receipts, each transaction is identified (various revenue sources), the fund affected is designated, the function of the receipt is coded, and the designation is made, if it is appropriate, to special cost centers, subjects, or operational units.

Full implementation of this kind of accounting system provides a relatively detailed picture of how revenues flow into the several programs and how they are expended

FUND	SPECIAL COST CENTER	FUNCTION	OBJECT	SUBJECT	OPER. UNIT	INST. LEVEL	JOB ASSIGN.	AMOUNT
: :	: : :	: : :	: :	: : : : : : :	: :	:	: :	: : : : : : : : :
: :	: : :	: : :	: :	: : : : : : :	: :	:	: :	: : : : : : : : :
: :	: : :	: : :	: :	: : : : : : :	: :	:	: :	: : : : : : : : :
: :	: : :	: : :	: :	: : : : : : :	: :	:	: :	: : : : : : : : :

SEND ALL INVOICES TO:

SOUTH-WESTERN CITY SCHOOLS
2975 KINGSTON AVE.   GROVE CITY, OHIO 43123

DELIVER TO: **PURCHASE ORDER**

TO:

SHIP PREPAID – VIA:
Material on this order is Exempted from the Ohio Sales
Tax and Federal Excise Taxes.

Numbers listed BELOW are required on all invoices for payment.

PURCHASE ORDER NO.

VENDOR No.

FOR DISTRICT USE ONLY

DATE _____
REQUESTED BY _____
FUNC./SUBJ.   INSTR. LEVEL

QUANTITY	UNIT	DESCRIPTION	PRICE @	AMOUNT	OBJECT

TERMS OR CONDITIONS: Time of delivery is of the essence of this contract. Buyer reserves the right to refuse any goods and to cancel all or any part of this order if seller fails to deliver all or any part of the goods in accordance with the terms of this order. This contract may not be modified or terminated orally, and no modification or termination, nor any claimed waiver of any of the provisions hereof shall be binding unless in writing and signed by the party against whom such modification, termination or waiver is sought to be enforced, and by the treasurer of the School District who shall affix a new certificate to such contract by reason of such change. **PLEASE ACKNOWLEDGE RECEIPT AND ACCEPTANCE OF THIS ORDER.**

TREASURER'S CERTIFICATE
It is hereby certified that the amount required to meet the contract, agreement, obligation, payment or expenditure for the above has been lawfully appropriated or authorized or directed for such purpose and is in the treasury or in process of collection to the credit of the fund free from any obligation or certification now outstanding.

_____
Treasurer, Board of Education

THE BOARD OF EDUCATION
South-Western City Schools

By _____
          Purchasing Agent
THE ORDER IS VOID UNLESS TREASURER'S CERTIFICATE IS SIGNED

FIGURE 11.4 Purchase Order

Courtesy of South-Western City School District, Grove City, Ohio.

in each. The specific processes of implementation are spelled out in the following description of the accounting procedures employed by a forward-looking school system of approximately 18,000 pupils.

The principal requisitioning materials for a given educational program initiate a typical transaction. The teacher who originated the request determines the item and price per unit from a vendor's catalog, and the quantity needed. The principal approves the request, giving consideration to its educational merit and the building's program allocation for such materials for that year. The combination requisition-purchase order form is completed, and the principal fills in the code number that reflects the planning, programming, budgeting, evaluation system (PPBES) accounting classification. (See Figure 11.4.)

If approved, the business administrator signs the purchase order as purchasing agent, assigns a purchase order number, selects a vendor (if none was designated on the requisition), and submits the document to the chief fiscal officer. Increasingly, all of the above functions are undertaken electronically, online, within the framework of a school district's automated and real-time accounting system.

At this point, the data describing the transaction are fed into the computer for verification. The computer program classifies transactions by codes, and, thus, compares unencumbered balances in a given account for the given building with the amount of the purchase order. If the computer program identifies an error (e.g., wrong coding, insufficient unencumbered balances), an error is indicated and corrections must be made before the order is submitted to the chief fiscal officer for his or her approval.

The chief fiscal officer's function is to sign the purchase order. By law, this obligates the district, and the computer encumbers the funds necessary to satisfy the contract with the vendor.

In this particular district, cash balances are deposited in several banks according to transaction codes. Bank balances and fund balances are automatically adjusted to reflect each approved transaction.

Up to this point in the accounting process, financial transactions have been reported (requisitions and purchase orders) and recorded (from the documents into the computer). A first step in the classification function has already taken place with the encoding of each transaction (date, purchase order number, fund, account, building, program object, and the like). The following steps illustrate how the computer further classifies, analyzes, summarizes, and reports the financial condition of the school district. (See Figure 11.5.)

Journalizing

With the data from transactions (requisitions and purchase orders in the example) stored in the computer memory unit, the accounting steps can be initiated. The program determines the way in which the data are processed. Because each program is discrete, no particular sequence of programs is necessary to complete the accounting process. However, in order to follow the logical sequence of steps described earlier, the initial step of journalizing is described.

Several programs produce reports that equate with the general journal. A Daily Audit Report displays each transaction in sequence by date. The Cash Disbursement Journal displays all the cash disbursements in daily sequence. The Purchase Order Update Report is a journal that reflects the daily aggregations of descriptions and amounts of purchase orders. The computer program in the example district has the capability of combining payment for several purchase orders to a single vendor into one check, thereby reducing

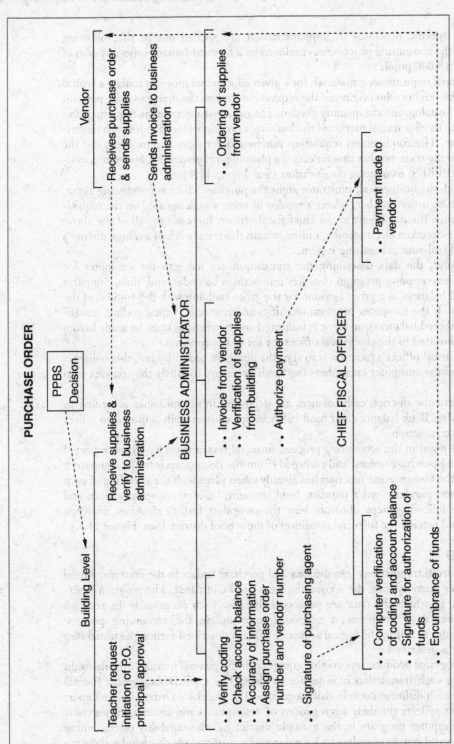

FIGURE 11.5 Purchase Order Flowchart

Courtesy of South-Western City School District, Grove City, Ohio.

the overhead costs of multiple checks to one vendor. The journals serve the function of reporting the daily sequence of transactions and take the form of computer printouts that can be aggregated for weekly, monthly, or yearly reports. The data from the journals are used to create the several ledgers used by the school district. The posting process (taking data from the journal and classifying and recording them in the ledger) is accomplished by the computer to produce various ledgers.

The General Ledger

The format of the ledgers generated by this particular accounting system reflects both state mandates and the unique needs of the school district. A computer printout provides the status of each fund and each account maintained by the school district. Specific data for each include the original appropriation, adjusted appropriation, year-to-date expenditures, unexpended balances, outstanding encumbrances, and unencumbered balances. These same data should be presented monthly to the board of education as part of the monthly financial report.

A second, but usually optional, general ledger classifies the same data by a program budget classification system developed by the district. This ledger shows the financial status by programs and cost centers (individual buildings). Modifications of this second general ledger can provide reports used by building principals and administrators of other cost centers.

Because the data fed into a computer include disbursements as well as purchase orders, checks to vendors are produced in a process parallel to the accounting process. Reports on checks issued include the check register which reflects the vendor, the check number, accounting codes, and amount.

The Cash Position Report is used in this chapter's illustrative district for purposes of cash-flow management. When checks are written and cash is received, the cash position of the district changes. The report reflects these changes and is thus considered a form of cash journal. Data on each fund include balances, cash disbursements, funds available, interim funds (which may be invested), and active funds (which may not be invested). Printouts of these data provide the bases for short-term investments. The report also reconciles cash-flow data with the amounts on deposit in each bank.

Balancing the Books

Balancing never stops. The function of balancing is a recurring activity as the accounting process progresses. By virtue of electronic verification and retrieval, a full range of balances can be programmed into the process. If imbalances or errors occur, the computer either rejects the transaction or records it on a special report. An example of the latter type is the Invoice Update Report, which provides a daily summary of all invoices. If negative balances emerge, adjustments in appropriations may be made.

Another example is the Invoice Validation Report that designates, on a printout, all instances in which vendors submit invoices in absence of, or at variance with, an original purchase order. This is particularly useful when partial payments are made on partial orders. The faulty invoice is rejected, and the business office can then initiate the audit trail to resolve the problem.

Each of the reports derived from the journals and ledgers contains balances such as cash, fund, and account balances—encumbered and unencumbered, daily, month-to-date, and year-to-date balances.

Generally Accepted Accounting Procedures

One of the obvious weaknesses in the above-described modified cash accounting system is that it concentrates only upon current assets and liabilities. The cries for reform in education have included accountability, but are usually limited to educational results and spending decisions. Only recently have states concluded that school systems should incorporate accrual accounting into their programs. Thus, long-term assets and liabilities should be reflected in accounting systems. Modified cash accounting does not accommodate the liabilities of a multiyear teachers' salary agreement, depreciation of capital, or an early retirement incentive program. It does not accommodate investment interest earned beyond the current year, long-term debt, or the value of investments.

An alternative or supplementary accounting procedure has been put in place in some states and school districts to remedy this weakness. Generally accepted accounting procedures (GAAP) have had a long and rich evolution in terms of the application to school accounting. Its chronology has been summarized by Bernard F. Gatti. He gave prominence to the report *Governmental Accounting, Auditing, and Financial Reporting* published by the National Council on Governmental Accounting in 1968, which specified generally accepted accounting procedures for state and local governments and ". . . defined the modified accrual basis of accounting and included a model financial statement reporting format, the initial version of the Comprehensive Annual Financial Report (CAFR)" (Gatti, 1987, p. 43).

The Revenue Sharing Act of 1972 provided substantial impetus for GAAP because recipients of these revenues were required to use a uniform accounting system mandated by the federal government. Since then, many agencies have developed specific accounting standards that, in turn, have been reviewed for approval by various governmental and professional organizations. Generally accepted accounting procedures provide for the establishment of fixed asset records, maintaining accurate inventory records, selecting an auditing firm, and completing a series of specific tasks.

An abbreviated description of the groups of tasks includes:

- Cash and investment detail with budgetary and bank reconciliations.
- Receivables such as taxes, accounts, and intergovernmental transfers.
- Prepaid expenses such as insurance premiums.
- Inventory and its valuation.
- Fixed assets, including general accrued wages, pension benefits, workers' compensation, and accounts payable.
- Long-term liabilities, including note indebtedness, bond indebtedness, bond and coupon account reconciliation, capital leases, claims and judgments, and compensated services.
- Budgetary presentations, including review of budgeted revenues and appropriations prior to year-end, fund consolidations, working-paper schedules for budget and actual data, statements, schedules, note reconciliation, and disclosures.
- Reclassification of cash transactions, including revenues, expenditures, capital outlay debt service, transfers, advances, and other financing sources and uses.
- Trial balances, journal entries, and posting of cash.
  (California Department of Education, School Fiscal Services Division, 2005)

▉ AUDITING

The concept of an audit is a logical part of the idea of the state's responsibility for public education and its accountability to the public. *Auditing is the study of an accounting system in general, and specific accounts in particular, to verify their accuracy and completeness.*

Because states specify much of the accounting system used in most school districts, audits usually include checks on the legality of expenditures as well as the accuracy of the many entries and calculations.

Audits can be classified by at least two criteria. In terms of time sequences, audits can be described as follows:

Pre-audits are conducted before a transaction is completed. In this type, accounts are checked to see whether expenditures are proper or within the appropriation. Initiating the encumbrance procedure is a type of pre-audit.

Post-audits are conducted after a series of transactions have been completed. Usually, the annual audit by a certified public accountant hired by the board at the end of a fiscal year or a periodic audit by a state auditor is considered a post-audit.

Continuous audits are conducted by very large organizations to ascertain net worth or cash flow. School systems with computer capability might conduct their own continuous audits, especially if unique fiscal problems require monitoring the flow of revenues and expenditures.

The organizational affiliation of the auditor makes possible two other classifications of audits: (1) internal audits, and (2) external audits.

Internal audits are conducted by individuals within the organization. In school systems, this might be done (and sometimes mandated by the state) by a designated official reporting directly to the board of education: for example, the secretary, clerk, treasurer, or comptroller. Usually, someone on the administrative team will verify the figures of the accounts in order to prepare various financial reports. Both of these constitute a form of internal audit.

External audits are conducted by individuals from outside the school system. These may be private auditors employed by the board or state, regional, and federal auditors checking on legal conformity to the particular governmental requirements.

Auditors' reports are not designed exclusively to identify criminals and embezzlers. Instead, they can be used by school officials to improve practices and build bridges of confidence with the community and professional staff. Educational needs can be evaluated with more confidence if this kind of assurance of validity is provided.

If computers are used in accounting and auditing, an audit trail must be established so that actual documents are available for each major step in the processing of the transaction.

In the News

Top Roslyn school officials and their friends and family siphoned off more than $11 million of district money in an elaborate scheme involving far more people and far more extravagant spending than had been suspected, a state report has found.

Those implicated allegedly made mortgage payments on six different homes—including two in Florida—

paid off personal loans, bankrolled vacations to the Caribbean, leased luxury cars and shelled out thousands of dollars at Tiffany's, Nordstrom's, Sharper Image, Coach and Rolex. "It's a sordid story," State Comptroller Alan Hevesi said yesterday in Mineola as he released the report. "It's a story of breathtaking diversity in the schemes that were utilized by numbers of people to take public funds and use them for personal benefits."

The Roslyn school scandal unfolded last year after an anonymous letter tipped off authorities that top officials had engaged in systemic misspending for a decade. So far, three former district officials—including the superintendent, the assistant superintendent for business, and the accounts payable clerk—have been arrested and pleaded not guilty to charges of grand larceny. Now auditors say as many as 29 people may have benefited from the scheme.

Auditors found that much of the fraud revolved around the abuse of district credit cards originally issued to the superintendent, the assistant superintendent for business, and the accounts payable clerk. Those three in turn handed out the cards to family and friends until 74 cards were circulating among 13 people. Between 1997 and last year, they charged $5.9 million for personal use. Supplemental findings, showing $3 million more misspent than first thought, were turned over to the Nassau district attorney's office. More arrests could come, authorities said.

The 64-page report blames everyone from the key administrators who blatantly misappropriated millions to the school board members and business officials who should have been watching, but weren't. Roslyn seemed gripped by a "culture of corruption,"

said State Sen. Michael Balboni (R-East Williston), who has sponsored legislation to strengthen oversight of school district finances. "This is New York State's Enron," he said.

A team of auditors worked 808 days reviewing 57,000 transactions from 1996 to 2004. Their report details an intricate conspiracy to defraud one of Long Island's wealthiest school districts. At least 26 other people were named in the report as benefiting from the district dime, including nine who got more than $100,000 each. Some got gifts—Palm Pilots and plane tickets—from those with access to district funds. Others received unauthorized salary increases that totaled $549,129. Among the most startling abuse of district funds included supplies purchased from Home Depot for a family member's construction business; payments on student loans, a car lease, a home mortgage, and cable TV bill with district funds; credit card purchases at various hair and nail salons; trips to St. Thomas, Morocco, Cancun, Puerto Rico, Thailand, Indonesia and Argentina; and cruises. The superintendent even asked the district to reimburse him for 65-cent bagels.

The report blames the fraud on those charged with stealing, but also on the "monumental failures" of those who didn't catch it. Much of the misspent money was hidden in unrelated accounts, such as maintenance. Spending in the accounts spilled over budget—sometimes by more than $1 million—but that went either ignored or unnoticed.

From: Vargas, T., & Laikin, E. (2005, March 3). Audit: Over $11 million siphoned from Roslyn schools. *Newsday, Inc.*, Retrieved January 29, 2007, from http://www.news day .com/news/local/longisland/ny-lirosl0303,0, 1972021.story?coll=ny-top-headlines.

Given the differentiation between internal and external auditing, the school business administrator's responsibility here is twofold. The administrator frequently has the responsibility of seeing that internal audits are conducted in order to ensure the adequate functioning of financial and business systems, and also to monitor the system's ability to accurately provide planning data to the administrative team. The status of pertinent funds, accounts, and cash flow will determine, for example, whether money should be borrowed to meet the October payroll or whether a short-term investment in Treasury Bills is possible.

The responsibility of the business administrator and other fiscal officers is indirect and supportive in cases of external audits. Especially in state-mandated audits, the business administrator's activities are usually limited to providing an external auditor with ready access to information needed. Auditors need not only accounts and previous financial reports, but also supportive information such as the vouchers, the minute book of the board of education (showing resolutions and authorizations for financial transactions), the school district policy manual and personnel records (showing certification and eligibility of personnel for various positions at given salary levels), and the insurance register (showing policies covering only insurable risks).

As of the turn of the twentieth century, state-mandated auditing has included student activity accounts, because these have been judged to be "public monies," even if not generated from public taxes. External audits of student activity accounts are made in essentially the same way as external audits of conventional school district funds. However, because of the involvement of many teachers, and even students, in the accounting process, the school business administrator needs to provide much care and supervision in order to prevent teachers from using loose accounting procedures that might result in subsequent auditors' findings being lodged against the student activities accountant.

▪ REPORTING

The accounting and auditing processes have to do with generating and verifying information pertaining to the financial status of the school system. Reporting concentrates upon disseminating information to persons or offices that can use it to improve their understanding and concomitant decision making in school matters. The reporting facet of accounting is extremely important: Without adequate reporting, nearly all else that goes before has little impact on understanding, decision making, or planning. As a result, the accounting system should be considered as part of a total information system. Accounting reports are output from the accounting subsystem and input to other sub- and suprasystems.

Recent years have brought a sharply increased demand for information in all facets of school affairs, particularly school business administration. The accountability movement demands answers to myriad questions. School administrators are thus faced with the general question: What is accountable to whom, for what, and in what way? This question suggests the necessity of developing a systematic overview of the entire school operation with responsibilities, roles, and relationships clearly allocated and delineated. In addition, it requires a management information system to disseminate appropriate information throughout the operation. Financial accounting and auditing data are important components of the lifeblood of the school organization. They supply critical information describing the schools' financial positions so that administrative decisions can be made.

Comprehensive Annual Financial Report

A standard format for reporting financial conditions of school systems was developed in response to demands for greater detail and clarity of financial data. Parallel to these demands was the concern for financial reports that also enabled reasonable comparability among school systems within and between states. These demands stimulated the publication of *Governmental Accounting, Auditing, and Financial Reporting*, known as the "Blue Book," by the Governmental Finance Officers Association (Gauthier, 2001).

Of particular interest to school systems is the comprehensive annual financial report (CAFR). The format of CAFR utilizes GAAP to ensure interschool system comparability. Because the report is not only comprehensive, but also interpretative, it is well suited to the general public and others who are not oriented to conventional accounting concepts and terminology.

Major elements of the report include:

- Introductory Section (developed by the school system), including
  - Letter of transmittal.
  - List of officials.
  - Organization chart.
- Financial Statements, such as
  - Combined—all government fund types.
  - Combining—all special revenue funds.
  - Individual fund schedules.
- Notes to the Financial Statements—explanatory materials.
- Single-Audit Section—schedule of federal financial assistance.
- Statistical Section—school system data presented in tabular form.

Supplementary information included in a CAFR provides a context for the reader that helps in the interpretation of the accounting data. This information includes:

- General governmental expenditures by function.
- General revenues by source.
- Property tax levies and collections.
- Assessed and estimated actual value of taxable property.
- Property tax rates of all overlapping governments.
- Special assessment collections.
- Ratio of net general bonded debt to assessed value and net bonded debt per capita.
- Computation of legal debt margin.
- Computation of overlapping debt.
- Ratio of annual debt service for general bonded debt to total general expenditure.
- Revenue bond coverage.
- Demographic statistics.
- Property value, construction, and bank deposits.
- Principal taxpayers.
- Miscellaneous statistics.

An illustrative CAFR developed by the River Forest Public Schools District 90 is characterized by this introductory statement:

> *The Comprehensive Annual Financial Report is presented in three sections: Introductory, Financial and Statistical. The introductory section includes the transmittal letter, the*

District's organizational chart, and a list of principal officials. The financial section includes the general purpose financial statements and the combining, individual fund, and account group financial statements and schedules, as well as the independent auditors' report. The statistical section includes a number of tables of unaudited data depicting the financial history of the District generally presented on a multi-year basis, demographics, and other miscellaneous information. (River Forest Public Schools District 90 Comprehensive Annual Financial Report for Fiscal Year Ended 2005, p. vi)

The increased intervention of, and hence accountability to, federal and state educational agencies have placed more pressure on school systems for accounting and auditing data. Developments within the local school system itself have also exacerbated the situation. Teacher organizations, in their negotiation processes, demand revenue and expenditure data. Citizens, clients, and taxpayer groups have taken advantage of long-standing public access and more recent sunshine law provisions.

School systems have acted to meet both legal and moral responsibilities to provide the data. As the administrative team and site-based management concepts are adopted and flourish, the increased interdependency among these units demands full and free exchange of information in order to make the best decisions within the given circumstances. Considering reporting from this posture, the next section looks at reporting to external agencies and internal units within the school system.

External Reporting

Federal and state laws, along with policy, dictate which data, and in which format, must be reported to external agencies. Federally funded programs usually specify the accounting procedure to be used in describing the financial status and transactions made in connection with their grants. Probably the most important decision for the school business administrator (once involvement in the federally funded program is ensured) is how the specified accounting responsibility is to be executed. The total information system perspective is helpful as the school business administrator plans for a flow of school system information relevant to the data required in the federal specifications. In essence, this process requires the integration of local data and data channels with the required data and procedures.

Much the same is true for state-mandated financial reports. However, in most school districts, the information system for the local district is structured around the state mandates. The monthly financial report for the board members usually uses the same data, format, and terminology as required in monthly or annual financial reports that the school system must file with the state education or finance department.

Financial reports to local agencies or groups are not usually limited to those mandated by the state. Thus, local boards and administrators have considerable freedom in providing data for their own design for these groups. Most school systems are required to publish or make available some kind of annual financial statement or report. In addition, school boards frequently integrate this with an annual or "state of the school system" report, to inform citizens of the status, problems, and accomplishments of the system. A considerable amount of interpretation of both program and finances is included.

Special reports of the fiscal status of the educational enterprise are frequently generated to illustrate the need to issue construction bonds, pass tax levies, and enact other public policy related to fiscal affairs. Unfortunately, the public often perceives such reports as attempts to inform only when the school has a predetermined solution and needs public ratification in the form of additional allocations. Out of this perception has grown the public demand for greater accountability on a continuous rather than a sporadic, crisis-oriented basis. With an understanding of school accounting, the school business administrator can satisfy the public demand for accountability by helping the administrative team design and develop meaningful reports that can relate the school system to the community in the most open and honest sense possible.

Public demand has had the effect of increasing the flow of mandated reports on programs in general and financial information in particular. At the local school district level, administrators have become sensitized to the fact that citizens desire information above and beyond that which is typically provided by the board of education and the administration. School business administrators are called upon to make information available (and understandable) to individuals and citizens' groups. Under sunshine and open-records laws, data are on the public record, available to all. This concept of responsible fiscal reporting is quite different from an earlier one limited only to meeting the letter of the law.

Other factors that call for the broadening of the reporting function are those related to increased involvement of the following processes in decision making: participative management, establishment of common databases in negotiation processes, the advent of new decision processes (such as PPBES) that call for different aggregations of data (costs by program rather than by object), and the necessity of making unusual and very difficult financial decisions (such as which schools should be closed because of declining enrollments and rapidly escalating costs). All the items of this incomplete list imply that much more financial and accounting data must be generated, ordered, and interpreted to ensure that needs and demands are met.

Internal Reporting

The internal reports that involve school accounting can also be perceived as one facet of an information system. It is in this form that accounting can best be described as a planning tool. If administrators think of themselves as a team and see their roles and behaviors in an interactive milieu, it follows that each must have access to the data as well as the thinking of the others. Thus, the accounting system must provide data of a financial nature to each member of the team. These data are: (1) indigenous to each member's responsibility, and (2) relevant to all other operations of the school system and sufficient to provide a financial context for their programmatic character.

Furthermore, it is important that information regarding the nature of all available data and the channels that may be used to obtain it be made available to the whole team. In this way, accounting information is accessible to but does not inundate a whole staff, many of whom do not want or cannot use it at a given time.

Planning and decision making can be expedited through optimizing the quality and availability of relevant data. The school business administrator fulfills team responsibility not only by providing appropriate information, but also by integrating data production processes into the larger information systems at federal, state, and local levels. A significant move in this direction has been made by the U.S. Department of Education with its development and publication of the *State Educational Records and Reports Series*. These handbooks establish uniform definitions and classification systems that provide help to state and local administrators who seek to upgrade quality and uniformity of data among the several levels of government.

For school systems and individual school units that have moved to site-based management, it is imperative that they adopt and utilize accounting systems that provide discrete site revenue and expenditure data. Such data can break down actual program costs. These can be used in cost-benefit analysis to determine program alternatives and priorities.

Summary

School accounting requirements and current practices have been drawn from the accounting arts and sciences developed in the business and public administration sectors. This chapter describes the function and objectives of school accounting. Principles of accounting are reviewed to afford an overview of the fundamental concepts and terminology, and, thus, provide a school business administrator with sufficient knowledge to understand the data and reports generated by the school system accountant. The accounting equation is reviewed to provide an understanding of assets and liabilities. The process of accounting is reviewed to acquaint the reader with the concept of debits and credits and the interaction in the flow of transactions. The ten basic steps in the accounting cycle are applied to school business transactions to give a sense of sequence. Adaptation of the principles to contemporary manual, automatic, or machine accounting results in complex and rapid processing. Few, if any, school business administrators have responsibility for actually operating such equipment. However, a knowledge of the accounting principles enables one to read, analyze, and interpret the data and reports produced by such machines. In this way, the school business administrator has the information needed to initiate, design, and implement plans in the school business sphere.

The accounting data generated provide the raw material for auditing and reporting. Audits are used internally (pre-audits) to monitor financial affairs. Post-audits are conducted after the fact to determine the accuracy of the system and the propriety of the transactions. Both audits and reports are important to maintain accountability and credibility in both the state and local communities.

Discussion Questions

1. Obtain a copy of your state system of classification of accounts and compare it with the accounting system being used by a local school system in your state. If there are variations between the two, try to account for them.
2. In many states, the accounting responsibility is vested in an office other than that of the school district official. Find out how this responsibility is designated in your state. How does this affect the responsibility of the school business administrator?
3. Obtain a copy of a monthly financial report of a board of education. From it, develop an interpretation that could be understood by a reasonably perceptive layperson.
4. With the cooperation of an accountant in a local school system business office, select a given transaction and trace an audit trail on it from its initiation to its final disposition.

Web Resources

Governmental Accounting Standards Board—
    http://www.gasb.org/
Government Finance Officers Association—
    http://www.gfoa.org/

U.S. Department of Education, *Financial Accounting for State and Local School Systems 2003—* http://nces.ed.gov/pubs2004/h2r2/

References

Adams, B.K., Hill, Q.M., Lichtenberger, A.R., Perkins, J.A. Jr., & Shaw, P.S. (1967). *Principles of public school accounting, state educational records and reports series: Handbook 11-B.* Washington, DC: U.S. Government Printing Office.

California Department of Education, School Fiscal Services Division. (2005). *California school accounting manual.* Sacramento, CA: California Department of Education Press.

Everett, R.E., Lowes, R.L, & Johnson, D.R. (1996). *Financial and managerial accounting for school administrators.* Reston, VA: Association of School Business Officials, International.

Gatti, B.F. (1987, October). ASBO's certificate of excellence program: 15 years of professional excellence. *School Business Affairs, 53*(10), 43.

Gauthier, S.J. (2001, June). Then and now: 65 years of the Blue Book. *Government Finance Review*, 1–3.

Montgomery, B. (2005). *Uniform school accounting system-users manual.* Columbus, OH: State of Ohio, Local Government Services Division.

River Forest Public Schools District 90 Comprehensive Annual Financial Report for Fiscal Year Ended 2005 (River Forest, Illinois). Retrieved January 29, 2007, from http://asbointl.org/Recognition/index.asp?bid=10379.

Tidwell, S.B. (1974). *Financial and managerial accounting for elementary and secondary school systems.* Chicago: Association of School Business Officials.

Note

1. See Tidwell, pp. 108–9, for a more comprehensive discussion of cash, accrual, and modified accrual systems.

CHAPTER TWELVE

Managing Money

◼ INTRODUCTION

Part of the role that school business officials assume is responsibility for productive use of financial resources. This responsibility includes not only expending resources to achieve programmatic and related goals, but also acting in a fiduciary or stewardship role with the school system's liquid assets. The latter role includes the productive and prudent investment of these resources. Local taxes, state and federal aids or grants, and miscellaneous revenues pour into school system treasuries at a rate that does not match expenditures on a day-to-day basis. Thus, "surplus" monies are frequently available for investment. For example, real property taxes may be collected every six months, so early in any six-month period there is often a large balance bulge in various funds. These are usually drawn down to small balances by the end of the period, and the cycle is repeated.

LEARNING OBJECTIVES

In this chapter a reader will learn about:

- Technical terms needed to communicate with experts when dealing with money matters.
- The nature of cash for investment.
- Cash flow and its analysis.
- Investment policy considerations.
- Investment strategies and tactics.
- The variety and characteristics of investment instruments.

Responsibilities of public finance officers include not only the provision of security, but also the productive and prudent investment of these monies. The rationale for investing inactive monies is to optimize revenue available for eventual expenditure. Thus, investment of available revenue retains or increases the purchasing power of public monies dedicated to providing an educational program. In this function, school administrators play the role of good stewards of public monies.

Major financial goals of cash management cited by Dembowski and Davey (1995) are:

- Availability—to ensure cash availability (liquidity) to meet daily needs.
- Investment—to increase cash available for investment purposes.
- Yield—to earn the maximum return on cash invested.
- Safety—to protect the assets of the school district against loss.

These goals conflict to the extent that cash invested may not be readily available to meet current obligations, and that the interest rates available on investments increase with risk.

The obligations and goals of cash management imply serious responsibilities. These are significantly impacted by the fact that the cash and credit market is highly volatile. Public officials who administer the education system especially labor under increasing scrutiny by the public.

For the public officials who were managing the finances of the education system, cash management was easier in the past. Inflation assured continually rising property values; tax levies remained constant; excessive portfolio earnings allowed for the funding of new programs and the hiring of new people; and the tax base increased continually. In short, to most every educator's delight, reaching financial goals seemed to be on automatic pilot. To complement all of this, banks (which are the source of well over half of the end investments used by institutional officials) were in excellent financial condition. Rates of return on investments were usually understated in budget projections, leaving plenty of cushion for the cash manager to meet any surprise financial shortfalls. All this created a relatively easy investing environment.

In the latter part of the twentieth century, matters were more regulated. "Rolling recessions" cut deeply into property values and assessed valuations, creating the need for increases in tax levies. As explained in Chapter Six, which concentrates on school revenues, the restrictive tax movements of the late 1980s have placed new pressures upon the public official (Flynn, 1990).

■ THE NATURE OF CASH FOR INVESTMENT

In its simplest form, cash for investment is stated as:

Revenues − Expenditures = Cash for Investment

School systems receive revenues from federal, state, and local sources. Federal revenue is tied largely to specific programs with discrete disbursement schedules. Typically, state revenue is transferred to school systems on a fixed and regular schedule that is reasonably predictable. Local revenue payments in the form of property and other taxes dedicated to school systems are also made on a relatively fixed schedule. Local taxes are less predictable due to the nature of changing tax rates, assessment procedures, tax delinquencies, and the like. Miscellaneous local charges, fees, and other sources are also subject to change. On the whole, the largest sources of revenue are relatively predictable, but only if underlying variables are taken into consideration.

The expenditure component of the cash for investment equation is governed by both policy mandates and school system discretion. School system obligations must be met on a fixed schedule, for example, tuition payments from one system to another, fees due to state agencies such as the auditor's office or the teachers' retirement system, and debt service payments to retire bond issues. School board and administration discretion, at least in part, govern the larger part of total expenditure.

Salaries and payroll procedures are usually negotiable items; although there are certain specific mandates, such as minimum salary provisions, pay periods, deductibles, and the like. The purchase of supplies, equipment, services, and capital assets is a permissive power granted to the school system within general parameters of state policy. However, the board and the administrative staff largely determine the timing of such expenditures. Many expenditures can be timed to coincide with the flow of revenue and thus even the cash flow.

■ CASH FLOW

The concept of cash flow is derived from the analogy that revenue flows into a pool and that expenditures flow out. At a given moment, the pool may hold a relatively large amount of cash if revenue exceeds expenditure. If, at the next moment, expenditure exceeds revenue, the amount of cash in the pool would be reduced. All organizations with fiscal systems experience the dynamics of cash flow. An important consideration, then, is how cash flow should be managed to maximize its benefit (or, perhaps, minimize its liabilities).

The initial step for such consideration in a school system is describing and analyzing the cash flow. This is a prerequisite to the development of both a management strategy and a set of management tactics to attain investment goals. Given the uncertainties and the systematic changes from year to year, multiyear analysis is necessary to obtain useful trend data. It is desirable to review several past years of revenue and expenditure data, and then forecast a year or two of anticipated revenue and expenditures. Cash-flow forecasting should be based upon explicit assumptions of enrollments, staffing, salary levels, program costs, and other expected expenditures. Revenue forecasting likewise should be based on explicit assumptions of local property valuation, tax rates, tax delinquency and abatements, and other local sources of revenue such as tuition, fees, and investment income. State and federal sources should also be forecast based on explicit assumptions related to the criteria or formula components used by the funding agency.

Table 12.1 is an illustration of an annual fiscal forecast for a general fund on a month-to-month basis. The forecast was developed by an analysis of the actual cash flow for each month of previous fiscal years. The same format is used to record actual receipts, expenditures, and ending cash balances.

The ending cash balances for each month offer insights as to cash that is available for investment. Using the same format but calculating the balance on a daily basis can obtain a more precise, but still not absolute, figure. Most school systems with aggressive investment policies have provisions for monitoring daily cash flow.

A careful analysis of cash flow can reveal several ways to increase or optimize cash available for investment. Prompt payment of bills from vendors who offer discounts is advised in order to minimize expenditures. Daily monitoring of the cashing of payroll checks reveals the "float" that is available for two, three, or four days of additional investment time. School systems can earn additional interest dollars if payment of large sums is made at the last possible moment. Examples of this practice include making payments to retirement funds and insurance programs by courier rather than by mail.

TABLE 12.1 Yearly Revenue and Expenditure Report

School District: Hilliard City School District Fiscal Year: 2006

	FTD Actual	July	August	September	October
BEGINNING CASH BALANCE RECEIPTS	5,522,954	5,522,954	31,401,324	24,874,450	22,416,624
FROM LOCAL SOURCES					
1 REAL ESTATE	68,823,119	30,680,825	18,670	149,640	—
2 PERSONAL TANGIBLE	16,576,507	2,059,312	734	(149,640)	10,595,118
3 INVESTMENT EARNINGS	1,214,723	74,892	143,535	153,035	142,174
4 PROCEEDS FROM SALES OF NOTES	—	—	—	—	—
5 OTHER LOCAL	2,555,879	119,226	296,701	398,504	175,840
FROM STATE SOURCES					
6 FOUNDATION PROGRAM	38,195,755	3,394,113	3,035,498	3,058,997	3,060,821
7 ROLLBACK AND HOMESTEAD EXEMPTION	7,936,801	3,389		4,366,020	
8 OTHER STATE	1,506,067			360,679	
FROM FEDERAL SOURCES					
9 PUBLIC LAW 874	—	—	—	—	—
10 FEDERAL	243,552	—	50,927	9,312	
FROM ALL TRANSFERS					
11 OTHER NON-OPERATING REVENUE	547,610	23,753	167,940	31,594	238,980
12 TOTAL RECEIPTS (LINES 1–11)	137,600,013	36,355,509	3,714,005	8,378,141	14,212,933
13 TOTAL RECEIPTS, PLUS CASH BALANCE	143,122,966	41,878,462	35,115,329	33,252,591	36,629,558
EXPENDITURES					
14 SALARIES AND WAGES	85,685,966	6,222,422	6,064,506	6,906,496	7,041,449
15 FRINGE BENEFITS	28,468,273	2,256,029	2,310,160	2,290,266	2,366,023
16 PURCHASED SERVICES	8,673,893	814,228	846,928	611,786	703,038
17 MATERIALS SUPPLIES AND TEXTBOOKS	4,788,755	138,996	638,908	706,237	343,500
18 CAPITAL OUTLAY (INCL., REPLACEMENT)	1,378,970	616,160	343,998	21,602	(561,792)
19 REPAYMENT OF NOTES	—	—	—	—	—
20 OTHER NON-OPERATING EXPENDITURES	2,701,848	429,303	36,378	77,200	258,796
21 OTHER EXPENDITURES	275,865	—	—	222,378	20,841
22 TOTAL EXPENDITURES (LINES 14–21)	131,973,569	10,477,138	10,240,879	10,835,966	10,171,854
ENDING CASH BALANCE (LINES 13 MINUS 22)	11,149,397	31,401,324	24,874,450	22,416,624	26,457,704

Source: Hilliard City School District, Monthly Revenue and Expenditure Data: Fiscal Year: 2006

continued

November	December	January	February	March	April	May	June
26,457,704	19,284,066	12,122,980	4,155,277	36,579,669	32,624,071	25,873,128	17,233,028
223,758	(223,758)	—	37,942,748	31,237	—	—	—
—	4	281,023	1,901,164	778	—	—	1,888,014
152,073	(53,174)	43,847	71,732	61,242	72,635	136,836	215,894
—	—	—	—	—	—	—	—
211,712	292,105	53,166	181,788	58,509	412,365	104,263	251,700
3,058,116	3,077,038	3,101,356	3,095,037	3,366,747	3,302,362	3,258,706	3,386,964
—	—	—	—	3,565,785	—	1,607	—
—	37,279	—	281,023	307,260	16,140	503,685	—
—	—	—	—	—	—	—	—
4,752	3,629	71,632	83,783	—	—	19,519	—
28,702	2,230	—	—	11,741	—	21,953	20,718
3,679,112	3,135,354	3,551,024	43,557,274	7,403,300	3,803,502	4,046,570	5,763,290
30,136,816	22,419,420	15,674,004	47,712,551	43,982,969	36,427,573	29,919,697	22,996,318
7,388,347	7,065,419	7,108,340	7,306,898	7,499,656	7,207,118	8,604,355	7,270,960
2,293,428	2,278,038	2,424,411	2,362,027	2,728,713	2,334,885	2,410,416	2,413,877
867,353	583,405	652,409	813,719	834,521	620,584	592,787	733,133
264,878	247,092	252,710	283,315	260,936	294,464	511,833	845,886
840	4,866	234	3,380	—	22,961	478,977	447,744
36,474	113,553	1,080,499	351,803	24,690	74,433	88,302	130,416
1,429	4,066	125	11,741	10,381	—	—	4,904
10,852,749	10,296,440	11,518,727	11,132,882	11,358,898	10,554,445	12,686,670	11,846,921
19,284,066	12,122,980	4,155,277	36,579,669	32,624,071	25,873,128	17,233,028	11,149,397

The same concept applies when receiving large amounts of revenue. School system agents frequently pick up checks for state reimbursement or warrants from the local taxation administrator for the system's property tax allocation. Even more sophisticated Internet-based methods have been introduced to expedite obtainment of these revenues. For example, a wire transfer service, whereby local or state government treasurers can wire-transfer the monies from the local or state agency account to the account of the school system, may be available. These transactions are nearly instantaneous. Such techniques are examples of cash concentration—providing for the prompt acquisition of revenue for investment purposes.

■ INVESTMENT POLICY CONSIDERATIONS

A successful school system investment program requires careful planning and a deliberate strategy. Although private-sector investment programs have some similarities to those found in school systems, there are marked differences. Private-sector investment is similar to school system investment programs in that both are sensitive to the market. The yield rates of both are related to supply and demand of investment money. The rates of return on U.S. Treasury notes and bills are reflective of the amount that investors are willing to commit to them, which, in turn, is related to the relative rate of return compared with other investment options.

All investments involve risks, and the degree of risk is related to the amount of yield as demanded by the market. Both private-sector and school system investments have an inherent risk-yield relationship, although the nature of it in each is somewhat different. This is discussed in more detail in a subsequent section.

Nearly all legitimate investments carry some restrictions. In the private sector, these may be characterized by the regulations of the Securities and Exchange Commission (SEC). School system investment programs are severely constricted by state policy because school systems are agents of the state. Additionally, local restrictions may be enforced by boards of education through their permissive powers.

Despite state and local policies to minimize risk in school system investment programs, school monies are frequently lost through less than judicious investment practices. In one example, several school districts in Ohio were in danger of losing millions of dollars on "interest-only" securities. In essence, districts bought the rights to interest on government agency securities, but when the interest rates fell, the value of the interest-only rights fell also. A security of this kind could not be cashed in for its original cost. A bulletin from Ohio's State Auditor alerted municipal officials to this problem and its consequences:

> It has come to our attention that several political subdivisions governed by the Revised Code have made high risk investments that may be in violation of the Revised Code. Section 135, Revised Code, specifically identifies the types of investments a political subdivision may purchase. The two major criteria outlined in this section require that the investments will mature and or be redeemable within two years from the date of purchase, or be obligations of or guaranteed by the United States, or those for which the faith of the United States is pledged for the payment of principal and interest.
>
> At this time, it is our interpretation that investments in "Stripped Backed-Mortgage Securities" (i.e., interest only) are not suitable and do not comply with the requirements as set forth in Section 135, Revised Code. Audits performed pursuant to Section 117, Revised Code,

will include a review of the investment policies and procedures to assure compliance with Section 135, Revised Code. Violations of Section 135, Revised Code may result in non-compliance citations and or findings for recovery. (Ferguson, 1993)

While safeguards are now in place in many school districts to avoid such situations, the most notorious examples of excess risk occurred in Orange County, California. In the closing days of 1994, an investment pool managed by the county on behalf of itself and scores of underlying units of government and school districts collapsed. Widely publicized postmortems of the county's ill-fated investment pool that was unwound in December 1994, with losses of some $3 billion, found a number of causes: an "out of control" investment manager, an overleveraged pool, lax statutory local government pool oversight, and the use of derivatives (Karvelis, 1995).

Differences between private-sector investment programs and those of school systems are observable when the basic premise of each is considered. In the private sector, investments are made on the expectation of future earnings. A private-sector investment cliché states that one should invest only what one can afford to lose. In school system investment programs, the premise is more related to retaining and protecting assets. It must be acknowledged, however, that private investors also seek the latter goal and that school system investment programs are designed to enhance the liquid assets of the system.

A second major difference is the range of investment instruments that may be used. Most states have relatively severe restrictions. These usually allow purchase of government issues backed by the full faith and credit of the federal or the state government. Some states permit school systems to purchase collateralized commercial paper. At the same time, they may prohibit speculative investments such as junk bonds or ventures into the futures markets. Investment strategies also vary in that school systems are not permitted to buy securities through leveraging or on margin.

The major considerations that guide a school system's investment program (list follows) are essentially the same as those used in private-sector programs, but they vary in specific applications.

1. *Does it conform to legal restrictions?* The fundamental restrictions are specified in state permissive legislation. Major provisions include permissive powers of school boards, sources of revenue from which investments may be made, and the term of the investment period, for example, within the fiscal year or beyond the fiscal year. State policy usually specifies the nature of the investment instruments, as previously described, and how the investment authority is exercised. Accounting and reporting procedures for investments are frequently incorporated in state policy as well.

   Local policy is an extension of state policy and tends to be procedural in nature. For example, the school board may authorize the business administrator to invest all balances of specific funds in repurchase agreements in a given bank over weekends or holidays.

2. *What is the nature and amount of risk to be assumed?* It is axiomatic that all investments carry risks. However, it also is generally accepted that school system investment programs are not speculative in nature. Thus, the risks are restricted by statute or policy. Bank deposits are backed by collateral, but the value of the collateral may fluctuate given changing market conditions. Treasury notes and bills are guaranteed by the federal government, but only at par. So there may be some risk if a note or bill were purchased at a price over par, because at maturity the principal repaid will be at par. However, if interest

earnings are considered, the return of principal plus earnings might far exceed the purchase price. Thus, the nature of risk is relative. It is incumbent on the school business administrator to be aware of the risks of doing nothing as well as the risks of developing an investment program to obtain maximum return on a minimized risk.

3. *What is the yield?* The yield on investments derives from either interest earned or appreciation (or depreciation) of principal or both. The most secure instruments (e.g., Treasury notes or bills) repay the principal at par, so the yield is derived from the interest. However, if the buying price were over $100 at par, the net yield at maturity would be reduced. If the buying price were under $100 at par, the net yield at maturity would be increased. If a security is sold prior to maturity, the appreciation or depreciation (difference in purchase price and selling price) would be calculated as a part of yield.

4. *What is the degree of liquidity?* Liquidity is an important consideration, for several reasons, in developing a school system investment portfolio. Because cash flow is irregular, invested cash may be needed before scheduled maturities or at the last possible moment before bills are paid and checks are cashed. Because market conditions change, the prices of investments may change. Interest rates, and, therefore, yields, may change because new issues reflect the current rates, which may be higher or lower than earlier ones. Consequently, it may be advantageous to "swap" issues. This tactic is discussed in a later section.

A volatile cash flow suggests the desirability of highly liquid investments. These might have disadvantages of lower interest yield but the advantage of less costly transactions. For example, certificates of deposit (CDs) may offer an interest rate higher than that of a repurchase agreement, but withdrawing a CD before maturity incurs a substantial penalty.

The following excerpt is an example of an investment policy that reflects these major considerations. It was developed by the Hilliard City Schools (Ohio).

It is the policy of the Hilliard City Schools to invest public funds in a manner which provides the highest return with the maximum security while meeting the daily cash flow needs of the District and conforming to the Ohio Revised Code governing the investment of public funds.

Objectives

The primary objectives, in order of priority, of Hilliard City Schools' investment activities are:

1. *Safety.* Safety of principal is the foremost objective of the investment program. Investments of the District are undertaken in a manner that seeks to ensure preservation of capital in the overall portfolio.
2. *Liquidity.* The District's investment remains sufficiently liquid to enable the District to meet all operating requirements which might be reasonably anticipated.
3. *Return on Investments.* The District's investment portfolio is designed with the objective of attaining a market rate of return throughout budgetary and economic cycles, taking into account the District's investment risk constraints and the cash flow characteristics of the portfolio.

Policy

1. The Treasurer of the Hilliard City School District (hereinafter known as "Treasurer") shall be bound in any and all investment transactions to those policies, rules and regulations provided by this document.
2. All investment activities shall be undertaken by the Treasurer, or those other persons assigned by the Board of Education to engage in investment activities.
3. The Treasurer shall be responsible for the daily investment activities, including reporting, monitoring, reviewing, and complying with the laws established by the Ohio Revised Code and the compliance regulations established by the Auditor of the State of Ohio.
4. The Treasurer shall invest in securities that have maturities of two years or less (except for repurchase agreements), or those that are redeemable at par, or above, within two years of the purchase date.

Criteria

1. *Safety*—The safety of the investment portfolio is of greatest concern to the Board of Education, thus regarded as the primary objective of the investment policy. At no time will the safety of the portfolio's principal investment be impaired or jeopardized. Safety is herein defined as the certainty of receiving full par value plus accrued interest, at the security's legal final maturity. The Investment Section of this policy will identify those securities eligible for purchase into the portfolio.
2. *Yield*—The Treasurer will consider yields attained by various investments. The primary goal will be to attain maximum yield possible per investment while complying with the policies and procedures established within this policy.
3. *Liquidity*—The Treasurer shall invest in instruments that give some flexibility to its portfolio to avoid unreasonable risks. Portfolio liquidity is defined as the ability to sell a security on short notice near the par value of that security. To assure desired liquidity, at least ten percent (10%) of the investment portfolio, with final maturities of 6 months or less, shall be maintained to accommodate unexpected cash needs of the district.

Authorized Investments

The following investments shall be permitted by this policy, and are those defined in section 135 of the Ohio Revised Code:

1. Bonds, notes, debentures, or other obligations or securities issued by the U.S. Treasury, federal government agencies, and federal government instrumentalities;
2. NOW accounts, Super NOW accounts or any other similar account authorized by the Federal Reserve's Depository Institutions Deregulation Committee, provided that such accounts are secured by collateral prescribed in the investment policy;
3. Interest bearing certificates of deposit and savings accounts only in financial institutions organized under the laws of this state, provided that any such deposits and savings accounts are secured by collateral as prescribed in the investment policy;
4. Before transacting a repurchase agreement with a particular broker/dealer, a master repurchase agreement must be entered into between the District and

that particular broker. Each master repurchase agreement provides for collateralization of each repurchase agreement, the market value of which shall not be less than 102% of the principal amount of each repurchase agreement, plus accrued interest;

5. The state of Ohio investment pools, otherwise known as STAR Ohio, is the only authorized investment pool in which the Treasurer may invest District funds;
6. Any no-load money market mutual funds as defined by the Ohio Revised Code;
7. Notes issued by any entity that is defined in division (D) of section 1705.01 of the Ohio Revised Code and has assets exceeding five hundred million dollars and all other limitations imposed by ORC 135.142;
8. Bankers' acceptances of banks that are members of the federal deposit insurance corporation to which obligations both of the following apply:
   A. The obligations are eligible for purchase by the federal reserve system;
   B. The obligations mature no later than 180 days after purchase;
9. Any obligation of the state of Ohio or Hilliard City Schools, without regard to length of maturity or interest rate as stipulated in the Ohio Revised Code, is an authorized investment instrument.

Competitive Bidding

The purpose of competitive bidding is to strengthen the investment program in terms of level and consistency of performance. When purchasing securities, the Treasurer obtains a minimum of two offerings on government securities and certificates of deposit.

Diversification

The Treasurer diversifies the portfolio to avoid incurring unreasonable risks inherent in over investing in specific instruments, individual financial institutions or maturities:

Diversification by Instrument	Maximum Percent of Portfolio
U.S. Treasurer Obligations (bills, notes, and bonds)	100%
U.S. Government Agency/Instrumentalities	75%
Certificates of Deposit/Bank Deposits (collateralized)	75%
Repurchase Agreements (REPOs)	25%
State and Local Government Securities	25%
State of Ohio Investment Pool	75%
Commercial Paper/Bankers' Acceptances	25%

Diversification by Issuer	
Commercial Paper/Bankers' Acceptances	25%
Certificate of Deposit/Bank Deposits	50%

Reporting

The Treasurer is charged with the responsibility of providing reports on investment activity and returns on the pooled balance of funds. These reports are prepared on a monthly basis and submitted to the Board. The reports provide a clear picture of the status of the current investment portfolio and include the following:

1. A listing of individual securities held at the end of the reporting period by authorized investment category; and
2. The percentage of the portfolio represented by each investment category.

2007 Ohio School Boards Association, Hilliard City School District, *Policies of the Hilliard City School District: Revenues from investment* (Hilliard City Schools).

▪ INVESTMENT STRATEGIES

Any investment strategy should be predicated on a policy dealing with investment and depository activities. State statutes usually cover the latter regarding both security for cash and other assets as well as the school system personnel who are responsible for investment decisions. Legislation specifies conditions under which cash may be invested. Consequently, it is crucial that local policy be developed to specify ways in which school system investment officers may choose to exercise these powers. Policy and procedural guidelines should include the following considerations:

- Objectives of the investment program.
- Designation of in-house and contracted investment counsel or services.
- Authority and responsibility of the investment officer or agency.
- Procedures to determine cash flow and other basic data necessary to make investment decisions.
- Procedures to determine the sources and amounts of investable cash.
- Designation of the minimum and maximum investment maturities.
- Investment instruments to be used.

A key step in developing strategies for investment is using cash-flow analysis to determine the nature of investment potential. This topic was discussed earlier and speaks to the question of when and how much one should invest.

Yield Curves

A second step concentrates upon the nature of yield on investments. As just mentioned, yields change as economic conditions change. A strategy must speak to the question of how to optimize the yield of a given or alternative investment instrument. The concept of the yield curve is central to this strategy. Investments with shorter maturities usually yield less than investments with longer maturities. A normal yield curve ascends as maturity is extended. Even within a fixed period of time, yields of related investments respond in different ways.

An inverted yield curve, the converse of the normal yield curve, is characterized by instruments with shorter maturities having higher yield and those with longer maturities having lower yields. For example, if the economy has the prospect of stagnation (and thus lowering corporate dividends and needing less capital), investors may flee the stock market

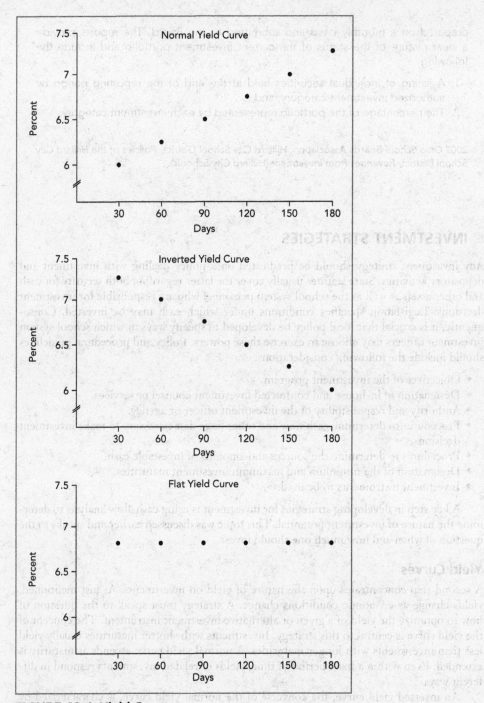

FIGURE 12.1 Yield Curves

and move into Treasury notes, bills, and bonds. This "oversupply" of capital may reduce the interest rate the government must pay to sell these securities.

A flat yield curve is no curve at all. Although an infrequent phenomenon in the absolute, yields on securities may tend toward a flat yield when there is little difference in yield between short-term and long-term securities. This situation is like a resting period within fixed-income markets. Factors that have contributed to a flat yield curve include actions by the Federal Reserve Board to increase short-term interest rates to decrease the money supply, and, in turn, dampen the threat of inflation. In recent years, these increased interest rates were also a part of the strategy to stabilize the value of the dollar against the currencies of other nations. Figure 12.1 illustrates the three types of yield curves.

Investment strategies can be built around yield curves and the periodic changes of yield for various investment instruments. Not all instruments respond in precisely the same way to changing economic and fiscal conditions. Thus, an analysis of yield curves may suggest several alternative reactions or tactics. One might shift investments from short- to long-term maturities or vice versa. One might "swap" treasuries for CDs or vice versa. One also might roll over short-term maturities. The nature of investment tactics is described later.

Benchmarking

A third premise for building an investment strategy is related to the determination of the goal for investment yield. Benchmark is the conventional term for this concept. School system investment officers and boards of education should base their investment strategy on the nature of cash flow and an explicit policy reference to risk-yield relationships.

In the News

Investment Benchmarking

The basic understanding of the benchmark concept and its implementation are described in a position paper by Jeffrey B. Flynn:

Chances are, your school board members or others in your district probably have many different ideas about what constitutes successful investing. To those who are adverse to risk, a six or seven percent return may seem quite reasonable. These folks likely are among the millions of people who invest their personal funds in passbook savings accounts.

Others who dabble in options or futures markets with personal funds may see anything less than double-digit returns as complete investing failure. One group or the other may perceive your investment performance as a failure whatever the level of investment return. In order to be judged fairly, you will need to establish some sort of guideline as an investment benchmark. In doing so, you will be setting forth a measure to which your performance can be compared.

The benchmark you select should be in keeping with your own individual investment philosophy. For example, if you employ a frequent short-term rolling approach to investing, chances are that your average maturity is also relatively short. However, if you prepare accurate cash flow forecasts, you may be able to invest in longer term maturities.

This approach generally rewards the investor with higher returns associated with upward sloping yield curves. Therefore, it is important to select a benchmark commensurate with the average maturity of the portfolio. This would represent a fair target for return comparison. If your investments have an average maturity of 176 days, for example, an appropriate benchmark might be a six-month Treasury bill.

Let's examine in general terms, how the benchmark can be used to evaluate relative performance (see Table 12.2). (Yields shown in the chart are illustrative only.) As you can see from the statistics, the weighted average maturity of the portfolio is 129 days and the weighted yield is 8.048 percent. If you select a benchmark with approximately the same maturity you may choose either the 120-day or 150-day Treasury note. As of the same date, these yields were 7.65 percent and 7.76 percent respectively. Therefore, the portfolio is roughly outperforming its benchmark by 10 to 30 basis points, depending on which benchmark you selected.

(Flynn, 1988, p. 56).

Diversification

Diversification, or "putting one's eggs in more than one basket," is appropriate for the short term as well as the long term. The former is important, given that banks and savings and loan associations with insured accounts have gone into receivership and federal insurance may not cover all the CDs held by school systems. In the long term, global economic systems are developing that will affect the financial market in the United States. As more investment options appear, there will be both greater competition and opportunities for investment. Money managers in school systems will need to monitor these trends carefully to select those instruments that provide suitable diversification.

TABLE 12.2 Selected Investment Instruments

Instrument	Minimum Amount	Issuer	Liquidity	Risk
U.S. Treasury Bill	$10,000	U.S. Government	Immediate	Least
U.S. Treasury Bond	1,000	U.S. Government	Immediate	Least
U.S. Treasury Note	5,000 1,000	U.S. Government	Immediate	Least
U.S. Government Agency Bonds	5,000	U.S. Government Corporations	Immediate	Little
Certificates of Deposit	Varied	Banks, Thrifts	Fixed Maturities	Limited Insurance
Repurchase Agreements	Varied	Banks, Brokers	Immediate	Little
Money Market Certificates	Varied	Banks, Thrifts	Fixed Maturities	Limited Insurance
Money Market Funds	1,000	Brokers, Mutual Funds	Immediate	Varies with collateral
Passbook Savings	Minimal	Banks, Thrifts	Immediate	Limited Insurance
Commercial Paper	Varied	Brokers	Immediate	Varies with the financial status of the corporation

Pooling

The investment pool is an investment strategy used in many small school systems where investments are small and short term, and where cash managers have neither the time nor experience to maintain an investment portfolio. Several states have developed such pools for state and local governmental units. Specific provisions vary, but most states, by aggregating the monies of large numbers of units, invest in Treasury bills or Treasury notes. The pool establishes its own cash flow and invests in high-liquidity instruments. Because the maturations are short, the returns are relatively low. The major benefit to school systems, is relatively easy access. The yield is determined on the basis of the amount of a school system's investments and the yield of the pool each day. (If a school system has invested 1 percent of the pool, it will have earned 1 percent of the interest for that day.) Cash managers can monitor the performance of the pool against that of alternative instruments. Liquidity, safety, and convenience appear to be the major strengths of these programs.

Contracting Out

A similar but almost universal strategy is that of a board of education contracting with a bank or other agent for cash management services. Not only does the bank assume responsibility for making the investments, but it also aggregates all school system fund balances into one investment pool, usually called a concentration account.[1] This has the advantages of the bank determining and monitoring cash flow on a daily basis and thus investing larger sums which usually command higher interest rates. A bank can theoretically invest every dollar every day because it has ready access to a whole range of investment instruments.

▮ INVESTMENT TACTICS

Because the financial and investment markets hold so many uncertainties, it is necessary, or at least opportunistic, to make adjustments in the way an investment plan or strategy is actually carried out. Investment tactics are the specific actions taken to implement an overall plan or strategy. It is not practical to describe here the full range of investment tactics available to the school system investment officer. The following are illustrative of some of the generally recognized types.

Riding the Yield Curve

A conventional strategy might call for investments in given instruments, Treasury bills or notes, for example, to be held to maturity. However, under some conditions, it may be advantageous to sell these securities before maturity. A study of yield curves is the means by which such decisions may be made. The tactic, known as "riding the yield curve," is exemplified by the decision as to whether it is more advantageous to buy a 90-day Treasury bill and hold it to maturity or buy a 180-day bill and sell it after 90 days. Investment agents can calculate the net return on these two options by considering the discounted purchase price of both and the discounted purchase price at maturity for the 180-day bill at the end of 90 days. If there were no interest rate changes, it would be concluded that the purchase of the 180-day bill would be advantageous, since the normal yield curve for longer-term bills is higher than that of short term.

One must remember that Treasury bills are bought and sold at discounts that determine their relative interest rates. In the case of the 90-day matured bill, there is no discount while the remainder of the 180-day bill would have the same discount as the 90-day bill. Thus, the school system would have the interest earnings on its 90-day investment at a substantially higher rate than the 90-day bill. However, for this tactic to be successful, the yield curve must be a stable, normal curve. If the discounts change, there is an interest risk.

The following example, again for illustration only, describes the concept of riding the curve.

> *Assume the purchase of a six-month T-Bill generates a 7 percent return if held to maturity. Assuming that rates stay about even, in three months, the original six-month T-Bill will actu-ally become a three-month T-Bill which . . . is yielding 6-1/2 percent. If that T-bill were sold after being held for three months, the actual return on that T-Bill for the time it was held would be 7.52 percent. (If the original amount invested was $96.63, the amount received when sold at 6-1/2 percent was $98.44.) [sic] When the difference is annualized and multiplied by the days held divided by 365, it equals a 7.52 percent return. This return is 52 basis points better than the original purchase yield. As a matter of fact, if interest rates are unchanged and the yield curve has a positive slope to it, selling T-Bills prior to their maturity will always offer a better holding period yield than the original purchase yield. Often, in the short amount of time left for investment of the funds, a Repurchase Agreement (REPO) would be a good choice. REPOs usually pay more than very short maturity T-Bills.* (Flynn, 1988, p. 57)

Spreads

A tactic related to changing yields rather than stable yields is that of "spreads." During peri-ods of economic instability, there are variations in interest rates between closely related instruments such as Treasury bills and Treasury notes. Generally speaking, in periods of uncertainty, risks are perceived to be greater and interest rates increase. When concerns of inflation are reduced, interest rates tend to go down. Treasury notes with shorter maturities in the latter situation need to be reinvested more frequently. If these economic conditions persist, they will be reinvested at rates lower than the longer-term Treasury bills. Thus, yield curves for these two treasuries will show a spread. Treasury notes, because of the interest risk, will be discounted more deeply and thus be purchased with higher interest rates.

Swaps

A somewhat more speculative tactic is the swap. In essence, a security is sold in order to buy another. The objective is to enhance the value of the overall investment portfolio by increasing the yield to maturity of these securities. The swap should not be consummated unless the yield to maturity is definitively increased. Factors such as different maturities and the direction of the yield slopes over the periods of both maturities must be consid-ered. The relationship of spreads over the two maturities must also be put into the analy-sis. A third factor that must be included is the direct and indirect costs associated with swaps. Direct costs are those related to brokers' fees while indirect costs are those related to time, information acquisition and analysis, and the like.

Short-Term Rollovers and Matching

Tactics appropriate to school systems with uncertain or uneven cash flows tend to center on a series of short-term investments. In many instances, these instruments, such as REPOs or CDs, are frequently rolled over when it appears that there will be sufficient cash for investment. The interest rate on these short-term instruments is relatively low, and the time expended for withdrawal and reinvestment is considerable.

A tactic providing greater yield is that of matching. Investment maturities are matched with anticipated expenditures by means of a well-designed cash-flow analysis. Such an analysis can reduce uncertainty and thus enable the investment officer to buy longer-term securities and avoid the short-term rollover. If necessary, the longer-term security can be sold before maturity, and, given a normal yield curve, will produce a greater net interest than that achieved by the alternative of short-term rollovers.

Odd Lots and Round Lots

A related tactic that is applicable on a much larger scale is buying odd lots or round lots. The former, in Treasury bills or notes, is an amount of less than one million dollars; the latter is one million dollars or more. Brokers' fees for odd lots are greater than for round lots, and thus a matching tactic is useful when purchasing these securities.

Arbitrage

The practice of arbitrage—for example, taking the proceeds from a sale of a school system bond issue and reinvesting them in securities that pay an interest rate higher than that of the bond issue—has long been an investment tactic in public school systems. School bond issues are usually exempt from federal and state income taxes; thus, they carry lower interest rates. The spread between interest on bonds and interest paid by Treasury bills or notes can be nearly two percentage points. In most cases, the proceeds of a bond issue are drawn down as construction is completed, so it is appropriate to calculate the cash flow for this revenue.

A simple example will show how this finance technique works. A school district issues $4 million in bonds for construction of school buildings. The bonds bear interest at the rate of 6 percent per year and the interest is exempt from federal income tax. The bond issue has a serial maturity over a ten-year period with the first bonds coming due in two years and the final at ten years. The construction work will be completed in stages and completed in approximately two years. Half of the construction costs must be paid in the first year and the other half in the second year. Half of the bond proceeds will not be needed until year two of construction and can be invested by the district at a higher rate than the bond issue rate during year one, thus yielding a fiscal gain for the district (Weldon, 1989). In essence, the school district is capitalizing financially on simultaneously borrowing and lending the same money by focusing on the yield.

Arbitrage was considered good cash management but the Tax Reform Act of 1986 contained limitations on arbitrage that had the potential of significantly changing school districts' borrowing and lending practices.[2]

Debt Management

School district treasurers or fiduciary agents can also reach the objectives of asset management through careful administration of the system's debt service. School district bonds, for example, are sold to finance construction of school facilities. The bonds are paid off by a tax levy to service (pay off the principal plus interest) the debt over a period of years. The interest rate is determined at the time the bonds are sold.

The market for school bonds varies over the years. In the early 1990s, with a stagnant national economy, interest rates fell. Treasurers or business administrators from districts with high levels of bonded indebtedness refunded bond issues carrying high interest rates with the proceeds from a new bond issue carrying a lower interest rate. An example of this would be a bond issue of $27.1 million with an interest rate of 8.62 percent. Five years later, this was refunded with a 22.5 million issue with a 6.0 percent interest rate. Thus, the net savings on debt service was an estimated $5 million, a significant savings for the district's taxpayers.

■ INVESTMENT INSTRUMENTS

A wide variety of instruments are available for school system investment programs. Each has unique characteristics as to risk, yield, and liquidity. Naturally, the school system official with investment authority must limit choices to those that meet state and school system statutory standards. In most systems, investment opportunities for large amounts over long periods of time are relatively few. Thus, shorter-term investment instruments suited to unique cash flows are the most popular. However, as the following sections dealing with investment strategies and tactics suggest, it is possible to sell, swap, or spread long-term securities and derive the advantages of relatively high interest, possible appreciation, and reasonable liquidity. Some of the major groups of investment instruments are described in the following subsections and summarized in Table 12.3.

U.S. Treasury Bills, Bonds, and Notes

Treasury issues are backed by the U.S. government and are considered the lowest risk investment. They are sold at government auctions and thus reflect the interest rates in effect at the time of sale. School systems usually buy and sell these instruments on the open market through brokers. Because the bond interest rate is fixed, changes in interest rates in the financial markets are reflected in the price on the face of the instrument. For example, a $7\frac{3}{8}$ percent 30-year $1,000 bond to mature in ten years may be discounted in the market.

Treasury bills have maturities of thirteen, twenty-six, and fifty-two weeks, and are issued in $10,000 denominations. Treasury notes of $5,000 denominations mature in two

TABLE 12.3 Example Investment Returns

Investment Type	Amount	Percent of Portfolio	Weighted Average Buy Yield	Weighted Average Maturity
Total Repurchase Agreements	$1,000,000.00	8.33%	7.900%	42 days
Total Bankers Acceptances	$984,100.00	8.20%	8.078%	72 days
Total CDs and Bank Investments	$3,000,000.00	24.99%	7.540%	31 days
Total Treasury Securities	$2,547,428.67	21.22%	7.980%	211 days
Total Agency Securities	$4,471,170.83	37.25%	8.453%	180 days
Total Investment Portfolio	$12,002,699.50	100.00%	8.048%	129 days
Portfolio Average Weekly Earnings at Buy Yield—$18,575.68.				

or three years, while $1,000 notes mature in four to ten years. U.S. bonds are issued for thirty years in $1,000 denominations.

U.S. Government Agency Bonds

A host of government corporations issue bonds to specific government-sponsored activities. Most familiar are the Federal National Mortgage Association (Fannie Mae), Government National Mortgage Association (Ginnie Mae), and Federal Home Loan Mortgage Corporation (Freddie Mac). These are largely secured by mortgages, but are not wholly insured by the full faith and credit of the government. They may be purchased through banks or brokers.

Certificates of Deposit

School systems use CDs in the same ways that other investors use them. However, the banks that issue CDs may make special provisions for large amounts with shorter maturities to serve the unique interests of the school system. A major criterion for selecting a bank to deal with is whether the CD is collateralized—that is, fully secured by U.S. Treasuries or other insured securities. School systems have encountered problems when CDs were secured by bad loans and the bank or savings and loan association went into receivership. Penalties are charged for early withdrawal (before scheduled maturation).

Repurchase Agreements

Repurchase agreements are used for relatively short-term investments (even overnight or over a weekend). A school system agrees to invest its funds for a given number of days and takes title to bank securities as collateral. At maturity, the bank repurchases the securities, and the school system receives the original investment, plus interest. These investments tend to be highly liquid, and the risk is governed by the quality of the collateral. The yield is relatively low but certainly greater than that obtained from a checking account.

Money Market Certificates, Money Market Funds, and Passbook Savings

These conventional instruments are designed for the general public but are sometimes used in school system investment programs. Yields reflect the going interest rate. Ordinarily, relatively small amounts can be invested because there is reasonably high liquidity. Risk is related to the collateral provided by the bank so this becomes a major concern.

Commercial Paper

Several states permit school systems to purchase commercial paper (e.g., corporate bonds). These instruments usually carry a relatively high rate of interest, and thus reflect a relatively high risk because they are not backed by government securities, but instead by the financial resources of the issuing corporation. An example of the worst selection is that of "junk bonds" used in leveraged buyouts in the corporate takeovers of the late 1980s. On the positive side, high-quality commercial paper is available with relatively little risk in AA-rated utility bonds and other similar issues.

Selecting among Alternative Instruments

School officials with responsibility for investment programs have many alternatives suited to the unique cash flow and investment objectives of their school systems. Investments may be made for the long or short term, for relatively high or low yield, and with varying degrees of liquidity. The investment program may be simple, with only REPOs and CDs; or it may be complex, with changing packages of investment instruments to fit the ebb and flow of available cash.

Summary

The investment of idle cash, or momentarily idle cash, in school systems is a legitimate exercise in the stewardship of public monies dedicated to providing public education. Investment protects or enhances the purchasing power of these dollars that will eventually be expended for educational services.

A cash-flow analysis is a prerequisite to determining the amount for and timing of investments. Such an analysis provides data necessary to make decisions as to the optimum kinds of investments to make. In most situations, a variety of instruments will provide the portfolio best fitted to the cash-flow analysis. Typically, long-term securities carry higher interest rates so these are well suited to the proportion of cash available for a relatively long term. Those parts of the cash flow over the given period of time that constitute small amounts and/or shorter terms of investment potential can be invested in instruments suited to maturity and amounts indicated.

Factors that must be considered in developing an investment program for a school system include legal constraints, risk, yield, and liquidity. The public nature of the gathering, use, and investment of school system monies is the most important concern because it guides all other considerations. Risk, yield, and liquidity are interrelated, and thus policies must be developed to guide investment decisions. High yields carry with them high risk—principal risk and interest risk. Liquidity also comes as a trade-off with risk and yield.

Investment policy also suggests alternative strategies that can be employed. Yield curve analysis, market analysis, and the establishment of an investment benchmark are useful in determining a general investment plan. In carrying out a plan, an investment officer has a host of tactics available. Tactics are employed to optimize investment in a changing market economy. Techniques of rolling or matching, riding the yield curve, and buying and selling on the basis of spreads are used in day-by-day investment decisions.

Every school system has some opportunity for investment. To achieve satisfactory results, it is necessary at the minimum, to develop a cogent and complete policy, a comprehensive cash-flow analysis, and an overall strategy. Investment tactics can be rather simple or very complex, depending on their components, risk, yield, and liquidity. Return on investment is an important bottom line. However, an even more important line is that the investment program is a means to the end of providing increased support for the educational program.

Discussion Questions

1. From your school system's fiscal and/or accounting reports, develop a cash-flow history over the past four or five years. Develop some general conclusions as to possibilities for the investment programs.
2. Based on number 1, develop a specific proposal for an investment program (compatible with school system policy) involving long-term (longer than one fiscal year) and short-term (shorter than one year) planning.
3. Survey several local banks and brokers to ascertain current interest rates, minimum amounts to be invested, maturity periods, and other data relevant to investment options.
4. Interview your school system's fiscal and/or accounting reports and develop a cash-flow history over the past four or five years. Develop some general conclusions as to possibilities for the investment program.

Web Resources

Texas Comptroller of Public Accounts, Texas School Performance Review offers a comprehensive overview of school district investing—
http://www.cpa.state.tx.us/tspr/inv/index.html

References

Dembowski, F.L., & Davey, R.D. (1995). School district financial management and Banking. In R. Craig Wood (Ed.), *Principles of school business management.* Reston, VA: Association of School Business Officials International, pp. 13.1–13.25.

Ferguson, T.E. (1993, October 12). Audit Bulletin AB No. 93-003, Columbus, OH: Auditor of State.

Flynn, J. (1990). *The art of investing school district funds: Rules of the games.* Reston, VA: Association of School Business Officials International.

Flynn, J.B. (1988, December). Ensuring investment success. *School Business Affairs* 54(12), 56.

Flynn, J.B. (1988, July). Investments—A "rolling" philosophy or "matching" philosophy? *School Business Affairs* 54(7), 57.

Karvelis, L.J., Jr. (1995, April). The "D" words default and derivatives in Orange County. *School Business Affairs* 61(4), 46–47.

Weldon, W. (1989). Arbitrage interest rules and school district borrowing. *School Business Affairs* 55(1), 10–13.

Notes

1. Zero-balance accounting is an implementing concept for developing the concentration account. All other accounts in the school system are established for given purposes. As accounts payable, they carry a zero balance, and all monies are aggregated in the concentration account from which investments are made. School officials write checks on the various accounts payable. When these checks clear with the bank, the exact amounts are drawn from the concentration account on a daily basis to cover each of them. Thus, cash balances are fully invested each day.

2. For a more complete explanation of the implications of the Tax Reform Act of 1986 see Weldon [1989] or contact the Internal Revenue Service of the United States.

CHAPTER THIRTEEN

Managing Personnel

■ INTRODUCTION

A school district's human resources responsibility, including collective bargaining for the district, may well fall under the aegis of the school business manager. Also, it is frequently within the school business administrator's purview that technically and clerically oriented persons and supervisors of skilled and nonskilled employees must come together to discuss and solve problems.

LEARNING OBJECTIVES

In this chapter a reader will learn about:

- The evolving personnel management context.
- The necessity of an organization having updated employee position descriptions.
- Major federal laws that influence personnel recruitment and selections.
- Personnel orientation, training, development, motivation, supervision, evaluation, promotion, discipline, termination, and retirement.
- Collective bargaining's statutory foundations.
- Bargaining issues such as scope, collective, and individual bargaining.
- Collective bargaining strategies, contract administration, grievance and dispute resolution tactics.
- School business official's role in collective bargaining and dispute resolution.
- Personnel budgeting matters such as salaries, performance pay, fringe benefits, and assistance programs.

■ THE EVOLVING PERSONNEL MANAGEMENT CONTEXT

Contemporary management orientation toward organized labor is typically less emotion-laden than the conflict-filled conditions that characterized the last quarter of the twentieth century. Findings from behavioral science research have contributed to an employee-centered management approach. Far wider worker expectations have been fostered by a new social climate derived in part from a growing level of education and the development of the world's most inclusive communications network. The old-time owner or manager holding a major or even exclusive proprietary interest in the business has now been substantially displaced and succeeded by hired administrators oriented toward management as a profession.

Another contemporary condition worthy of note is that inclusion of women in the labor market expanded dramatically during the twentieth century. By 1990 more than 70 percent of all U.S. women between the ages of 25 and 65 were in the labor market, and more than 50 percent of all new persons added to the labor force have been women. Consequently, new insurance concerns, flexible work schedules, and family leave provisions are major parts of most new labor contracts. Finally, the right of workers to organize and bargain collectively, free of employer restraint or coercion, has been protected by statutes since the mid-1930s (Sloan & Witney, 2004).

Additionally, the concept of site-based management often conflicts with general provisions that unions wish to include in contracts to cover services to the district as a whole. As will be seen in other sections, site-based labor-management conflicts often flow from contracted differences and from the attempt to use grievance procedures to extend (from a union perspective) or to loosen (from a management perspective) basic contract provisions.

However, not all labor-management challenges reside within the immediate sphere of the business manager. Labor, too, has issues that it must resolve. Unions, outside of education, are faced with declining numbers and changing membership characteristics. The interests of older and younger union members often differ, with older workers frequently preferring increased benefits, while younger workers often are most interested in higher wages. Minorities are frequently less committed than are longer-standing union members in seniority systems that are perceived as a hindrance to promotions and wage increases. Members of some professional groups value their status as individuals more than they do communal membership in a union.

An effective school business manager education recognizes all the above-mentioned complexity and is mindful of the goals of the organization, the needs of people, and the effects of social and technological change in organizing a plan of operation that allows for variability among groups and simultaneously displays a concern for the individual employee.

Naturally, dynamic context within which the school business manager operates generates conflict. The school business is often engaged in managing conflict relative to the distribution of resources, including budget allocations, assignments of service staff, allocation of space, and issues of autonomy.

■ PERSONNEL PLANNING, RECRUITMENT, AND ASSIGNMENT

The school business administrator can be of significant assistance to the total school district in the area of personnel planning and recruitment. Few conditions benefit more from detailed analysis than the general question of what transpires in a school district—from the local school to the operations at the central office. It is imperative that district personnel constantly evaluate the requirements and responsibilities of each particular employee position. Below are management considerations about which a school business official must constantly be conscious.

Job Descriptions

A detailed job description is a must for each specific position within a school district, from data entry personnel to superintendent. Certain job descriptions are more routine, more easily established, and involve fewer nebulous statements than others. However, all job descriptions must be as detailed as possible and be written clearly, so that the interviewer and the interviewee are able to evaluate the requirements of the position.

Job descriptions are developed from job analyses and detail the specific activities, responsibilities, and requirements of the position. These guidelines include skills necessary, types of responsibility, and limitations imposed by the job. Federal, state, and local fair employment practices must always be considered when developing job descriptions. The more detailed the job description, the less conflict thereafter develops. Following is a description of custodial duties for a large school system.

I. Custodial Duties
Custodial personnel of the public schools are responsible for:
A. Cleaning, heating, minor maintenance, and maintaining . . . .
B. Providing services (cooperatively determined by the principal and head custodian) to the faculty and student body.
II. Custodial Responsibility during the School Year
A. During the school year, the head custodian is directly under the supervision of the principal. In schools where there is more than one custodian, custodial helpers and maids are responsible to the principal through the head custodian. The head custodian is responsible to the principal for:

   1. Cleaning and minor maintenance of the building.
   2. Heating the building.

B. During the school year, custodians are responsible for providing certain services to teachers and the student body that are listed.
III. Custodial Responsibility during Summer Months
All custodians who are on duty during the summer months are under the direction of the Director of Plant Operations and Maintenance, who will deploy them to address various responsibilities.

The final composition of a job description can be influenced by the results of union agreements or civil service contracts in effect within the district. In areas of high unionization, the slightest alteration in a job description may require union agreement or at least becomes a subject for negotiation at the time of the next bargaining session. Until that time, the job description usually has to remain unchanged. Legislation has restricted such statements as "male only" or "under twenty-five years of age" in job listings and descriptions.

Personnel Selection and Recruitment

Supply and demand often influence personnel selection. The adage "select the best person for the job" is certainly not wrong, nor is it to be cast aside. It may be better to leave a position unfilled than to fill it with an improperly trained individual or an individual with a poor or unrealistic attitude toward the job or the world of work in general. No effort should be spared to select competent personnel and to compensate them adequately.

Personnel selection procedures should be detailed and available for review as part of general school board policy and procedures. Proper affirmative action practices must always be followed. In several states, laws have been adopted requiring that selected city school districts secure classes of candidates from approved civil service lists. These lists are constructed from test results and personnel records for use by all governmental units. This phenomenon most typically is a function of a fiscally dependent school district, one that is an administrative arm of a municipal or county government.

Where appropriate, some positions, for example, nurse or engineering technician, require an applicant to hold a state license. Also, some positions may be covered under union agreements requiring the appropriate apprentice, journeyman, or craftsman designation. This brings about uniformity of pay scale across all agencies and is generally combined with a detailed employee classification structure.

Depending on the type and use of local board policy, building principals' counsel in the selection of noncertified staff will vary. In those systems in which major site-based expenditures are authorized by the principal, selection of personnel may be a major responsibility.

If personnel selection is a local function directed by the building principal, then the role of the school building administrator may be one of advertising, initial screening, and contract interpreting, as opposed to actual selection and placement of personnel. The varying responsibilities dictated by the two different roles certainly require different administrative application by the school business administrator.

■ MACRO POLICY CONSIDERATIONS

Major federal laws that impact recruitment and selections include:

- Equal Pay Act.
- Title VII of the Civil Rights Act.
- Age Discrimination in Employment Act.
- Equal Employment Opportunity Act.
- Vocational Rehabilitation Act.
- Executive Order 11246.
- Vietnam Era Veterans Readjustment Act.
- Americans with Disabilities Act.
- Title IX Act.
- Family Leave Act.
  (Webb & Norton, 2003, p. 280)

Below is a summary of several of these federal acts promoting equal employment opportunity.

Title IX Act

The application of Title IX and affirmative action guidelines to the selection of employees of school districts clearly revolves around the need to avoid discrimination claims relative to gender and minority group hiring practices established by state, federal, and local authorities. Adherence to the published standards of affirmative action developed by the local school district and approved by the appropriate governmental bodies provides the basis for the school business administrator's selection process.

The nondiscriminatory factors of Title IX relative to equal facilities, equal opportunities, and equal access for both male and female participants in any kind of selection process, as well as the necessary affirmative action hiring practices relative to race, gender, and handicapping conditions, must be strictly adhered to by the school business administrator. Care must be taken to inquire only about appropriate information from a potential employee. Certain questions, such as those concerning marital status, life style, and expected length of employment, cannot be asked. However, questions related to job skills are appropriate.

Age Discrimination in Employment Act of 1967

This act is designed to protect individuals who are at least forty years of age, from age discrimination in terms of replacement by younger workers or in terms of reduction of benefits or loss of tenure time and pension support through discriminatory firing practices.

Family Leave Act of 1993

School business administrators and school districts must be alert to the provisions of the 1993 Family Leave Act and the possible impact on staffing patterns. Maternity leave has been in place (either in board policy or professional agreement) for some time. However, the new provisions of the Family Leave Act permitting leave time for fathers of newly born or adopted children may create new pressures on staffing. The provision also provides extended leave time for illness of parents, children, or spouse. This will add even more pressure to the already complex staffing patterns of school districts.

Although only in place for a limited time, this act influences current staffing patterns and may be a major issue relative to professional negotiations. Most government mandates—good or bad—often come with stiff requirements and little or no funding support.

Americans with Disabilities Act of 1990

In general, the provision of the Americans with Disabilities Act is a broad-based effort to avoid discrimination of individuals who are physically challenged or who have a handicapping condition. This act prohibits systematic denial of access, job opportunities, and other activities based solely on a handicapping condition.

Equal Pay Act of 1963

Amending the Fair Labor Standards Act, the Equal Pay Act prohibits wage differentials based on sex. In passing the bill, Congress denounced sex discrimination for the following reason:

- depresses wages and living standards for employees necessary for their health and efficiency.
- prevents the maximum utilization of the available labor resources.
- tends to cause labor disputes, thereby burdening, affecting, and obstructing commerce.
- burdens commerce and the free flow of goods in commerce.
- constitutes an unfair method of competition.

Few conditions are more damaging to a school district's reputation than a board of education that personally intervenes in personnel selection, recruitment, and retention of staff members, instead of setting policies for these activities. A school business administrator should exert maximum professional influence to ensure proper personnel policies are established at the board of education level and that proper personnel selection is pursued within the school business department.

Recruitment involves the need to plan for both short- and long-range personnel needs of the district. A current need for qualified personnel must be addressed, while long-range planning must be designed to ensure a continued supply of qualified personnel. The difficulty of recruitment is measured by the difference between the demand for and the supply of qualified personnel. The school board administrator must provide the school board with sufficient data on the recruitment alternatives and practices so that an evaluation of the impact of each can be made.

■ ORIENTATION, TRAINING, DEVELOPMENT, AND MOTIVATION

Job Orientation

Job orientation is a key element of success in any employment program. Proper instructions, job descriptions, and job analyses all provide a newly hired staff member a way to orient to what is expected and required to be successful in the position. An organization of virtually any size should have a detailed orientation program. A specific plan should be implemented to introduce new employees to the various functions of the organization. This gives the individual a sense for who does what, why it is done, and how a function fits into the overall operation of an effective school district. It is imperative that the orientation program be developed to such an extent that the newly employed individual is made to feel important, as a viable part of the organization, rather than just a certain anonymous person at a certain desk in a certain row.

Material covered in an orientation session includes information on employee welfare, such as the district's fringe benefit package, insurance, sick leave and maternity policy, vacation schedules, and medical and hospital benefits. Additional points to be covered include job-related information on promotion policy, grievance procedures, and the manner in which jobs are classified and defined. A copy of the school board policy manual should be available to all employees. Detailed information as to the nature of the specific position being filled and its role in the system should be offered.

Job Training

The training of employees to be efficient in the school district is an important element of any successful program. The most basic and perhaps simplest training program is orientation for new employees. Usually, little job-related material is presented; emphasis is on introductory information and housekeeping procedures, with the main purpose being to make employees feel comfortable in adjusting to their new employment surroundings, particularly in the department or area to which they are assigned. The most important facet of training, however, may be that which goes beyond the orientation phase and becomes a complicated process of technique and motivation as employees are persuaded to discard inefficient practices and learn new, more productive skills.

A logical beginning point at which to determine training requirements is the labor planning process. This is accomplished through job analysis that defines appropriate knowledge in skill areas and performance appraisals, and also indicates how adequately these have been attained. Yet another approach in determining training needs is to review other organizational records, such as accident reports; grievances; principal, student, teacher, and parent complaints; and employee attitude surveys, assessment center results, and skills text analyses.

Once a training needs analysis has been completed, the question of priority always arises. Because no school system has unlimited financial resources, the human resources department can cope with only a restricted number of training programs. When the school board or superintendent's staff has set priorities, the next step is to choose the appropriate training methods.

Perhaps the most widely accepted training method is on-the-job training, usually conducted by a supervisor in the particular area in which the training is to occur. Pretraining steps include establishment of timetables to learn the skills, disaggregating the job into learning segments, having all materials available, and arranging a workplace as the employee would find it.

The general induction process for any noncertified (not licensed) staff member must be directed at helping newly assigned personnel subject to their new work environment. It is important to remember that time spent in the induction process is often a beneficial investment because much turnover occurs during the initial weeks of employment. Because change and turnover often cause hostility or resistance, and because frustration often develops when new employees find a difference between job expectations and job realities, a smooth induction process is essential to maintaining an organization's effective functioning. Additionally, these concerns have cost implications, because the recruitment, selection, induction, and data training costs are major considerations for the school business administrator and school districts.

Internships combining on-the-job training with classroom instruction, ranging from local classes taught by in-house personnel to those taught by university and technical school faculty, are another method of instructing and conducting training. Apprenticeship training is similar to training occurring separate from the actual workplace but with similar equipment. It is often referred to as vestibule training, in that it involves both on- and off-job-site learning.

Probably the newest and most efficient, as well as one of the most promising, training techniques is Internet-based and computer-assisted instruction. The majority of such computer programs adjusts the instruction to the level of the student, and material is selected to provide a student with the most beneficial format. The flexibility of computerized learning and computerized training is limited only to the effectiveness of the software that can be developed. In many instances, computerized training can be developed for use with regular employees, learning-disabled employees, and employees with physical disabilities.

However, after a training program has been accomplished by whatever appropriate methods selected, the final step is to evaluate what has been accomplished. A training program should have taught the desired knowledge, and the new skills should result in the anticipated outcome at the workplace.

Employee Development

As important as personnel planning and recruitment are to the overall development of an effective program within a school district, the development of employees once they are members of the organization is even more significant. The expenditures made on staff selection, orientation, and recruitment can be wasted if an effective development program is not established for the total school district and for those specific areas considered. These functions can be reinforced through the effective implementation of evaluation procedures and through proper overall personnel supervision.

Staff development changed markedly during the 1990s. Emphasis shifted to interactive and interdependent programs rather than isolated projects, to site-based plans rather than centralized plans, to emphasis on technology and unlimited methods and types of delivery rather than limited use of technology and state methods of delivery, and, finally, to more staff involvement in identification, planning, and implementation rather than the use of top-down, predetermined, "outside"-directed plans (Webb & Norton, 2003).

Job obsolescence is a recent phenomenon for school districts and is directly related to the fact that more and more jobs have become technically oriented. Many of the operations responsibilities of the school district now are highly technical or involve at least a minimum amount of technical ability. The need for more general-purpose custodial staff and simply more people to do a job has vanished from public school settings, as it has from other industrial and private sector situations. Many of the jobs performed by receptionists, telephone operators, clerks, sweepers, cleaners, and painters, that required little or no technical capability, have now been replaced by positions for which much more technical expertise is required.

Economic necessity and better health care have combined to extend the work career of many school system employees. The desire of many employees to retire early has been tempered by the economic challenges of retirement living. Furthermore, many people who wish to work at a second career are unable to find such employment and are keeping jobs for longer periods. While this reduces the cost of recruitment and training, it increases basic payroll costs and reduces the flow of new ideas (through personnel) into the organization.

In-service training, while as old as the concept of the professionally trained teacher, continually challenges school districts to select meaningful and rewarding experiences for its employees. Such programs are generally planned for the central office professional personnel and the teaching staffs of school districts, but are often overlooked for classified and technical personnel.

In-service training, or, more properly, staff renewal (given the proper philosophical and managerial foundations), can be quite useful in upgrading skills and developing knowledge that staff members lack when they come to an organization. Release time may be provided for the attendance of these functions, and incremental pay schedules may be based on completion of certain predetermined courses or experiences. While specific prerequisites for every step of upgrading staff cannot always be identified as precisely as those for the Certified Professional Secretary (CPS), rewarding and meaningful experiences can be provided when some thought and preparation are involved in their selection.

It is important that staff members be involved in determining areas for staff in-service or staff renewal activities. Current employees may have sufficient expertise to conduct certain classes or demonstrate use of certain types of equipment. It is not an unusual practice to invite selected personnel from other divisions within a school system to provide presentations in the staff renewal process. Cost and time considerations may make the use of in-house personnel desirable.

With continued pressure to maximize use of scarce school system resources, the concept of shared resources for staff renewal activities is widely used. This can entail cooperation by educational cooperatives, boards of cooperative educational services, and independent districts or can simply be a shared experience between two adjacent districts.

Often, experiences can be structured to use key personnel for larger groups at no additional cost or to use local personnel as team leaders for group discussions.

A feature of staff renewal programs that has gained national attention is the point system, or variable unit program. Under this plan, numerous opportunities—short courses, college credit work, travel, regular in-service days, and so forth—are assigned "points" based on a determination by a coordinating body of staff and administrators. Some experiences are mandatory, while others are chosen by each participant until a specified number of points are obtained. Individualization is a key consideration, and all participants generally welcome the flexibility of choices.

Employee Motivation

The area of employee motivation concerns all administrative personnel. A school business administrator is concerned not only with the day-to-day operations of a division, but also with staff motivation to perform assigned duties. Motivation is directly linked to good personnel practices. For example, most employees perform more efficiently if predetermined goals are established within a job description and if basic procedures for accomplishing goals are established. If a list of available staff renewal opportunities is posted and policies on coffee breaks and lunch hours are spelled out, most employees function more effectively.

Motivation is also enhanced by the existence of salary increments based on predetermined and established criteria. Established goals and responsibilities that are rewarded by promotions and pay raises are important to almost all employees. Small increments, awarded frequently, are generally more effectively used with clerical- and technical-level personnel than are yearly increments, which are more often awarded to professional-level personnel.

Personnel Supervision

There is little question that supervision is necessary for all employees, whether it be specific, direct, and continuous, or a part of the general personnel policies of an organization. The supervision of any staff position is directly related to staff evaluation, and, therefore, staff retention or termination. Insofar as possible, supervision should be a direct, responsive condition of an organization in which supervisory communication lines are reciprocally open for two-way communication. Supervision is more effective when the supervisor and the boundaries of supervision are clearly identified.

While supervision is distasteful to many classified personnel, it is essential to establishing an effective and well-ordered program. Supervision of any employee is always based on the job or position (as defined by the job description) for which the employee is hired. The basis of evaluation forms and questions must be found in the job description as presented to the employee.

Veto powers of a building-level administrator are directly related to the amount of site-based control that board policy permits. With major site-based budgeting, principals traditionally have primary control over custodial and, to some degree, operational staff at their site.

A school business administrator should document efforts regarding the manner in which staff, faculty, students, and other school-related personnel are trained to address sexual, social, ethnic, or other areas of harassment. Problems dealing with all levels and types of personnel and varied situations need to be in place, in action, and regularly evaluated.

Staff Evaluation

All staff members are evaluated at periodic intervals. Much staff member evaluation occurs on a day-to-day basis, is informal, and is nonstructured. However, any well-structured organization has predetermined patterns for the evaluation of staff members. Whether evaluation takes the form of interviews, rating sheets, tests, or a combination of several of these, it must be done on a periodic and established basis.

Staff evaluations should be a cooperative venture. Under no circumstances should an evaluation become a "witch-hunt" in which a supervisor is searching for faults in a staff member's performance. As with student evaluation, the goal is to determine areas of strength upon which to build and areas of weakness to be improved.

One productive way to establish an evaluation policy is to provide a degree of self-evaluation. Proper emphasis must be placed on the central activity within the staff member's job description. To give too much weight to an activity that is not defined or understood by the employee to be a prime area of responsibility is unfair to the employee and is damaging to total employee-employer relations. The evaluation method must mirror activities that are specified in the job description.

The evaluation on the part of supervisors and staff members should be viewed as a constructive effort directed at the improvement of the performance of the particular staff member and toward the betterment of the supervisory process under which that staff member operates. In keeping with this idea, it is useful to consider that other resources beyond the local division, or even the department, may be called upon to facilitate the evaluation procedure.

Job targets, work plans, and other organized schemes for planning what needs to be accomplished by individual staff members have emerged as a major activity for many school districts. The development of each administrator's own job target or work plan for the year has become a major feature in the evaluation of most staff members within a system. The development of the work plan is a cooperative effort between the administration and the individual staff member. The supervisor and staff member determine what is expected from the staff member throughout the coming year. The year-end evaluation conference determines how successfully these goals have been met. First evaluation efforts may lead to over- or underestimation of employees on the part of staff members, but after one or two efforts, staff members come "on target."

Management by objectives (MBO) represents an umbrella approach for managing an entire organization. The key to effective MBO deployment by the school business administrator and other members of the school administrative team is that all levels of the organization have goals from which the objectives can emerge. Goals must be available from the very top (board) to the very bottom (employee) to be effective.

A major feature of the MBO process is that an individual employee and immediate supervisor agree on what the job responsibilities are and on written objectives to meet these responsibilities. A review of these objectives follows. Finally, the appraisal process occurs. The employee provides factual data on which performance can be judged. The degree of success in presenting these data then determines the reward (positive or negative) for the employee (McGregor, 2000).

Promotion

Promotion policies in a school district should reward competence and experience on the part of employees and should specify qualifications such as seniority and skill levels needed for promotion. The school business administrator and the planning team may cooperate to determine promotion policies for certified personnel, while the administrator alone is often directly responsible for promotion policies affecting a large number of noncertified personnel.

In many districts, union agreements determine most of the ground rules for promotion, both within a section and across division lines. Stipulations as to training, seniority, and pay schedules are covered in all union agreements insofar as these affect promotion policy. In districts where noncertified personnel are not covered by union agreements, a set of personnel policies should be established that guarantee rewards for those deserving them, yet protects the district against unfair exploitation. Some employees can be covered under civil service, with the attendance rules and regulations associated with civil service appointments.

Employee Discipline

Employee discipline issues are a part of most negotiated contracts. Contract provisions discuss the types of conduct that are seen as inappropriate and specify general codes of expected conduct, including specific behavior and the consequences of specific behaviors (e.g., arrests, convictions). These provisions are part of the basic labor agreement, which also enumerates provisions for grievances.

In the News

The following is an example of a basic labor agreement taken from the Staff Handbook of the Metropolitan Nashville Public Schools.

An employee of the District shall not engage in any conduct, behavior, activity, or association that discredits the employee and/or the District. Each employee is expected to exhibit behavior, both on and off the job, which will reflect credit on both the employee and the District.

It shall be the duty of each employee to maintain high standards of cooperation, efficiency, and economy in his/her work. Department heads or supervisors shall organize and direct the work of their units to achieve the objectives. When work habits, attitude, production, or personal conduct of an employee fall below a desirable standard, supervisors should point out, where possible, the deficiency at the time it is observed. Any disciplinary action resulting from a deficiency will take place as soon as possible but at most within 40 working days.

No employee may be terminated, suspended, or demoted in pay grade, except for just cause and after a hearing before the department head/principal or other appointing authority.

Whenever possible a department head/principal should conduct an investigation (including all parties involved) to whatever extent possible before proceeding with a disciplinary hearing.

Charges for any disciplinary action against an employee must be initiated by the department head/school principal or another employee.

From: Handbook for the support personnel of the metropolitan public schools, Nashville-Davidson County, Tennessee, 2005, pp. 25–28.

Causes for Disciplinary Action

An employee may be disciplined for just cause for the following actions (among others):

- Neglect of duty.
- Failure to perform one's duties.
- Inefficiency in the performance of one's duties.
- Insubordination.
- Positive test result from alcohol/drug test.
- The possession or carrying, whether openly or concealed, any weapon on any school property, real or personal.
- Giving false information on employment application or on application for promotional positions.
  (Metropolitan Nashville Public Schools, 2005, pp. 25–28)

Clear policies relative to sexual harassment have become major issues in education. Several concerns are noted as follows:

- Does your district have clear policies regarding sexual harassment, both verbal and physical (harassment of students by other students, harassment of students by staff, and harassment of employees by other employees)?
- Is the guiding principle of these policies creating a safe, respectful environment for learning?
- Do the policies:
  - Define harassment?
  - Require staff to report harassment and intervene to stop it?
  - Identify people who can receive harassment reports?
  - List possible consequences for harassers?
- Is an officer appointed to coordinate prevention efforts and receive harassment reports?
- Are parents, students, and staff members aware of the policies?
- Are staff members assigned to respond to harassment reports appropriately instructed in how to conduct thorough investigations?
- Is the district prepared fully to document the scope and findings of any investigations?
- Is the district prepared to deal with privacy concerns?
- Does district staff know which incidents must be referred to law enforcement in your state? (Hardy, 2002, p. 16)

Personnel Termination

Generally speaking, personnel terminations are not pleasant. However, some terminations are routine and should be viewed as such. Terminations that carry out board policies having to do with health and residency requirements are viewed as routine policy actions and are carried out accordingly. There should be no ill will involved, nor should there be any reluctance to specify the policy as the reason for termination of the employee.

As with many facets of promotion, termination procedures are often covered in union agreements. If this is the case, most of the reasons for termination and the avenues open to both parties are outlined in detail. Alteration or abandonment of these procedures becomes a point for litigation and union-management bargaining, and all situations remain static until negotiations can be conducted and completed.

In some school districts, where employment of noncertified personnel falls under civil service, provisions and regulations associated with termination are specified. In some cases, noncertified personnel may have tenure status in the school district.

In any situation involving employee termination, the school business administrator and the system's legal staff must ensure that due process is granted to the staff members. An employee has every right to due process, and the school system is obligated to see that the individual is informed of rights and the avenues of appeal that may apply.

When applicable, a severance pay package can be available. Again, board policy dictates circumstances and amounts of severance pay. Read the textbook that follows for a typical example of a school district's severance policy.

Severance Policy Statement

Employees who are laid off will be provided an allowance (severance pay) based on length of continuous service with the Board. Employees who resign, retire, or are otherwise terminated prior to being identified for layoff are not eligible to receive severance pay.

Severance pay is calculated as follows:

Length of Service	Weeks of Payment
Less than 1 year	1 week
1 year but less than 3 years	2 weeks
3 years but less than 6 years	3 weeks
6 years but less than 10 years	4 weeks
10 years or more	6 weeks

Severance pay given to employees will follow these guidelines:

- Payments will be at the employee's base rate of pay at the time of layoff. Supplements will not be included.
- Payment to eligible employees will be made in a lump sum.
- An employee who has been paid a lump sum and is then reinstated prior to the expiration of the period represented by the lump sum payment shall be required to return to the Board that portion which covers any period following reinstatement. Repayment may be made either in a lump sum or by payroll deduction.

(Memphis City Schools, [1995]."Severance Pay," *Personnel Policy Manual*, Policy 4110.)

Terminations become unpleasant when a lack of productivity, a lack of ability, or an unwillingness on the part of the supervisor or the employee to resolve a difference of opinion necessitates the employee's termination "with cause." The key word here is, of course, *cause*. To replace persons summarily in nonunion systems without justifiable cause is damaging to the total morale of a school system. Though not issued formally, this kind of information will "spread among employees." Proper review and appeal procedures should be built into board policies to cover any differences between professional and nonprofessional terminations within the system.

It should be made clear to the individual at the time of employment that there are avenues of appeal and that grievances can be pursued through legal channels. This action is a rare occurrence, but it can happen, and parties are under obligation to apprise each other of the situation.

Termination within a fixed probationary period is a general feature of most employment contracts. The administration has an initial period to determine whether the employee exhibits the necessary traits and skills to perform the job properly.

Generally, the provisions for dismissal during the period are oriented toward management and are not as stringent as during a later term of employment. As always, however, dismissal should be based on concrete, documented reasons.

In the event of discharge, the following provisions regularly apply: (1) the employer will only discharge employees for just cause; (2) the employee being discharged has the right to meet with a union representative before leaving the employer's property; and (3) if the employee or the union representative considers the discharge to be improper, a complaint normally shall be presented in writing through this representative within a specified number of working days. Generally, concerns have centered on procedural rights of persons terminated rather than on the authority of schools to terminate or what is identified as substantive due process.

Contractual arrangements usually state that the employer has the right to discharge any employee for such actions as: (1) not returning from sick leave or leave of absences, (2) being under the influence of intoxicants or drugs, (3) falsifying records, (4) moral offenses, and (5) stealing board and/or other employee property.

In general, the employer sends written notification to the employee at the last known address stating that the employee has lost seniority and the individual's employment has been terminated. In case of discharge for one of the reasons listed, a review may be possible in a special conference at a time agreed upon between the union and the employer.

Declining enrollment, fiscal and economic reductions, reorganization, reduction or elimination of positions, and other "just causes" have been ruled as appropriate reasons for a reduction in force (McGregor, 2000). Generally, courts have held that a school board's good faith determination in these issues is sufficient ground for supporting the action. Strict adherence to affirmative action and Title IX guidelines is also important in termination activities.

In all situations, the employer must provide the application of due process to the employee. Both persons have an obligation to participate in due process, and all efforts should be aimed at providing both sides with proper protection.

Retirements

An activity of business administrators that has peaks and valleys is the early retirement of staff members (certified and noncertified). Changes in state laws and economic conditions may result in early retirement opportunities offered by school districts. These permit employees to take either reduced benefits or full benefits based on service rather than age. In general, early retirement and the associated costs have become a part of contracts or board policies.

Cash incentives for early retirement are generally limited to personnel within a fixed number of years of retirement in terms of age and/or service. They provide a partial salary and continued insurance coverage. The success of these programs has been limited, with lukewarm acceptance by staff (and faculty). The impact of potential changes in Social Security retirement age limits is a concern for school business administrators, but is not likely to affect most people currently employed. If changes occur, they will be phased in over time and be of limited concern for several years.

One of the basic concerns of retirement is that the benefits of the retirement package are protected under the negotiated contract and that any school mergers or other alterations of the basic structure of the school system protect persons who have invested years of service in the organization. Many city or special school districts that have later merged with county or governmental units to create larger- and broader-based school districts have faced this problem.

An additional problem caused by budget reductions has been the need to carry an ever-increasing portion of the resources allocated to the school district to provide for the retirement, and, incidentally, medical and other fringe benefit packages of the large number of aging teaching and noncertified staff personnel in a district. The costs have become increasingly large as persons have held jobs for longer periods of time and as turnover in a job area has lessened. In order to deal with the problems of "riffing" faculty members, many school systems have elected to suggest to personnel within a given period of time prior to a normal retirement cycle that they take early retirement. This arrangement creates a job opening for a younger employee and reduces the overall payroll, because younger employees generally make less money.

■ PROFESSIONAL NEGOTIATIONS

Negotiation activities on the part of one group of employees can effect changes in the day-to-day activities as well as in the thinking of all groups within the district. The interaction of one group with another cannot be denied, nor can the direction the interaction takes be predicted. Success on the part of one group may not ensure success on the part of another group, nor does failure in one area by one group guarantee failure in that area by other groups.

Lieberman and Moskow (1966) define professional negotiations as:

A process whereby employees as a group and their employers make and counter offers in good faith on conditions of their employment relationship for the purpose of reaching a mutually acceptable agreement, and the execution of a written document incorporating any such agreement if requested by either party. Also, a process whereby a representative of the employees and their employer jointly determine their conditions of employment. (p. 418)

Negotiations have become regular features of personnel administration for the majority of school boards. School boards must be alert to the possibility of multiple kinds of negotiations as well as the ramifications they all have for the short- and long-range operation of the school district.

Negotiations generally fall into the "piecemeal" or "total" approach. In the piecemeal approach, one issue at a time is considered; while in the total approach, everything is settled or nothing is settled. The school business administrator may be a key member of the negotiation team of the local district.

Teacher collective bargaining is a highly legalized area of education practice. School employer-employee labor relations represent a dynamic, changing relationship operating within a legally defined framework. Often, state legislatures have created challenges for employee boards and for the courts by failing specifically to define the terms of bargaining. In addition, a growing number of legal challenges are emerging from the arbitration process. No other aspect of public school administration is subject to the number and complexity of rules and regulations as is collective bargaining (Webb & Norton, 2003).

The data for the negotiating of contracts are specified in the master contract. On the date named, the local educational agency or union and the board begin negotiations for a new agreement covering wages, hours, and terms and conditions of employment.

A contract often specifies that neither the local educational agency nor the union shall have any control over the selection of the negotiation or bargaining representatives of the other party and that each party may select its representatives from within or outside the district. In some instances, a state statute defines what can/cannot be negotiated. It is often recognized that no final agreement between the parties may be executed without ratification by a majority of either membership. However, the parties present have the necessary power and authority to make proposals, consider proposals, and make concessions in the course of negotiations or bargaining, subject only to ultimate ratification. Normally, the agreement may be modified only with the voluntary mutual consent of both parties in writing, signed as an amendment to the agreement.

In the News

Relationships between school districts and teachers' unions used to be primarily adversarial. Union leaders and negotiators saw their role as advocates for the teachers, whom they needed to protect from the actions of the school board and administration. They did this by taking a hard-line stance in negotiations, refusing to yield to any district proposals, and aggressively pursuing their own interests.

Negotiations generally were conducted in the traditional format of a single spokesperson, often an outside representative, who spoke for each negotiating team. The result was little more than a battle of wills, with the union occasionally appealing to the public or—if state law allowed—resorting to work stoppages or slowdowns. More often than not, negotiations were lengthy and difficult. But times, and relationships, have changed, and so have attitudes on both sides of the table. The parties more often find they have common interests in areas where previously they could see only conflicting interests. In the best cases, they have become partners rather than adversaries.

Two external factors have provided strong motivation for teachers' unions and school leaders to join forces rather than battle each other. Primary among these factors is the difficult financial situation of public employers generally, and schools particularly. Rising costs that are largely outside the district's control—such as new program mandates, the growing need for special education services, and rapidly increasing health insurance costs—contribute to this situation. A corollary is greater public scrutiny of school district expenditures.

Many school and union officials now realize they must work cooperatively to make the most of the limited resources available to the district. The unions have recognized that with gains in teacher salaries and with generally higher levels of fringe benefits than private sector employees, the public is no longer an ally when it comes to renegotiate the teachers' contracts. Rather than locking horns in a battle to see how much of the district's resources the teachers can pry from the hands of the board and administration and how much the district can hold on to, both parties recognize that they need to find ways to control expenses.

Contract settlements are changing as a result. It used to be that most teacher negotiations ended with a listing of the raise the teachers received, the improvements in fringe benefits, and the additional restrictions on how the district could manage its teaching staff. But in today's political climate, that kind of result is no longer acceptable. Today, contract settlements usually include provisions that are there for the benefit of the district—changes to contain health insurance costs, for example, or more teacher work time and more flexibility of teaching assignments.

Traditionally, most school district bargaining has involved teams of negotiators on each side, each with a designated chief spokesperson. Negotiations begin with an exchange of each party's proposals, which usually consist of specific modifications, deletions, or additions to current contract provisions. Counter-proposals are exchanged, with the discussion devoted to the merits of each side's proposals—or what's wrong with them. This process continues until each party has "convinced" the other that its proposal should be accepted, or that the other side's should be withdrawn. The negotiations are completed when all proposals have been resolved or withdrawn.

But just as there have been changes in district-union relationships, the negotiation process has also changed. On both sides, there are efforts to stop hiding—or at least disguising—the party's true interests at the table and to be more open about the goals the party seeks to achieve in the negotiations. This helps eliminate the traditional posturing as the parties put forth proposals they want the other side to accept without disclosing their true interests.

Assuming both district and union want to eliminate wasted time and energy and deal openly with the real issues, is it really necessary to change the negotiations process? It depends. In some districts, the parties will have reached a stage in their relationship where the discussions can take place on a more open and meaningful level without a process change. In other districts, a change will be necessary if for no other reason than to make it clear that the parties are indeed dealing with each other differently. If things do not at least look different, people may not believe the parties really are committed to a changed way of handling negotiations. The greater the level of trust, the less the need for visible process changes.

From: Farmelo, D.A. (2004, September). "Finding common ground." *American School Board Journal*, 56–59.
Reprinted with permission from *American School Board Journal*, September 2004.

It is difficult to imagine a school district involved in complex negotiations without the assistance of the school business administrator. While titles vary and responsibilities differ, the school business official is an important player in the negotiations process.

Because so many union proposals have such a direct and often substantial impact on the local school budget, every school board must be sure it knows what the price is before agreeing to any proposal. Unions usually minimize the cost of proposals, hoping that a school board might not take the time to identify what it is being asked to pay out. For example, proposals for a comprehensive family dental plan, an improved longevity schedule, or payment for accumulated sick leave upon retirement can become expensive. The school business administrator is in an excellent position to explain to the board about the cost of these proposals.

Legally, the right to bargain has statutory roots and procedures legislated by most states. Since Wisconsin enacted the first bargaining statute in 1959, most states and the District of Columbia have had some form of legislation on collective bargaining for employees in public schools. Yet, due to local differences, the permissive and mandatory scope of bargaining varies by state. Thus, it is imperative for negotiating teams to be current on state requirements and those components of a master contract that may supersede state law.

Despite the importance of the collective bargaining process in the allocation of resources and the operation of the instructional program, many school districts: (1) do not have adequate data upon which to make informed decisions, (2) do not develop well-conceived bargaining objectives, and (3) do not have a good bargaining strategy. In addition, board members and administrators make the same predictable mistakes that are counterproductive to a successful bargaining outcome.

 CASE 3 REVISITED

School Business Office Meltdown, and the Band Played On

Recall the challenges faced by John Sample, the newly elected school board member, as he and other board members confronted an impending crisis stemming from an unexpected fiscal deficit. Given the filing of grievances and lawsuits by teachers in protest of the proposed salary decrease, how should the school board respond? Should it enter into a legal wrangle or try negotiating? If negotiations are on the table, how do you envision the school board and the teachers will approach the negotiating process? What suggestions would you give to the school board for achieving a successful outcome?

The National Labor Relations Act

The main body of law governing private-sector collective bargaining is contained in the National Labor Relations Act (NLRA). It explicitly grants private-sector employees the right to bargain collectively and to join trade unions. Provisions of the National Labor Relations Act often serve as the foundations adopted by states to cover collective bargaining in the public sector. Hence, the significance for schools of the NLRA.

Originally enacted in 1935, the NLRA is applicable to most private nonagricultural employees and employers that are engaged in some facet of interstate commerce. Decisions and regulations of the National Labor Relations Board, which was established by the NLRA, greatly supplement and define the provisions of the act.

The NLRA established procedures for the selection of a labor organization to represent a unit of employees in collective bargaining. The act prohibits employers from interfering with this selection. The NLRA requires the employer to bargain with the appointed representative of its employees. It does not require either side to agree to a proposal or make concessions, but it does establish procedural guidelines for good faith bargaining.

The Scope of Bargaining

Proposals that have the prospect of violating the NLRA or other laws may not be the subject matter of collective bargaining. The NLRA also establishes regulations about which tactics (e.g., strikes, lockouts, or picketing) a side may employ in negotiations to advance its bargaining objectives. State laws further regulate collective bargaining and make collective agreements enforceable under state law (Bolton, 1999).

Where there is a legal requirement to bargain, the scope typically includes wages, hours, and other conditions of employment. Since the last quarter of the twentieth century, courts and labor relations boards have attempted to clarify which matters are subject to permissive negotiations.

The price tag on all negotiated union agreements must be known so that the total impact on a local budget, both short and long term, can be predicted. Proposals for a comprehensive family dental plan or an improved leave plan, and provisions for accumulated sick leave payments or career ladder payments can have substantial cost consequences for the next fiscal year and on into the future. These costs are generally fixed up to certain limits (e.g., cost of a system's share of family health insurance), but can be influenced by state legislative mandates. For example, state legislatures often pass enabling legislation dealing with payments for "climbing" career ladders and providing early retirement options. This legislation often allows for but does not fully fund the activity. These legislative mandates clearly affect the activity of the local school business administrator.

In many states, public agencies have established guidelines for which terms or subjects of concern appropriately fall within the scope of representation of a collective bargaining contract and what must be negotiated. Although the list is extensive, the most commonly negotiated items (from California as an example) include:

- Affirmative action plans.
- Grievance procedures.
- Seniority.
- School calendars.
- Hours of work.
- Transfers.
- Class size.
- Preparation time.
- Working conditions.
- Discrimination.
- Early retirement.
- Salary.
- Dues deductions.
- Safety fringe benefits.

Regardless of which approach to collective bargaining a school district chooses to employ, negotiating salary and fringe benefits is usually the most difficult item within the scope of representation and clearly the most emotionally charged. When negotiating monetary issues, there must be a relationship between the district and union that promotes trust and teamwork. There must also be procedures in place that ensure that agreements will be fair, clear, enforceable, and owned and understood by constituents. Although not widely used, formula-based compensation systems are being used with some measure of success by some school districts. Formulas vary, but the concept of mutual cooperation and shared interests exists in each. Some formulas rely on the annual Cost of Living Adjustment (COLA), while others operate on the basis of revenue sharing for all financial increases coming to the district, including lottery, equalization, and categorical dollars (Sears & Picus, 1999).

Ten Tips for Successful Negotiating, by Ed Brodow, gives a brief look at the issue of negotiations. These include:

- *Develop "negotiation consciousness."* Successful negotiators are assertive and challenge everything. They know that everything is negotiable.
- *Become a good listener.* Negotiators are detectives. They ask probing questions and then examine information prior to the negotiation. What are their needs? What pressures do they keep shut up? The other negotiator will tell you everything you need to know—all you have to do is listen.
- *Be prepared.* Gather as much pertinent information as you can. What options do they have? Doing your homework is vital to successful negotiation.
- *Aim high.* People who aim higher do better. If you expect more, you'll get more. Successful negotiators are optimists. A proven strategy for achieving higher results is opening with an extreme position. Sellers should ask for more than they expect to receive, and buyers should offer less than they are prepared to pay.
- *Be patient.* This is very difficult for Americans. We want to get it over with. Whoever is more flexible about time has the advantage. Your patience can be devastating to the other negotiator if they are in a hurry.
- *Focus on satisfaction.* Help the other negotiator feel satisfied. Satisfaction means that their basic interests have been fulfilled. Don't confuse basic interests with positions: Their position is what they say they want; their basic interest is what they really need to get.
- *Don't make the first move.* The best way to find out if the other negotiator's aspirations are low is to induce them to open first. They may ask for less than you think. If you open first, you may give away more than is necessary.
- *Don't accept the first offer.* If you do, the other negotiator will think they could have done better. (It was too easy.) They will be more satisfied if you reject the first offer, because when you eventually say "yes," they will conclude that they have pushed you to your limit.
- *Don't make unilateral concessions.* Whenever you give something away, get something in return. Always tie a string: "I'll do this if you do that." Otherwise you are inviting the other negotiator to ask you for more.
- *Brodow's Law:* Always be willing to walk away! Never negotiate without options.

(Retrieved February 8, 2007, from http://www.brodow.com/Articles/NegotiatingTips.html.) Ed Brodow is a motivational speaker and negotiation guru on PBS, ABC News, Fox News, and Inside Edition. He is the author of *Negotiation Boot Camp: How to Resolve Conflict, Satisfy Customers, and Make Better Deals* (Doubleday).

Individual Negotiation

In total number of persons affected, the individual negotiation is one of the procedures least used by school districts. The vast majority of certified personnel and a similar sized group of technical and supporting personnel in most systems are subject to some type of union, civil service, or local predetermined salary schedule. Whether the schedule is restrictive or flexible, a large percentage of persons in virtually all entry-level positions are covered by a set salary schedule. If such a schedule does not exist, it can be implied that the school board is in the business of administering the schools, rather than setting policy for its administrators to follow.

Individual negotiations have a valid place in most school districts but usually pertain to key personnel such as the superintendent, selected other staff personnel, and possibly some technical employees. In elementary form, individual negotiations can be distilled into a decision between "What am I offered?" and "What will I accept?" In most districts, there is a predetermined salary and fringe benefit range, and key exceptions provide override capabilities. The employee has in mind a basic salary determined by the job market, geography, and salaries of peers. Other compensation in terms of activities, membership, and other "perks" is often a major consideration on the final selection and negotiation process.

Final terms of the agreement should be subject to board approval and should be a matter of public record. Individual contracts are few, but they often cover the key employees within a district. It should also be remembered that individual negotiations often involve expenditures of funds in excess of selected fringe benefits paid directly to or for the employee as well as extra or expanded auxiliary services such as clerical assistance, office space, or transportation.

Group Negotiations without Outside Consultation

The ability of groups of school employees, either certified or noncertified, to organize and act effectively without outside consultation is severely limited. Rarely can a single uniform goal or set of goals override personal differences to a degree that equals the cohesion and disengagement that outside consultation brings to personnel negotiations. It is unrealistic to assume that a board of education can enter into negotiation without readily available, expert consultation services. The group pursuing this avenue may soon find itself in the same position as the person who chooses to present him- or herself in a court of law, virtually without representation.

Groups without outside consultation may prepare points for initial consideration, and key points for further consideration or confrontation may be identified, if not resolved. If time permits and the atmosphere allows, this avenue may be pursued. However, the group seeking to negotiate should not be shocked if this approach fails to bring expected results.

Group Negotiations with Outside Consultation

Outside consultation services provide expertise that is generally unavailable within most local employee groups. Professional negotiators usually have a background that is useful in discussion with board representatives. Consultants can arm themselves with the pertinent information and then condense it to a set of goals and alternatives, including the extent of the demands a group is willing to seek.

The school business administrator is intimately involved in these negotiations because each result affects the funding of the school district for subsequent years. The results may be seen in salary figures, fringe benefits, and a multitude of other ways.

Additionally, the business administrator is a prime information resource for the board throughout all negotiation considerations. The administrator's organization must be able to respond rapidly with accurate fiscal information and predictions.

The role of the school attorney in the negotiations process has taken on considerably more importance. The major function served by the attorney in these areas is to interpret negotiated contracts and to certify that procedures followed are correct and appropriate. The chief negotiator for the board, often the school business administrator, must give attention to these rulings as well as have a view of the larger needs of the district. Just what can be negotiated from a budget and educational program position provides the information base for future contract work.

Administration of the Agreement

Any labor agreement establishes only a general framework for labor relations in the school system. At the time of contract signing, emphasis shifts to application and administration of the contract and away from the rhetoric associated with its signing. As most negotiators agree, contract language is often broad, and, to a degree, purposefully vague to allow agreement to be reached and to provide some flexibility for each side. Thus, the real success of a labor agreement rests with the day-to-day application and administration of what was signed.

The climate of labor relations in any organization will, to a large degree, be determined by the extent to which the parties—the school district and whatever unions are involved—discharge their day-to-day understanding and application of the contract. The administration of the contract usually allows some flexibility on both sides, but flexibility can create problems. Problems are then handled and settled through the grievance procedures of the labor contract. If, however, the bulk of bona fide labor problems cannot be solved at some level of the grievance procedure through the process of negotiation, the next step must occur—mediation or arbitration (Sloane & Witney, 2004).

Dispute Resolution

Conflict resolution techniques range from relatively weak to very strong, starting with the fairly mild form—mediation—and ending with the strongest—arbitration.

Mediation. Mediation has its success in settling disputes without duress. However, there are few generally accepted rules as to how to reach this resolution. Good mediators are persons who listen well; both parties agree upon selection of a mediator. Techniques of mediation are as varied as the characteristics of the mediator. The basic requirement of the mediator is that the individual be a good listener and work from a sound, basic approach to the task. Whether to meet with both sides together, how to discuss issues, what proposals to provide for consideration, and when to say an impasse exists are some of the areas with which mediators must deal. Mediators come from various sources, but all must be agreed upon by all parties. To assist both parties, the federal government provides—on a voluntary basis—the services of its Mediation and Conciliation Service (U.S. Equal Employment Opportunity Commission). Some states have added "fact finding" as a second step in the conflict-resolution process.

Arbitration. Arbitration is the referral of a dispute by voluntary agreement to some person judged impartial for determination of a final result (Sloane & Witney, 2004). The arbitration is based on information provided and arguments presented by both sides. In general, arbitration becomes an agreement by both parties that all other avenues, including mediation, fact finding, and negotiation, have failed. Either side may call for arbitration. Thus, the arbitration is an agreement by both parties that they are willing to submit information to a disinterested third party whose decision will be considered acceptable to both parties. The costs of arbitration cover the preparation/presentation of the case, a report of the testimony, the arbitrator's fee, and administrative expenses. The major item of any arbitration is, of course, the cost of the arbitrator. These expenses generally are shared between the two parties. This is a negotiable fee depending on a variety of factors.

There are two kinds of arbitration—binding and nonbinding. Compliance with the award is compulsory in binding arbitration, whereas, in nonbinding arbitration, compliance is optional. In nonbinding arbitration, each party considers the award and makes the decision whether or not to accept it. Principally, nonbinding arbitration varies little from mediation if no final determination must be made. Because many employees fear reprisal from their employer, a no-reprisal clause has become a common part of most grievance procedures. State law must be considered as the beginning point for the determination of any arbitration strategy.

School Business Official's Role in Collective Bargaining and Dispute Resolution

An early prerequisite and responsibility for the school business administrator is the presentation of accurate data. Sunshine laws and other court decisions (e.g., *Oldbaur v. Drummond, Board of Education*, 1975) indicate that all parties have the right to know and have access to certain kinds of data. What is supplied to one side must properly be supplied to the other. Information readily accessible to union negotiators must be equally accessible to the system negotiators.

The negotiated contract is designed to provide a "blueprint" for both parties. Major features of most contracts include district rights, staff and association rights, features of professional negotiations activities, and grievance procedures as well as specifics such as vacations, transfers, leaves of absence, qualifications and assignments, conduct, disciplinary procedures, and seniority.

Contract provisions may limit management's prerogatives in personnel administration. Decisions on what can be done without union consultation or approval often are seriously limited by the agreement. The school board administrator must plan according to these limitations in all facets of contract-personnel work.

Denny Bolton, a former president of the Pennsylvania ASBO and the ASBO International, has offered the twelve most frequently made mistakes by school business officials and boards in the total negotiations process:

1. Failure to differentiate rhetoric and reality in teacher bargaining.
2. Willingness to negotiate every teacher demand.
3. Taking the bait too soon (making the best offer too early).
4. Inability to resolve intraboard conflict.
5. Permitting unions to define the comparison base.
6. Circumventing the bargaining team.

7. Board's failure to hire someone who is knowledgeable.
8. Failure to learn the bargaining language of the teachers.
9. Waving the "red flag" (using inflammatory remarks).
10. Negotiations by board members.
11. Failure to give authority to the negotiating team.
12. Trusting the mediator.
   (Bolton, 1999, pp. 4–8)

As a final word, every school district is different, and the variables make it impossible to make observations and suggestions to cover every situation. In general, Bolton has offered some suggestions as to how to improve the probability of success by diligent preparation and the careful selection of the bargaining team. Also identified are what the author believes are costly mistakes that inhibit board negotiating teams from realizing bargaining objectives.

Civil Service-Union Association

Any or all forms of negotiation noted previously can be used by employees working under union agreement, using their professional associations as a bargaining agent, or by employees operating within civil service salary guidelines. The school business adminis-trator is concerned with the activities of both groups because of the previously established or potential impact on the budget. The administrator must constantly keep the board apprised of future trends in the budget produced by contract items and/or the impact on the budget if requested items are granted.

■ GRIEVANCE PROCEDURES

Most states have established a grievance resolution process to ensure that negotiated con-tracts are interpreted and properly implemented. The procedures usually call for several progressive steps to be taken within the school district in an effort to resolve a dispute once an employee or a group of employees has filed a grievance complaint.

More than twenty states have enacted statutes permitting school districts and unions to adopt grievance procedures that culminate in binding arbitration. This type of arbitration is commonly referred to as grievance (or rights) arbitration. Several states mandate binding arbitration as the final step in the grievance resolution process. In other states, the issue of whether to end the grievance resolution process with binding or advisory arbitration is left to the various parties. In grievance arbitration, the interpretation and applicability of the collective bargaining agreement is in dispute; that is, labor grievances arising out of the col-lective bargaining agreement are submitted to a neutral arbitrator for final determination.

However, the general legal rule is that arbitration is the preferred means of resolving disputes over the interpretation of collective bargaining agreements. The U.S. Supreme Court decisions have promoted the use of arbitration as a means to resolve grievance dis-putes. The Supreme Court has concluded that judicial reviews or arbitration awards are limited, and courts are to uphold arbitrators' awards as long as the award draws its essence from the collective bargaining agreement.

A claim by the bargaining unit or individual is often sufficient to initiate a grievance procedure if there has been an alleged violation, misrepresentation, or misapplication of the provisions of a contract applicable to wages, hours, or conditions of employment.

Grievance procedures provide for due process for both representatives, the naming of a local representative for each side, the maintenance of grievance committees for the purposes stipulated, and the number of days indicated for each step of the procedure. Penalties are also set forth for failure of an aggrieved party to proceed from one step of the procedure to the next within the time limits. In general, grievance procedures specify a series of steps or activities that must be completed, in sequence, within a specified period of time. Both parties agree to be bound by the decision of an arbitrator, if one is called in, and agree that either party may enter judgment thereon in any court of competent jurisdiction. The use of an arbitrator is normally a last resort in the grievance procedure. Miscellaneous items occur in most grievance procedures, all of which are concerned with due process for the individual.

Each union negotiates its own grievance procedure. While there is variability in the language of contract clauses, there is much commonality in the fundamental features of a grievance procedure. Features generally specified include the following:

- What is the definition of a grievance?
- Who may initiate a grievance?
- How long does the grievant have to decide whether or not to file a grievance?
- What is the union's role in the process?
- Where should the grievance be filed?
- What are the procedural steps to follow?
- What are the timelines and deadlines?
- What is the final step?
  (Nolan, 2007, pp. 13–14)

Because any contract can become the focus of a dispute, ideally the grievance process provides a quick and inexpensive resolution of contractual disputes. Employees are given an opportunity to protest management decisions without fear of retribution and to do so with the assistance of a union advocate. As has been noted, all parties to any labor contract have a vested interest in enforcing compliance of the terms and conditions of the agreement. While management has various disciplinary measures to ensure that employees honor the terms of the contract, a union often must rely on the grievance procedure to enforce the contract. The union must enforce the control or it will have little value and the union will have lost power. Grievances also provide a vehicle for the union to react to management decisions and to protect the rights of employees.

The public also benefits from the grievance process because grievances are settled without disruption to the school schedule. Strikes, pickets, slowdowns, and other disruptive practices are not needed, because employees accept the grievance procedures as a legitimate method of resolving differences. Consequently, disruption of the school calendar and the daily schedule of parents and students is greatly minimized.

While the benefits of grievance procedures are substantial, critics have identified several key problems. The process can be costly, time consuming, and legalistic, and it often fails to meet the needs of individual employees. This is especially true when binding arbitration is the final step. Because this quasi-legal process often involves lawyers and transcripts, a single arbitration may cost a union several thousand dollars, and a small union may not have the funds to arbitrate many legitimate grievances. When the legitimate grievances are not taken to arbitration because of cost consideration, both the arbitration process and the union lose credibility.

If the best efforts of both sides fail and there is a strike, the system must be in a position to provide essential student, staff, and faculty support services necessary to maintain the health and safety of all parties. If a bus mechanics' strike makes the safe operation of buses questionable, then the buses should not operate. The inconvenience of no bus service does not override the safety of the child on an improperly serviced bus.

Strike contingency planning is but another role of the school board administrator. The availability of a detailed plan for dealing with the issues is the best way to ensure that the school will operate as successfully as can be expected during this emotion-charged time. Basic educational needs must be met, and every effort should be made to keep the instruction as close to normal as possible.

▪ PERSONNEL BUDGETING

The establishment of detailed, written salary policies for all levels of employees within a school district greatly facilitates the solution of numerous personnel problems. A set salary policy for both certified and noncertified personnel is a must for effective and truly efficient operation of any school district.

Step-increment salaries comprise the type of policy used by most school officials. Regardless of the system used, a detailed picture of the personnel budget plan is a must. Salary projections for general budgeting purposes are little better than guesses without an established framework within which to work. Staff turnover, court actions, annexation, and union agreements all have an influence on salary policies within a school district. However, none of these can be allowed to set salary policy. Established policies for both certified and noncertified personnel have been identified as priority items. As previously discussed, salary policy and its implementation are important elements in staff motivation. An established and published board policy relative to salary and fringe benefits also assists a school business administrator to work more efficiently and effectively.

All states provide salary schedules for certified personnel that take training and years of experience into consideration. A bachelor's degree is the usual minimum training requirement. In lieu of a bachelor's degree, a journeyman union card or some other evidence of training and experience is often required of vocational/technical teachers. Doctorates must be from accredited colleges or universities. In general, the schedules indicate minimum salaries, which tend to be augmented in most districts. Augmenting of the state salary schedule normally occurs with increased training and experience, or increased responsibilities such as coaching, music direction, or yearbook coordination.

Performance for Pay

Eighty-six percent of private-sector employees are rewarded, at least in part, based on their job performance. This is seldom true in education. Indeed, public schools are almost alone in the American economy in not paying employees based on performance. It is estimated that in 95 percent of public schools, teachers are paid from the single-salary schedule described in the above paragraph. However, in the early part of the twenty-first century, added attention has been given to paying teachers and other education employees based on student achievement or some other measure of performance. In 2007 the federal government provided funding to selected local school districts through Teacher Incentive

Fund (TIF) grants for pilot projects involving teacher pay for performance. A school business official should keep appraised of this development.

Fringe Benefits

As union agreements are negotiated, as civil service contracts are set, or as general employee contracts are established, the total dollar value of fringe benefit packages continues to grow. These benefits include vacations with pay, paid holidays, medical insurance costs for the employee and family, group life and disability insurance, sick pay (leave), tax-deferred annuities, and many others. It is often possible for professional negotiators to use fringe benefits as a trade-off against wages when a quantity discount would benefit both parties.

For example, in an insurance plan in which family coverage is offered but most persons choose single coverage, the value of the benefit for contract negotiation purposes may be calculated at the higher rate. In some systems, a fringe benefit is available in terms of a sick leave incentive cash payment plan for persons who do not use accumulated sick leave. Extended medical care in areas such as dental services also has become a popular item. Continual attention to the direction and quantity of the growth in fringe benefit packages is an important responsibility for the school business administrator.

Some of the fringe benefits for noncertified personnel include supplementary pay; license and dues allowance; maternity leave; personal leave; jury duty leave; military leave; health, life, accident, retirement, and disability insurance; and miscellaneous items such as meal allowances, uniform allowances, equipment usage, housing, credit union membership, automobile allowance, in-service training opportunities, and conference visitations.

In negotiations with groups of certified and noncertified personnel, the trade-off of fringe benefits against wages is a major concern. In many instances, the tax advantage of selected fringes allows the employee to realize ten or more cents on the dollar rather than the dollar value realized after taxes for each dollar negotiated in wages.

Employee Assistance Program (EAP)

These are programs that grow from a base of caring for persons and also of concern for job performance and its relation to the individual employee. Under most conditions, it is more desirable to rehabilitate a current employee than to recruit and train a new employee. While EAPs have greatest visibility in areas such as professional basketball drug and alcohol rehabilitation programs, they are a feature of many collective bargaining agreements.

Summary

Personnel management is a multifaceted feature of the school administrator's position. New developments in personnel policies and major changes in the role responsibilities of the school business administrator have created a new working environment. Also, changes in legislation, restructuring of collective bargaining units, and technological growth have had a significant impact. A lead role in personnel planning and recruitment as well as actively engaging in all areas of personnel development must be assumed. Participation in personnel budgeting and instructional support is visible but is seldom easily accomplished. The professional negotiation role has undergone major changes, and no end is in sight, as labor and management ideas must be blended with the ability and willingness of the public to pay. New ideas, new challenges, and new experiences are all part of the school business administrator's role in personnel and payroll administration.

Discussion Questions

1. What would be the role of the school business administrator in setting performance standards for classified positions within the district?
2. How does the school business administrator function as a part of the professional negotiations team? Should such a role be part of the school business administrator's responsibilities? Why or why not?
3. What elements are needed in plans for a reduction in force of maintenance personnel within your school district? Is it possible to have a "one-size-fits-all" plan? Why or why not?
4. How is due process provided in personnel terminations in your district or school? How do moral, racial, and gender issues factor into such considerations?
5. How do school business administrators plan for the institution of collective negotiations in their area of responsibility? For impasse situations?

Web Resources

American Federation of State, County & Municipal Employees, Public Sector Collective Bargaining Laws for each state—
http://www.afscme.org/publications/11157.cfm

Federal Mediation & Conciliation Service—
http://www.fmcs.gov/internet/

References

Bolton, D. (1999). Collective bargaining: Successful practices and the baker's dozen mistakes. *School Business Affairs*, 65(4), 4–8.

Farmelo, D.A. (2004). Finding common ground. *American School Boards Journal*, 191(9), 56–59.

Hardy, L. (2002, June). Trust betrayal. *American School Boards Journal*, 189(6).

Lieberman, M., & Moskow, M.H. (1966). *Collective negotiations for teachers: An approach to school administration*. Chicago: Rand McNally.

McGregor, D. (2000). *The human side of enterprise*. New Jersey: Wiley.

Metropolitan Nashville Public Schools. (2005). *Handbook for the support personnel of the metropolitan public schools*. Nashville-Davidson County, TN, 25–28.

Nolan, D.R. (2007). *Labor and employment arbitration in a nutshell* (2nd ed.). St Paul, MN: Thomson.

Sears, D., & Picus, L. (1999). Formula-based compensation. *School Business Affairs*, 65(4), 20–23.

Sloane, A.A., & Witney, F. (2004). *Labor relations*. Englewood Cliffs, NJ: Prentice-Hall.

U.S. Equal Employment Opportunity Commission. (n.d.). *Facts about mediation*. Retrieved February 28, 2007, from http://www.eeoc.gov/mediate/facts.html.

Webb, L.D., & Norton, M.S. (2003). *Human relations administration*. Upper Saddle River, NJ: Merrill-Prentice Hall.

CHAPTER FOURTEEN

Managing Facilities

■ INTRODUCTION

One of the key roles of the school business administrator is in the maintenance and operation of the plant, equipment, and service facilities. Billions of dollars have been spent for constructing and equipping currently operating school plants in the United States. Additional amounts have been spent on rehabilitating older facilities to make them more energy efficient and environmentally safe; adding equipment to meet current demands of instructional programs, such as special needs education, vocational-technical education, and science; and providing more comfortable, usable, and safe facilities in terms of thermal and physical environment, lighting, and noise control. These facilities and expensive, complex equipment must be maintained and kept operational.

LEARNING OBJECTIVES

In this chapter a reader will learn about:

- Ensuring long-term use of school facilities through strategic planning and preventive, predictive, recurring, and emergency maintenance.
- Organizational strategies for maintenance and operational activities, including the prospect of outsourcing selected endeavors.
- Maintenance performance measures and maintenance records.
- Selection, evaluation, and continued training of maintenance and operations personnel.
- Organization and oversight of custodial personnel.
- Efficient energy management.
- Security strategies, tactics, and equipment.
- Environmental hazard and fire safety maintenance.
- Added considerations in the construction and retrofitting of school buildings.

As a part of an administrative team, the school business administrator conventionally joins with other staff members to determine a philosophy of maintenance and operations and advocates its adoption by the board. The philosophy should allow for the development of policies for maintenance and operations, and provide the framework for developing procedures to execute these policies.

Decisions to delay capital improvements such as new roofs or new boilers and to reduce general maintenance by painting less frequently or budgeting less for preventive maintenance for computers and audio and video equipment are initial results of reduced budgets.

Because most educational institutions are as much as 85 percent salary-intensive, the tendency to apply the budget ax to maintenance and operations is quickly seen. While a "fair share" cut is reasonable, short-term budget savings can be easily transferred to long-term major costs for replacement of poorly maintained facilities and/or equipment. The concept of using a cost stream—the cost flow of a project—is a major management tool for the school business administrator. Figure 14.1 presents a cost stream showing such cost factors as research, investment, operation and maintenance, and phaseout.

A plan like this presents a quick, graphic representation at the idea of cost concepts as related to maintenance and operations (Hentschke, 1975). It also depicts the interrelationships among the several factors (e.g., irresponsible purchasing decisions could result in extraordinarily high maintenance and operations costs).

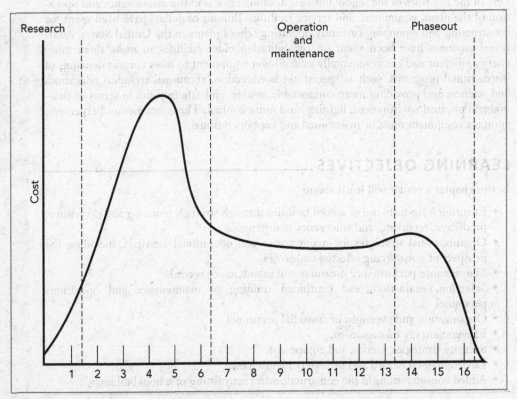

FIGURE 14.1 Sample Cost Stream

Source: Hentschke, Guilbert C. (1975). *Management operations in education.* Figure on p. 211. "Sample Cost Stream," reference to pp. 205–28. Berkeley: McCutchan Publishing Corporation. Permission granted by the publisher.

■ MAINTENANCE

Maintenance is the function of the school system components associated with upkeep, repair, and replacement that ensures continuous usability of the physical plant, equipment, and service facilities. Ensuring availability for continuous use is the key priority in any maintenance program and is the essential point illustrating the need for planning on the part of the school business administrator. The development of the system's maintenance philosophy and the establishment of policies necessary to implement this philosophy in daily operations are vital to a successful maintenance program.

Besides the maintenance philosophy developed by the district, the school business administrator must adhere to the legal responsibilities of state and local building codes. In many instances, specified worker accident laws do not apply solely to schools, but are also a part of the overall operational policies of a district.

With a stronger emphasis on site-based budgeting, local building administrators have major responsibilities for maintenance and operations. These responsibilities extend to making broader decisions in funds' usage, activities' scheduling, and personnel administration. The extent to which site-based budgeting for maintenance and operations is implemented is a function of local policy and philosophy. In many instances, the school business administrator is charged with responsibility for systemwide and local building projects. These shared responsibilities are a major feature of decentralization in many school districts and provide an opportunity for collegial efforts.

Maintenance operations are among the first targets of privatization efforts in public facilities for two reasons: (1) maintenance tends to be well outside the core operations of any government facility, and (2) public facilities for years have grappled to fund maintenance adequately. Some have not performed well, as evidenced by huge sums of deferred maintenance and the subpar conditions the public sees regularly in many buildings, most noticeably in public educational facilities.

Privatization remains an emotionally charged issue in many school districts but continues to grow each year. The majority of school districts that outsource use one to four services. Many schools find that they can save money by contracting out certain services and operations to private companies. Whether outsourcing will be more cost effective than self-operation depends on factors that vary from service to service and from institution to institution. Some schools have efficient in-house operations in place and would not benefit from privatization. Many schools have brought in private contractors to operate their transportation services, food preparation, and custodial operations.

Transportation, HVAC maintenance, food service, and office equipment repair are outsourced by approximately one-third of the districts. Data in the following lists illustrate frequently noted sources for using or not using privatized services.

Use	Not Use
Save dollars	Threatens job of loyal employees
Improve operations	If they can make a profit, we ought to be able to do it for less
They could do a better job	Too expensive
Save management time	Union contracts make it too difficult
Provide greater accountability	Not necessary; we can do the job as well

This is an illustration of where a cost stream analysis is an invaluable tool for the school business administrator. Low-cost, high-success maintenance can often be ensured with proper advance planning, which can affect the choice of materials used in the construction of buildings; selection of equipment for HVAC systems, student workstations, laboratories, shops, and cafeterias; and purchase of consumable supplies for the operation of equipment, plant, or grounds.

Low cost of initial construction is not always the best solution if it is recognized that many school buildings have an expected life span in excess of fifty years. The actual construction cost of a building is generally considered inversely proportional to the cost of maintenance of that facility. For example, it can be expected that a poorly or improperly constructed building will cost much more than the average 2 to 3 percent maintenance figure generally accepted for overall school building maintenance. Maintenance costs are often in excess of 7 to 10 percent for poorly constructed buildings. Future maintenance costs are significantly influenced by decisions made at the time of construction.

The school business administrator, as a team planner, must seriously consider the problem of educational obsolescence versus physical obsolescence of school plants. This question addresses the point at which, regardless of the effectiveness of continued maintenance programs, the building ceases to be viable for use in the instructional program of the school district. The function rather than the maintenance of the facility becomes the issue. Structural alterations, program changes, and so forth are an integral part of such considerations, but the ultimate decision to dispose of a property will probably be made on both a programmatic basis and a maintenance and operations basis. Decisions to abandon well-maintained buildings are hard, but an objective look by all members of the team allows the proper interchange of data that can facilitate a consensus decision.

It is generally false economy on the part of a school board to reduce outlays for maintenance programs when a budget squeeze eventuates, because deterioration of a building improperly maintained is potentially more costly than the current expenditure necessary to maintain it at an acceptable and usable level. Occasionally, budget considerations do require that maintenance programs be curtailed or even halted in certain areas. The key centers in the time lapse and the selection of items to be curtailed.

School people agree that the success of academic programs is hard to "see," unlike the physical appearance of school facilities. The basic approach to good public relations through good maintenance is really common sense. Keep paper and other litter removed; keep entrances and exits free of clutter; keep interiors painted and cleaned, water fountains cleaned, and all areas well lighted. Inside public areas should be clean, neat, and safe. The equipment used in maintenance and operations activities should be in good repair. Uniforms should be clean, and workers should be clean and as neat in appearance as possible considering the job situation. Because many visitors see ball fields and other sports facilities on their initial arrival, outside ground appearance is especially critical. All restrooms, but especially those used by visitors, should be checked regularly, with strict attention to the provision of adequate supplies and proper security.

Public relations makes sense for schools, and physical appearance is where public relations is easiest to showcase.

In the News

The debate was as civil as humanly possible, but at the end of the day, it was still a teacher going up against the school treasurer. The Collinsville school district board met Monday night, hearing a 10-minute speech from Webster Elementary schoolteacher Pat St-Germain. St-Germain, who has worked in the district for 33 years, provided the board with a litany of complaints, detailing many of the improvements she said are sorely needed at Webster. "We have areas in the school where mold is starting to show, where repairs are badly needed," St-Germain said. At times, she said, neither the teachers nor the custodians are able to regulate the amount of heat or cool air coming into the building.

In responding to her comments, school district treasurer Bill Jokerst said that while he is aware of many of the improvements that could be made to Collinsville's schools, he is concerned with the financial health of the district. "We have to separate the needs from the wants," Jokerst said. "If you are looking for someone to blame, blame me." Jokerst said that at the start of the school year, the district was still facing a nearly $3 million cumulative deficit in the education fund. The school board has worked hard to decrease that deficit by nearly $1 million, and perhaps in a few years, that debt could be completely wiped out, he said. "The only way to do that is to keep spending down," Jokerst explained. "When you try to balance the budget of a school district, you don't have much control over income. The only thing you can control is spending."

Jokerst also responded to comments made by a Caseyville woman who said that children who attend the newly built Collinsville Middle School have limited choices during recess, as the school district failed to install basketball hoops or other playground amenities. Jokerst said that the district chose to invest its limited resources into the building, which would benefit students the most. "We can't have everything," Jokerst said. St-Germain said she was disappointed by the treasurer's comments, adding that she would like to see the district do more to show that they value both the teachers and the students in Collinsville.

From: Morelli, C. (2006, April 26). Jokerst tells teacher "blame me." Reprinted from the Collinsville (IL) Herald, April 26, 2006.

Organization of Maintenance

All maintenance programs are concerned with the basic elements of safety, serviceability, energy conservation, and general economy. There are basically three plans of maintenance for school district consideration: (1) the local system maintenance program, (2) the contracted or outsourced maintenance program, or (3) a combination of these. For example, some districts service their own office machines and computers (both for staff use and for instructional purposes), while others contract with outside vendors for the service. The economics of each plan must be examined in all maintenance and operations programs.

Scheduling of maintenance activities on the second or third shift should also be considered for improving building security. Management concepts such as cost utility are a major asset in determining the "best" program.

There are a number of factors to be considered in examining a district-operated maintenance system. If a school district operates its own maintenance program, it can avoid delays and costs associated with taking bids, opening them, and perhaps negotiating for services or materials of equal quality. Overhead costs charged by companies performing maintenance functions can be eliminated. An additional factor that might influence the decision on contractual versus no contractual service is that there need be no time delay with a local (i.e., in-house) maintenance system, although time delays do occur locally and must be part of local contingency planning. Other advantages of local maintenance systems are that it may be possible to make more efficient use of personnel in terms of scheduling peak-load or peak-time operations and that local district employees can often be required to provide higher standards of workmanship than can the contractor working for a profit.

However, there are problems associated with implementing an in-house maintenance operation. Many maintenance functions require specialized procedures that may not be needed more than two or three times a year, and the skilled employees necessary to accomplish this work may be too expensive to include in the local staff. Specialized equipment or tools that require a physical structure or materials not generally associated with a local school district maintenance program may cause problems.

Another factor is maintenance scheduling. For example, some types of school repairs cannot be made under certain weather conditions. An additional factor in favor of contracted services is that while time and money may be saved at the bid phase of work by having local personnel perform the job, the costs related to matters such as equipment, depreciation of maintenance buildings, special insurance, and sick leave pay add to the budget. The scheduling of needed seasonal work may also require that a district consider contracted services for periods such as summer vacations. The use of these services is dictated by workload and local vacation schedules.

Capital outlay projects are another cause for policy decisions regarding contracted versus no contracted services. To use maintenance crews to build bookcases or lay sidewalks may cause the routine maintenance program to be neglected. Again, if the school business administrator uses the planning function in a proper manner, one can determine approximate amounts of time when crews can be used on capital projects, scheduled projects, or emergency requests.

Whatever type of maintenance program is used, some trade-offs are made. Relations with unions, establishment of a plan for dispatching personnel, and organization of work units are some of the features of maintenance programs that vary with the type of program used.

Regardless of the organization of the maintenance program in the district, an individual plan for each structure and item of equipment must be established. A replacement schedule for bus engines, a plan for roof upkeep on each building (including a replacement cycle), and a painting plan for each building are musts for effective planning and allocation of scarce resources.

Cost Analysis

A competent school business administrator should be able to predict, within an acceptable range, the year-end balance for maintenance projects. Cost data for each job for which funds are encumbered should be compiled for the current year and used in making budget projections. Records for several years should be maintained for use in long-range planning. Accounting problems often occur in unfinished jobs when, for example, materials on hand are used without appropriate requisition records or when materials to be purchased cost more than estimated. Funds for maintenance should be allocated on a systemwide basis rather than on a building basis. This provides for flexibility in the use of funds and does not allow needed services to be omitted at one site while "make-work" projects are being accomplished at another.

Types of Maintenance

The key element in any maintenance program is not its complexity, its cost, or its organizational scheme, but simply its effectiveness. This effectiveness is measured each day in many ways in numerous locations, from central office to athletic dressing rooms to laboratories. The major types of maintenance fall into four classifications: (1) preventive, (2) periodic, (3) recurring, and (4) emergency. The divisions overlap to a degree, but each has a separate function. Often a combination of two or more operations must be made to ensure adequate service.

The use of private maintenance contractors when services are obtainable at a fixed price through competitive bidding often can be more cost effective than employing special workers within the district. Several factors can influence the decision to purchase maintenance. These include:

- The difficult task of keeping the optional number of employees with specific skills under contract.
- Reduction in collective bargaining problems.
- Fixing of contractor's fees for supplies and materials for a specified time.

Additionally, the provision of this support service is guaranteed for the life of the contract. The expertise of the contractor also can be determined and successful work guaranteed with performance bonds. Because every agency has an obligation to provide the best possible service at the lowest possible cost, contracting for maintenance could be the way to go. However, each situation has unique variables involved, and decisions should be based on individual circumstances. The recent influx of a large volume of computers and other electronic devices has given a new dimension to maintenance, electrical, and security issues.

Preventive Maintenance. Preventive maintenance is the program for servicing machines, systems, and structures that is devised to prevent a breakdown of the total system or any one of its component parts. For example, a preventive maintenance plan is set up to inspect all parts of a shop's lathe or band saw for specific points of stress or wear, which could indicate possible failure in the future. Checking for proper tension of belts and springs on various machines is another example of preventive maintenance. The purpose of preventive maintenance schedules is to maximize the useful life of a piece of equipment, a structure, or an operating system, and, therefore, preclude or at least delay a breakdown that could render it unusable. In terms of cost return, one of the most worthwhile items in a school budget is the cost of a properly planned preventive maintenance program.

Preventive maintenance has not been practiced in many schools because workforce needs are so acute in other areas—there is not time for this function. Second, preventive maintenance is often not practical due to lack of an easily administered inspection service.

The planning function that provides accurate control records and schedules is a necessary part of a successful preventive maintenance program. Recordkeeping is discussed later in this section.

Preventive maintenance—performing the tasks that keep the "place" operational—has become a greater concern, in part, due to increased federal safety regulations, rising insurance costs, and the increased cost of equipment. Implementing a preventive maintenance system as a part of a system's long-range management program is of major importance. In general, a good preventive maintenance system should have effects such as:

- Producing a complete and accurate inventory of building components and equipment.
- Reducing the frequency and number of emergency repair responses.
- Providing cost collection and analysis tools to assist in budget preparation.
- Increasing the effectiveness of facility maintenance.
- Implementing a flexible and easily operated system.

The main goal of a preventive maintenance system is to fix something before it requires emergency repairs, which are often costly, time consuming, and disruptive to academic programs. Preparation to implement a district preventive maintenance program means an examination of existing criteria for selection, construction of the automated system, analyses of the pilot program, refinement of elements and criteria selected, and implementation of procedures needed to operate the program.

The preventive maintenance schedule (PMS) is planned so that condition monitoring and inspection can take place in a programmed way through an automatic checklist. This allows good management techniques and an improved overall environment for risk managers to present well-documented information to insurance underwriters. It is important to note the relationship between risk management and this particular area of management and operations. In the final analysis, this management tool provides a strong element of accountability and a basis for budgetary decisions. The PMS system takes care of the routine decisions and allows maintenance staff to focus on more creative activities that increasing effectiveness and productivity.

Periodic Maintenance. Periodic maintenance is scheduled on a recurring or a contractual basis for equipment and facilities at predetermined times. Generally speaking, a PMS is set up to be accomplished on specific days or at specific times. Performance of periodic maintenance is often associated with equipment in school office and in teaching areas such as computer labs and business education, home economics, and/or trade and industrial programs. However, building maintenance functions such as painting can also be scheduled on a periodic basis.

Predictive Maintenance. Predictive maintenance can be defined as the ability to estimate the likelihood of an equipment failure over some future time interval so that problems can be identified and maintenance performed before the failure occurs.

Recurring Maintenance. Recurring maintenance is more closely related to the daily operation of facilities and use of equipment. Where PMSs are not in force, or where the need to have repairs made in a short period of time is important, a recurring maintenance plan is needed. This plan provides that equipment be maintained at full operational status regardless of the number of service calls needed.

Emergency Maintenance. Emergency maintenance means, of course, fixing or repairing equipment or systems that have ceased to function. The basic differences between recurring and emergency maintenance are the time frames in which they occur and the cost factors. For example, an emergency maintenance plan for a computer system that is in operation twenty-four hours a day is always in effect. With recurring maintenance, several hours might lapse between the breakdown of the item and the arrival of maintenance personnel.

Many useful references are available that detail school building maintenance procedures. These sources provide reference lists and explanations beyond the scope of this chapter and should be examined carefully by the school business administrator.

Maintenance Performance Measures

Whether maintenance is provided in-house or through outside contractors, maintenance managers can use these suggested performance measures to evaluate the quality of maintenance operations:

- Custodial—general cleanliness, quality of cleaning equipment, quality of supplies used in cleaning, employee training.
- Maintenance—equipment breakdowns, response to emergency maintenance needs, quality of preventive maintenance, adequacy of information regarding status of maintenance work orders, employee training.
- Grounds—quality of grounds work; frequency of mowing, edging, and trimming.
- Employee training.
- Cost measures—overtime expended; cleaning/maintenance cost per square foot; cleaning by one custodian per square foot; administrative time taken by upkeep, on, over, or under budget. (Hounsell, 1996, pp. 16–19)

Selection and Training of Personnel

As is true with any other function of the school operation, the selection and training of maintenance personnel have a significant impact on the success of the maintenance program. Different patterns of selection and training emerge in school districts of different sizes and geographic locations. As noted in a previous section, larger school systems often have union agreements covering both maintenance and operations personnel. Under these circumstances, some of the elements of training and selection may be covered by union assignment stipulations based on union membership, journeyman workers status, and so forth. Stipulations in most, if not all, union agreements detail specific competencies to be expected from each employee; at the same time, the scope of each position is defined. Actual selection is generally left to local systems, but qualifications are spelled out.

Where the size of the school district warrants, a supervisor should be employed to direct the maintenance program. The supervisor should report directly to the school business administrator and/or the assistant superintendent for buildings and grounds. The supervisor's responsibilities include recommendations concerning personnel selection, evaluation and retention, and training for all maintenance personnel. The supervisor also has major responsibilities in scheduling staff and providing data for effective recordkeeping in areas of materials and supplies.

In a small district, the school business administrator may be charged with planning the maintenance function and also may act as the direct supervisor. In small districts, the problems of personnel selection may be compounded by the scarcity of competent persons available locally. Extensive training programs may be needed to gain the level of competence necessary. However, factors such as cost, time, and staff turnover might make extensive individual training impractical.

Extreme care should be exercised in a district's decisions about using student employees in both the operations and maintenance programs. Insurance regulations, union agreements, and federal and state laws are three areas of concern to all maintenance and operations employers. The types of maintenance service (local versus contracted) established by the local district also affect the role of the school business administrator and the nature of the maintenance staff.

Maintenance Records

One of the most important parts of any maintenance program is keeping adequate and complete records. It is imperative that an exact record of all maintenance functions within a school district be kept and that this information be available to the appropriate personnel within the district. Only through the proper selection of maintenance forms and the proper completion of these forms can the cost-effectiveness of a maintenance program be determined with any accuracy. These data provide the day-to-day record of the maintenance of each building and of each item of material used. Work schedules also provide useful data for planning staff usage and reflect what is to be accomplished over a specific period of time. These facts are important in the determination of cost-effectiveness and current maintenance fund balances, and for advanced planning within the school district.

The accuracy and completeness of maintenance records have become a major concern of school business administrators. Accurate custodial equipment inventory records allow for cost-effective purchases, while eliminating inefficient warehousing of surplus materials. Bulk purchasing of custodial supplies, for example, is only efficient if the use cycle warrants such purchases. Accurate inventories also allow effective use of tools and equipment at multiple sites, thus avoiding costly duplication in purchasing.

Maintenance Management Systems (MMS)

Many schools are using technology to assist in monitoring facilities maintenance programs more efficiently. A maintenance management system allows maintenance workers to keep track of ongoing work orders, job costs, preventive maintenance schedules, and equipment and supply inventory. It also can provide a historical record of completed work. Recent MMS packages have become available through application service providers, in which a service provider uses its computers to maintain computer applications and institution data, and school maintenance workers connect to the system over the Internet (Kennedy, 2003).

■ PLANT OPERATION

Plant operation consists of day-to-day activities such as cleaning, heating, and grounds care. Generally, the term plant operation is limited to a specific building (or set of buildings) located on one site. The basic element of any quality plan for plant operation is the establishment of cost estimates for item implementation and completion. As discussed in the foregoing section on maintenance, a school district's philosophy of operations is a determining factor in the success of any program. Establishing an acceptable level of cleanliness, delineating staff responsibilities, developing personnel policies, and describing the role of the custodians and other operations staff members must also be understood and supported by the board.

School buildings often represent a million dollars or more in construction costs, plus a comparable amount in furnishings and equipment. Thus, funds expended on the daily operations should provide high-quality plant care. Funds allocated for custodial services for each school building should be sufficient to provide a level of building care appropriate to its operation, thus increasing the useful life of each building.

The roles of the principal and systemwide personnel in plant operations are determined by board policy. The degree to which the concept of site-based management is implemented determines the scope of each participant. Some responsibilities of local building administrators and system personnel are similar. Supervision of personnel and responsibilities for implementation of negotiated agreements are critical elements for both levels of administration. Procedures must be known and responsibilities understood for effective plant operation. An interesting consideration that may need to be undertaken at some point is the cost-effectiveness of relocation rather than the operation of an existing facility.

The goal of educators, those creating policy and those operating a school, is to promote learning for all the children in the district. Facilities are provided to help promote the best learning situations. With this goal in mind, at least five questions need to be asked:

1. Do the facilities still provide for all necessary current and future learning programs?
2. Are current facilities located in appropriate proximity to students?
3. Is the physical condition of a building safe?
4. Is the building worn out? Does the equipment need replacement?
5. Is it cost effective to sell an old building and construct a new one at little or no added cost? (Ovard, 1992)

Under a site-based management concept, the role of the principal in effective operations practices is greatly expanded. While hiring and training usually will remain centralized functions, the majority of the daily responsibilities for custodial use and supervision rests with the principal. These responsibilities include the distribution of time (within district guidelines) and conflict resolution. The principal is also responsible for cooperative use of time, prioritization of jobs, and the maintenance of appropriate standards.

Organization of the Custodial Department

Individual school building operations may be part of a systemwide program or may operate independently under a supervisor appointed by the central office. The difference depends on district size and operations philosophy. When a systemwide plan for providing custodial services is used, the director of operations (or maintenance) is charged with the responsibility of providing services for all schools in the district. The use of head custodians or supervisors is a necessary part of this program and any other plan in which several employees work in the same building.

Proponents of systemwide plans say better use of staff can be accomplished, while opponents say it violates the basic management theory that the principal is responsible for a building. Both plans have merit, and consideration should be given to each.

Custodial Standards

Assignment	Production Rate (Avg)	Normal Frequency
Locker Bays Includes policing floor areas, benches, etc., of loose paper and trash; sweeping, wet/dry mopping floors; dusting exterior surfaces of lockers, wall tile, ledges, shelves, cabinets; spot mopping, scrubbing, stripping, refinishing floors; washing/polishing lockers inside and outside	Sweeping: 70 sq.ft./min. Dusting: 140 sq.ft./min. Locker dusting—72 sq.ft./min. Locker washing—2 min. ea. Ext. Locker washing—3 min. ea. Int.	Daily Daily Daily Three (3) times/year Annually
Shower and Dressing Rooms Includes policing all areas, hosing down showers and disinfecting area; wiping, washing, polishing mirrors, fixtures	Hosing and disinfecting—25 sq.ft./min.	Daily when in use
Gyms, Multi-Purpose Areas Includes policing area of loose paper and trash; spot mopping as needed; dry/damp mopping as needed; dusting bleachers, chairs; spotting walls; clean offices, game rooms, toilet rooms as needed	Sweeping gym floors—200 sq.ft./min. Dusting gym floors—400 sq.ft./min.	Daily when in use

FIGURE 14.2 Custodial Standards

Courtesy of Alexandria City Schools, Virginia.

Figure 14.2 displays custodial standards, including assignment, production rate, and normal frequency of occurrence.

Maintenance and operations are closely associated. Because of this factor and the related factors of cost, storage, and training, a single director of maintenance and operations may best serve a school district. District size will determine the best organizational scheme, but policies related to control are key elements in whatever organizational plan is followed. The person(s) responsible for maintenance and operations may report to the assistant superintendent for business or (in a small district) to the superintendent. Whatever the maintenance and operations plan, the centralization of services, materials, procurement, and personnel selection is essential to the effective operation of a school district.

Team maintenance allows the district to reorganize its total maintenance workforce into teams, each with a working-crew leader. The teams are each assigned to special areas—preventive maintenance, plumbing and heating, electrical and electronics, carpentry, and security work.

No single group of activities is as important to the success of the overall operations program as the selection, training, assignment, and supervision of staff. As was discussed in the introductory section of this chapter, union agreements regarding operational and custodial personnel often determine the qualifications of persons to be selected, job definitions, and the scope of assignments. Thus, responsibilities for operations functions or maintenance functions are fixed. Again, the size and the geographic location of the system play significant roles in determining requirements for staffing.

Staff Selection. All staff members in the operations areas should be selected according to criteria established by the board of education and administered through the superintendent's office. The selection process should be inclusive enough to ensure that the school district "gets its money's worth." Factors such as health, skills, character, and attitude should serve as a basis for establishing selection criteria. Figure 14.3 illustrates the duties; job features; examples of work; required knowledge, skills, and abilities; and acceptable experience and training for a custodian.

The implementation of Title IX guidelines relating to sex discrimination in hiring practices and the Privacy Act relative to collecting data on such factors as sex and marital status have had a significant impact on hiring practices for custodial and maintenance personnel. Factors of health, skills or competencies, and so forth are still of major importance, but the application of traditional sex roles has been affected by the implementation of the Title IX guidelines.

In school systems with a decentralized operations model, the principals select school building custodians. However, the principals should work within guidelines established by the system and with awareness of the previously identified factors of sex discrimination, privacy, and so forth. In general, the building principal relies on the school business administrator as a key resource person; thus, the school business administrator may become involved in hiring practices even in a decentralized model. It is often the school business administrator's responsibility to coordinate any policy revisions or policy changes that might affect hiring practices through the district. Also union agreements must be reviewed to ensure that they are properly explained and honored.

Under no circumstances should the awarding of custodial positions be viewed as a reward or established as a patronage system. However, criteria for selection of custodial staff should not be viewed by the board as a mandate to interview all potential employees at any level. The member of the superintendent's staff should recommend the actual selection to the board with this assigned responsibility. In many districts, a supervisor is charged with the responsibility of administering the total program of maintenance and operations.

Because buildings need to be maintained twelve months a year, building custodians and maintenance personnel need to be employed year-round. Some reassignment to other operations areas is a possibility, but twelve-month employment is necessary to attract and keep quality personnel. A reasonable package of fringe benefits also serves as a positive factor in attracting competent personnel. A high turnover rate among personnel at this level is as costly as high turnover in teaching staff. The cost may be even more pronounced if key skills are involved.

Staff Training. Even though staff members with specific skill levels are hired, in-service training affords the opportunity to sharpen general skills in building operations as well as to introduce new techniques and products to a large group. Group training and demonstration is a most effective method of providing necessary and useful information.

DUTIES OF THE CUSTODIAN

GENERAL STATEMENT OF DUTIES

Performs routine building cleaning and semiskilled maintenance tasks and related
work as required

EXAMPLES OF WORK (illustrative only)

Sweeps and mops floors and stairs
Dusts desks, woodwork, furniture, and other equipment
Washes windows, walls, blackboards, sinks, and other fixtures
Polishes furniture and metal furnishings
Empties waste baskets, collects and disposes of rubbish
Clears snow and ice from walks and driveways
Mows lawns, trims shrubs, rakes leaves, and performs a variety of other ground-
keeping tasks
Operates a coal or oil low-pressure heating system, including firing and removing
ashes
Delivers packages and messages
Checks operation of clocks and bells
Puts out and takes in traffic safety signs
Arranges chairs and tables and other equipment for special use of school buildings
Repairs window shades, replaces lightbulbs, soap, and towels
Paints rooms and equipment, repairs furniture and makes minor plumbing, electrical,
and carpentry repairs
Prepares and maintains a variety of records and reports

REQUIREMENTS (illustrative only)

Knowledge of building cleaning practices, supplies, and equipment; working
knowledge of the operation and maintenance of heating equipment and ability to make
minor plumbing, electrical, carpentry, and mechanical repairs. Ability to follow oral and
written directions; willingness to do custodial and other manual tasks; good physical
condition.

DESIRABLE EXPERIENCE AND TRAINING

One year of maintenance experience, or equivalent training

FIGURE 14.3 Duties of the Custodian

Pre-school workshops, at which a wide range of activities is discussed, play a valuable role
in a school district. At these sessions, the entire operations plan for the year can be
reviewed, questions answered, and new techniques or refinements of old plans introduced.
Care should be taken to secure input from present custodial and maintenance personnel
for use in planning future training programs as well as for improved efforts in decision
making, procedures, and work practices.

Staff Assignment. The assignment of custodial staff to individual schools should be made in accordance with established board policies. Criteria for assignment should be determined by members of the superintendent's staff and recommended to the board. These professional staff members are better able to provide specialized inputs and to apply general personnel criteria useful in avoiding charges of patronage or favoritism at certain schools or with certain persons.

An appropriate number of custodial persons should be assigned to each building to maintain each building at an acceptable level in accord with board policy. Figure 14.4 shows a custodial assignment formula. As noted earlier, it is inappropriate to construct a building and not maintain it at an acceptable level. That acceptable level of maintenance also will indicate what central office services need to be allocated. Through these activities, the proper cost factor can be projected for long-term budget work in areas of personnel, purchase of supplies, and maintenance scheduling.

Assignments are determined in a number of ways; one of the more common is by some type of square-footage measure. It is important that the school business administrator give some consideration to a factor-weighing scheme based on the type and use of the facility rather than on size. Laboratories, auditoriums, gymnasiums, and athletic dressing rooms all have unique cleaning problems, and size may not be an effective common denominator in assigning work to a group of custodians.

Staff Supervision. Day-to-day supervision of a custodial staff occurs at the system or at the building level, depending on the operating plan adopted by the board. As previously discussed, if the principal has direct responsibility for the condition and maintenance of the facility, it is necessary that the custodial staff be responsible to this position. If maintenance responsibility is assumed at the system level, an operations manager is responsible. If more than one custodian is functioning at a single facility, one should be designated as head custodian.

Enrollment ÷ 250 = Number of full-time positions (N_1)

N_1 × 16,000 Sq. Ft. = Sq. Ft. covered in N_1

Total Sq. Ft. − Allowance above = Remaining Sq. Ft.

Remaining Sq. Ft. ÷ 25,000 = Number of part-time positions (N_2)

or

E ÷ 250 = N_1 (12-month positions)

N_1 ÷ 16,000 = X_1

Sq. Ft. − X_1 = X_2

X_2 ÷ 25,000 = N_2 (10-month positions)

FIGURE 14.4 Custodial Assignment Formula

Courtesy of Chattanooga Public Schools, Tennessee.

The head custodian, the principal, the general maintenance operations supervisor, and other appropriate staff should design work schedules on a short- and long-range basis. Whenever possible, each staff member should be involved in evaluation of one's own competence. This facilitates explanation of work expectations and assists in producing a sense of accomplishment in daily work assignment. Plans should be made for exceptions in custodial requirements, because special cases do arise for additional services.

Continuous evaluation should be made of all maintenance and operations personnel in the district. Annual efficiency reports should be prepared on each person by an immediate supervisor. General supervisory evaluations should be made where appropriate, and the sum of all ratings should serve as a basis for retention, transfer, and merit salary adjustments.

When a school system changes from systemwide to site-based management at the building level, the principal's role and responsibility change in both maintenance and operations of the physical plant. The principal becomes more accountable for the day-to-day applications and for the operations plans and has more input into the overall operation of a school facility than under total central administrative organizational plans.

Scheduling of Custodial and Maintenance Services

Routine custodial services and selected maintenance activities are performed during the school year. Housekeeping chores, small repair projects, and selective replacement activities can take place without disrupting the instructional program. Some major capital projects may be undertaken or finished during the school year if proper safety standards can be met and if construction can be combined effectively with noise control to allow the normal continuation of classes. Of course, emergency repairs may need to be made at any time during the school year, with a certain amount of inconvenience resulting.

In isolated instances, a one-day interruption or rescheduling of classes (e.g., to accomplish an inside task such as ceiling repairs or lighting corrections) is not out of the question. The staff available to the system cannot accomplish these activities if all such tasks are left to periods when school is not in session. Even if additional personnel were available, the cost could prove prohibitive. Another factor to be considered is that staff members under full-time contract must be continuously utilized.

Planned maintenance activities not accomplished during the school year must be accomplished during periods when schools are closed. Activities that must be carried out during closed periods are those that create major disruptions or require that utilities be suspended or that no persons be allowed to use facilities for an extended period of time. Work such as sanitary facility replacement, replacement of water systems, major painting, carpeting or retiling of an entire building, or the paving of access roads must be scheduled when school is not in session.

Reduction in Force

While not as common as in the mid-1990s, the need to reduce staff by greater numbers than those due to natural attrition may occur in some districts. Any reduction in the maintenance and operations workforce has a serious impact on the general care and usability of all facilities and equipment. As major items such as painting and roofing are delayed, the question of how much delay is possible becomes an important issue. At what point does delay cause significant structural damage? More efficient scheduling of personnel and better care by staff and students will help, but a certain level of care and maintenance is required for general usage of all facilities and equipment.

Union Agreements

Union agreements cannot be overemphasized with regard to establishing maintenance and operations programs within a school district. The role of the union is crucial in many districts and is becoming an increasingly important aspect of all school business administration functions. In general, union agreements provide features such as recognition rights, seniority, job shifting, vacancies, regular and overtime pay, and fringe benefits, including hospitalization, vacations, leaves of absence, and military leaves. Other elements of a union agreement include negotiation rights and specific considerations for grievance procedures.

Energy and Resource Conservation

As all school business administration personnel know, energy costs are a major factor in operating any school system, community college, or university. The school business administrator, other central office staff, and local school staff should continually assess energy and resource conservation opportunities within the district. Opportunities for conservation are widespread and should be examined in terms of total system and individual building application.

Energy/Supplies. A recycling program for consumable supplies should be implemented. In general, the school business administrator, who has knowledge of the expenditures of the district for consumable supplies, energy, transportation, and other factors, is the logical officer to undertake a serious examination of all areas of possible conservation. This should not be a one-time-only operation, but an ongoing, regular process that is implemented at all times by all employees and users. For example, it is possible to facilitate a 25 percent reduction in energy consumption in a particular school building and system-wide. School systems should explore the area of alternate energy resources where appropriate. For example, use of passive solar heating in areas of the South and West should be considered when new construction occurs. Savings in HVAC costs and consumable supplies are feasible and should be examined in terms of their impact on programs throughout the district.

An energy audit is a major item in determining energy usage and needs and in projecting potential savings. A survey of all physical facilities should be made to determine the current usage, conditions, and estimated costs of any upgrading to bring facilities into the most energy-efficient state. A plan can then be developed for usage, capital improvement, and the identification of specific needs requiring further evaluation. While not a "cure," this plan will provide direction in determining trouble areas warranting further exploration. Of course, some facilities will require more work than initially indicated, but, generally speaking, these estimates will prove a reasonable guide. It is realistic to expect implementation of this plan to be phased over time.

A representative team competent in areas of specialization should conduct the audit. A detailed project schedule should be developed that allows multiple checkpoints and provides target dates. The school business administrator is probably the logical team leader. Current cost records should be readily available, as well as other pertinent data, so that an early overview of project needs can be made and appropriate administrative bodies notified.

In the News

The San Diego Unified School District (SDCS), the second largest school district in California, with more than 15,800 employees serving almost 136,000 students, has initiated a photovoltaic roofing project that converts the sun's energy into electricity and reduced energy costs. As of January 1, 2007, a total of 24 solar systems are installed and operational. Plans are underway for 16 more, for a total of 40 facilities.

SDCS estimates the overall project will result in a potential savings of more than $37 million in avoided costs during the next 20 years.

From: Dolan, T.G. (2007, January). Solar roofs in San Diego: SDCS has found an innovative way to save energy and cut costs, and they plan to expand it to all of their facilities through time. *School Planning and Management*, 46(1), 19–21.

Energy Management. While administrators are properly concerned with many important day-to-day issues of program implementation, data manipulation, word processing, and budgetary applications, the nonglamorous responsibilities and concerns of energy management often pass through offices and by boards without a thorough understanding of their impact on budgeting resources and facilities use. One of the best ways to conserve is to use a microcomputer-based unit designed to provide control and energy management functions for HVAC systems.

The bottom line of energy management is that when computer technology and energy demands are merged, the potential for substantial dollar savings is high. Basic management systems, for which there are several major vendors, operate from an energy control unit, a microcomputer, visual display terminals, a printer, and a power line communication system for controlling all energy-consuming equipment. In general, energy management systems utilize a set of control points for which parameter bands are established. These parameters are monitored by a computer to determine whether the system is operating within the predetermined limits of each of these parameters.

Remember that each school should have a plan for energy savings involving the ever-expanding number of computers in use. The energy used by each monitor (greater than that of the CPUs) can be substantial when examined over a period of weeks and months.

Energy Upgrades. Money can be saved by altering behavior, such as turning off lights in unoccupied areas, shutting down unused computers, and installing more energy-efficient equipment. Replacing an antiquated, inefficient heating, ventilation, and air-conditioning (HVAC) system with a modern system also reduces maintenance costs and lowers long-term energy costs.

Schools that cannot afford the initial expense of new equipment often use performance contracting to partner with energy service companies. The company pays the initial cost of an upgrade, and the school pays for the new system with the savings generated.

Operating Schemes. Any of the accessible areas or items in a management system that can be accessed have parameter levels that can be altered. For example, starting time for building cooling or heating is a flexible feature of any system and is controllable based on decisions about when school activities start or stop, the level of cooling/heating desired, and time pattern variability for weekdays and weekends and holidays. Decisions also may be influenced by the number and type of activities that take place in a particular area (e.g., computer laboratory versus general instruction).

Cost Reductions. Cost factors of energy management systems are always major considerations. Some vendors offer "paid-from-savings programs" in which building owners may pay for purchase, maintenance, and financing of energy management and building automation systems with funds to be realized from savings after system installation. Length of payback depends on how well (or whether) the user was maintaining thermostats and time clocks prior to system installation. Two major decisions must be made when installing an energy management system either as a retrofitting of an existing structure, as the addition of facilities to an ongoing operation, or as a "ground-up," basic installation. The first decision concerns the type of energy management system that is to be installed, and the second concerns the installation of the appropriate devices, sensors, monitors, and the like, through which the program can function. An appropriately designed and utilized energy management system is a cost-effective investment.

To the extent that energy commodities are not predictable in their price volatility, school district budgets are vulnerable to rapid increases in energy commodity costs. School district budgets are often established and approved a full year in advance of actual expenditures. Any item that was budgeted based on a trend line of gradual increases will be underfunded if there is a sharp increase in cost between the time the budget is adopted and the costs are incurred.

Creating Financial Incentives. Many districts budget utilities at the school site. Savings from energy as well as other activities, such as use of substitute teachers, are then permitted to be carried over to subsequent years or can be shifted to alternative activities.

In the News

Elementary students in Fort Collins, Colorado, stay warm all winter with a little help from recycled blue jeans that insulate school buildings. "The kids love the fact that we use blue jeans for insulation," says Stu Reeve, energy manager for the Poudre School District. Poudre capitalizes on the "blue jean factor" with the Truth Wall, an exposed cross-section where kids can see the denim at work, look at pipes and electrical systems, and check school energy use.

Welcome to the green schools movement, when even the buildings teach. The movement is spreading because it is cost-efficient, and there are many successes. Building a new-high-performance school designed to save energy and reduce environmental impact can save districts as much as 50 percent in operations costs when compared to traditionally designed schools, according to the U.S. Department of Energy. Energy-efficient renovations—such as the replacement of inefficient boilers, lighting and other systems—can save up to 30 percent annually.

Each year, taxpayers spend $6 billion on energy for American public schools—about 25 percent more than necessary due to waste and inefficiencies. Not only can green schools save on operation costs, but districts that build them are eligible for a variety of state and federal grants.

From: Shorr, P.W. (2004). It's so easy being green. Retrieved March 1, 2007, from http://www.asbj.com/lbd/2004/inprint/shorr.html.

Fire Safety

At times, it seems as if fire drills are more of a nuisance than a needed safety precaution. Children return to the building distracted, and teachers lose valuable time in the classroom. Nevertheless, reasonable practice and preventive measures can help schools stay within fire safety codes and prevent a potential disaster.

The most common violations to fire safety codes are:

- Flammable materials affixed to walls (holidays, such as Thanksgiving and Christmas, are a particular problem time).
- Storage of combustible materials under stairs and elsewhere in stairwells.
- Exits wholly or partially blocked by combustible materials.

To keep the school from becoming a potential fire trap:

- Have a monthly locker cleanout. Student lockers crammed with papers, notebooks, and other combustible materials are a hazard, especially when lockers are stored against walls.
- Do not cover more than 20 percent of the wall space with papers, projects, and decorations.
- Store flammable liquids and gases, such as those found in a science room, in an approved fireproof cabinet. (Laboratory Safety Workshop, 1992)

Inspections

Safety inspections should be planned as a regular part of the maintenance and operations schedule of a school district. A detailed plan for this procedure should be established for each building in the district. Implementation of this plan should be coordinated with manufacturer recommendations for items of equipment so as to comply with local fire, disaster, and civil defense regulations. Inspection teams should be established, trained, and granted adequate fiscal resources and time to function. The use of manufacturer representatives, local governmental personnel, and/or community members should be encouraged, but the responsible representative of the local school district should handle the supervision of these persons.

Inspections should be made promptly of potential safety hazards noted by parents, school personnel, students, or others. Necessary corrections should follow or adequate warning procedures be initiated until such time as proper repair or removal of the potential hazard can be made. General health inspection procedures may fall in the area of maintenance and operations, but adequately trained personnel must augment the general staff if these inspections are to be made effectively.

Environmental Hazards

The location of a school site should be determined on the basis of educational needs of the host community. Careful planning of the learning environment during this phase of development includes the identification of present and future needs. Health or environmental educators note that chemical, biological, and physical environmental health hazards at school sites are concerns of the school business administrator and the school district. Basic environmental health considerations used in selecting a school site include proximity to sources of air, noise, and water pollution, and potential for earthquakes, tornadoes, severe wind storms, and floods.

Environmental factors may not determine a school location, but awareness of their influence plays a major role in the comfort, health, and safety of personnel who spend time there. Evaluation of potential redevelopment of existing sites to improve energy use, grounds utilization, and safety is also a part of the school business administrator's overall concern.

The maintenance and operation of laboratories are examples of major concerns in terms of providing appropriate health-safety systems in which faculty and students work and study. Indoor air pollution is another factor facing schools. The inhalation, ingestion, inoculation, and absorption through the skin or mucous membranes of chemical contaminants can be a major factor in health concerns.

Computers are particularly vulnerable to electrostatic discharge (ESD). These machines are unable to differentiate between a command pulse and the random pulse of ESD. Environmental area treatment using appropriate floor coverings seems to be the most likely (and the most cost-efficient) remedy.

Radon. Unlike the asbestos threat, the hazard posed by naturally occurring radioactive gas, more commonly referred to as radon, is not yet well identified. The main questions, of course, concern how much of a problem it is in the schools and what can be done to rectify the situation.

Radon is a colorless, odorless, tasteless gas that occurs as a result of the natural breakdown of uranium found in almost all soils. Radon seeps into buildings through holes and cracks in foundations and is generally a threat only in an enclosed space, where concentrations can soar to unacceptably high levels. Some studies have shown that extended exposure to high concentrations of radon can lead to lung cancer. Unlike asbestos, however, the money and time needed to detect radon are minimal. Short-term tests can be performed in less than a week and generally cost less than $20. The cost of making a school nearly radon-free can be as little as a few thousand dollars.

A key to radon elimination, or at least control, is to prevent its entering a building or to dilute it. Because many school are well ventilated, their air-exchanging systems have managed to dilute any potential threat. The major areas of concern include basements and first floors, especially when these areas are used for the placement of younger children (i.e., kindergarten, nursery school, pre-school programs).

Mold and Asbestos. Indoor air quality has become one of the latest buzzwords in the construction trades. School board members are quickly learning of its significance as well. Schools across the nation have been plagued by mold that can make students and staff members sick, particularly if they already suffer from a respiratory illness such as asthma. Fixing leaky roofs, cleaning carpets, and scrubbing air-conditioning ducts can avert many air-quality problems.

The Environmental Protection Agency (EPA) has taken an increasingly active role in improving school air quality. The EPA found that schools built during the 1970s energy crisis have some of the worst air problems. The buildings were designed to retain warm air in the winter and cool air in the summer, but those energy-saving measures also limited air circulation.

The EPA has assembled a Tools for Schools kit to help educators protect indoor air quality. The kit includes checklists for teachers, maintenance workers, principals, and other school officials, along with background materials (see Web Resources on page 334).

Likewise, planning and preventive maintenance can help schools keep asbestos under wraps. The mineral itself isn't necessarily harmful, but microscopic asbestos fibers released into the air can have long-term health effects if inhaled. Many older schools still struggle with an asbestos problem, and the Education Department guide says school officials must identify any asbestos in their buildings, inform the staff and parents, and train employees to work in affected areas (School Facilities Maintenance Task Force, 2003).

HIV/AIDS. Some fundamental knowledge is required by school officials that will not only enable them to maintain regulatory compliance, but also actually minimize environmental hazards at far less cost. Each issue should be addressed in a systematic, logical approach. Key issues are blood-borne pathogens and lead in paint and water.

In the mid-to-late-1980s, legislators became aware of the need for guidelines and regulations to protect workers from blood-borne pathogens, those microorganisms found in human blood and other potentially infectious body fluids that can cause disease in humans. The concern for protection began with the recognition of the human immunodeficiency virus (HIV) in 1981 and rose as scientists recognized the potential of HIV to infect health care professionals.

HIV is only one type of blood-borne pathogen. Numerous sexually transmitted diseases and other viruses, including the hepatitis B virus (HBV), are included in this category. Although HIV received the most attention initially, hepatitis B has become an increasing concern.

Training is the key element of a universal precautions program. Universal precautions training briefly explains the facts to personnel and renders them more aware of circumstances that possess the potential for exposure. This type of training, reinforced periodically, could minimize, if not eliminate, the exposure risk to building personnel.

Housekeeping is an integral part of minimizing the risk of exposure. Areas with blood-contaminated surfaces or restrooms with bodily fluids of unknown origin must be treated as potentially infectious. At this point, the level of dealing with blood-borne pathogens becomes an "occupational exposure." The custodian whose job requires cleaning a blood-soiled area is at a potentially greater risk of exposure than are other employees. A more extensive program of protection may be warranted for employees who fall into this category. These employees might include, but are not limited to, school nurses, custodians, special education teachers, athletic trainers and physical education teachers, bus drivers, and perhaps sports equipment managers. Depending on their particular responsibilities, these individuals may require specialized training, personal protective equipment, and possibly an immunization program for HBV (DiNardo, 1996).

Lead Poisoning. Anxiety, weakness, headaches, and excessive tiredness are some of the initial symptoms of lead poisoning. However, these symptoms are also the daily complaints of numerous school children for a variety of other reasons. It is imperative to understand that even children with no clinical symptoms of lead poisoning, but with elevated levels of lead in their blood, may experience a drop in their expected cognitive abilities by as much as five or more IQ points.

How is lead poisoning recognized? It is a common misconception that children who acquire lead poisoning are children who eat paint chips. Most lead exposure to children occurs from lead dust ingested from normal hand-to-mouth activity.

Some common sources of lead exposure in school settings are lead-based paint and lead-contaminated drinking water. Lead dust can be caused by activities and conditions such as paint deterioration, water damage, chalking, renovation activities (sanding, etc.), window or door replacement, paint stripping, or the simple abrasion of painted windows and doors. These types of activities are frequently so routine in schools that the risk of lead exposure is often overlooked (DiNardo, 1996).

Pest Control. Another area often overlooked in custodial services is pest control. In urban locations, this is usually a contracted service; while, in more rural settings, local personnel deal with the problem. Under the terms of most contracts with outside sources, each building would be serviced in its entirety once each year during the summer months. Monthly treatment is provided to designated areas within each building-food service areas, restrooms, and so forth. Other areas are treated on an "as-needed" basis. Thus, it is important that on-site staff include preventive pest control measures in the regular building maintenance program.

Pesticides. School districts are faced with an increasingly difficult issue relative to the uses of chemical pesticides, including even those that can be bought locally "off the shelf." In general, chemical pesticides are a fact of life in most school districts and in most school buildings, but increasing concerns have been raised relative to the widespread and generally uncontrolled use of chemical pesticides. As a result, many school systems have adopted policies that required officials to monitor and record each pest population, to determine pest infestation levels that can be tolerated before any action is taken, and to identify all nonchemical alternatives to pesticides that can be used to control a particular pest. This would include items such as use of traps, or, in some instances, the introduction of the pest's natural enemies.

Clearly, one of the major factors of pest control is pest prevention. By placing emphasis on preventive education and good housekeeping measures at all levels, the numbers and varying types of pests can certainly be reduced. The centerpiece of all policies relative to integrated pest management programs is clearly the close monitoring of pest populations and the use of nontoxic pest control methods. In instances in which the situation is a major problem, many techniques that can be used have been around for a long time but have not been used because of a reliance on pesticides. In addition, other procedures that can be performed routinely and as part of a regular maintenance program can save a school system several thousand dollars by reducing the need for pesticides, which are a large expenditure in many districts. However, in some instances, chemicals are necessary, and their use is determined by weather, climate, and humidity levels in a particular area rather than by practices under the control of the business administration or the board.

Plant Security

Detailed descriptions of what areas are to be secured and how they are to be secured must be determined for each building in the district. Proper locking devices, alarm systems, and surveillance systems must be decided upon by the local boards and installed at appropriate locations.

Current school security needs are substantially more complex compared even to recent years. The possibility of physical threats to faculty, staff, and students has been added to the recurring concerns of threats to property from theft and vandalism. These threats come from both inside the building (e.g., students attacking faculty or other students) and outside the building (e.g., nonschool persons entering the school grounds to sell drugs or to abduct children). School locker and hall monitors are one method of security, but, as time tested as these are, they may not be sufficient for today's problems.

In the News

School Security and Emergency Planning Trends

School violence, especially non-fatal shootings, stabbings, and gang activity, will likely continue to rise in 2007. Expect ongoing challenges with athletic event security, especially at high school football and basketball games, and violence on school buses. As problems grow, public demands for accountability on school safety issues will also rise. Parents and the media are increasingly frustrated and skeptical of the adequacy of safety measures in schools. The cost of doing nothing, or the bare minimum, is increasingly greater than the cost of doing things properly.

Budget cuts for security and prevention programs will continue until at least 2010. Even if federal and state safety dollars are restored, districts will have to incorporate safety into local budgets more in the long haul. School safety can no longer be viewed as a grant-funded luxury. Educators increasingly recognize that using fill-in-the-blank crisis "templates" does not work. Relationship

building and emergency planning with police, fire, medical, and emergency management partners will rightfully grow.

While full-scale drills are informative, they are also too time and labor intensive for many schools. Yet more school leaders recognize the need to get plans off shelves and into practice. Professional evaluations of school emergency plans and tabletop exercises to talk through hypothetical scenarios with public safety partners will continue as popular best practices. School tabletop exercise allows school participants to examine the roles, responsibilities, tasks, and overall logistics associated with managing a similar real-life emergency situation and make subsequent adjustments in their school emergency/crisis plans.

Various school districts' tabletop exercises have also revealed some common, interesting "lessons learned" including:

1. Many school crisis teams have unrealistic expectations of their public safety partners in a crisis.

For example, school teams often mistakenly believe the number of police officers who would respond to their school in an emergency is much greater than the police department staffing levels can actually immediately provide.

2. A number of school crisis teams have a tendency to jump into lockdown modes faster than what may be necessary based upon the threat at hand.

3. Managing parents and the media will typically be the two biggest "crisis after the crisis" matters school teams must deal with following an emergency incident. Yet crisis plan evaluations and tabletop exercises consistently find these components of school emergency guidelines to be the weakest parts of school plans.

4. School crisis plans too often lack adequate backup levels of leadership and planning.

5. Parent communication and parent-student reunification plans are typically not well developed.

6. Crisis media protocols, especially joint agency protocols, and crisis media training are often lacking.

Each school district and individual schools within the various districts must develop their own school crisis preparedness plans and school emergency plan guidelines. A "cut and paste" approach using other school emergency plans will typically not lead to full ownership and successful school crisis planning within one's school. In fact, it could lead to increased liability for school officials.

Adapted from: Trump, K.S. (2007, January). Trends in education: What's ahead for educational facilities planning? *School Planning and Management*, 46(1), 16–19; and National School Safety and Security Service's web site—http://www.schoolsecurity.org/consultants/tabletop.html.

Designing on the Outside. Every facet of design, including security, relies on the proven fundamentals of educational facility planning. The same process that administrators, planners, and designers use to create effective learning environments also can be used to create safe, secure school facilities. This process begins by engaging all stakeholders to discuss what is important for their community. An architect can serve as a facilitator and provide knowledge gained from experiences with other schools. This process establishes a level of awareness and expectations that serves as the basis for an effective design.

The planning process should begin by involving all stakeholders and posing two fundamental questions:

1. What are we securing against?
2. What levels of security do we need—and what are we willing—to provide? (Young, 2003)

Planning for a Special Event. Planning security for special events at schools can seem daunting. However, a balanced approach to a security program can help the event come off smoothly. All forms of security planning involve three aspects:

1. Natural—using basic crime prevention through environmental design techniques.
2. Organizational—training and preparing the security staff and instructing participants.
3. Mechanical—using security equipment to assist the security program.

When schools plan security programs using only one of these aspects, the result is that the school does not get the best bang for its security buck, and the event may encounter problems. But a serious attempt at addressing all three can prove successful.

Basic security is a major concern of all school personnel. However, there are indicators that reactions to a series of random events have created a situation in which possible overreactions have occurred. Statistical data support the position that schools—in general—are safer than they have ever been. This, in no way, should lead to a false sense of security or reduction in diligent, exhaustive approaches to maintaining and improving the safety level of all schools.

Districts and local school sites need to be encouraged to review all safety and security plans and to be especially cognizant of opportunities to work with local law enforcement groups. Far too often, school districts have had a "knee-jerk" reaction and form independent police safety units with little or no interaction with other government agencies.

While the safety of students, staff, and family should never be compromised, the cost-effectiveness and general effectiveness of such efforts are often questionable. Selection, training, administration, and review/evaluation produce recurring costs that possibly could be shared among multiple governmental groups. Collective bargaining issues also arise as to possible conflicts between student, parent, and teacher privacy rights and the need to provide a safe, secure environment in which to learn and/or work (Safe Schools, 2000).

School police officers need to be trained in strategies for deterring criminal behavior. That includes knowing how to make school buildings inhospitable to criminals and criminal activities. School security personnel should understand the importance of physical security and crime prevention measures through environmental design making sure that windows and doors are locked and that security equipment is functioning, and requiring that visitors and employees are identifiable. For example, officers need a working knowledge of criminal law and school law, and how the two relate; an understanding of what the courts permit in terms of search-and-arrest procedures at school and the use of force; and knowledge of how to perform first aid and CPR procedures (Kennedy, 2003, January).

Clearly, school size, location, and demography affect issues of security. In areas of high crime, schools are no less vulnerable than convenience markets, gasoline stations, liquor stores, or houses. The decision to fence school grounds or to add locking devices and lights is based on identified problem frequency. Determining what security services are needed and how these will be provided has a major impact for the school business administrator. The basic reason, as is often the case, is that effective security costs money, but a lack of adequate security can cost substantially more.

Security Technology. Continuing technological advancements and lower costs mean that more schools can afford high-tech solutions to security problems. Surveillance equipment such as closed-circuit cameras, access-control systems, metal detectors, and alarms can help many schools provide a safer environment for their students and staff without breaking their budgets. Advancements such as digital video recording allow schools to record and archive their surveillance without having to label and store space-gobbling videocassettes.

While VHS-based surveillance technology and real-time closed-circuit TV monitoring are widely used in schools today, selected districts have taken their surveillance systems into the digital age. Unlike traditional videotape recorder surveillance, which requires someone on-site to review tapes and handle recording equipment, remote digital-surveillance recording technology enables users to watch and record real-time surveillance footage of school grounds utilizing a personal computer. The PC-based technology works by transmitting live data from school cameras to networked computers via an Internet or intranet connection.

The PC-based systems digitize, compress, and store surveillance video on the PC's hard drive for up to thirty days. Video files then can be accessed and reviewed on the computer monitor by typing in dates and times. The video files also can be backed up onto a Zip disk or CD-ROM; and, if necessary, individual screen shots of video can be saved as evidence to a floppy disk. Digital recording technology also allows for more defined images than those captured on VHS surveillance systems (Joiner, 2002).

Contracting for certain types of security services may make good financial sense for some school systems, especially smaller ones, rural systems, or those without major security difficulties. It is often cost effective for large school systems, especially urban ones, to establish their own security forces. A possible cost-efficient alternative is to employ a private security firm to provide the support needed. The type of services and the degree of expertise sought are functions of what must be protected in terms of property and personnel.

Search and Seizure. All school officials who conduct student searches or seizures should be aware of the potential civil penalties for violating the Fourth Amendment rights of students. Students can make a tort claim against officials in both state and federal court for declaratory or injunctive relief, and for compensation and punitive damages. In some cases, students can even recover lawyers' fees. In *New Jersey v. T.L.O.* (1985), the U.S. Supreme Court imposed practical limits on the scope, intensity, and methods of a search. Overall, students do not have a right to resist or prevent lawful searches.

Zero Tolerance and Profiling. On-campus shootings over the past decade have led schools to adopt a number of safety measures. The most visible—and extreme—responses are zero-tolerance policies and student profiling. These measures have led to unintended consequences, and now educators and school safety experts are having second thoughts about both measures.

Zero-tolerance policies can contribute to school safety, but the key is in "striking an appropriate balance in keeping schools safe and not being draconian." The policies can be helpful to school administrators, but there needs to be some provision for discretion to fit all circumstances in all situations. Zero-tolerance policies have been adopted because of pressure to deal with school violence, but the policies often have had a negative effect, especially on low-income or minority students, who seem to be overrepresented in the percentage of students expelled or suspended. The policies have painted schools into a corner and taken human judgment out of decisions. "Zero tolerance means zero understanding. It is applied in irrational ways and creates a sense that the system is unjust." This criticism has led some districts to reexamine their policies so administrators can have more discretion.

Another antiviolence measure that is coming under scrutiny is student profiling, in which school officials use a checklist of characteristics associated with youth who have committed violent acts to gauge a student's potential for violence. A 2000 report by the U.S. Secret Service found "there is no accurate or useful profile of the school shooter." The report showed that student shooters ranged in age, racial and ethnic backgrounds, and academic achievement. "There is no system around that will predict with 100 percent accuracy whether a youngster will conduct an act of violence."

The improvement of school security is a complex task that often requires physical security measures and the involvement of trained personnel. The goal of any security system plan is to both deter crime and provide additional safety measures. The service may be directed at ensuring surveillance and crime reporting, not necessarily the capturing of persons caught in the act. Other security systems may provide physical protection from bodily injury or harm. Electronic monitoring systems (e.g., television cameras, listening devices), expanded lighting, new locking devices, and securing background checks on appropriate personnel, especially those who have access to the buildings at times other than normal security hours, may well be reasonable expenditures of funds.

A continuing problem facing local school districts is lost or stolen keys. The cost of replacing locks and keys in a building can amount to several thousand dollars. One successful approach has been to charge these costs to the loser of the keys.

A goal of each system should be an antivandalism program. Whether this is an educational program, a community assistance program, or a combination of a number of approaches, the entire administrative team should assume shared responsibility. Input from various sources should be welcomed, and no avenues should be closed.

Vandalism prevention measures considered to be major contributions to plant security include extra outside lighting, extra inside lighting, night custodians, use of plastic glazing material, school citizenship programs, and security patrols. Another major factor in plant security is proper planning for security measures while the building is still on the drawing board. School plant planners must work with architects to identify features that will lessen vandalism in future buildings. An alarm system, whether local, central station, or direct connect, is still seen as a first line of defense in any plant security program. A review of educational facility planners' designs can be important to business administrators as they plan the renovation of current facilities and the construction of new ones.

Some specific approaches to security for school facilities include implementation of programs using students and community members as patrol groups. The use of an "internal" or an "external" security force has helped many school systems. Both systems may alienate students if personnel are not carefully screened. Both of these methods are costly. Another method of curbing vandalism is cooperating with the staff and students. Development of an *esprit de corps* can help to reduce vandalism. This is a rather inexpensive system that works with varying results.

Other physical security measures include audio alarm systems, magnetic door contacts, window foils, and vibration detectors. Closed-circuit TV is a possibility in the plan calling for scheduled maintenance during the second and third shifts. The presence of personnel is always a major deterrent to crime.

The training of systems-level personnel in security procedures is often overlooked in many school districts. A key feature of a security program can be the training of central staff, who, in turn, train building-level staff. Through this procedure, systemwide policies can be transmitted and understood at all levels, which facilitates the flow of personnel across all levels and provides a consistent operations policy.

■ A GROWING FACILITIES NEED

Despite the building boom, facilities needs remain great. The baby boomlet increased enrollment by an average of almost 100 students in each elementary school from 1982 to 2000, according to the U.S. Department of Education. At the same time, inexpensive—and in some cases, inadequate—schools built during the 1950s and 1960s started to show severe wear and tear.

About three-fourths of the nation's 80,000 schools need repairs, renovations, or modernization to be in good condition, according to the American Society of Civil Engineers. The average cost per school is $2.2 million, or $3,800 per student. That brings the price tag for the nation's school facilities to somewhere between the $127 billion estimate from the National Center for Education Statistics (NCES) and the National Education Association's $268 billion figure. U.S. school districts' construction projects completed during the 2005 school year totaled $21.6 billion for new buildings, additions to current facilities, and modernization of present structures (McMilin, 2006).

The task ahead for the school business administrator, other administrators, school boards, and academic program planners is to begin the process of retrofitting buildings for the future. The enormous cost of constructing new buildings will make it necessary for most districts to retrofit, remodel, and add to existing buildings. In making these facility realignments, sufficient amounts and types of space will have to be dedicated to technology use. Wireless networks, personal notebooks, year-round schooling, providing programs to severely disabled students, and substantial power upgrades, new lighting, carpeting, and furniture are all unknown needs.

These and other technology challenges are forcing districts to carefully plan future budgets for both technology and facilities. Unfortunately, in many districts and states, it appears very unlikely that adequate amounts of tax dollars will ever be available for both facilities and technology. Structural shells for school buildings will have to be well designed for the twenty-first century. It is quite likely that school facilities in the future will be used for longer periods of time. The school year will be lengthened, as will the school day. Additional use will increase wear on the physical plant and reduce the summer days available for heavy maintenance (Glass, 1997).

Construction for the Future

The evolving world of technology is changing not only educational programs, but also the facilities in which they are housed. School business administrators need to become key participants in planning efforts to ensure that classrooms and buildings facilitate technology-based learning. In addition, they need to be the lead planners in understanding how facilities must be physically adapted to become adequate places of working and learning for the twenty-first century.

Site-Specific Issues

Many site-specific issues have influenced the evolution of school design. Each plays an important part in providing a safe and secure school facility. Here are examples of ways that school administrators, facility planners, and architects have responded to these challenges:

- *Building sites*. Land availability and costs are the main factors dictating the size and location of a school site. Conducting a site analysis, inclusive of security issues, will allow districts to consider such important security-related issues as perimeter and setback.
- *Perimeter and setback*. Over the decades, traditional school designs created a well-defined perimeter; it was clear when one had made the transition from community to school property, and one had to walk a distance through the schoolyard before reaching

the front door. Today, many urban school buildings are set close to the street, and the front door may be just a few steps from the sidewalk. As a result, some schools are left without a safe perimeter.

- *Planners and designers need to create safe zones as buffers around the building; where they cannot, they have to erect a hard barrier, such as a fence.* The building often becomes the buffer between the street and sidewalk, and the schoolyard, playground, and other recreational areas are situated behind the building.

- *Vehicular and pedestrian circulation and access.* Traditional school design provided for building setbacks that allowed cars and buses access to the front of the school, often via circular driveways. At many schools today, the drop-off of passengers from cars and buses into the building occurs within a limited space. The design needs to provide a buffer. The creation of a vehicular courtyard can provide a secured transition space that serves as a deterrent for threats such as car bombs and maintains distance from other undesired street activities.

- *Front door.* Over the years, the symbolic value of a school's front door has eroded. Buildings designed in the last thirty years often have multiple points of entry. This creates confusion as well as security challenges. (Young, 2003, p. 556)

Education administrators do not deliberately seek potentially hazardous land when choosing sites for new schools, but often that is the unintended result. A 2002 study by the Childproofing Our Children Campaign, "Creating Safe Learning Zones," looked at only five states—California, Massachusetts, Michigan, New Jersey, and New York—and found that 1,195 schools are within a half-mile radius of a known contaminated site. Why is it that schools frequently end up on contaminated sites? Often, it is too difficult to find an uncontaminated site, especially in a developed urban area, that meets all the other qualities desired in a school location: adequate acreage, appropriate topography, neighborhood acceptance, potential for joint uses, and reasonable cost (Kennedy, 2003, May).

A major impact of technologies is that generally associated with learning in the classroom via use of personal computers, laptop/notebook computers, CD-ROMs, interactive multimedia, laser disks, the Internet, local area networks, long-distance learning, CAD, VCRs, and satellite links. This partial list of technology is augmented by use of computers for controlling HVAC systems, building communications, security systems, and numerous applications in school and district business offices.

There are approximately 88,000 school buildings in the United States—probably two-thirds more than thirty years old—which places them in the pre-computer age. In general, most were constructed on minimal budgets that translated to less than roomy classrooms and support spaces. The primary criterion for judging good school design is flexibility. Unfortunately, low construction budgets and flexibility in design are not usually partners on many projects.

Retrofitting

Each district must decide the best way of dealing with the older buildings. In doing this, the school business administrator and others must consider each school's educational needs, community reactions to the replacement and upgrade of any facility, and the financial resources of the community/district.

A discussion of the impact of technology, and all of the needs for wiring, HVAC upgrades, lighting, security, and so on, occurs elsewhere, but it is safe to say that technological considerations are a major component of any decision to retrofit a building or to replace the structure. Cost savings in new construction techniques, energy-saving materials, and the ability to be electricity-current are major factors, but they should be considered against enrollment trends for an area and cost comparisons between renovating/upgrading and new construction. Cost and program needs are key elements, with some estimates placing new construction and a progress/extensive renovation closer in costs than might initially be thought. Retrofits for school facilities most often include work for HVAC, lighting, ADA compliance, electric works, and painting. Expenditures for security/life safety and technology infrastructure are lower on the list.

A final consideration is the Americans with Disabilities Act concerns. When it is not technically feasible to meet the act's accessibility standards, alterations that could affect the usability of a facility must be made in an accessible manner to the maximum extent feasible. The regulations define technically infeasible as building alterations that have "little likelihood of being accomplished because existing structural conditions would require removing or altering a load-bearing member which is an essential part of the structural frame" or that have other physical or site constraints that prohibit modifications (Kennedy, 1999).

Summary

Advanced planning and scheduling by the system's administrative team are the keys to an effective maintenance and operations program, as with all system activities. The board must establish a philosophy of maintenance and operations, and policies to implement the philosophy in the day-to-day school setting must be established. Decisions concerning contracted services versus system-provided services; procedures for selecting, training, and retention of staff; and budget priorities are all related to a successful maintenance and operations program. Clearly, concerns relative to energy usage and conservation are paramount for the school business administrator. Costs continue to rise, and supplies are "iffy" in some areas. The need to monitor energy programs is of continuing importance. Additionally, environmental concerns ranging from noise pollution to asbestos removal are increasing. Costs for building modifications or improvements and possible litigation are of more than passing interest. Safety and security issues are more than ever under review by the board and the school business administrator.

The school business administrator should supply the cost-analysis data representing many facets of maintenance and operations needed for effective decision making. Planning is the key for the successful merger of these needs with other needs throughout the district.

Discussion Questions

1. How can school business administrators ensure that they are operating a cost-effective maintenance/operations program under a site-based management plan?
2. How should decisions be reached regarding use of contract versus system-supplied operations/maintenance services?
3. What is the value of staff development for school site and system-based custodial personnel? How should these programs be organized and evaluated?
4. Develop a plan for the maintenance of each facility in your district (including buildings, fields, etc.). What records are necessary? How does/could the MIS facilitate this plan?

5. How should a maintenance program be organized in a time of reduced funding and increased responsibilities due to advancing technology requirements and usage?
6. Develop a plan for community and other group use of your site. Who would be permitted to use the school facility and when? Who would not be permitted to use the school facilities and why?

Web Resources

United States Department of Energy—
http://www.eere.energy.gov/buildings/program_areas/rebuild.html
United States Environmental Protection Agency's Tools for Schools Kit—
http://www.epa.gov/iaq/schools/

References

DiNardo, C. (1996). Environmental hazards: What you need to know. *School Business Affairs*, 62(11), 22–23.

Glass, T.E. (1997). Schools built for technology: The effects of technology on educational facilities. *School Business Affairs*, 63(2), 11–17.

Hentschke, G.C. (1975). *Management operations in education*. Berkeley, CA: McCutchan.

Hounsell, D. (1996). Privatizing maintenance. *School Business Affairs*, 183(2), 16–19.

Joiner, L.L. (2002, March). Life saving lessons. *American School Board Journal*, 189(3). Retrieved February 10, 2007, from http://www.asbj.com/2002/03/0302expresslines.html.

Kennedy, M. (2003, January). Cutting costs. *American School and University*, 75(5), 20.

Kennedy, M. (2003, May). What lies beneath. *American School and University*, 75(9), 20–25.

Kennedy, M. (1999). Ensuring upgrades meet ADA standards. *American School and University*, 71(11), 50.

Laboratory Safety Workshop. (1992). Elementary Newsletter. *American School and University*, 65(2), 42.

McMilin, E. (2006, June). Maintenance program. *School Planning and Management*. Retrieved July 23, 2006, from: http://www.peterli.com/archive/spm/1165.shtm.

Ovard, G.F. (1992). Should your school be sold? *American School and University*, 64(5), 443–44.

Safe Schools, supplement 2. (2000, February). *American School and University*. Security, CO: Ingersoll-Rand, 551–58.

School Facilities Maintenance Task Force. (2003). *Planning guide for maintaining school facilities* [Chapter 4]. Washington, DC: National Cooperative Education Statistics System.

Young, D.M. (2003). Designing on the outside. *American School and University*, 75(6), 556.

CHAPTER FIFTEEN

Managing Materials

■ INTRODUCTION

This chapter covers topics such as purchasing, warehousing, distribution, and other matters related to the acquisition and distribution of physical materials. These include large items such as furniture and heating, ventilating, and air-conditioning (HVAC) equipment, and small items such as paper and pencils. It involves purchasing of recurring items or consumables such as food, and of more enduring items such as school buses. Regardless of size, value, or frequency, purchasing of goods deserves careful attention. These items represent a small part of school district budgets, about 5 to 10 percent. Still, nationwide, they comprise billions of dollars in economic activity.

LEARNING OBJECTIVES

In this chapter a reader will learn about:

- Materials management relative to the overall operation of an educational institution.
- Purchasing procedures.
- Relationship of purchasing to accounting.
- Inventory control.
- Warehousing of purchased items.
- Distribution of supplies and materials.

■ PURCHASING—THE CONTEXT

Purchasing involves the management of materials in a continuous flow, from the establishment of sources and shipping, through inventory and warehousing, to the ultimate delivery at instructional venues. At every stage there are decisions to be made as to quality, quantity, timing, source, and cost. These decisions must be keyed to a constantly changing educational business and to economic conditions that alter the immediate objectives and policies of purchasing from month to month.

Innovations in purchasing include the just-in-time (JIT) practices adopted by industrial leaders such as IBM, Motorola, and Harley-Davidson. JIT advocates suggest that it produces better quality while lowering inventories and cutting costs. It does require close collaboration between purchaser and supplier, and results in a smaller number of suppliers who benefit from a more stable and predictable production schedule. Among the benefits noted by practitioners of JIT purchasing are bare-bones inventory, reduced acquisition and handling costs, improved quality, and sometimes lower costs.

State Regulation

Whatever purchasing authority a school district possesses is granted by the state. Purchasing power is not inherent, but must be delegated to the local district through statutory law passed by the legislature or by rules and regulations of the state department of education and other agencies. Thus, the state frequently mandates purchasing responsibility and authority, purchasing limits, procedures, and forms.

Before engaging in a purchasing activity, the business administrator must become familiar with statutory law governing purchasing in the public sector. Many states have regulations requiring that all purchasing beyond a specified amount be procured by sealed bids, meeting state bid-advertising and bid-allocating procedures. Other states require purchasing from state lists at stipulated prices. The various state requirements make it problematic, at best, for a local school district to pursue JIT practices.

Some states have specialized personnel to assist with purchasing procedures. Sample specifications for particular items are made available. Quality-testing procedures have been established by some states. Computer programs that integrate purchasing, inventory, and delivery planning systems are available from some states. Before developing a system, a business administrator should check to see what commercially prepared programs are presently available.

Federal Mandates

Restrictions imposed by particular federal grants must be read carefully and followed closely. Many require that a district or other agency purchase from organizations that employ fair labor practices. Others may require an agency to cooperate with agencies that practice affirmative action in personnel policies. Other policies may suggest that a district purchase from minority-owned business or service agencies. Some policies necessitate renting rather than purchasing equipment. If the equipment is to be utilized by the school system after the ending of a contract or grant, a rental-purchase agreement may be a wise consideration. Court decisions have made some affirmative action programs obsolete, so a review and updating of purchasing policies are urged.

Centralized Activities

When bidding is centralized at the district level, more standardized purchasing criteria can be utilized and personnel can be more specialized as to function. However, central purchasing personnel should avoid sacrificing educational qualities needed in order to have larger consolidation of orders.

Even when centralized purchasing is utilized, the determination of quality and quantity of educational supplies should, within reason, be made by the user. This allows adjustment of supplies to the individual programs to be conducted at the site. Purchasing can be handled effectively at the site if the purchasing officials at the central office serve in an advisory, consultative, and coordinating role.

Districts that have adopted site-based management as a functional tool for decentralization have found that purchasing is more productive when done in a highly centralized way. These districts have utilized site educators to develop minimum specifications for the many items used and to assist in evaluating the utility of particular items, but they have generally standardized the bid process as a central function. The sites actually prefer this, for it provides top quality while still maintaining the principle of site-based decision making.

Relationship of Purchasing to Educators

Ultimate responsibility for the type, quality, and quantity of materials to be bought should rest with those who use them and are responsible for results—the educators and support personnel. In this sense, the using departments are the customers of the purchasing department, and they must be satisfied. This does not place the responsibility or authority for selection in the hands of the educators or the support personnel. Rather, their responsibility is to define accurately the product in terms of formula or analysis, accepted commercial standards, blueprints or dimensional tolerances, the intended purpose of the material, or, in some cases, the identification of a product in the vendor's catalogue.

Most educational materials, supplies, and equipment are procurable in competitive markets from a variety of vendors, and it is the function of the purchasing department to select the particular materials and source most advantageous to the school system. Patronizing two or more alternative sources is desirable to stimulate competition or ensure continuity of supply, provided always that the essential quality requirements, as defined, are met. Some believe that purchases must be made from local vendors, because they are taxpayers. This should be discouraged unless local vendors meet competitive prices and other vendors are aware of this purchasing practice.

A purchase request for materials states quantity needed and the date or time of delivery. The purchasing agent must check quantity ordered against need, particularly if an order deviates from past experience. It is part of the purchasing agent's duty to avoid duplication, excessive stock, and unnecessary rush orders that may disrupt the procurement program and cause unnecessary expense.

Once quantity and delivery requirements are established, it is the responsibility of the purchasing department to decide whether the goods are to be bought in a single lot, in a series of smaller transactions over a time span, or in a single long-term contract with delivery schedules specified according to needs.

Commercial facets of the transaction negotiations, such as price, delivery, guarantees, terms and conditions of contract, and adjustments for over- and under-shipments or deficiencies in quality, are the responsibilities of purchasing. For most school systems, the purchasing function includes following up on delivery, reconciling receipts and vendors' invoices with purchase orders, and passing invoices for payment.

The person or persons responsible for purchasing should also handle inspection and quality testing of purchases. The purchasing department is also responsible for storekeeping, warehousing, and complete accountability for materials until they are issued to the using department. With most purchases under federal titles, this is not an easy task.

Large Systems

In large systems, a purchasing department will include buyers in specialized areas, for example, supplies, equipment, and capital equipment. The total operation may be computerized, with reorder points, purchase orders, and normal order follow-up handled through an automated system. The process may be highly formalized and regimented, sometimes to the detriment of the educational programs. Purchasing must remain a support role and not become the primary role in material selection. In large systems, the process may become greatly isolated from the educator.

Small Systems

One of a business administrator's many responsibilities in a small system may be the purchasing agent function. The process may not be as formalized and regimented as in a large system. With the advent of desktop computers, the process can be highly routinized. On the other hand, material specifications, advertising for bids, bidding, placing orders, order follow-up, invoice approval, delivery, and warehousing may be handled clerically. The educator may be more highly involved in the selection process. Increasingly, small school districts are banding together into purchasing cooperatives in order to gain the benefits realized from quantity purchasing. In Iowa, for example, the Area Education Agencies (AEA), as the regional service centers are known, coordinate and administer purchasing activities for member districts. (See "Purchasing Cooperative or Consortia" on page 347 for more detailed information on purchasing cooperatives.)

Site Based

Purchasing at the site level allows greater adjustment for program differences. Faculty and staff may feel much more accountable for selecting items as well as for prioritizing purchasing when funds are scarce. The central staff can continue to assist in a consulting and coordinating role. Without proper coordination, purchases may be made in inefficient quantities. The central staff should still do follow-up on purchase orders. If too much of the purchasing procedure is handled at the site, the district may have to consider staff duplication or have generalists handle specialized functions.

In the rapidly emerging e-commerce age, it is anticipated that most purchasing will be done at the site in those districts that have adopted the site-based management approach to district organization. It becomes the duty of the central office purchasing personnel to establish minimum requirements and specifications for items to be ordered as a service to the campus that will ultimately order the item.

The role of the central purchasing department has undergone great change with the advent of the site-based management form of educational organization. Rather than being the sole decision maker in terms of purchasing school equipment and supplies, the purchasing department is now a coordinator of purchasing items the campuses want for the instructional programs. Personnel in the purchasing department search for and approve vendors, determine the quality of the item requested, and verify price, but the campus initiates the direct purchase. This is a marked change from the traditional method of operation of the purchasing department.

Legal Facets of Purchasing

In an industrial or manufacturing setting, a purchasing agent is authorized to make valid contracts of purchase for the agency. Many vendors are aware of the role of the industrial purchasing agent and assume that the same relationship exists within the educational setting. This is seldom so in public schools. Thus, school administrators should develop comprehensive job descriptions for their purchasing personnel, with definitive statements as to authority and responsibility.

A primary rule for purchasing personnel is to consult the school's legal counsel on any doubtful or controversial points in the analysis of unusual or obscure legal terms in the vendor's forms and in the phrasing of clauses and conditions that are to be incorporated into purchase agreements. Because purchase orders issued or contracts signed are legal documents, it is not sufficient that a purchase be economically sound; it must be legally sound as well—both the agreement itself and the way it is carried out. Many governmental requirements regarding labor conditions, employment practices, fair competition, and the price and distribution of goods have legal implications.

Unless a purchase order is issued in acceptance of a specific bid or offer by a vendor, it is not a contract; it is an offer and only when it is accepted by the vendor will it become a contract. This is the reason that "acknowledgment copies" of purchase orders are sent with the original order, to be signed and returned by the vendor. It has been held in courts that a signed order given to a traveling salesperson is not valid until accepted by the employer. Salespeople are not agents of the company and are generally legally allowed a degree of "puff" about their product. A contract, to be valid, must impose an obligation upon both parties. The obligation is on the buyer's part if the demand is hypothetical or the quantity to be delivered is conditioned solely by the will of one of the contracting parties. Date and time of delivery and price should be integral parts of the contract.

Warranties are of two types: express and implied. In the absence of express warranties for quality, fitness, or performance of a product by a seller, an implied warranty is in effect if the buyer relies on the seller's judgment and skill to determine that the goods shall be reasonably fit for the purposes described. In invoking the warranty clauses of a contract, the purchaser is under obligation to take action as soon as deficiency of goods or breach of warranty is observed.

Making a purchase involves a transfer of title to the merchandise from vendor to buyer. If goods are sold and shipped f.o.b. (free on board)[1] from the vendor's location, the purchaser automatically takes legal title, thereby assuming full responsibility for accidents, contingencies, damage, loss, or delay by the carrier. Once the goods arrive at the predetermined destination, such as a port, the purchaser determines the best means and route for transport, suitable insurance, and installation or handling of materials. If goods are shipped f.o.b. to the buyer's location, title passes to the buyer when goods are delivered by the carrier.

Legal fraud has been defined as any act, deed, or statement made by either a purchaser or vendor, before the purchase contract is formalized, that is likely to deceive the other party. A vendor is not liable for fraud if the evidence proves: (1) that the vendor or the salesperson made a false statement after the contract was signed, (2) that the vendor or salesperson did not know that the quality of the merchandise was not as claimed in the contract, or (3) that the buyer did not rely on the vendor's statements concerning the product. If a buyer inspects merchandise before entering into the contract, the buyer, if experienced with the merchandise, is expected to practice good judgment in decision making.

If a contract agreement is made on the basis of fraudulent acts or statements, the contract is not valid. A delay in claiming fraud or a payment made after fraud is discovered may destroy the basis for rescission and damages.

There are many more facets of law that affect purchasing. In planning the purchasing routine, the person responsible should cooperate closely with the school board's attorney in preparing procedures, purchase forms, and contracts.

Relationship of Purchasing to Other Administrative Divisions

The purchasing function is an integral part of the administrative milieu. In the area of budget planning, whether short or long term, the purchasing group can be instrumental in costing out educational programs. Purchasing personnel, because of training, experience, and current understanding of costs, can be extremely beneficial in the development of program budgets. The purchasing agent can assist educational personnel in exploring possible new instructional materials and media.

In maintenance and capital outlay programs, purchasing personnel can perform the costing function. As cost-benefit analysis and cost-effectiveness analysis become common evaluative planning procedures in the educational world, purchasing personnel can provide valuable operational inputs. In buying for a hospital, a university, a school system, or some governmental unit, where the profit motive and competitive factors are absent, the goal should be to obtain maximum value for the expenditure of a fixed budget appropriation.

Purchasing efficiency in institutional and governmental administration helps to make the materials dollar go further, thereby either reducing the necessity of raising additional funds by taxation and appropriations or releasing available funds for an extension of services.

■ PURCHASING—THE PROCESS

The fundamental objectives for a purchasing department are:

- Plan a program of educational materials and equipment procurement that optimizes the system's educational outputs.
- Maintain continuity of supply to support the educational program, with the minimum in inventory consistent with educational need, safety, and economic advantage.
- Avoid duplication, waste, and obsolescence of materials and equipment.
- Maintain standards of quality in relation to suitability of use.
- Acquire materials and equipment at the lowest cost consistent with quality and service required.

Purchasing personnel must remember that they are serving a support function for the educational system. They must not become so involved with the purchasing act itself that the process becomes cumbersome.

Requisition

In a purchasing procedure, the first step is to determine the need and authority necessary for the purchase. Essentially, the individual, school, or department initiates a standardized requisition that implies a need. An administrator is delegated the authority to determine the validity of the expressed needs. Typically, one copy of the requisition will remain with the initiator. Multiple copies will flow to an approving authority.[2] A copy will be returned to the initiator, indicating whether the requisition was approved. If approved, a copy will go to the warehouse to see if the item is already on hand. If the item is not on hand, a signed copy of the requisition will flow to the purchasing department. The purchasing department should standardize purchases whenever this does not negatively influence the educational process.

Specifications

There are many reasons to control the quality of purchased items. Correct quality improves the morale and efficiency of those in the system utilizing the purchased items. Without a clear statement of why or how the purchased items are to be utilized, legal responsibility redounds to the buyer if the vendor ships under an honest misunderstanding. The buyer may then be responsible for all or part of the defective goods if quality requirements on the purchase order were incomplete or unclear. The purchasing department must:

- Know what is wanted and convey the information to the vendor.
- Ensure that a vendor performs according to the purchase quality specifications.
- Take necessary steps to protect the school system against financial loss from materials or parts that do not meet the purchase specifications.
- Utilize vendor suggestions where they promote desirable quality and reliability.

Vendor notification of rejected items should be handled by the purchasing department because: (1) the buyer is instrumental in the negotiation of a mutually acceptable agreement—that is, the purchase order has been placed by the buyer, and the buyer is more familiar with the entire picture; and (2) vendors are more likely to resolve quality problems and negotiate quick turnaround or replacement if they are dealing with the person responsible for additional business.

Quality must be defined. It is, specifically, the sum or composite of the properties inherent in a material or product. Every definition of quality is predicated on some unity of measurement understood by purchaser and vendor.

An example of one method of measuring quality is chemical analysis. The formula of a cleaning compound measures its usefulness and safety on various types of materials and its efficacy in removing various types of dirt or foreign matter. The sulfur, ash, and BTU contents of coal indicate the suitability of a fuel for use in a particular power equipment installation and its measure of heat efficiency. The school system may need to employ outside testing agents for this type of quality control.

Another possible quality measurement is to buy products meeting federal purchasing specifications, for example, motor oil, floor waxes, ink, cleaning solutions, and lunchroom detergents.

Physical tests provide a measurement of quality in respect to properties such as the tensile and shearing strength of metals and fibers; the bursting, folding, and tearing strength of paper; and the elasticity, ductility, opacity, resistance to abrasion or shock, and resistance to sunlight or moisture of other materials. Performance or guaranteed output may be a basic measure of quality, and the purchaser's proper description of intended use makes this the responsibility of the vendor.

If purchasing is done by brand name, the phrase "or equal" should be added to the statement, or there occurs the serious disadvantage of limiting procurement to a single vendor, and thus eliminating the competitive element, except insofar as competition may exist in distribution.

The actual description or definition of quality is sometimes avoided by inviting prospective vendors to match a sample submitted by the purchaser. This practice is justified under certain conditions—in the case of special, no repetitive items when absolute quality requirements are not a significant factor, or when the size and importance of the purchase do not warrant the effort and expense of formulating a more definitive buying description.

In many commodity fields there are well-established grades or quality designations that are known to vendor and purchaser. Where this is the case, the commercial description of desired qualities is simplified by reference to the appropriate grade.

There are some items, usually of a technical nature, the quality of which cannot be sufficiently defined by any of the preceding methods, so that formal bid specifications must be prepared. The specifications should state the means or basis for testing purchases. Nonessential quality restrictions should be avoided because they can add to cost and difficulty of procurement without adding to utility or value. Definitions that unnecessarily restrict competition should be avoided. Conformation to established commercial and industrial standards should be encouraged. Analysis of function to be performed should receive primary consideration in preparing specifications. Minimum standards should be stressed so that anything meeting the standards can be considered. In summary, it cannot be stressed too strongly that the quality requirements of purchased goods are properly determined and defined by those who are responsible for their utilization.

Before an order is placed or a quotation is requested, the purchasing official must specify what is desired so that prospective vendors can intelligently quote prices and fill orders. Specifications may be very simple or considerably detailed, as shown in the following examples:

- *8d common wire nail* is a generally understood term and requires little explanation.
- *Smooth-on no. 4 plane* or equal is also generally understood.
- *Ink, writing, blue-black* to meet federal specifications #TT-1-563b of October 1, 1968, is more detailed.

Items of office equipment may require a lengthy description of type, style, material, and, sometimes, method of construction. In addition to the description, specifications should state "or equivalent."

Quotations

Price is meaningless unless it is predicated on adequate quality and quantity, assured delivery, reliability, and continuity of supply, maximum efficiency in educational utilization, and minimum downtime because of service needs. To establish a right and realistic price, buyers properly insist on firm bids. Competitive bids are almost mandatory in government purchasing because of possible charges of favoritism and patronage and the need to conserve taxpayers' money. Negotiated prices are not necessarily incompatible with competition. In almost all cases, negotiation starts with a firm bid, but many further modifications may be made before the optimum balance is achieved among quality, service, and cost.

Discounts

There are three types of discounts that concern a buyer in the consideration of price. Trade discounts are established on a graduated scale that is applicable according to the vendor's classification of customers. The purchaser's responsibility is to see that the school system is in the most favorable customer classification possible. This is a proper subject for negotiation with the prime supplier, distributor, or both.

Quantity discounts offer lower unity prices on large-quantity orders. The buyer's responsibility is to adjust ordering practices to the most advantageous quantity price break. (See Figure 15.1 for a sample price quotation request form.)

REQUEST FOR BID OR QUOTATION

DISTRIBUTION:
White & Canary–Purchasing
Pink–Originator

TO: _____ FROM: Donald Frye, Purchasing Agent

FROM: _____ TO: _____ Date _____
Director, Supervisor, Principal

It is requested that bids or quotations be obtained for the following equipment or material.

To be delivered to _____ By _____
                  Location, Street Address, City, State   Zip Code   Date

Budget Account Number	Article, Description (Complete detailed specifications. Use additional sheet if necessary.)	Quantity	Unit	*Estimated Cost

*If estimated cost requiring installation is to exceed $25,000 Public Hearing required.

On bids requiring installation, the following information is required:

    Work to be started _____ Date

    Work to be completed _____ Date

    Project Superintendent _____

Suggested companies who may be interested in submitting Bids or Quotations.

Company Name	Street Address	City, State & Zip Code

FOR PURCHASING DEPARTMENT

Bid or Quote No: _____   Copy of Tabulation sent _____ Date

Date Issued _____ Date Due _____

Note: QUOTATIONS (Estimated cost under $4,000.) The minimum time before an order can be placed is fifteen (15) working days.
BIDS (Estimated cost over $4,000.) The minimum time before an order can be placed is fourty five (45) working days.

FIGURE 15.1 Sample Price Quotation

Courtesy of Des Moines Independent Community School District, Des Moines, Iowa.

Cash discounts are an inducement to prompt payment of invoice charges and are earned only when payment is made in accordance with stipulated terms. The purchaser's responsibility for this potential saving includes: (1) seeing that proper cash discount terms are incorporated in the order, (2) securing invoices promptly from vendors, (3) processing invoices promptly and getting them to the proper paying agent, and (4) securing extended discount privileges when unavoidable delays are encountered.

The objective evaluation and rating of vendor performance have lagged behind the measurement of other factors in purchasing. The buyer is aware in a general way that some vendors require an excessive amount of expediting effort and are consistently late in deliveries and that rejections for inadequate quality are more numerous for some than with other vendors. Many times, these same vendors are slow to assemble or service equipment or may do so incorrectly. A computer for which downtime due to lack of service is measured in days rather than hours can make the initial purchase price a rather insignificant portion of the total cost. Purchasers should establish a system of vendor evaluation and consider the results in determining the lowest responsible bidder. (See Figure 15.2.)

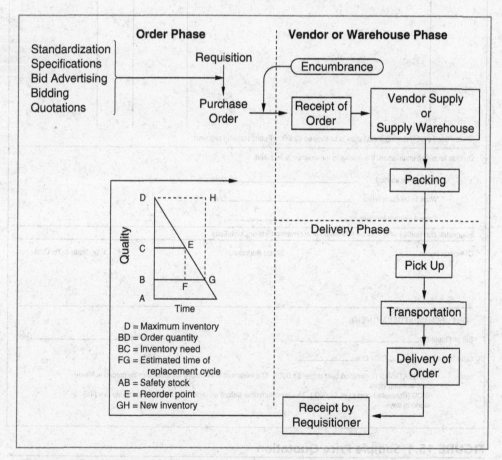

FIGURE 15.2 Three Phases of Planning for Educational Continuity

Bidding

There are formal and informal bids. Formal bids necessitate: public advertising, public opening, and award to the lowest responsible bidder. Award is culminated by the issuance of a contract document. Informal bids are the telephone quotation and the (preferred) written quotation when the dollar value is less than the required statutory limit.

Formal bid procedures should be followed unless exceptions are defined by regulation or are bona fide emergencies. Complete openness and impartiality are essential to protect the bidder and the school system.

Advertising. Public advertising for bids is an open invitation to all qualified potential bidders to participate. All common advertising media should be utilized. Newspaper advertising is a must and is usually required by law. Because advertising has its limits, invitations to bid should be sent directly to all interested potential bidders. School systems can cooperate with each other and other governmental agencies to develop potential bidder lists.

Bidders should be evaluated. A performance record should be compiled for each vendor listing late deliveries, noncompliance, rejection, and other problems.

Bid and Contract Documents. These must be clear, logical, and as standardized as possible in order to produce the greatest number of low qualified bids. The document set should include:

- A copy of the legal advertisement.
- Instructions to bidders.
- General bid conditions.
- Special bid conditions.
- Item specifications.
- Bid proposal forms.

Each bidder should be furnished two complete sets of documents, one set to be returned with proper documentation execution and signatures, and the other to be retained by the bidder for reference.

Bid Processing. Formal bids should be submitted in sealed envelopes, color coded or otherwise easily identifiable. Bids should be placed in a locked receptacle until official bid opening.

Bid Opening. Both the opening and the tabulation of bids should be under the control of the person responsible for the purchasing function. Bidders, reporters, and interested citizens should be invited to attend bid openings. Bids should be opened and read aloud for the benefit of those attending.

Late Bids. Reasonable time should be set for the submission of bids. Bids received beyond the time limit should be returned unopened.

Bid Errors. Bidders making genuine errors should be allowed to withdraw bids without prejudice. However, the withdrawals should be noted on the vendor's evaluation records.

Repeated withdrawals may indicate shoddy practices. Courts generally allow withdrawal of bids on the following conditions:

1. That a mistake of a clerical or mechanical nature was made.
2. That the bidder was not guilty of culpable negligence.

Award. Most statutes on purchasing require that the award be made to the lowest responsible bidder. Making correct value judgments when considering awards is a primary purchasing management responsibility. Impartial professional judgment is necessary, and thorough documentation of reasons for awarding to any other than the lowest dollar bidder is prudent, because the notion persists that governmental agencies should take the lowest bid regardless of related factors.

Award is usually confirmed for a contract or purchase order. The basic elements of legally enforceable contracts are:

- Offer and acceptance.
- Parties competent to contract.
- Legality of subject matter.
- Sufficient consideration.

Security Requirements. Bid deposits in the form of certified or cashier's checks, money orders, or currency are more common than bid bonds. Performance bonds[3] do not necessarily guarantee the faithful performance of contracts; they simply provide for responsibility by a third party. If the vendor defaults, the bonding company becomes responsible and may be sued for relief by the school system. Aggressive action by the school's legal representative can serve to improve a vendor's fulfillment of a contract.

Vendor Evaluation. Each competing supplier is evaluated on quality, price, and service. Quality evaluation is simply the supplier's record with respect to meeting required specifications; it is measured as the percent of its material that is rejected. Quality evaluation can be secured from quality control if this group is performing its proper function. Price evaluation in its simplest form is the figure quoted in each bid. Service evaluation includes prompt submission of data, response to inquiries, delivery performance, special services rendered, and other intangibles. Under ordinary purchasing situations, these factors, properly weighed, should be sufficient to evaluate vendors.

Ethics. Ethics are probably more critical in educational than in industrial purchasing. This is especially true because of increasing interrelations among business, government, and institutions. Control of attempts at "backdoor selling" is frequently more difficult in institutions than it is in industry. In theory, collusion should be easier to control in schools and hospitals than it is in industry; in practice, this is often not the case. Trustees, donors, board members, and alumni on occasion bring great pressure on institutions to purchase their companies' products. Normally, such purchases (if made on any basis other than quality, service, and price) should be resisted.

Purchasing Cooperatives or Consortia

Many states with a multitude of small districts may want to form purchasing cooperatives or consortia. The consolidation of orders into larger units may bring about more competitive bidding. Orders can be consolidated into more efficient order quantities. Truckload or carload lots can be more economical with present high freight rates. Deliveries can be routed to individual districts or buildings. In some purchasing cooperatives, warehousing may also become a joint venture.

Site-Based Purchasing

This is useful if the district maintains many unique programs at the building level. Particularly with larger units, optimum order quantities may be generated at the site. The central purchasing personnel should still serve in a consultative role. The central office will serve a coordinating role for smaller site orders.

▮ OVERVIEW OF PURCHASING

The establishment of centralized purchasing is a reflection of overall school board philosophy and policy. It immediately entails a series of interdepartmental policies related to lines of authority, channels of procedure, and departmental relationships. These interdepartmental policies should be carefully defined and made a matter of record, for they determine the scope and responsibility of the purchaser. Policies might include such matters as authorization to make requisitions, permission for vendor representatives to contact school personnel, final responsibility for specifications, and value analysis.

The Requisitioner

The first step for the requisitioner is to advise the purchasing department of a need, defining it in sufficient detail for ordering purposes, and supporting the request with the necessary approvals to authorize a purchase. Definition of the need includes a description or code identification of the material wanted (this may be as simple as giving an item number in a specific vendor's catalog), the quantity requested, and the date by which it will be needed. School policy should explain carefully the procedure for approving requisitions initiated at any place in the educational system. Some larger school systems develop a system catalog that includes all standard items used in the educational systems. The teacher then simply lists the catalog and item number on the requisition. (See Figure 15.3 for a sample requisition.)

The Purchase Order

This is the instrument by which goods are procured to fill a requirement. Essential information on every purchase order includes name and address of the school system, identifying order number, date, name and address of the vendor, general instructions (marking of shipment, special shipping information, number of invoices required, and so forth), delivery date required, shipping instructions (destination, type of carrier, traffic routing, packaging requirements, and receiving hours), terms and conditions of the transaction, description of materials, quantity, price, appropriate discount information, and signature. (See Figure 15.4 for a sample purchase order.)

CENTRAL STORES REQUISITION NUMBER

INSTRUCTIONS FOR USE OF THIS FORM	USE THIS FORM FOR ORDERING FROM CENTRAL STORES CATALOG ONLY

TYPEWRITER ONLY PLEASE–RETAIN ORIGINATOR'S COPY (PLY 4)
AND THE PRECEDING CARBON PAPER–FORWARD REMAINDER OF SET INTACT TO CENTRAL STORES, 1800 GRAND AVE.

REQUESTED BY	APPROVED BY	SCHOOL OR DEPT.	ROOM NO.	ACCOUNT-NO.	REQUISITION DATE

SCHOOL NUMBER	JOB NUMBER	SERIAL NUMBER	ANNUAL REQUISITION		REGULAR REQUISITION	

CLASS NUMBER	ITEM NUMBER	DESCRIPTION	QUANTITY ORDERED	UNIT OF ISSUE	UNIT PRICE	COST TOTAL	QUANTITY FILLED	BACK ORDERED

PERSON FILLING ORDER (INITIALS)	TOTAL COST

DES MOINES INDEPENDENT COMMUNITY SCHOOL DISTRICT • DES MOINES, IOWA 50307

RECEIVED ABOVE ITEMS _____   DATE _____
ACCOUNTING OFFICE

24-87971 Form 945

FIGURE 15.3 Sample Requisition

Courtesy of Des Moines Independent Community School District, Des Moines, Iowa.

IF AVAILABLE, UNIT PRICE AND TOTAL COST SHOULD BE INDICATED. A SUGGESTED SOURCE OF SUPPLY, TOGETHER WITH IT'S COMPLETE ADDRESS SHOULD BE SHOWN. REMOVE LAST PLY FOR YOUR FILES AND FORWARD THE REMAINDER OF THE SET INTACT TO PURCHASING DEPARTMENT.

REQUISITION

NAME (SUGGESTED VENDOR)	ADDRESS	CITY	STATE	ZIP

No. 390062

REQUESTED BY	APPROVED BY	SCHOOL OR DEPT.	ROOM NUMBER	ACCOUNT NUMBER	REQUISITION DATE

SCHOOL NO.	JOB NUMBER	SERIAL NUMBER	PURCHASING DEPT. USE			
			VENDOR NO.	QUOTATION OR BID DATE	BID NUMBER	LEDGER DESCRIPTION

PURCHASE REQUISITION / ORDER
DES MOINES INDEPENDENT COMMUNITY SCHOOL DISTRICT
1800 GRAND AVENUE • DES MOINES, IOWA 50309–3399
PHONE 515 – 242 – 7751

PURCHASE ORDER

No.

THIS NUMBER MUST APPEAR ON ALL INVOICES, PACKINGS & CORRESPONDENCE

NOT A VALID
PURCHASE ORDER
UNLESS NUMBERED ABOVE
AND SIGNED BELOW

PURCHASE ORDER

INSTRUCTIONS TO THE VENDOR

1. DO NOT CHARGE IOWA SALES TAX
2. BE SURE TO USE PURCHASE ORDER NUMBER ON ALL INVOICES, PKGS. & CORRESPONDENCE
3. SHIP TO CENTRAL STORES AT ABOVE ADDRESS UNLESS OTHERWISE INDICATED
4. BILL TO ADDRESS SHOWN ABOVE–ATTENTION: ACCOUNTS PAYABLE

DIRECTOR OF PURCHASING

THIS AREA FOR PURCHASING DEPARTMENT USE ONLY

SHIP TO

NAME
ADDRESS

CENTRAL STORES

AUTHORIZED SIGNATURE

AT ABOVE ADDRESS UNLESS INDICATED BELOW

IF SHIPMENT CANNOT BE MADE WITHIN 30 DAYS ADVISE SHIP DATE

QUANTITY ORDERED	UNIT	DESCRIPTION OF ITEMS (DOUBLE SPACE BETWEEN ITEMS)	ORIGINATOR USE ESTIMATED		PURCHASING DEPT. USE ONLY	
			UNIT PRICE	TOTAL COST	UNIT PRICE	TOTAL COST

NOTE: PAGE 1 OF   PAGES   TOTAL THIS PAGE

TOTAL OF ORDER ❯

FIGURE 15.4 Sample Purchase Order

Courtesy of Des Moines Independent Community School District, Des Moines, Iowa.

The purchase order should be prepared in multiple copies. The original is the vendor's copy. A second copy should also be sent to the vendor, to be signed and returned as acknowledgment and acceptance of the order. Additional copies are useful for the following purposes:

- Copy to the receiving department as notice that a shipment is expected and to facilitate identification.
- Copy to the accounting department as notice of the commitment, to be reconciled later with the invoice and receiving reports as authorization for payment and also to encumber the account for the amount of purchase order. This will be adjusted when an invoice is received.
- Copy to the requisitioning department as confirmation.
- Copy for follow-up or revision purposes. The use of color-coding facilitates routing and processing. (See Figure 15.5 for sample purchase order revision form.)

The Warehouse

The warehouse department is responsible for receiving incoming goods; signing and checking the carrier's delivery notice; identifying and recording incoming goods; reporting receipt to purchasing, inventory control, and quality control personnel; and making prompt disposition to the appropriate department.

Institutions have the same two reasons for storing items as do industries—economy and service. However, institutions also have a third reason—campus congestion. Using vendors' storage can alleviate overcrowding of supply facilities. Using the vendor as an extension of the institution's storage system can free funds for other purposes and contribute to procurement efficiency.

Accounting

The purchasing department's copy of the invoice is checked against the purchase order number to identify shipment and avoid duplication. Prices and terms, f.o.b. point and transportation charges, quantity and quality are verified, and prices are extended. When all of this is done, the invoice is passed along from the purchasing to the accounting department and serves as a voucher for payment through the disbursing office. An earlier copy would have been sent to accounting for encumbrance of funds in the proper account.

Inventory Control

For some time there has been a growing awareness of the importance of inventory control as a planning and policy function of the school administrator. The school administrator must strive for maximum utilization of school equipment and supplies and prevent the breakdown of the educational process from lack of school supplies. The size of the school system's inventory depends on the delivery service of vendors. When vendors carry complete inventories, school systems need not do so.

With the advent of JIT ordering, the need for huge warehouse and distribution centers has passed. However, because many school districts (especially large ones) may still have such centers, the rapid phase out of all warehouses is probably not going to occur. There is an advantage in utilizing warehouse space: The school district can take advantage

PURCHASE ORDER REVISION

DES MOINES INDEPENDENT SCHOOL DISTRICT
1800 GRAND AVENUE / DES MOINES, IA 50307
PHONE: 515/242-7751

VENDOR:
ADDRESS:

PURCHASE ORDER # _____
DATE OF ORIGINAL P.O. _____
DATE OF REVISION _____
BID/QUOTE # _____ DATE _____

QUANTITY	UNIT	DESCRIPTION OF ITEMS	UNIT PRICE	EXTENDED COST
		PLEASE MAKE THE FOLLOWING CHANGES TO OUR ORIGINAL P.O.:		
			TOTAL	
			MODIFIED EXTENDED TOTAL OF ENTIRE P.O.:	

AUTHORIZED BY

FORM NO: 1020   500 SETS 7-87   CAMPUS PRESS

WHITE – VENDOR'S COPY
BLUE – ACCOUNTING DEPT. COPY
GREEN – PURCHASING DEPT. COPY
CANARY – RECEIVING DEPT. COPY
PINK – POINT OF DELIVERY COPY
GOLDENROD – ORIGINATOR COPY

FIGURE 15.5 Sample Purchase Order Revision Form

Courtesy of Des Moines Independent Community School District, Des Moines, Iowa.

of quantity purchasing to keep costs competitive while following the Deming point of buying for quality rather than price.[4]

Flow of Materials

Having a current and long-range storage plan is one key to a consistent and efficient warehouse operation. Some questions that must be asked in planning proper warehousing and flow of materials are as follows:

- How much space is required to store items properly?
- How many units are normally withdrawn in an order?
- What is the maximum number of items to be stored at any one time?
- What type of storage is best (considering weight, shape, and handling)?
- What handling equipment is necessary to transport the item?
- How often is the item withdrawn from stores?
- Where is the item most frequently used in the education process?

Storeroom Layout

Good storeroom layout attempts to achieve eight objectives:

- A straight-line flow of activity through the warehouse.
- Minimum handling and transportation of materials.
- Minimum travel and wasted motion of personnel.
- Efficient use of space.
- Provision for flexibility and expansion of layout.
- Security against pilferage.
- Ease of physical counting.
- Minimum material deterioration.

Control

Efficiency and economy in inventory control can greatly enhance the educational program. As individual learning processes require greater and more complex planning, the acquisition, storage, and delivery of educational materials and equipment become more important. Some advantages of efficient inventory control are that it:

- Expedites educational planning throughout a system.
- Promotes buying economies by determining needs systematically.
- Prevents duplication in ordering because it offers a clear picture of present materials available throughout the system.
- Facilitates exchange of materials and equipment throughout a system.
- Minimizes losses from damage due to transit.
- Reduces losses from mishandling and theft.
- Aids cost accounting and the development of a program budgeting.
- Aids in cost comparison between and among programs and departments.
- Provides data for perpetual inventories, and therefore can lead to reduced insurance costs.
- Minimizes the investment in inventory.

Inventory control can be expedited through computerization. All material receipts and issues for each stock item are fed to the computer daily. There is no hand posting of stock records. The computer performs all the additions and subtractions so as to show the current inventory status of each item at all times and automatically compares this figure with a previously established reorder point. The computer signals when an item reaches reorder status so that purchasing action can be taken to replenish stock in accordance with predetermined inventory and ordering quantities.

The ordering quantity in a system is fixed in the machine memory. It is possible to program a system for: (1) fixed ordering quantity with variable ordering frequency; (2) fixed ordering frequency with variable ordering quantity; or (3) at the expense of some additional computations and running time, variable quantity and variable ordering frequency. The first system is deemed advisable, because the fixed ordering quantity achieves the advantages of ordering in full package lots rather than broken package quantities, ordering in the most favorable quantity discount brackets, and ordering in lots conforming to full pallet loads.

If the reorder point and quantity are set with accurate consideration of lead time and safety stock requirements, and if all vendors keep their delivery promises, the system is completely automatic. If an emergency arises because of failure in delivery or abnormally heavy use of an item, the machine signals the emergency and the buyer handles it manually, either by expediting an open order or by placing an emergency order to supplement the normal flow of material.

Provision is also made for automatic consideration of stock status within "families" of items—related items procured from one source. Thus, stock items frequently go on order without manual assistance of any kind.

Salvage

Efficient purchase and inventory control limits the generation of surplus and scrap items. Requisitions must be screened carefully to avoid overbuying. If surplus occurs, a centralized purchasing system can often meet the needs of one particular school through the salvage from another school.

Selling

To dispose of surplus or salvage, one should first contact the original vendor. Many times, a vendor may have an outlet for extra materials or equipment. Second, there is the established trade of surplus and used equipment dealers. If the surplus items have any general utility and marketable value, such dealers constitute a logical outlet. Another possibility is direct sale to other possible users. Many business publications and association bulletins have sections devoted to the listing of surplus materials and equipment.

Leasing

An alternative method of procuring equipment, one that circumvents the salvage problem, is leasing instead of outright purchasing. Leasing of equipment that reflects continuous innovations due to technological advancement (e.g., computer hardware, photocopiers) is especially advantageous. Additional advantages of leasing are as follows:

- It postpones large capital outlay but permits the use of modern equipment at low initial cost.
- Equipment can be tested in actual use, bypassing the risk of buying the wrong machine or equipment.

- Maintenance costs are minimized or can be included as a part of the leasing arrangement, thus reducing the need for highly specialized personnel within the system.

Destroying

Almost every school system has had, at some time, the sad experience of destroying obsolete texts, library books, equipment, or educational materials. Before considering destruction as a solution, all salvage alternatives should be considered. If these alternatives have been considered and costs are prohibitive, then destruction may be a possible answer. However, even if economically sound, destruction may be a poor alternative from a public relations standpoint.

Educational Materials En Route—Distribution

Distribution is the way teaching materials and equipment move from one place of need to another. A steady, constant flow of materials between learning stations is important. Time spent in transit is time wasted as far as optimal use in the learning process is concerned. Use of teachers or school administrators to deliver materials to the next point of use is an inefficient utilization of high-cost professional personnel. Clerical or hourly employees can perform this function efficiently and economically.

Scheduling

In smaller school systems, materials and equipment may need to be moved throughout the system on request. Some of this movement can be done during the hours when schools are in session. Directions to the messenger must be explicit to ensure pickup of materials at the correct location and delivery to the proper place for optimal utilization the next day. (See Figure 15.6.)

Larger school systems may have regular delivery routing between schools within the system. Studies should be made to determine delivery priorities. General supply deliveries can be scheduled to avoid peak periods of educational materials movement. Flowcharts and linear programming techniques can be used to plan optimal distribution of educational supplies and materials.

Central versus Decentralized Storage

Many authorities advocate decentralization of supply storage. Decentralized storage is complementary with site-based management. If a system has chosen the site-based model, it would probably enhance its operation with decentralized purchasing and receiving, storage. With the increased cost of transportation, it is cheaper to decentralize storage. Supplies can be made available much more quickly, particularly if deliveries are not made on a routine, short-interval basis. Alternative supplies may be more readily recognized by the person doing the requisitioning. Conscientious employees may exercise more care in seeing that supplies do not become obsolete.

Authorities favoring the centralization of storage argue that decentralization adds to the supply management problem. They argue that under decentralization it is much more difficult to keep accurate inventory records and cost supplies to various departments, and also to keep supplies current and fresh. Supplies may tend to become the sole property of the particular building where they are housed and not be moved to meet needs throughout the system. It may be more difficult to protect against pilferage under the decentralized system.

VEHICLE LOG FOR MAIL AND DISTRIBUTION AND WAREHOUSING DATE: _____				
DRIVER'S NAME	TRUCK NO.	DESTINATION	TIME OUT	TIME IN

FIGURE 15.6 Vehicle Log for Mail and Distribution and Warehousing

Courtesy of the Memphis City School System.

Most systems of fairly large size try to balance the centralized-decentralized storage issue by providing storage space for a limited amount of supplies at the building level while still achieving economies of purchasing scale by storing greater quantities centrally. In this manner, buildings are charged for consumables as they order and use them, control is much more effective, and the economies resulting from mass purchasing can be achieved.

▪ EVALUATION OF PURCHASING, INVENTORY, AND DISTRIBUTION SYSTEMS

The purchasing function must have as its primary objective the provision of high quality materials, supplies, and equipment of the right quantity, on time. If this objective is not accomplished, economies and technical efficiencies become worthless. Bearing this objective in mind, however, does not mean that one conducts the purchasing function without consideration of economical methods of purchasing and distribution. It should be recognized that through effective and economical procurement, more and better equipment and supplies can be provided. This efficiency is important, as very few school systems have all they need of instructional supplies, materials, and equipment of the proper quality.

The inventory group is responsible for seeing that educational items are stored at the lowest possible cost that does not detract from the quality of items. Item obsolescence, pilferage, and deterioration must be avoided so as not to inflate the cost of the good. Cost of handling items should be compared with similar school systems with comparable costs. Evaluation of the distribution system focuses on the time between requisition arrival and delivery as well as the cost of daily deliveries throughout the system. Cost must be prorated to the total delivery system. If supplies do not arrive in time for an educational activity to take place, the system has failed. The educational process is the primary function of an educational system as well as the support system.

Summary

Every principle of good procurement applies to purchasing, inventory control, warehousing, and salvage in all types of institutions. Good purchasing follows the same guidelines for industry, government, and institutions. However, nonprofit institutions often lack the motivation for cost-control efficiencies that may exist in competitive industries and institutions.

The purchasing, warehousing, inventory, and distribution functions in schools involve more than the acquisition of materials to keep them running. Instead, they are perceived as determining how schools are operated and this implies a function that is directly tied to the purposes of schools. As such, purchasing should not be viewed as a peripheral service but as an integral part of the educational program. The difficulty arises when considerations of economy, efficiency, and cost-effectiveness are introduced. The function of school business administrators, as introduced in Chapter Three, characterizes this dilemma. In short, both instructional and business considerations (and personnel) must be involved in these decisions.

In decisions related to purchasing, teachers and instructional personnel must be involved in determining the nature of instructional materials necessary to carry out the teaching strategies most appropriate to reaching instructional objectives. This is operationalized by involving teachers and instructional personnel (especially site-based administrators) in the development of educational specifications for the materials and the estimated or requested quantities. Considerations of economy, efficiency, and cost-effectiveness involve school business administrators who use their expertise to locate materials to meet the established specifications, submit requests for bids, evaluate the bids, and submit recommendations for purchase.

Many of these decisions are formulated in conjunction with the budget development and implementation processes. A prime example is that of evaluating the purchase in terms of its effectiveness: Was this a good buy? Cost-effectiveness relates cost to the degree that objectives were met as a result of the particular purchase. These data are then considered in the budget for next year.

Warehousing in the school business administration context is more than merely storing materials until they are needed. A major cost component of any material is related to providing accessibility—having what one needs when one needs it. School business administrators must balance optimum accessibility with cost. What is the cost of warehousing a whole year of supplies as opposed to warehousing only a week's supply through the year? To what extent does the discount of large-volume buying offset the costs of warehousing a year's supply? Concepts of just-in-time purchasing and economic order quantity described in this chapter speak to management techniques useful to the school business administrator.

Distribution is closely tied to warehousing and inventory. These concepts also relate to having materials available to the user at the appropriate time and at the least cost to the organization. Because the flow of needed materials in classrooms and other school departments is often uneven and unpredictable, the problem for the school business administrator is planning a distribution system that has considerations of both flexibility and cost effectiveness. Instructional personnel involvement can again be useful in designing the system. Teachers, for example, can understand that if they plan and adhere to weekly warehouse requisitions, they can reduce these overhead costs, and, subsequently, have an argument for a larger budget for instructional materials the next year.

Salvage of obsolete, damaged, or surplus material is an important topic for school business administrators, as it revolves around the concept of optimum use of resources. By definition, these kinds of materials are not contributing to reaching educational objectives. Thus, these assets should be liquidated and then be used in a productive manner.

Discussion Questions

1. List and discuss the essential elements of a contract.
2. When a purchase (or sales) contract is created, what specific actions constitute the offer and the acceptance?
3. Explain in some detail why purchasing goods and services for large institutions differs from doing so for a small institution.
4. Diagram and discuss an automated purchasing and inventory system. What are the benefits and shortcomings of such a system?
5. The uninformed person sometimes envisions an automated purchasing system as one in which most purchasing personnel are simply replaced by a huge computer. This is not true. What jobs do people perform in operating an automated purchasing system? Discuss the importance of these jobs.
6. Explain how the just-in-time ordering procedure can and should replace the existing huge warehouse type of storage and distribution now so widely used in school districts.

Notes

1. Free on board (f.o.b.) means that the seller pays for transportation of the goods to the port of shipment, plus loading costs. The buyer pays freight, insurance, unloading costs, and transportation from the port of destination to the factory. The passing of risks occurs when the goods pass the ship's rail at the port of shipment.
2. The individual steps involved in the particular system will vary, such as how many copies are retained and to whom the copies will be distributed.

3. Performance bonds submitted by the successful bidder upon award of the contract guarantee faithful performance of the contract and payment of materials and labor by the contractor to all subcontractors and material suppliers.
4. See "Managing an Organization" on the website for a discussion of Deming's management theories.

Web Resources

Examples of school district b:d requests, requests for purchase and auction—
http://www.irvingisd.net/purchasing/default.htm

Example of school district distribution center services—
https://www.roundrockisd.org/home/index.asp?page = 92

Purchasing and integrated waste management information—
http://www.ciwmb.ca.gov/schools/wastereduce/purchasing

CHAPTER SIXTEEN

Managing Risks

■ INTRODUCTION

Risk involves variability in a series of possible outcomes that can occur in a specific situation over a defined period of time. *Risk* is used to describe any situation in the future that is unknown or highly uncertain (Harrington, Harrington, & Niehaus, 2003). Risk management is the acceptance of responsibility for recognizing, identifying, and controlling the exposures to financial loss, legal action, or personal injury that is created by the activities and actions of the organization.

LEARNING OBJECTIVES

In this chapter a reader will learn about:

- Definitions and classifications of risks.
- Circumstances under which risks can be mitigated through insurance.
- Types of insurance available to education agencies.
- Government regulations regarding insurance companies.
- Means for acquiring insurance.
- Employee insurance matters.
- Occupational Safety and Health Act (OSHA).
- Workers' compensation.

In this chapter, the idea of a comprehensive risk management program for school districts is presented so that the proper balance between cost of protection and the degree of risk a district is willing to assume can be generated. Due to federal and state mandates, negotiated contracts, and a wide range of other concerns, achieving a proper balance involves more than the decision to simply buy insurance.

■ RISK AND THE ROLE OF THE SCHOOL BUSINESS ADMINISTRATOR

Risks are a day-to-day concern but assume greater meaning when related to choices in planning and purchasing specialized insurance coverage for a wide variety of responsibilities for the district or other educational unit. Several factors influence the implementation of an effective risk management program. In general, risk management includes the identification and measurement of risk as well as the processes for dealing with losses in all areas—from property to people.

School business administrators should be concerned with identification of potential risks in all areas for which the school district has responsibility, the potential for loss (in hard dollars), possibilities and costs for reduction or elimination of these risks, and a plan for regular review of potential and actual losses. Risk management consultant Jean Paul Louisot states (2003):

> The traditional reactive approach of the insurance purchaser to protect the assets of the organization should be replaced by a dynamic and proactive vision aimed at achieving the organization's mission, goals, and objectives under stress or surprise. The modern risk manager must look beyond the organization's frontiers to include all the economic partners, indeed all the stakeholders, of the organization. (p. 26)

One interesting, and pertinent, statement relative to risk management for schools is "Never risk a lot for a little." In other words, be smart about big loss potential and high probability of frequency of loss. Also, be alert to the best deals—low probability and high severity—and to the worst deals—high probability and low severity. This concept is illustrated in Figure 16.1.

Experience suggests that lawsuits against schools generally arise in response to one or more of three categories: (1) a failure to provide adequate supervision or instruction, (2) a failure to provide safe equipment, and (3) employee misconduct. A district goal should be to make sure that none of these conditions exists in any area of school operations (Williams, 1996).

In addition to being meticulous, risk identification should be regular and ongoing. The district's risk managers should be included in the planning of all new programs, facilities, and events because each new endeavor brings with it the potential for new, unidentified risks. The need to identify, evaluate, and eliminate risks is the purpose of such a plan (Loving, 1996).

Risk management includes both financial management and the use of physical and human engineering techniques. Risk management is a coordinated effort to protect an organization's human, physical, and financial assets. The three key steps in this area are:

- Identification of risks.
- Analysis of their probable frequency and severity.
- Loss control.

Therefore, the risk manager must be able both to isolate areas of risk in programs and facilities and to appraise the cost of reducing potential risks by installation of safety equipment, appropriate modification of facilities, and employee training. When a decision is made to take a risk, either because it is unavoidable or because it is essential to system objectives, the risk manager normally attempts to reduce the chances of loss by taking

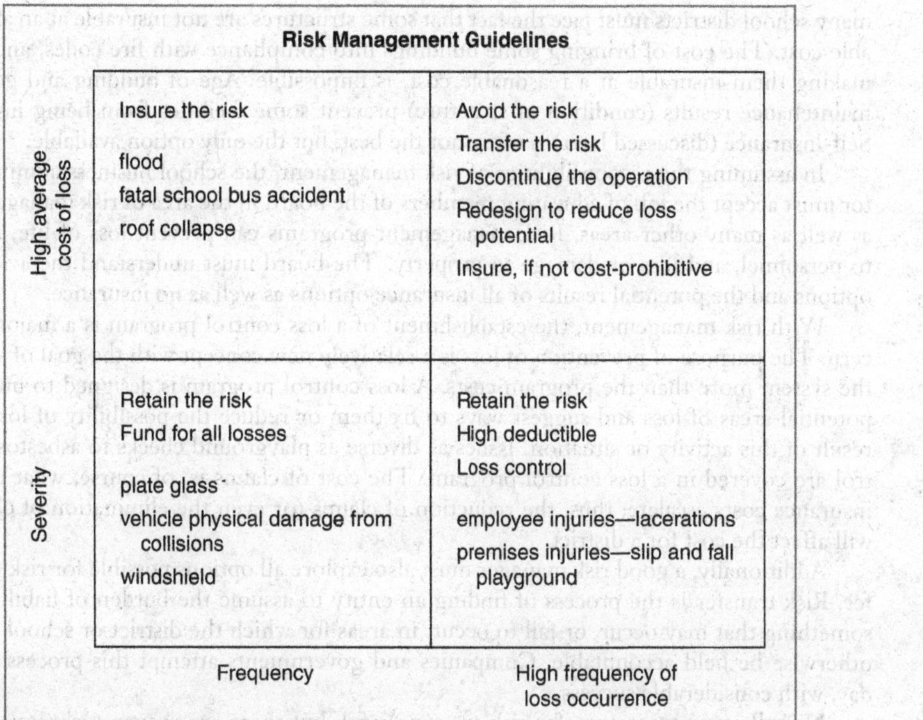

Risk Management Guidelines

High average cost of loss	Insure the risk flood fatal school bus accident roof collapse	Avoid the risk Transfer the risk Discontinue the operation Redesign to reduce loss potential Insure, if not cost-prohibitive
Severity	Retain the risk Fund for all losses plate glass vehicle physical damage from collisions windshield	Retain the risk High deductible Loss control employee injuries—lacerations premises injuries—slip and fall playground
	Frequency	High frequency of loss occurrence

FIGURE 16.1 Relationship between Severity and Frequency of Loss in Risk Management

countermeasures or by transferring the financial effects of the risk to others through the use of insurance or other hedging procedures.

As the risk manager of a school system, the school business administrator or the designated risk manager should determine which incidents should be reported to the insurance carriers. Failure to report occurrences and events to a carrier can often cause problems when one attempts to make a claim under an existing policy.

The concept of risk management is a key element for the school business administrator to consider in the area of insurance planning. Of course, the concept requires the system to analyze its needs and requirements and assign the level of risk it is willing to assume. Beyond this level of risk, based on an actuarial acceptable standard, the system must be prepared to pay for insurance protection.

The degree or amount of risk a system is willing to assume is determined by a number of factors. In property insurance, factors include the age, condition, and usage of buildings, equipment, and motor vehicles; possible natural disasters; and history of loss. The business administrator must weigh the costs of protection against the costs of replacement and recommend a plan for insurance procurement. In some instances, the school business administrator must consider "insurability at all" with regard to property. For example, many school districts must face the fact that some structures are not insurable at an afford-able cost. The cost of bringing some buildings into compliance with fire codes, and thus making them insurable at a reasonable cost, is impossible. Age of building and general maintenance results (condition of structure) prevent some facilities from being insured. Self-insurance (discussed later) is often not the best, but the only option available.

In assuming the responsibilities of risk management, the school business administra-tor must accept the job of educating members of the board in the area of risk management as well as many other areas. Risk management programs can prevent loss of life, injury to personnel, and loss or damage to property. The board must understand the available options and the potential results of all insurance options as well as no insurance.

With risk management, the establishment of a loss control program is a major con-cern. The purpose of prevention of loss is a relatively new concept with the goal of saving the system more than the program costs. A loss control program is designed to uncover potential areas of loss and suggest ways to fix them or reduce the possibility of loss as a result of this activity or situation. Issues as diverse as playground checks to asbestos con-trol are covered in a loss control program. The cost of claims is, of course, what makes insurance costs escalate; thus, the reduction of claims (or even the elimination of claims) will affect the cost for a district.

Additionally, a good risk manager must also explore all options possible for risk trans-fer. Risk transfer is the process of finding an entity to assume the burden of liability for something that may occur, or fail to occur, in areas for which the district or school could otherwise be held accountable. Companies and governments attempt this process every day, with considerable success.

Not all attempts to transfer risk are successful, but there are proven techniques that work for schools. Transfer of risk away from a school district requires:

- Proper execution of a contract or lease agreement.
- Incorporation of the proper language in the agreement.
- Receipt of certificates of insurance or other assurances that properly document the transfer.
- Verification that the documents provide the protection that the district requires.

Opportunities for risk transfer exist in many places—with outside contractors, in rental agreements for use of school facilities, in rental of buildings and equipment on a long-term basis (for unused facilities and surplus equipment), and for school trips. The risk is transferred through a "hold harmless" agreement[1] and a specification of limits and types of coverage. The hold harmless agreement is written in language that conforms to state statutes and should be reviewed by counsel. Although the wording of the agreement varies by type of contract, the extent of protection required and the scope of activities cov-ered should be clearly stated.

The specification of limits and types of coverage must also be stated in the contract. The desire to set high standards must be balanced against the likelihood that the contrac-tor or organization will be able to obtain the coverage and at a reasonable cost. For some contracts, a state may impose statutory minimum requirements (Williams, 1996).

An aggressive risk management program is characterized by these activities:

- Identification of risk.
- Measurement of risk.
- Risk-handling techniques.

- Risk control.
- Risk funding.

As with maintenance and operations, the availability of data for establishing a good risk management program can best be supplied through the development of an effective management information system. With accurate, regular data collection and a means of processing, school business administrators can review, plan, and predict an effective program.

■ THE STRATEGIC ROLE OF INSURANCE

The most popular method of managing risk is that of purchasing insurance. For practical purposes, insurance is defined as a promise by an insurer to an insured of protection and service.

Protection means making good a financial loss, and service means rendering aid of various sorts in connection with the promise of protection. The promise is made only to the extent that the loss may be caused by fortuitous events, and, with certain exceptions, promised protection is legally enforceable only to the extent of actual loss. The insurer is the person or organization making the promise; the insured is the person or organization subject to loss to whom the promise is made.

To clarify further the concept of insurance, a discussion of insurable risk is appropriate. There are many risks of economic loss that no insurance company would be willing to accept. Conversely, there are a number of conditions that make a risk insurable. While some kinds of insurance are written in which one or more of these conditions is not present, their absence acts as a danger signal to the insurance company that then must take extra precautions to protect itself.

The following are some conditions that make a risk insurable:

- The peril involved must be characterized by a definite loss not under the control of the insured.
- There must be a large number of homogeneous exposures subject to the same peril.
- The loss must be calculable, and the cost of insuring it must be economically feasible.
- The peril must be unlikely to affect all the insured simultaneously.
- The loss, when it occurs, must be financially serious.

The major techniques for eliminating risk exposure include:

- Avoidance.
- Reduction.
- Assumption.
- Transfer.

Although there is no commonly accepted definition of the terms soft market and hard market, they represent a function of coverage availability and affordability. It is not news to say that the insurance market is tough. During the first half of 2001, rates were already climbing 20 percent to 40 percent. After September 11, 2001, and the failure of huge firms such as Enron and WorldCom, insurance rates soared to over 400 percent for some lines of coverage.

In addition to rate hikes, available coverage is shrinking. Manuscripted forms are a thing of the past as carriers focus on conventional off-the-shelf products. New exclusions are being introduced often across all lines. The most common of these is the terrorism exclusion, first introduced on property, but has been adopted in policies with no terrorism exposure such as errors and omissions (E&O). Multi-year policies, too, are becoming increasingly rare.

As a result, risk managers are being forced to accept higher deductibles and self-insure risks at heretofore unseen levels. Carriers are highly selective about the type of companies they want to insure, which in some cases translates into whichever company is willing to pay the most for coverage.

School business officials must dedicate much effort to identify the appropriate level of coverage for their organizations. It is essential that school districts develop a sound risk management plan that limits their exposure to losses from fires, bad investments, accidents, injuries, lawsuits, tornadoes, embezzlements, and a host of other calamitous events (Young, 2000). In addition to these traditional insurable risks, school districts face increasingly complex factors that must be addressed in order to protect their assets.

One of the key factors in the complex area of risk management for schools and school districts is criminal noninsurability. It is not possible to purchase insurance against criminal acts by a school employee or anyone else. If an employee were to engage in such activities as theft or child molestation, for example, insurance against these acts by the district cannot be purchased. No criminal claims can reasonably be made against the district, but civil claims can be initiated. If civil claims are made, then the school or district should react as with any other lawsuit.

The issue of the actions of district employees, volunteers, or students in areas of violation of civil rights and inappropriate personnel conduct is an area of growing concern. The protection of students from either other students or staff and faculty volunteers has surfaced as a major concern in recent years. Much like issues faced in sports, churches, or businesses, the school business administrator—in the role of risk manager—must be prepared for issues of civil rights violations and negligence in the performance of duties by staff and faculty. Additionally, the school system may be responsible for the actions of volunteers working with the school district in the instructional, athletic, or enrichment areas. More discussion of this area is focused in the section on liability insurance.

In many instances, the school district employee purchases a personal or professional liability policy to cover such instances. The National Education Association and the Council for Exceptional Children both provide such coverage, often as part of the dues package, to members or other persons willing to join. Another method of individual coverage is through riders for homeowners' policies. These, however, are often weakened by substantial exclusions to the coverage.

A second contributing factor to the complexity of risk management has been the increase in the tort liability regarding negligence in the proper maintenance of school buildings, property, and equipment. As with litigation in general, school litigation in areas associated with proper maintenance is on the increase.

In typical negligence suits, courts have described the hypothetical prudent person as one capable of average knowledge and ordinary skills. However, because of the special relationship between the school and students and the professional status of educators, courts have held schools to a higher standard of care than is expected of average persons.

Negligence is any action falling below a certain standard that results in an injury to another person. If nonpreventable, the accident is not the result of negligence. Usually four elements must be present to constitute actionable negligence: (1) a duty must be owed, (2) there must be a failure to perform this duty, (3) a close connection between this failure and the injury must exist, and (4) actual loss or damage must result.

To avoid this problem, school business administrators must be responsible for the proper maintenance of equipment and facilities under their control. Courts have long been concerned with issues covered by areas such as:

- Knowingly having or providing a dangerous environment likely to be frequented by children who, due to age or inexperience, do not realize the danger.
- Providing an attractive nuisance situation (i.e., playgrounds) that attracts children but is not properly maintained.
- Maintaining grounds, buildings, and equipment in an improper manner.
- Failing to provide proper inspections for all school-related items.

The best alternative to litigation is, of course, the avoidance of injuries through precautions. To reduce the risk of litigation and to protect the health and safety of students and others, policies and procedures should be developed that demonstrate reasonable care.

The search for possible areas of loss must be meticulous. The person in charge of risk identification must be able to imagine the dark side of all people and events and must be able to envision all sorts of failures and conditions. Often, a professional consultant is needed for this pessimistic task; administrators tend to see their own operations and those of their colleagues through rose-colored glasses.

In addition to being meticulous, risk identification should be regular and ongoing. The district's risk manager should be included in the planning of all new programs, facilities, and events, because each new endeavor brings with it the potential for new, unidentified risks. Once a board is armed with a list of potential losses, the superintendent can set about planning how to manage risks (Loving, 1996).

In the News

They've been covered for broken windows, vandalized walls and slips on the playground. School districts took out property- and liability-insurance plans that covered anything from accidents to weather-related mishaps. But that's not enough anymore.

There's no longer such a thing as simple property and liability coverage for schools. Now, districts are insured to cover situations considered rare 20 years ago: sexual misconduct or molestation of students by teachers or school staff members; wrongful-termination complaints by teachers; lawsuits by parents over an educator's teaching style.

School shootings, natural disasters and terrorist attacks have spurred further action, forcing district officials to look at ways to safeguard their students and insure their buildings. "You try and cover as many possible catastrophes as you think might happen and you try to prepare for that," said Reynoldsburg business manager Ron Strussion.

Property insurance covers damage sustained by schools and facilities, typically for wind, hail and vandalism, officials said. Liability coverage foots the bill for slips and falls on school property, as well as claims by teachers related to discrimination, wrongful termination and sexual harassment against school-board members or administrators. Insurance also covers legal costs for districts under fire by parents of special-needs students who think schools don't meet their children's educational needs.

Though school officials said the cost of property and liability insurance has fluctuated—it's more than tripled in cost since the Sept. 11 attack—they said it still is a pretty good deal considering it costs a fraction of the district's budget and can see the district through potential budget-busting situations.

"I don't think the cost-benefit analysis is out of line at all," said Dublin schools Treasurer Chris Mohr. He said Dublin currently pays $350,000 a year in property insurance to cover all district buildings. That's not much, considering it would cost about $300 million to replace all of those buildings.

High-profile molestation cases have attracted more attention, and caution, from schools, said Jeff Junkas, spokesman for the Chicago-based Midwest bureau of the American Insurance Association. "Twenty to 30 years ago, you would never expect a teacher or a coach would do that," Junkas said. "Today, there is probably a greater awareness of the potential dangers. Schools are taking a closer look at that."

Now, sexual misconduct and molestation coverage has become a standard in a district's coverage, officials said. Columbus Public Schools currently faces a lawsuit from the parents of a developmentally disabled girl who said she was sexually assaulted by other students at Mifflin High School last year. The lawsuit, filed in Franklin County Common Pleas Court, seeks unspecified damages in excess of $25,000 from Columbus schools, the school board, and the faculty and administration at Mifflin. It alleges 14 counts of negligence and breach of duty.

Another policy up for consideration by school districts is terrorism insurance, employed by a handful of Franklin County. "We don't believe schools are a high-risk terrorist target, but we think it's prudent to look at the coverage," said Dublin's Mohr. Dublin has continually renewed its coverage since insurance carriers started offering the plan in 2002. This year, the district spent about $12,000 for the plan, which covers damages on district property.

Mohr said the plan applies to acts of terrorism regardless of whether they are defined that way by the U.S. secretary of state and attorney general. Under the Terrorism Risk Insurance Act, which requires insurance groups to offer terrorism insurance, a terrorism attack is defined by an individual or group acting on behalf of "any foreign person or foreign interest." That would mean, he said, that the Sept. 11, 2001, attack on the World Trade Center is classified as an act of terrorism, though the Oklahoma City bombing in 1995 would not be identified as one under the Terrorism Risk Insurance Act. "It's the world we live in today," Mohr said. "We don't write that script."

Mohr said the district also was quick to respond to the Columbine shootings in 1999, spending $7,500 to add an "act of violence" policy to Dublin's liability coverage. Ken Carey, an insurance agent, recalls a time when schools were given governmental immunity for some of these situations. But changes in the Ohio courts during the early 1980s reduced the amount of immunity, requiring officials to buy liability insurance.

Though terrorism insurance makes sense for some districts, others don't think they can afford the cost. With 139 schools and 14 district-owned buildings, terrorism coverage would cost Columbus Public Schools $33,000 a year, said district spokesman Michael Straughter. "While there is a need because of the world we live (in), $33,000 can go along way in terms of

purchasing books or hiring another reading specialist," he said.

From: Roduta, C. (2006, July 10). Schools diversify insurance coverage: Policies for sex misconduct, terrorism more common. *The Columbus Dispatch* (Ohio), p. 01A.

▪ INSURANCE ACQUISITION

The insurance buyer for a school system has direct contact with the insurance field and its limitations. In selecting an agent to handle insurance for schools, the administrator must explore abilities of the possible agents to determine which can best meet the schools' needs. Familiarity with the market and ability to cover unusual risks are evidence that the agent or broker is well informed and is keeping abreast of developments in the field.

Many school districts have made it a practice to award school insurance business to local agents regardless of the cost. The explanation for this practice has been that the local board should do business with local taxpayers. However, the board does have an obligation to make the best use of local tax dollars. Indeed, the board must maximize risk reduction at minimum cost. The board should examine the possibility of using a competitive bidding process for insurance acquisition as it does to secure supplies and materials.

Care should be taken if a sealed bid approach is used. Such a procedure may obligate the district to award a contract to the lowest responsible bidder. Informal bids can allow more flexibility in the determination of the quality and extent of insurance services needed. There is no easy answer for reconciling these differences, because local situations often provide the best guidelines for selection of services.

Because some of the major pressures on a local board are in the area of insurance placement, an appropriate board policy should be established. The board should set guidelines for who can bid, the amount of insurance that can be placed, and specifications of the insurance program. These guidelines, along with a decision to seek appropriate assistance, place the process on the necessary professional level.

Many district risk managers often prefer to view insurance as a service rather than a product. By viewing insurance as a service, they argue that the relationship between an agent or a broker is substantially more important than a few dollars saved when all insurance is purchased on a low-bid basis. As in purchasing procedures, service is an important consideration. Many risk managers are viewing contracts of three years or more as a minimum to have with one company. This time frame allows development of long-term relationships and may avoid unnecessary delays and long-term litigation of some claims.

Risk managers generally believe that long-term relationships are especially important in the area of bus fleet insurance. The possibility of "locking in" coverage for specific rates for a specific period of several years is also a popular option.

Some insurance carriers are exploiting their position in the market. Most underwriters acknowledge that, to some degree, price is determined by what management wants across their book of business. Risk managers have enjoyed a soft market for the past several years, so certain price increases are to be expected. But if a district can partner with its insurance carrier, assuming the right partner, a district will be able to confront difficult times with less angst than others who shop on price alone.

Coverage of "what you should have" compared with "what you might have" and "why" is presented in Table 16.1. This illustrates only a few of the many risk management issues facing school districts and school business administrators (Sherman, 1985). In this table, the first column displays a desirable type of coverage, while the second suggests what a goal should be. The third column explains why the "should have" is a good idea.

Agents and Brokers

An agent is an individual, or sometimes a partnership or corporation, licensed to represent a particular insurance company in a specified geographic area. The agent may be a general agent, allowed to hire and supervise other agents, or a soliciting agent, responsible only for individual production, and may represent more than one company. When a school system places business with several agents throughout a district, coordination of the insurance program can be become cumbersome. Under these circumstances, the district may appoint an agent of record who will then assume a coordinating role with all other agents involved. This arrangement can be a substantial time-saver for the district.

When buying property insurance particularly, it is sometimes better to deal with a broker. A broker is the representative of the insured; it is the broker's responsibility to place the insurance on the most advantageous terms for the client. Brokers can do business with any company licensed in the state and strive to obtain maximum protection of the client's property for the lowest premium.

Although a broker represents the insured rather than the insurer, the insurer compensates this individual on a commission basis. Despite the possible conflict of interest that

TABLE 16.1 Insurance Coverage

What You Should Have	What You Might Have	Why
Property		
Blanket limit for real and personal property	Scheduled limit for building Scheduled limit for contents	One limit applies (administrative ease)
Blank limit for all locations	Scheduled limit for individual locations	One limit applies (administrative ease)
General Liability		
Combined single limit for bodily injury/property damage	Separate limits	One limit applies to bodily injury and property damage
Broad Form CGL endorsement provides 13 ext: i.e., contractual liability, personal injury, etc.	Not provided	Fills many gaps in the general liability policy

this entails, brokers are useful to buyers of large amounts of insurance, because they are expert in fitting the various types of available insurance policies to the needs of the buyer, and they know which company's policy is most appropriate in a given situation. In nearly all states, the law does not recognize the existence of life insurance or health insurance brokers, though many property insurance brokers also hold life insurance agents' licenses.

Insurance Contracts: Legal Requirements

The same basic laws that govern all types of contracts also govern insurance contracts. Specific legal requirements vary from state to state, and care should be exercised to secure correct advice in the wording and stipulation of insurance contracts. There is actually a special body of law regarding legal problems associated with insurance. One key point is that insured parties (such as a school district) rarely participate in the drafting of the actual contract. In some instances, the state, not the insurer, drafts the contract. A final point of concern is that many insurance options are valid in only one state.

Tort Liability. A major concern for school business officials is tort liability. A tort is a civil wrong (other than a breach of contract) for which an award of damages is appropriate. (See Chapter Five for additional information on tort liability.) School boards generally become involved in tort liability as the result of an injury or accident. Through the years, courts have held school boards as corporate entities to be immune from liability as long as they were operating within the scope of legislative authority. Individual board members are not protected when they exceed their authority and act in a nonresponsible manner.

Legislation is such a variable and school system situations are so change oriented that school business administrators need to be alert to current legal changes. Again, fees for a top-flight risk management consultant and an attorney are generally money well spent.

Fortunately for the consumer, insurance contracts are highly standardized as a result of statutory or administrative directives, voluntary agreements, or customary practice. Otherwise, choosing among the policies issued by thousands of insurers would be extremely difficult.

For example, in most states, the standard fire policy is prescribed word for word by statute. All insurers, domestic or foreign, writing fire insurance in those states must use the prescribed policy. Consequently, (1) the insured need not consider differences in policy language when selecting an insurer, (2) all the insured are subject to the same treatment, (3) policy conflicts do not arise when two or more insurers are required to provide the necessary protection or become involved in the same loss, (4) court interpretations of the contract become more meaningful, (5) the insured and insurance agents save time and energy in contract analysis, and (6) loss experience can be pooled for rate-making purposes.

Structure of the Insurance Contract

All insurance contracts, whether consisting of policies, plus forms, or policies only, contain provisions that can be classified as: (1) declarations, (2) insuring agreements, (3) exclusions, (4) conditions, and (5) endorsements. In many property or liability insurance contracts, the provisions are grouped into these five categories and labeled accordingly, but in other lines, the provisions must be rearranged to achieve this grouping:

- Declarations are statements by the insured, on the basis of which the insurer issues the contract.

- Insuring agreements are the provisions that distinguish one contract from another.
- Exclusions are perils, persons, property, or situations not covered by the insurance contracts (some are absolute; others may be nullified by endorsement).
- Conditions are provisions in the contract with which the insured must comply in order to enforce the insured's rights under the contract.
- Endorsements supersede provisions in the contract with which they are in conflict.

■ TYPES OF INSURANCE OPTIONS

Property Insurance

The term property insurance encompasses coverage for buildings and their content. It also covers physical damage to any kind of real property, such as buses and equipment. Coinsurance clauses in most property policies state that the insurer must pay only the part of the loss the amount of insurance bears to the amount required to escape any penalty.

General methods of valuing property, real estate or personal, vary from area to area. However, certain basic patterns of this valuing are used most often by the risk manager individually or in combination with others. These methods include: (1) original cost, (2) market value, (3) tax value, and (4) replacement value. Each of these methods includes variations based on local situations.

The value for which any structure should be insured is the sound replacement cost after such conditions as depreciation, site acquisition, and architects' fees are taken into account. Because costs of construction and general replacement costs for furnishings and equipment change frequently, district personnel must make every effort to keep records current. Accurate and frequent appraisals are the surest method of having the proper information available for determining the appropriate insurance program. Insurance companies often take local appraisal at purchase, but reserve the right to have commercial appraisal when a claim is filed. For the same reason, frequent appraisals help prevent needless expenditure of district funds for excessive insurance on uninsurable interests.

Replacement cost insurance for buildings should be considered where appropriate, especially in the case of relatively old buildings. To fail adequately to cover the replacement costs of equipment and furnishings or to purchase amounts of insurance far in excess of what will be an acceptable replacement cost is not economically sound practice. A "rule of thumb" is that full replacement cost increases the insurance premiums by 25 to 40 percent. These increases are influenced strongly by type of structure (e.g., a technical school building) and age of structure.

All school districts are faced with many insurance needs other than those previously noted. Burglary, robbery, theft, glass, and boiler and machinery insurance are some of these needs. Limited coverage and broad coverage are available for boilers, with specifics determined by state and local regulations. Glass insurance is generally restricted to plate or other special types. Coverage for burglary, robbery, and theft is determined by the legal definitions of each of these items. All-risk insurance may be used rather than certain specific coverages.

Property insurance contracts often have specific modifications made to reflect special situations. One of the more common is the addition of an endorsement covering vandalism, from glass breakage to total building destruction. School systems may elect to add this endorsement or to have insurance cover a percentage of the replacement costs because full coverage is too expensive.

One area that has created a large number concerns for school business officials is insuring computer equipment and large collections of software. These items are easily removed, easily sold, and easily damaged in a purposeful attack by vandals. These also are subject to extensive damage through negligence, and, to some degree, misuse. This simply adds another concern to the "risk management" skills of the school business officer. Special exclusions may apply or specific riders may need to be added to current policies.

Fire and Casualty Insurers

In the United States, these types of insurers write school property insurance: stock companies, mutual companies, and reciprocals. Stock companies have a major share of the business, with approximately three-fourths of all property insurance, with five percent of the total capital and surplus available for protection of policyholders.

Stock Companies. In these companies, stockholders, who are desirous of profit, like any other corporation, own a stock life insurance company. It is managed by a board of directors elected by the stockholders and by officers chosen by the board. If the company realizes a profit, the stockholders receive dividends; if business is unprofitable, reserves are depleted. Many stock insurance companies issue nonparticipating policies; these companies charge a fixed, definite premium, and the policyholders share through dividends in the profit of the company (Trieschmann, Gustavson, & Hoyt, 2001).

Mutual Companies. There are four types of mutual companies: (1) assessment mutuals, (2) advance-premium mutuals, (3) factory mutuals, and (4) "specialty" and "class" mutuals. Many write only fire insurance and allied lines. In some companies, all members participate in the management of the company. Many advance-premium mutuals charge a lower initial premium than do stock companies, while others pay out the profits from their lower operating expenses in the form of policyholder dividends (Harrington et al., 2003). Though policyholders receive dividends in profitable years, they cannot be asked to pay anything additional in years when operating results are poor. Because mutual companies operate on the ability to assess policyholders, many states will not allow insurance purchases from mutual companies, as these assessments are considered a noninsurable risk. State law for schools often specifies that only nonassessable purchases are possible.

Reciprocals. A reciprocal, or interinsurance exchange, is an insurance carrier without any corporate existence. The members pay an advance premium and are also liable for assessments of a stipulated amount. Theoretically, a reciprocal should be able to provide low-cost insurance for its members, because its cost of acquiring business, a major expense of most insurers, is so low. This may be an excellent form of insurance coverage for school districts.

State Insurance. Some states operate school insurance programs. North Carolina covers elementary and secondary schools. Some of the state programs are handled through the State Department of Education, while others are handled through the state insurance department. Many programs parallel self-insurance (discussed in another section) in that the local districts do not pay premiums. If administered correctly, these programs are much more economical than insuring through private agencies because they lack the high overhead common to many insurance firms. This practice has not spread, primarily because of the political power of insurance lobbies in most states.

Self-Insurance. Many administrators in large school systems recognize that because of district size, risk has already been spread, and thus money might be saved by adopting a program of self-insurance rather than buying insurance from commercial companies. Self-insurance is pretty much self-explanatory. With a self-insurance program, entities choose to "go it alone" and retain the risk of loss within their own budgets (usually with some level of catastrophic insurance protection). In the mid-1980s, many entities were forced to choose self-insurance when the insurance industry abandoned the market. There is a distinct difference, however, between having no insurance and being self-insured. Self-insurance is becoming, for the most part, the risk financing alternative of choice for medium to larger entities (Johnson, 1993).

Normally, when a self-insurance fund is established, small annual appropriations are made into the fund, the accumulated reserve is invested, and the earned interest is added to the reserve. As the accumulated reserve increases through adding the annual appropriation and interest, the system gradually phases out policies held in commercial companies.

Ordinarily, the first buildings phased out of the commercial policies are the relatively low-risk units; conversely, high-risk buildings are the last to have commercial policies dropped. Only when the business administrator and the school board are convinced they have adequate reserves to cover the reasonable probability of loss should the school system become completely self-insured.

Self-insurance may also operate on a deductible basis, whereby the district pays a basic value and any additional amount is covered. This allows lower rates, yet provides coverage for the major loss.

Because there is never complete assurance that the point of adequate reserves to cover probable risk has been reached, boards and business administrators must exercise considerable judgment. Considerations that must be entertained in determining whether an adequate reserve is in place are:

- The magnitude of the spread of risk.
- The general comparability of value of the several buildings in the system, so as to prevent distortion in the spread of risk.
- The general comparability of risk of the several buildings in the system, so as to prevent distortion in the amount of risk.
- The geographic separation of buildings to avoid multiple losses from a single fire.
- Transition of coverage from commercial companies to self-insurance in the low- to high-risk sequence.
- The probabilities and magnitude of future expected losses based on current risk exposure rather than on past loss records.
- The fiscal alternatives available to the school system to replace a loss exceeding the revenue available in the self-insurance fund.
- The ability of the school system to maintain the self-insurance fund at the level necessary to provide adequate protection.

Pooling. Pooling, a collective effort of public entities to jointly share the risk of loss, was a major response to the insurance charges and fluctuations of the mid-1980s. Many pools provide services such as risk control and claim management, and are generally credited with advancing the concept of risk management among school personnel. Many schools participate in pools for at least one line of coverage, with many participants having joined in the late 1980s. Price is, of course, a key reason for joining, while unavailability of coverage and nonresponsiveness of commercial agents are other reasons for closing a pool management. The future of pools will depend largely on the results of prices from commercial vendors and the availability of the product (Johnson, 1993).

The structure of the pool is very important. Most pools are structured with the loss fund followed by an aggregate loss fund protection policy. An illustration of a pool structure appears in Figure 16.2.

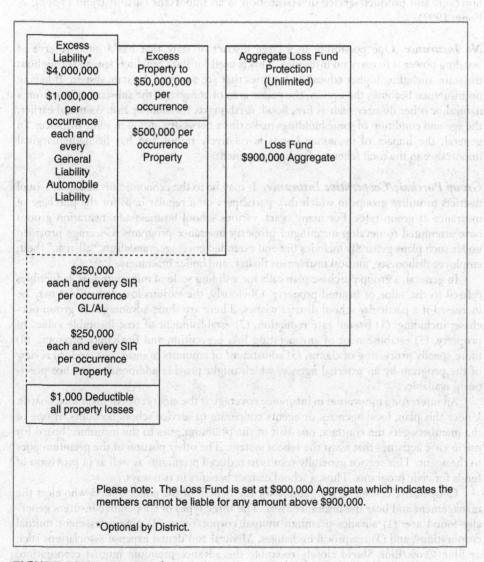

Excess
Liability*
$4,000,000

$1,000,000
per
occurrence
each and
every
General
Liability
Automobile
Liability

Excess
Property to
$50,000,000
per
occurrence

$500,000 per
occurrence
Property

Aggregate Loss Fund
Protection
(Unlimited)

Loss Fund
$900,000 Aggregate

$250,000
each and every SIR
per occurrence
GL/AL

$250,000
each and every SIR
per occurrence
Property

$1,000 Deductible
all property losses

Please note: The Loss Fund is set at $900,000 Aggregate which indicates the members cannot be liable for any amount above $900,000.

*Optional by District.

FIGURE 16.2   Loss Fund

The pooling movement in the United States is well into its fourth decade, and, although pools face some significant challenges, there is no indication that the movement is nearing an end. Approximately 400 pools operate throughout the nation, providing coverage for between 30,000 and 35,000 public entities (about 40 percent of the total market). Formed mainly to respond to hard-market cycles for government liability insurance in the mid-1970s and mid-1980s, they have outlasted the crisis that spawned them. In contemporary school finance practice, pools most commonly provide liability and workers' compensation coverage. Broader risk management services are provided to a much lesser degree. This emphasis is changing, however, and product/service diversification is an important current trend (Young & Fone, 1997).

No Insurance. One possibility in a large district or state that has a good reserve of bonding power is to carry no insurance. This is used for state buildings spread throughout the state, including higher education facilities that are a part of the state system. If having no insurance becomes the option, the major area of concern is the substantial loss from a natural or other disaster such as fire, flood, earthquake, tornado, or riot. As noted earlier, the age and condition of some buildings make this a necessary option in some instances. In general, the impact of insurance bonds is relatively minor and has been of marginal importance in the total scheme of risk management.

Group Purchase/Cooperative Insurance. It may be to the economic advantage of school districts to utilize groups in which they participate on a regular basis for the purchase of insurance at group rates. For many years, various school business administration groups have attempted to develop meaningful property insurance programs. Coverage provided under such plans generally includes fire and extended coverage, vandalism, "all-risk," theft, employee dishonesty, musical instrument floater, and boiler machinery.

In general, a group purchase plan calls for a sliding scale of minimum loss deductibles related to the value of insured property. Obviously, the various loss deductibles may be increased if a particular school district wishes. There are some advantages to group purchase, including: (1) overall rate reduction, (2) establishment of true insurable values of property, (3) establishment of an operating loss prevention and fire safety program, (4) more speedy processing of claims, (5) adjustment of amounts of insurance, and (6) review of the program by an external agency, which might provide additional input not previously available.

An interesting innovation in insurance coverage is the emergence of insurance boards. Under this plan, local agencies or agents cooperate to service school accounts. If one of the members gets the contract, one-half of the premium goes to the insurance board for use in civic activities that assist the school system. The other portion of the premium goes to the agent. This service generally results in reduced premiums as well as in provision of funds for civic programs. Thus, a school district benefits in two ways.

Cooperative insurers are organized for the benefit of the policyholders who elect the management and bear the insurance risks. The three types of cooperative insurers generally found are: (1) advance-premium mutual corporations, (2) pure-assessment mutual corporations, and (3) reciprocal exchanges. Medical and dental expense associations such as Blue Cross/Blue Shield closely resemble the advance-premium mutual corporation. A detailed discussion of the technical differences among the groups is too lengthy for inclusion here. An interested reader can secure information from the insurance board representative, broker agent, or insurance publications.

Liability Insurance. Liability insurance is written to cover any insured party's responsibility for damages due to bodily injury, death, and dismemberment. Two areas of liability—general liability and vehicle liability—are covered in most school district policies. (Vehicle liability is discussed in another section of this chapter.)

Liability insurance is a complex area for any school district and should be closely studied by the administrative team. An overall comprehensive insurance plan to cover the district is preferred over scheduled plans. Workers' compensation (see next section) is designed to cover injuries to school employees, and such injuries are generally not covered in liability programs. Liability insurance is not an accident policy, and payment of a claim need not be made until damages are awarded in a court. State statutes and the determination of what constitutes neglect affect decisions to such a degree that a board must insure for self-protection.

In most states, school districts may not be held liable for injuries to pupils or other persons. This legal position has led to the establishment of nominally priced pupil accident insurance plans, wherein parents purchase coverage. Group rates apply, and coverage is usually restricted to the school day and time spent traveling to and from school. Competition in interscholastic athletic events is usually excluded in these policies. Athletic departments or parents for the specific sport in which the pupil participates purchase insurance covering these athletic events. Teachers, administrators, and other school personnel are turning to personal liability insurance at a rapid rate.

All school districts must maintain an effective security program for staff, faculty, and students. The school site and district as a whole have an obligation to provide as "risk-free" an environment as possible, but it is not possible to guarantee the safety of all people at all times. The risk must be reduced, but it cannot be removed.

There are very few workplace issues that have captured the attention of the public as has sexual harassment. Employers and employees have been forced to become more aware of both the issue of sexual harassment itself and their responsibilities under the law.

When dealing with the issue of sexual harassment, administrators and teachers have to wear many hats. Administrators must administer and provide guidelines to prevent sexual harassment from taking place. Administrators and teachers must be the conveyors of knowledge to students and staff regarding what sexual harassment is and how to protect themselves from falling victim to it.

Sexual harassment is legally defined as any unwelcome sexual advance, request for sexual favor, or other verbal or physical conduct of a sexual nature if: (1) you have to submit to sexual demands to keep your job; or (2) submission or rejection is a basis for employment decisions about you; or (3) the conduct makes your working or learning environment intimidating, hostile, or offensive. This definition can apply to teachers, administrators, staff, students, and volunteers. The school business administrator must remember that all groups of stakeholders can put the district at risk.

One area of concern in school is the responsibility for properly managing volunteers in order to protect pupils from negligent acts. While volunteerism provides many unique services that contribute to the mission of educating students, it requires proper supervision and management to work effectively.

To reduce risks associated with use of volunteers, a school system should consider the following:

- Development of relevant management policies and procedures.
- Development of descriptions and responsibilities.
- Appropriate screening of applicants.
- Provision of proper orientation and training.
- Adequate supervision of personnel.
- Maintenance of adequate and appropriate liability insurance. (Harshfield, 1996)

Another equally vexing issue for school business administrators is that of changes relating to child molestation. While the number of claims is still low, the potential for coverage is still a major concern. Generally limited to younger children, the claims can be made until the child reaches the age of majority (a year determined by each state, but generally eighteen or twenty-one years of age). This is the so-called long-tail issue and can result—much like asbestos claims—in suits years after the actual or alleged event. While the full legal ramifications are not totally clear, the issue of physical or psychological damage resulting from child molestation or abuse must be a serious concern of the risk manager. Individual teachers may opt to carry such coverage, but the system still is extremely vulnerable to long-tail suits.

Even fewer in nature, but of substantial importance, are the issues related to claims made for AIDS exposures to students, faculty, or staff. Although, as a health-related issue, much of the coverage concerns will be limited, the opportunity for exposures to a known HIV-positive person at a school-sponsored event is a major concern for the school business administrator. Again, product policies must be in place to protect the infected worker, student, or faculty, and, at the same time, protect the other members of the school community and others associated with them.

One of the more important developments in the area of commercial general liability (CGL) policies is the changes required by a shift to the "claims-made" form of coverage from the traditional "occurrence" basis of coverage (McConnell, 1986).

Occurrence policies cover all losses that happen during the time the policy is in force, even though a claim is not presented until a later time. Under the claims-made type of policy, the coverage would be provided by the policy that was in effect when the claim was made or the lawsuit was filed. Although not in widespread use, the claims-made policy raises four basic issues:

1. Inclusion of an annual aggregate policy limit.
2. "Retroactive date" feature.
3. Notice of claims and occurrences from the insured to the carrier.
4. Primary policy's tenure with terms of excess or umbrella policies.

Items related to these concerns will become a larger problem as more districts switch to this type of policy. Perhaps the key difference—and most interesting feature—is the fact that under a claims-made policy, the carrier of record at the time of claim filing is the responsible company. With questions such as long-term effects of asbestos exposure or child molestation, for example, a company has a difficult time projecting losses or potential claims. Newer forms exclude some coverages altogether. Finally, injuries sustained by large numbers of persons at a school event must be reported. However, notification of injury does not substitute for a claim and would not trigger coverage. If notification is not made, the carrier could cancel coverage or require some type of exclusion.

Section I—Coverages
Coverage A. Bodily Injury and Property Damage Liability

1. Insuring Agreement

 a. We will pay those sums that the insured becomes legally obligated to pay as damages because of "bodily injury" or "property damage" to which this insurance applies. No other obligation or liability to pay sums or perform acts or services is covered unless explicitly provided for under SUPPLEMENTARY PAYMENTS—COVERAGES A AND B. This insurance applies only to "bodily injury" and "property damage" which occurs during the policy period. The "bodily injury" or "property damage" must be caused by an "occurrence." The "occurrence" must take place in the "coverage territory." We will have the right and duty to defend any "suit" seeking those damages. But:

 (1) The amount we will pay for damages is limited as described in SECTION III—LIMITS OF INSURANCE;

 (2) We may investigate and settle any claim or "suit" at our discretion; and

 (3) Our right and duty to defend end when we have used up the applicable limit of insurance in the payment of judgments or settlements under Coverages A or B or medical expenses under Coverage C.

FIGURE 16.3 Commercial General Liability Coverage

Source: Includes copyrighted material of Insurance Services Office, Inc., with its permission. Copyright, Insurance Services Office, Inc. 1990.

Architects and engineers generally are excluding services related to asbestos removal from their contract and are requiring owners (i.e., school boards) to hold them harmless from any claims. While not usually a problem with K–12 systems, hazardous waste is also routinely excluded. Issues related to excluding pollution-related claims are not as clear, but also are generally excluded.

The Insurance Service Office, the insurance organization that prepares recommended policy forms for use in the United States, has made substantial revisions to its commercial general liability policy. Three major issues are covered in these sweeping changes:

1. The change from occurrence basis of coverage to claims-made basis of coverage.
2. Exclusion of coverage for all forms of pollution.
3. Including the costs of defense within the coverage limits of the policy.

As with all insurance policies, care must be taken to read and understand policy provisions. Figure 16.3 illustrates the differences between policies addressing the issues noted in the previous paragraphs. It shows material provided by the Insurance Service Office, Incorporated—"Commercial General Liability Coverage"—and the same form providing "claims-made coverage" (McConnell, 1986).

■ EMPLOYEE INSURANCE

Employee insurance programs constitute one of the major insurance items for a school district. Workers' compensation and medical insurance are the two major items of employee-related expense and are major items for consideration in the planning role of the school business administrator.

Workers' Compensation

In most situations, district employees, both certified and noncertified, are covered under provisions of the state workers' compensation law. Any particular exclusion to this law should be noted in negotiated contracts between the individual and a particular bargaining unit. Generally, in cases in which physical disability resulted from compensable accidental injuries sustained while on the job, employers augment payment employees receive from workers' compensation.

Many contracts state that beyond a specific day, in this case the seventh, the employer pays the employee the difference between the workers' compensation payment prescribed by law and a regular weekly income to the extent and until such time as the employee has used accumulated sick leave. In many instances, payments are provided beyond this period and can be charged against compensable leave on a prorated basis, computed on the relationship of differential pay to the regular weekly pay, until compensable leave is exhausted. Any further payments would have to be negotiated as a part of the individual contract.

Rates for insurance coverage are determined by the dollar value of past claims. As claims increase, rates for coverage increase. The school business administrator, site personnel, and other central administrators can play a key role in avoiding increased rates through a vigorous accident prevention and risk management plan. A regular plan of inspections, preventive maintenance, and risk avoidance through education can assist in holding the line against rate increases across several insurable areas. A team effort to identify risks and reduce them is necessary for an effective program. In some school districts, especially in larger urban areas, self-insurance for workers' compensation coverage is often provided.

No benefits are payable in the case of injury resulting from willful intent. Specific injuries, medical expenses, disability, and death are covered in workers' compensation programs. In several states, workers' compensation is required for all public employees, while in others, the school district is held to be liable for the risk. Rates for workers' compensation are based on employee compensation, and the risk value associated with specific jobs within the district, and any special cases may be covered by adjusted rates. A good accident prevention program, coupled with regular physical examinations and strict adherence to safety rules, is an effective method of reducing workers' compensation claims for any school district.

Substantial increases regularly occur in claims and substantially larger numbers of persons have been involved in litigation. To counteract the difficulties this increased activity has produced, many groups, such as School Boards Associations, have formed self-insured trusts (SITs). In essence, the SITs operate like an insurance pool, but without the worry of dealing with assigned risk problems. The assigned risk issue, a function of many legal entities, was required for states and has always required that a portion of all funds be set aside for noncovered personnel. SITs have alleviated this problem.

The use of stress (generally that produced by administrative directive) as a covered claim has opened many doors, as have the growth of sexual harassment and child abuse claims for liability coverage. In general, the area of stress as a basic claim could add literally thousands of claims to a basic set for a given year. Many companies, of course, have raised premiums for basic coverage, and, in some instances, companies have withdrawn coverage.

To prevent this loss of underwriters, state courts have often held that a company cannot withdraw coverage based on only one year of claims. In other instances, companies have been told that in order to write some high-profit coverage areas, they must write their "fair share" of the nonprofitable coverages. These issues continue to be unresolved and are an ongoing concern of the school business administrator (Trieschmann et al., 2001).

Medical Insurance

Group medical insurance programs with options to cover both the employee and the individual's family (spouse and children) are features of virtually all plans. This coverage is often an integral part of union agreements or other negotiated packages. Coverage has increased in recent years to include major medical and disability or income-protection programs as well as death benefits. More recent program additions have included dental, optical, and psychological services.

Prepaid health plans that offer comprehensive medical care for a fixed fee have become a feature of a large number of school-based medical plans. These are most commonly characterized by the term health maintenance organization (HMO). HMOs are established to provide medical coverage for a single fee and cover a wide variety of services, outpatient to major surgery.

HMOs are of two major types:

1. Group practice plans provide medical services at centers staffed by salaried physicians. Laboratories, X-ray facilities, and pharmacies are on the premises so members can obtain outpatient services at one central location.
2. Individual practice plans offer medical care in the private offices of physicians under contract to them. One advantage is a wider choice of physicians. These physicians sometimes receive a monthly payment for every member who has enrolled with them.

HMO packages are criticized because of reductions in services due to revenue loss, but most often due to the list of doctors or service providers available. Since 2000 broader coverage plans—local groups opting to join state systems—and an upgraded list of service providers available have stabilized many plans. The newer Preferred Providers Organizations (PPOs) are gaining in popularity, and both PPOs and HMOs have become more "user-friendly."

One key feature often overlooked by risk managers is a possibility of organizing a wellness program for employees, both faculty and staff. The general effects of wellness programs nationwide have been good, with results attained in the lowering of some health insurance premiums, reduction in absenteeism, increased productivity, and enhanced faculty and staff morale.

Early identification of an employee's health problem is vital for the effectiveness of the wellness program. Early identification and treatment of a problem are substantially in the interest of the school district because they may eliminate long-term recovery or loss of job performance capability by faculty or staff members. Some systems may also provide payment or partial payment for memberships in a health club and as a part of the wellness efforts. Many other benefits accrue to a school district having an established wellness program, but one of the most important is that the tangible costs of health care may be reduced.

Coping with COBRA

The Consolidated Omnibus Budget Reconciliation Act (COBRA) of 1995 made history in June 1999 when the Supreme Court issued its first COBRA decision, ruling that employees whose job-based health benefits were ending could elect COBRA coverage even if they already had group health insurance. Meanwhile, the Health Insurance Portability and Accountability Act of 1996 expanded the scope of COBRA coverage. It also marked a serious shift in thinking. Before the Supreme Court decision, consultants and lawyers routinely told employers that the law did not require them to offer continuing coverage to those with other insurance; not anymore.

Justice David Souter noted that COBRA does not say "if the beneficiary 'is' covered or 'remains' covered . . . ," but when the beneficiary becomes covered. The high court's unanimous conclusion: The right to this continuing coverage ends when the beneficiary signs on with another group policy after electing COBRA, not because of preexisting coverage. The implications for the school business administrator are important, especially when facing negotiations for the next set of contracts (Trieschmann et al., 2001).

Prior to the mid-1980s, many health plans were really reimbursement for the first dollar of expenses and for most coverage areas (certain psychological services were often excluded). Since this time, there has been a rather steady erosion of benefits to include—at best—coverage of a 60–40 split between systems and employee, increased deductibles, stop limits for certain coverages, maximum benefits for entire families over a year or lifetime, and stiff preexisting condition clauses. These restrictions have been for both licensed and nonlicensed personnel in the district.

Many new health programs take advantage of the PPO approach, which are generally considered more flexible, especially in doctor selection than HMOs. PPOs, complete with some self-pending (system pays a fixed dollar value before insurance reimbursement is requested) and modest copayments, have been shown to be extremely cost effective. For both licensed and nonlicensed personnel, the PPO is the apparent plan of the future.

Unemployment Insurance

The implications of recent court decisions have made school employees eligible for unemployment insurance in cases that were not previously covered. For example, in some states, teachers who were considered to be eligible for unemployment insurance during periods of unemployment or layoff became eligible for unemployment fringe benefits of a magnitude not previously experienced by local districts.

State plans for unemployment insurance coverage are at best heterogeneous. Some are liberal and others are very restrictive. Problems abound with regard to covered groups, especially part-time employees. The risk manager must keep abreast of current legislation at both the state and federal levels. The school business administrator and planning personnel have to consider the burden these payments place on the annual budget and plan to meet them. Because expenditures occur after the fact, the school business administrator has a major problem with allocation of the funds for this expense. The watch phrase here is adequate planning so that the proper compensation units can be built into the budget.

■ ALTERNATE FINANCING FOR RISK MANAGEMENT

If, as many risk managers believe, the insurance crisis of the mid-1980s is not the last such upheaval, alternative forms of risk financing may be needed. One such form is the capital assets market. This approach is characterized by a district's administrator analyzing its exposure to loss, conventionally insuring some loss potentials, retaining (self-insuring) some loss potential, and creating a quasi-insurance entity by borrowing in the capital assets market to replace some types of coverage. In short, the district has established its own insurance company.

The capital market's approach to risk financing has four goals:

1. To stabilize the cost of risk financing.
2. To stabilize the availability of coverage.
3. To stabilize the availability of limits of liability.
4. To provide control over the district's destiny.

■ INSURANCE RECORDS, MAINTENANCE, AND PROTECTION

It is imperative that all school district records are maintained in a safe and yet accessible manner. Insurance records and all other records within the school district must be protected to the degree that the value of the documents warrant. For example, there are crucial, important, useful, and nonessential insurance records. It is imperative that each type of record is classified by category and that appropriate procedures are established to ensure that vital records are protected. Proper security measures must also be maintained when transporting data to and from vaults. Insurance records are maintained on various kinds of electronic memories and stored at a separate location. It is important the insurance records are designed to feed back into the fiscal accounting procedures so that the school business administrator can direct these materials into the day-to-day flow.

■ PERSONNEL AND CONTRACTOR RISK MANAGEMENT CONCERNS

Negotiated Contracts

Expanded insurance benefits—dental, optical, psychological, and so forth—have become a major issue for negotiations. While the need for increasing wages is still of paramount importance, many employee groups (and employees) see fringe benefits, such as insurance and vacations, as fruitful areas to use for bargaining. The actual benefit to the employee may be several times the equivalent percentage increase in wages.

Riffing of Staff

Riffing is the reduction in force (RIF) that occurs when staff is discharged. The determination of insurance coverage when staff riffing occurs is a matter of serious concern to both school system and employees. A general position has been that the language of the contract set by collective bargaining will determine any insurance provisions for persons affected by a RIF. The issue is one of policy and contract. In those systems without contracts, school board policy should be in place to avoid suits and other legal problems. COBRA issues also need to be considered, due to the potential cost consideration.

Retirement Changes

Many school districts include early retirement incentives to reduce riffing effects. Under many plans, persons within a specified number of years of retirement are given a "bonus" to retire early. This prevents dismissal of a new faculty or staff person and also lowers the general employee total for the system. The extent or full impact of this practice is not fully known.

Surety Bonds

A surety is a person, group of persons, or company guaranteeing that other persons will fulfill a valid obligation to the school district. There are several kinds of surety bonds available to public school districts and to the school business administrator. These include: (1) contract, (2) court, (3) license, and (4) permit bonds. Each of these bonds guarantees that under a particular situation, such as a performance contract, failure to perform a specified activity or to produce an acceptable level of work will be covered for the completion of that contract in accordance with its terms.

Contract bonds help to eliminate incompetent and dishonest contractors from bidding because a contractor without a good reputation is unlikely to be able to secure a bond. The advantages of bonding in general include the district's assurance that its contract will be completed, or that the surety company will have the contract completed; that incompetent or dishonest contractors will have difficulty in obtaining contract bonds; and that construction progress will be aided because payment of bills is guaranteed in a performance bond or in a separate payment bond.

Bonds affecting individuals are aimed at ensuring performance or faithfulness of another party under an "honesty of the employee" bond. Under such a bond, if a public employee is careless or dishonest, any losses incurred by this activity will be covered. These are generally referred to as fidelity bonds, although they are technically a type of surety bond.

Vehicle Insurance

Insurance coverage associated with school transportation is a multifaceted component of a school district's total insurance program. Planning on the part of the school business administrator in order to recommend coverage requires input from many school district sources, including the district's legal counsel, the personnel supervisor, union representatives, the purchasing agent, and the transportation director. Policies in a vehicle insurance program might include, among others, comprehensive, collision, fire, theft, liability, medical, and extended coverage. Additionally, the school business administrator, as part of the administrative team, has the responsibility of providing information to all involved in the use of private automobiles for school-related functions. A business official may also be expected to give suggestions as to types of insurance coverage needed or recommend additions to existing private coverage necessary to provide adequate protection.

Drivers of school buses are, of course, liable for negligence that causes personal injury or property damage. Negligence may also apply to the school board. Different insurance needs apply when buses are leased. The school business administrator must know the extent of coverage permitted or required by the state. Questions must be answered about the extent of coverage provided for drivers, passengers, and property. Safety training programs for drivers related to a reduction of insurance premiums, efforts to regulate pupil conduct for the protection of equipment, and other safety considerations may well be a partial responsibility of the school business administrator.

■ OCCUPATIONAL SAFETY AND HEALTH ACT (OSHA)

A major concern of all business administration personnel is the implementation of and the reaction to federal and state laws. One of the major pieces of legislation now affecting school systems and likely to continue to do so over the next several years is the 1970 Occupational Safety and Health Act, which mandates specified operating standards for various kinds of activities, structures, and job situations. For example, activities in the areas of transportation, maintenance, and school plant management all contain features covered under the Occupational Safety and Health Act. Thus, the necessity of providing adequate documentation and attention to detail in accident prevention, while it has always been present, is of paramount importance.

The application of the Occupational Safety and Health Act is a key feature of any safety program within a district. When applied to the environment of workers, OSHA standards address not only accident prevention, but also noise and air pollution. The intensity enforcement of the act is subject to the prevailing attitude of the federal administration in office at any particular time.

The implementation of this legislation, while probably causing an extra outlay of funds, may provide an advantage in terms of insurance premiums. The establishment of a rate structure that supports these particular innovations may well provide significant rate reductions. Many boards do not avail themselves of the opportunity to negotiate insurance rates. Thus, the opportunity to examine insurance programs in detail and to negotiate rate structures is an advantage that the introduction of OSHA may bring into sharper focus.

The OSHA regulations of the early 1980s included a right-to-know law designed to help employees reduce and prevent adverse health effects from exposure to workplace chemicals and other hazardous substances. School districts are responsible for identifying such materials and substances, for providing information concerning employees' rights, and for providing necessary training and retraining of all employees in these areas. While often considered "another law, another form," school districts must consider the risk factor of such issues and take appropriate steps to educate and inform their employees of possible problems. The laws are designed for the protection of all employees, and are thus a concern of the total district and especially the school business administrator with responsibilities of risk management and loss control. Investment in the safety, health, and welfare of employees and also students makes the implementation of such laws a must (Harrington et al., 2003).

Summary

This chapter discussed the major planning responsibilities of the school business administrator in the insurance program of a school district. Insurance contracting, including such facets as declarations, exclusions, conditions, and endorsements, was presented. Aspects of insurance acquisition, property insurance, fire and casualty insurance, state insurance, self-insurance, and their interrelationships were discussed. Information on insurance record-keeping and valuation, and discussions of employee insurance, surety bonds, vehicle insurance, and other kinds of insurance was provided. It is clear that because a major part of the school business administrator's role is to maximize returns on educational dollars spent, protection of school funds, persons, and property is an integral part of this function. Wise protection is a vital part of effective planning.

Discussion Questions

1. Design and conduct a risk management survey for your school district.
2. Under what circumstances could competitive bidding for insurance not be desirable?
3. What are the major strengths and weaknesses of insurance for a school system?
4. What are the conditions in your school that could make a risk insurable? Uninsurable?
5. How is insurable value determined? By whom?
6. Would self-insurance, coinsurance, or no insurance be suited to the district in which you work or last worked? If so, how? If not, why not?
7. What are the key issues in insurance acquisition, and how would you weigh the various options to determine the necessary coverage for your site or system?

Web Resources

U.S. Department of Labor Health Plan and Benefits information for COBRA—
http://www.dol.gov/dol/topic/health-plans/cobra.htm

U.S. Department of Labor Occupation Safety and Health Administration information for OSHA—
http://www.osha.gov/

Workers' compensation information for each state—
http://www.workerscompensation.com
http://www.dol.gov/esa/regs/compliance/owcp/wc.htm

References

Harrington, S.E., Harrington, S., & Niehaus, G. (2003). *Risk management and insurance* (2nd ed.). New York: McGraw-Hill/Irwin.

Harshfield, J.B. (1996). Liability issues of using volunteers in public schools. *National Association of Secondary School Principals Bulletin*, 80(581), 61–63.

Johnson, B. (1993). Walking the tightrope, balancing risk finance options. *School Business Affairs*, 68(6), 4–9.

Louisot, J.L. (2003). What makes an effective risk manager? *Risk Management*, 50(6), 26–30.

Loving, J.P. (1996). Reducing risk. *The American School Board Journal*, 183(5), 27–29.

McConnell, J.G. (1986). The claims-made policy. *American School and University*, 58(12), 19–25.

Sherman, J.A. (1985). Do you understand your insurance program? *American School and University*, 57(8), 61–63.

Trieschmann, J.S., Gustavson, S.G., & Hoyt, R.E. (2001). *Risk management and insurance* (11th ed.). Cincinatti, Ohio: South-Western College Publishing.

Williams, T.L. (1996). An integrated approach to risk management. *Risk Management*, 43(7), 22–27.

Young, P.C. (2000). Managing risk. *The American School Board Journal*. Retrieved February 19, 2007, from http://www.asbj.com/schollspending/young.html.

Young, P.C., & Fone, M. (1997). The future of pooling. *School Business Affairs*, 63(2), 48–52.

Note

1. *Hold harmless* means that one party agrees not to hold the other responsible for certain acts or under certain circumstances (e.g., events beyond the control of the parties, unforeseen circumstances). Usually the agreement should spell out what those acts and/or circumstances are in some specificity.

CHAPTER SEVENTEEN

Managing Auxiliary Services

■ INTRODUCTION

Auxiliary services generally provide the school business administrator with most of the severe day-to-day problems encountered in the typical school system. While these services are not directly related to the teaching-learning situation, their absence makes it impossible for the primary function of the school to continue. Because auxiliary services are so important to the normal operation of a school system and because the efficient operation of these services enables the educational process to proceed with a minimum of distraction and disruption, considerable planning effort must be devoted to their appropriate injection into the total operations of the school system.

LEARNING OBJECTIVES

In this chapter a reader will learn about:

- The operation of school district transportation systems and related matters, such as outsourcing the service, safety regulations, staff training, maintenance, and routing and scheduling.
- The operation of school food services, including related matters, such as government regulation, menu planning, purchasing, portion control, staff training, and health and safety issues.
- The organization and operation of school security personnel, including related issues of possible outsourcing, recruitment, staff training, principal, student and community relations, and performance evaluation.
- Tangential issues, such as use of school facilities by community groups and the sale of school services.

In planning auxiliary services, the school business administrator must first adopt the premise that these services are support services to the teaching-learning situation and not ends in themselves. Additionally, the function of auxiliary services is to enhance the educational environment and to make possible the most efficient learning situation. Therefore, auxiliary services personnel must see themselves as support personnel and must be able to make adjustments as needed to accommodate the learning process. Because auxiliary services often involve the provision of a specific service at a specific time, such as food services and/or transportation, careful planning of the logistical details is crucial to success. Optimum use of expensive equipment also requires careful attention to logistics.

With the rapid increase in collective bargaining across the country, business administrators must develop expertise in contract management as it pertains to those departments over which they have direct line responsibility, such as food services, transportation, and operations. Because of the crucial nature of the business role in the negotiations process, the business administrator is an important member of the management bargaining team. The dual realities of collective bargaining and contract administration add importance to the strategic planning function of the business official.

There are a number of school systems across the country that are developing alternatives to the traditional manner of providing for auxiliary services. Increasingly, school systems are going to the private sector for the provision of auxiliary services. The rationale is that auxiliary services are not the main function of the educational system, that those services most efficiently and effectively provided by the private sector, that by getting competitive bids for these services they are provided at minimal cost to the taxpayer, and that the educational system has enough to worry about without becoming involved with auxiliary services.

Of course, the down side of the argument is that the local system loses control when these services are privatized and that the quality of the service may be compromised as a result. For the business administrator, privatization reduces the burden of being responsible for several employee groups, each with unique needs and demands. In addition, the school system gets out of the fringe benefit business, the cost of which is increasing dramatically with no sign of letting up.

While auxiliary services include items such as attendance services, health services, student activities, and community services, the services that most often become a part of the school business administrator's direct responsibility are security, food service, and transportation as well as maintenance and operations of facilities, which are covered in Chapter Fifteen. These are services over which the business administrator is apt to have direct line responsibility, as opposed to a staff relationship in the instructional support activities. It is therefore appropriate for a school business administration to deal in some depth with the planning of food services and transportation programs. When discussing these functions it is practical to be aware that nuances of region and geography and variables of local and state policies make generalizations hazardous.

The move from a traditional pattern of organization to a site-based management emphasis further complicates the provision of auxiliary services. Rather than develop a standard, inflexible set of auxiliary activities, the business office must now consider local unit needs in the development of transportation schedules and food services. Consideration of local preferences and needs may cause some deviation from traditional unilateral decisions, but once physical and financial constraints are identified, the process does simplify. Strategic planning requires that the clients, in this case the building principals, be involved participants. While more time consuming, it ultimately leads to better understanding of the limitations, more unity in the final decision, and a better service for the students.

■ TRANSPORTATION SERVICES

What was once a rural phenomenon has become an accepted service provided to over half of the public school children in the United States. In addition, a sizable proportion of parochial school pupils is provided transportation services. The transportation of schoolchildren began at a time when the country entered the automotive age, and was a real stimulus to the development of consolidated school systems. The breakthrough in transportation led to the elimination of small, inefficient school systems and greatly assisted in the establishment of the comprehensive school systems of modern America.

As paved highways and improved vehicles were developed, the service area of a school system could be expanded, until today it is not unusual for children to be transported many miles to schools suited to their educational needs. Indeed, in some of the more sparsely populated sections of the country, it is quite common for children to be transported over fifty miles to school. The sight of fifty, one hundred, even two hundred school buses parked on a school transportation site is no longer unusual. The big yellow vehicle going down the road has become a common sight to most American drivers.

As the nation's highways became more highly developed and as the variety and size of vehicles increased, many other important uses of the transportation services were introduced. With the advent of smaller (six- to fifteen-passenger) and more specialized vehicles, moving particular children to special schools (e.g., handicapped, gifted) became economically feasible. The use of buses as mobile classrooms and as learning laboratories was also introduced. More recently, cities and newly emerged suburbs have come to depend on transportation services for a number of tasks besides basic transport between home and school.

Even more recently, the use of transportation services for desegregation purposes, including transportation to alternative schools, magnet schools, and for court-ordered student transfers among regular schools, has expanded the use and scope of the typical transportation department. Emerging "schools of choice" legislation in many states will add to the complexity of strategic planning for the transportation system.

Among the more demanding state mandates requiring school business administrator action and concern are the following:

- Seat belt requirements.
- Bus safety requirements.
- Changing eligibility for transporting students.
- Bus driver requirements.

Actions to be taken by the business administrator must be predicated upon federal law and statutes for the particular state and should reflect an ongoing concern for the safety of children. For example, Public Law 94-142 requires that vehicles used to transport students with certain disabilities meet certain requirements and capacities. These requirements, for example, hoists, wheelchair capacity, ramps, and so forth, call for unique specifications and attention from the business administrator.

In the News

Let's assume 2-point lap belts are required in school buses nationwide. What effect will that have? And what will it cost?

Assuming the requirement applied only to new buses, and that retrofitting would not be required, about 25,000 to 30,000 large buses would be equipped annually. That's how many large school buses are manufactured in a typical year. At an estimated cost of $1,500 to $2,000 per bus to install lap belts, which is about 3% of the cost of a typical $60,000 school bus, the additional cost to install lap belts on all new large school buses would range between $37,500,000 to $60,000,000 annually. Historically it takes about 12 to 15 years to convert the entire fleet, though a small percentage of pre-1977 buses (now more than 20 years old) remain in service. During the transition, the total cost to install lap belts would range between $450,000,000 and $900,000,000, and this leaves aside annual maintenance and replacement costs.

When the transition would be complete, assuming ridership remains at about the 55 percent level and the K–12 student population grows as projected by the U.S. Department of Education, we'd have more school buses on the road. That's because lap belts reduce the capacity of the three-across, 39 inch wide seat. So, instead of 475,000 school buses in the U.S. in 2006–2007 there would likely be 500,000 school buses upon completion of retrofitting the entire fleet.

The question of who would pay for seat belt installation is unknown. If the U.S. Congress—the only legislative body with the power and authority to do so—were to enact legislation to require seat belts nationwide on all school buses, its record with unfunded mandates is well known. On the other hand, if Congress required states or local education authorities to foot the bill, it's an open question whether the cost would be borne by the states in their education budget or some other revenue source.

From: School Transportation News. Retrieved February 20, 2007, from http://www.stnonline.com/stn/occupantrestraint/seatbeltfaqs/index.htm#Assume.

The school business administrator's task of planning to meet the transportation needs of a school system becomes a complex, often frustrating endeavor. Not only must the primary function of moving children to and from school be attended to, but the important tasks of moving children for purposes of educational quality and educational equality must also be addressed. Recent decisions mandating the "mainstreaming" of students previously assigned to special schools further complicate the logistical difficulties involved in planning transportation services.

Because the planning and implementation of transportation programs are neither exotic nor desirable chores compared with the spectrum of duties normally assigned to the business office, the service dimensions must be emphasized and rewarded. There are many considerations that must be resolved in order to implement a transportation program.

Planning Considerations

Crucial decisions as to what kinds of transportation are important to the educational programs of a school district must be handled at the policy planning stage. Questions to be addressed include the following:

- Is the transportation system to be used only for moving children to and from school?
- What are other legitimate uses of the transportation system?
- What are the constraints (legal and otherwise) on the transportation system?
- What benefits can accrue to the students through expanded use of transportation systems?
- What federal, state, and/or local regulations affect the transportation system?
- How do children qualify for transportation services? Is distance the only criterion or are physical traffic concerns also important?
- What portion of the educational resource is most profitably invested in the transportation system?

The transportation policy of a school system should evolve from decisions made concerning these and other questions. As the policy questions are resolved, operating rules, regulations, and procedures are developed. Periodic, systematic review of the transportation policy must be a part of the planning-implementation cycle because variables change, and so must policy dealing with the variables. As policy shifts are made necessary by changing conditions and/or new educational goals, rules, regulations, and procedures for implementing policy must be modified. The overriding concern must always be to provide the best possible support and service to the learner and to the school system.

Contract versus District-Owned Equipment

One of the early planning decisions to be made is the resolution of the question of contract versus district-owned equipment. There are many advantages and disadvantages to either approach to pupil transportation, and the decision is often one of convenience rather than one based on careful planning and analysis of alternatives.

There are a great many considerations to be assessed in reaching a decision on contract versus district-owned equipment, not the least of which is capital equipment expenditure.

Convenience to the learner is another important criterion for deciding the contract versus district-owned issue. If, for example, there exists a well-developed public transportation system that has the capacity to service the needs of the school system while meeting the health, safety, and convenience criteria established for students, the decision to contract is relatively simple. But if use of the public transit system places an excessive burden on either the system or the clients, then other alternatives must be explored. In many instances, the use of the public transit system provides for optimum use of that system while meeting the educational needs of the school district at the same time. In such cases, it is to the advantage of both the school and the transit authority to enter into a cooperative effort to ensure that total utilization of community resources is being implemented.

In other locales, there is no public transit system and the decision is more difficult. Contract opportunities with private carriers provide alternatives to district-owned equipment. Once again, health and safety needs, convenience, and cost benefits must be assessed before a decision is made. Among the advantages the private carrier offers to the school business administrator are the following:

- No large investment is required.
- A large administrative management task is eliminated.
- The school district is not in competition with private business.
- The enormous tasks of maintaining and operating a bus fleet are not the school district's.
- Transportation personnel are not added to the complement of school district employees.
- Many of the criticisms can be directed to the contractor rather than to the school administration.

Conversely, there are advantages inherent in school district-owned transportation systems. These include the following:

- Operating costs are usually less than with private contractors.
- Buses are available for use for other aspects of the school program.
- There is greater control over matters of health, safety, and convenience.
- The transportation program can be planned as an integral part of the total educational experience for the learner (as in the use of school buses for field trips).
- In many states, state subsidy is available to assist the local district in the capital expenditure.
- Transportation personnel can be selected and trained to ensure an appropriate level of both driving and educational competency (bus drivers are considered to have instructional roles, as they can influence children in areas of citizenship, human relations, good manners, responsibility, cooperation, and so forth).
- There is far greater flexibility inherent in a district-owned and -operated transportation system.

While there are many contract agreements in operation across the country, well over 70 percent of the school transportation systems are district owned and operated. Careful cost-benefit analysis of all options should lead to the best decision.

In the News

NARRAGANSETT—Spending more to bus its students than any other community in the state, the school department is considering privatizing its bus fleet.

At a joint meeting last week the Narragansett Town Council urged the School Committee to look into the potential cost savings of hiring an outside contractor to bus the town's children. The town currently owns its own buses and has a transportation staff of 34 people, including 17 drivers and 11 bus monitors, according to Ron DiFabio, the school business manager.

"I think the transportation department does a great job," said Schools Supt. Albert E. Honnen. "But there's probably a reason not too many communities have their own transportation departments."

The School Committee subsequently directed Honnen to gather information in preparation for seeking bids from private companies.

"I think the town deserves to know what a privatized contract would cost us," said School Committee President Ann E. Masterson.

Facing declining enrollment and seeking voter approval of a $21.5 million bond referendum next year for repairs to school buildings, the School Department has been looking for ways to cut costs. Earlier this year the School Committee voted to eliminate more than 20 teacher positions, but its per student spending, nearly $15,000, remains the second highest in the state (after Block Island).

A significant portion of that spending, more than $1.2 million, is being spent on transportation, according to figures compiled by Town Manager Maurice J. Loontjens, a figure that is likely to increase this year given the high price of fuel.

At $723 per student, the cost of busing Narragansett children is by far the highest in the state and more than $300 above the state average.

One of the central concerns is the condition of the Avice Street barn where the school buses are maintained, which is badly in need of repair. The Town Manager estimated the cost of renovating the barn at $900,000. The bond proposal does not include funds for the transportation department.

"If we're going to look at cutting costs and being fiscally smarter, it's something that we at least have to investigate," said School Committee vice chairwoman Nancy Devaney. "I'm in favor of gathering the facts and doing a really good study of all the pros and cons of the issue."

Douglas Wardwell, chairman of the Narragansett Property Owners Association and one of the few residents to regularly attend school committee meetings, applauded the move.

"For many, many years we have been questioning the cost of having our own fleet," he said. "Let's do a real study on the cost to lease versus the cost to own."

It may be a difficult discussion.

Some parents are likely to point to the personal relationships that are formed with bus drivers as an intangible that benefits the community, said Honnen.

Others may point to financial benefits. Ownership of the buses facilitates school field trips, and the Parks and Recreation Department, which runs a day camp for residents, also uses the buses frequently during the summer months.

Devaney said she would like to see a committee established to explore the options. Masterson said any discussion would include representatives from the union, which still has two years left on its contract.

One possibility, should the committee decide to seek a private vendor, would be to require the company to offer current drivers and employees positions as a condition of the contract, said Honnen. He conceded that he did not know how this would affect possible cost savings.

"I have mixed emotions. I think we are very fortunate to have our own buses and the bus drivers are really members of the school community," said Devaney. "By the same token, it's a very expensive proposition."

Narragansett transportation supervisor David Correira is on vacation and could not be reached for comment.

Routing and Scheduling

Without question, one of the more demanding and frustrating aspects of transportation system planning is the development of routes and schedules. Techniques range from maps identifying each student to be served (required by law in many states) to computer programming of routes and schedules, sometimes with questionable results. The difficulty of programming the variables of human behavior and the problems encountered when dealing with weather conditions and machinery make the development of routes and schedules additionally sensitive.

Problems of routing and scheduling are compounded by population sparseness or density, traffic conditions, road quality and conditions, school schedules, and the variables of weather. Planning decisions on routes and schedules involve determinations as to appropriate roads to travel, what distance youngsters may walk to converge on a pickup point, services provided to the disabled, effects on property owners of pupils congregating at a certain point, traffic flow and congestion, safety of pupils, time constraints, size of buses, geography of the route, and so on. Another important consideration is how to make the most efficient use of vehicles; that is, should routes be planned so that buses can make more than one trip, and, if so, should age ranges of pupils play a major part in the route development?

As transportation systems become a more important component of the educational program, the problems of scheduling for educational use become more complex. Field trips of every description are valuable educational experiences, and the meshing of these activities with the primary home-to-school-to-home obligation presents severe logistical problems. The routing and scheduling of a fleet of buses to provide safe, economical transportation, as well as to support the variety of educational experiences possible with extended use of vehicles, requires thoughtful, resourceful, and sensitive planning.

Recent developments in the use of computers to assist in scheduling have permitted much more efficient schedule development. Many districts have moved to a three-tier schedule whereby buses are utilized for three runs as opposed to two, giving a fifty percent increase in capacity. Computer scheduling permits a variety of options to be considered and allows many route configurations to be examined. With the dramatic increase in fuel costs affecting all fleet operators, efficient scheduling becomes a must. The bus fleet must be utilized as effectively as possible in order to minimize the strain on the educational dollar. Careful examination of all bus usage is important in ensuring optimum program opportunity.

Inspection and Maintenance

School bus accidents, while rare, are tragic specters for school personnel. Accidents due to mechanical failures are especially tragic and often involve negligence on the part of those responsible for transportation systems. When a school district commits itself to the purchase of a transportation fleet, at the same time, it commits itself to a planned, systematic inspection of the maintenance program.

It is unfortunate that many maintenance programs are of an emergency nature, when the use of orderly, periodic inspection procedures can lead to a preventive maintenance program that will not only provide greater safety and service to users, but also return savings to the school district.

Typically, the school system finds itself with a growing fleet of school vehicles, but with little or no equipment to use in the care of these vehicles and with no trained personnel to assign to the maintenance of moving stock. The care of the transportation fleet is contracted to local garages that attend to simple (e.g., gas and oil) needs on a regular basis and to other needs as they are requested. Because of the harsh reality of school budgets, vehicular maintenance is usually on an emergency basis and typically occurs only upon major breakdown of the vehicle. This is, in fact, false economy and leads to the inconvenience of the failure of transportation services. Occasionally, this method of operations leads to mechanical failures that result in tragic and avoidable accidents.

Regular inspection and planned maintenance of vehicles are crucial to the health and safety of users and permit the optimum utilization of the transportation system to the advantage of the educational program. Inspection and maintenance are closely interrelated and mutually dependent. Inspection is accomplished daily, weekly, monthly, quarterly, and annually, depending on the need of the vehicle.

Maintenance, too, is accomplished according to a short- and long-term schedule. Inspection checklists filled out by the driver, mechanic, supervisor, and other personnel give information relative to maintenance needs. Daily inspections, usually performed by the vehicle driver, are mostly visual and are intended to act as safety checks on the vehicle. Examining of tires, testing turn indicators, checking braking power, testing lights, checking engine warm-ups, reviewing gauge readings, and examining fuel levels are routine and perfunctory inspection tasks for the driver. Scheduled inspections by mechanics become more minute and intense as use time of the vehicle grows. Periodic lubrication efforts and minor engine tune-ups are performed on a regular basis. Annual inspections involve major repairs and replacement of worn and used parts.

Certain maintenance tasks are the result of seasonal weather changes and may differ according to geographic location. Certainly in the northern regions, winterizing of vehicles must be planned and accomplished well in advance of winter weather conditions.

The realization of an adequate vehicular maintenance program is the result of careful planning and resource allocation. Equipment, space, and personnel must be provided for such a program to succeed. It is not unusual for school transportation fleets of from fifty to eighty vehicles to employ four to six full-time mechanics and to have garage facilities that provide indoor workstations for at least six to ten buses. In addition, the stocking of sufficient parts, tires, tools, and equipment calls for an investment of thousands of dollars. It must be recognized that the typical fleet of fifty to one hundred buses represents a capital investment of well over a million dollars and an annual operating expenditure of significant size. If supply and equipment stocking is based on sensible prediction of need and the advantages inherent in volume purchase, great benefits can accrue to the school district.

With the advent of just-in-time purchasing procedures and with the increasing use of e-commerce, the capacity to order needed replacement parts quickly and efficiently is enhanced and should negate current warehousing needs for bus parts and materials. Most important, of course, is the savings involved with curtailment of vehicle downtime. While actual dollar savings cannot be computed in terms of downtime, the fact that the transportation system can meet its obligation in terms of service to the user is of tremendous importance. In addition, the dollars saved by district-performed maintenance enables the expenditure for transportation to be a high-benefit expenditure.

An important part of the inspection and maintenance program is keeping adequate records on each vehicle. Routine and periodic maintenance operations depend on records. Records can also provide the basis for ordering equipment, parts, and supplies on an annual basis to encourage additional savings. Annual bids on fuel, oil, and other consumable materials can add to the savings. The annual bidding on fuel alone can result in enough savings to enable the costs of fuel pumps and storage tanks to be amortized over a very short time. Certain regional accommodations are also appropriate to realize optimum return on investments. For example, the use of antifreeze additives in fuel is desirable in northern climates. It can also be a direct savings if head bolt heaters are installed in subfreezing climates. Installation of such devices will guarantee cold-morning starts and save countless hours of driver and mechanic time. One school district known to the authors calculated that the use of head bolt heaters on its fleet of eighty buses saved over $25,000 per year in driver and mechanic overtime, all for an initial expenditure of $3,800.

To conclude, if a school district determines that the transportation system should be school district owned and operated, then plans for adequate inspection and maintenance procedures must also be formulated. Such a program must include adequate provision for regular inspection and preventive maintenance, conducted by trained personnel backed by appropriate equipment, space, and supplies. Such planning not only provides safe, timely service, but also is reflected in significant savings to the school system.

Staff Supervision and Training

The supervision and training of transportation personnel is another of the difficult tasks facing the school business administrator. Because the number of persons involved in the transportation system can range from very few to upward of several hundred, general statements can be misleading. Generally, large bus fleets are under the direction of a director of transportation who is responsible to the chief school business administrator. In smaller systems, the school business administrator assumes direct control of the transportation system, sometimes with the help of a supervisor or the head mechanic. However the system is organized, some office must assume training and supervisory responsibilities.

The training of drivers is an important and demanding task. Not only must school vehicle drivers have driving ability and the capacity to exercise good judgment, they must also have personal characteristics and qualities that make them positive influences on children. Qualities such as tolerance of noise, firmness, fairness, and love and understanding of children are as important as reaction time, driving ability, physical stamina, and good eyesight.

The training of drivers must reflect the need for transportation personnel to relate well to young people. Many districts have developed concurrent programs that couple classroom instruction with on-the-road training with experienced drivers. Classroom instruction covers such items as child growth and development, safety, psychology, vehicular law, negligence, district demography and geography, and driving regulations. Aptitude and personality tests designed to measure adaptive capacity and stability are also used. Actual driving, first with the supervisor and/or mechanic, is used to develop appropriate driving habits and to learn the handling of large vehicles. When the neophyte gains in ability and confidence, he or she is permitted to accompany other drivers on trips and to actually drive the loaded vehicle. After a series of such experiences, the novice is given certain "short" route responsibilities prior to assignment as a regular. Periodic ratings and test drives are part of the training sequence for drivers.

Many school systems encourage and even require transportation personnel to participate in periodic staff development programs in which safety procedures, driving techniques, child psychology, and so on, are reviewed. In addition, periodic physical examinations are required for personnel to retain their positions.

While much rhetoric has been produced concerning the amount of court-ordered busing now being mandated, the reality is that the bulk of the pupil transportation provided is due to distance between home and school and not a court-ordered desegregation plan.

In some instances, mandated busing plans reduce time and distance for many pupils. Busing is, nonetheless, a negative term to many educators and parents, while pupil transportation carries a positive connotation. After a dramatic increase in federal court intervention on desegregation issues during the late 1960s and the decade of the 1970s, it appears that the political pendulum has swung to a posture of no longer requiring busing in such cases. The judicial process continues to be the focal point of the desegregation issue.

Utilization and Evaluation of Services

When examining school districts, one often finds beautifully developed auxiliary services divisions that are so underutilized that it is difficult to justify their existence. This is true in the case of many school-owned and -operated transportation systems. Vehicles are used for pupil transportation to school in the morning and home in the afternoon and then sit idle the remainder of the time. In addition, routes are often planned so that vehicles must cover an area a number of times to accomplish what could be done more efficiently in a single trip. Low utilization of transportation services not only makes its continuance questionable, but also, more importantly, negates one of the more compelling rationales for the value of a highly developed vehicular capacity: the availability of buses for use as educational tools for the classroom teacher.

Highly skilled and creative curriculum developers plan cooperatively with the school transportation administrators to incorporate the use of the bus fleet into the continuing educational experience of the student. Regularly scheduled field trips, ranging from visits to the farm or dairy or fire station at the primary level, to high school-level visits to the museum or library or art institute and specialized visits to the university or architectural firm or machine shop, are important components of the program and cannot be left to individual whim or chance. Many sophisticated and innovative school systems provide a series of such trips at each grade level, and, in addition, allow individual teachers the opportunity to plan further experiences calling for transportation.

In addition to field trips, appropriate uses for the transportation system include the movement of students between schools for particular programs to encourage optimum use of particular equipment and talent (e.g., a planetarium located in one school, an advanced math program, a technical offering). Also, the use of vehicles for extracurricular and cocurricular activities further optimizes the transportation system. It is important that the transportation division of the school system recognize that as a service arm of the school it must stand ready to provide transportation services as the demands for such services are generated.

Although pupil transportation costs vary greatly from district to district, depending on a great many factors, extended use of vehicles to provide additional educational benefits invariably reduces the pupil-mile cost ratio. This is because the added service provided is most efficient in terms of load factor and single destination. The gains in terms of educational enrichment are not as easily evaluated, but all indications point to greatly expanded opportunities for the learner.

Standards and Specifications

The setting of standards and specifications for school vehicles is closely related to the purposes and aims of the transportation program as well as to the demography and geography of the school district. Minimal standards of safety and health are often prescribed by the state department of education. If not, one can call the U.S. Department of Education for assistance in determining such standards.

Because of the minimal nature of the typical state and/or federal standards, many local school systems develop their own specifications to incorporate particular standards they deem necessary. Given the ease with which seemingly innocent specifications can eliminate desirable and reputable manufacturers of vehicles, great care must be exercised in their development.

National standards of safety must be made an important part of any specification, but beyond that, there are a variety of considerations that must be faced. These include such items such as:

- *What size vehicle is appropriate for the kind of use envisioned?* If basic uses involve transporting children short distances, and if density of population is such that large numbers of riders are gathered in a short time, then the larger capacity vehicle is most appropriate. If, however, the travel distance is great and children are quite scattered, then a smaller vehicle might be more feasible.
- *What kinds of road conditions exist in the area to be served?* The type of vehicle to be specified must enable optimum satisfaction to the user. Excellent four-lane highways and fully developed, paved secondary roads warrant different usage than do gravel roads and rutted, ungraveled trails found in some locales.
- *What is the geography of the area?* Level, flat terrain calls for different vehicles than does uneven, mountainous territory. The type of bus, its engine, its capacity, and its size will depend on the kind of terrain it must negotiate. Decisions on power equipment, engine capacity and horsepower, tires, gear system, and suspension system are all somewhat dependent on geography.
- *What is the climate of the area?* Heating and/or cooling capacity of the vehicle, types of extra equipment needed, engine size and power, and vehicle configuration are all related to weather conditions.

Answers to these concerns, coupled with strict attention to national safety standards, can lead to specifications suited to the needs of the particular school system. While it is important not to underestimate the need for a transportation system, it is equally important not to overestimate the need. Judgment and careful planning are crucial to the development of standards and specifications. Bidding procedures and specifications vary widely among states, ranging from state-developed and -mandated procedures to state-approved procedures and specifications to complete local option.

Contracting Services

With continued increases in the cost of energy and the difficulty in providing transportation services at a cost-effective rate because of equally rapid increases in labor costs, many school systems are seriously examining the possible impact of contracted transportation services. Contracting for either the entire service or for the more highly specialized portions of the service, like special education and vocational education, can reduce the drain on local staff and budget in terms of logistics, capital replacement, labor contracts, and client pressures. A number of firms have become very large providers of transportation services throughout the country. These firms have excellent records and are capable of providing the amount of service requested. Additionally, the contract approach eliminates the need for the local education agency to get involved with all the details that are part of caring for full-time employees.

In some cities, the local education agency contracts with the local transit authority to provide transportation services. This seems to work well as long as the needed services fall along established routes and do not require too much deviation from those traditional patterns. However, because peak demand of normal ridership and the school system often coincide, the use of the public transit system is not as attractive as it might be. Still, many school systems utilize public transit for such special activities as field trips, athletic events, shuttle services, and other off-peak-demand opportunities.

The Energy Factor

The energy crisis is forcing careful rethinking and reordering of many of the plans developed in the past. It is possible that a number of previously discarded notions will be utilized to reduce the impact of the accelerating costs of energy. Such technological developments as cable television and data processing may provide activities that will help reduce the need for some transportation services. Some futurists expect that school-home audiovisual contact will become the norm rather than the exception. The implications for the business office in the provision of the myriad transportation services are great. Care in providing the best possible service at the lowest possible cost is an important charge.

■ FOOD SERVICES

Another of the auxiliary services that is fast becoming one of the important support services of the school system is the food service operation. Realization that the hungry child has severe learning impediments, and that for many children the only balanced meal of the day is the school breakfast and/or lunch, has served to emphasize the importance of the food service program. Until recently, federal support has grown steadily, from the provision of surplus foods at minimal (storage) costs to recent aid in the form of direct grants to provide hot meals to needy children. In many urban areas, one-third to one-half of the public school children qualify for the subsidized food program. Increasingly, the pressures of an urbanized society, with its demands on the family and the continued expansion of the workforce to include more and more women, have generated greatly expanded demands for school food services. What was once a phenomenon unique to school districts serving consolidated schools, which had to provide food services because of the distance traveled by the students, has become a common service extending to many of the neighborhood schools of the country.

Originally a means to utilize surplus foods, the food service program has become recognized as a most valuable component of the school system. Increasingly, school systems are using the food service operation as an important sector of the educational program. Health, diet, consumer economics, ecology, nutrition, aesthetic development, chemistry, and an introduction to the service industry are all important contributions that the food service program can make to the curricular efforts of the school. However, the primary role of the food service operation is that of providing tasty, tempting, balanced meals at reasonable cost to the students.

Planning the food service operation is sometimes a daunting experience to the average school business official, who has little knowledge or appreciation of the complexity of such an effort. Often such planning is left to a local person who, because of some culinary skills, has been named head cook. While such people are experts in providing excellent meals for a family, the mass feeding of hundreds and even thousands of children requires skills far beyond those of persons responsible for food preparation in the home. The food service operation is as complex as that of the largest restaurant chain with split-second demands for service. Such an operation must be carefully planned and developed according to the food needs of the school system.

Decisions to be made include those related to contracted preparation versus local building-level food preparation, and fixed menus versus flexible menus. Because food and labor costs continue to mount and because state/federal subsidies are being curtailed, more efficient delivery is essential.

Additionally, the need to dramatically reduce the waste being experienced in many lunch operations gives still another conflicting charge to the business office: How to serve food that meets nutrition requirements while still meeting student preferences so that the food is not wasted? Flexible menu planning to reflect prevailing student food preferences is but one of a variety of ways to address this issue. Ethnic preferences must also be considered as menu planning proceeds. The most successful food service operations provide choices for children, with such niceties as salad bars, soup and sandwich, and soup and salad, which are increasingly popular.

Most school food service operations are incorporating various ethnic foods and healthier choices into their menu planning. Fast food favorites such as pizza, french fries, hamburgers, tacos, and hot dogs are not uncommon in school lunch offerings. Devising a cost-effective manner in which to serve food that meets the many demands of various student preferences and societal pressures for healthier eating is a challenge in which the school business administrator may be involved.

In the News

The Seven Hills School Food Service Director Jan Alford has been named as one of the four winners nationally of the 2005 Golden Carrot Award by the Physicians Committee for Responsible Medicine for "innovation in school food service and an exceptional job of improving the healthfulness of school lunches."

In announcing the award, the Physicians Committee for Responsible Medicine stated that Jan Alford "recently over-hauled her school's kitchen, tossing the deep-fat fryer, eliminating all foods with trans fat, and making organic soymilk and rice milk always available." Following discussion with consulting chefs, who held idea sessions with students, faculty and parents, Seven Hills made dramatic changes in its food service, starting in March, 2005. In addition to removal of the deep fryer and food that was hydrogenated, bleached and refined or contained trans fat, preservatives and high sodium, these changes included employing Master Chef Jimmy Gherardi as a full-time member of the food service team; using fresh, organic and natural foods in creating new dishes and menus; adding a salad bar; and conducting culinary education classes for faculty, staff, and students.

To comply with a new emphasis on culinary diversity, Chef Jimmy Gherardi introduced new dishes like Penne Pasta with Asparagus and Fire Roasted Red Peppers, and Turkey Meat-loaf with Latino Flavors. Student favorites like tomato soup and grilled cheese, hot dogs, hamburgers, chicken fingers, and pizza remained on the menu, but now the tomato soup is homemade—with organic tomatoes—and the "grilled" cheese sandwiches are baked on organic 12-grain bread. Hamburgers are low-fat organic beef. Chicken "fingers" and pizza are made in house.

Seven Hills is not only offering healthy, innovative lunches; it is doing so at a savings to the School. The food service program is self-supporting. The income from food sales (plate lunch $3.00, plus other à la carte items) wholly pays for the food service program and its team. The School has cut expenses in the program by preparing its own healthy, homemade meals, rather than employing a food service company which involves management fees and commitment to certain vendors.

From: *The Seven Hills School Magazine,* Fall 2005. Retrieved February 24, 2007, from https://www.7hills.org/podium/default.aspx?t=44908.

With reductions in commodities and in federal subsidies, contracted food services become more attractive. However, the local education agency (LEA) must recognize that complete control over menus, over variety of meals, and other issues is no longer possible and that the contractor can make decisions previously housed in the LEA. In many cases, the contract service does provide food service at a lower unit cost because of the efficiencies of mass purchasing and mass production, and more effective use of a trained workforce.

Increasingly, school districts are going to the private sector to provide all food services to the schools. These national concerns, often operators of gigantic food service operations as well as hotels and restaurants, are superbly prepared for the task of planning and operating a food service program. They have been involved in mass-feeding operations over the years and have specialized in producing low-cost meals that meet all requirements for quality, attractiveness, balance, and taste. Many of the concerns have operated food service operations for the universities and colleges of the country for decades and have just recently focused on public school systems as potential customers.

As with the use of the private sector in other auxiliary areas, the contracting of school food services imposes some restrictions on the local district. The contracts drawn for the provision of the service should explicate as many of the expectations as possible so that there are few surprises for either party down the road. For example, if the school expects the food service provider to provide services at extracurricular activities and PTA meetings, these must be stated in the bid document.

Advantages in contracting with the private sector for the provision of food services are many. They include the obvious advantage of relieving the school system from the burden of providing fringe benefits and insurance benefits to a whole segment of their former workforce. With private-sector contracts for food service, the problems associated with managing a workforce are no longer the primary responsibility of the business office, which in highly unionized areas can have a salutary effect. While there are few formal evaluations of private-sector versus school-operated food service operations, consensus seems to be that it is worth careful consideration by the business office in the effort to provide the best possible service to the students of the school system.

Policies, Rules, Regulations, and Procedures

Policies established by the board of education become guidelines for the development of rules, regulations, and procedures for the operation of the food service program. Food service policies attempt to establish broad parameters for the operation and include determinations such as the following:

- Is the school food program to be available to all children or just to those who meet certain specified criteria?
- Is the school food service program to be a systemwide centralized operation or is it to be a building-by-building procedure, with each building principal, in effect, administering a lunch program?
- Is the program to be a hot foods program or a sack lunch?
- If the program is systemwide, should à la carte menus be available? What about snacks? What provisions are made for children who carry sack lunches?
- What provisions are to be made for feeding indigent children?
- Is food to be prepared at each building or is central preparation with "hot cart" delivery more desirable?
- Shall the schools observe "open" or "closed" lunch periods? If closed, what about requests for children living close to school to be allowed to go home for lunch?
- Shall breakfast programs be initiated?
- What educational benefits can accrue from the food program?
- What is the line-staff relationship between food service personnel and building principals?

The development of rules, regulations, and procedures from policy statements leads to creation of an operating manual for day-to-day operations of the food service division. Standards and expectations for personnel and methods of operations are defined. Procedures for collection of monies, use of children as helpers, serving of food, dining room regulations, special food service capability, use of lunch facilities by outside groups, amortization and replacement of equipment, and so forth, are important planning functions.

Increasingly, contracts with various school employee groups, that is, teachers, clerks, custodians, and lunch personnel, become important in the development of rules and procedures. The use and effectiveness of the dining room as an educational resource depend on the availability of staff during the dining hours. Minimum standards of health, cleanliness, and decorum are important to the food service operation and must be well defined.

Because of the severe time constraints imposed by the school day, operating procedures have very real logistical implications. Delivery schedules, serving schedules, preparation schedules, and efficiency are very important for the food service program that must quickly accommodate large numbers of children during a short time span. Delays and confusion must be minimized in order to provide optimum service to children. Rules, regulations, and procedures must be explicit and direct while allowing sufficient flexibility to meet unique and unforeseen needs (for example, certain groups may periodically need picnic lunches provided, or may have to eat early or late on a particular day, or may invite a group from a different city for lunch).

Staffing and Supervision

Planning for the staffing and supervision of the food service operation requires that close attention be given to educational considerations as well as to the culinary qualifications of applicants. Compatibility with children, health standards, temperament, adaptability, personal habits, energy level, and general appearance all contribute to the desirability of prospective staff members.

In districts numbering several thousand students housed in a number of buildings, it is desirable to engage a school food service director (and, if size and volume warrant, several persons) to administer and supervise the food service program. This person is generally trained as a dietician and/or mass-feeding specialist and brings a background in food service work to the school system. Sometimes, a certified teacher trained in food service (home economics) is available, and, with appropriate support, develops the capacity to administer the program. It is a great relief and benefit to the school business administrator to have such a person available to handle the daily administration of the food service program.

The determination of the type and size of food service staff needed depends on a number of variables. Immediate concerns are the following:

- Is the program to use central food preparation or is each building to have its own preparation capacity?
- What is the projected number of meals to be prepared either centrally or by building?
- Are silverware and dishes (plastic or china) to be used or are throwaway utensils and dishes to be used?

If, for example, a centralized food preparation system is projected, with hot-cart delivery to individual buildings, the preparation center is staffed very differently from the individual-building preparation kitchens. In centralized preparation, specializations such as salad chef, meat chef, vegetable cook, baker, and dessert chef might be in order, while in decentralized preparation, categories such as head cook, assistant cook, and cook's helper are more common.

In the News

Some of the same technologies that allow adults to access their bank accounts and enter secure buildings are now being used to collect school lunch money and track students' eating habits. A growing number of cafeterias are installing computerized cash-register systems that let students pay for school meals using personal identification numbers, school badges, and even scanned images of their fingerprints.

The lunchroom uses of those technologies are proving to be a sweet deal for many food-service employees, who say that the new approaches have helped them cut administrative costs and increase student enrollment in the federal free- and reduced-price lunch

program. "It's saved us a lot of man-hours," said Cathy Graham, the food services director for the 2,300-student Pewaukee public schools in Wisconsin, which began using a computerized cashier system in 1998 to ease the daily burden on staff members. It upgraded its system this fall to include touch-screen technologies and digital photos of students.

Before the system was installed, food-service workers had to manually count the money collected for student lunches each day, tally the total number of students who purchased meals, and then record the number of subsidized lunches served so that the school could submit a reimbursement request to the federal government. The process could eat up more than 10 hours a week, and was open to a number of human counting errors.

Now, instead of counting out crumpled dollar bills or fumbling for raffle-size meal tickets, students use a touch screen to enter a four-digit PIN number before every school meal. A computer then shows the student's picture and a list of meal selections, and deducts the cost of what is bought that day from a prepaid account.

The system keeps a record of all the meals served and calculates the number of free and reduced-price lunches. What's more, it allows parents to use the Internet to pre-pay lunch fees online, review what their children are eating, and even to restrict the types of food items their children can buy. "We're in a technology age," said Ms. Graham. "So we're just moving along with the world."

But while technology offers students and parents a convenient alternative to cash or meal tickets, such systems don't come cheap or problem-free. The average system costs $4,000 per unit. In many cases, that cost doesn't include the scanning or decoding devices needed, support services, and software. And with most schools needing between two to eight checkout units per building, the expense adds up to thousands of dollars just to get started. Price is a huge issue and that's what is keeping it out of a lot of school systems, plain and simple—price.

Debra Foulk, the coordinator of business-support services for the 27,000-student Akron, Ohio, school district, says price was a serious concern when her district began looking into cash-register systems in 1998. The district spent $700,000 to install a system called iMeal, which uses a scan of each student's fingerprint to create a 39-digit number that deducts lunch costs from a prepaid account. "My board had some very serious discussions on going in this direction," said Ms. Foulk. "This was a big effort to get this up and going."

From: Hurst, M.D. (2004, October 27). School lunchrooms take digital twists and turns. *Education Week*, 24(9), 8. Editorial Projects in Education.

In-Service Training and Coordination with Educational Program

As in most school-related activities, there is a continuing need for staff training and development for food service employees, many of whose experience is limited to cooking in the home. These employees, while usually very fine family cooks, are not attuned to mass feeding, and therefore must be encouraged to learn the techniques appropriate to such an endeavor. In addition, the use of the food service program as an important component of the educational program suggests other special talents that must be present and highly developed in food service personnel. The planning for, preparation of, and serving of food to several hundred persons for each meal is very different from the preparation of a family meal. Staff development activities include such items as recipe preparation and use, food display, health standards, reporting procedures, youth culture and preferences, actual preparation and seasoning of new recipes, ordering techniques, storage techniques, cleanliness standards and objectives, staff relations, student relations, and so on. Operating rules, regulations, and procedures are reviewed and adjusted to meet current needs and expectations. Objectives and goals of the food service program are emphasized as part of in-service activity.

Also related to staff development efforts is the coordination of the food service program with the educational program. There are certain constraints and time obligations that must be met if the food service program is to operate in schools. Children must eat at an appropriate time, and they must be fed quickly and efficiently so that the program of education is not unduly interrupted or disrupted. Additionally, the food service program has a great opportunity to become an important part of the educational program and can complement and support curricular efforts at every grade level. Health, safety, nutrition, food chemistry, economics, service vocations, and aesthetics are but a few of the potential areas to be supported by the food service division. Opportunities to provide such fringe services must be nurtured and expanded by making available the total food service resource to the educational staff.

Food Preparation Systems

Food service needs and the policies of the school system to meet these needs will dictate the specifications for food preparation areas. There are several alternative systems to serve individual situations. Among the alternatives are:

- The central kitchen.
- Individual/independent kitchens.
- Manufacturing kitchens.
- Satellite kitchens.

Each system has strengths and weaknesses, advantages and disadvantages. Rationale as to which is most appropriate rests with individual districts and should be an outgrowth of local policy.

In centralized food service operations, provisions for trucking hot food on a very rigid time schedule are most important. Additionally, there must be personnel provided at the receiving schools to serve and distribute food, to handle the cleanup and dish return or disposal chore, and to supervise the dining room operation. While centralized food preparation is generally considered to be more efficient and while quality is more easily controlled in such a scheme, other considerations also enter into decisions on centralized versus decentralized food preparation. Obviously, quality control and administration are easiest in the central food preparation arrangement.

Other advantages include savings in capital equipment and space costs and lower unit costs due to quantity preparations as well as potential for specialization in tasks. Still other advantages include the capacity to develop special foods production (such as baking, butchering, salad prep, and so forth), the capacity to accomplish long-range planning, and savings that accrue from volume purchasing and storage.

However, certain disadvantages are also present. These include the loss of the food service operation as a component of the educational program, rigidity in terms of schedules and timing, loss of jobs for neighborhood people, loss of food service resources for community groups, dependence on transportation systems for delivery of foods, and limited capacity to meet local food service needs and tastes.

A difficulty that usually arises in decentralized food service operations is the conflict over who has line responsibility over kitchen personnel—the principal or the school lunch administrator. Generally, it is decided that although the food service administrator sets rules and procedures that pertain to food preparation, menus, distribution, and so forth, the principal has line responsibility, as it pertains to the ongoing program of the school. In this sense, the principal determines serving schedules, collection procedure, dining room expectations, and such. As a service to the teaching-learning process, the food program must meet the established overall educational needs of the school.

Menus, Prices, and Portion Control

School lunch menus are the result of careful long-range planning efforts. Seasonal harvests, market fluctuations, government surplus offerings, unique tastes, ethnic and racial group preferences, talents of preparation personnel, and regionality all play a part in menu planning. Most menu planning is based on cyclical rotation of a basic number of meals so that daily, weekly, and even monthly variety is provided. Past experience and records as to what meals are most accepted are also valuable planning tools.

Generally, menus are planned for the entire system, or at least subsystems of the total school district. The basic lunch is known as "Type A," and if Type A lunches are served there is little deviation from the menu. If, however, in addition to Type A lunches there is to be provided an à la carte menu and perhaps snack or sandwich opportunities, the planning task is more complex. Usually such questions are resolved by insisting that the one-basic-meal menu be adhered to at the elementary school level, with variety and flexibility allowed at the secondary school.

Prices can and do vary greatly from area to area. The main objective of the food service program is to provide balanced, tasty meals at the lowest possible cost. Labor costs and food prices differ from place to place. Urban centers tend to reflect higher costs because of the highly unionized labor market and because fewer foods are grown locally. In spite of this, it is often possible to provide food at lower unit costs because of savings realized through mass production of foods.

It is important that the food service operation provide the greatest service at lowest possible cost to the user. It is equally important that the food service division consider such expenses as amortization of capital equipment, replacement of equipment, utility costs, custodial costs, and overhead when determining the real cost of the program in order to establish a price structure. If the school board must subsidize the service, policy should provide for it.

Portion controls are usually established by regulation, and U.S. Department of Agriculture (USDA) minimum standards are used to determine the amount and variety of food to be served. Differences in age level should be reflected in both the size of the portion and in the price charged. Portion control is relatively easy in centralized operations that prepackage the meals. It becomes more difficult when food is served cafeteria style. Many systems use scales to weigh meat portions and sized serving utensils to determine vegetable portions. It is important that adequacy and consistency of portions be maintained.

Federal and state guidelines are used to determine qualifications for reduced and free food services. Each LEA provides the forms for parents to use in determining the validity of their request. Family income, number of family members, and local cost considerations are involved in the resolution of this serious problem. As costs increase, participation in the paid lunch program decreases and requests for reduced and/or free service increases.

Purchasing

Analysis of food purchasing practices among the school districts of the United States reveals a complete spectrum of purchasing practices. This spectrum covers a wide range, starting with the practice of the cook calling the corner grocer to place an order for the day's food needs, to very sophisticated bidding procedures that involve the cooperative efforts of forty to fifty school systems. The use of the corner grocer to supply all the food needs of the neighborhood school is fast becoming a trend of the past. Food service has simply become too big an operation to neglect the development of sophisticated purchasing procedures.

For example, the medium-size school district that feeds an average of 10,000 students per day generates a total operating budget of over $2 million. This is apt to be the single largest departmental budget in the entire school system, which demands that careful planning be utilized in its expenditure. Because food costs, supply costs, and other purchases typically involve 50 to 75 percent of the total budget (depending on the current availability of federal surplus foods), and because there is a wide variety of different items needed in the food service operation, purchasing is fast becoming recognized as an important function in the administration of the food service program.

The purchasing procedure applicable for school food services is illustrated in Figure 17.1. It contains the essential elements of a general purchasing procedure, but it also highlights certain features relevant to school food service purchasing.

The development of bid procedures and of standards and specifications requirements for food service purchasing is a highly specialized task to be performed by someone well

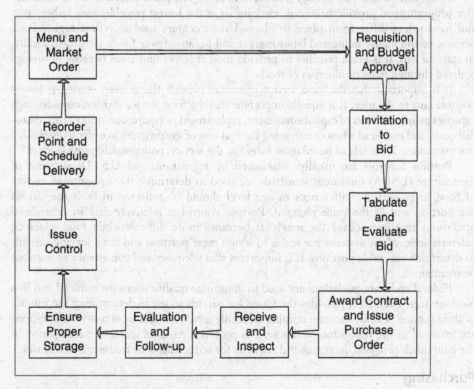

FIGURE 17.1 Flowchart for Purchases

Source: Flanagan, T. *School food purchasing guide.* Evanston, IL: Association of School Business Officials, 1961, p. 120.

versed in mass feeding. Decisions as to canned foods versus fresh and/or frozen foods invoke such variables as freezer/refrigerator space, cold-storage capacity, dry-storage capacity, seasonal variance in food stuff availability, market conditions, and other difficult-to-predict conditions. In addition, the determination of quality standards, container and lot size, quality-control procedures, and delivery schedules has to be made by highly skilled food service personnel.

Because savings of significant proportions can accrue to the school district through intelligent purchasing practices, the school business administrator must provide the support and talent needed to initiate such an effort. Examples of specific techniques include the purchase of paper goods in carload lots, the timing of bid requests to correspond to seasonal production of specific foods, realistic appraisal of quality (fancy labeled canned goods are premium priced and often not essential to high-quality food service), development of sufficient storage space to enable volume purchasing, contract purchasing of perishable foods to ensure price stability (milk products, baked goods, and so forth), group purchasing plans involving a number of school districts to provide volume, and many other creative and money-saving ideas.

Purchasing is an important component of the planning effort of the food service operation. Menu planning, projections of numbers to be serviced, and prediction of items needed all contribute to the purchasing process. Initiation of the purchase is only the start, however. Delivery schedules must be established to ensure that supplies and materials are available when needed. In addition, quality-control procedures must continue to ensure that standards and specifications are maintained at expected high levels. Skill in purchasing often determines how successful the food service operation will be, for the savings effected here will make possible the stabilization of costs to the user at a reasonable level.

Accounting, Reporting, and Cost Analysis

The amount of discretionary tolerance in terms of resource utilization is so slight in the food service operation that very careful and minute accounting, reporting, and cost-analysis procedures must be followed. Because, in most school systems, the food service operation is designed to be self-supporting, and because unit costs must be kept to a level that will encourage participation by all clients, the recordkeeping, planning, and implementation tasks are crucial to success.

Many states have well-established accounting manuals for the food service operation. Most recommend a modified encumbrance system that greatly assists in the planning effort. Because of the unique daily cash-flow process found in the food service operation, daily income accounting procedures are desirable. Records showing number of meals served, income received, food and usable supplies consumed, worker-hours of labor required, and peripheral costs incurred are usually required for each cafeteria.

Providing forms indicating these and other data, along with bank deposit slips and statements with the daily, weekly, and monthly report forms, is a task of utmost importance to the person charged with responsibility for the food service program. Encumbrance of wages, food costs, supplies, utilities, and so on, will enable the reporting system to be meaningful and current.

Because most income is on a cash basis (except for billing procedures for special functions and/or organizations) and because all expenditures are in the form of salary vouchers or payment of invoices submitted for goods and services, the use of daily records, purchase orders, and work orders is most important to the accounting process. Periodic audits, both internal (performed by the business office) and external (performed by an audit firm), require accurate data. Responsible management also requires that recognized accounting practices be followed.

The use of daily, weekly, and monthly records and accounting practices to generate needed reports to a variety of persons is recommended. Reports indicating the overall status of the food service division, along with building-by-building breakdowns, are important information to be shared with personnel of the food service program as well as with principals and central office personnel. Data such as number of meals served, percentage of student participation, variance of participation with menu, special food services provided, and so forth, are important items to be reported. Reports including these and additional interpretive cost data (e.g., unit costs, labor charges, and food costs) are useful in the cost-analysis requirement and can provide valuable planning data.

Many states require reports for participation in state and federal programs. Such reports can be the basis for generating a variety of in-house reports providing specific data of interest to specific groups. Certain informative data (participation, menu implications, labor, and material use) should be reported on a daily basis, while other more interpretive reports can be made on a weekly and monthly cycle. Also important are legally mandated annual reports and audits that are to be submitted to the board of education.

Constant analysis of income and expenditures is most important to the continued health of the food service operations. Decisions and plans developed as a result of careful cost analysis will encourage optimization of the food service program. Given regional labor cost differences and the fluctuations in costs of foods and supplies, the analysis of food service operations must be a continuing effort to ensure maximum benefits for the user.

Comparative cost data will help determine the most efficient and well-operated components of the food service division. If, for example, elementary school A is consistently averaging out to forty cents per plate for labor as compared with fifty cents per plate for elementary school B, and if the total number of meals served in each school is comparable and each school offers the same menu, then it is probable that school B needs some help in organizing its food service operation more efficiently. Similarly, cost data can provide information leading to reduction of waste or to improvement in menus, or give clues to deficiencies in certain units. Careful cost analysis should lead to increased benefits for the children of the school system in terms of tastier foods prepared in the most efficient, economical manner possible.

Remembering that the goal of the food service operation is to provide attractive, tasty, well-balanced meals to students at the most economical rate possible leads to full utilization of sophisticated accounting and reporting procedures as a means of generating data upon which to base cost analysis.

■ SECURITY SERVICES

The latter decades of the twentieth century saw a marked increase in the need for security services in all school systems. The dramatic rise in the number and intensity of youth gangs, the spread in the use of drugs, and the continued decline in the influence of the family and of social agencies and the church all contributed to the increase in violence in the schools. The general breakdown in society was coupled with pressures brought on by the education reforms of the 1980s and 1990s, with their call for increased requirements and heightened standards that were often rigid and lacked a corresponding requirement for viable alternatives. As a result, school became an impossible situation for many students, who then engaged in deviant behavior to satisfy their need for recognition.

Statistics on juvenile crime rates show that while adult crime is leveling off and declining, the rate for youth crime is continuing to rise. Reasons for this are many and varied. Among the prime factors are the realities that the opportunity for gainful employment for youth not achieving a minimum of literacy has become virtually nil. The focus on high school completion as the minimum acceptable level for entry into the job market has served to place yet another burden on the school.

The drug culture and all that it implies is another factor in the dramatic increase in school-related crime. With the sharp increase in the availability of hard drugs at relatively low cost, the young people of America are increasingly trapped into dependence on drugs, and schools have become places for conducting drug transactions. Drugs are no longer for just the affluent; young people of every economic level and ethnicity are involved in the activities related to drugs. Not only are various drugs, such as cocaine, heroin, uppers, and downers, actively marketed on many of the school campuses of the country, but youth are increasingly turning to alcohol as an easily obtainable substance to abuse.

With the annual cost of vandalism now approaching $1 billion, school systems have had to develop a number of ways to deal with the effects and causes of school vandalism. Approaches ranging from the use of dogs to sniff out the presence of drugs in lockers and cars, to reward systems for classes and campuses that reduce vandalism, to community patrols of the various campuses as a means of controlling possible trouble elements are being tried. Formal police patrols and even school system security forces in uniform and carrying firearms are being used in the effort to curb school crime rates. Elaborate security systems tied to local police stations are now common in most urban schools. The use of special forces to infiltrate the campus and pose as students is also becoming common.

Typically, responsibility for the establishment and conduct of a security system falls on the business office. It is crucial, in planning for security services, that the business official work cooperatively with the campus administrators to devise optimum plans for a particular campus. This will also create a more accepting posture on the part of the principal as plans for the protection of the school campus are identified.

Approaches to Security Services

School districts across the United States use a variety of mechanisms to provide security services, ranging from large, internal security divisions to contracted services exclusively. Many provide security through some mixture of the two concepts, while others work closely with and depend on the local police department for the bulk of the service.

As school districts enter into the development of a school security force, a number of important issues arise. Included are those dealing with the type of persons to be employed, their training needs, their duties, and how the force is to be deployed. Typically, the security function falls into several types of discrete activities. These include:

- Routine patrol activities that are carried out during nonschool hours and vacations. Building checks, routine site visits, and monitoring of devices to alert the staff when someone enters a building are part of this activity.
- Campus monitoring and patrol activities that are conducted during the school day and are intended to maintain order and ensure student and staff safety.
- The monitoring of various metal detectors installed to prevent the carrying of weapons into the school.
- Investigative activities that are conducted to resolve security issues and other crime-related concerns. Included here might be student-related concerns such as child abuse, excessive absence, and similar problems.

- Activities to ensure school safety and student safety, which include OSHA concerns as well as traffic and vehicle-related matters.
- The ongoing task in every school system of monitoring drug and substance abuse concerns.
- School-police liaison activities that attempt to utilize the local police acting in concert with school staff to provide support services to schools, students, staff, and parents.

In addition, many variations of these approaches are being utilized, including a number that call for volunteer and parent as well as student participation. It is generally accepted that uniformed police are used in situations in which crowd control is necessary, for instance, at interscholastic activities, concerts, and so forth.

Security Planning Considerations

Board of education policy generally begins with a statement of intent to provide educational services to all qualified students in an environment that protects individual rights while ensuring the safety of all participants. Protection of property and of persons involved is strongly suggested as a primary responsibility of the school system. Indeed, organization of staff and allocation of resources are often predicated on safety and security concerns.

Staffing and Supervision

As security concerns in recent years grew and became focused, specialized staff needs emerged and training activities became more visible. Indeed, a number of institutions of higher education now offer degree programs in school system security, while others incorporate such course offerings as part of the general law enforcement and criminal justice programs.

Many larger systems have developed sophisticated in-service efforts, often in cooperation with a local college or university. Generally, a security staff is selected under a variety of criteria, ranging from ability to relate to students to physical stature and strength. After a period of time, concerns about formal training in security skills arise, and efforts are mounted to provide a program for existing staff. Additionally, a supervisory staff is recruited from various security agencies, ranging from local police departments to graduates of formal degree programs in security.

Deployment of staff ranges from a centrally controlled and assigned staff that responds to particular requests to staff assigned permanently to specific units for overall security services. As the staff becomes more sophisticated and better trained, specialties emerge and specific staff can be assigned these duties.

Relationship to Building Principal

Because most student-related security needs revolve around school buildings and/or school-related functions such as athletics, drama, and dances, the security personnel must be on a close working relationship with building principals and local staff. The principal, under site-based management concepts, has ultimate responsibility for security and safety. The principal must rely on trained staff for advice, counsel, and support as particular concerns are addressed.

In matters requiring investigative procedures, the principal can be invaluable to the security staff, for as the chief building administrator the principal knows the student body and its concerns and needs. The use of trained security persons to assist principals in investigative efforts is a major support service. Security staff assigned to the building report to the principal, as do all others who are a part of the building staff.

Relationship to Students

The most successful security personnel are those who are respected and liked by the students they serve. Many act as quasi-counselors, with a firm grasp of prevailing value systems and student jargon and preferences.

As students develop trust and respect for security personnel, they tend to keep them informed of the nuances and rumors that spread around the campus. Additionally, students solicit the assistance of security personnel as potential difficulties arise. An important planning consideration is the potential ability for the security applicant to relate to the various groups that make up the student body as well as to adult personnel.

Under site-based management particularly, the security person must observe dual reporting relationships. If assigned to a campus, the person is an integral part of the building staff and must respond to the principal, while at the same time being sensitive to districtwide needs as they arise. This, of course, implies a reporting relationship to the central security office as well.

Reporting encompasses not only the direct superordinate/subordinate relationships, but also the gathering and sorting of statistical data related to security. Such data, when examined on both a campus-by-campus basis as well as a districtwide basis, can provide valuable planning information and assist in anticipating problems before they become serious confrontations and/or disturbances. In addition, data will assist in planning the total security operation with staff deployment and with preventive actions.

While many of the larger school districts have developed their own security divisions as an integral part of the non-instructional support services, there is valid and consistent support for entering contractual agreements for school campus security provided by the local police agency. This places the responsibility for school security with the agency best suited to this unique and difficult task and is often a much more efficient and less costly service when provided by the local police department, especially when the specialized training and equipment needed to offer this service are considered.

■ OTHER AUXILIARY SERVICES

Among other auxiliary services are the community use of school facilities, sale of specialized services, and sale of excess property and materials. The first of these, community use of school facilities, is probably an auxiliary service in the purest sense of the term. The others could be considered quasi-auxiliary in nature.

Community Use of School Facilities

Board of education policy must explicate the district's approach to community use of school facilities. Typically, a fee schedule is developed by the business office for implementation. Fees are predicated on several factors, among them the type of group needing the activity, the type of activity planned, whether there is a profit motive involved, out-of-pocket expenses for personnel and utilities, and the definition of a school-related group.

Usually, school-related groups are not charged a fee, but, in some instances, are expected to cover the out-of-pocket expenses for utilities, cleaning, security, and so forth.

School-related groups such as booster clubs, PTA, and such fall into the category of school organizations and are generally welcome to use facilities as the need arises. Other community groups are generally charged a usage fee depending on the plan for use of the facility. For example, a service club using a room for meeting purposes would be charged less than a private organization using an auditorium to present a program from which a profit is expected.

Other factors that determine the fee include whether security is needed and the size and type of the facility. School board policy usually dictates the need for security, providing parameters for how much security is needed based upon type of event and the number of expected attendees. In setting a usage fee for special facilities such as swimming pools, gymnasiums, auditoriums, and cafeterias, one must consider the equipment and potential for damage. Some school districts require a bond to cover breakage as part of board policy.

Generally, community groups are encouraged to utilize facilities to the maximum, and fees are kept at the lowest level possible. Because schools are public facilities and because citizens of a community are the people who pay for schools through the property tax, every effort should be extended to encourage community use of schools.

Priorities for facility use must be established, with definite guidelines to be used in scheduling. School groups have top priority. After this come community groups, and, finally, private parties. Scheduling is always a difficult task, and if there are no policy guidelines, the process becomes very cumbersome and confused. Policies must be clear, concise, and definitive as to processes used.

Sale of School Services

Many school systems enter into contractual arrangements with other districts and other agencies for the provision of specific and specialized services. These can range from special programs, such as special education and vocational education, to data-processing services to evaluation services to other activities, such as tax appraisal. Obviously, such interagency and multi-school district cooperation leads to more efficient use of scarce resources and provides an opportunity to share in the cost of highly specialized and expensive activities. It also enables the service costs to be spread over a wider area and extends sophisticated activities to more users of the particular services.[1]

Summary

Auxiliary services are important to the success of the school system. While they are not directly involved in the teaching-learning process, their absence makes the educational process very difficult, if not impossible. Auxiliary services are part of the board's scope of activities grouped under non-instructional services, without which the school system cannot exist. These services provide support to the instructional program in order to make possible the most effective delivery of instruction to student.

The presence of auxiliary services proceeding unobtrusively and unnoticed is probably an indication of the service being most effective and appropriate. As the directing force behind all non-instructional services, the business office can take great pride in the ongoing and important role auxiliary services play in the total operation of the school system.

The three auxiliary service divisions most commonly under the direction of the business administrator include transportation, food services, and security. Each of these divisions involves specialized activities requiring talented and highly trained personnel. The staffs of the three divisions must not only possess abilities in the specialized activities involved (e.g., vehicular or food service), but also need to have added talents and strengths in working with children. It is therefore very important that ongoing staff development programs be provided in each of these areas. Success in each of these areas rests on the development of adequate policies that lead to rules, regulations, and procedures governing the daily activities of the three divisions. Supervision and administration of transportation, food service, and security often require specialized personnel and are considered full-time activities.

The school business administrator must adequately and carefully plan for auxiliary services. This includes a need to recruit well-trained supervisory personnel for the routine operating tasks involved, because each of the services described is a highly specialized, demanding activity. As the chief business planner, the school business administrator must have a working knowledge of each service, but cannot hope to assume the actual operating responsibility of such diverse activities.

Discussion Questions

1. Design a pupil transportation survey in a school having such a program. Try to find out such information as number of pupils transported, number of pupil-miles traveled per day, number of miles traveled by each bus, the amount of driving time each day, and so forth.
2. Determine the state requirements regarding pupil transportation for your school system. To what extent are these requirements exceeded by local policy enacted by your school system?
3. Develop a plan for food services to meet the needs of your school system. Incorporate regional and/or ethnic needs that must be reflected in order to make the program successful. What considerations will you give to healthy choices?
4. Identify the most severe security problems facing your school system. Develop a positive response to each of them.

Web Resources

National Association of State Board of Education Healthy Schools displays state-by-state school food services/school food environment policies—
http://www.nasbe.org/HealthySchools/States/Topics.asp?Category=C&Topic=1

School Bus Information Council—
http://www.schoolbusinfo.org/index.html

Note

1. As an example, one district known to the authors provides data-processing services to eighty school systems in a region of the state. This enables the operation of a most sophisticated data-processing system with modern hardware and the capacity to develop software, as users request, yet provides the service at a modest per-pupil expenditure because the costs are distributed over such a broad base.

CHAPTER EIGHTEEN

Managing Information

■ INTRODUCTION

Data and information continue to proliferate at a daunting rate that makes both their management and use difficult. However, a school business official cannot run away from this modern phenomenon; it will not go away. The challenge is to reduce vast quantities of data and continually evaluate volumes of information in order to facilitate critical decisions of continuing concern to all administrators and certainly to school business administrators.

LEARNING OBJECTIVES

In this chapter a reader will learn about:

- Defining data and distinguishing data and information.
- Information system language.
- Business officials' roles in information management.
- Computers and data.
- Systems concepts applied to computing.
- Networking, Internet, e-mail, electronic bulletin boards, weblogs, and chat rooms.
- Computer system selection, management, and security.

Data refers to facts and figures—about people, things, ideas, and events. Information is the result of processing data in ways that make the underlying trends and conditions useful to people. Computers are, of course, the machines that power data to produce information. A data-based information management system is a computer-based information system for the storage and retrieval of data (Shelly, Cashman, Gunter, & Gunter, 2005).

Specifically, a database is a collection of data files tied together by keys or identifying names. This eliminates the need to store redundant data in several files or sets. Data sets represent an organized collection of data items. Reduced enrollments and shrinking funds in a period of decline increase the importance of managerial decisions and the data on which they are based.

When little up-to-date data or information was available, decisions were based on experience, intuition, or some other less-than-exact system. Today, decision makers are inundated with data. Computer printouts, graphs, charts, cost projections, demographic profiles, and columns of governmental and private statistics are available for minimal cost. The problem then becomes one of managing these vast resources of data and information.

In the News

Just as workers in the nation have Social Security numbers, students in many states have individual statewide student ID numbers that can be used to track them and possibly identify their academic needs. Florida has, for about two decades, used a special number that follows a student through school and into the work force. But Pennsylvania long has been reluctant to keep information on individual students at the state level. Even the individual results of reading and math tests are off limits to the state. They are held by the contractor, who scores the exams, and then sent to the local school districts.

Now, Pennsylvania officials are talking about the idea of a state student identification number as well as other ways to improve the quality of school data. The pressure comes from the federal No Child Left Behind Act, which requires the state to keep track of how students are doing. Getting the data right is important because if students aren't doing well enough, schools face sanctions under the act. And it's harder to target help if it's uncertain which student needs what.

"Without student ID numbers," said Michael Golden, the state's deputy secretary for information and educational technology, "we're at a disadvantage to be able to create the resources and tools and to consolidate the information about students to help them reach proficiency." For example, one student could be counted in more than one

place without an ID. "To us, it's not important who that person is. To us, it's just important to understand there is a person and these characteristics, and we need to help that student achieve," Golden said.

Deborah Newby, director for data quality for the Council of Chief State School Officers, said student ID numbers are becoming a necessity, adding that most states have them.

"What's driving it all is instructional improvement," she said. "The more you can zero in on student needs, student performance, and connect it with different aspects, you can start identifying how to improve instruction." With specific information, she said, "it will make their data systems far more powerful in producing reports not only to satisfy federal and state reporting requirements but to look at instruction."

She said some have concerns about privacy, but "there are methods that states can use to prevent access to the records, to mask the IDs in such a way it would be difficult for somebody to get into a system and identify student-specific information." She said the systems needed in each state vary, depending in part on how the current systems of data collection are set up. "It's not a cookie-cutter solution. That means it's not a cheap thing to do," Newby said. "Some states might say we did it for just under $1 million. Others say it takes us $10 million to do it." Aside from the lack of student ID numbers, Pennsylvania has other problems which hamper its ability to use data effectively to help students. The state Department of Education requires each school district to file more than 150 reports to more than a dozen sub-agencies each year, according to Ken Sochats, director of the Visual Information Systems Center at the University of Pittsburgh.

Yet those reports often ask the same questions, such as race, but use different definitions and codes for those same questions on different reports, he said. Sochats estimated as much as 75 percent of the information on the reports is repetitive. Even something as simple as gender may be coded as x or y; male or female; M or F; 1 or 2; 0 or 1; or plus or minus. The result is a bunch of reports that are time-consuming for school employees to fill out and quite difficult to compare so that information helpful to students can be gleaned.

The center at Pitt is working to improve the quality of data through Project VIPER—Visualizing Information for Pittsburgh Public Schools Evaluation

and Research. With help from both the district and the state Department of Education, the center, which has already produced an atlas of city schools, is working on ways to streamline reports school districts are required to file. The first step is to figure out what is in each report, what the definitions are for each item and how the reports are the same or different.

The center later will develop tools for reaching into the data to get information needed for educational strategies. Such tools, for example, may be able to identify students who are doing well but haven't been tested for the gifted program. "We're trying to make sure all of our data is comparable and forms a good basis for making decisions," said Sochats.

From: Chute, E. (2004, September 8). ID numbers considered for students; streamlining data collection to pinpoint instructional shortfalls. *Pittsburgh Post-Gazette*, p. A-12. Copyright 2004 P.G. Publishing Co. *Pittsburgh Post-Gazette* (Pennsylvania).

■ THE LANGUAGE OF INFORMATION SYSTEMS

One of the key elements of an information network is the ability of varied audiences within the system to utilize the database and retrieve the information needed to perform the tasks desired. The search strategy used by a system developer has major impact on the usability of the system.

A vital concern of any information system designer is how to employ the words and phrases of individual users while maintaining the general nature of a system that may be used by many people. The use of key-word searches or table look-up information may be useful ideas for consideration. For example, the school business administrator's need in the area of budgeting and accounting requires use of specified terms and parameters that will influence the way the system is built and accessed. The user must recognize the special needs required in construction of the system to accommodate multiple users, but the system designer needs to provide a "user-friendly" scheme for each user.

All information system applications should be accompanied by thorough, well-written, easily understood documentation. The three general types of documentation include tutorials, user's manuals, and reference manuals. Tutorials lead the new user through examples of the program's capabilities and usually involve demonstration programs. A user's manual documents the system's features and functions in a systematic and comprehensive manner. The reference manual provides in-depth, technical descriptions of the program's capabilities and functions.

Users also need procedures for an operation's activities. These concern the use and maintenance of system components, including the installation of hardware, installation of programs and data files, and instructions for performing basic equipment maintenance. Procedures should also describe how to manage data files and how to maintain security of the system.

▌ THE CONCEPT OF SYSTEMS

Effey Oz, in a book entitled *Management Information Systems*, states: "Managers and other professionals plan, control, and make decisions. As long as an information system supports one or more of these activities, it may be referred to as a management information system (MIS)." Clearly, the key to the effectiveness of an information system context for the school business administrator is the manner in which usage occurs. Educational professionals generally use three levels of data analysis: the individual; the group, school, or school site; and the total organization.

The school business administrator is a key individual in the MIS context of a school district or system. School business administrator usage is related to departments or groups throughout the district, including instructional personnel, all support departments, and units such as the superintendent's office or the board. Responsibilities to the total organization—from parents and pupils to board members and fiscal and political support groups—affect the MIS context for the school business administrator. Planning, organizing, and controlling within the MIS context are the driving forces for the school business administrator. The integration of the three elements of individual, group, and total usage into the MIS context is a likely determinant of the school business administrator's success.

To manage the use of information (i.e., knowledge coming from data) through the structure of the system (a group of components, individuals, or the total system) is the major role of the school business administrator.

All facets of information—accuracy, timeliness, and pertinence—are moot if the system structure for management is not in place and utilized. A system's being in place is not sufficient. The system must be used, reviewed, and modified as needed. The school business administrator, in the role of supporting the key instructional goals of the system, must utilize information in its upward and downward flow for the success of various groups and the total system.

A good information system strategy for many school business administrators collaborating with superintendents, other key central office administrators, as well as site-based administrators is stated in these objectives:

- Bring all users to required information.
- Overcome and manage the burdens of information requests on both central administration and school-site personnel.
- Provide faster, better, cost-effective technologies to serve all users.
- Be alert to rapidly changing needs.

Clearly, the central administration of a school system is concerned with the management of its resources. This umbrella concept of management includes both a process and people to implement that process. Generally, a plan for management must first be established. Then, a structure through which implementation can occur must be developed. Staff must be selected and resources allocated. Finally, overall direction and control must be established. Site-based administrators are vitally concerned with the successful implementation of a data-based management system. The need for local data is of primary importance at each building.

The business functions of a complex organization such as a school system are an integral part of a data-based management system. The capability to store and retrieve data on a variety of personnel, facility, equipment, and supply expenditures is essential to efficient and effective budget planning. Raw data and derived elements produced over a five-year period (ranging from individual salary figures to total costs for glass replacement) allow decisions to be based on hard information.

Even the smallest school district can have access to some type of computer system. Several manufacturers provide electronic equipment with monthly rental prices that fit within the budgets of any school district. Additionally, manufacturers, data-processing or leasing companies, and software houses have developed remote data-processing capabilities to such a degree that they are available for relatively small monthly expenditures. The introduction of low-cost personal computers, or PCs as they are often called, has added yet another dimension to data processing. Development activities are continuing at a rapid rate in all areas of computing.

Emergence of extensive competition is reducing the total cost for many facets of computer systems. Hardware costs are lower each year and performance continues to increase. Software development has proceeded at a rapid rate. Generally, software for any business or administrative function is available from a large number of sources. Hardware manufacturers, user groups, and software houses all provide programs for specific machines. Costs range from zero to hundreds of thousands of dollars.

Clearly, the amount of hardware available determines appropriate applications and thus software selection. These considerations are discussed in a later section. Thus, the relationship between a data-based management system and business functions allows raw data gathered from multiple sources to provide meaningful information to a wide variety of users. This information is then available to be used in making decisions on significant issues.

The need to receive and transmit data to state and regional offices has also grown rapidly in the last few years. Finally, some data are being transferred electronically from agencies such as the U.S. Department of Education and downloaded to local sites as appropriate. One note is the rapid increase of such delivery systems as e-mail and websites for communications. These types of communication dramatically reduce the time for response and make information available to large numbers of people at the same time.

Failure Recovery

All information systems fail at one time or another, and components likewise can fail. The hardware can malfunction, programs can have errors, data can be lost, procedures can be misunderstood and misapplied, and people can make mistakes. The time to consider such possibilities is before the failure. Users must know what to do when the system fails and how to proceed when the system is restarted.

First, users must know how to detect that a failure has occurred and know what is normal and abnormal behavior for the system. When a failure does occur, users need to know how to bring their activity to a halt. Then, users need instructions stipulating how to proceed. This may involve calling for assistance or initiating file recovery for themselves. Secondly, users need to know how to proceed to identify and fix the problem. Furthermore, users need to know the possible costs in terms of time and money for each response.

Even when their systems are performing well, users should anticipate failure. Periodic backup of the data needs to be made. Additionally, some form of the workload processed since the backup must be kept so that during recovery the files can be restored from the backup data. Procedures must exist not only for making the backup copies, but also for executing the recovery. During a failure, time is the most critical factor.

■ SCOPE OF INFORMATION FLOW RELATED TO DATA-BASED MANAGEMENT: MIS CONCEPTS

A *MIS* is generally defined as a computer-based system that provides management with useful information for decision making within an appropriate time frame. The MIS should process day-to-day business, personnel, and educational data generated by the system in an effective and efficient manner. A MIS generally provides regular reports of school issues (e.g., payrolls), special reports (e.g., number of teachers certified in Spanish), and summary reports (e.g., pupil population projections). These reports need to be timely, relevant, and complete. To be effective, a MIS must operate from a sound database. The selection of database items (e.g., age, race, certification, immunization records) is the key to report production. Accurate information cannot be derived from incomplete or inaccurate data.

The means of collecting data are as varied as their applications. One of the concerns facing school business administrators is the type of collection procedures to use. The options vary from the traditional written report that must be keyed into a system to direct terminal input at remote sites. Grade sheets and student tests can easily be scored by high-speed equipment such as optical character recognition (OCR) machines and many times online data forms can be used for data transmission. The less often data have to be transmitted through a human interface, the less often a human has to input data into a system, the more accurate data are likely to be.

Because data are the raw materials used in decision making, the determination of hardware and software to be used in processing is of major importance to the school system. Communication links with the ability to "talk" from one terminal to another are another feature of current computer systems.

As site-based management becomes more widespread, the need for an effective MIS becomes paramount for building-level administrators and school business administrators. As noted in other chapters, the necessity of maintaining relationships between centralized management functions and site-based management functions becomes critical for the day-to-day operations of an instructional program. The periodic reports necessary at both levels require access to data and adequate processing capabilities. Purchasing, inventory control, and personnel records represent some areas where a MIS would be of major importance. Since selected items are purchased at the user site and others are purchased at the system level, an automated inventory and accounting control makes purchase, warehousing, and payment decisions easier and more accurate. The merging of accounts administered at the system level and those administered at the site level is accomplished more easily and with a greater degree of accuracy through up-to-date, correct data from a MIS.

Because school business administrators—as well as all other system and site-based administrators—are users of information and database services, "linkage" among these users and access to the various data sources become critical. As is noted in the section on types of hardware, the ability for local sites and the central office to be connected through the use of a terminal or personal computer (PC) is a simple, relatively inexpensive operation with currently available hardware.

The ability to access database information dealing with fiscal and instructional applications allows rapid, accurate flow of vital information for decision making and the sharing of alternative planning strategies. When all involved parties are working from the latest set of information, the possibility of error and miscommunication is reduced. By having online presentations and interactions, proposal modifications can be tested, evaluated, and then either integrated or discarded as the result dictates.

Linkages also facilitate reciprocal flows of information and directories from the central office to local sites and from local sites to the central office. Additionally, school-to-school linkage permits the productive flow of student records and appropriate faculty and staff records information.

Networks

Local administrators are able to access database information dealing with fiscal and instructional applications, so decision making is improved and a number of key people can share in planning. Involvement of multiple parties working with the latest set of information avoids the possibility of error and miscommunication. For example, interested parties can develop proposals online with a round of electronic reviews; proposal modifications can be tested, evaluated, and then either integrated or discarded as the situation dictates. Additionally, curricular information and software exchanges can be made using network capabilities.

There are two categories of networks—local area networks (LANs) and wide area networks (WANs). These are generic terms referring to two basic types of networks. A LAN is a system of computers and associated peripherals such as printers that are physically connected by cable within a limited geographical area—often in a single building or general area. LANs use fiber optics or coaxial cable to connect computers, and each computer must have special communications software installed on a hard disk. Software has been developed that allows PCs to coexist and exchange data on the same LAN. A LAN system can consist of a few computers or as many as fifty. LANs are often used in computer laboratories or to connect the principal's office with the bookkeeper's office and the food service office within a school building.

WANs connect computers in separate geographical areas, using telecommunications methodologies such as telephone and satellite transmission. The Internet is an example of a WAN system. An example of how a school district might use a WAN is to distribute educational computer programs on demand from a state agency to local school districts, or to file reports originating at local sites on a central state computer. WANs can be used to record instruction taking place in one facility and beam it by satellite to other facilities.

A dedicated computer, called a file server, manages many networks. This network design is referred to as a centralized network. A file server has a large-capacity hard disk and special software that manages access to files on the network. It controls the sharing of data and databases among users on the network, and controls how users access master copies of data and applications software on the centralized hard disk. The file server makes sure that two users do not accidentally try to update a file at the same time and thus scramble the data. The file server may also manage access to a piece of hardware, such as a laser printer; set up a queue (list) of jobs waiting to be printed when more than one user sends files to the printer at the same time, and can be programmed to give priority to certain tasks or jobs.

When a file server is used on a LAN, large databases are stored on the server, and users may store all of their work files there as well. This operation is analogous to someone manually collecting all the data each day, placing it in a file drawer, and then redistributing these data to the workers as needed. A centralized file server is the most common network design.

An alternative to a centralized network is the distributed network. In this design, data are stored on individual micros, but data files can be shipped around the network so that other users can review them, update the data, or use the data in other documents or applications. Distributed networks allow PCs more autonomy, but there may be less control over access to data.

The Internet

The Internet is a "network of networks" that connects computers across the world into one gigantic global communications system that allows all the computers on the Internet to share and exchange data. In computer-speak, the Internet is a wide area network (WAN) composed of many LANs. A LAN is simply two or more computers wired together so that each can communicate and share information with the other. Think of a computer on a LAN as a house with telephone service. A WAN, therefore, is a network of networks. Table 18.1 compares LANs and WANs.

Table 18.1 Comparison of LANs and WANs

	Local Area Networks (LANs)	Wide Area Networks (WANs)
Common connection types	Ethernet, Token Ring, FDDI	Leased lines, serial links, ISDN, X.25
Advantage	Speed	Distance
Cost center	Dense installation (about one interface per room)	Length of long-haul lines (about one interface per 100 miles)
Current speed	10–100 Mbps (mostly 10 Mbps)	0.01–45 Mbps (mostly clustered around 1 Mbps)
Common uses	File sharing	E-mail and file transfer (including Web)
Common problems	Cable disruption by users	Cable disruption by backhoes
Conceptually	A bunch of lines hooking users together	A bunch of lines hooking cities together

Created in 1969 by the U.S. Department of Defense, the Internet (or ARPAnet, as it was then called) was designed to link a number of military sites to form a research network. However, computer networks at that time were rudimentary; that is, if one link or computer failed, the entire network might collapse. The military needed a "bombproof" network that could still function even if parts of it failed. In order to accomplish this, a computer on the ARPAnet had multiple connection paths to the other computers on the network so that even if one (or several) of these paths was not working, another one could be used.

The unfortunate reality is that nothing as powerful as telecommunications can exist without unique problems. Although the problems, dangers, and concerns are not sufficient to abandon the use of this powerful tool, the educational community must explicitly address these issues, and districts have the obligation to ensure that these new tools and methods are actually a step forward. One controversial issue in telecommunications (among many) is the accessibility of pornography. Pornography exists in the culture and also exists as an electronic representation of that culture. The reasons that pornography is available through telecommunications are the same as those that allow its availability in other media.

When classrooms are opened to the world, which is the appeal of telecommunications, they are opened to both the good and the bad. Controlling what children read, view, and hear through telecommunications is much the same as controlling their interaction with the print environments—by monitoring what children are doing. Legal implications are a continuing concern of the school business administrator and other school personnel (Lockard & Abrams, 2004).

E-mail and Instant Messaging

E-mail and instant messaging are the most important applications for networks in allowing communication between computer users. E-mail allows users electronically to transmit and receive messages, text, or data. E-mail functions rather like a mailbox: users can send messages whether or not the intended receiver is currently on the network, and the message is stored along with a signal for the receiver that indicates that there is a message waiting. These electronic communication systems are said to be asynchronic, meaning that a sender and receiver need not simultaneously be engaged.

The network software can detect whether the receiver is present when the message is sent, and, if so, whether the receiver is willing to accept a message at that time. For example, a user who is working on a report to be presented at the school board meeting that night may not want to be interrupted. The network sends messages to the correct user, manages transmission at the appropriate time, checks and corrects for transmission errors such as garbled or incomplete messages, and stores messages for people who are not currently online.

E-mail has replaced the telephone for many messages. Users can respond when it is convenient, without being interrupted, and can get their messages either on-screen or in printed form. Without the need for personal conversations, the "telephone tag game" is bypassed. Messages can be sent when it is convenient, received when available, electronically filed, or responded to with annotations and distributed to names on a previously created mailing list.

A note of caution is in order, however: Others can read e-mail because unauthorized users often can discover passwords.

Electronic Bulletin Boards, Discussion Boards, and Weblogs

Electronic bulletin boards, discussion rooms, and weblogs (usually shortened to *blogs*) are other interesting applications for networks. These allow users to post and retrieve messages that are not directed to a specific user, much like announcements that are posted on an office bulletin board. These communication forums are used on PCs that have access to the Internet. An example of a discussion board is the Association of School Business Officials International's *Academic Efficiency Web Forum*.[1]

Organized by topic, electronic bulletin boards and discussion boards can be structured vertically (one subject) or horizontally (a broad range of applications). Discussion boards, chat rooms, or e-rooms are generally used to conduct online, real-time discussions whereas bulletin boards are used more for information posting.

A weblog is a website that consists of dated entries presented in reverse chronological order so that the most recent entry appears first. Weblogs take three common forms: (1) personal blogs are usually the work of one person writing about personal views; (2) internal organizational blogs are used by groups, such as teachers in a school, to communicate internally; and (3) commercial blogs are used by businesses or organizations as a marketing tool. The National School Board Association's *Boardbuzz* is an example of a blog provided by a professional organization (Brooks-Young, 2006, p. 67).

E-Rate Subsidy[2]

According to the National Education Association's (NEA) Center for Education Technology, young people without adequate computer literacy, including fluency in Internet and World Wide Web navigation skills, will be unlikely to function as competent employees in the workforce. The Telecommunications Act of 1996 calls for schools and libraries to receive discounted access—known as the e-rate—to the Internet and to a wide range of telecommunications services and internal connections.

Thousands of schools and libraries have submitted applications for e-rate discounts. Technology is now the real environment shaper of school design. Students can have around-the-clock access to instantaneous information. They can stay in touch, stay connected, and research any topic they wish at their own pace. However, as mainstream as computer technology may seem, it is out of reach to students without power and data access. Convenient and safe plug-in ability, safe and neat wire management systems, flexible and comfortable tables, desks, and seating, as well as durable and versatile components, can make all the difference to computer-literate students. Educational facilities that do not recognize the importance of such key design issues will be left behind.

A technology plan must be developed to ensure that a school has the ability to use the services once they are purchased. Technology plans should specify how schools plan to integrate use of these technologies into their curricula and programs. Once requests for services have been developed, they must be posted to make the information available to potential service providers. The long-term impact of this is difficult to judge, but the school business official and other district administrators need to follow these developments carefully.

In the News

Twitchy-thumbed school leaders have a new reason to like the federal E-rate program: It will now help support their BlackBerry habit. The Federal Communications Commission has cleared the way to allow money from the $2.25 billion program of subsidies for school technology to apply to e-mail service for mobile, wireless devices, such as the BlackBerry, which are increasingly popular among administrators for keeping tabs on their schools while on the go.

School users of wireless e-mail services on Palm TREOs and other mobile devices, including some cellphones, will also benefit from the FCC'S recent changes to its "eligible-services list" for the E-rate, which the commission approved and posted in October.

In another significant change, the FCC for the first time made Internet-based voice services that use school broadband networks and connect to regular telephone networks eligible for funding under the E-rate. Those services, known as interconnected Voice over Internet Protocol, or VoIP, and offered by providers such as Vonage and Skype, are cheaper and offer more features than regular phone service, school officials say. Just last month, the 437,000-student Chicago school system announced that it was switching its entire phone system—24,000 phones in all—to VoIP.

E-rate discounts will make the wireless e-mail and interconnected VoIP services even cheaper. The decade-old federal program collects fees paid by telephone customers into a universal-service fund that covers from 20 percent to 90 percent of the cost of eligible school telecommunications services, depending on the poverty level of the district's students.

The discounts are available to all school districts that make valid applica-

tions. Other services financed by the E-rate program, such as the wiring of classrooms, are generally available only for the poorest districts.

The E-rate—short for education rate—generally supports direct classroom learning, such as by providing access to the Web for classroom computers. It also supports certain expenditures designed to benefit districts as a whole, such as telephone service. But by funding the e-mail service that underlies the BlackBerry—or, say, the Palm TREO—the E-rate is now helping pay for something administrators can get their own hands, or thumbs, on.

"All our administrators use BlackBerrys," said Frank R. Buck, the curriculum and special education supervisor for the Talladega, Ala., city school district. He said that last year the 2,700-student district bought BlackBerry devices for principals and assistant principals at each of its seven schools, as well as for five district administrators. Their model, he said, has a built-in cellphone, a walkie-talkie feature, "push e-mail," and capabilities that include an electronic calendar and storage of "all kinds of reference material." The district has received E-rate discounts covering about 80 percent of the devices' cellphone service.

Sorting out eligible from ineligible services and equipment is part of the complicated process of applying for E-rate discounts. Originally, the discounts under the program were supposed to go only for educational purposes. Yet as telecommunications services have become more mobile, the distinction between educational and other uses has been harder to make. And the FCC has recognized that school administrative functions have an educational impact.

As a sign of growing interest in the technology, the Mitel Networks Corp. announced an agreement early this month with the Chicago school system to deploy an interconnected VoIP system throughout the district's 700 schools and administrative buildings over the next four years. The $28 million cost will be funded in part by the E-rate program's support for internal wiring. Under the eligible services list, the district will be able to apply for discounts on the service costs as well.

Robert W. Runcie, the chief information officer of the 437,000-student school system, said in a statement that the VoIP system would allow the district "to reduce our operating costs and improve safety." It is unclear whether such claims will defuse the critics of the E-rate program, who for years have argued that the subsidies encourage school districts to purchase telecommunications services that they don't need and to be heedless of waste and fraud that have afflicted the program.

From: Trotter, A. (2006, November 15). E-rate to support wireless e-mail, Internet calling. *Education Week*, 26(12), 1–2.

▪ UNIQUE ROLE OF THE BUSINESS ADMINISTRATOR

The school business administrator has a unique role in hardware and software selection and use. This person will be involved in the bid process and in evaluation of specifications and proposals from vendors. School business administrators must understand the concept of MIS/data flow and its relation to decision making.

The results of the 2004 *Digital Leadership Divide* survey[3] of 455 school district decision makers for technology reveal important considerations for school business administrators:

- Forty-five percent of all school leaders surveyed cited planning and budgeting as the key challenges to the effective use of technology.
- Sixty-six percent of surveyed districts do not consider or use return-on-investment (ROI) calculations when they buy or evaluate technology.
- Fifty percent of school leaders cite lack of training as the most serious barrier to more effective data-driven decision making.
- School leaders identify a multitude of other barriers to data-driven decision making, including:
  - Incompatibility of computer systems (42 percent).
  - Lack of data collection priorities (36 percent).
  - Lack of uniformity in data collections (35 percent).

Although school business administrators may or may not be directly responsible for management information systems, they have an influential role in district technology decisions via the budgeting, planning, data collection, and professional development processes. The long-range potential and the current concerns of managing information in a cost-effective manner are real considerations of the school business administrator.

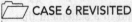

CASE 6 REVISITED

Determining What a District Continually Needs to Know about Itself

Chief business officer Hilao Bama faced the daunting task of completely overhauling and upgrading the district's data system. As you read through this chapter, devise a plan for tackling this challenge. Provide details in regard to how the plan should be implemented and evaluated. Give consideration to issues such as how will the data needs of personnel be determined? Where will the data system be housed? How will the budget be determined? and so on.

How technology will be used and how much of the budget will be dedicated to technology and management information systems are administrative decisions linked to the long-range goals of the district. Each school system has goals that dictate how and to what extent computer technology will be applied. Examples of goals that affect computer implementation are those that set standards for the cost-effectiveness of the school's operation, the teacher/student ratio, and the curriculum content itself. These system and site goals should be articulated and regularly reviewed by local faculty, central office administrators, parents, and board members.

These goals may be said to fall into two categories: those that relate to school administration and those that define the instructional programs. Educational computer applications likewise fall into those two categories, and each school's computer applications should be designed to meet system and local goals for administration and instruction.

Administrative goals are concerned with the operation and staffing of the school district and local sites. These range from broad-based, system-oriented goals for administrative excellence to site-based goals for implementing programs and utilizing staff and resources. Instructional goals are concerned with implementing a quality instructional program and utilizing the instructional talents of faculty. A school business official has major input into both administrative and instructional goals.

Although not the responsibility of each business official, an effective school administrator, business official, superintendent, or site manager should be able to:

- Select hardware or software for administrative applications.
- Develop plans for computer facilities for a site and the district.
- Develop a plan for teacher, staff, and administrator computer training.
- Describe how existing administrative applications could be improved.
- Conduct a feasibility study of a specific administrative application at a school site or district level.
- Evaluate multiple software sources for a specific application.
- Develop a network plan describing how computer equipment and databases could be shared.
- Write a proposal for funding of administrative or instructional applications.

With flexibility, speed, and low cost as advantages, computer use will enhance the decision-making potential of all administrations. The amount of information that needs to be managed at a school site and within a school system has grown tremendously. Decisions regarding the utilization of staff and faculty, of physical plants, and of fiscal resources are a constant concern.

 CASE 5 REVISITED

Overcoming Fiscal Failures and Facing Future Challenges

Business manager of North Harbor, Howard Tremble, is tasked with addressing the three scandals for which the Board failed to take responsibility: overstatement of district usage of buses, inaccurate attendance figures, and discarded classroom books from a warehouse. Reflect on how Tremble could use a management information system to resolve these scandals. In addition, how can the use of technology and data facilitate parental involvement at North Harbor?

■ EFFECT ON STAFF, ADMINISTRATORS, AND FACULTY

While there is a clear need for business officials and site-based administrators to make use of the computing power that is available to them, a word of caution is in order. If acquisition and implementation of computer systems are not carefully planned, the system may not successfully meet the goals it was designed to support. Here are five examples of common administrative planning oversights that create unnecessary problems after the system is in place:

1. Planners fail to include staff and community representatives in decision making.
2. System components are purchased independently, without regard to system integration.
3. Purchase decisions are made without a complete understanding of hardware and software capabilities.
4. Administrators fail to design an implementation plan that takes all user groups and needed results into account.
5. There is no plan to train or acquire computer-literate personnel.

The training and education of administrators, faculty, and staff designated to work with this new technology are major considerations in planning for computer acquisition and use. It is the responsibility of administrators to ensure that school personnel are adequately trained to carry out assignments involving use of computers. The kind of training required differs among three district personnel groups: faculty members who teach computing courses, faculty members who use computers in classroom instruction and administration, and noncertificated staff members who use computers to support administrative and instructional goals.

The average school system has numerous computers in the central office, at each school site, and in the homes of most of the administrators and teachers. Data are routinely transferred from school to school and from school to central office site. The school business official depends on computer systems to address much of the day-to-day work of the office. Budget projections, risk management and insurance data, and school bus routes are processed or run each day. Personnel files are available on disk or can be accessed from online computer files in a routine manner.

Clearly, the business of school business administration has changed. The role of computers is well defined and growing in both the administrative realm and the instructional realm. New applications and demands of the system come up each day. Teachers want more computers and more software to use on them. The building maintenance and operations staffs require additional funds to update building codes for electrical needs and to rewire and evaluate the lighting in some structures to accommodate the increased use of electronic elements.

The downside effect on staff has been reduced from previous times because the computer is such a ubiquitous part of the daily work of most teachers, and all administrators— both central office and site based. Most systems and many schools have a technology coordinator and access to the needed expertise from the state department or other educational organizations.

Effect on Administrators

Conflicts may arise within the central office when a central data-processing facility is established in a school district. Inadequate thought is often given to the placement of the data-processing center, which, in turn, leads to future problems. The fact that a data-processing facility is to serve the entire school system is often overlooked at installation time. The school business administrator should advocate placement within the district where the computer can serve all areas of the program. Two possible top-level organizational schemes are shown in Figure 18.1 and Figure 18.2.

The use of microcomputers at a local school site will have a limited effect on a large central facility's operation. However, as remote processing and the use of remote terminal input increase, the use and control of the main computer might become a shared problem. This problem centers on the distribution of resources necessary to serve all possible users effectively. It is at this point that scheduling and prioritization of job selection become major concerns.

Either of the organizational patterns shown in Figures 18.1 and 18.2 allows the flexibility necessary to provide service to all areas of a school district with a minimum of conflict among departments concerning control and allocation of funds. Both types of organization provide a structure for distribution to the proper location within the

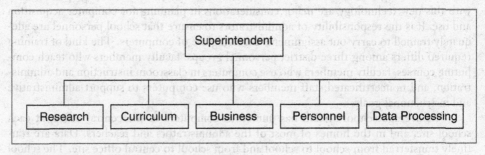

FIGURE 18.1 Organizational Scheme I

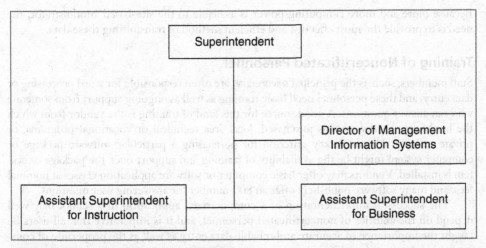

FIGURE 18.2 Organizational Scheme II

organization without some of the problems of clearing data sources with various groups throughout the central staff.

The need to ensure necessary information and data are available within the district cannot be overemphasized. The flow of information and data to various areas of the district is the only logical base for decision makers to use in working through key problem areas. As will be discussed later, the computer can serve as a key provider of planning information when correctly applied within any school district.

The business administrator and other key administrators within the district must consider the concepts of data processing in terms of systemwide use. A full understanding of the uses of data processing systemwide is a major step toward its proper utilization. A continual search for more and better uses of the data-processing system is an objective for all concerned. The business system must be consulted as scarce resources are allocated.

Problems associated with the placement of a computing or data-processing facility often revolve around fiscal control. It is natural to associate the control of the hardware with the area of fiscal responsibility. However, it is imperative that the tremendous resource represented by an "electronic school system" will have proper access to the hardware. It is to be expected that the school business administrator will have responsibility for the implementation of many of the general uses of the machine once it is available. In many districts, the school business administrator is the logical person to head the long-term strategic planning group for the district. If the school business administrator does not lead the group the expected practice is that he or she will participate as a key member of the committee. This committee, or one similarly constituted, must be in operation well before installation time and should continue as an integral part of the system's organization. Generally, the time frame of an academic year is best, because many nontraditional activities often occur during the summer period.

With the increasingly large emphasis on site-based management and a parallel emphasis on the usage of greater volumes of data, the school business administrator's role in management of the district's computer facilities takes on an increased degree of importance.

Because more and more computing power is available to the site-based administrator, the need is to provide the most effective and efficient method of transmitting these data.

Training of Noncertificated Personnel

Staff members, such as the principal's secretary, are often responsible for word processing or data entry, and these personnel need basic training as well as ongoing support from someone who can answer questions. A good source for this kind of training is the vendor from which the hardware or software was purchased, local area technical or vocational programs, or private training schools. A key criterion for purchasing a particular software package or computer system might be the availability of training and support once the package or system is installed. Vendors may offer basic computer or software application classes at nominal fees, and many software publishers offer an 800-number for answering user questions.

The successful implementation of a computerized application in a school may well depend on the abilities of noncertificated personnel, and it is imperative that all users be taught the importance of accurate and reliable data entry as well as the proper use of computer equipment and applications.

A well-planned staff renewal program involving all levels of staff affected by the computer will increase the acceptance of the hardware and the new staff roles. An open discussion of what the machine can and cannot do and of the important role people play in the successful use of computers is a valuable part of staff training. Another method of reducing fears is to have staff members at various levels in other districts with data-processing systems visit with the local system's personnel. These face-to-face visits will do much to dispel fears.

Discussion of data security, privacy of information, and the multitude of factors of operation and management is a key element to incorporate into staff training programs. The problem of security occurs for information produced, personnel records, and hardware. The establishment of realistic goals and objectives, built with the involvement of local personnel and consultants, will provide direction.

Proper procedures for the review and rewriting of goals and objectives, as well as for a review of the operating procedures, are vital for effective implementation of a system. The more fully staff members understand the implementation of computer systems, the more they will cooperate. The new functions required of each staff member should be thoroughly understood by all staff.

Personnel Recruitment and Selection

The recruitment of sufficient personnel for work in a data-processing system may well be an expensive and laborious task for school districts. The selection of proper staff for systems in which the need for members is small requires that the data-processing/computer staff have varied skills, including competence with hardware and the interpersonal skills to work with a wide variety of people.

The school business administrator may be charged with the initial selection and recommendation for hiring of the entire staff. This includes the operators, programmers, and management personnel necessary to develop a smooth and well-functioning organization. Again, the size of the computer center operation is crucial. In an organization serving small school systems, perhaps only one or two people are needed. In larger systems, staff needs are magnified. A small staff may need more flexibility to do more things with more people, especially in relation to contacting individuals, as opposed to those organizations in which large numbers of people can be employed and only selected professionals need to talk with other members of the school administrative and teaching staffs.

Retention of any staff member in the data-processing center should reflect the staff retention policies applicable across the entire district. While unusual hiring practices may have to be used when securing data-processing professionals, the policies for retention of these professionals should in no way violate established school board policies relative to promotion and retention of any staff member.

As with any group of employees, attention must be given to union/nonunion personnel problems. General contract situations cover most issues, but specific language may be needed to protect the sensitive records or critical operations facets of a computer center.

▌ LEGAL CONSIDERATIONS

Recordkeeping systems and their use must provide the level of security required by federal privacy laws and Freedom of Information Act requirements. Therefore, the requirements for privacy of information on disk files, hard drives, or preprinted reports is no different in structure from that used in other recordkeeping systems within the district. For example, the security necessary to determine who has access to computer files is a primary concern when persons have access to online data files or to stored files, including information on individual students. Thus, it is very important that passwording sequences, security clearances, number identifications, and the like be made a part of any system in which files are addressed through the use of terminals or accessed with programs.

The information stored in personnel files and student files must be protected in the same manner. All data of a privileged nature must be afforded the security required of a paper document and should be protected and accessible only to qualified and authorized personnel within the district and only to authorized agents outside the district. Additionally, the distribution of printed information, whether student records or personnel records, from computer files must be carefully screened and only appropriate information provided. It is imperative that the same procedures for data security be applicable for all records within the district.

Passwords

One of the most widely used and effective measures for providing computer security is passwords. A password is a secret word or number or combination of letters and numbers that must be typed in on the keyboard before the system will allow any activity to take place. What normally occurs in passwording is that the computer user or group of users having access to a particular data file (such as student test records or individual fiscal information) must provide a certain predetermined code before that file can be unlocked.

When that password is implemented, it allows access to any authorized user. Most computer systems work so that the password entered at the keyboard does not appear on the screen or on typed copy anywhere. This is to avoid unauthorized distribution of the password and to prevent any unauthorized casual observation of a particular password used by an individual. Passwords become even more effective when they are changed on a regular basis and when the individual users do not share their password with unauthorized persons. One of the problems with passwords is obvious—if a person is authorized to use the file but does not have access to the password, the file remains locked and cannot be accessed by that user.

Rules of Thumb for Safe Computing

To protect school computers from new threats, teachers and administrators need to work with information technology (IT) personnel to understand how to protect themselves with technology and common sense. The following tips provide a great deal of protection and should be considered basic rules of thumb for safe computing in the classroom and computer lab:

- When using e-mail, do not open attachments that are unexpected, even if they come from someone you know.
- Never open attachments from unknown sources.
- Run a good antivirus program and firewall at the desktop level.

IT administrators should look at and thoroughly understand the security strategies that are currently in place. Enlisting a comprehensive approach, creating a defensive barrier that comprises antivirus, content filtering, firewall, vulnerability management, and intrusion detection measures will make systems extremely difficult and costly for intruders to compromise.

■ COMPUTING AND SOFTWARE SELECTION PROCESSES

Because hardware and software selection will lead to a major expenditure, whether on a lease, purchase, or some combination plan, care must be exercised from the beginning. Appropriate persons from the central office, local building sites, the community, and other areas need to have input. This approach presents a potentially difficult situation. The committee must establish a time frame for decision making and adhere to it. "Lobbying" by staff or others for a specific brand of hardware is another potential problem. The identification of all educational needs of the district must be made prior to final selection. Appropriate funds should be budgeted for the selection process.

Need

Need for data-processing equipment should be established on a day-to-day basis, for several years in advance, and in close cooperation with representatives of all phases of the school program. The services will be offered across several, if not all, aspects of the school program—business, instruction, and research—and should involve representatives from these areas in the planning phase. As stated before, it is necessary to start planning early, and it is not unusual to plan in detail for at least three years, and in one or two five-year blocks after that. These plans provide the director of technology with current as well as long-range systemwide goals to consider.

Representatives of each of the groups should establish a hierarchical arrangement of services needed. It is to be expected that one of the functions associated with school business administration (payroll, inventory, budgeting) will be among the first identified and the first selected for implementation. Cost figures should be computed, as should time commitments and data security for each identified need. Needs cannot always be computed in cost terms, because it is not always possible to know the value of rapid turnaround of information if none has been available in the past. Detailed cost figures for machine utilization, software development, personnel expenditures, and supplies should be maintained for the various facets of the school program. Data security should receive high priority in order to maintain the privacy of the individual student and staff member and to ensure the maintenance of correct and accurate data.

Selection Factors

It is impossible to provide a formula for machine selection. The variables involved in this decision are many and complex. As has been noted previously, visits to other school districts, regional facilities, and university centers have merit. Discussion of need with data-processing consultants is another valuable source of information. Vendors' information can be used profitably when several companies offer solutions for the same problems. These solutions should be based on hardware configurations. Another source of information is the varied technical reports researched by reputable firms or national data-processing organizations. Backup provisions for hardware utilization are important for all types of data processing.

The actual selection of a computer system, time-sharing service, or service center is a laborious and time-consuming task. The discussions of core size, computer speed, cycle time, compiler languages, peripheral devices, new personnel, expensive physical facilities, and the thousands of other details that must be examined to produce the best possible recommendation for board action are complex and onerous. Decisions as to what features can be cut without hampering proposed operations are difficult to make. Service and software (program) support are especially difficult to evaluate. Some maintenance plans include a certain number of service calls, others provide for unlimited calls, and some require a fee for each call.

Costs of machines are sufficiently low enough to warrant serious consideration of initial purchase—at least for some components. The place of micros in a line purchase plan must also be considered. Lease purchase plans are still important when growth potential cannot be predicted for a five-year period. If major changes will occur in less than five years, costs of replacement may outweigh the difference in purchase versus lease arrangements.

Security

As has been noted, the computer center or data-processing center is generally under the direction of the school business administrator. Thus, the issue of computer and software security is yet another responsibility of this person.

Basic consideration for hardware security includes the physical protection of the machines and the environment in which the hardware is located. Special locks, security codes for workers, and limited access are general, well-known means of protecting computer centers. Cameras and sound monitoring may also be used. Additionally, potential losses from disasters such as fires, floods, earthquakes, and tornadoes must be considered in locating a computer center within a district and in selecting accessibility and limiting ease of ingress and egress. The installation of prior detection systems and fire extinguishing systems as well as burglar alarm systems is a must. The threat of vandalism and purposeful destruction of computer data systems must always be the concern of the school business administrator.

Software and data file protection include all of these measures, plus some special efforts. Basic features of data protection include the age-old but extremely successful practice of making backup copies of sensitive data files and archival information that is then sorted at other sites. Also, where appropriate, copies of key software should be physically secured as the hardware is protected. One of the best methods of protecting software on the local site is to make copies and locate them in fireproof containers within the building.

Physical Protection

Trainor and Krasnewick (2000) provide a list of physical controls to secure computer systems in their book, *Computers.* The suggestions are extremely useful for school business administrators to consider as they work through protection of hardware and software. The suggested physical controls to secure computer systems are:

- Outside access to computer hardware is limited.
- Equipment is physically secured to tables and floor.
- Identification numbers are on all equipment, manuals, and software.
- Physical access is provided only to authorized people.
- Computer centers are built to withstand natural disasters.
- Smoke-detection and fire-extinguishing systems that do not harm electronic equipment are installed.
- Unused storage media are placed in a secure library.
- Access to hardware is password protected. (p. 473)

Computer Viruses

While initially a problem in governmental and industrial settings, the issue of a computer virus is also a critical consideration for schools. A computer virus is really a tiny program purposefully introduced by a computer programmer (commonly called a "hacker"). A virus is a parasitic program intentionally written to enter a computer without the user's permission or knowledge. The word *parasitic* is used because a virus attaches to files or boot sectors and replicates itself, thus continuing to spread. Though some viruses do little but replicate, others can cause serious damage or affect program and system performance. A virus should never be assumed harmless and left on a system. A virus can be told to attack certain things (e.g., remove names of all teachers making $21,000 or more), modify items (e.g., add $5,000 to each salary figure), or just create a nuisance (e.g., flash a message).

School sites and school districts continue to be vulnerable. Additionally, the use of content blockers is a major issue for school facilities as they determine appropriate content for students to access. Two of the most effective measures for protecting against a virus attack continues to be: (1) a good password security system, changed often and creatively developed; and (2) antivirus software—no program finds or cures all viruses, but many can be of help to the school business administrator in the fight to maintain secure, usable files. Perhaps the most important protection against viruses is backing up files on a daily basis. Finally, remember that there is no single fix for all viruses and that constant vigilance is a key part of avoiding severe damage.

Utilization

The need to utilize properly the vast potential of the MIS is of major importance. Decisions as to what functions are to be automated, how data will be collected, how persons will obtain information, how information will be protected, and what areas have the greatest need are all part of proper utilization of the MIS. The concerns of the various publics and the real considerations of costs are important areas of attention.

■ DEVELOPMENT OF SUITABLE SOFTWARE

The previous section indicates that while there are problems with machine selection, solutions are available that will allow these problems to be attacked by the district with the likelihood of success. The larger problem for study in the area of school business administration is the acquisition of suitable software.

Strategic planning is integral to the successful operation of any school site or district. The computer is one of the key tools in providing access to large databases useful for strategic planning. The computer also allows relatively easy reduction and manipulation of these databases through simulations, graphics, and projection programs.

The simple data-processing system is a transaction-oriented system designed for the express purpose of producing reports from a set of data. These reports include the attendance, grade reporting, and general bookkeeping functions associated with the areas of school business management and student personnel work. The value of an integrated data-processing system is to go beyond these transactions, use the collected data on many facets of the school program, pose questions of a sophisticated database, and utilize these data to discover alternative courses of action.

No area of computer data-processing applications is in more flux than that of software applications packages. Thousands of software packages are available in financial planning, word processing, graphics, insurance, computer-aided instruction (CAI), and hundreds of other specialized areas. However, some few dozen have emerged as industry standards for use with each type of machine. A major problem for school business administrators and other education professionals is to realize that a distinction must be made between applications software packages that provide solutions and those that provide users with tools to solve problems. Unlike most statistical applications, most business applications are complex, without an accepted method for solution.

These procedures may even vary from building to building. Thus, the selection of an applications package may only be the beginning of work for the school business administrator. The idea of a perfect fit for specific software applications is probably a myth. Many software professionals agree that if a package does 70 to 80 percent of what is desired, it is worth serious examination.

Proper documentation of any program and training in its use is essential for error-free operation at a new site. Any modification of purchased, free, or locally developed software requires some programming staff. Even with packaged programs, many systems have specific needs that require software modification or development. These needs affect staff costs and support costs.

Hardware and Software Purchases

Common pitfalls of buying technology are likely to cause long-term problems for the school business official. Some of the most common problems include:

- Making grandiose purchases of software or hardware with no provisions for user training, maintaining the hardware, or technical support.

- Allowing software decisions to precede hardware purchases. Software should be the determining factor in purchasing technology.
- Purchasing the latest and greatest without regard for instructional need.
- Being different from everyone else, which often provides highly customized software with little or no regard for cost and long-term benefits.
- Acting on enthusiasm for doing everything at once.
- Thinking bigger and faster is better; which is not necessarily so, although it certainly is more expensive.
- Becoming dependent on a single brand or single vendor.
- Planning inadequately for backup procedures for important data; not providing network and physical security, and not planning for recovery in the event of a disaster.
- Feuding among teachers, administrators, tech coordinators, and even parents over the direction of technology efforts. (Painter, 2002)

Standardization and Maintenance Procedures

Schools and school districts should, if at all possible, avoid applications software that is proprietary in nature. Using software that can run only on one company's system can restrict options and access to resources and lead to higher costs. Software vendors using open system technology in order to reach the greatest number of prospective clients are conducting development.

Single-shot, special-purpose programs should be avoided if at all possible. This approach tends to be wasteful of scarce resources and produces a type of unstructured working environment not conducive to efficient operation. The areas where this general rule may not hold are in the activities of research and instruction sections. The needs for processing in these two areas are variable, and, on occasion, require special applications.

Software formats should be standardized across all units of a district. For example, if a reporting format for costs in transportation can be used by food services, the costs of software development and maintenance can be kept to a minimum. Reporting formats should be standardized where possible and used on both output and input documents.

Some printed reports can become "turnaround" documents for divisions and thus create savings in time and supplies. Self-mailer forms for grades and attendance can be printed and mailed directly from the data-processing center or from a site using desktop publishing options available with many microcomputers. Numerous other applications are also possible.

The standardizing of terminology used in all system and site reports is a major feature of an efficient, effective MIS. Consistent use of terms such as per-pupil costs, average daily membership, assessed valuation per pupil, achievement, and instructional level allows effective communication to all school audiences. The standardization also allows for reduction in number of forms and in unnecessary (and expensive) alternation of software for use with the MIS.

Another argument favoring strict standardization and maintenance procedures is the necessity of a control process. Without strict control of programming and machine-use records, it is difficult for the business administrators to get an accurate picture of costs. These costs are invaluable to the business administrator for projecting areas of growth and the attendant growth costs. The minute details required for each subset of the operation to contribute successfully to the total scheme are evident, as is the need for proper documentation of each subset and for the total system.

Types of Equipment

The choice of types of equipment represents a key decision for the school business administrator and other system staff members. Identification of the district's needs, growth potential, and cost considerations is input for the decision process. Whether to lease or purchase, types of peripherals, personnel selection, and the like are all involved in the decision process. Again, input from a variety of sources is needed to provide a sound basis for final selection. Other considerations are that most computer systems are modular and that growth and change are to be expected and must be considered. The decision must serve central office and site-based needs in a multitude of areas and for wide-ranging applications.

Trends in Computing

Several trends have occurred during the history of computers and computer implementation in schools. Some have had more impact than others, but all have affected, or are affecting, the way the school business official approaches computer utilization, purchase, and maintenance by the school district.

- *Decrease in size*—Early computers were room sized, low powered, and clumsy to use. Today's machines are small, extremely powerful, and user-friendly.
- *Increase in power/speed features*—What a computer can do and the speed at which it can do it have increased exponentially, and it is expected that this trend will continue.
- *Decrease in costs*—Costs have been reduced relative to speed and power almost each year. In many instances, school business officials—because of cost reductions—consider compliance a regular expense (like books or paper/pencils) and not a major capital expenditure item.
- *Increases in costs*—While decreases have occurred in costs for hardware and software, not all trends have been down. If the number of units goes up, the cost of maintaining these units goes up. Even though the cost of maintaining an individual computer may be small, maintaining large volumes of computers is not a small cost. Secondly, the cost of new software titles must be considered, as must the cost for training of more personnel to use the machines. Standardization of platforms continues and has the major potential of reducing replacement costs, the costs of inventory of multiple parts for multiple machines, and the need to have specially trained personnel for different machine types (Maurer & Davidson, 1998).

Assistive Technology

The educational equity gap also affects students who are disadvantaged by disabilities and handicaps. Fortunately, broad ranges of "assistive" devices are available, ranging from special computer keyboards and mice to software designed to compensate for visual, hearing, physical, or mental disabilities. Such technology allows students with disabilities to participate fully in class activities (or perform a job) and have learning opportunities similar to those enjoyed by their nondisabled peers.

While initially slow to adopt assistive technology due to its high cost and the small numbers of students, teachers and other staff members (including those with special education backgrounds) have become increasingly supportive of IT applications. Prices are decreasing, and availability is growing rapidly (Mason, 2005).

Maintenance

With many computer centers and individual sites using hardware from a number of vendors, the determination of the cause of a problem is often difficult for data-processing managers. The interface among different machines and component parts (including telephone connections) often creates mechanical difficulties that are hard to pinpoint. Controller units, telephone connections, and remote entry devices are especially vulnerable.

Maintenance contracts are most often written in two forms—contract option and per-call basis. Contract-option agreements are sold in blocks (usually eight hours, although after the initial block, smaller segments may be offered). The per-call client pays for service on the basis of need and is billed for service time, including travel to and from the site. Per-call clients are generally serviced after contract-option calls, regardless of when the contract-option call is received—that is, contract-option customers are serviced even if a per-call client has logged a request previously. Basic package upgrade can occur under most agreements. This allows service calls to be completed once started.

Another concern for all customers is to determine what levels of maintenance support are available—for example, local office to regional office to national office. Established companies have several levels of personnel support, and equally important, an adequate supply of spare parts. Recommendations for services from satisfied users are a good way to determine if local offices are providing acceptable services.

Other Equipment Needs

The installation of a computer system in a school district affects the selection of peripheral equipment and the disposition of equipment that may be currently in use in the school district. As is evident from the previous discussion, supporting devices are necessary for any computing system.

A complete review of equipment requirements within a district provides an opportunity to look critically at how monies are spent on equipment of this type and at how efficiently it is being used to further the overall scheme of district operations. Therefore, some machines may be sold or turned back to the company because of cost-effectiveness considerations.

Computer Security

The allure of the Internet, the rapture of surfing the Web, and the excitement of contacting people around the world through e-mail and chat rooms are excellent experiences for students. But these areas also appeal to a "darker" element. Anonymity enables people to misrepresent themselves and to post information that is inaccurate or even harmful. In response, filtering products have emerged to prevent users from gaining access to inappropriate sites.

That said, few people have neutral feelings about filtering. Many see the Internet as a dangerous place, where children need to be protected. Exposure to sexually explicit material, pedophiles, and information that supports discrimination and violence is the most often cited reason in support of filtering. This concern is underscored by media coverage on children who have had bad experiences using the Internet. Others, however, see filtering as a step toward the demise of the First Amendment and freedom of speech, and view it as a misguided attempt to regulate the Internet and stem the flow of information to the public. Critics of filtering also contend that its use may lull parents and educators into a false sense of security that children will not be exposed to inappropriate information. They feel it is better to teach children how to be responsible and discerning users.

No piece of software or hardware, however, can substitute for good training and common sense. Adults and children need effective strategies for using the network and the Internet, and schools have a duty to see that material presented to students supports the instructional program (Shelly et al., 2005).

Disaster Recovery

There is a clear need for a comprehensive disaster recovery plan for computer centers and local site machines in the contemporary operating environment. The increasing dependence on automated systems and technological activities in most school districts mandates this protection. Certainly, the possibilities for disaster, including natural calamities such as earthquakes and floods, human errors, and purposeful destructions such as the introduction of a computer virus, make all educational computer systems vulnerable. Because many of these events cannot be prevented, it is imperative to devise a strategy that can be utilized in the event of a disaster of any sort.

The most important initial activity for a school system is the development of a comprehensive, consistent statement of all actions to be taken before, during, and after a disaster occurs. The plan should include documented and tested procedures that will ensure the availability of critical resources and guarantee that facilities maintain operations at some acceptable level. Such a plan must provide minimal disruption to operations in the event of major problems and/or interruptions, ensure organizational stability, and provide an orderly plan for recovery.

Clearly, a multiphase plan is important. The first step is to obtain the support and involvement of top management officials. The second step is to appoint a group that will be in charge of guiding the development of the plan, setting the scope of the plan, developing procedures to cover business disruption, restoration plans, and what happens to PCs, and any telecommunications networks. A risk analysis that includes a range of possible disasters should be determined, and each component of the system, both hardware and software, should be analyzed against these risks.

The identification and prioritization of processing applications to be recovered and reinstituted after a disaster plan must then be made. A final step in this plan is to determine the most practical backup operations for the data entry, which includes facilities most likely to be used as backup, those having a secondary backup possibility, multiple computers, data centers, vendor-supplied equipment, and so forth—in other words, all the options that are available for backup systems, both in terms of hardware and software. These procedures should be in written form and provided to all personnel with a need to know. Funding must be secured, and the plan must be tested, evaluated, and, if necessary, revised.

Consumable Supplies

The consumable supplies needed in any computing facility or for any staff member certainly include paper products such as daily attendance records, checks, transfer vouchers, invoices and other billing materials, personnel reports, charts, and graphs as well as other administrative information. Standard computer printer paper is intended for general-purpose reports, for testing, and for production of rather limited amounts of material. Preprinted forms on which material may be printed in special blanks are widely useful. Some uses of these special forms are payroll checks, W-2 forms, monthly reports, class registers, invoices, transfer vouchers, and other material in which header information can be given routinely, lines can be drawn, and certain columns can be preprinted to save both time and money.

It should be noted that costs for consumable supplies will rise as an instructional cost where large number of labs are implemented at local sites. Printer cartridges are also a major cost factor. This is especially true with the use of color in many areas. In addition, supplies that are not always considered in relation to computer facilities but that generate expense are standard office items. All centers do not use all types of materials, but as any school administrator knows, many kinds of supplies must be available in order to make the operation run smoothly enough to justify the cost of computer installation.

Nonconsumable Supplies

Consumable supplies make up a rather large expenditure for a computing center, but expenditures for nonconsumable supplies and equipment must also be considered. Such items as computer desks, storage carts, extra phone or Internet connections, and so on are all cost factors that can quickly grow.

Office Procedures Operations

By the time the school business administrator has participated in the decision-making process described in the previous sections of this chapter, it is doubtful that the individual would wish to take on more reorganization or alteration projects. However, the opportunity to examine the totality of office procedures will never be better. Staff reorganization, filing processes, and record management can be logically examined at this point.

With the introduction of computer processing, many of the filing and recordkeeping procedures are automatically altered. Current records, permanent files, transfer vouchers, purchase orders, and the like can all be generated by the computer system. This causes a restructuring of filing procedures and may call for the removal of certain files, such as the online inventory control system. Files of computer output differ from current files and may produce more detailed records requiring more space, but they will be organized so as to facilitate data retrieval.

Security of data, including personnel and financial records, is a current concern and will remain so. If data are maintained online, this is especially crucial. Centralization of responsibility is a vital part of any look at the current organizational scheme. Both the "owner" and "user" of sensitive computer files have responsibilities to control access to data.

Computer-generated output will grow as the school system's ability to use the system grows. Remote inquiry stations are an integral part of financial and personnel records. Storage locations for printed material are needed, and an access scheme or system for this material must be devised. Most computer system costs must be prorated to many areas within the system, and a machine program and accounting scheme must be developed to perform the task.

Output will build up rapidly, and a procedure for retention and disposition of all levels of records—nonessential, useful, important, and vital—must be established. Microfilming is a useful technique for producing more easily retrieved material. Personnel must be taught to interact with the machine and to get production as needed without becoming subjugated to the system.

In the News

A good school district management information system can be the crown jewel of your education resources. It's already an indispensable tool in managing and generating the mountains of data required by law and grant programs. But the technology has the potential to do more than data processing: it can produce invaluable information for critical and strategic education decision making.

With the growing popularity of charter schools and vouchers, your school district is competing to attract and keep students. That means you must view students and their parents as customers—which in fact they are, since such a large part of district revenue is pegged to student enrollment. Your district can gain a competitive advantage by creating a management information system that is student centered and capable of generating real-time information on demand for individual students, classrooms, schools, and the district as a whole.

What does a properly designed, developed, and maintained management information system look like, and what can it do? It should be able to manage and marshal appropriate district resources—such as assessment tools, online courses, and curriculum materials—to address the immediate education needs of any student. At the touch of a mouse button, the system should be able to track the current progress—not last year's history—of schools, classes, teachers, and students. From their classrooms or homes, teachers should be able to quickly locate teaching resources to help with classroom or individual instruction and to match resources with students without encountering bureaucratic intervention and delay.

In school districts that are hard-pressed to come up with the staff time and expertise to perform such tasks themselves, a good management information system can compensate for inadequate resources. Even as simple a task as correctly reporting attendance can be automated at the classroom level. At the school level, student information can be stored on a computerized database system, making real-time student data such as grades, test results, and attendance information easily available to principals, teachers, and parents alike.

But just as a management information system can be a dream come true for your district, when things go wrong, it can be your worst nightmare. Your system might be state of the art right now, but you must make a commitment to champion new systems developments and to endure the necessary upgrades and conversions. And you must be vigilant in monitoring the system's development, implementation, and maintenance.

Consider just a few of the possible pitfalls. The much-publicized insolvency of the Oakland, Calif., public schools in 2002, for example, can be traced to a poorly configured management information system that could not produce accurate financial figures. A more common problem is cost overruns that go way beyond planned budgets. Worse still is the information system that never gets completed and is eventually abandoned before it ever becomes operable.

Another disaster scenario is a breakdown in the student information system that stores transcripts, evaluations, and attendance data. The breakdown could be the result of poor system design, bad implementation, lack of maintenance, or it could be caused by a security breach by a malicious intruder, either physical or online.

When information systems fail, the most likely culprits are ineffective system leadership and ineffective communication. To guard against system failure, my advice is to identify the people accountable for the management information system, beginning with the superintendent, and assess whether they possess the requisite

technology leadership and communication skills.

From: Chan, L. (2004). Preventing problems. *American School Boards Journal.* Retrieved February 23, 2007, from http://www. asbj .com/specialreports/ 0904SpecialReports/ S3.html.
Reprinted with permission from *American School Board Journal*, September 2004. Copyright © 2004 National School Boards Association. All rights reserved.

■ THE FUTURE OF EDUCATIONAL TECHNOLOGY: ADMINISTRATIVE AND INSTRUCTIONAL

Few areas of school business administration and school system work have experienced more changes or have as much potential for improvement or change as the area of educational data processing and computing. The regular use of computers throughout school districts has really just begun. States are spending more each year, and the integration of the computer into the business and instructional program is growing dramatically. Utilization of broad-based data systems and the expanded hardware resources at the disposal of the school district provides excellent opportunities for improving services and is today's norm rather than an option.

The California K–12 Technology Challenges Survey asked about ten potential challenges for IT administrators and coordinators. The following are the five most important challenges faced by California K–12 IT administrators and coordinators in public school districts:

1. Managing the budget and funding (97 percent).
2. Adequate student information systems (95 percent).
3. Software licensing verification (95 percent).
4. Network security (92 percent).
5. Student and staff e-mail account management (92 percent). (Jennings, 2003, p. 16)

Summary

The school business administrator's role in planning within the local district involves many applications of management tools and processes. However, no tool is of more potential assistance in decision making and management operations than the computer. Computers facilitate the storage, manipulation, and retrieval of vast amounts of data on a multitude of subjects.

There is little doubt that the availability of the computer is an asset. However, as previously noted, the true value of the computer is in the combined use of the machine by several key staff members, including the school business administrator, and the creation of imaginative software to make proper use of the hardware. As was stated previously, personnel to do these jobs are difficult to locate, but are invaluable in assisting with conceptualization and application in a school system.

The school business administrator is one key member of the administrative team charged with properly charting the progress of the local district. This is a relatively new role for the school business manager. It requires that the school business official serve in an analysis and planning role as well as manage the day-to-day operation of the office. This new role gives the proper emphasis to the planning and initiating theme of the position.

Personnel, administrative control, hardware and software selections, and space allocations are but a few of the challenges to be faced in the operation of a computer facility. Machine activities must be monitored and evaluated on an ongoing basis throughout the system and across the various types of activities within the district. Yet, no single development can have as much impact on the district as the computer.

Discussion Questions

1. What will be the role of the MIS in decision making in your school system? In your administrative area?
2. Discuss the role of the computer in administration, research, and instruction for your system and for individual elementary and secondary schools. What are some innovative uses for utilizing computers to aid instruction, administration, and research?
3. Design a plan for the selection, utilization, and maintenance of computers in your school district and at each local site.
4. Review the "In the News" article, on page 418, regarding student ID numbers. Discuss whether schools should be permitted to track individual student progress with an individual ID number. Is this practice a violation of a student's privacy? Elaborate on the advantages and disadvantages of such a practice.

Web Resources

International Society for Technology in Education's website provides information on improving teaching, learning, and school leadership by advancing the effective use of technology in PK–12 and teacher education—
http://www.iste.org/

North Central Regional Educational Laboratory has an annotated collection of links to resources related to using or planning to use technology in schools—
http://www.ncrel.org/sdrs/areas/te0cont.htm

U.S. Department of Education National Education Technology Plan—
http://www.ed.gov/about/offices/list/os/technology/plan/2004/site/edlite-default.html

U.S. Department of Education Office of Educational Technology—
http://www.ed.gov/about/offices/list/os/technology/index.html

Youth Technology Support Cooperative helps decision makers define the type of program best suited to their student and school needs based on the best practices of current practitioners—
http://www.studenttechsupport.org/

References

Brooks-Young, S. (2006). *Critical technology issues for school leaders*. Thousand Oaks, CA: Corwin Press.

Jennings, J. (2003). IT in a time of budget cuts. *T.H.E. Journal*, 30(6), 16.

Lockard, J., & and Abrams, P.D. (2004). *Computers for twenty-first century education* (6th ed.). Boston: Allyn & Bacon.

Mason, C.Y. (2005). The future of technology in schools. *Principal Leadership*, 5(8), 46–52.

Maurer, M., & Davidson, G. (1998). *Leadership in instructional technology*. Columbus, OH: Prentice-Hall.

Oz, E. (2006). *Management information systems* (5th ed.). Boston: Thomson-Course Technology.

Painter, J. (2002). Purchasing pitfalls. Retrieved February 20, 2007, from http://www.electronic-school.com/2002/01/0102f5.html.

Shelly, G.B., Cashman, T.J., Gunter, G.A., & Gunter, R.E. (2005). Integrating technology and digital media into the classroom (4th ed.). Boston: Thomson-Course Technology.

Trainor, T.N., & Krasnewick, D. (2000). *Computers* (5th ed.). New York: McGraw-Hill College.

Notes

1. http://my.asbointl.org/emodules/source/communities/userhomepage.cfm?section= communities.
2. See the following website for more information on the e-rate: http://www. computerlearning.org/articles/ERate.htm.
3. The online survey was conducted by the Consortium for School Networking and Grunwald Associates. See full report at http://cosn.org/resources/grunwald/ index.cfm.

Glossary

Abatement A reduction of a previously recorded expenditure or receipt item by such things as refunds, rebates, and collections for loss or damages to school property or resources.

Account A descriptive heading under which are recorded financial transactions that are similar in terms of purpose, object, or source.

Accounting The procedure of maintaining systematic records of events relating to persons, objects, or money and summarizing, analyzing, and interpreting the results thereof.

Accounting Period A period at the end of which and for which financial statements are prepared; for example, July 1 to June 30.

Accounts Receivable Amounts due an open account from private persons, firms, or corporations for goods and services they ordered.

Accrual Basis The basis of accounting under which revenues are recorded when earned or when levies are made, and expenditures are recorded as soon as they result in liabilities, regardless of when the revenue is actually received or the payment is actually made.

Administration-Dominated Budget A budgeting process that is monopolized by management, and more specifically, the central office.

Administrative Unit, Intermediate A unit smaller than the state that exists primarily to provide consultative, advisory, or statistical services to local basic administrative units, or to exercise certain regulatory and inspection functions over local basic administrative units.

Ad Valorem Taxes Taxes levied on the assessed valuation of real and personal property that, within legal limits, is the final authority in determining the amount to be raised for school purposes. Separate accounts may be maintained for real property and for personal property.

Advertising Sale In selling bonds and in assuming passage of any school bond issue, a notice of sale is required by state statute. Bonds can be advertised in a newspaper with general district circulation.

Affirmative Action Practices Require an employer to increase the employment and promotion of certain protected classes of people.

Amortization of Debt Gradual payment of an amount owed according to a specified schedule of times and amounts.

Appraisal The act of making an estimate of value, particularly of the value of property, by systematic procedures that include physical examination, pricing, and often engineering estimates.

Appropriation An authorization granted by a legislative body to make expenditures and to incur obligations for specific purposes.

Appropriation Ledger A ledger containing an account for each appropriation. Each account usually shows the amount originally appropriated, transfers to or from the appropriation, amounts charged against the appropriation, the encumbrances, the net balance, and other related information.

Appropriation, School Money received out of funds set aside periodically by the appropriating body (district meeting, city council, or other governmental body) for school purposes; which funds have not been specifically collected as school taxes.

Arbitration Mandatory settlement of a dispute between groups by an agent specified as a part of the negotiated agreement.

Assessment, Special A compulsory levy made by a local government against certain properties to defray part or all of the cost of a specific improvement or service that is presumed to be of general benefit to the public and of special benefit to the owners of such properties.

Assets The things of value a school system owns.

Audit The examination of records and documents and the securing of other evidence for one or more of the following purposes: (a) determining the propriety of proposed or completed transactions, (b) ascertaining whether all transactions have been recorded, (c) determining whether transactions are accurately recorded in the accounts and in the statements drawn from the accounts.

Balance Sheet   A formal statement of assets, liabilities, and fund balance as of a specific date.

Benefit-Cost Analysis   *See* Cost-Benefit Analysis.

Bond Discount   The excess of the face value of a bond over the price for which it is acquired or sold. The price does not include accrued interest at the date of acquisition or sale.

Bonded Debt   The part of the school system debt that is covered by outstanding bonds of the school system.

Bond Premium   The excess of the price at which a bond is acquired or sold, over its face value. The price does not include accrued interest at the date of acquisition or sale.

Bond Rating   Dun and Bradstreet, Moody's, and Standard & Poor's are major raters of school bonds. A borrower who obtains an AAA rating has the best rating.

Books of Original Entry   The record in which the various transactions are formally recorded for the first time, such as the cash journal, check register, or general journal. Where mechanized bookkeeping methods are used, it may happen that one transaction is recorded simultaneously in several records, one of which may be regarded as the book of original entry.

Budget   A plan of financial operation incorporating an estimate of proposed expenditures for a given period or purpose, and the proposed means of financing them.

Budgetary Accounts   Those accounts necessary to reflect budget operations and conditions, such as estimated revenues, appropriations, and encumbrances, as distinguished from proprietary accounts.

Budgeting   Pertains to budget planning, formulation, administration, analysis, and evaluation.

Buying on Margin   *See* Leveraging.

Capital Outlay   An expenditure that results in the acquisition of fixed assets or additions to fixed assets that are presumed to have benefits for more than one year. It is an expenditure for land or existing buildings.

Capital Project Fund   A fund to account for all resources used for acquisition of capital facilities including real property.

Cash   Currency, checks, postal and express money orders, and bankers' drafts on hand or on deposit with an official or agent designated as custodian of cash; and bank deposits.

Cash Basis   The basis of accounting under which revenues are recorded only when actually received, and only cash disbursements are recorded as expenditures.

Cash Discounts   Allowances received or given by vendors for payment of invoices within a stated period of time.

Cash Flow   The cycles of revenue entering and expenditures leaving an account.

Categorical Aid   Educational support funds provided from higher governmental levels and specifically limited to a given purpose.

Cathode Ray Tube Terminal (CRT)   A device that contains a television-like screen for displaying data. Most CRT terminals have a typewriter-type keyboard.

Central Processing Unit (CPU)   Electric component that causes processing on a computer by interpreting instructions, performing calculations, moving data, and controlling the input/output operations. It consists of the arithmetical/logical unit and the control unit.

Centralized Budget   A budgeting process that treats all schools in a system alike. Though efficient in a sense, little consideration is permitted for differing needs among the various communities served under this type of process.

Certificate of Deposit (CD)   Issued by a bank or thrift, this is an interest-bearing term deposit that comes due at a specified future date.

Chart of Accounts   A list of accounts generally used in an individual accounting system. It includes the account title and an account number that has been assigned to each account.

Coding   Distinguishing among items and categories of information by assigning numbers or other symbolic designations so that the items and categories are readily identifiable.

Cohort Survival   A method of short-term enrollment projection utilizing the percent of change of cohorts within the immediate past.

Coinsurance   Insurer-provided coverage for the portion of a loss relative to the amount required to avoid penalty.

Compiler   A program that interprets computer statements in symbolic form and converts them into machine language instructions.

Comprehensive Planning   Planning usually done through a comprehensive survey that reveals future goals, needs, and resources.

Computer   A device that can perform computations, including arithmetic and logic operations, without intervention by a human being.

Concentration Account An account that is the aggregation of all of an institution's other accounts for investment purposes.

Conditions Provisions of a contract indicating areas and/or items with which compliance is essential to enforce the rights of the contract.

Contingency Fund Assets or other resources set aside to provide for unforeseen expenditures or for anticipated expenditures of uncertain amounts.

Continuous Budget Under this concept of budgetary development, educational plans are conceived on a long-range basis and attempts are made to budget accordingly. Budget development is considered an integral part of daily operations.

Contracted Services Services rendered by personnel who are not on the payroll, including all related expenses covered by the contract.

Cost Accounting A method of accounting that provides the assembling and recording of all the elements of cost incurred to accomplish a purpose, to carry on an activity or operation, or to complete a unit of work or a specific job.

Cost-Benefit Analysis An analytical approach to solving problems of choice that requires the definition of objectives and identification of alternatives, and that yields the greatest benefits for any given costs, or yields a required or determined amount of benefits for the least costs.

Cost Center The smallest segment of a program that is separately recognized in the records, accounts, and reports. Program-oriented budgeting, accounting, and reporting aspects of an information system are usually built upon the identification and use of a set of cost centers.

Cost-Effectiveness Analysis Primarily a post-evaluation technique used to help determine program effectiveness, failures, and ways of improvement.

Cost Stream Includes the costs associated with the researching, purchasing, financing, operating, and repairing of a system or piece of equipment.

Credit Opposite of debit. An entry into the right side of an account, reflecting a decrease in an asset or an increase in a liability or fund balance.

Critical Path Method (CPM) A type of network analysis. Its analytical emphasis is to determine the programming strategy that will satisfy schedule requirements at minimum costs.

Current The term refers to the fiscal year in progress.

Current Assets Those assets that are available or can be made readily available to meet the cost of operations or to pay current liabilities. Some examples are cash, temporary investments, and taxes receivable that can be expected to be collected within one year.

Current Expense Any expenditure except for capital outlay and debt service. Current expense includes total charges incurred, whether paid or unpaid.

Current Funds Money received during the current fiscal year from revenue that can be used to pay obligations currently due, and surpluses reappropriated for the current fiscal year.

Current Liabilities Debts that are payable within a relatively short period of time, usually no longer than a year.

Database A comprehensive collection of data composed of files relating to specific areas of information such as pupils, staff, property, finance, instructional programs, and the community.

Data Processing The activities of collecting and organizing data, sorting for future use, and preparing statistical reports.

Debit Opposite of credit. An entry into the left side of an account, reflecting an increase in an asset or a decrease in a liability or fund balance.

Debt Service Expenditures for the retirement of debt and expenditures for interest on debt, except principal and interest of current loans.

Debt Service Fund Used to finance and account for payment of interest and principal on all general obligation debt.

Decentralized Budget A budgetary process that especially applies to large school systems. Each school in a system establishes individual budgets and establishes its own educational priorities within the parameters of the total system. The process fosters a high degree of participation by a wide variety of persons.

Delinquent Taxes Taxes remaining unpaid on and after the date on which they become delinquent by statute.

Delphi Process An intuitive methodology for eliciting, refining, and gaining consensus from individuals within an organization regarding a given issue.

Depreciation Loss in value of service life of fixed assets because of wear and tear through use, elapse of time, inadequacy, or obsolescence.

Disbursements Payments in cash.

Double Entry A system of bookkeeping that requires for every entry made to the debit side of an account or accounts an entry be made for the corresponding amount or amounts to the credit side of another account or accounts.

Dynamic Programming A technique used for solving multistage problems in which the output of one stage becomes input for another stage.

Educational Budget The translation of educational needs into a financial plan that is interpreted to the public in such a way that, when formally adopted, it expresses the kind of educational program the community is willing to support for the budget period.

Emergency Maintenance Plan for servicing equipment and/or facilities, with no restrictions on number of calls, time, or costs.

Employee Assistance Programs Established by organizations to help employees resolve personal problems (stress, chemical dependency, depression, financial, family, and so forth) that affect job performance by reducing absenteeism, turnover, tardiness, accidents, and medical claims.

Employee Benefits Compensation, in addition to regular salary, provided to an employee. This may include such benefits as health insurance, life insurance, annual leave, sick leave, retirement, and Social Security.

Encumbrances Purchase orders, contracts, and salary or other commitments that are chargeable to an appropriation and for which a part of the appropriation is reserved. They cease to be encumbrances when paid or when actual liability is set up.

Endorsements Provisions added to a basic contract to increase or decrease the scope of the contract.

Endowment Fund A fund from which the income may be expended, but whose principal must remain intact.

Entry The record of a financial transaction in its appropriate book of accounts. Also the act of recording a transaction in the books of accounts.

Equipment Any instrument, machine, apparatus, or set of articles that (a) retains its original shape and appearance with use and (b) is nonexpendable; that is, if the article is damaged or some of its parts are lost or worn out, it is usually more feasible to repair it than to replace it with an entirely new unit.

Equity Equity is the mathematical excess of assets over liabilities. Generally, this excess is called *fund balance*.

Exclusions Areas, items, or actions causing insurance coverage to be omitted.

Expenditures Charges incurred, whether paid or unpaid, that are presumed to benefit the current fiscal year.

Express Warranties Explicit statements as to the quality, fitness, or performance of a product by a seller.

Fidelity Bond A bond guaranteeing against losses resulting from the actions of the treasurer, employees, or other persons of the system.

Fiscal Year Any period at the end of which a school system determines its financial condition and the results of its operation and closes its books. It is usually a year, though not necessarily a calendar year.

Fixed Assets Land, buildings, machinery, furniture, and other equipment that the school system intends to hold or continue to use over a long period of time.

Fixed Charges Charges of a generally recurrent nature that are not readily allocated to other expenditure categories. They consist of such charges as school board contributions to employee retirement, insurance and judgments, rental of land and buildings, and interest on current loans. They do not include payments to public school housing authorities or similar agencies.

Floppy Disk A mylar-coated plastic disk about six inches in diameter that can be used for magnetically storing data.

Flowchart A symbolic way of representing information about the relationships of discrete parts or steps in a process.

Flow Models The generic term for models that lay out the facilities on the organizational chart and enable managers and administrators to see the flow of material, equipment, personnel, and information.

Food Services Activities involved with the food services program that include the preparation and serving of regular and incidental meals, lunches, or snacks in connection with school activities, and the delivery of food.

Formal Bids Bids requiring public advertising, public opening, and award to the lowest responsible bidder.

Friable Asbestos Airborne asbestos that may have carcinogenic qualities.

Function An action that contributes to a larger action of a person, living thing, or creating thing.

Functional Budget A type of budgetary development that considers the educational objectives of a school district. The educational plan is translated into a budget for presentation to the community for reaction.

Functional Overlap These modifications of flow models depict contacts that occur where specialized information is sought. Most typically, these contacts happen when a specialist or intellectual leader expects influence without direct responsibility.

Fund An independent accounting entity with its own assets, liabilities, and fund balances. Generally, funds are established to account for financing of specific activities of an agency's operations.

Fund Accounts All accounts necessary to set forth the financial operations and financial condition of a fund.

Fund Balance The excess of the assets of a fund over its liabilities and reserves, except in the case of funds subject to budgetary accounting where, prior to the end of a fiscal period, it represents the excess of the fund's assets and estimated revenues for the period over its liabilities, reserves, and appropriations for the period; also called *equity*.

Game Theory A technique for analyzing choices between alternative strategies and competing decisions.

General Fund Used to account for all transactions that do not have to be accounted for in another fund. Used to account for all ordinary operations of a school system.

General Ledger A book, file, or other device in which accounts are kept to summarize the financial transactions of the school system. General ledger accounts may be kept for any group of items— receipts or expenditures—on which an administrative officer wishes to maintain a close check.

Grants-in-Aid Contributions made by a government unit and not related to specific revenue sources of the respective government, that is, general; or if related to specific revenue sources of the governmental unit, distributed on some flat grant or equalization basis. Grants-in-aid are made by intermediate governments, state governments, and the federal government.

Hardware, Computer Physical equipment, as opposed to the program or method of use. For example, mechanical, magnetic, electrical, or electronic devices.

Implied Warranties In the absence of express warranties, there is usually an implied warranty that the goods are reasonably fit for their purpose.

Improvements Buildings, other structures, and other attachments or annexations to land that are intended to remain so attached or annexed, such as sidewalks, trees, drives, tunnels, drains, and sewers. Note: Sidewalks, curbing, sewers, and highways are sometimes referred to as *betterments*, but the term *improvements* is preferred.

Informal Bids A telephone quotation or (preferred) a written quotation whose dollar value is less than the statutory limit.

Input, Computer Data to be processed by a computer.

Input-Output Analysis A method for analyzing the consequences of alternate spending plans throughout a governmental unit. Educators can use it to help determine optimum levels of school financing within a city or community.

Insuring Agreements Provisions distinguishing one contract from another.

Interfund Transfers Money taken from one fund under the control of the board of education and added to another fund under the board's control. Interfund transfers are not receipts or expenditures of the school system.

Internal Auditing Activities involved with evaluating the adequacy of the internal control system, verifying and safeguarding assets, reviewing the reliability of the accounting and reporting systems, and ascertaining compliance with established policies and procedures.

Internet A "network of networks" that connects computers across the world into one gigantic global communications system that allows all the computers on the Internet to share and exchange data. The Internet is a wide area network (WAN) composed of many local area networks (LANs).

Inventory A detailed list or record showing quantities, descriptions, values, and, frequently, units of measure and unit prices of property on hand at a given time.

Investments Securities and real estate held for the production of income in the form of interest, dividends, rentals, or lease payments. The account does not include fixed assets.

Invoice An itemized list of merchandise purchased from a particular vendor. The list includes quantity, description, price, terms, date, and the like.

Job Analysis A study to determine the constructs underlying successful job performance and important or critical duties.

Job Description A detailing of specific activities, responsibilities, and requirements of the position. These guidelines include necessary skills, types of responsibilities, and limitations imposed by the job.

Journal The accounting record in which the details of financial transactions are first recorded.

Judgment An amount to be paid or collected by the school system as a result of a court decision.

Land A fixed-asset account that reflects the acquisition value of land owned. If land is purchased, this account includes the purchase price and costs such as legal fees, filling and excavation costs, and other associated improvement costs that are incurred to put the land in condition for its intended use. If land is acquired by gift, the account reflects its appraised value at the time of acquisition.

Least Cost Estimating and Scheduling (LESS) A variation of CPM and PERT. LESS resolves the problem of at what time and hour each and every job should be done in order to complete the project at minimum cost and within a specified time.

Ledger Contains all the accounts of a particular fund or all those detail accounts that support a particular general ledger account.

Legal Opinion (1) The opinion of an official authorized to render it, such as an attorney as to legality. (2) In the case of school bonds, the opinion of a specialized bond attorney as to the legality of a bond issue.

Leveraging Using equity in one security or asset to buy an additional asset or security.

Levy To impose taxes or special assets. The total of taxes or special assessments imposed by a governmental unit.

Liabilities Debt or other legal obligations arising out of transactions in the past that are payable but not necessarily due. Encumbrances are not liabilities; they become liabilities when the services or materials for which the encumbrances were established have been rendered or received.

Liability Insurance Expenditures for insurance coverage of the school system, or its officers, against losses resulting from judgments awarded against the system.

Linear Programming An operations-research technique useful in specifying how to use limited resources or capacities to obtain particular objectives. It has been used to determine school transportation routes, location and number of warehouse and maintenance facilities, and the best location of schools.

Liquidity Refers to the ease or difficulty of using assets that are invested.

Local Education Agency Educational agency created by the state to carry out state policies and operate schools.

Long-Term Loan A loan that extends for more than five years from the date the loan was obtained and is not secured by serial or term bonds.

Maintenance Functions associated with repairs and/or replacements to ensure continuous usability of the physical plant, equipment, and service facilities.

Maintenance Personnel Personnel on the school payroll who are primarily engaged in the repairing and upkeep of grounds, buildings, and equipment.

Management by Objectives (MBO) Process wherein management provides a structure of individuals and subsystems of the organization to relate their objectives to those of the larger system in a cooperative mode and to be evaluated on the achievement of the results.

Management Information System (MIS) A method for improving the quality of and access to information pertinent to an enterprise. The method consists of defining management decisions, explaining decision-making policies, determining the information needed to make decisions, and developing techniques for processing the information.

Mechanical Budget Under this concept, budgeting is viewed as a revenue-and-expenditure operation—a bookkeeping chore required by law. This type of budgeting forces expenditures to fit income expectations and pays no attention to needs.

Mediation Process for settling differences between groups by consent or agreement of both parties.

Microcomputer A complete computer on a single miniature circuit board.

Minicomputer A stored program computer, generally having less memory and a smaller word size than larger machines.

Needs Assessment A basic procedure for determining the quantitative and/or qualitative extent of the discrepancies between what is and what is required.

Negotiations Processes for exchange between groups for the purpose of reaching mutually acceptable agreements.

Network Analysis Generic term for a tool of analysis. Two basic types of managerial technique used in design, planning, and control are critical path method (CPM) and program evaluation and review techniques (PERT).

Notice to Bidders Form that exists for the purpose of giving prior and proper notice to potential bidders. By means of the form, bidders can record their prices for specifically described articles.

Object The commodity or service obtained from a specific expenditure.

Object Classification A category of goods or services purchased.

Obligations Amounts that the school system will be required to meet out of its resources, including both liabilities and encumbrances.

Operation, Plant Those activities that are concerned with keeping the physical plant open and ready for use. They include cleaning, disinfecting, heating, moving furniture, caring for grounds, operating telephone switchboards, and other such housekeeping activities. They do not include repairing.

OSHA Occupational Safety and Health Act.

Output Material generated by the computer on tape, paper, disk, and such for current or future use.

Participatory Budget A budgetary process that attempts to involve school staff and lay public in the various levels of budget making. This process uses a combination of formal and informal methods to get persons involved.

Payroll A list of individual employees entitled to wages or salaries, with the amounts due to each for personal services rendered. Payments are also made for such payroll-associated costs as federal income tax withholdings, retirements, and Social Security.

Payroll Deductions and Withholding Amounts deducted from employees' salaries for taxes required to be withheld and for other withholding purposes. Separate liability accounts may be used for each type of deduction.

Periodic Maintenance Work on buildings and/or equipment scheduled at a specific time or for a specific number of times during a given period.

Petty Cash A sum of money set aside for the purpose of paying small obligations for which the issuance of a formal voucher and check would be too expensive and time consuming.

Planning approach The selection or identification of the overall, long-range goals, priorities, and objectives of the organization, and the formulation of various courses of action to be followed in working toward achieving those goals, priorities, and objectives.

Planning, Programming, Budgeting, Evaluating System (PPBES) A formal procedure for determining budgets. Some distinctive characteristics of this procedure are identification of the basic objectives of the enterprise,

determination of future-year implications and inclusion of all costs in budgetary considerations, and systematic analysis of alternatives with a view toward determining the relative benefits and costs.

Plant Security Program for protecting each site against damages, vandalism, loss of keys, and so forth.

Posting The act of transferring to an account in a ledger the detailed or summarized data contained in the cash receipts book, cash register, journal voucher, or similar books or documents of original entry.

Post-Sale Planning Planning done after the sale of bonds is accomplished. Prompt payment of principal and interest, and the notification of bond owners, rating agencies, and underwriters about the financial status and progress of a school system are very important.

Premium on Bonds Sold That portion of the sale price of bonds in excess of their par value. The premium represents an adjustment of the interest rate.

Preventive Maintenance Program for servicing machines, systems, and structures devised to prevent a breakdown of the total system or any one of the component parts.

Principal The amount of money that is invested.

Principal Systems and Priorities The main systems of an information system in an educational enterprise might be a student information system, materials information system, administrative and financial information system, and instructional system.

Privacy Act of 1974 Public Law 92-583, designed to protect citizens from unwarranted use of personal data.

Program A plan of activities and procedures designed to accomplish a predetermined objective or set of allied objectives.

Program Evaluation and Review Technique (PERT) A type of network analysis used in cases in which there is no established system for doing the task and therefore no exact basis for estimating the required time to complete each task.

Programming Preparation of a logical sequence of operations to be performed by a computer in solving a problem or processing data; the preparation of coded instructions and data for such a sequence.

Programming Language Sets of instructions or codes to communicate with a computer. Examples include FORTRAN (Formula Translation), COBOL (Common Business Oriented Language), and BASIC (Beginner's All-Purpose Symbolic Instruction Code).

Property Insurance Expenditures for all forms of insurance covering the loss of, or damage to, property from fire, theft, storm, or any other cause. Also recorded here are costs for appraisals of property for insurance purposes.

Proprietary Accounts Those accounts that show actual financial conditions and operations such as actual assets, liabilities, reserves, surplus, revenues, and expenditures, as distinguished from budgetary accounts.

Prorating The allocation of parts of a single expenditure to two or more different accounts. The allocation is made in proportion to the benefits that the expenditure provides for the respective purposes or programs for which the accounts were established.

Pupil Accounting A system for collecting, computing, and reporting information about pupils.

Pupil Activity Fund Financial transactions related to school-sponsored pupil activities and interscholastic activities. These activities are supported in whole or in part by income from pupils, gate receipts, and other fund-raising activities. Support may be provided by local taxation.

Pupil Transportation Consists of those activities involved with the conveyance of pupils to and from school activities, as provided by state law. This includes trips between home and school or trips to school activities.

Purchase Order The document by which goods are procured. Every purchase order must include such information as name and address of school system, order number, date, name and address of vendor, description of materials, quantity, price, and signature of authorization.

Purchasing Acquiring supplies, equipment, and materials.

Quadratic Programming A technique having applications similar to those of linear programming. This technique is able to compute nonlinear relationships.

Queuing Theory (Waiting-Line Theory) A mathematical technique for reducing lengths of waiting lines and for reducing time lost to waiting.

Real Estate Land, improvements to site, and buildings; real property.

Rebates Abatements or refunds.

Recurring Maintenance Plan for servicing equipment and/or facilities regardless of the number of service calls needed and at the convenience of the contractor.

Redemption of Principal Expenditures from current funds to retire serial bonds, long-term

loans of more than five years, and short-term loans of less than five years.

Refund A return of an overpayment or overcollection. The return may be either in the form of cash or a credit to an account.

Refunding Bonds Bonds issued to pay off bonds already outstanding.

Register A record for the consecutive entry of a certain class of events, documents, or transactions, with a proper notation of all of the required particulars.

Reimbursement The return of an overpayment or overcollection in cash.

Remodeling Any major permanent structural improvement to buildings. It includes changes of partitions, roof structure, or walls. Repairs are not included here but are included under maintenance.

Remote Entry Ability to communicate with a data-processing system from a location that is time, space, or electrically distant.

Rental-Purchase Agreement A contractual agreement for the rental of property with the option to apply all or part of the rental monies toward the eventual purchase.

Repairs The restoration of a given piece of equipment, a given building, or grounds to original condition or completeness or efficiency from a worn, damaged, or deteriorated condition.

REPO (Repurchase Agreement) Relatively short-term investments (even overnight or over a weekend) whereby the investor takes title to bank securities as collateral. The bank repurchases the securities at the end of the term, paying back principal plus interest.

Requisition A written request to a purchasing officer for specified articles or services. It is a request from one school official to another school official, whereas a purchase order is from a school official (usually the purchasing officer) to a vendor.

Resource Allocation and Multi-Project Scheduling (RAMPS) A variation of CPM and PERT. By considering various restrictions and requirements, RAMPS is able to determine the schedule that satisfies various prescribed criteria and minimum costs.

Revenues Additions to assets that do not increase any liability, do not represent the recovery of an expenditure, and do not represent the cancellation of certain liabilities without a corresponding increase in other liabilities or a decrease in assets.

Revolving Fund A fund provided to carry out a cycle of operations. The amounts expended from the funds are restored by earnings from operations or by transfers from other funds so that it remains intact, in the form of either cash, receivables, inventory, or other assets. These funds are also known as reimbursable funds.

School System All the schools and supporting services operated by the board of education, by a specified administrative unit, or by another organization that operates one or more schools.

Securities Bonds, notes, mortgages, or other forms of negotiable or nonnegotiable instruments.

Sequential Planning A family of techniques whose purpose is to sequence the various operations of an enterprise in order to reduce waste.

Serial Bonds Issues redeemable by installments, each of which is to be paid in full, ordinarily out of revenues of the fiscal year in which it matures or out of revenues of the preceding year.

Short-Term Loan A loan payable in five years or less, but not before the end of the current fiscal year.

Sinking Fund Money that has been set aside or invested for the definite purpose of meeting payments on debt at some future time. It is usually a fund set up for the purpose of accumulating money over a period of years in order to have money available for the redemption of long-term obligations at the date of maturity.

Site-Based Management Managerial decisions and processes carried out at the school site rather than at a higher organizational level.

Sociometric Overlap Modifications of flow models that describe relationships within the organization that are purely social. These may be positive or negative relationships.

Software Set of instructions for communicating with the computer. Also used to refer to all programs, whether locally produced or vendor supplied, for operating the computer system.

Staff Accounting Services rendered in connection with the systematic recording, filing, and storing of information related to staff members employed by the school system.

Stakeholders Individual and/or group representatives who share common interests in the educational process directed by a school district or building.

Statements (1) Used in a general sense, statements are all formal written presentations that set forth financial information. (2) In technical accounting usage, statements are presentations of financial data that show the financial position and the results of financial operations of a fund,

a group of accounts, or an entire governmental unit for a particular accounting period.

Stock Insurance Company An insurance company owned by stockholders and managed by an elected board of directors. Company profits are shared among stockholders in the form of dividends.

Stores Supplies, materials, and equipment in storerooms and subject to requisition.

Student Activities Direct and personal services for public school pupils, such as interscholastic athletics, entertainment, publications, clubs, band, and orchestra, that are managed or operated generally by the student body under the guidance and direction of adults or a staff member, and which are not part of the regular instructional program.

Supply A material item of an expendable nature that is consumed, worn out, or deteriorated in use or loses its identity through fabrication for incorporation into a different or more complex unit of substance.

Supporting Services Activities that provide administrative, technical, and logistical support to a program. Supporting services exist to sustain and enhance the fulfillment of the objectives of other major functions.

Surety Bond A written promise to pay damages or to indemnify against losses caused by the party or parties named in the document, through nonperformance or through defalcation; for example, a surety bond given by a contractor or by an official handling cash or securities.

Surplus The excess of the assets of a fund over its liabilities; or if the fund also has other resources and obligations, the excess of resources over obligations. The term should not be used without a properly descriptive adjective unless its meaning is apparent from the context.

Systematic Analysis Evaluation of alternatives that are relevant to defined objectives based on judgment and, wherever possible, on quantitative methods; the development of data-processing procedures or application to electronic data-processing equipment.

Tax Anticipation Notes Notes issued in anticipation of collection of taxes usually retirable only from tax collections, and frequently only from the tax collections anticipated with their issuance. The proceeds of tax anticipation notes or warrants are treated as current loans if paid back from the tax collections anticipated with the issuance of the notes.

Taxes Compulsory charges levied by a governmental unit for the purpose of financing services performed for the common benefit.

Taxes Receivable The uncollected portion of taxes that a school system or governmental unit has levied and that has become due, including any interest or penalties that may be accrued. Separate accounts may be maintained on the basis of tax roll year and/or current and delinquent taxes.

Term Bonds Bonds of the same issue, usually maturing all at one time and ordinarily to be retired from sinking funds.

Time-Sharing A computing technique whereby several terminal devices utilize a central computer concurrently for input, processing, and output functions.

Title IX Federal guidelines relating to sex discrimination in hiring practices.

Tort A civil wrong (other than a breach of contract) for which an award of damages is appropriate.

Trial Balance A list of the balances of the accounts in a ledger kept by double entry, with the debit and credit balances shown in separate columns. If the totals of the debit and credit columns are equal, or their net balance agrees with a controlling account, the ledger from which the figures are taken is said to be "in balance."

Unencumbered Balance That portion of an appropriation or allotment not yet expended or encumbered; the balance remaining after deducting from the appropriation or allotment the accumulated expenditures and outstanding encumbrances.

Unit Cost Expenditures for a function, activity, or service divided by the total number of units for which the function, activity, or service was provided.

Unit Record Equipment Wired board-controlled machines without memory, basically used for accounting-type operations.

Valuation Sound replacement cost of structures, equipment, and/or furnishings.

Voucher A document that authorizes the payment of money and usually indicates the accounts to be charged.

Vouchers Payable Liabilities for goods and services received, as evidenced by vouchers that have been preaudited and approved for payment but that have not been paid.

Voucher System A system that calls for the preparation of vouchers for transactions involving payments, and for the recording of such vouchers in a special book of original entry, known as a voucher register, in the order in which payment is approved.

Warrant An order drawn by the school board to the school system treasurer ordering him/her to pay a specified amount to a payee named on the warrant. Once signed by the treasurer, the warrant becomes a check payable by a bank named on the warrant by the treasurer.

Word Processing The manipulation of certain types of data—words, sentences, reports, and so forth—to express ideas and distribute them in hard copy (paper) and/or visual copy (CRT screen).

Work Order A written order authorizing and directing the performance of a certain task, issued to the person who is to direct the work. Among the information shown on the order are the nature and location of the job, specifications of the work to be performed, and a job number that is referred to in reporting the amount of labor, materials, and equipment used.

Workstation A general-purpose computer designed to be used by one person at a time and which offers higher performance than that normally found in a personal computer, especially with respect to graphics, processing power, and the ability to carry out several tasks at the same time.

Yearly Budget A type of budgeting process that is little more than a refinement of the mechanical type. The yearly budget forces quick decisions on expenditures and revenues, with little effort made to evaluate the impact of these decisions.

Zero-Based Accounting Implementing concept for developing the concentration account. Regular accounts are established as accounts payable. All carry a zero balance, with all monies kept in the concentration account until needed for a particular account.

Zero-Based Budgeting (ZBB) A process emphasizing management's responsibility to plan, budget, and evaluate. It provides analysis of alternative methods of operation and various levels of effort. It places new programs on an equal footing with existing programs by requiring that program priorities be ranked, thereby providing a systematic basis for allocating resources.

Index